LILY OF LAMORANTH

The Legend of Lamoranth
Book One

HANNAH LOWRY

Lily of Lamoranth is a work of fiction. Names, characters, places, and incidents are the products of the author's imagination or are used fictitiously. Any resemblance to actual events, locales, or persons, living or dead, is entirely coincidental.

ISBN: 978-0-9903965-0-5 (paperback)
978-0-9903965-1-2 (e-book)

First published in July 2015

I dedicate this book to my Little Mama,
whose independent nature and unconditional love
inspire and encourage my life in so many ways.
Mama, thank you for everything.
Love you forever.

CONTENTS

Creation Myth

The Beginning of the Unknown 1
A Death in the Tribe of Nather 10
Amadel Flight 19
Secrets Revealed and Secrets Kept 25
Elucidation 37
The Bane of the Fae 48
Xydolem 51
Alder 64
Out of the Great White Desert 78
Pillar of Sun and Ashes 91
Getting Acquainted 108
Blades, Bows, and Throwing Stars 123
Mirror, Mirror 135
Into the Grasslands of Ropaz 155
Honesty 168
Inner Magic 179
Plight of the Shepitan Coven 192
Maturity 208
Iron-Bound 223
Martial Magic 232

Dreams and Nightmares 252
Resolute 259
The Philosophy of Night Magic 268
The Gongoozler 285
Concerns and Confidence 303
Travelers' Travails 316
A Warrior's Mind 326
A Meeting of Minds 347
Goddess's Retreat 355
Disappointment and Deception 364
Revelations 375
The Antechamber 386
The Battle Begins 409
Crossing the River Ward 431
Sunrise at Golden Court 455
Gildenthrone 466
Sunset at Silver Court 485
In the Shadow of the Throne of Stars 509
Mourning by the Willows 521

Map 544
Pronunciation Guide 546

Acknowledgments 549
About the Author 551

In the beginning, there was balance.

When a beautiful Goddess came into being,
she spread her peace and her love,
and her white light shone down on the budding world
that did not yet have a name.

So too did the Dark ones come to exist,
Creating chaos and hate,
putting the world in darkness
by conceiving of the night.

She made the earth. They made the air.
She brought about water, and they brought about fire.
The Goddess spun magic from her spirit,
and the Dark Creators responded with a power
that could turn everything into nothing at all.

Where she sowed harmony, they grew discord.
While the Goddess embodied generosity, they became selfishness.
And in so doing, the Dark ones began to want more,
while the Goddess wished only to give.

The Beginning of the Unknown

As the striking rays of the fierce desert sun crested the horizon and began a glorious day, Lily rose from her nest of blankets as drowsily as usual. Unaware of what the dawning day would bring, Lily began her morning routine in semi-somnolence, gathering firewood from near the doorway of the spacious tent she shared with her mother. Known as Healer Rose to the people of their tribe, Rose was considered by one and all to be a gracious and melancholy woman who was highly competent in her vocation. Lily smiled at the thought of her only and cherished family member, her beautiful and loving mother, and wondered where she might be.

Ordinarily, they both woke and began their tasks at dawn, to escape laboring in the worst of the heat, yet her mother was already up and about in the near-darkness of first light. Lily guessed that she had been summoned in the night to tend to the impending birth of the chieftain's second child, and she resigned herself to completing the entirety of their little household's chores herself. Not that she cared about extra work, Lily reminded herself. Much. No one was as aware as Lily that her mother had an important role to play in the smooth functioning of their nomadic tribe, and that many of the members, particularly Chieftain Nather, were not easy to please. It was just that Lily always hoped for enough spare time to find a quiet place, outside of the bustling campsite, to recreate her dreams amidst the ever-shifting white sands of the Joquobon Desert.

After relighting the banked cooking fire with ease, Lily left the tent to fetch the day's water. She strode through the circular encampment toward the outermost and largest ring of dwellings, where the amadels were tethered. The shaggy-haired pack animals stood placidly in clusters, occasionally shifting their weight upon their six spindly legs. Due to camp having been set up many days before, the long-eared, short-necked beasts were allowed to rest, and so their concave backs were readily discernible. Though their smell was rather pungent in close proximity, Lily had always liked the even-tempered amadels and admired their considerable strength. Without them, the tribes traveling the desert would have no way of transporting their belongings or their vital burden of water.

A short line had already formed in front of the regimented rows of water casks, and it included not only some of the tribe's other teenage girls, but the chieftain's son Pather as well. When they noticed Lily, the girls hushed for just a moment before simultaneously bursting into poorly smothered giggles and whispers. Though the sting of their softened voices and hardened eyes still had some power to wound her, Lily put her mask of polite nonchalance in place and resolved to keep it from slipping. At least Pather, the future leader of their tribe, had never gone out of his way to do Lily harm. Not that he had ever tried to protect her from the cruelty of the other boys and girls, but Lily was grateful for small mercies. He certainly had the influence to make her life a great deal more difficult if he chose.

Lily had become resigned, though never truly accustomed, to the scorn of the tribe's other members. They mocked her for being inattentive, if not outright vacant, never realizing or caring that Lily had a propensity to spin daydreams out of virtually every chore. That, and her unusually pale skin, had always marked her as different and set her apart from the rest of Nather's tribe. Though such ridicule had been the cause of many childhood tears, she had grown fairly impervious to the unpleasant remarks, her hard-won poise a shield from even the most reproving scolds of the elderly tribespeople. After all, she had a secret. Lily focused on her wonderful discovery of years ago, and soon she had left the water line far behind her.

When she was just eight years old, a tiny girl who still believed in the fairy tales her mother told to help her fall asleep, Lily had fled the cruel jibes of the other children, running beyond the widest circle of Chieftain Nather's camp. She stumbled up and down bright white sand dunes, blinded by the harsh desert sun and the salty tears that streaked her face, some of the firewood she had been carrying still in her arms. When at last her shaking legs gave out beneath her, Lily wiped her eyes, took in her surroundings, and realized that she was thoroughly lost. There, collapsed on a pale mound of sand, somehow even more alone than ever before, she suddenly felt a desperate, burning anger in her chest. She was furious with the other children for the words and rocks they flung at her so painfully and so often. She was even angrier with herself, for succumbing to their unrelenting cruelties.

In a moment of pure rage, Lily grabbed a handful of the endless sand and hurled it, along with the pieces of wood she still held, away from herself in a moment of heated emotion. As they sailed through the air, tongues of crimson flame actually burst from her palms for a protracted moment and burned the airborne sand and wood. Something fell to the ground, an object that was neither sand nor wood, even as the flames flickered before sputtering out. Lily approached cautiously, hardly believing what had happened as a result of her temper. Not sure what to expect, Lily was shocked to see that the incinerated sand and wood had coalesced into a small, shapeless mass, both hard and clear. She had created glass!

Her anger momentarily forgotten in her utter amazement, Lily spent the rest of the day attempting to create more, without success. She was still trying to conjure the mysterious fire from her hands when her mother had appeared, more frightened than Lily had ever seen her. Though profound relief had crossed her face, Rose was soon furious at Lily's absence from camp. Upon their return, she had given Lily a number of onerous duties as punishment. While Lily had found helping in the collection of amadel chips rather unpleasant, she had worked to hide her smile as she cleaned each and every one of her mother's many glass jars of healing herbs and roots.

Lily had never forgotten the pain she had caused her mother that day, but neither did she dismiss the excitement of making something beautiful with her bare hands. She hadn't told her mother about the fire or the glass, unsure of how her mother would react to a reminder of that day. From then on, Lily had taken every opportunity that arose to go out into the desert with a bag of wood ash and attempt to mold her emotions into a tangible form. When the other children made fun of her pale skin or golden eyes, Lily had quietly retreated into the unrestricted, imaginative spaces in her mind, deciding what shapes her glass would take next. Always she selected the beings of the fairy tales, figments as far from the stark realities of her life as possible.

She made full use of all her free time over a period of years, eventually learning how to use the air around her to add a wealth of detail to her artwork. Lily had reached a level of skill with the sand, ash, fire, and air, such that her statues seemed almost imbued with life. Some of her best glass figures even occasionally took on a golden tinge in their depths, though Lily did not know why, other than her passion for the chosen subject. Lily's art allowed her to forget for a time the heat and harsh sunlight of the desert for the cool glades of the Forest of Ancients, where elves and tree sprites acted as guardians of the woods and its other fantastical inhabitants. The mirages of water caused by the mischief of the sun became Molten Mirror Lake, which protected the fairies of the Fae Wood from the trolls whose dwellings were in the Volcano Crescent. Even the ever-shifting sand dunes were transformed into the tidal waves of the Ocean of Fintilles, where mermen and mermaids were fabled to abide in the deep among coral reefs and sunken ships.

Lily had just decided to attempt a sculpture of a dwarf from the Grandfather Mountains, carefully holding his people's treasured Soul Cup, when she was brought back to the water line with jarring abruptness. Ignis, the amadel keeper and water distributor with a long and bumpy nose, was impatiently waiting for her to hand over her container.

"What are you waiting for, clouds and rain?" he barked. "Hand over that jug, or have you got knotted amadel hair for brains?"

Lily felt her cheeks heat. She reached up to adjust her black cloth hair wrap in a feeble attempt to mask her lack of attention and ensuing frustration with the disagreeable man. Ignis observed her nervous gesture with open amusement, looking down his bumpy nose at her as the countless iron bangles on her arm tinkled to her elbow and back down to her wrist. Lily immediately regretted her display of embarrassment and felt a small bubble of rebellion expand in her chest. Why did he take every opportunity to mock and insult her? Why, in fact, did everyone in the tribe seem to slight her with humiliating regularity?

"I will need the jug completely filled, please," Lily said curtly. "I plan to wash our clothes this afternoon, and my mother and I will, of course, need enough for cooking our food and brewing the medicines needed for the birthing of our chieftain's child. Or should I tell Chieftain Nather that you refused our request?"

Lily watched with satisfaction as the smug look vanished from Ignis's long-nosed face. He hastened to fill her container to the brim, marking the amount next to her mother's name in his account book and wishing her a good day with an oily smile. Laden with her heavy burden, Lily left the distasteful man and his bowl-backed charges. She retraced her path through the circles of tents to the third smallest ring, where she and her mother resided. When Lily had been young, they had always set up their tent in the bigger rings. Over the years, however, Rose's gift for healing had earned her a place in the smaller, more prestigious circles. They were now quite close to Chieftain Nather's large tent in the very center, which all the other tribespeople's smaller dwellings enclosed.

Lily was nearly home when she overheard a wisp of conversation through the door flap of Old Fripda's tent that brought her to a complete halt.

"Have you heard the latest news from Nather's tent, Mingeldi, my friend?" asked Fripda. "I have it on good authority that things are not going well for the chieftain's wife, not at all. Just when we need that healer woman's skills the most, it seems she will fail. Nather's wrath will be considerable, but none will suffer more than Rose, I can tell you."

Lily waited with baited breath for Mingeldi, the second oldest woman in the tribe after Fripda herself, to respond. As the painful words passed through the thin amadel-skin walls, Lily pictured the two old crones sitting on their woven mats, hunched toward each other near their cooking fire. Their deeply tanned, well-lined faces would be alight with glee at the transferal of the latest tribe gossip. Fripda's thin lips would be curved in a malicious smile, just as surely as Mingeldi's dark brown eyes would be conveying a look of haughty, thoroughly feigned indifference.

"Well, we all knew Nather's wife was going to have trouble, what with the treatment she gets from the likes of the chieftain, Fripda," Mingeldi replied. "Too thin by half to be bearing children in my opinion. If there are any other complications, I doubt even Healer Rose will be able to deliver the second son that Nather desires."

"Oh dear, wouldn't it be a pity if Rose and that garishly pale daughter of hers got cast out, Mingeldi? Did you know, I heard a rumor that her hair is as yellow as her eyes under the head wrap? Imagine, hair nowhere near brown! I tell you, those two aren't normal desert outcasts."

"I agree with you, Fripda. Strange and unnatural, the pair of them. Do you think there's a chance they might have, well . . ."

Mingeldi paused, question suspended in the air for long, agonizing moments. Lily was certain, even in her desperation to hear the rest of their conversation, that the fallacious indifference usually apparent in old Mingeldi's eyes would have temporarily vanished. The old crone finished her sentence in a whisper.

". . . the Anathema?"

Old Fripda let out a scandalized, and utterly thrilled, gasp.

"Why Mingeldi, what a thing to say! Just because they are both so fair in their features, you think them wrong to dwell in the Desert of Outcasts? Answer me this, then: Why would a woman like Rose give birth and raise a daughter all on her own for sixteen years if she could use the Anathema out in the rest of Lamoranth?"

"I'm certain I don't know," answered Mingeldi, "but it's not just their pale skin and light eyes. Have you ever known a healer to last this long without being accused of having the Anathema? And under the rule of Nather, no less! The man is suspicious of everyone and even more ruthless than his father Kather before him. In my opinion, Rose is doomed either way. If the babe dies, Nather will be enraged. If she manages to keep it alive, it will be so miraculous that even the most thick-headed of our tribe will be questioning exactly how she succeeded. I don't care how many herbs she buys from the traders in Japeta—"

"Oh, I think you may have a point, Mingeldi," interrupted Fripda. Lily could picture, with a kind of sick clarity, that malicious, thin-lipped smile spread wide across the crone's craggy face. "It's like I always say, 'Act normally, or suffer the consequences!'"

Lily stumbled away from the tent, unable to listen to the venomous slander of the two old hags a moment longer. Unsteadily, she made her way home, half afraid and half angry, nearly spilling the forgotten jug of water she was carrying. Dazed, Lily made a largely futile attempt to gather her thoughts. What could those two old gossips mean by accusing her mother of the most despised taboo in the Joquobon Desert? Perhaps the worst thing about it was that she didn't even know what it was. Such was the prohibition that even speaking of the Anathema was supposed to be forbidden. Lily entered her tent completely distracted and fearing greatly for her mother. Those under suspicion of the Anathema rarely lived.

And how had they found out about her honey-blond hair? Lily was so very careful to keep it covered at all times, especially outside of her own tent. She never took it down to sleep, only to wash it, and only then in the safety of her mother's tent. Her mother had always insisted on this, and Lily had complied, if for no other reason than that most girls of a certain age covered their hair in black wraps, just as most of her teenage peers also wore black or brown knee-length, sleeveless tunics with leggings and sturdy slippers. Lily had never minded the plain, utilitarian clothing, for it was comfortable and convenient for desert life. Besides, Lily had more iron jewelry to embellish her drab wardrobe than any other marriage-eligible girl in her tribe. Every year for her birthday, her mother had gifted Lily with armbands, bangles, necklaces, anklets, and even, on her thirteenth birthday, an iron belt with a width the span of her thumb. Lily had the distinction of being the only girl in Nather's tribe with a piercing in each ear, and she took quiet pride in the pair of earrings that dangled just below her hair wrap. Though it all got a bit heavy at times, Lily was secretly pleased with her mother's rare and expensive gifts. In this way, at least, she could choose to stand apart from the others, rather than being forced to the fringes.

Lily turned her troubled mind back to the puzzle of the Anathema and its threat to her mother, all the while cutting vegetables and heating some of their water supply on the cooking fire she had lit at dawn. If her mother didn't return in the next hour, Lily decided to bring the meal to the chieftain's tent. She could perhaps see for herself if Old Fripda and Mingeldi spoke any truth, while making sure that her mother got something to eat during the long and often arduous birthing process. Lily added some bits of carefully saved dried meat into the kettle, followed by a few seasonings her mother always kept in ready supply on their cooking shelf.

As she waited for the stew to finish, Lily tidied up the tent. She folded her nest of colorful blankets into a proper bed and did the same for her mother's sleeping space, which had obviously been left in haste sometime during the night. Lily swept sand from the sitting mats near the cooking fire, as well as from the top of her small traveling trunk, which contained all of her meager possessions. Pausing over the egg-shaped trunk a moment, Lily impulsively opened it and surveyed her belongings.

She saw her clothing first: extra tunics, leggings, and underthings conveniently on top. Lily shifted the garments aside and found her old pair of slippers, which had a hole in the left sole. Beneath those articles of clothing lay her warm amadel-hair jacket for the occasional less-than-balmy desert nights and a few of her treasured childhood toys, including a spinning top. Next to these items was a medium-sized bag that she usually kept full of wood ash, for her precious glass-making hours in the desert. At the very bottom, some of the iron rings for her fingers had found their way. Lily seldom wore them, for they often caused her knuckles to swell and inhibited her everyday tasks.

Finally, she uncovered her favorite birthday present, from her fourteenth, which was carefully wrapped in her bright blue, special-occasions-only hair wrap. Lily slowly unwound the cloth and drew out a circular mirror, encased in a delicately carved wooden frame with two small handles on opposite sides. On the back was a picture of a startlingly life-like flower with a mysterious script flowing around it. Lily gazed at the looping symbols, mesmerized as always by their enchanting elegance. Her mother had told Lily that the mirror had first been given to her as a gift many years ago, and that she wanted to bequeath it to Lily in turn now. When Lily had inquired about the carvings on the back, her mother had said that the flower was a rose, in honor of her name, and that it was spelled out by the unknown runes. Her mother had given the mirror to Lily, she claimed fondly, so that Lily could be sure that all of her shining golden tresses were covered before leaving their tent.

"More than for such a practicality, my darling, I also think every young girl ought to have a way to stare vanity in the face and overcome it. Remember, Lily, knowing yourself on the inside is far more important than being aware of your exterior, however beautiful you are growing to be. Let this mirror remind you to reflect on your mind and your soul, any lady's most vital assets. Felicitations on your foundation day, child of mine."

Her mother had looked so lovely as she spoke, her large silver-gray eyes timeless and wise, a small, wistful smile playing about her full lips. Lily had sensed that this gift was very different from all the others, all of the jewelry to be worn on the outside. This was one of her mother's few treasured possessions, and Lily had thanked her exuberantly, even as she pondered her mother's advice.

Lily carefully rewrapped the hand mirror and put it back in her trunk. As she did so, another flash of iron caught her eye, and she suddenly recalled the gift she had received for her sixteenth birthday, nearly a year ago now. It was a dagger in an ornately inlaid sheath, which could be easily attached to her iron belt. Lily had been uneasy about this present, and she had shoved it toward the bottom of her trunk as soon as politely possible. She didn't doubt for a moment, though, that her mother saw and understood her uneasiness, for Rose knew how gentle her daughter usually was, how much Lily tolerated from the people of Nather's tribe. However, Lily was also aware that, deep inside of her, there was a ferocity, a proud force that would refuse to tolerate just a small number of things. One of these was the integrity of her mother. Though she was frightened by the snippet of conversation she'd just overheard from Old Fripda's tent, Lily also felt angry with the two old crones who had called into question

Rose's exceptional healing abilities. Lily was disturbed by the intensity of her feelings, particularly those of animosity, just as she had been a number of times in the past. It had seemed unwise before to arm herself with a dagger when she was capable of feeling such anger. Given the threat of the Anathema now, however, Lily was suddenly glad for this small measure of protection, and she resolved not to ignore it from then on.

She closed her oblong trunk and turned back to the stew, which appeared to be ready. Lily carefully ladled it into two bowls until she was scraping the bottom of the kettle. She ate her share before it had even properly cooled, burning the roof of her mouth in her haste to visit her mother in Chieftain Nather's tent. When she had finished, Lily carefully covered the top of her mother's steaming bowl of stew and gathered her courage as she set off for the center of the campsite, her heart much more troubled than it had been with the sunrise.

A Death in the Tribe of Nather

Lily quickly made her way to the large central tent of her tribe, reminding herself to hold fast to her composure as curious glances peeked out from behind door flaps and around the curves of conical abodes. Upon reaching Nather's tent, she explained her errand to the guard who was usually on duty, Phepin, and was admitted into the first room of the spacious chieftain's tent. It was the only dwelling in the whole tribe allowed to have more than one room. The space was comfortable, with a central cooking fire and many colorful woven sitting mats for guests. The chieftain's goffir, apparently returned from flying messages to other leaders in the desert, sat perched in its cage, an elaborate construction of very thin amadel rib bones. Its head had sunk forward into the sky-blue plumage of its breast in sleep, leaving its sand-white wings, back, and three long tail feathers visible. A few steps away from the goffir's cage, Lily noted that wood had been laid out for a fire, but as yet remained unlit. This probably confirmed that her mother hadn't had anything to eat. Normally, Phepin's wife, Chafa, cooked and cleaned for the chieftain's household, but it was more likely that she was assisting with the birthing today. The dim room and break in routine made Lily uneasy.

Suddenly, Lily heard a terrible moan of pain from the adjoining room. A frisson of fear struck down her spine like a bolt of lightning, eerily akin to the rare flashes she had once seen far to the north of Jeridoff. Lily had helped her mother act as midwife for many other women of the tribe, and she knew that the chieftain's wife wasn't making the measured sounds of a lady in labor, but whimpers of fright and exhaustion. Lily crossed the guest room and stood before the door flap to the bedroom. She paused just a moment to make sure her voice would be steady.

"Mother? May I enter?"

Lily heard her mother giving hurried instructions to Chafa before she emerged from the birthing room, quickly closing the flap behind her. Rose's fine features showed her fatigue and concern. Her gray eyes looked weary and troubled, and the skin of her face seemed somehow tightened with stress, making her cheekbones even more prominent than usual. Though Lily was prepared for it, the blood and fluids staining her mother's tunic from the birthing still made her cringe slightly.

"Mother, I brought you some stew. I thought you might be hungry. I also wanted to offer to help. Do you need me to brew any of your medicines?"

Over the years, Rose had taught her a considerable amount of healer's knowledge, and Lily often made the drafts and salves for minor complaints when her mother was busy with more serious illnesses. Her mother smiled just a little, but it only briefly lit her eyes before the worry returned.

"Thank you, darling. I must eat quickly. If you could make the draught for lowering fever, that would be a help."

Rose then lowered her voice and whispered the words Lily had been dreading.

"The birthing is not going well." Her mother took several swallows of stew, then continued, still in her softest voice. "There is a good chance that you and I will have to leave Nather's tribe very soon, Lily. I know this is frightening for you, but I need you to be brave and keep a cool head for me. Make the fever draft, and pack your essential things and all of our non-perishable food in my big haversack. Then open my trunk and pull out a spare pair of clothes for me, as well as the sword and sealed scroll you will find at the very bottom. Put these items inside my medical pack, the one I usually take when I visit patients. Go, my darling, and return quickly."

With that, her mother finished the stew, handed the bowl back to Lily with more thanks, and returned to the birthing room. Lily stood for a moment, rooted to the spot, just as she felt sure the trees of a forest clung to the ground when the wind blew fiercely about them. Then she shook herself into motion and walked as quickly as possible back to her own tent, barely acknowledging Phepin along the way.

What was happening? Were the outcasts actually going to cast her and her mother out in turn? They hadn't even done anything wrong! Lily felt a flare of anger, and her palms grew slightly warm, just as they always did when she spun fire out of her hands and sculpted glass. Then a terrible idea occurred to her: What if her ability to create fire and control the sand, wood ashes, and air was the Anathema? What if someone had found out her secret and the danger she was in, that she had put her *mother* in, was all her fault? Lily felt sick, so much so that for several protracted moments, she was hardly aware of being back inside her tent, still clinging to her mother's empty bowl. It was the innocuous bowl that propelled Lily to action a few moments later. Her mother had given her instructions, and she would carry them out to the letter. If Nather's wrath and their subsequent punishment was in any way due to her own actions and separate from the birthing, then it was her responsibility to do whatever she could to find safety for their little family of two again.

First she scrubbed the bowl and the little kettle clean, then put them on their customary shelf near her mother's trunk with the other cooking supplies. Lily could hardly believe that a sword was inside her mother's battered brown trunk, that it possibly had been for years, and she had been none the wiser. Her mother was a profoundly peaceful person. Why then did she have such a deadly weapon? Had she been expecting trouble? Lily shoved her countless questions to the back of her mind and focused on only the most immediately vital ones. Should she do the packing first? Or the fever draught? The potion would need to steep for a quarter of an hour, so Lily decided to start it and pack while she waited for it to mature.

After she had put two cups of water in the kettle and set it over the fire once more, Lily opened her mother's healing trunk. It was the same egg shape as their travel trunks and sat in its normal place at the head of her mother's bed. She pulled out the glass jar full of yarrow for the fever draught. Lily measured the amount of the herb needed with a practiced eye, then ground it into pieces with her mother's mortar and pestle. She then removed the kettle from the fire and carefully poured the boiling water into a clean bowl. Lily put the prepared yarrow into the hot water, covered the bowl, and left the simple infusion to steep as she turned to do the packing.

Lily went to her mother's travel trunk and lifted the lid. She felt slightly guilty as she began rifling through the contents, as if she were intruding on her mother's privacy. Lily quickly grabbed a spare tunic, leggings, and head wrap, as well as a pair of gloves that her mother favored. Setting the clothing aside, she dug in the trunk until she found the sword and scroll at the very bottom. Lily grasped the sheath covering the blade, which was entirely plain but for a few of those mysterious foreign runes. It felt heavy as she lifted it out of the trunk, as though it weighed a great deal more than it possibly could, given its size. Lily felt the sudden urge to drop it, allow it to fall, forgotten, back into the depths of her mother's trunk, but she resisted the urge and wrapped it in her mother's extra set of clothing.

After closing the lid to the traveling trunk, Lily returned to the healing trunk, taking the more convenient medical pack out of it that her mother used every day. She opened the rectangular case that held the most commonly needed roots, herbs, and barks securely in their glass jars, restocking anything that was running low from the more extensive supplies in the healing trunk. Lily then reached for the scroll and the swaddled sword, carefully placing them inside the pack by a couple of spare glass containers. The sword didn't quite fit, and the handle of the blade protruded from the padded top flap of the pack. She felt slightly dazed by the incongruous mixture of the new with the familiar. There were the healing things beside the mortiferous weapon, along with a scroll written in a language Lily may very well not even be able to read.

Finally, she turned to her own trunk, unable to put off the inevitable. Her mother had told her to bring only what was essential. Lily didn't have much, and she felt reluctant to part with those few things she called her own. Yet the situation seemed desperate, and the fear and confusion she felt on account of the Anathema and the birthing seemed to make her task more urgent. Lily selected two full sets of clothes, the jacket, her half-full bag of wood ash, the mirror, her rings, and the dagger with its sheath. The last she attached to her belt, seeing a greater advantage in being armed from that moment on. Lily had never worn it before, and it felt inordinately heavy, much as her mother's sword had when she'd briefly held it in her hands. She closed the lid decisively, then turned to put her selections in the haversack, along with the two loaves of bread she'd baked the day before, all the vegetables and dried meat on their cooking shelf, and the container of water. Despite her unease, Lily smiled at the thought of the look on Ignis's long-nosed face when he discovered he had willingly given her and her mother enough water for a journey of several days' duration.

Finished with the packing, Lily turned back to the covered bowl and found the fever draft ready. She strained the herb matter from the tea, ladled a generous portion of it into their largest drinking bowl, and covered the top once more, this time for the walk to the chieftain's tent. With a final look at the haversack and medical pack, both of which looked bulky where Lily had set them against the curved wall near the doorway, she quickly carried the draught back to the chieftain's dwelling at the center of the tribe. Along the way, Lily was keenly aware of the eyes following her every step as she passed the two shrinking rings of tents. Unlike the curious glances of a short while ago, Lily could feel the tribe's suspicious glares like sand scraping against her skin, the abrasions making her feel raw and vulnerable. She forced herself to ignore all of their growing animosity and focus her attention on her task, walking with a brisk and steady tread, though she wanted much more to run from the mistrust and mounting hostility. Everyone knew that Nather was on the brink of one of his rages. No one wanted to be his scapegoat if they could possibly avoid it, or deflect it onto someone else on even the flimsiest pretense.

Lily, her sense of dread and impending danger building, approached Phepin a second time. The trepidation must have shown on her face, for the guard inclined his head ever so slightly toward the tent, the warning in his eyes putting Lily on further alert. Had the condition of the chieftainess deteriorated so quickly? She entered hurriedly and immediately came face to face with Nather himself.

"What are you doing in here?" Nather snarled at her.

Lily, in her rush, had interrupted his impatient pacing. She looked upon him and suddenly felt all her childhood fears of Nather come back in full force. He was tall and powerfully built, with the tan skin, brown eyes, and dark hair of all respectable desert dwellers. What made him so intimidating, however, was not his bulky muscles or broad frame, but the malice carved in every line of his face. Nather was a pitiless predator waiting for prey to stalk and capture. As his eyes, so full of seething hostility, roamed freely over her, Lily knew herself to be in danger and did not know what to do. Carefully casting her own eyes onto the doorway beyond him, Lily spoke quietly into the stretching, menacing silence.

"My mother bid me make a fever draught to aid the chieftainess."

"Did she now? I told her I could care less about my wife. The child is my only concern, and it should be your mother's as well."

Nather sneered and slowly advanced, his calloused hands flexing open and closed at his sides. Lily reached for a calm she did not feel as her apprehension mounted. She had to be brave. Panicking only made things worse. Lily stood her ground.

"Please, Chieftain, may I pass? I would like to do all I can to help with the birth of your child."

"Oh you would, would you?" Nather shot back. "Do you really think that will save your mother after she used the Anathema on my wife? I let her into my tribe, all those years ago, alone, pale, and already heavy with child. She was a complete liability, without even a tent or kettle to her name, and this is how Rose repays me? She has brought the forbidden into my tribe, and for that, she must die. What will become of you, I wonder, when Healer Rose is gone?"

Somewhere through the haze of her rising terror, Lily saw the look of cruel enjoyment flash across Nather's raptorial countenance, a look that promised something horrible for her, the quarry that now had his fixed attention. Nather's hand suddenly snaked out and grabbed Lily's upper arm with frightening agility and speed. If not for her iron armband, Lily felt sure he would have left bruises. The fever draught was flung to the ground, the liquid splattering everywhere. The goffir let out an indignant screech as the bowl clattered against the base of its cage, even as Nather wrenched Lily toward him.

Just as she caught the unpleasant smell of his breath much too close to her, a baby's cry split the air. Nather swung in the direction of the sound, his attention momentarily diverted. Lily's heart, which had frozen in shock, stuttered a few beats, then thundered fully back to life. She seized Nather's moment of distraction, which had slackened his grip on her arm, to rush toward her mother and the child she had just brought into the world. Lily pushed aside the door flap and burst into the bedroom, immediately noticing the air close and heavy around her. She beheld a huge pile of soiled blankets, on top of which lay the wasted form of the chieftainess, who did not appear to be breathing. Chafa was holding the baby, silently crying as she cast frequent looks at the lifeless woman upon the bed. Rose had just severed the cord that connected the infant to the chieftain's wife and was cleaning the newborn's head with a soft, damp cloth.

"Mother, the draught, it spilled, I'm sorry—"

"It is no longer needed. The chieftainess is dead. Are you alright?"

"Yes, I don't know, did you hear what—"

"Yes, it is as I feared. I have been accused of the Anathema," Rose stated calmly. Her gaze flicked to the weeping Chafa and back to Lily before she spoke in a softer voice. "We must leave. Here is what we will do: I will present Nather with his son. You will stay behind me and remain completely silent. Once we have gotten the packs from our tent, we will leave camp immediately. It is imperative that we steal an amadel to ride so that our flight will be swift enough to evade pursuit. Do you understand me, Lily?"

Her head spinning, both from her desperation for safety and with her concern at the countless opportunities for disaster in the plan, Lily met her mother's flashing silver eyes and simply nodded. Without another word, Rose gently took the baby boy from Chafa and strode toward the bedroom's only exit.

Nather was still waiting impatiently in the receiving room, his eyes greedily taking in the sight of the tiny child in Rose's arms.

"Is it a son?"

Though Lily couldn't see her mother's face, she knew the complete disapproval that would be written there. She stuck closely to her mother's back, keeping a hand on the rough brown tunic, as much to assure as to be reassured.

"The baby is a boy. He is healthy," Rose said, handing the newborn directly to Nather.

The chieftain's smug face became startled as the infant was thrust into his arms, followed quickly by annoyance as the tiny boy began to cry with hunger. Not wasting a second, Rose continued out the door, Lily still grasping a handful of her tunic. Phepin watched them leave, allowing them to pass unchallenged. Lily was certain that Nather would get over his surprise and order them back, with his guard's assistance if necessary, yet the sounds of pursuit did not come.

"I imagine he is being told about his wife just now. That, and perhaps the question of a wet-nurse, may grant us some time," Lily's mother whispered in her softest tones.

Before Lily knew it, they had arrived at their own tent. Her mother thrust the door flap aside and looked about, quickly eying the haversack and medical pack with approval.

"Did you manage to get water, Lily?"

"Yes, our whole container. I told Ignis I was doing laundry."

"Excellent, we needn't worry about that on the way out then."

Rose hefted her pack, grimacing slightly.

"This sword is always so heavy," she said on a sigh. "Let's go, darling."

Lily looked once more upon the inside of their tent, the only home she'd ever known, then turned and followed her mother back outside.

They were met by hostile stares, though no one dared approach them. Lily wondered if it was their fear of the Anathema or the fact that Nather had not yet publicly pronounced their guilt. She wondered if her mother really had used what was forbidden on the chieftain's wife. Was that why she had died? Lily's mind rejected the thought immediately. No, her mother would never willingly kill another person. Besides, Lily knew her mother would never do anything to put her only daughter in danger. The chieftainess had several other potential causes of death, not least among them a monstrous husband. Lily felt a moment of sadness for the downtrodden woman who no longer lived, hoping she was more at peace now than she had been since her marriage into their tribe.

Lily's frantic thoughts flicked back to the cause of their flight. If her own control of fire and sand was Anathema, the taboo might not necessarily be something frightening or evil, as she had always assumed. Lily wondered when she would have time to question her mother. Why had she never asked before?

"See Bepo, tethered third to the left, Lily?" her mother asked, snapping Lily out of her distracted thoughts. "We're going to try to take him. He's accustomed to obeying us, and he's certainly strong enough for our long journey."

Lily chastised herself for her lapsed attention at such a critical juncture in their escape, trying to atone by searching for the unpleasant figure of Ignis among the herd of amadels. She spied the water distributor on their far right, checking the hoof on a middle leg of a smaller amadel. It was his responsibility to guard both the herd and the water casks, and he could not let either out of his sight until someone else took up his watch. Ignis seemed wholly absorbed in his task, another stroke of good fortune in their precipitous departure.

"Ignis looks distracted. I say we take Bepo now," Lily answered. Then she hesitated, finally saying, "We're not going to leave payment for him, Mother?"

Though her brisk pace never slowed, Lily's mother glanced at her daughter's open face, then solemnly said, "I will consider it the tribe's payment for seventeen years of excellent healing services rendered, Lily. However, even if that were not the case, your life is worth far more than a stolen amadel. Your safety is paramount to me, and if theft is necessary, I will not hesitate to commit it in order to ensure your well-being. This might very well happen in the weeks to come, for we have a lengthy journey ahead of us. I have raised you with a strict sense of honor, but know that I have my reasons for putting you before all else. Let us take only the dishonest opportunities we greatly need when we cannot otherwise provide for ourselves, beginning now."

With that, Lily's mother ducked into a graceful crouch and made her way, with all possible stealth, toward the amadels farthest from Ignis. Lily followed, her heart pounding against the confines of her chest. When they had reached the pack animals, they slunk past a cluster of females, carefully skirting their many legs, and finally arrived beside Bepo, their predetermined amadel. Rose helped Lily mount and settle into the shallow depression of his bowl-shaped back, then easily jumped in front. She immediately grabbed Bepo's long, floppy ears, which made ideal reins for such a short-necked animal. As soon as they both sat cross-legged, just as they always did on their tent's woven mats, Lily's mother urged him into a brisk trot. When they were clear of the rest of the herd and entering the open desert, Rose urged Bepo into his fastest pace, a decent canter. Lily grabbed her mother's waist around the medical pack, which she hadn't taken the time to remove, and held on tight.

Amadel Flight

Though they were absconding with all possible haste, Lily wished they could grow wings and fly far away. It would be a smoother journey, Lily was quite certain, for the large amadel's many-legged gait was rather jarring for his riders. They had only made it up the first large sand dune when the infuriated shouts of Ignis reached their ears. Lily's heart sank, even as they crested the mound of sand and began descending the other side. Though briefly out of sight, their escape had not gone unnoticed. Within moments, most of the tribe would see them heading north, straight for the permanent town of Jeridoff, if they hadn't already.

Lily pondered their direction. The Joquobon had only three unmoving settlements, which were situated around the only three sources of water in the desert. Most of the desert dwellers belonged to nomadic tribes that constantly journeyed in the triangular path that connected those fixed cities of Jeridoff, Japeta, and the Oasis of Julast. Nather's tribe was currently camped just a few days north of the smallest and southernmost town, Oasis of Julast, having come from Jeridoff, the moderately sized city of craftsmen. Lily had assumed they would make their way east to Japeta, for it was not only the largest settlement but the one with a bustling market. Her mother always traded for her healer's supplies in that town, due to the fact that merchants from the grasslands of Ropaz always carried what she needed. If they were being forced to leave the desert, that would be the most expedient route that led to other people, at least as Lily understood things. No outsiders had ever been seen in northern Jeridoff, and certainly not in the Oasis of Julast, which was deep in the Joquobon.

Though she didn't want to break her mother's concentration, Lily felt she at least deserved to know their general plan of escape. Just as she was about to ask, however, Rose began speaking over her shoulder.

"Because they have seen us leaving, we must attempt to deceive them from our true goal. I think we should travel north today, and possibly tomorrow, to make Nather and his men believe we are heading for Jeridoff," her mother explained. After a brief pause, she continued. "So far, I have told you nothing of what you now need to know, Lily. Be patient just a bit longer, and I will tell you things of importance and answer some of your questions. For now, suffice it to say that we are ultimately traveling a considerable distance east, and a stop in Japeta will likely prove necessary for supplies. Let us focus at present on losing our pursuers."

With that, Lily's mother fell silent, leaving Lily herself to ponder what lay to the east that was so imperative for them to reach. Were they going to seek refuge in Ropaz, perhaps with some of the merchants who were allowed to enter and trade in the desert? Lily realized that she had very little reliable information on the world outside of the Joquobon. What if there were greater dangers inhabiting the rest of Lamoranth than the likes of Chieftain Nather? Certainly it would have taken something extreme for Lily's mother to travel into the desert all those years ago, pregnant and completely alone. Lily had often wondered about her father, if he had perhaps been cruel enough to force Rose to flee, and had even asked her mother about him once, years ago. Rose's face had filled with pain, and her eyes had held some other emotion that Lily did not understand. After a moment, Lily's mother had simply said, "I'm so sorry, my darling, but I cannot bring myself to think of him. It is just too difficult."

Lily had felt guilty for making her mother suffer, however unintentionally, and she had never brought up the subject of her father again. Though she still longed to know if he was the one who had forced them to become outcasts, it had never seemed worth making her mother so terribly sad. Lily wondered if her mother would talk about him in the days to come, if he was somehow a part of their plans now that their life in the desert was coming to an end. Would they have to continue to avoid him, or could he be counted on for help?

Lily's thoughts scattered as she heard shouts from somewhere behind her. She turned and saw a half dozen men pursuing them a good distance back on large amadels, following the path that Bepo had forged across the rolling dunes. They were all armed with short swords that glinted in the sun, and one man also carried a bow with a quiver of arrows. Chieftain Nather was in the lead, and even with a decent expanse of sand between them, the look of rage contorting his features was completely clear, as was his deadly intent. Lily faced forward once again, wondering how they were going to outpace Nather and his men when their amadel was doubly burdened.

"Mother, Nather and five others are following us, all armed. I've never seen the chieftain so livid," Lily reported, only the slightest tremor in her voice giving her away.

Lily felt more frightened than she ever had before. Though she had accepted her place on the fringe of the tribe, never making friends and forced to cope with a great deal of loneliness, she had never thought her life was in danger. Lily's longstanding preoccupation with their animosity seemed so trivial when death itself felt so near. If that man got within arrow's range, she saw no way to defend herself. Though the haversack hung diagonally and covered much of her back, her head was fully exposed and swathed in black cloth, starkly contrasting with the white sand that swirled about them from the westerly winds. For once she was grateful for Bepo's bouncing, lurching gait, for it would make her a more difficult target.

"Lily, do they have packs of any sort with them?"

Surprised by the question, Lily turned about and looked carefully for any bags or sacks.

"I see nothing but swords, except one man who has a bow and arrows as well."

"Who is the bowman?" her mother queried urgently.

Lily turned quickly once again to scrutinize the bowman's face.

"He is Phepin, Nather's regular guard. It's the man who was on duty this morning, I'm certain."

"Then we may yet have a chance," replied Rose. "They left in haste and brought no supplies with them. They assume that they will overtake us sometime today. If we can keep our distance or get out of their sight for long enough, they will most likely have to return to camp by nightfall."

"But what about Phepin?"

"I do not think we need to fear him. Just two months ago, Nather gave that man a serious injury in one of his foul tempers, and his wife Chafa came to me desperate for aid. Though the wound was fairly serious, I managed to heal him. They have since considered themselves indebted to me. That is probably why Chafa handed Nather's son over to me so readily, and distracted him right afterward. Phepin let us pass unchallenged as well. This leads me to think that they have no strong allegiance to the chieftain, while they seek ways to help us in our time of need."

Lily recalled Phepin's subtle warning the second time she had approached Nather's tent, and she felt a glimmer of hope. He was the only one who could harm them from a distance, and it seemed possible that he might take the opportunity to save them as he had been saved by Rose. Lily's main concern became Bepo, who already seemed to have slowed a bit in pace. How long would the chase last if their mount tired too quickly?

"Will we be able to elude them, Mother?"

Rose did not respond, but leaned forward slightly and spoke gently into their amadel's long ears to urge him on. Lily felt a surge of affection for their long-time pack animal as Bepo gave a snort, as if in acknowledgment, and sped up at her mother's request.

The next several hours proved highly nerve-wracking for the two runaways. Lily couldn't remember a time when she had been in such a terrible state of suspense. At several points, Lily thought they might be pulling ahead and out of sight of their enemies. At other times, however, it seemed Nather gained on them, coming dangerously close. When this happened, Lily wondered what she could possibly do to assist in their escape. Should she jettison her haversack? Though it was tempting to lighten the load for Bepo, Lily knew that finding themselves without food or water in the Joquobon would soon prove disastrous.

What else could she do? Lily was struck by the realization that she could move sand, create fire, and control the air. Why hadn't she thought to use her talent before? Lily hesitated, unsure of what to do. What if she was using the Anathema? Until now, Nather had only been assuming her mother had used it, without proof and for his own ends. If Lily revealed her strange ability, what would the consequences be? Perhaps if she could use it in a way that wasn't completely obvious . . .

Turning around, Lily allowed her emotions, her fear at being caught, as well as her strong underlying anger at being hunted down like this, to burn in her chest. Focusing that powerful feeling, Lily ignored the fact that Nather and his men were getting perilously near, refused to cower as Phepin loaded an arrow in preparation to shoot at her and her mother. Lily concentrated exclusively on determining the most inconspicuous way to lose their six pursuers.

The men were just cresting the large hill of sand that their own faithful Bepo had left behind. If she could make the gentle western wind blow harder, then use it to help pick up the sand on that neighboring dune . . . Lily tried to remain calm, to focus her complete attention on her task. The only things that mattered in that moment were the weight of the sand, the strength of the wind. The key was to let the elements do as much of the work as possible, just like when she sculpted glass.

Lily realized, however, that this was going to take considerably more effort than creating a glass statue, and as she slowly built up the force of the wind, she tried to keep herself from total exhaustion. Their escape from the desert would take endurance, and Lily knew she couldn't afford to overtax herself now. Instead, she turned her mind to memories of the countless sandstorms that had blown upon Nather's camp, always without warning and most often from the west in this part of the desert. The wind usually picked up considerably, and minutes later a great deal of sand gusted through, landing on everything, coating the sides of tents and creating a gritty white layering on anyone unfortunate enough to be caught outside their dwelling. Lily attempted to imitate that natural pattern, and soon the air behind them became thick with stirred-up sand.

Unfortunately, this didn't seem to be slowing Nather and his tribesmen. Though they had covered the lower halves of their faces with cloth, they appeared to be pushing their amadels to the limits of their endurance, knowing they needed to get north of a storm that would blow west to east. Lily wasn't sure what else to do, or even how to do it. She quickly decided to attempt to slow the amadels specifically by tossing sand at their heads. She lifted a portion of sand with the strength inside of her, picturing herself lifting a full container of water with her body in the ordinary way for guidance. Lily had selected the sand from the side of a dune just ahead and to the left of their enemies. Drawing on that inner strength more consciously than ever before, Lily cast the sand she had lifted directly toward the faces of the amadels. Though the effort was distinctly lacking in finesse, Lily watched as, with the additional sand churning amidst the storm she had already created, the six men and their mounts were entirely lost to sight.

Lily slumped forward and rested her head against her mother's slightly bulging medical pack. She felt more fatigued than she ever had before, even compared to the times when Nather ordered the camp to pick up and move quickly and she had to haul their bundled tent and trunks onto Bepo's back unassisted. Her arms and neck in particular felt painfully sore, as if she had seriously overexerted herself with physical labor. Though she felt a bit dizzy, Lily still heard her mother's voice clearly over the wind that swirled about them.

"Lily, are they still following us? Are you well?"

Lily concentrated on lifting and turning her sore neck, looking carefully at the huge formation of sand that continued to storm just behind them. She examined the entire area, staring intently, seeing neither man nor beast. Suddenly, a lone amadel lurched into sight, its rider barely remaining on its back. The frightened amadel collapsed almost immediately, its sides heaving as it violently attempted to snort sand out of its nose. Lily focused her attention on the rider, who was hastily dismounting the fallen amadel. He was holding a bow and notching it with an arrow. As Lily watched, her heart sank. After all she had just done, would Phepin still be able to shoot at them? Lily was fairly certain that they were within his range.

Phepin assumed a shooting stance, aiming straight for Lily and her mother. He quickly fired an arrow. It fell far short of them. Lily's spirits began to lift when his next arrow completely overshot them, falling to their right. Rose turned in her seat and looked momentarily stunned at the scene unfolding behind them. Phepin notched a third arrow, glanced behind his wheezing amadel at the storm, then deliberately turned his body and pointed the bow and arrow due east. He held the stance for several long moments, then lowered his weapon and turned to care for his mount. Lily faced forward once more, smiling into her mother's pack as they crested another dune and lost sight of Phepin, his winded amadel, and the storm that was just barely beginning to blow itself out.

Secrets Revealed and Secrets Kept

"Mother . . . I created that sandstorm," Lily quietly admitted.

Though it had taken her a little time to speak up, Lily had come to the conclusion, not long after they had left the sandstorm behind them, that she needed to be entirely honest with her mother about what she was capable of doing. She had kept her secret more than long enough.

Rose abruptly turned around to look at Lily directly. Her face held surprise, but her reaction was certainly calmer than Lily had anticipated. Shock or astonishment, perhaps, but not the predominating concern. Her response caused Lily to be taken aback in turn.

"Lily, which elements exactly do you feel you have a measure of control over? Does it cause you pain to manipulate them?"

Lily forced herself to speak, to explain the secret she had been keeping, hoping her mother wouldn't be angry or hurt over her evasion.

"I've been going out into the desert alone for years, making glass out of our campfire's ashes and sand heated by fire. I think I do basically control the sand and wood, and definitely the fire. At some point, I also discovered how to use air to add more details to my glass sculptures . . . It's never hurt me before, it just makes me tired sometimes."

Lily stopped, hardly believing that she had just divulged her big secret, and that it had hardly surprised her mother at all.

"Fire, earth, and air . . . painlessly?" Rose murmured contemplatively. Then she addressed Lily once more.

"What about water? And have you ever generated darkness, brightness, or a colored light? Tell me about this, Lily."

Lily searched her memories, trying to recall if she had ever controlled water. Then she remembered, from the depths of her childhood, a day when her mother had been out of the tent, visiting a sick member of the tribe. Lily had accidentally lost her grip on the handle to the water container, spilling every drop they'd had. She had been extremely upset, for their journey to one of the permanent cities, all three of which had the desert's only accessible water sources, had been delayed by frequent sandstorms, and everyone's water allotment was severely rationed. Lily remembered wishing with all her might that she could just suck all the water back out of the sand and woven mats it had spilled on, and before she knew it, that was exactly what she'd done. An amorphous globule of water, perfectly clean, had floated a hand-span above the ground, and Lily had instinctively directed it back into the container. She had been immensely relieved, but soon distracted by something else, as small children often were. Lily had completely forgotten about the incident until now.

"Yes, water too. I can remember at least once, when I was little. I haven't practiced with it though."

"And the darkness, the brightness? Any colored light . . . silver or golden light, perhaps?"

Though Lily was still feeling a little unnerved by her mother's questions, she felt more certain of her answers to these.

"My sculptures are sort of tinged with gold sometimes . . . usually when I'm trying to make a statue of you, or when I really feel as though I've captured my subject. The brightness I'm not sure about, but the darkness I haven't ever made. But, you know how I was worried about the dagger you gave me? Well, it was because I was worried about having a weapon when I feel . . . ferocious sometimes. Like when something makes me angry, and that part of me wants to retaliate. And I've always worried that it was a sort of . . . darkness inside me. Is it, Mother?"

Lily suddenly felt anxious for her mother's reply. She had never voiced her fear so directly, and she wanted reassurance that it was unfounded.

"If you regularly incorporate love element into your artwork, Lily, I do not think you need to fear the Void yet, though all magic users must be extremely cautious of the darkest element. I think your ferocity is something else entirely, and it is something you must try to keep inside yourself at all costs until we reach safety. I'm sorry I cannot explain that to you further, but the less you know about certain things just now, the better."

Lily wanted to protest against deliberate ignorance. Hadn't she gone long enough without knowing anything? Magic users! Magic was real . . . unbelievable. Did that mean that all the fairy tales of powerful beings were true? Were there actually elves, mermaids, dwarfs, and trolls? Where then was the Forest of Ancients, the Grandfather Mountains, the Volcano Crescent? Were they beyond the Ropazian grasslands, or closer to Lily than she had ever imagined? Then something else occurred to her, something that was glaringly obvious now.

"Is magic the Anathema? Why do the desert dwellers despise it?"

"Magic is called the Anathema in the Joquobon Desert, for its people are not able to wield it and thus greatly resent it. When the witches and wizards of Ropaz produce non-magical children, those individuals are labeled 'outcasts' and sent to the desert to live out their lives. This is because the Joquobon is a land without natural magic, and so unwanted by magic users. For protection, and also out of resentment and anger, the desert dwellers forbid magic wielders to enter their territory without permission, just as they themselves are forbidden to venture into Ropaz without summons. Though I have scrupulously avoided using any of my magical abilities while living in the Joquobon, it suits Nather's motives to place suspicion of magical use on me now. We've been forced to leave the desert sooner than I'd have liked. It would have been easier for you if you had been given more time to grow up, but that is no longer possible. You have been kept safe, and that is the most important thing. Now the time has come for me to take you back home."

With her mother's epiphany about magic slowly sinking in, Lily was silent as they rode Bepo for the entire afternoon and into the evening, still heading north. While her mother focused on the well-being and direction of their mount, Lily eventually concerned herself with stretching and relaxing her aching body. This was no easy task, given that the journey seemed to become increasingly uncomfortable with every jarring, many-legged step that Bepo took.

She gradually concentrated on turning over the events of the morning in her mind, trying to make sense of everything that had occurred and all of the revelations concerning Lamoranth that had been made known to her. Lily also attempted to determine more practical concerns. How safe were they now? What had Phepin meant by pointing east without shooting his arrow? She felt overwhelmed. After a time, Bepo slowed to a walk, finally coming to a complete stop a short distance later and refusing to take a step farther.

Rose sighed, clearly feeling tired, and slid from Bepo's back. After giving the amadel an affectionate pat on his side, she turned and looked up at Lily.

"Do you need help getting down?"

Lily nodded as she unfolded her cramped legs and swung them over Bepo's side. She began to slide down, and had intended to hold out her arms for her mother's assistance, but found herself unable to move them from her sides. Lily's feet hit the ground and her legs buckled before she could speak a word. Her mother, seeming to anticipate this, caught her and broke Lily's fall, then slowly lowered her to the sand. She proceeded to take the haversack from Lily's back and lean her against the amadel's side, only then removing her own medical pack with obvious relief. Rose opened Lily's luggage and brought out the water container, carefully drinking some herself before giving Lily and Bepo a slightly larger amount.

Lily continued to simply watch her mother as she next brought out one of the loaves of bread, attentively tearing off a crusty end portion, the part Lily favored, and handing it to her to eat. Lily accepted it without comment. She could see that her mother was gathering her thoughts, preparing herself for the important conversation they both knew was upon them. They both chewed their bread thoughtfully, giving their bodies a much-needed rest.

At last, Rose swept the crumbs and sand from the front of her soiled tunic, seeming to brush aside her hesitation as well. She turned to her daughter, and Lily knew, in some strange yet indubitable way, that her life would never be quite the same after her mother spoke.

"My darling Lily, there is much that I have kept from you, quite a bit of which I still feel is unsafe to reveal. However, now that we are returning to our rightful home, it is time that you do know some of the things I have so long sought to keep a secret."

After a brief pause and a deep breath, Rose continued.

"Every fairy tale I have ever told you is truth. All of the magic, all of the races of magical beings, all of the places that they claim as their own, is largely fact. There are even some I did not speak of, for they were too close to the desert for me to acknowledge comfortably, such as dragons and vampires. Though their numbers are fewer than they once were, the dragons are huge, scaly beings who breathe fire and make their home inside Mount Brimstone. This mountain is only three hundred miles north of Jeridoff, an easy distance for any but their hatchlings to fly. The vampires exist in the Cave Kingdom, which is on the western border of Ropaz, where they drink the blood of witches and wizards for sustenance. We must be extremely wary of vampires, for they are powerful Void wielders living just north of the Magentay Canyons, of which you know due to the witches and wizards of Ropaz who are permitted to trade in Japeta. These merchants must make their way through those rocky formations to arrive at the Joquobon. It is through the canyons that we must pass to reach the grasslands of Ropaz. I have chosen this route because I wish to avoid the Volcano Crescent as much as possible, for the countless trolls who live in their molten depths are the enemies of the Fae."

At this point, Rose paused, looking at Lily's face as though to gauge her reaction. Lily was too busy attempting to accept the fact that, on top of dwarfs, elves, giants, tree sprites, goblins, mermaids, and all other manner of magical races and their homes of which she had always known but never credited as real, there had been other dangerous beings whose existence was now critically important to her life. *Vampires?* Would they want to drink her blood too? Utterly stunned, with no idea how she felt about the recasting of her world, Lily simply returned her mother's steady gaze and waited for her to continue. Rose took another deep breath and went on.

"Lily, you and I are fairies, and our rightful home is the Fae Wood. I was born into a very old family that always abides in Silver Court, one of the two royal cities established by the fairy race countless millennia ago. After I met your father, I went to live at Golden Court, which was and still is his home. I believe it is time for the two of us to return there."

At this mention of her father, Lily's eyes widened in surprise. It sounded as if she would be able to meet him soon . . . Her emotions felt tangled about the prospect. What would he think of a daughter who knew nothing of her heritage? Lily didn't have time to dwell on her conflicted feelings, however, for her mother was still speaking.

"I plan to turn east tomorrow, pass through Japeta for supplies, and leave the desert by way of the trader's route through the Magentay Canyons. From there, we will follow the southern border of the Ropazian grasslands, traveling well north of the Volcano Crescent until we see the River Ward. Over time, our people have placed many protective enchantments on this length of water, which flows from the Ocean of Fintilles west until it reaches Molten Mirror Lake, a body of water also well-spelled to keep the trolls out. These protected waters separate the Fae Wood and its inhabitants from the rest of the world of Lamoranth. The only way to pass through the dome of defensive magic by land, water, or air, at least without the assistance of either the Captain of the Court Guard or the Captain of the Waters, is the bridge city of Ford-upon-Ward. We must make for this town with all haste, and then on to Golden Court, the largest Fae city in the Wood and the location of an immense fairy castle built on the edge of the sea."

Her mother stopped speaking for several moments, as though recalling her homeland, seeing the trees and castle in her mind's eye in every loving detail, and her face grew wistful. At length, she went on, her voice lower and full of intensity, choosing her words carefully.

"If ever we are separated on our journey home, Lily, this is the route I wish for you to take. It is very important for you to make it past the Wardens and into the Wood, where you should then have little trouble on the road to Golden Court."

At these words, Lily finally stirred from her attentive silence. The mere thought of being apart from her mother, whom she had never lived without a day in her entire life, was too daunting to consider, especially now that they were leaving behind the only home Lily had ever known.

"Why is it so important for us to make it to Golden Court?"

"It is much more vital that you, rather than I, return to the Fae Wood alive," Rose replied. "Alas, though I wish to be forthright with you, I firmly believe that it is not yet wise to tell you why this is so critical, in the event that we are captured by the wrong beings. Suffice it to say that a malignant force gathers in the north, and I have reason to believe that this destructive being should not know of your existence for as long as it is possible. That is why I wish to use as little magic on our return to the Fae Wood as possible, to avoid detection by those who might be watching."

Though Lily was dissatisfied with her mother's answer, it also brought up another pressing concern on her part.

"Mother, if we're traveling through the rest of the world, the places in Lamoranth where magic is not Anathema, why can't we use it, especially if we are in danger? I don't really know how much control I have yet."

Lily's mother sighed, rubbing slow circles on her temples, as was her habit when she was worrying about something.

"I have told you before that the Joquobon Desert is a place without magic, which is why the witches and wizards of Ropaz find it a fitting place for the non-magical people of their race. They have many ways of detecting the amount of magic within the people who use it as they cross the grasslands, most of them unavoidable for us. You see, Lily, fairies are unique among the races of Lamoranth, because our very bodies constantly produce and hold magic. We are additionally able to manipulate the magic of this world where it exists in the elements, just as the other magical beings are able to do. We are therefore extremely valuable captives to those who would enslave us, which is why most fairies stay within the safety of the Fae Wood unless they are strong enough to overcome any opposition. By avoiding the use of magic on our journey, we will simply appear as desert dwellers much out of place, but largely undetectable while we do not actually conjure our magic. I believe the greater danger will almost always lie in using magic, rather than abstaining from it. It is one of my primary concerns that you have already demonstrated powerful magic, and that it may be impossible for you to avoid invoking it before reaching the Fae Wood."

As Lily digested this new information, she grew both uneasy and just a bit excited. From what her mother said, she was quite possibly a huge liability. What if she got angry and spouted fire from her hands without a thought? Then the witches and wizards in their vicinity would know where they were and might give chase, and these people were another thing altogether from the malignant northern force. On the other hand, it was quite possible that Lily was a reasonably strong fairy, and she considered this reassuring as she found herself leaving the desert, embarking on a journey through the vast magical remainder of Lamoranth. This realization, however, brought up yet another question in her mind.

"Mother, if there is no magic in the Joquobon, have I been using the fairy magic inside me to control the elements?"

"Yes, Lily, you have. This surprises me for a number of reasons. First, because most fairies' inner power manifests much later than their teenage years. The second is that almost every fairy born in the past several ages has grown up in the Fae Wood, or else, in rare instances, other magical places in Lamoranth, such as the Forest of Ancients among the elves. Thus all Fae for many, many thousands of years have been surrounded by magic outside of themselves from birth. As a result, fairies often find it easier to use that outer magic before growing to understand the magic within. You have discovered and begun teaching yourself how to use your inner magic completely unassisted, without the benefit of accessing any outer magic beforehand. I find this exceptional. You already have the sophistication not only to make glass, but glass artwork, a respected talent among the Fae. Additionally, your skill is evidenced by the considerable sandstorm you raised this morning, which made you merely weary. My final reason for surprise, which I tell you with a little reluctance, is this: though fairies have as many foibles and faults that result from our minds and emotions that the other races possess, we have but one great physical weakness. If exploited, it can completely debilitate all of our outer and inner magic abilities. Can you guess what it is, Lily?"

Lily was unprepared for any questions, due in part to the fact that this was the strangest conversation of her life, and also from the fatigue resulting from the day. She couldn't remember the last time her muscles had been so sore, not only her neck and arms, but even, to a lesser degree, her lower back and the area between her hips, under her large belt . . . and with that, Lily suddenly thought she had an answer.

"My jewelry? Is it iron that makes fairies uncomfortable?"

Her mother smiled faintly, though her eyes remained very solemn.

"It is far more serious than discomfort, Lily. Though I always knew that you would be strong, I could never have anticipated how much you would flourish, even alone in the desert with me. I have been forced to keep you a secret over the years by giving you a larger and larger amount of iron to wear. There were days when you would begin to glow with a soft white light, as all Fae children do, though you already wore bracelets and necklaces. I even feared, when you became a teenager, that you would realize that it was not the glare of the desert sun and sand that made your fair skin appear to give off a light of its own, though at that point you were also wearing anklets and armbands. I gave you the belt. When even that cumbrous item didn't seem to completely diminish the light of your inner magic shining through, I gave you the dagger, as well as the rings. I noticed that you wore them hardly at all, and I knew it was because you sensed their effect on you more than anything else I'd given you. As we travel through the magical lands of Lamoranth, you may have to wear some or all of your jewelry directly on your skin, for you will be encountering outer magic for the first time, and that after you have already gained a measure of control over your inner magic. I am sorry for this, for it will almost certainly cause you pain."

Here, her mother looked troubled. After a moment, she spoke again.

"Can you grant me forgiveness, Lily, for the iron I have inflicted upon you when you did not know its harm to you? That I will, in fact, ask you to continue wearing it until we reach the Fae Wood? For I see no other way to prevent your magic from being detected and keep you safe along the path we must forge."

Lily carefully thought through her answer, so that her mother would know it came from her heart. After absently drawing a pattern of circles in the sand before her, Lily responded.

"I enjoyed having the jewelry. It never seemed more than a bit heavy. I can forgive you, because you gave me the iron to wear for the same reason you have ever done anything for me: because it was ultimately in my best interests. If I must wear it under my clothes, then I will do so. I don't relish the thought of pain, but I'll endure it the best that I can. I promise you, Mother, I will only take it off if I am certain it is safe to do so."

With that, she looked up from her sandy sketches into her mother's face. It was full of relief, approval, and profound, unconditional love.

"Oh child of mine, how lucky I am to be the mother of a daughter so much wiser than her tender years. I have never been more proud of you, Lily, than I have been today, and right now. In the words of a well-known fairy scribe, 'May you go on as you have been though the rain will surely fall, and may the sun beam down to light the way unto your homely hall.'"

With that, Lily's mother embraced her, conveying something more, the feelings that neither of them had words for, yet both felt all the same. If it was trepidation for the journey ahead and the dangers in their new lives, it was also relief that they were going together and leaving a place disliked for a home where they could belong. When at last they parted, both mother and daughter were smiling.

"Well, Mother, I hope you remember how 'wise' I am when I'm complaining about iron every other step of the way to Ford-upon-Ward," Lily teased.

Rose laughed, a beautiful sound that Lily had rarely heard.

"You forget, my darling, that I will be carrying an iron sword and sheath across my back at all times for this venture, as much for protection as to quell my own magic. I found it useful seventeen years ago when I had to find a way to make sure my wings couldn't come out."

Lily's eyes widened in astonishment, and she felt her mouth drop open before she could prevent its descent.

"You have wings? *Wings*, Mother? Do you think I have them too? Or will have them someday?"

Rose smiled, then looked at the sun, whose dying rays seemed to surprise and even sadden her. Then she seemed to recall Lily's exuberant questions, and she smiled once more.

"Do you not remember your fairy tales, Lily? I tried to acquaint you with some of the history of our people in that way, though they were certainly not in the manner of lessons young fairies traditionally receive. Most Fae have one or two pairs of wings, which come with their own sets of magical abilities. It is largely a matter of how many wells of power, or inner magic depths, they possess. I have four wells of power, two that are deeply full of inner magic, and two in which my magic is more shallow, allowing me to fill them with outer magic when needed. As for you, I am certain you have, even now, a powerful pair of elemental wings. To be able to control fire, earth, and air elements consciously, and water and love elements with less awareness, is impressive for a number of reasons, as I have told you.

"Today, I actually briefly considered flying the two of us back to the Fae Wood, after the sandstorm made your power so apparent. However," and she held up a hand to halt the sheer jubilation that had shone on Lily's face, "I have decided against it. I am simply not strong enough to take your weight while I fly alone for any length of time. Drawing the attention of other beings is not worth the brief spurts of flying I would be able to manage, at least not until we are approaching Ford-upon-Ward and able to summon help."

"Is there any chance you could teach me how to fly now, Mother?" Lily asked, incredibly excited by the prospect of taking wing and soaring through the air. They would be able to reach safety so much faster that way!

"It will not be possible for you to fly yourself, my darling. It takes years for most fairies to learn how to fly, and even that instruction must wait until a fairy's inner magic has allowed his or her wings the chance to erupt from their upper backs. These wings are not physical, after all, but magical, and you must be allowed to grow into each pair of magical wings that you possess just as surely as you have needed many years for your body to mature. Even though you show obvious signs of being ahead of what is normal, your wings most likely will not conveniently break forth in the next few weeks. Even if they did, you would tire easily and often, especially if we are flying into a brisk eastern wind. That will certainly be the case as we near the Ocean of Fintilles."

Lily's extreme disappointment must have been showing more clearly than she meant it to on her face, for Rose smiled slightly, and just a touch indulgently, then gave Lily more reasons to set aside her sudden and fierce desire for flight.

"Even if you could fly, child of mine, or I could fly carrying both you and our packs, it would still be too dangerous to risk. In using magical wings, it is absolutely certain that the witches and wizards of Ropaz will detect us, and those unfriendly with the Fae will see an excellent opportunity to capture us. We are, after all, two ladies unguarded by any warrior Fae, all of whom have extensive knowledge in weaponry for the express purpose of protecting all within the Wood. I know how to wield a sword, but I have not a warrior's wings. It will be almost impossible to make our way home without confrontation or fighting once we have been in the air for even a short time, and a battle off of the ground is the worst place to match magic with witches and wizards: their strongest element by far is air. It is for these reasons that I would much rather risk a long, non-magical journey before a shorter, violent trip with failure being much more likely than success. Can I depend on you to keep your promise to me, Lily?"

Though Lily was disappointed, strongly and almost irrationally so, her mother was obviously much more informed than she was on what they faced, and Lily knew it made little sense to argue with the choices of the one person she trusted in all the world.

"I will, Mother . . . as long as I get to learn to fly in the Fae Wood!"

Rose nodded, a small smile once more playing on her full lips.

"Thank you, child of mine. I know this is a great deal to understand all at once, and I am proud of your perseverance in the face of such a challenging day. Would that you could have learned these things gradually, under more propitious circumstances. It is fortunate indeed that you are strong in more ways than one. And now, though I'm sure you are still full of questions, I believe we should rest as the sun does, and hope our amadel is up to another long canter in the morning. Try to sleep, and I will wake you when it is time to continue."

Lily leaned over and kissed her mother's cheek. She was about to wish her mother a good night when she recalled one question she really thought needed to be asked.

"Mother, did you see Phepin after he came out of the sandstorm? Why do you think he pointed that third arrow away from us, without shooting it?"

Rose frowned, causing the slightest of creases to appear between her eyebrows.

"I am not sure, Lily. Perhaps another warning of some kind? I will ponder this as I watch over your sleep. Sweet dreams, my darling."

Rose then gently kissed the center of Lily's forehead. Her mother's kind night-time words and kiss, the same she had given every night before bedtime that Lily could ever remember, soothed Lily as nothing else could. She looked out at the hills and valleys of sand completely surrounding her. The setting sun was just gilding them with a glorious array of colors, and Lily felt momentarily captured by the beauty of it.

For a short time, she watched the soft western wind create ripples in the briefly sun-tinged sands, destroying and rebuilding the landscape before her very eyes. If there was one thing about the Joquobon she would miss, Lily knew it would be the sunsets, which had never failed to lift her spirits. She waited until the sun had set completely, taking its colors with it beyond the horizon, leaving Lily in a darkened world of ordinary white sand once more. Feeling comforted by those familiar things, Lily laid her head down on her lumpy haversack, careful of her sore neck. Her last thought before falling deeply asleep was that the desert might have just a bit of its own magic after all.

Elucidation

Lily woke to the sound of her mother's voice shortly after sunrise. Though she was as groggy and incoherent as usual at this early hour, she became increasingly alert as Rose's words filtered through her semi-consciousness. She could hardly continue to slumber, after all, when reminded of yesterday's uncharacteristically varied and generally harrowing events, interspersed with almost completely unbelievable information. All of which was true, Goddess help her.

"Time to get up, Lily darling. I'd like to go as soon as we've eaten a bit of breakfast from your haversack. I think our amadel will be alright. Bepo's had a good night's rest and proven himself an admirable example of his desert-dwelling species."

Bepo gave a snort that for all the world sounded indignant, which made Lily smile even as she slowly attempted to rise from her prone position. Despite leaving her lumpy pillow, she found herself regretting even that much movement as her body seriously protested. Groaning, Lily carefully stretched her miserably sore muscles, then successfully nudged the haversack toward her patiently waiting mother. After a small repast with careful portions of their food and water supply, Lily and her mother mounted Bepo once more and resumed their escape from the Joquobon. Lily quickly noticed that her mother gently directed the amadel straight at the rising sun.

"You don't think we need to continue north now that we've shaken off Nather and his men, Mother?"

"Correct, child of mine. Though we could travel to Jeridoff to resupply and head east from there, I am reluctant to take a route that will keep us in the desert and within Nather's reach any longer than necessary. Jeridoff is out of the way, and we were last seen heading in that direction. I would rather stop in Japeta, as it is both on our way and a source of much-needed information."

"Information?" Lily asked, not sure what her mother meant. She would rather not see or speak to anyone regardless of where they stopped. It just seemed safer, given their fugitive circumstances, to avoid other people altogether.

"I have made a couple of friends over the years whom I believe to be trustworthy, a life-partnered witch and wizard from one of the Ethic-faithful covens, who can tell us important things about the state of Ropaz and the movement of races we might encounter as we pass through it. I would be especially grateful to know the recent activity of the trolls and vampires, for my intelligence is many months out of date."

Lily shivered just a little at the thought of encountering such beings. It was daunting to think that Nather could never hope to be as big a threat to her as many of the races outside the desert.

"Will we be safe if we can just avoid them? Can we go around the areas where they live?" she asked.

Rose gave a small shake of her head.

"Remember that we are going primarily through Ropaz, and witches and wizards are our greatest concern. While some covens adhere to the Ethic and worship the Goddess faithfully, many others are far less scrupulous. You should know that my greatest worry once we are out of the desert will be those very few wizards and witches capable of wielding the Void. Their pursuit of the darkest element leaves all of them corrupted by their greed for power. They are willing to obtain it by even the most unpalatable means, especially within the grasslands. It is their home and the place where they are at their strongest. We must be very wary of all Ropazians due to them, for I know not how to recognize friend from foe."

Lily's heart sank at the reminder of more danger. It put her in mind of the warning Phepin had seemed to give them in the midst of the sandstorm.

"Do you think Phepin pointing with his bow and arrow was indicative of the direction we should go or the way we shouldn't?" Lily asked. This was something they needed to decide sooner rather than later. With her hands loosely wrapped about her mother's waist, Lily could feel the deeper breath Rose took before answering.

"I have carefully considered the actions of Nather's guard and his use of the bow and arrows as well. I am still inclined to think that it was some kind of warning, for he and Chafa most certainly helped us multiple times yesterday. Unfortunately, we cannot ask him if he was indicating danger in the east, or rather pointing us in the safest direction in which to travel. I have decided to proceed with all possible caution to Japeta, as I've always planned. We can only hope that, even if Nather suspects we will turn east at the first opportunity, he will be slowed enough by the sandstorm to remain too far behind us. Between his newborn son and his responsibilities to his tribe, I think we can be cautiously optimistic that at this point, he would arrive in Japeta after we have already come and gone. Once in the Magentay Canyons, Nather cannot follow us, and we need worry about him no longer. So, child of mine, do you agree with my reasoning and this decision?"

Lily was both startled and pleased that her mother wanted her opinion on a matter of such importance. Though Rose had occasionally asked Lily for her ideas related to the healer's tasks that had arisen with the sick and injured of their tribe, Lily sensed that her mother wanted her to be more involved in their new life. After weighing what she knew against her instincts, Lily felt uncertain as to her reply.

"Well, we know that Nather can't possibly arrive in Jeridoff before us," Lily began slowly. "So it seems the safer choice, except that it will keep us in the desert longer than our supplies are likely to last. Taking the route north will also keep us from gathering information that might prove invaluable later. Nather must know about how far we can go. He has also probably guessed that you'd prefer a route through Japeta, because he and everyone else in the tribe know that you get your healer's supplies from Ropazian merchants there."

Lily paused a moment, then went on, a little more hesitant than before.

"Personally, I have this . . . feeling that Japeta is unsafe. Nather must be betting on our haste and our need, and he knows that you're smart enough to avoid directly heading in your true direction when your enemies are watching. However, if you're sure that Nather won't be able to precede us . . . I suppose I agree with your decision. I don't see what other viable choice we really have, except to head north right out of the desert and ask the dragons for a ride to the Fae Wood."

Lily briefly savored the image of soaring with amazing speed through the air on the back of a huge, magnificent dragon, a being who easily breathed fire that burned air-and-Void-element-using wizards right out of the sky. She had only been trying to get her mother to smile, but Lily was surprised by the thoughtful silence that met her rather flippant suggestion instead.

"More than six millennia ago, the fairies made a pact with the dragons, that one race would always come to the aid of the other, despite living on extreme opposite sides of Lamoranth, if their need was great. However, I do not think it would be wise for you and I to seek help from the dragons now. A mere three centuries ago, the trolls nearly made a serious incursion on the Wood. The Fae invoked the dragon pact, for if weaknesses in the protective dome were to be exploited, particularly on multiple fronts, the Wood and all of its inhabitants would be in great jeopardy. Of even greater concern was the fact that if the trolls found any measure of success, the witches and wizards of Ropaz could then also attack the Wood from the north if the defensive spells were weakened or damaged. However, the dragons did not come. They sent an elven messenger, who had been paid a great deal of gold, to inform the fairies that the dragons were too few in number to sustain losses in battle. The Fae managed to repel the trolls with the aid of the elves in their stead, though with much more loss of life than there would have been had our dragon allies heeded the call for help earlier.

"I think that if the dragons gave up their sacred pride and failed to fulfill the pact, no matter how long ago it had been made, then they really must be facing extinction. If that is the case, then I do not think they will help the two of us. They have already given up their honor, and have nothing else to lose but the last members of their race, who are nearly unassailable if they remain in Mount Brimstone. I do not think, even if the elder dragons allowed us near enough to speak, that we could convince them to leave that safety, for which they have made such a great sacrifice.

"I am impressed with your reasoning though, Lily. In all my years of planning, I never gave the dragons a thought. Other than the vague sense that they have become untrustworthy pact-breakers, I didn't consider them seriously enough to be a feasible option. Until fairly recently, though, they would have been. It is reassuring for me that your young mind may realize things that mine, encumbered as it is with certain prejudices and inclinations, may not. We make good partners, don't we?"

Lily smiled and gave her mother's waist a small squeeze of affirmation, feeling more grown-up than she ever had. She did seem to be making a good cohort for her mother so far. Hadn't they successfully evaded Nather and his men yesterday? Lily knew she should still be afraid of all the dangers that they faced, yet she couldn't help a slowly growing sense of excitement for the long journey ahead. She and her mother were fairies, full of magic, and they were going to their homeland at last. Lily would have a chance to learn all about her inner power and how to use it. Maybe she would be able to do something special, something that would benefit other people in some way. And what about her father? Perhaps she would meet the one she had always wondered about. Had she gotten her blond hair or golden eyes from him? Though her features were much like her mother's, Rose had gray eyes and shiny silver hair. Would her father approve of her? Come to love her? Lily realized that he might not even know she existed. Again she wondered about her mother's numerous secrets. What else didn't she know? What questions could she ask? Lily decided to start with easy ones first.

"How long will it take to reach Japeta, do you think?"

"I hope to make it in three days. If Bepo can maintain this pace and avoid injury, we should be able to reach Japeta by nightfall of the day after tomorrow. I think coming and going under cover of darkness will be best."

Bepo gave a huff as he cantered along, as if offended at the doubt regarding his stamina. Lily nearly laughed, but was too preoccupied with thoughts of their stealthy pass through Japeta. She wondered how they would buy food if all of the stalls were closed for the day. Would they have to steal again? Perhaps they could pay her mother's befriended witch and wizard for both tidings of Ropaz and the supplies they would need?

"Do your coven friends have a camping place in Japeta we'll be able to find in the dark? How do we know they'll be in the city and not back in Ropaz?"

Her mother didn't answer right away, and Lily wondered at the delay, feeling slightly uneasy. She was again reminded that Japeta was somewhat of a gamble in their plans, though they had just decided that it was a necessary stop. Would it be worth the potential danger if they couldn't gather any information about Ropaz, though? Bepo's many hooved feet and their steady rhythm against the bright white sand had lulled Lily into relaxing a little when Rose finally responded.

"For the last decade or so, the witch and wizard I've told you about, Gerrita and Thondir of the Ruchip coven, have considerately timed their trips to Japeta to coincide with the times of the year that Nather brings his tribe to that city. This is due in part because I am one of their best customers. Though our former tribe is not due in Japeta for another month or so, I know that they often arrive early and stay until all of their wares have been sold, which can take some weeks. There is a chance, then, that they may have arrived. Even if that is not the case, they are almost certainly on their way, and we will be able to meet up with them, perhaps in the Magentay Canyons. That will make our stop in Japeta even more brief, a fact that comforts me."

Lily accepted this, though a small part of her had been hoping to find a reason to avoid the potential danger in Japeta altogether. She gave herself a slight shake. Their journey would be long and full of obstacles. There was no way to avoid all of the things that could go wrong, and they would simply have to make the best out of whatever did come their way. Lily resolved to cease her worrying and ask her mother more questions. She hardly knew where to start. There had been so many revelations from the day before that she wanted her mother to elaborate on, and Lily realized that the greatest had been the fact that she was a fairy. Finally, a reason for her treatment in Nather's tribe, as well as her ability with the elements. Would she fit in among the other inhabitants of the Fae Wood, having been raised in the desert? Would she be taught how to use her magic by her mother, or by others? Rose had taught her how to read and write the language of the desert dwellers, which she knew was the same for the people of Ropaz, as were many other customs, such as their belief in the Goddess. Did the Fae speak differently? Would Lily even be able to talk to anyone? Lily found that she really wanted to fit in better in her new home. She was being given a chance to start over, and she resolved then and there to make the best of this extraordinary opportunity.

"Mother, I know that there is much you haven't told me for my safety, and I accept that. But is there anything you can tell me about being a fairy that I really need to know? I'm sort of worried about . . . what the other Fae will think of me when we get there. Will they think that my desert clothes and speech are strange? Can you tell me things like that?"

Her mother answered without hesitation this time.

"I have no doubts that you will be welcomed and accepted among our people, Lily. You will be shown a respect that the desert dwellers of Nather's tribe never gave you, something that always angered me, even if it was unavoidable while we were in hiding. It has shaken your confidence in yourself, even more perhaps than the iron has affected you. I want you to know that your concerns are those of the very young, which can, and will, be taken care of with time."

Lily had noticed the stiffness that had infused her mother's spine as she spoke, belying her anger. Lily decided to remain silent while her mother recovered from her small lapse in composure.

"The things I most wanted you to know about the Fae I conveyed to you in your childhood with the bedtime stories, my darling. I had always planned to teach you the basics of the Fae language along the way to the Wood, once you knew your true heritage. It is not, as many in Lamoranth mistakenly believe, an inherently magical tongue. The words themselves hold no power, and as such, I see no reason for you to be kept from learning them at this time. Would you like to have your first lesson now?"

"Yes, I would love to!"

Lily was elated. Here, at last, was something she could do to prepare herself for her new life. She could learn something worthwhile now that wouldn't be dangerous to know immediately, still outside of the Fae Wood. She waited impatiently for her mother to begin, squirming slightly in her cross-legged position atop their faithful Bepo. Her mother seemed to sense her eagerness, for there was a smile in her voice as she began to explain.

"The Fae language is more similar to the language of the elves than the speech commonly used in Ropaz and the Joquobon, which many different races have learned out of necessity, due to the size, population, and central location of the grasslands," Rose said, her voice taking on the tone she used whenever she instructed Lily in the healing arts, as well as other subjects that none of the other desert children ever learned.

"However, there are certain aspects universal to intelligent communication, and I would have you look for those linguistic tendencies and keep them in mind as we begin. I think it will be easiest to start by giving you vocabulary words and working on pronunciation, then explaining the most basic sentence structures. We can work on conjugating verbs after that. I want to see how quickly you pick up that much, and we can adjust your lessons from there. How does that sound?"

"Like a challenge," Lily responded with relish, "but I can't wait! Would you say something for me first, like a common phrase that fairies use? Please?"

Lily could hardly contain her excitement, though she realized that learning a whole new language was not going to be easy. She would probably still be far from fluent when they arrived at Ford-upon-Ward, but at least she would have an idea of what the other Fae were saying, and that would be something. Lily leaned forward over her mother's medical pack, the better to hear her very first fairy words. Her mother turned her head slightly to the side, and she smiled as she spoke.

"I love you, child of mine."

Slightly exasperated, Lily tried to mask her impatience.

"I love you too, Mother. I'll love you more, if that's even possible, when I can start speaking some of the Fae language."

Rose turned around, her eyes open wide in astonishment.

"Lily, can you understand what I'm saying right now?"

Lily frowned, confused. Her mother's meaning was clear, but . . . the sounds had been different to her ears, the words more lilting and fluid than any she'd ever heard.

"Yes, I can understand what you're saying," Lily responded, totally perplexed. "Mother, what's going on?"

Rose seemed to ponder her answer, still looking back at Lily with a startled expression.

"It would seem that you may have, or will eventually develop, wings of elucidation."

Lily sat back and digested her mother's statement for a moment.

"Well, you said yesterday that most fairies have one or two pairs of magical wings. Mine are probably elucidation and elements, right? It will be kind of nice knowing that ahead of time, actually."

"It's a bit more complicated than that, Lily. Again, I can hardly believe you could understand me, as young and as burdened by iron as you are, and in the desert no less. However, a pair of language wings, as they are also called, especially fully developed, is one of the more rare abilities of the Fae. I'll be interested to know, once we are in the Wood, and you are unhindered, if you can not only understand what is said to you, but if you can speak, read, or write the Fae language, or any language of Lamoranth. Some of those Fae with wings of elucidation have an instinct for the customs of other magical races, and there is a legend of a fairy who could even understand . . . Ah, but that is something that perhaps would be disastrous in the wrong hands. If only I could be assured that we would not be captured and tortured for information, then I would tell you so many things, with relief . . ."

Lily didn't know whether to be happy or terrified by her mother's words. On one hand, she had demonstrated another potential gift. On the other, however, her mother had now presented the possibility of torture, and that on top of mentioning enslavement yesterday. Just how many dangerous, un-Ethical witches and wizards lived in the Ropazian grasslands? Or was her mother thinking more of that northern force, which she had so vaguely alluded to before? Lily felt frustrated and confused, and her thoughts and feelings only became more muddled as she and her mother lapsed into silence.

It was only when they stopped for a brief rest and a modest meal of hardy vegetables and water many hours later that Rose spoke once more.

"Lily, your potential for wings of elucidation has added yet another layer of urgency to our journey. There are already aspects of your being that I find critical to conceal outside of the Fae Wood. However, if you carry an inherent knowledge of our people, secrets of our history, and . . . abilities that have been kept from the rest of Lamoranth, then your safety has become even more important than ever. I want to consider some additional methods of protection for you, for I am worried that my skill with a blade may not be enough with so many miles between us and home. I hope you will accept that whatever I decide is best."

Lily hardly knew what to say. What other protection was there? Should she feel guilty that the situation was so serious, that she was worrying her mother so much? Was there anything she could do to help? Lily's mind spun in circles, getting her nowhere. They spoke very little for the rest of that hot, windy day, and Lily slid off of their persevering amadel at sunset with her mind and heart just as confused as they had been since the earlier conversation. After another small meal of bread and some dried meat, Lily laid down next to Bepo, appreciating the warmth that still clung to his shaggy coat. After a moment, she wished her mother a good night. Rose kissed her softly on the forehead.

"Sweet dreams, my darling."

Lily was certain, even as she drifted off, that no desert dweller had ever spoken words so fluid or melodic.

Lily's mother seemed a bit more cheerful the next morning, clearly determined to keep Lily from worrying overmuch.

"Have a bit of breakfast, child of mine. We can finish off the bread and have some water before we proceed."

Lily was back on top of Bepo, inwardly complaining with verbosity, a very short while later. She wasn't sure who was more unhappy, her or poor Bepo, but they both attempted to endure their circumstances as her mother set a brisk pace east once again.

"I think we should begin your instruction in the Fae language this morning, Lily. Even if it turns out that you don't immediately require it in the Fae Wood, it will give you something new to occupy your mind for now. You have always loved learning new things, ever since you were a small child. You used to get into my healer's chest and go through all of the jars, smelling the herbs, feeling the texture of the barks and roots, asking me where they were from. It always made me wonder if you'd have healer's wings like me . . . But why don't I start giving you some Fae words? Knowledge without understanding or wisdom is no true gift, after all."

Lily was dying to ask about her mother's healer's wings, for she hadn't specified what wings she had when they'd talked about Fae magic before. However, Lily could tell, just by the stern way her mother was sitting on the amadel in front of her, that she wasn't going to get to ask any questions just now. Lily had learned early in life how to wait for the right time for certain things, and Rose usually rewarded her patience. She began to dutifully recite the lilting words her mother uttered, carefully and slowly, focusing on what she actually heard as opposed to the translations her magic provided.

Lily quickly became absorbed in the lesson. She soon discovered that if she pictured the word in the desert language as she spoke the corresponding word in Fae, she remembered it every time her mother used it after that. It was as though her mind had a comprehensive list of desert words in one long column, and she was simply beginning a new column and matching the new sounds to her base of knowledge. This method didn't always work, however. Lily completely stumped her mother when she asked for the Fae words for 'drought' and 'amadel', and her mother had to give her words that only approximately matched the meanings for concepts such as 'tribe' and 'nomad'.

Over a lunch of their dwindling food supplies, Lily wondered if it would be possible to question her mother further, but Rose kept up their language discussion, delving into the different parts of speech and word order in Fae. All too soon, they were continuing their eastern path, with Lily's mother insisting on attempts on her daughter's part to form very short and simple sentences. By that evening, she was struggling with the different verb tenses, but making notable progress. This was in part due to the fact that her mother often simply repeated whatever Lily said, and Lily could then understand where she had gone wrong each time and make corrections.

Rose called a halt to their travel shortly after sunset, and the two of them ate the last of the vegetables and a small piece of dried meat each. Their water container felt miserably light as Lily took the tiniest amount possible, wondering if her mouth would feel anything but dry and gritty ever again. Certainly her lips felt cracked beyond repair, despite applying a balm her mothered proffered at regular intervals throughout the day. Lily formed an indention in the sand to lay in, again next to Bepo, and then kissed her mother's cheek as she wished her good night. Her mother kissed Lily's forehead in turn.

"Sweet dreams, child of mine."

Lily fell into peaceful slumber the instant her head touched the haversack.

6 The Bane of the Fae

Rose's attempt at an earlier start the following morning was met with an unforeseen complication: Bebo absolutely refused to budge. Rose tried coaxing him to his feet with small portions of water, but apparently even amadels reached a point at which water alone was insufficient. Lily and her mother next fed him a piece of dried meat and a few of their remaining vegetables, which was almost all of the food they had left. By the time Bepo was satisfied enough to stand on his many legs and allow them to climb on his back, the sun had risen free of the horizon and begun to cast its blistering rays upon both sand and travelers.

For most of the morning, Rose continued with Lily's language lessons, though she seemed more distracted than the previous day. Their midday break served to cast a more definitive pall on Lily's learning, however, for they ate the last of their food and emptied the container of every last drop of their water. With nothing left to sustain them, both Lily and her mother turned their thoughts to the possible events of the night ahead. Japeta was now completely unavoidable, unless they wanted to risk finding food and water in the Magentay Canyons beyond. When Lily timidly suggested this, though, Rose slowly shook her head.

"I'm sorry, my darling, but we just can't take that chance. We would lose time skirting around the perimeter of Japeta, and it will still be two or three days until we reach the canyons from the settlement. We need supplies, at the very least."

Lily sighed. While she had known what the answer would be, she wasn't any happier with this decision when it was spoken aloud.

"I have also decided on a method of additional protection for you. Because it is now more crucial than ever to hide your magic while we traverse the south of Ropaz, I must insist that you wear as much iron as you possibly can. This will both eradicate any chance that your inner magic will flare and prevent you from subconsciously manipulating the outer magic that will grow stronger the farther from the desert we travel," Rose said solemnly.

Lily only just refrained from sighing again. More iron would undoubtedly be a heavy burden, and their expedition was already difficult enough. This did not sound promising.

"I spent most of the night considering several other possibilities, but in the end I did not feel that we could risk any of them. All other means aside from iron involve intricate and powerful magic or very special magical tools. We are still in the desert, and any magic we use so blatantly will prove without doubt that we are fairies utilizing considerable inner magic. The magical means of mind shielding are also time-consuming, involving the gradual build-up of a sort of wall around your thoughts, memories, feelings, and all else that resides in your head. I do not have the time to instruct you on such a delicate process, and it is almost impossible to shield the mind of another for more than an hour or so, or I might have attempted to do so for you. I see no other way but to risk thoroughly incapacitating you with the Bane of the Fae."

The Bane of the Fae? Thoroughly incapacitated? No, this was definitely sounding worse and worse. The sense of unease Lily had been feeling grew, her apprehension no longer something she could overlook.

"I am so sorry for this, Lily. If there was any way I could make this journey easier for you, I would, but it seems to be your lot to endure the hardships that often result from being gifted. It is fortunate that you have such resilience and courage. If you discover nothing else in the course of our travels, I hope you realize that putting forth your greatest effort often results in favorable or unexpected outcomes. I hope you also believe me when I say that, at least in my experience, being selfless, no matter how difficult at the time, is rarely regrettable."

Lily sat on the sand, completely still and silent, in the small bit of shade that Bepo afforded. She didn't know what to say, how to feel. She felt inadequate somehow, as though she could not possibly live up to the high standards her mother held her up to with such confidence. Lily had never really endured intense, sustained physical pain. What made her mother think she could wear a nearly lethal amount of iron for weeks, possibly even months, of living on the run? Could she really do this?

For several long moments, Lily wrestled with what her mother was asking of her. Why had she spoken in such a strange and almost distant tone, as if she were a chieftain spurring on fighters? Where was the healer who took away pain, or her loving mother who always had a gentle word and a soft touch? Lily struggled for several long minutes with this new side of her mother and what was being asked of her, feeling confused and a little upset. Slowly, however, Lily's logic reasserted itself.

She had already agreed, and actually promised, to wear the iron until she was safe. Lily didn't have to struggle with a decision she had already made and committed to, especially where her mother was concerned. She was really just testing her own resolve, searching for some reassuring thought to hold on to as she painstakingly made her way to the Fae Wood. Lily thought the idea of the Wood and the new life it symbolized might be a strong enough lure. She wouldn't have to hide her magic there, or live a life fettered and without prospects. Lily also knew that her mother would not imperil her life, would instead help her gauge the amount of iron that was necessary to stay both undetected and alive. With that, Lily knew she could do what she must, because she would not be alone.

"I have promised you, Mother, and I will not fail you," Lily said simply, her voice surprisingly steady.

Rose looked for several minutes into Lily's eyes, and it was her mother who finally looked away, seeming more at peace than Lily had seen her in a long time, or perhaps ever.

Without another word, they remounted their amadel and kept the intense afternoon sun at their backs, both now wholly focused on the night in Japeta before them.

XYDOLEM

SEVERAL HOURS LATER, LILY CAUGHT HER FIRST glimpse of Japeta over her mother's shoulder. The large, permanently erected tents shimmered in the desert's white heat. They were the first sign of civilization Lily and Rose had seen since leaving Nather's tribe. After drawing a bit closer, her mother brought the weary, enduring Bepo to a halt.

"I think we should stop here and rest," Rose said. "We've made good time, and there will be no sleep for either of us tonight. If you manage to nod off now, I'll wake you at sunset so that we can continue."

Lily nodded, happy for any respite she could get from Bepo's uncomfortable gait. She was afraid she might actually start dreaming of his six-legged canter soon. She also tried to ignore her feeling of disquiet about Japeta. It was only natural to wish to avoid danger, and the greatest hazards in their journey were running into people in general and sinister magic wielders in particular. Lily reminded herself that Nather was their greatest concern in the desert, and he couldn't have arrived in Japeta before them. Though her internal arguments were well-reasoned, Lily only managed to doze fretfully as the blinding desert sun beautifully closed another day.

She finally sat up, unable to really rest with their foray into Japeta drawing so near. After a moment of looking about, Lily caught sight of her mother leaning against Bepo's other side. Rose was just rolling up the scroll Lily had put into the medical pack in the midst of their hasty departure from Nather's camp. Lily hadn't given it a second thought, for she had been much more surprised by the sword and sheath at the time. Was that roll of paper some sort of map? Her mother couldn't have been writing anything on it, for Lily knew she had neither a quill nor a bottle of ink.

Before she could question her mother, however, Rose preempted Lily's curiosity by holding up one finger, silently requesting patience. She then began to trace designs around the tightly rolled scroll, and they glowed faintly before vanishing, seeming almost as though they had sunk into the paper itself. Lily realized that if it was a written form of the Fae language, she had not been able to read it. She looked back up at her mother with undisguised wonder. Rose didn't make her wait any longer for an explanation.

"You have just witnessed me placing a very special seal on this scroll, Lily. It is now impossible for anyone but the King of Golden Court to open. This scroll contains information I have gathered on behalf of the Fae, as well as an explanation pertaining to your life in the desert, that he will need to know for the difficult days that I believe our people must soon face. I have chosen the King because I know that once you are in his presence in Golden Court, there is no safer place for you to be," Rose said, watching Lily carefully.

Lily nodded, not sure what her mother was looking for exactly.

"This scroll must reach him for the sake of our people, Lily. Though I am loath to make you promise me anything more, I would have your word that you will do anything it takes to reach the Fae Wood and deliver this scroll to the King personally. I want you to be in his presence when he opens it, to guarantee that he knows its contents. Will you promise me, Lily, that whatever happens to me, if I cannot make it to the Wood to speak with the King of my sojourn, that you will deliver the scroll in my stead?"

Lily couldn't speak for several moments, she knew such terrible fear. How could her mother talk like this? How could she assume the worst, and deal with it so calmly? And how in the wide world of Lamoranth could Lily promise what her mother was asking? Lily tried to pull herself together, to look at the situation as rationally as possible. Her mother was merely preparing against the worst-case scenario. Rose was an intelligent, resourceful woman who had survived the last seventeen years on her wits alone. She was just being thorough, as she was in everything she did, from healing the injuries of others to calmly executing escape plans. Lily could just throw the scroll in her haversack and let it sink to the bottom, never to be thought of again, never doubting that her mother would live to see the golden fairy castle by the sea and take care of Lily along the way.

But Lily knew that this didn't truly encompass all that her mother was asking of her. Rose wanted Lily to accept her death as a real possibility, and to promise to keep living, even if that meant living alone. Even if that meant traveling well over one thousand miles in lands full of enemies whom she might not even recognize. The world had never seemed so big, and Lily had never felt so small. She raised her eyes to meet her mother's, summoned every grain of courage within her, and took the scroll from her mother's hand as she spoke the words she knew her mother needed to hear, and Lily herself had to believe.

"Mother, I promise that I will reach Golden Court, no matter what happens. If you do not make it," Lily swallowed hard, and then forced herself to finish, "for whatever reason, I will live to watch the King read your scroll."

Rose heard the sincerity in her voice, read the realization in Lily's eyes, and immediately pulled her into a fierce embrace.

"Thank you, child of mine," she whispered.

Lily wasn't certain how long her mother's arms stayed wrapped securely around her, but she resolved never to take her for granted again. At last, they parted, and Rose straightened her back before hefting the medical pack onto her shoulders. Lily carefully placed the scroll in her haversack, wrapping it in a spare tunic and situating it right beside her generously swaddled hand mirror. The empty water container went back on top, for Lily assumed that getting enough water for the next stage of their journey would be of the highest priority. As she lifted the single diagonal strap of her sack over her head and into place, Lily felt as though she had just put the weight of the world upon her own back.

Her mother was already seated on Bepo, his long ears cradled gently in her hands. Lily climbed up behind her mother, and they started off under the cover of darkness. The silence lasted a few long moments before Rose began to speak.

"Our first stop will be one of the two blacksmith's buildings. I hope to find pieces of armor that will be a close enough fit for you to wear. Then we will see if Gerrita and Thondir have arrived. If they have, we will barter medical supplies for their food and water. If they have not, then we will have little choice but to get water directly from the well and hope that it will be reasonably easy to steal some food nearby. Just stay close to me, and do exactly as I say. If we're fortunate, we'll be in and out of Japeta in less than an hour with no one the wiser."

After Rose had given her instructions, she lapsed into a concentrated silence, which Lily easily imitated. All too soon, her mother was slowing Bepo and gently steering him toward the southern curve of the settlement. Even in the darkness of the night, Lily could tell that there were very few traveling merchants currently camped in Japeta. Her mother seemed to be scanning for a particular tent or landmark. After a few long-drawn moments of slow riding, she shook her head in disappointment.

"They are not here," Rose whispered. "They always camp just across the road from the row of amadel hitching rails, in a striped tent. That spot is vacant," and she indicated the location with a tilt of her head.

Lily's heart began to sink. Already, the trip into Japeta was not going well. She strained to see a telltale black anvil in front of any of the permanent tents they were now passing, determined to accomplish one of their other goals. Eerily, not a single person was outside at that late hour. Lily was surprised by how unfamiliar she was with this part of Japeta. Usually, the children of Nather's tribe were all watched by a select group of adults within their own encampment, who supervised their tribe's youngest members while everyone else purchased what they needed, then came back and took their turns watching. Lily had few fond memories of such days, for she had never had anywhere to go to escape the taunting of the other children. At least she understood now why her mother had always refused to bring Lily along with her: she had been collecting information along with her roots and barks, herbs and spices. There were times when Nather had lengthened their tribe's stay to correspond with a desert trading fair, and it had been only those times when Rose had taken Lily around to see the food stalls and colorful displays. Lily hoped she would be of more use to her mother tonight once they reached that area of Japeta. It was then that Lily espied an anvil at last, situated prominently next to the door of a sturdy-looking, uncharacteristically square building, made out of a solid-looking, light-brown material that Lily did not recognize.

"Mother, an anvil!" she whispered with a mixture of fear and excitement. Rose nodded in agreement, then steered Bepo right up to the anvil and quietly uttered a few words in his long, floppy ear. Whatever she said, Bepo seemed to understand, for he stood rooted to the spot, looking far more alert than any amadel normally did. Lily's mother then beckoned her to the side of the building, where she coaxed open the shutters of a window without a sound. Lily watched in a state of mingled disbelief and admiration as her mother removed her pack and sprang agilely onto the sill of an establishment closed against the night, clearly ready to steal whatever they needed. Rose helped Lily up onto the windowsill after she had reluctantly parted with her haversack, and they both quietly dropped inside.

The first thing Lily did when she slipped down from the ledge was nearly upset a veritable dune-sized pile of beaten metal, which stood stacked on top of a low table almost directly beneath the window. Breathing her relief at the near miss, Lily watched as her mother began hunting through the pieces of armor that were scattered upon various tables spaced throughout the shop, pausing to pass a critical eye over several of them in the moonlight. Without further delay, Rose motioned for Lily to come stand beside her.

"Take off your tunic and leggings," she whispered on a breath of air into Lily's ear.

Lily immediately began undressing, taking off her belt and attached dagger so that she could doff her sleeveless tunic. Leaving on her undergarments, as well as her earrings, necklaces, armbands, and bracelets, Lily next removed her slippers, anklets, and leggings. Rose began strapping on the armor she had chosen as quickly as possible. She murmured the names in Lily's ear, as though this would somehow make all of it a little easier to bear.

"Cuirass," and on went a thin breastplate that connected to a covering for the back of her torso via leather straps over her shoulders and just under her arms, shielding her from neck to waist.

"Plackart," and Rose attached another thin sheet of iron to the bottom of the breastplate with rivets, effectively covering Lily's abdomen.

"Coulet," she said as she attached a smaller piece to the lower edge of the backplate, providing protection to Lily's lower back.

"We'll dismiss the fauld because it will inhibit your movements and won't fit under your clothing easily. I also think it would be best to skip all of the arm coverings, such as the pauldrons, couters, vambraces, and gauntlets, because of your bracelets and armbands. Now for the legs . . ." she said, turning to a different table and soon coming back with four more pieces.

Lily had been feeling all right up to that point. Though it was clearly much heavier for her than for the wealthy, high-status desert boy for whom most of this armor had been intended, she had been reasonably confident that permanent misery was not her lot for the width of the Ropazian grasslands. That optimism was soon crushed by "cuisses" on her thighs and "greaves" covering her shins and calves. Lily felt slightly ill, as though she had eaten something that disagreed with her, and her skin crawled with stinging pain wherever the iron directly touched her, just as the rings for her fingers always had. She tried to accept the pain, which seemed to be getting worse just gradually enough that Lily wondered if it was simply her overactive imagination at work.

"You're doing so well, Lily . . . almost there," her mother murmured encouragingly. "I want you to put your clothes back on now. We have been very fortunate here. The materials necessary to refine iron into steel are prohibitively expensive for desert dwellers to acquire, and so they only purchase them for the production of their short swords. They so rarely use armor that it was entirely impractical for these pieces to undergo that process, and while that makes for armor that is not as hard or durable, it suits our purposes perfectly. These iron pieces will have a much more potent effect on your magic than steel armor would have, enabling you to wear less than I'd planned."

Rose paused and considered for a moment, then nodded to herself and continued softly.

"I believe it will be fine to forgo the poleyns on your knees and sabatons on your feet. I think, however, that I will also put some of these small pieces that he has polished like the rest and roped at the edges in your hair wrap. I suppose they are sort of circular lamés . . . We really are quite lucky that this suit of armor has been fitted and finished, but not yet padded or engraved. Without any distinctive markings or embellishments, no one who sees this armor will know where we took it from, and hence where we have been."

Lily complied with her mother's request to don her clothes once more, surprised by how sluggishly her body was responding to what she wanted it to do. How was she going to run away from danger like this? She found herself worrying, even as she slipped her sleeveless tunic back on. As her mother rewrapped her hair cloth, now significantly heavier, Lily began to pull her leggings back on. There had been a bit of slack in the fit before, but they were more snug now that the thin pieces of iron armor added a layer to her legs, almost like a nightmarish second skin.

Lily was shocked by how the fairly loose tunic seemed to cover her thin iron additions without effort. She was so much heavier! How could a change so drastic be invisible? Lily tried to stay calm and collect her panicked thoughts. She grabbed her belt and sheathed dagger and cinched them back in place, then replaced her anklets and slippers, all the while trying to rationally work through the inchoate fear that constantly buffeted her. It was as if the mounting terror was trying to shape her into one of the star dunes so common in the northeastern part of the Joquobon.

She felt bad, increasingly so. Her legs had never been hindered by anything more than the anklets. Now, though, she felt as if she had been buried up to her hips in sand. Lily didn't know how she was ever going to breathe easily again, and she could already feel a serious headache forming. She tried to focus on the positive. For example, her arms felt about the same as usual. They certainly seemed more inclined to move than the rest of her body. Lily had been hoping that more iron would sort of feel like the aftereffects of the sandstorm she had created the other day. Sore muscles would have been manageable, even if they continued to feel like they had been seriously overexerted in the weeks and months to come. This, however, was so strange because she felt not only pain, but fear. Lily hadn't quite realized what a mental battle the extra iron would prove to be, and she wished there had been some way to prepare for this unforeseen complication. Before she could dwell on it any further, her mother was at the windowsill once more, motioning for Lily to precede her out and down.

When Lily was sitting on the sill, she was surprised and relieved when her mother grasped her waist and lowered her down, where she managed to stand without falling over. Mere seconds later, Rose was out, and the window shutters were closed. They put their bags on again and turned the corner of the blacksmith's shop to find Bepo still patiently waiting, seeming so attentive that it was almost as if he knew he had been guarding their packs and acting as a lookout. They climbed up on top of his indented back and were soon on their way to the very center of Japeta.

Though a part of Lily's mind wanted desperately to continue helping her mother, most of her head seemed to be battling the fear and pain of the iron. She soon quit looking out for the water well around which all of Japeta revolved in favor of retaining her lucidity. It was because of this that Lily didn't question her mother when Rose reached behind Lily and removed their water container from the haversack, then slid down off Bepo's back just a few curving streets before the water well.

"This ring has the largest number of food stalls, Lily. Just be careful not to wake up any of the vendors, because many of them sleep on pallets set up in the back room of their little businesses. Be silent, and try to grab only food that will keep for a while. After you think you have enough, stay near here and out of sight. I'll be back from the well with water soon."

With that, Lily found herself gently placed on the ground deep in the shadows between a bread stall and a jewelry shop, one ear of the amadel placed in her hand. Had her mother just left her? What was happening? Lily realized that she wasn't able to focus on her task properly, and that frightened her even more. What had her mother just told her to do? Lily stood perfectly still in the darkness, vision blurred, feeling faint. Slowly, she pushed back her fears and awareness of physical pain in order to recall her mother's words. Get nonperishable food. Quietly. Then stay put, presumably with Bepo. Alright, that wasn't so difficult. Hauling the water up from the depths of the well would have been much more so, Lily was certain. She turned toward the bread stall, wanting absolutely nothing to do with jewelry of any kind, perhaps ever again. Lily was vaguely surprised to find that nothing more than a flap of cured amadel-skin stood between her and several loaves of bread. With her arms still able to move and bend fairly easily, Lily silently snatched the three loaves closest to her, feeling only the slightest bit guilty amidst the roiling turmoil in her mind.

The next stall sold candles and matches, and the one after that appeared to be full of blankets. Lily wasn't as worried as she might have been ordinarily, preoccupied as she was with waging a mental battle with her emotions. The next little shop contained piles of vegetables and some fruit. Lily gladly shoved some of the longer-lasting varieties into the mouth of her haversack, too physically miserable to remove it from her back first. Fruit was a luxury in the desert. Lily didn't even want to consider the worth of all the things she was stealing. This, surprisingly, created a different, though smaller, pain in her mind, remorse she didn't have the energy to feel. Try as she might, however, Lily couldn't seem to dismiss the items taken from this stall as she had the loaves of bread. Their need was great, but that excuse seemed hollow in the face of endangering the livelihood of merchants she didn't even know. Without pausing to consider the consequences, Lily slipped off a fine, thin bangle from her right arm and placed it where the pilfered vegetables had been.

Just as she was leading Bepo away from the stall, Lily was bombarded by yet another feeling inside her mind. There it was, that illogical sense of dread at being in Japeta, back yet again. Lily tried to focus on that one very deep apprehension, to separate it from the fear and pain of the iron that was closer to the surface, leaving enough of her mind open to concentrate on her situation. She couldn't afford to collapse at the first true test of her endurance. Lily knew she owed her mother so much more than a paltry effort. And suddenly, Lily was certain that something was about to happen to her mother. She didn't know how she had become aware of this, or why it caused a huge surge of pain from the iron-dominated area of her thoughts. Lily just knew that she had to get to her mother, and get them both out of Japeta, right now.

Without stopping to give a thought to her mother's instructions, Lily began walking as quickly as she could in the direction of the water well, Bepo's ear still in her hand. She thought briefly of returning to his back, but quickly discarded the idea due to how impossible it seemed for her to accomplish just at that moment. After walking past three curving rings, Lily paused in the shadows at the edge of the circular commons, where the well was prominently featured in the very center. Her mother was standing with her back to the well, their water container brimful at her feet. But she was not alone.

Rose was surrounded by a dozen tall, hissing beings. They were little more than skeletons, hairless, with countless teeth as sharp as blades, and just enough stretched, mottled red skin to supply them with grotesque wings on their backs. What disturbed Lily the most, however, were the thick, twisted black ropes that wrapped around their torsos, necks, and limbs, so tightly that the oily black shine of their bindings seemed almost a part of their deeply crimson flesh. The very worst thing about the cadaverous creatures, however, was that they were threatening Lily's mother.

As soon as Lily comprehended what she was seeing, her mind made yet another radical change. She still felt guilty for stealing. She was still afraid of the iron, aware of the pain it caused her with her every movement, her every thought, and how it was debilitating her from the inside out. Yet Lily was absolutely certain that she had no greater fear, and faced no greater pain, than losing her mother. Nothing, no amount of iron, no threat of torture, no promise of enslavement, could possibly scare or hurt Lily more than the thought of living without Rose, the best mother any daughter could ever hope to have. And with this newfound certainty, Lily was able to push the effects of the iron, both mind and body, aside, for they would forever be in second place to a fear that went much deeper, a pain more profound in every conceivable way.

Lily cleared her mind of everything but what she should do about the unfolding scene, her worst nightmare coming to life in the darkest hours of the night. Lily listened, for the emaciated beings who had apparently ambushed her mother had begun to speak. Their words became a hissing, whistling distortion upon leaving their mouths, making them sound as sinister as their bodies appeared. Lily listened to their words through a pain-filled haze of growing horror.

"Long hasss the Missssruler sssssssearched fffor you fffairy Rosssssse."

"Yessssss, our masssster hassss been interessssssted in your whereaboutsssss ever sssssinccce fffinding out you were missssing from the Wood."

Her mother remained silent, holding her ground, clearly searching for a way out of her dire predicament. Lily hesitated, certain that her mother wouldn't want her to come rushing into the open.

"We will posssstpone your binding, Healer Rossssse, iffff you will jussssst tell ussssss what you have been doing in the dessssssssert. Chieffffftain Natttthhher sssusssspected you were up to ssssomettttthhhing when he reported you a missssing perssson yearsss ago, but he hassss never ffffound out what. Tttthhhough we contacted him monttttthhssss ago about the old report, hissss many messsssagesss ssssinccccce tttthhhen have not been ussssefful at all."

"You cccccccertainly didn't make a ffffffriend of Nattttthhhhher, Fffffae lady. He believed ussss insssstantly when we hinted ttthhhat you were an esssscaped criminal, and he told ussss all he knew about you, ssssight unssssseen. He wassss eager to sssssend hissss bird to warn usssss of your abrupt departure befffore giving you chassssssse tttthhhhhree daysssssssssss ago."

Lily quietly gasped at the mention of Nather. Could he really have colluded with beings such as these? Believed the worst about Rose and exposed her to these creatures? Lily was hit with remorse when she realized that they had never given a thought to Nather using his goffir to exchange messages with someone ahead of them on their escape route. With its plumage as camouflage, the bird of prey could have flown right over them and they would never have known.

Rose, still continually scanning her surroundings for escape, finally caught sight of Lily in the shadows. Their eyes caught, and her mother held her gaze for a moment, her silver eyes like moonlight in the darkness. Rose gave the slightest shake of her head. Then the barest of smiles flitted across her lips before she drew her sword from her medical pack and finally responded to the beings menacing her for answers to their questions.

"I have heard that xydolem are the souls of the dead who return to the living world by Void-binding themselves into a corporeal form. Surely, though, this is not actually done in a desperate attempt to save a surviving loved one from destruction? If such an incredible myth proved to be true, then I pity every last one of you. No afterlife with your mates or family, or no afterlife at all when the bonds that hold you to such grotesque forms consume and destroy you in turn."

A terrible shrieking and wailing filled the air, for nearly every xydolem around the well was enraged beyond reason at her mother's audacious words. They began to attack Rose at once, biting, slashing with the hooks on their wing joints, and clawing with their feet. Her mother began parrying their blows immediately, swiping at their bodies with the sharp blade to keep them at arm's length. She succeeded in giving one foe a deep slash on his chest, then nearly cutting off the arm of another. The xydolem, however, fought with desperation, anything to keep her words in abeyance, to deny the terrible fate Rose had uttered. Only one of the xydolem held back, one who was larger than the rest, and had a startling splash of silver skin across his chest. Lily only vaguely wondered if he was the leader, or if he was simply intelligent enough to realize that his efforts were not needed.

Her attention didn't stay on him more than a moment, however, for her mother began to fight her many opponents with an even greater intensity. Rose's skill with the blade was formidable, readily apparent as she caused yet another of the creatures to wail in pain. What was equally plain to Lily was that, however skilled a blade wielder her mother might be, she stood no chance against so many enemies. Lily still stood in the shadows, physically incapacitated but no longer controlled by the iron's fiery pain and chilling fear. She wanted, with every fiber of her being, to rush into the fray and save her mother. Lily knew nothing of fighting, of magic, of these xydolem, but for a moment, none of her ignorance mattered. She drew the dagger from the sheath on her belt and took a step toward the fight, absolutely desperate.

"NO!"

Lily froze, jerking her gaze back up at the sound of her mother's shout. Rose's attention seemed to be entirely focused upon the fight for her life. Lily took another step forward, more anxious than ever to do whatever she could to help her mother.

"STOP!"

Lily stilled, looking up again in time to see Rose glancing away.

It was at that moment when Lily knew she had a choice. It was very simple, and yet so painfully complicated. She could either keep her two promises to her mother, or break both of them. To stand any chance in a fight, Lily would have to remove all of her iron and try to control the elements around her, when it was clearly not safe to do so. She would then rush into battle with no real plan of action or likely chance of success, and then the scroll would never reach the fairy king of Golden Court. Neither would she. Neither would her mother. And then this malignant northern force, perhaps this Misruler, would continue to send the terrible xydolem after innocent people like her mother. Her mother, who had foreseen something just like this happening on their journey, and had told Lily clearly what her wishes were if it did. Lily had to live. *I promised her, I promised.* And in that, Lily knew what she had to do, or rather, not do. She could not fight. She had to watch her mother lose from the shadows, while a part of her own heart was annihilated.

The end came quickly. The blood-colored xydolem, sensing the approach of the desert dwellers they had roused from sleep with their screeching and wailing, rushed her mother simultaneously. Unable to fend them all off at once, Rose cut off a wing from the nearest frenzied xydolem, then struck out courageously at another, nearly severing its neck from its body. It was then that yet another xydolem attacked from behind, burying his claws deeply into Rose's unprotected back, a couple of them piercing her mother's body clear through. Rose's grip on her sword slackened, and her weapon fell to the sand, which began to soak up the xydolem blood she had drawn.

The people of Japeta were just beginning to arrive to investigate the noises. A few screamed in terror at the sight of the monstrous, shadowy forms of the xydolem, who took flight abruptly. It was as if they did not wish to be seen by the masses, even if only in the faint moonlight. Lily waited until she was completely certain the xydolem had gone, even the injured ones who flew slower than the others. When only a few Japetan people were milling about in the dark, confused and uncertain of what had just happened in the center of their home, Lily made her way to her mother's body, the ear of their faithful amadel clutched in her hand.

She could see that her mother struggled to breathe, as though she was holding on to life by the barest thread, waiting for Lily to come. Lily dropped to her knees beside her mother's heavily bleeding body, wounded beyond any help. Lily took her mother's hands in her own and brought her face directly in front of her mother's line of vision. Her mother saw her, tried to speak, and failed. Lily spoke to her, loudly and clearly, even as a pain too deep for words or expression altered her forever, making her feel irreparably broken. The iron she wore was only the vaguest discomfort now compared to this.

"Mother, I promised you. I will keep those promises, no matter what it costs me. Mother—" Lily's voice broke. A sob escaped her. And then she pushed the last words out, before it was too late. "Mother, I will love you forever."

Her mother's beautiful silver eyes seemed to glow for an instant, then they softened with love, accepting Lily's and conveying hers. Then the glow vanished, like a candle being snuffed out. As Rose's darkened eyes closed for the last time, her final breath left her lips, forming one short word on the barest of whispers: *Oak*. Lily barely heard, for she had put her ear directly over her mother's heart, listening for a beat in the profound quiet of the night. When the smothering silence had stretched interminably, Lily knew that her mother was gone.

Alder

Lily had just enough presence of mind to collect her mother's medical pack, bloodied sword and sheath, and the container of water, which had come at such a terribly high price. She couldn't afford to let herself fall apart here, now. Lily wanted to be alone, and she didn't want to be in Japeta, now or ever again. Lily started to climb onto the amadel, then stopped. She just couldn't bear to leave her mother's body behind. After returning to Rose's bleeding remains, Lily hesitated. She knew she needed to leave, before dawn, before any more Japetans woke up. Looking around, she saw that the few who had lingered were returning to their homes, dismissing the noise out of their own sleepy sense of security, and failing to see her or her mother in the night's intense darkness.

Lily waited until the last of them had gone, leaving the commons vacant, except for herself. She wanted, somehow, to take her mother with her. Finally, Lily decided to burn her mother's body and keep the ashes. The burning of a body was tradition in the Joquobon, though the ashes were usually scattered as laments were sung by the tribe of the deceased. Lily, however, would certainly not be scattering her mother's remains in this place. She summoned her inner fire, ignoring the peripheral discomfort it caused, and concentrated on her mother's body. Lily fumbled in her mother's medical pack until she found the few extra containers her mother had always carried along. She selected the largest of the empty jars, which seemed about big enough, and gently used her ability with air to begin sweeping her mother's ashes into the glass container. When none of her mother's body remained, Lily channeled the last of her ashes into the jar and replaced the stopper carefully. Except for a few scorch marks on the well-trodden sand, not so much as a drop of Rose's blood remained. Lily clutched the glass jar to her chest, against her broken heart, for several long moments. She watched as the wind blew away the burned sand, erasing the last evidence of her mother having ever been there. Then Lily reverently placed the jar in the medical pack, tucking it against the sword and sheath that still had xydolem blood upon them.

Lily climbed atop the amadel and rode out of town, her heart still aching fiercely as she left Japeta behind. The world was still cloaked in darkness, though Lily thought that dawn was nearing. All Lily could allow herself to think of was her need to continue east. She forced herself to focus only on riding, only on her direction, only on making good on her promises. Lily would not think about who she had just lost, or how. She rode through the brief remainder of the night and well into the next day, keeping all the pain in abeyance, until it was safe to let it run amok in her shattering mind.

Bepo stopped and refused to budge in the early evening. Lily gave him some water and a piece of bread, then forced herself to eat. She'd never make it to Ford-upon-Ward, and the Fae Wood beyond, if she allowed her body to grow weak. It was nothing more than reflexive action, however, and Lily soon realized that the needs of her mind could no more be denied than those of her body. Lily curled into a tiny ball next to the shaggy-haired Bepo, and she allowed the pain and despair that she had just managed to hold back to fill her mind and very soul as she cried endless tears and sobbed helplessly.

Lily relived the terrible battle, watching those huge black claws sink into her mother's back over and over as the pain of her loss grew exponentially. She couldn't survive this. This was not something she could endure. Lily felt as though her soul had been broken into pieces when the portion bearing her love for her mother had been violently gouged out. How was she ever going to hold herself together, to live with that gaping hole, long enough to reach Golden Court? Lily began calling in vain for her mother, like she had as a child upon waking from a nightmare, but nothing happened. She was alone in the desert where no one could hear her. She cried out again and again from the pain, begging her mother to come back for her. Lily could feel a strange, almost comforting numbness encroaching upon her, and her fear at the thought of having to live without Rose mounted, even as the numbing relief tempted her to succumb. Eventually, Lily's voice grew hoarse, then disappeared completely— yet she never stopped calling for her mother inside her mind.

It was just then, when Lily didn't know how she could endure another second of agony, that a warmth touched the outer reaches of her mind, then slowly came further inside. Though she felt lost amidst the pain and fear inside of her, Lily had to wonder at this warm visitor, who looked something like a piece of unformed glass, giving off the slightest hints of color around the edges. Softly, so quietly she wasn't sure she had really heard it, a voice seemed to emanate from the glass-being.

"Hold on."

I can't, Lily told it. *It hurts too much.* Couldn't it understand? She had lost everything.

"Hold on, please! I am here, I will help you."

The voice was stronger now, and Lily thought for a moment that the glass-being was male, and perhaps fairly close to her in age, though she didn't know how she knew. Lily felt him slowly making his way deeper into her tribal mind, past the outer, less prominent rings where she had pushed all of the iron pain and fear. He left a trail of warmth in his wake, making everything seem infinitesimally less terrible, forging a path of something like hope. The glass-being continued on, floating past her ring of recent memories where the battle of the night raged, going around other memories from the past few days without examining them closely. Lily had the sense that he was looking for something in particular, but was not entirely certain where to look.

Lily suddenly felt angry. He was intruding, and she did not want him here. She didn't want anyone to see how much she hurt, how much she feared.

"I'm sorry for entering into your mind uninvited. Just let me help you, let me go deeper into your mind, just for a while. I want to help you survive, to keep you from breaking. I can't let that happen, not when I've waited so long for you."

Lily couldn't understand all that he was saying, though she didn't see how he could possibly keep her from breaking when she already felt shattered inside. Lily followed his progress, but even his remarkable presence didn't distract her from the pain for long. It never seemed to lessen, never felt for one moment like it would decrease or become something Lily could tolerate. The glass-being was passing by the ring that contained Lily's bodily awareness now, and he seemed to struggle with her deteriorating condition.

His forward progress stalled again as he tried to pass through the ring of Lily's more cherished memories and accumulated knowledge, all of it irrevocably entwined with Rose. It caused Lily even more pain as she realized her mother would never again contribute to this part of herself. He gasped with worry and a fear all his own, seemingly shocked by the sheer enormity of Lily's loss.

"Please, don't give up! I see all the pain you're in, I can sense your fear, but just hold on, and I'll do whatever I can for you."

Lily thought this was a lot for a complete stranger to ask, yet she fought off the image of her mother's blood-soaked body, eyes closing in death, with the weight of her unfulfilled promises. She used those promises, her mother's last wishes, as a sort of shield against the temptation to give up. This seemed to work for a time. Lily felt the glass-being going ever deeper, past increasingly smaller rings that held her strongest emotions and innermost thoughts. He refused to turn back, though he clearly suffered. A part of Lily felt bad about this, but she had no idea what to do about it. She was beginning to feel upset with him again, for he was now moving into a part of her mind that Lily herself had never consciously considered or explored.

Suddenly, he came to the most prominent, circular place that shone with a soft golden light. At first, Lily didn't understand what she was seeing. She felt the vaguest embarrassment, though that was soon eclipsed by everything else she was feeling. The golden light was emanating from the tops of what appeared to be nine separate water wells, arranged in three rows of three, like a tilted square. The thought of water wells made her think of Japeta, causing another wave of pain to wash through her, weakening her resolve to continue her struggle with despair.

The glass-being was transfixed by the sight of the wells.

"A diamond of gold," he marveled, his voice filled with amazement and joy.

Lily felt simultaneously furious and relieved, on top of everything else. She was unbelievably angry that the stranger was so happy in the midst of the worst, the very darkest, hour of her life. At the same time, it was a relief to even sense joy through all of her pain, even if it wasn't her own. From the depths of the central golden well came a loud, rumbling growl, and Lily suddenly realized that the glass-being had just found the very core of her ferocity, the often-dormant turbulence that occasionally seized her when she was angry.

"Magnificent," the glass-being said, his tone both excited and full of respect. With a bit of reluctance, he tore himself away from that place in

Lily's mind and went further, beyond all that Lily really knew of herself. He went past all of the rings that circumscribed her nomadic desert mind to a place that was open and vast and indistinct.

Lily gradually became aware of him in a slightly different way. It made her nervous. Soon, before she was ready, he would be in a most important place, she was somehow certain. Then he would see the broken pieces of her soul, and the hole where her mother's love had so recently been. That thought caused her more pain than any she had yet suffered, and Lily's grip on her promises began to slip. The visitor passed with all speed through her mind's uncharted plains and further yet, to a place that had trees as Lily imagined them to be. He cast about anxiously amidst the blurry stands of trees, desperately searching, knowing Lily could do no more all alone. He came upon a small dappled mirror of space and gasped, utterly stunned. The glass-being had arrived at last.

He saw Lily's perfectly spherical glass-like soul, brilliantly colorful around the edges and full of golden light in the center. He seemed to realize that this was her final struggle. He saw, with all of Lily's painful clarity, the image of her mother's bloody body, eyes closing in death, which was battering against her soul, causing many small cracks in the glassy surface. And then he spoke to Lily directly, soul to soul, in words brimming with emotion.

"Nothing is missing."

Lily didn't understand, and she wanted more than anything to give up. It would be a relief to stop feeling altogether, there by the tree partially shading the cloud-filled reflection of a blue, blue sky.

"Nothing is missing," he repeated. *"You are still beautifully whole. Do you know what that means? I went past your mother's battle earlier, I heard your last words to her. You think there is a gaping hole inside of you, that you have lost your mother's love because she is dead. But that isn't true. Nothing can take away the love she gave you all of your life, that you hold inside of you, here in your soul. I see it. I see your soul, cracked from pain and fear, but complete. You have the most beautiful soul I could ever imagine. If you really will love your mother forever, then somewhere, somehow, she will love you forever too."*

And suddenly, Lily knew that he was right. No xydolem, no Misruler, no one and nothing in Lamoranth or beyond, could ever take her love for her mother away. Her love was timeless, eternal. She would always have her memories, would always be able to cherish them and the love her mother had given her. Lily reached for those memories and pulled them close. Her mother, head tilted back in a rare laugh, happiness in her eyes at something clever Lily had said. Her mother the healer, who would never hesitate to bind a wound or give Lily words of comfort when others were cruel. Her mother the warrior, who had faced those xydolem squarely and without fear, to keep Lily safe and to give her a chance to live.

Lily's soul began to glow, and the image of her mother's dead body slowly floated off, back to the concentric circles of her mind. It was not forgotten, but it was now without the power to shatter her with unbearable pain and loss. Lily knew that she could never see her mother alive again, and the pain of that realization was immense. Now, however, she knew that she hadn't lost the most important things: their mutual love and their bond as a mother and daughter. Strengthened by that knowledge, Lily believed she could live on, continuing to feel the love that had always connected them, stretched less than gossamer thin with immeasurable distance though it was now.

Lily focused her attention on the visiting soul, wondering how she could ever thank him enough. Though the cracks in her own soul hurt terribly, she tried to convey her gratitude to him.

I'll be able to keep my promises to my mother because of you, Lily told him, and she hoped he understood what that meant to her.

He seemed suddenly very shy.

"I was so afraid. I thought I was going to lose you before we'd even met. I heard you screaming . . . and I knew I had to try to find you, to help you if I could. I'm not even really sure how I got out of my body. I was so desperate to get to you that I didn't pay attention. I can just barely sense it, still sleeping at home. Where are we, anyway?"

Lily could hardly believe that this total stranger had gone to such lengths for her. She worried about his body. Would he be able to stay alive without his soul? Would he just sleep until his soul returned? Lily was deeply troubled at the thought of him in so much danger because of her. Then she realized that he had asked her a question, and she was rudely not answering.

We're on the edge of the Joquobon Desert.

Lily felt his astonishment at her reply.

"This situation should be impossible for so many reasons. I've heard of Fae who could leave their bodies in dire need, but it happens very rarely, and never over such a vast distance. I must be a thousand miles from my body!"

Lily suddenly wondered, a bit uneasily, who and what he was, and where he called home. Here he was, in her mind and in the presence of her very soul, probably able to read her like an unrolled scroll, and she knew nothing about him at all.

"A moment ago, you were feeling worried, and now you seem uneasy. What's wrong? Is it because of me?"

Lily could sense that he was anxious, and she hastened to reply.

I was worried about your physical form, and I didn't want you to endanger yourself because of me. I guess I'm uneasy because . . . well, I've never met another soul before, and no one has ever been in my mind except me. I was wishing I could know more about you, since you probably know everything about me by now.

"Oh, definitely not," he quickly reassured her. *"Mind-reading, in the sense that a person's memories, thoughts, feelings, abilities, and other functions are organized like an ink-written work and are as easily understood is a complete myth. How often do we even know our own minds when it comes to making a decision, for example? I sort of got visual impressions of the things that were consciously bothering you when I was near them, and while I'm in your mind, I feel your emotions almost as strongly as I'd feel mine in my own body. But even now, with my soul so close to yours, I can't really tell what you're thinking until you project it at me deliberately. I felt all of your pain and fear, but I didn't know the cause until I got to the heart of the matter, so to speak. How does your soul feel, by the way? Some of those cracks are rather large . . ."*

He trailed off, seeming a bit uncomfortable, as if he'd asked too personal a question. Lily didn't feel offended, though. He was the reason she wasn't in pieces, after all.

Well, it's like you said. I'm still whole, and that's because of you. The cracks I can live with. Maybe I'll even be able to fix them, someday, when more of this pain goes away. But thank you, so much, for saving me. My mother's death would have been for nothing if I hadn't lived through it.

Though Lily was definitely feeling pain at the thought of failing her mother and breaking her promises, she hoped he could also feel the depth and breadth of her gratitude. Her soul began to glow just a bit, and it surprised her as much as it did him. Lily had always been aware of her soul in a general way, but she had never been *this* conscious of it. She had never actually explored this deeply inside of herself before, to the core of her very heart. Lily could feel his emotions, as varied and conflicting as her own, as his soul glowed a bit as well.

Suddenly, a fine golden thread slowly spun itself out of Lily's soul, steadily approaching her unexpected rescuer. Lily could sense his shock, as though he couldn't quite believe what was happening, followed by happiness so monumental that she felt just a little humbled by it. A thin silver thread began to spin itself out of his soul, and Lily could clearly detect his intense longing, though she didn't understand why he felt it. After a moment, their respective threads met in the middle of the intervening distance between their souls and started twisting around each other in tight spirals. When Lily's thread had spun and twisted itself across the entire distance between them, it gently pushed through his corona of colors and latched onto the glass-like center of his soul. Lily was immediately able to feel his emotions with greater clarity, and she was also able to understand, somehow, what kind of person he genuinely was, without any modesty or prevarication. He was very patient, and deeply kind; a bit reserved, but quietly generous. His word was his honor, and his honor was sacred. He was truthful, protective, and profoundly trustworthy. Lily thought he was extraordinary. Though the cracks in her soul ached, fresh open wounds that would be slow to heal, Lily thought she might be all right in the future, especially if there were more people in the world like him.

Just as Lily came to this realization, his thread latched softly onto her own spherical soul. Though she didn't know if he understood her better now too, Lily felt a sense of commencement, the beginning of something important. Here was the foundation for something solid, as promising as a day that started with a beautiful sunrise, silent but colorfully brilliant. Lily felt that things were as they should be, and it comforted her in ways she could never have imagined before.

Both souls were quiet for a time, not wanting to alter anything with words. Finally, Lily bestirred herself, knowing that life had to go on, even if she would never forget what had just happened as long as she lived. Had she just begun a life-long friendship? She hoped so, wished with all she had left that she wasn't alone after all.

What just happened? We are connected . . .

"We just had our first bonding . . . experience," he said, his voice soft with awe.

Is it a fairy custom? What does it mean for us now?

"I believe . . . that it is a communion of souls. The Fae definitely bond this way, but I can't speak for other races of Lamoranth in this regard. We are certainly . . . true companions now."

Lily could tell that the term 'companions' wasn't quite right, but she felt too much pain and fatigue to examine her tie to this newcomer any further. She did want to ask him questions, to begin trusting him, but she wasn't sure where to start. Lily could sense a mixture of emotions from him, including some uncertainty, and she finally landed on something to say.

My name is Lily. I will always proudly be the daughter of a healer and fairy called Rose. It's so good to meet you.

Lily felt his shock at her words, as well as a tenderness, and admiration.

"My name is Alder. I am the pupil of Pine and Iris, both beloved. My parents are Linden and Hyacinth, whom I respect and obey." He hesitated, then inquired, *"May I ask how old you are, Lily?"*

Lily could feel his deep contentment as he spoke her name, as well as considerable curiosity.

I am sixteen years old, she answered, wondering why that was the first question he had chosen to ask. She herself had just recalled, with concern, that he was endangering his body.

Shouldn't we be worrying about your body now? If something happens to you because of me . . .

"Well, I don't know exactly how I left, so now I don't really know how to get back, either. I sort of cast myself out and followed the sound of your . . . voice. It took me a while. I'm not sure that I can find my body when it won't be calling for me, especially since it's so far away. The Joquobon!"

Lily could feel his astonishment, and just a tiny bit of pride. He didn't seem overly worried, however.

Alder, isn't this a potentially dangerous situation for you? What can I do to help keep you alive?

"Don't be anxious, Lily. Iris has healer's wings, and it is easy for her to magically help fairy bodies in many forms of distress. I think it is possible to live without one's soul, at least for a time, though why anyone would want to under ordinary circumstances is beyond me. She will watch over my body and be able to keep me healthy, at least for a month or so, until I am able to return. You don't mind traveling to the Fae Wood, do you? What did you promise your mother to do? I might be able to wait if you need to do that first . . ."

Lily ached at the thought of explaining her promises, for that would force her to think of her mother and their last days together. At this point, however, she believed Alder had a right to know, stranded as he was in her mind. Lily slowly pulled the events of the last several days from one of her outer rings, the one with her short-term memories, carefully showing him all of the conversations she'd had with her mother about fairies and magic, Lamoranth and danger. When she got through the xydolem battle and finally to his arrival, Lily let the memories float back into place within the desert of her mind. She could feel that Alder was stunned by much of it, though he was also clearly thinking all of it over very carefully.

"You didn't know you were a fairy until four days ago?"

My mother thought that it would be dangerous if I knew too much about myself. You saw how she would cut herself off, stop speaking, when she thought something important could be tortured out of me by wizards in Ropaz or that 'malignant force.' Do you think she meant the Misruler that the xydolem mentioned?

Alder hesitated, as though he wasn't sure of his answer.

"I have heard only whispers about the Misruler. If that is the evil in the north, and I think it probably is, then your mother must have known something about it to which few others are privy. Perhaps that is what she wrote about in the scroll. Lily, I . . . have begun to put certain things together, though much of this entire situation still baffles me. I will share some of my ideas with you on these matters, if you wish. I only hesitate to say some of what I know with certainty because of the reasons your mother gave. If only I had my body! I would be able to protect you on your journey, and be completely open with you."

Alder was clearly projecting wistful and anxious feelings. Lily thought about what he had said, and although she realized that Alder would be able to satisfy her curiosity about being a fairy and living in the Fae Wood on a number of points, Lily knew it would be just as dangerous for her to know those things now as it had been all of her life. Perhaps even more so now, as she would be traveling alone, at least physically so, for a number of weeks. Lily hadn't yet thought about the fact that she now had to complete the majority of this journey by herself, and she struggled to accept it now, knowing she would be leaving the desert quite soon, perhaps forever.

"Lily, are you upset with me?" Alder asked, misinterpreting the reason for her feelings.

I still have so far to go, Alder, and now I have to do it without my mother. How will I ever make it? What if I can't deliver the scroll as my mother wanted? How can I protect myself in Ropaz, especially with all of this iron on? It's really going to slow me down. You saw how I was around the market stalls, so unfocused and weak . . .

Lily could actually see Alder's soul shudder when she mentioned the iron jewelry and armor. Then she felt him summon courage and reassurance before he replied.

"Lily, I will be with you the whole time, so you'll never be completely alone. I can't protect you with my warrior's wings or . . . other abilities, but we can fully utilize my soul's knowledge and training on this trek. I've completed

a mission in the grasslands of Ropaz with a select group of Wardens, and I've been to the Forest of Ancients several times. I'll do everything I can to get you through this. Then you can present yourself at Golden Court and fulfill your promises to your mother. I am most anxious to get you there, where you can take all this iron off. Lily, . . . I truly find it unbelievable how much iron you can tolerate. The Fear has failed to penetrate anywhere except that peripheral desert-like area of your consciousness. It takes a very strong mind and soul to exercise that kind of control. I think as we travel that it should be one of your top priorities to remain completely aware of where and how much the iron is affecting you. Seeing as I will be in your mind for the duration, I'll keep watch on the Fear's inner status, but you'll have to pay attention to your body's response to the pain that it causes. Does this sound like a good strategy to you?"

Lily was relieved that Alder would be able to help her in the difficult days and weeks ahead. It was a huge comfort that he would know what to do at times when Lily would be at a loss. She wondered, however, why he was so unaware of her body. She was still fully in control, simply from a new perspective. Lily had allowed her body to sort of fall asleep shortly after their bonding, in order to rest up for another long day of amadel riding. She also knew that dawn was near, and she would soon rise and make for the Magentay Canyons.

Alder, if you're not aware of my body, will I just have to tell you when I see a potentially dangerous situation? I'd like to have a plan for disasters ready before I start riding.

Lily could tell he was pondering the problem, and she kept silent as he thought it through.

"I am only aware of your mind, not your body, at the moment. However, your mind and soul control your body from somewhere in your head. I think I may have passed it in my rush earlier . . . So if it won't bother you, I might float about until I relocate the part of your mind that absorbs and controls your sensory awareness. When you wake up and start riding, how about I move around until I become accustomed to how your mind works?"

Though Lily still felt a bit nervous about giving someone free rein within her mind, she knew that she could rely upon Alder. He not only needed her to succeed to return to his body, but she could also clearly feel that he had her best interests at heart. Hadn't they made a bond of friendship almost immediately upon meeting? As lonely as Lily had been in her life thus far, she knew that she had never needed a friend more than she needed one now. She would have to learn how to trust him.

That's fine with me, Alder. It's about time to get up anyway. If we make good time, I think we should be seeing the Magentay Canyons by the end of the day.

Lily detected a surge of happiness from him, so she decided to project her curiosity about it in his direction and see if Alder would explain.

"Well, you just started thinking in terms of 'we', instead of 'I', and that made me happy. I feel joy every time you say my name, too."

He was feeling shy and a bit hesitant again. Lily felt a tenderness for Alder begin to flower in her soul, and she started to emit a soft golden glow once more. Lily thought that he was sweet, but she didn't think most beings of the male persuasion wanted to be thought of as sweet, so she wasn't sure what to say to him.

I don't feel so alone anymore, I guess that's why I started thinking of 'us'. Alder, I think I'm going to set myself little goals, to keep myself focused on what's possible day by day, rather than the journey as a whole. If I ever let myself dwell on the entire one thousand miles, I think you'll have to distract and encourage me, just like if my iron trouble starts to get out of hand. Will you help me with those things?

"I'll be right here. Just let me know, though, if ever you think I'm being too authoritative . . . Male Fae are always strongly cautioned against the tendency to be domineering. Most of us have warrior wings, and that comes with a certain . . . sense of command and obedience. I'm fairly powerful, and perhaps a little too accustomed to being obeyed as well. I hope you'll speak up if it bothers you. Perhaps we could start traveling soon? The faster you get to the Fae Wood, the happier I'm going to be. What's the name of this animal we're going to ride, by the way?"

Lily didn't answer right away. She had just caught herself wishing that her mother was here now so that she could ask all the questions about the mysterious other gender she had never voiced. Alder was worried about ordering her around? She wondered how he compared to someone like Nather . . . The desert men had rarely respected her and had never been kind. It had been a source of sadness for her for years, but Lily felt hopeful for the first time in quite a while. Her unique new companion seemed much more considerate than she was used to being treated . . . Lily was pulled from her thoughts by Alder's slowly growing nervousness. Hadn't he asked her a question?

Sorry Alder, I was just thinking about my mother and . . . some of the things you just said. I'd really like it if you felt a little more comfortable with me, because so far, I think you're amazing. It surprises me every time you feel worried about my reactions, because you've done nothing but help me and be patient. Truly, you are one of the best people I've ever met. I'm just a bit of a mess right now, and apparently being rather rude. What was your question again?

Lily watched as his soul started to glow considerably.

"Oh, I just asked about the strange beast you've been riding. I'm sorry if I seem so nervous around you . . . I'm not used to being this open with anyone, even my parents. Usually I mask my emotions from others quite a bit, except for Captain Pine and Iris. Generally, though, I'm perceived as rather aloof. I always knew I'd have to let down my guard considerably when I . . . made a friend like you. It's just that our situation hasn't allowed me to do it gradually. I just don't want to make a mistake with you, that's all. I'm glad that our first meeting has gone so well. I already think highly of you as well . . . so loving, so strong. To take your promises so seriously . . . I feel honored, even now, to know you. I'll try to relax more, it just might take me a bit of time."

Lily was surprised, and pleased, in turn. He felt honored to know her? How strange, and wonderful, to be both liked and respected just for being herself. The Joquobon seemed easier to leave, somehow, knowing that Alder was at the end of her arduous travels. One more reason to make it to the Fae Wood, to get up and push on every day . . .

Thank you for saying that, Alder. I'll be happy when you feel able to relax, especially as you are a guest of sorts. As for now, I really think we ought to try to ride out of the desert today. I have no idea if we'll still be able to communicate this easily, but if not, I'll come check on you later and make sure you've found my eyes and ears. Is that agreeable to you?

"Oh certainly. Have a good morning, Lily."

Lily then woke herself up and took careful stock of the sand and sky about her. Bepo seemed to be rested and ready for another long day. She gave him some water, then ate a small meal herself out of the haversack. Lily decided to consolidate her bags, so she took the medical pack, first removing the sheathed sword, and leaving only the medical supplies and her mother's ashes within, put it inside the bigger haversack, where she had already stowed the water container once more. The sword and sheath she slung sideways across her body, then put the haversack on over top, strapped on the opposite shoulder. The sword's iron weight registered on her body and mind, but Lily was able to keep the additional Fear and pain under tight control. She had only to think about her mother to determine how shallow the effects of the iron were upon her by comparison. Finally, Lily climbed onto Bepo's scooped back, took careful note of the sun's position, which was just now reaching above the horizon, and steered him directly at the dawn.

Out of the Great White Desert

A few hours later, Lily began to wonder about how Alder was doing. She could sense his presence in her mind, so she decided to try to talk to him while still riding and observing her surroundings.

"Alder, can you hear me?"

She paused, startled by the raspy hoarseness of her voice, and also to listen for him. Lily thought she might have heard a response, but she wasn't entirely certain. She thought about the times when she occasionally argued with herself and tried to bear that in mind as she tried again.

Alder? Have you found my body's senses yet?

"Yes, just a little while ago. They're in one of the middle circles, near your long-term memories. I thought the sand was going to blind me, figuratively speaking. It's so white! The edge of the Fae Wood has beaches along the Ocean of Fintilles, but the sand is much darker. It is sort of tan, an almost light brown color. I know a few artists who would give much to have sand of the Joquobon's quality."

Lily thought about her own ability to make glass out of the elements, and she wondered if that was the kind of art to which Alder referred. She suddenly wanted to make one more statue in the Joquobon, a memento to carry with her wherever her life might lead. Lily wanted it to be of her mother, a tribute to Rose and a lasting image that Lily could keep, even if her memories faded over time. She wondered if it would be safe. They weren't in Ropaz with all of its witches and wizards yet. Even if any were traveling through the canyons, they probably weren't close enough to either their powerful grassland home or her isolated place in the desert to detect her. There had been very few of them in Japeta, so this might not be the time of year in which the merchants were attempting long-distance trade. Her mother hadn't chastised her for conjuring that sandstorm when only the desert dwellers could see, for they couldn't detect Lily's power at all. She decided that it was safe enough to try, for the work she was already shaping in her mind wouldn't take long.

Lily gave Bepo's ears a gentle tug, and he immediately slowed and came to a stop. Lily slid off his side, then took her half-full, medium-sized bag of wood ash out of her haversack. She was happy now that she had decided to bring it, and she sat with it on the hot desert sand. Lily was more in tune with Alder now, and she could sense his curiosity about her actions. Usually, Lily grasped a handful of ash and sand each, then, bringing her hands together, summoned the fire to her hands to begin a piece of glass. She would then use one hand at a time to lift and add the proper amounts of her ingredients, firing them as needed and using air around her to shape and detail her piece. Lily didn't know how her iron accessories and armor were going to affect her capability with the elements, at least not now, when she wasn't desperately fleeing for her life, so she proceeded with caution.

She attempted to draw the familiar ability from inside herself, deciding that it might come out of her iron-free hands more readily than most of the rest of her body. Lily felt the pain in the outer areas of her tribal mind immediately flare up and intensify, but it was just bearable. She began to search her memories for one particular day, a year or so ago, when she had made her mother smile and laugh.

Rose had asked Lily to do some extra chore or other, and Lily, desirous of some time for herself at the end of that day to work on her art, had displayed an uncharacteristic show of rebelliousness. "No! That's not fair. I've already done a lot of work today, and I want to be alone! Just leave me be, Mother!" It was one of the only times Lily had raised her voice and shouted at her mother, and she regretted her fit of pique almost immediately. Rose had surprised her, however, by throwing her head back and laughing for several long moments, leaving Lily temporarily dumbfounded. "You reminded me so much of myself at your age just now, Lily," she had said, smiling widely. "I didn't mean to laugh at you, my darling, it's just that I remembered my own mother rolling her eyes once in the midst of my own teenage dramatics, which, by the way, were far more frequent and exuberant than yours. It took me so aback that my mother laughed for several minutes at the expression on my face. My father actually came to investigate what was going on when he became aware of her merriment, and he was a very busy person at the time." Rose paused in fond remembrance before focusing again on Lily. "Why don't you go out and do your thinking, or whatever it is that you do, for a while in the desert, child of mine. Next time, when you wish to do so, just say so, and we'll work it out, all right?" Lily had sheepishly thanked her mother and left their tent, returning early to do the chore her mother had asked her to accomplish, only to find it already completed.

Lily focused on her mother's smiling face from that day, and her glass began to take form as she manipulated the air around her like sharp-edged tools. She could feel Alder's conflicted emotions as she worked, and Lily thought she could guess at some of his thoughts. His first reaction to her drawing on her magic had been anxiety, for he had seen, and probably even felt, the spike in iron pain that had resulted. He also knew that in doing so, she risked exposure to witches or wizards and a physical condition weakened still further. Alder had also been watching her memory, and Lily knew that if he had seen it while in his body, he would have been chuckling aloud. Lily also thought she could detect admiration, and she wondered if he was a little impressed with her elemental control. She was surprised to discover that she wanted Alder to think well of her, to think she was talented in some way. Perhaps she was showing off for him, just a little . . .

Did I detect a bit of amusement at my expense just now, Alder?

Lily could tell she had startled him with her teasing, but he quickly seemed pleased about it.

"Oh, I just thought your mother handled the situation well, allowing you to express your feelings without getting mad at you. I was also thinking that I'll have to remember that you have a bit of a rebellious streak."

Lily felt another soul-chuckle, and then sensed Alder grow more serious.

"It seems wise of your mother to have given you some personal space, especially as I can see how artistically you used your free time. You really have a gift, Lily. I have seen very few glass statues with such minute detail. Your talent is remarkable, your elemental skill exquisite."

Lily felt herself blushing at his high praise. Alder was the only person who had ever seen her making and working glass. She hadn't known what his reaction would be, and she had been a bit worried that perhaps he would think her hobby childish. Lily was relieved that he thought better of her for it instead.

Thank you. I just wanted to make a sort of statuette of my mother, to help me remember her as she was. I shouldn't take too much longer.

"I think this is probably the best time and place, outside of the Fae Wood. I hope it makes you feel a little better to have a memorial to honor her. Are you able to inscribe words with air? Perhaps you could write an epitaph of sorts on the base."

I think that would be nice. My mother would have appreciated that, I think.

Lily paused, then kept her forming glass figure suspended in the air in front of her as she carefully took out the medical pack, and then her mother's jar of ashes, from the haversack. After carefully removing the stopper from the mouth of the container, Lily used all of her finesse with air to gently draw out some of her mother's remains. She proceeded to fire those very special ashes with more sand, until she knew she had made enough glass to spin just the right size and shape for her statuette. It would be about as tall as her forearm was long, and not much wider than her forearm's circumference.

Lily then set to work in earnest, critically watching as her mother's tunic and leggings-clad body became perfectly proportioned. She took a long time on her mother's hands, trying to convey Rose's gentle healer's touch. Lily set to work on her mother's long, silvery hair, having decided to leave it down, though it rarely had been during Lily's own life. When she felt that she had gotten the waves of hair flowing down Rose's back just right, Lily finally began chiseling her mother's face. She remembered her mother laughing, her arms wrapped loosely around her sides in her mirth, her silver eyes shining with happiness.

It was her eyes that took the longest and kept Lily fully occupied even after the full smiling lips, prominent cheekbones, delicately arched eyebrows, and all other features were perfect. Lily pulled from that well of power inside of her, the one that must have her elemental wings within, and drew forth a measure of love element, ignoring the throb of pain it caused her. She wanted to try to give the statuette a hint of her mother's shining soul, which Lily hadn't seen or fully appreciated until the moment of Rose's death. Lily took her time, trying to make the color turn from gold to just the right shade of silvery gray, finally capturing it and placing it gently inside the head portion of her glass memorial.

Remembering Alder's suggestion, Lily began to carefully use air element to carve words onto the small circular base beneath her mother's feet. She had thought about the words she wanted, and decided that something short and simple would be best. When she was done, it read:

Beauty without vanity,
Strong-willed against her foes,
Sharing wisdom, lovingly,
The fairy healer Rose.

At last, it was finished.

Lily left it suspended in air to quickly finish cooling.

"It is masterful, Lily. It is just as your memory recalls. What do the words say? I cannot read the desert language you used."

Lily quietly told him. Alder seemed to feel that it was just right.

"I think that is who she really was, at her core. You have chosen your words well. I am surprised that you didn't sign your name. That is customary, though I suppose you would have no way of knowing that."

Lily was a bit startled, and then hesitant. This was about her mother, not her. After thinking it over, Lily decided it would be admissible. She gently tilted the statue, still hovering in the air, and etched 'Lily' in the more decorative script of the desert dwellers. On impulse, she sketched a four-sided diamond around her name, gently imbuing the lines and name with her golden love element. Lily could feel Alder's amazement as she turned from her artwork to pack up what she had withdrawn from her haversack. Before putting away the half-empty bag of wood ash, Lily filled it with sand. As strange as the thought was for her, Lily knew that soon sand would become a rare commodity. It seemed prudent to take some with her, just in case she wanted or needed to make glass again on the journey. She then removed her mother's spare tunic from the haversack and wrapped the small commemoration with it after the statuette was completely cooled and ready for travel.

After Lily had clambered back into the bowl of Bepo's back and continued east for a time, she decided to project some of her thoughts toward Alder.

You seemed surprised when I signed my name. I had just been thinking of what you said, when you found where my wells of power were in my mind, and I just sort of added the 'diamond of gold' at the last minute. Did that bother you?

"No, not at all. I thought it was very fitting, although your modesty was surprising. Most artists I know sign their names in a prominent place, and most of them don't have near the skill you already possess. It will be interesting to see how you can use the elements on a larger scale, once your iron has been removed in the Fae Wood and you can be tested to determine your full potential."

Lily thought that over briefly, feeling both excited and slightly intimidated by the prospect, then decided to ask another question.

You said that you couldn't read the desert language I used, Alder, but my mother told me long ago that the Joquobon Desert dwellers use the same language and script as the people of Ropaz. Are fairies not taught any language but their own? Will I have to use my wings of elucidation to communicate when we finally get to the Wood?

Lily sensed sheepishness from Alder, and worried that she might have been rude somehow. Just as she was about to offer an apology, however, he responded.

"I admit that languages are not my strong suit, though I certainly understand that being multilingual is a useful skill, to be highly valued. I can speak the language of Ropaz, and several others, fluently, after a great deal of studying, but I cannot seem to learn the corresponding glyphs to any of them, though goodness knows I've tried."

Lily hastened to commiserate.

It can be quite difficult to learn a language not your own. I had to really make an effort when my mother was instructing me in the Fae language. I think you should be commended for persisting in learning languages that did not come easily to you, Alder. You probably need speech more often than the ability to read other languages anyway, I would imagine. It's also going to be a good thing that you can speak and understand the language that I know the best, at least when we first arrive in the Fae Wood. It's a relief to me that we'll be able to converse easily, just as we are now.

Lily felt Alder's happy warmth as he responded.

"It makes all of my struggling with Ropazian vocabulary, grammar, and pronunciation entirely worthwhile, then, Lily. Though many Fae choose to study the elf language exclusively, I opted to learn the speech of the witches and wizards, the Sea Speak of the mer-people, and the tree dialect of Sprite, which is one of the older languages spoken by the elves, in the course of my studies. I insisted on learning Ropazian because it is the most widely used and understood language in Lamoranth. Most beings speak it in addition to their own, due to the High Priestess's realm being both centrally located and quite large. I thought that learning it would be the best way to enable myself to communicate with the greatest possible number of individuals. Though my parents advised otherwise, I certainly feel vindicated by my choice now."

Just as Lily was about to comment on this, she felt, quite abruptly, a strong sense of . . . something from inside herself. Climbing, she needed to climb . . . up. After looking about her surroundings and seeing nothing but wind-rippled white sand, as always, Lily was puzzled.

Alder, did you feel that?

"Feel what?"

Lily could then clearly sense his alarm, which was quickly tempered with a strong determination and a sharpened focus on her sensory awareness.

No, not an outside disturbance, an internal . . . feeling. Just now, I felt like I should start 'climbing up' . . . What do you think that means?

"Did you notice where it came from inside you? Your mind? A memory perhaps . . . I wasn't paying attention to most of your mind, your eyes and ears have kept me busy."

Lily had never 'climbed up' anything except an amadel in her life, and she didn't think that was it. She began to consciously explore her mind, looking for the origin of that feeling. It seemed very important to Lily to find out. That feeling had been just like the dread of Japeta she'd experienced before they had entered the settlement last night. Lily wasn't going to ignore forebodings like that again anytime soon.

I'm pretty sure it came from the same place as my instinct against Japeta. Alder, we need to figure this out quickly. It might mean something bad is going to happen again.

Lily felt a bit panicked. She couldn't afford to have strange inner senses about things unknown that caused sharp, distracting iron pains all the time. Now that she was inside herself more deliberately, Lily was conscious of the Fear creeping slowly inward from the circular periphery of her more settled mind. She didn't think making the statuette had given it that much leverage to encroach. The effort she began to put forth to keep the pain as far as possible out of the rings of her memories, body control, thoughts, and emotions, as well as her nine wells of magic, left Lily feeling worn out. She felt a little comforted, however, by how far the iron effects still were from her innermost soul where it remained sheltered amidst the amaranthine trees.

When she thought she had a solid grip on the Fear once more, Lily went to her wells of power, where she had so recently been to access her elemental magic. She thought briefly about how her mother had told her that she herself had possessed four wells of power. Was Lily very unusual to have so many more than her mother? Perhaps she had inherited extra from her father . . . But Lily was distracted by the need, almost a desire, to climb, and she saw the well at the top of her diamond glow considerably brighter than the others, seeming to pulse the imperative in Lily's direction.

Alder, I found the climbing feeling. It's coming from one of my wells of power.

He arrived in the prominent circle of her tribal self as she projected the thought in his direction. Alder seemed pensive, and a bit concerned.

"I thought it might be this, especially when you ruled out the possibility of a memory. Lily, though there have only been two Fae seers alive in the Fae Wood for a very long time, I think you will soon be adding to their number."

Lily felt unnerved by Alder's pronouncement. She would have been perfectly content with elemental magic and wings of elucidation, and perhaps eventually growing healer's wings like her mother. In her frustration, the middle well of power emitted a loud, rumbling growl, just as it had when she had last been here with Alder. Lily felt exasperated. What, was that a disgruntled pair of warrior's wings, wanting to get out and have a stretch?

"Try to calm yourself, Lily. You definitely don't want to stir up that middle well yet, trust me. If anything, your strong possibility for wings of prophecy justifies your mother's caution, and her sacrifice to help you get to the Fae Wood. It would be a disaster for our people if you fell into the wrong hands, as gifted as you are. The Fae are currently the only beings in Lamoranth who have somewhat reliable oracles and future-telling. Well, except for some beings who reside in the Forest of Ancients, perhaps. Not only that, but you speak the language of souls as well, as you have so amply demonstrated with me . . . The sooner you are in the Fae Wood, the better. We should use your glimpses of short-term prediction as you get them to help us along the way. How many days in advance of Japeta did you dread entering the city?"

At first, I just wanted to find an alternative route. I suggested Jeridoff, and then jokingly mentioned the dragons, though my mother took that seriously. It came down to the absolute necessity for water and food, and still I tried to justify skirting around Japeta. The real dread arrived the day preceding the night we went in, or the day before yesterday about this time.

"So, we will need to 'climb up' sometime tonight, or perhaps tomorrow? Do you think the change in the amounts of iron you are wearing now compared to then will make a difference?"

Lily considered this, then shook her head in uncertainty.

Though I wear more now, I think the fact that we will be reaching the Magentay Canyons tonight is important. The outer magic of Lamoranth might be a factor as we approach the desert's edge, and the canyons will give us something to actually climb up as well. I would feel better if we could arrive before nightfall, the better to anticipate potential enemies in the basin of the canyon.

Once again, the prophecy well pulsed the injunction to climb up, and Lily could detect Alder's surprise as he clearly felt the magic this time.

"Amazing . . . no one ever really asks Quince or Eustoma how their wings work, how it feels . . . They are truemates, so perhaps they discuss it alone together . . . but it is impossible to mistake the advice of your magic here and now. I wonder what you will see of the future when you can safely bring your wings out . . . but I suppose I shouldn't tell you too much about this, just in case . . . I hate not being able to speak freely about such things with you though, Lily."

I understand, Alder. I need to go push the Fear back again anyway. Then I think I should focus on riding and making good time to the canyons. Why don't you go back to the ring with my eyes and ears and help me look for beings to avoid? I'm just assuming they'll be in the basin, since my instincts are telling me to climb up to the rim . . . Does that seem right to you? I think the Ropazian merchants take a path through the canyons. It would make sense for them to camp down low, out of that western wind, which might take out any tents not designed for use in the Joquobon . . .

"Your logic seems sound to me. Let's go cautiously and take conditions as they come."

Lily pushed back the Fear and the extra pain from the pulse that had affected all of her iron-covered skin. They had taken advantage of her distraction at her power wells, but Lily shoved it all out to the peripheries of her mind with a concentration of thoughts about her mother. Now that she could focus on both losing Rose and retaining her mother's love, those most profound events eclipsed the devious workings of the iron upon her. Lily then fully surfaced, only struggling now with her sadness, to steer the faithful Bepo, who was listing slightly to the north. It was on this gently altered course that Lily began to notice the ground gradually hardening into a substance that clearly did not shift about as sand did. Alder must have noticed Lily's wonderment, for his next words to her were tinged with amusement.

"The ground appears to be solid rock here. All the sand of the Joquobon was probably this compact countless years ago, but time and the wind have eroded it as surely as a river formed the Magentay Canyons over the ages. How do you feel as you leave the desert? A bit sad, perhaps?"

Lily explored her feelings, but found no real sadness. The desert was familiar, with its blazing sunlight, shifting sands, and arid heat. Yet Lily left nothing behind her: no friends, no family, no prospects. Only memories remained, and there were enough upsetting and downright sorrowful remembrances of Nather's tribe and Japeta that Lily couldn't find it in her heart to really miss the Joquobon.

Though I feel a bit unsure venturing out from all that is familiar to me, I can look ahead with more hope and less sadness than I leave behind. I could never stay where my mother was killed, where I was always an outcast among the Outcasts. It was so often an unbelievably lonely way to live. No, I will at least have you in the Fae Wood, and I want to look for my father there, too, after I fulfill my promises and return you to your body, of course.

Lily felt a tangle of emotions from Alder resulting from her words. Though she wanted to ask him about that, a glance around her new landscape quickly made Lily realize that Bepo had just cantered into and begun to follow a deep, straight groove in the solid ground. Had her amadel possibly found the Ropazian merchants' route? If so, Lily quietly marveled at a path that didn't disappear with the western wind, but rather grew deeper with continual use.

Alder, do you think Bepo just found the Ropazian traders' route through the canyons?

"Is that his name? Well, he found either a well-established route, or the bed of a river long dried up. They might very well be one and the same, given what you said earlier about the witch and wizard merchants camping in the basin. We must be getting close. Do you think we should follow this path until we reach the Magentay Canyons and there's something around for us to climb?"

I think so. This path is kind of north and east, though. Do you think that's all right?

"Yes. Going directly east from the desert would have you arriving at the Volcano Crescent and dealing with trolls, which would be highly undesirable. At some point, you were going to have to travel a bit north to go around them and actually into the southern reaches of Ropaz. Might as well do it as we pass through the canyons. Legend has it that they have been uninhabited since the ancient Fae Magentay himself practiced his magic and foresaw many things alongside a powerful river. He claimed that it flowed all the way to him from the Forest of Ancients, and before that from the snow-covered summits of the Grandfather Mountains north of the elven woods. If no one has lived in the canyons for that long, well before it became necessary for the Fae to remain in the safety of the Wood, it's a good place to travel for people like us, who don't wish to be seen or noticed. We can probably avoid a group of merchants fairly easily, although I hope I don't have to take back such words later."

Lily accepted Alder's confidence in their direction, then turned her thoughts to the legendary Magentay for a time. Had he lived all alone in the canyons, which perhaps had only just begun to form in his day? Lily wondered what he had predicted, and if any of what he'd seen had actually come to pass. How did wings of prophecy work, exactly? Surely the future wasn't set in stone, as the past seemed to be. Were some things inevitable, fated, immutable, while other events were as changeable as the minds who made decisions about them? Could Lily have prevented her mother's death if she'd been allowed to explore her own inner abilities, to see more clearly the dangers in their journey and help avoid them assiduously? Lily shied away from such thoughts after working her mind into knots. There was no point in agonizing over how she might have been able to do one thing or another. Lily knew she had made the right decision, the one and only choice her mother had wanted from her, and she was just going to have to keep living with the consequences and hope she could fully accept them with time.

Lily swayed and rocked in the scoop of Bepo's back well into the evening. They followed the indention in the ground as it continued a more or less straight path to the northeast, stopping once for Lily to eat and rest her persevering amadel. As dusk approached, the rocky ground on either side of their route began to rise steadily higher. Lily slowed, unsure if they should begin their 'climb' now that they seemed to have reached an outer portion of the canyons. She directed this inquiry to Alder, who hesitated a bit as well.

"Can you tell if we need to ascend the right bank or the left bank? Perhaps your prophetic instincts will be more specific if you concentrate them on what you want to know . . . although it's not at all worth you suffering unnecessarily or producing any kind of detectable magic."

Lily revisited her inner magic, focusing on their minor dilemma in the hope that she would get further information without actually pulling any golden light from the well of prophecy. All she felt, even after Alder floated close to offer quiet support, was that she needed to listen.

'Listen', it says. 'Climb up' and 'listen'. I think I might fully surface and see what Bepo thinks. He was right about the path, maybe he will be about this, too.

"Ultimately, either side will get us to approximately the same place at the opposite end of the canyon. Let's not waste any more of this fading daylight. You and the amadel will need it to climb anything safely. I'll let you know if I see something. Could you try looking around more, scanning behind yourself occasionally? I'd prefer a more panoramic view to scout for trouble."

Lily felt slightly chagrined by this lapse in her knowledge of even basic survival tactics against the external dangers she faced. She had to focus so much energy on her interior, on the iron pain and the Fear, and in using thoughts of her mother against them, that she felt exhausted in a different, deeper way. Lily had thought she had been doing well to keep up the pace and direction of her amadel and in remembering to eat; in keeping her attention focused only straight ahead, however, she had forgotten that external danger could come at her from any direction. Lily resolved to do better on observing her surroundings from then on.

After carefully looking all the way around herself from atop Bepo, who had come to a stop in the trail while she had conferred with Alder, Lily saw no one and nothing astir. She realized she wasn't the best person to determine if anything was out of place, seeing as everything was going to be strange to her now that she had left the Joquobon. Lily felt deeply grateful for Alder's presence once more, then sat quietly for a moment, listening. After several minutes of hearing nothing but the wind, Lily thought she heard something else, ahead and to her left. Had the wind just sighed a bit more loudly, or had Lily actually heard a voice calling out for an instant? She directed Bepo out of the deeply grooved ground and began their ascent of the inclining left side of the canyon.

Lily soon began to appreciate the way the light of the slowly setting sun struck the sides of the canyon walls. The colors were like the edges of Alder's beautiful silver soul against the variegated vertical stone, and Lily found it lovely enough to rival the pretty desert sunsets of which she had always been fond. She was a bit worried, however, when their new, unmarked trail leveled out and they began simply following the rim of the canyon's left side. That hadn't really been a climb. Lily had half expected the necessity of walking alongside Bepo and his spindly legs for steep portions of rock, yet that had not been the case so far.

All too soon, the sun had set completely, and Lily brought her amadel to a halt. Though she was wary of danger, Lily was extremely tired, both physically and emotionally, and the need to rest felt paramount just then. Alder agreed that Lily needed to get some sleep.

"I can tell how fatigued your eyes are, Lily. They've been drooping since we started up the left bank. It's nighttime now, at any rate, and probably not the best time to be traveling along the rim of a canyon we can barely see. You rest, and I'll stay by your bodily senses. Perhaps I'll be able to hear something and wake you if needed."

Lily projected her gratitude in Alder's direction, then simply said, *Good night, Alder.*

After a brief hesitation, Alder said, very gently, *"Sweet dreams, Lily."*

Though that phrase caused Lily to remember her mother in an intensely personal way, she still felt a mixture of pain and happiness that surprised her. It was comforting to have Alder wish her a pleasant sleep, though she didn't think it would have felt that way if anyone else had spoken those words to her. Lily drifted off to the deepest slumber she'd had since the night before Japeta, thinking that she was lucky to have her first real friend be someone like Alder.

Pillar of Sun and Ashes

It was Alder who woke her up shortly after sunrise the next morning. Lily felt fairly well rested, although she knew she could have slept a lot longer. With a groggy *Good morning,* Lily sat up stiffly and reached for her haversack. After eating some fruit and bread and drinking some water, then giving some to the greatly deserving Bepo, Lily repacked her bag slowly. Her mind was gradually turning fully to the day ahead, and Lily began to wonder about the climbing problem they would likely face.

"Not much of a morning fairy, are you?" Alder commented, sounding both interested and slightly amused.

Lily tried to appreciate his sense of humor, but she couldn't help feeling a bit grumpy about it instead. It had taken a great deal of strength to resist the pain and Fear that had penetrated further into her mind, near those critical inner circles, as she slept unguarded. It would probably take her until midday to push it all back to the edges of her mind, for Alder couldn't control it or keep any of it in check while she was unconscious. Lily envied him the luxury of simply floating into portions of her mind that remained unaffected by the iron.

No, waking up isn't much fun for us iron-clad fairies.

When Alder immediately expressed remorse for his teasing query, Lily felt a bit guilty for her own words. She hastily sought a peace offering of sorts for her snide remark.

So, did you think about the climbing feeling from yesterday? Any new ideas on what that might mean, Alder?

Alder seized on the change in topic with relief, accepting it for what it was, though he had little to say about it that they hadn't already discussed.

"Though I'm a little concerned that the timing of the actual climb didn't occur yesterday evening, I think that just means we really need to prepare ourselves for it today. I also think it wouldn't hurt to glance over the rim into the basin occasionally, to see if any witches or wizards are traveling below. We'll see them well in advance if they're up here, as it appears to stay fairly level now, though the basin must get considerably deeper."

Just as Lily was about to speak her agreement, she heard a sound, perhaps a voice. It was little more than the whistling of the wind through the canyon, though she was certain that it was in fact more than just wind. Was this the same noise she had heard last night? It was barely more audible, though Lily was less tired now than she had been when she'd chosen the left side of the canyon. She tossed her haversack and the sheathed sword into Bepo's back, then climbed in as well. After grasping his ears gently but firmly, Lily began the day's ride, keeping the basin rim in sight on her right.

They rode all morning, making good time and checking stealthily over the edge periodically. When Lily stopped briefly for a meal and a rest from her amadel's gait, she had heard the sound several more times, each a little bit louder than the last. Lily was certain now that it was a voice, saying the same thing repeatedly. She wondered what Alder thought about it, but he didn't bring it up during their midday break, so Lily pondered it in silence, even after resuming their travels.

Hardly another hour had passed when Alder spoke up.

"Do you see something directly ahead? A sort of rocky projection?"

Lily stared more carefully in front of her, and she quickly saw what Alder had pointed out. Though it would be late afternoon before they reached it, that column of rock was obviously the only thing in sight that Lily would be able to climb up today.

Do you think the voice is coming from that stone spindle, Alder?

Lily sensed Alder's surprise.

"What voice are you hearing, Lily?"

Alder couldn't hear it with her ears? How was she hearing it then? Lily worried for several moments, but before she could say anything more, she heard the voice again, even louder this time. Had it sounded troubled just now? Was someone stranded and in need of help? Ordinarily, Lily wouldn't have hesitated to give aid to someone who required it, yet she had to be much more cautious now that she had to negotiate her way through much of the southern half of Lamoranth.

I hear a voice, and I think whoever it belongs to is in pain, or in trouble. It's coming from somewhere ahead of us, and it's been getting easier for me to hear all morning.

"Is it causing you more iron pain when you hear the voice?"

Lily paused, testing her mental strength against the Fear. She found that it was a little more intense, though that small fluctuation had been lost amidst the considerable pain she already felt while her mind was distracted with her external observations and exertions.

Yes, a bit.

"It may be possible, then, that you are hearing a soul in distress, Lily. I can't use your magic without my body, or your express permission, so it might be your wings of elucidation at work here. We should look out for this being, as well as whoever is responsible for causing its pain."

Lily returned to worrying about whether or not she would be able to help the owner of that voice, or even if she should aid a potential enemy in these isolated canyons, as the unnatural structure came more and more clearly into view. Several hours later, Lily gentled tugged Bepo to a stop at its base. The column was about five times Lily's own height and perhaps twice her height in width, made of deliberately stacked blocks of rock, clearly cut and placed in this spot by someone for a specific purpose. Lily could make out what the voice was saying now. It was calling out "Vabiri, Vabiri!" with such heartrending agony that Lily forgot all her previous misgivings and immediately began climbing up the small stone tower.

She was aware of Alder's concern, both for her and for the distressed person still above them. Lily concentrated on finding hand holds and foot holds as she deliberately made her way toward the suffering being. At last, arms straining and legs wobbling, Lily pulled herself up the last portion of steeply stacked rocks and reached the flat top of the structure, only to become perfectly still with shock.

In the exact center of the tower's topmost slab, with his arms and legs tied far apart to four stakes deeply embedded in the rock's surface, was a pale-skinned, dark-haired, fine-featured male, clad all in black, who appeared, at least to Lily, to be in his middle years of life. Though clearly near death, he still gave off a distinct aura of power and age that belied his situation and visage. He was writhing in agony, struggling with all his depleted strength against his bonds, a crazed look in his very dark brown eyes. Though his mouth was closed tightly, Lily could hear a profoundly sorrowful voice emanating from him, still calling out with all the remainder of his vitality the word "Vabiri." Lily sat on the edge of the tower, completely awed and deeply troubled, as Alder's mixture of sympathy for the being and terror for her safety washed over her inner awareness.

"Lily, you have to get away from him, right now. He must be a vampire."

Despite Alder's dire warning, Lily couldn't bear to leave him to suffer and surely die. What did "Vabiri" mean? Lily wondered if vampires could speak in some way without their mouths, or if her linguistic magic really was enabling her to pick up on the word he was calling out.

Alder, do you know why he would be saying "Vabiri," or what it means? I can't stand just leaving him like this, it's not right. We have to do something, please.

Though Alder was still incredibly anxious, Lily could feel his growing curiosity as well.

"Lily, I still can't hear him saying anything. That means you definitely aren't hearing the word with your ears, but with your inner magic. Vampires speak with their mouths, as the majority of sentient beings in Lamoranth do, so it's almost certainly his soul you're hearing. In which case, you would understand the word, just as you comprehend the actual words I say to you, instead of just feeling my emotions, as is usual for fairies. Perhaps it is a name . . . that would still sound like the vampiric tongue in the language of souls . . . But Lily, regardless of that, vampires are extremely dangerous. The witches and wizards of Ropaz have despised them for ages, because the inhabitants of the Cave Kingdom drink their blood to live, and it's said that they absorb their victims' magic when they do so. They are the only magical race in Lamoranth whose power rivals the Fae . . . except they are fully our opposites, for they can only invoke Void magic, while we eschew the black power and utilize our inner fairy magic, the love element. They are a mysterious and dangerous people, and you would be safest by keeping your distance."

As if on cue, the vampire seemed to catch Lily's scent from her position on the edge of the tower's summit and began mindlessly snapping his mouth in her direction, as though to sink his teeth into some part of her and begin drinking her blood.

Although this frightened her, Lily still carefully thought over what Alder had just told her. She remembered her mother telling her to be wary of vampires, right before she told Lily that she was a fairy. Rose had also stated that vampires were powerful Void wielders. Lily had been curious about the Void ever since she had first been told about it, though much had happened to distract her from thinking about it since. Was it darkness and evil? Or something else? It didn't seem quite right to Lily to assume that the Void was hateful, simply because it wasn't like the 'love' element. She checked on her wells of power, where her prophetic magic was still making her feel the need to listen, and her wings of elucidation clearly picked up the despair-filled word "Vabiri" over and over. Lily knew better than to ignore this part of herself. That meant the only thing she was certain of was the importance of speaking with the vampire and hearing what he had to say.

I'm going to talk to him, Alder. It's important. He's dangerous, but he is also bound and weak. I will just stay a bit away while I try to find out if he's able to converse with me.

Alder clearly felt upset by her decision, but Lily waited until she sensed his grudging acceptance and sharpened focus before crawling closer to the vampire, who was still biting the air with a crazed look suffusing his face.

Just as Lily was about to speak, the vampire stilled, then arched his back involuntarily from some extraordinary pain. Then, before her very eyes, the vampire began to dissolve. When Lily saw the ashes his body was slowly becoming, the image of her mother's dead body disintegrating in flames seemed to superimpose itself with an awful clarity over the horrific vision before her. Without another thought for her security or her promises, Lily sprang toward the dying vampire, unsheathing her dagger and cutting a shallow slice in the skin of her left forearm, safely above the bangles around her wrist. Lily grabbed the vampire's head by the hair and held him steady as she put her bleeding arm to his lips. The vampire latched on to her and swallowed reflexively once, then twice. The ashes immediately ceased to continue forming, and instead seemed to float back onto his exposed skin, becoming a part of his body once more. With a third swallow of Lily's blood, the tortured look faded from the vampire's eyes, and he became calm and aware, though still a trifle dazed. When he then raised his eyes and looked into Lily's face, the vampire released her arm in complete astonishment.

Lily staggered back, a little dizzy and still bleeding from the cut and small teeth punctures on her arm. She watched as the vampire turned his head to follow her movements. When he saw that she was clearly not going to attempt to run away from him, the vampire easily broke his bonds, actually pulling all four stakes from their deeply embedded places in the top of the stone tower. He stood, obviously at his full strength once more, then tore his gaze away from Lily's face and looked directly at the sun, holding his hand up to the late afternoon light experimentally.

When the vampire returned his steady gaze to Lily, she knew a moment of fear and uncertainty, though it was nothing to the absolute horror that Alder was feeling on her behalf. Lily realized that she had failed him, had failed her mother, in helping the vampire escape certain death. She wondered if this powerful Void-user would spare her if she begged him, if she could somehow convey to him the absolute necessity of fulfilling her promises.

The vampire paused, as though waiting for her to speak. Lily stood and looked him full in the face, refusing to cower if she was about to die. She sensed Alder's pride in her courage, and Lily realized that he felt just the same, unwilling to flinch from the very real possibility of imminent death.

At last, the vampire broke the silence, speaking the language of Ropaz with an unusual accent that was unmistakably urbane.

"Please do not fear me, little fairy child. I will not harm you."

Lily stood completely still, not able to process the swift change in her circumstances right away, or if she should believe that they really had. In some small portion of her mind, she felt just a bit miffed at being called a child. Understanding this feeling more than anything else in her morass of confused emotions, Lily clung to it.

"I may be young, but you are not the most frightening being I have ever seen."

That, at least, was completely true.

At the vampire's surprised and then gently amused expression, Lily felt compelled to elaborate.

"Well, perhaps I was a bit frightened when you pulled the stakes from the rock just now. I was so terrified for you, but that intimidated me instead. Now I'm just really . . . confused."

Still rather unsettled by the last few minutes, Lily absently reached up to straighten her hair wrap. The tell-tale sign of her nervousness, however, caused her to still when she noticed the blood still dripping from her arm.

"This isn't bothering you, is it? I can wrap it with some medical supplies in my pack if it is."

After a short pause, the vampire spoke again.

"No, your blood is not affecting me. There is a myth among vampires that just one drop of fairy blood will quench the Thirst indefinitely, and any more than that can quell it permanently. That certainly seems to be the case. I crave no more of your blood. I Thirst for it not at all, though it appealed to me so strongly just moments ago. Please forgive me if I frightened you with my actions or offended you with my words. I was able to become acquainted with you, after a fashion, when you gave me your blood, and so I know that you have not yet lived two decades. I am nearly three thousand years old, and so you seem a child to me."

Lily was stunned by this information, though she could tell that Alder was not as impressed. His horror for her safety seemed to have diminished somewhat, although he was still keenly observing the vampire. Lily asked the imposing being before her the first question that came to her mind.

"What else did you find out about me? How does that work?"

The vampire inclined his head in thought, as though considering how best to explain.

"It is one of the mysteries of our race, the ability to read certain aspects of character from the blood we drink, and no satisfactory explanation for how it is possible has ever been discovered. Many witches and wizards believe we can consume their powers when we drink their blood, which is a falsehood. Even if their race possessed magic within, it would not be accessible through the blood of their veins. I took none from you, though I was able to see that your inner magic is stored in your mind, and it is of astounding proportions. I also learned that you taste of the very essence of kindness, such as I have never encountered. You also seem to possess . . . either one very large soul, or two souls, inside you."

Lily's eyes widened as the vampire continued to shower her with his incredible words. She grew uneasy, however, that he had detected Alder in her mind. Given her egregious lack of judgment earlier, Lily felt determined to protect Alder's soul better in the future. She remained silent as the vampire paused again. Finally, he asked a question of her.

"May I ask you what your name is, young Fae lady?"

Slightly startled by his query, Lily nevertheless answered without hesitation.

"I am Lily," she said. Then she softly asked him, "What's yours?"

"I am the vampire Vadom."

He hesitated, as if he usually introduced himself with some sort of additional information, then fell silent. Lily heard his soul quietly say "Vabiri" once more. Though Lily wanted to ask about this, she still wasn't entirely certain about Vadom's intentions, so she asked a less risky question.

"What happened to you?"

Vadom grew very solemn before Lily's eyes, looking more reserved than he had a moment ago.

"I was staked here by my enemies to greet the sun."

"Did you deserve it?" Lily asked bravely, wondering if he would be honest with her.

He paused, weighing his response, looking troubled.

"My enemies wanted to make a decision that I thought very unwise. I voiced my apprehensions, as I felt I must, for the decision would impact all in the Cave Kingdom. Later, they threatened to harm my otherwing if I did not follow them to these canyons. I had no choice but to do so, knowing they would kill her if I showed the slightest hint of hesitation. They said that they would spare her life if I gave up mine. Again, I felt I had no other way to keep her safe, and so I complied. Perhaps I am deserving of death, but personally, I do not think so."

Alder, this sounds like the truth to me. What do you think?

"I think it must be true. He is far too old and powerful to be caught and staked without the least sign of a struggle. And to think, he was willing to become ashes for his mate . . . Perhaps we should perform a small test. See how he responds to the name Vabiri. I think it will be safe to mention her, for I don't think he means to harm you. He could have done so by now and probably would have if that was his intention. He already knows you are powerful, but he cannot draw your inner magic from your blood as I thought. He might also just think your knowledge of "Vabiri" is somehow a normal fairy ability, for our races have not met formally anywhere in Lamoranth for years uncounted."

Lily decided to take Alder's advice and focused fully on the vampire once more.

"I don't think you deserve death for protecting your life-partner. Was it her name you were calling out before? Is she Vabiri?"

The vampire appeared surprised again, though it was soon eclipsed by a look of intense longing. Lily was strongly reminded of her mother and the mixture of love and pain on her face the only time Lily had ever asked about her father.

"Yes," he whispered. "How do you know such things, Lily? How do you come to wander so far from your home? Rarely do the male Fae venture into Ropaz, and never do their ladies or young. It is very dangerous for you. Your blood smells and tastes better than anything I have ever encountered before, and you must know that few witches or wizards will befriend you in the grasslands."

Lily was certain he spoke the truth now, and it did him credit in her eyes to say things that were less than ingratiating.

"I have never been to the Fae Wood before, though that is where I wish to go now. I know there are many dangers to me, but I have made promises that I must keep. You seem to be an honorable being, Vadom, so I think you will understand why I must risk my safety to keep my word to one most dearly loved."

The vampire looked at Lily more closely than before, with something like respect in the depths of his gaze.

"I think you have an interesting story to tell, Lily, though your years are still few. First, however, I feel obligated to tell you certain things that now pertain to you, in regards to me. Though this information is common knowledge among the inhabitants of the Cave Kingdom, you cannot be aware of it, young Fae lady that you are. You saved my life, even as my body was being slowly turned to ash after nearly two days in the sun, and I now owe you a life debt. Furthermore, you freely gave me your blood, asking for nothing in return and risking your own life to be near me when the Thirst was so strong upon me. The fact that you have given me Fae blood, which has prevented my death, made me immune to the sun, and quenched the Thirst, makes this an extraordinary blood debt. Though I have had few debts at all in my past, and none coming close to this magnitude, I think I am fortunate to be bound to one such as you, Lily, for you are clearly both kind and honorable."

Lily, and Alder as well, were both struck temporarily speechless by this pronouncement. Lily could hardly believe that such a powerful, experienced, and noble being considered himself deeply in her debt, especially because she was greatly in need of one such as Vadom. Before Lily could ponder the matter further, however, Vadom gently broke in on her amazement.

"I feel that it is unsafe for me to attempt to return to the Cave Kingdom at this time. Better to let my enemies think I am dead, for that will almost certainly keep my otherwing safe. They will not make an attempt on Vabiri's life without a serious cause, as they felt my betrayal was to their inadvisable decision. Usually, our females and young are never to be harmed, but rather to be protected from danger at all costs. This being the case, I wonder what I can do for you now, young Lily, while I am unencumbered by my duties in the Cave Kingdom, to begin repayment of my debt to you."

Lily knew exactly what she needed, but she thought the matter over carefully before she finally spoke.

"Vadom, I can't tell you what a relief it is to find an ally in someone like you. I mentioned before that I made promises to a person I loved, but I worry that I will not be able to keep them because of certain limitations placed upon me. I would be extremely grateful if you could help me reach Ford-upon-Ward, the bridge city leading into the Fae Wood, alive and unharmed. I know that I will hardly be able to recognize an enemy in Ropaz, let alone fend them off if they try to imprison me. If you agree to take me that far on my journey to Golden Court, there is something else I would ask of you, if you are willing. When my mother died," and here Lily paused, swallowing hard, trying to remain composed in front of this near-stranger, "I knew nothing of fighting, of weapons, of even the most basic ways to defend myself. I still don't, for it was just a few days ago. Vadom, if you know anything of such practical matters, I would ask you to instruct me on our journey, so that I never again have to stand by and watch, completely helpless, as someone I love dies for me."

Lily stopped speaking as terrible pain washed over her. Just when she thought she had grown to tolerate the iron, the pain of her mother's loss would strike, deep inside of her where indistinct trees shaded and sheltered her very soul. The iron had never been beyond the tribal circles of her mind or escaped the confines of her sizable white desert, and hence it could never cripple her so profoundly. Lily clung to the glowing comfort Alder projected for her, using his presence as a reminder of love undiminished, waiting until the pain of her loss receded enough to look up at the vampire Vadom once more.

He had been carefully watching her, and the respect in his eyes remained, though there was a new softness in his gaze that Lily wondered about. When she had fully regained her equilibrium, Vadom spoke into the silence between them.

"Such suffering, and such responsibility, in one so young is difficult for me to witness. I will do what I can to alleviate your cares, Lily. Perhaps it will comfort you to know that all male vampires live the life of a warrior. We begin with the strenuous training of youth, then enter a predominantly militaristic culture upon maturity, when we have completed the traditional warrior's education. I was fully trained, by the *vapa* who adopted me, after five centuries of tactical study; practical application and mastery of an extensive array of weaponry; and comprehensive tutelage in magic, with a large focus on the night element. I believe I will be able to provide you with adequate protection across the southern reaches of Ropaz. Though I am not familiar with the city or the river that you mentioned, I know of the magical boundary to the lands of the Fae. It is farther south than I have been before while hunting, for it is an inconvenient distance from the Cave Kingdom.

"Escorting you to the forest of your people, however, scarcely begins to repay either of my debts to you, Lily. I think, for my blood debt, that initiating you into the life and knowledge of a warrior will be a useful service to you, and bring you some peace of mind. I must warn you now, though, that this is not lightly undertaken among vampires. We must perform a small ceremony, formally acknowledging our joint commitment to your warrior's education. I will be taking responsibility for you in very personal way. It is strange," Vadom said, looking pensive, "for I have long considered adopting a *vipin* to raise into a warrior and a mature adult. Most vampires of my age have taken in at least one, if not two. Yet it is not only my decision, but my otherwing's choice as well."

Here Vadom paused, looking as if he was focused on something far away, but very dear.

"Long has my Vabiri desired to become a *vama*, to take in a *vipin*. Yet now, quite exceptionally, I will adopt a *vipina* instead. And a fairy child, no less . . . Yet I feel that, could she be here now, if she knew what you have just done for me, the exquisite rarity of your taste and smell, and your incredible kindness of spirit, my otherwing would approve of you, Lily."

Still looking wistful, but with the relaxed gravity of one who has just made an important decision, Vadom refocused on Lily's stunned, and slightly awed, countenance.

"I think that once I am your *vapa*, and you my *vipina*, the life debt I owe you will begin, gradually, to be repaid as well," he added softly.

Lily hardly knew what to say. She was amazed by this ancient being, by everything that he was, that he represented, that he loved. Some part of Lily's mind realized that he was about to do her a great honor. She wondered if she would be worthy of it, and resolved to give Vadom her very best effort.

Alder? Lily whispered, and he seemed to know what she was asking.

"This is so extraordinary, Lily, I don't even have words for it. To learn the ways of a vampire warrior . . . Lily, I didn't tell you this before, but when

I said they rival the Fae in magical power, I wasn't really conveying the depth of their formidable abilities. Male vampires are the ultimate opponents for Fae warriors, and very few engage them willingly. They are either too young to stand a chance or they are older and skilled, but truemated, and cannot risk inflicting their ladies with the pain of losing them. I can't believe we're going to learn from one so old . . . Though our sources are few and often unreliable, it is said that vampires grow more powerful with time . . ."

Even as Alder's words increased Lily's wonderment, she also felt troubled by what he was saying. Vadom wasn't committing to teaching both of them. Lily didn't want to begin such a relationship with dishonesty. She looked up and began to speak, but hesitated, worried for Alder's safety. The conflict must have shown on her face, for Vadom was carefully watching her, and he softly spoke to her once again.

"I hardly need to tell you, Lily, that I will be revealing many of the secrets of the Cave Kingdom in the course of your warrior's training, which I must ask you to share with no one else. It might compromise the safety of the otherwings and young living in my underground home, which I cannot knowingly or willingly do. Once you speak the words of the ceremony, I would expect you to keep what I tell you between us, even if your style of combat eventually indicates vampiric origins."

Lily paused once more, asking Alder for permission with her feelings.

"This is what you felt troubled by just now, Lily? I think your honesty becomes you. I don't think I will be in danger from Vadom now, and you are right: he does deserve to know that I am here. It's fine with me, and the only honorable thing to do. Go ahead."

Relieved, Lily's face cleared of conflict, and she met Vadom's gaze directly.

"Earlier, Vadom, you said that you could taste two souls within me. You should know that is indeed true."

Vadom's eyebrows raised. He seemed to ponder what Lily had confirmed, though he also seemed satisfied about something.

"Would you be willing to explain who else resides in your body, Lily?"

Lily hesitated just a second, then looked at Vadom very solemnly.

"Can you promise me something first? Will you help me keep him safe?"

Vadom responded with equal gravity.

"While his soul is a part of you, I will protect him as I will protect you, absolutely and without hesitation. I will accomplish this by any means necessary, whether that entails utilizing magical force or simply employing discretion."

Lily was completely appeased by Vadom's pledge, and when she felt Alder convey his own reassurance, Lily began to tell Vadom about him.

"I told you that my mother . . . didn't survive a battle a few days ago. She was outnumbered by a dozen dark red creatures, the xydolem—but she was still able to distract them from my existence. I left Japeta with all the supplies I needed, but . . . the next night, I started crying and couldn't stop. I called and called for her . . . but I knew she couldn't come. I was giving up, it was too much, it just hurt so terribly . . . and then there was a new light in my mind, and it was beautiful beyond compare. It was Alder. He's a fairy who cast his soul from his body in the Fae Wood to try to find me in time to save me. He did, he kept me from shattering, and now we are traveling to the Wood to fulfill my mother's last wishes and to return Alder to his body. I'm sorry I didn't tell you about him sooner, Vadom. I wanted to, but I feel protective of him, and I didn't know if I could trust you with my new friend, who is so vulnerable now because of me."

Lily stopped herself, then waited to see what Vadom would say. Inside of her mind, Lily could feel Alder glowing very brightly.

Vadom's expression gave away little, but Lily thought she caught a hint of approval, and perhaps understanding, in Vadom's fathomless dark-brown eyes.

"Can Alder hear what I say now?"

When Lily nodded, Vadom continued. Lily could sense Alder's complete concentration.

"Then hear this, Alder of the Fae Wood. Because of your body's absence, I will act as Lily's protector in your stead. You know of my debts to her, and how she wishes them to be repaid. Do you find it acceptable that I will be teaching her the ways of a warrior, though both of our races prefer a nonviolent, peaceful existence for our ladies?"

Alder deliberated carefully, then asked Lily to speak his words aloud.

"Alder says, 'I gratefully accept your protection of Lily on this journey. I also accept that she will be enduring the rigors of a warrior's training, and I will try not to interfere with your instruction. Given the considerable power of her inner magic, of which you know from her blood, this was already inevitable. She has a soul with the strength to endure what most of our Fae ladies could not, and I had planned to begin training her myself when she reached the Fae Wood. Please know this, however: I do not want her to suffer any more than is necessary. Lily has already been forced to cope with the emotional loss of her mother, and she bears a heavy burden of iron that incapacitates her physically in the extreme. I ask that you adjust your lessons accordingly.'"

Vadom stared into Lily's eyes for several long moments, and she was a little unnerved by the certainty that he wasn't really looking at her.

"Your concerns have been heard and will be taken into account. Will you also agree, Alder, to keep the knowledge I impart to Lily strictly between the two of you? I think that if any two Fae could understand my desire to protect the innocent, and a loved one, it would be you and Lily. Therefore, I am willing to teach her in your presence, if you will maintain the same circumspection that I will ask of her, even after you have been returned to your body."

"'I will repeat nothing that you speak of, except alone with Lily, and I will only practice your style of weaponry and magic with Lily, in the event that you are absent. Though I cannot give my word that my own warrior's magic will not adjust to incorporate what you will impart, I do swear never to use anything you teach against the ladies or children of the Cave Kingdom.'"

After Lily had repeated Alder's words as solemnly as she could, she breathed a small sigh of relief. Lily was pleased, though perhaps also a bit embarrassed, that they were taking her training so seriously. The only person who had ever taken pains with her safety and education before was her mother, and now she had a friend and a teacher who were both ranking those things among their highest priorities.

The three of them were silent for a short time, digesting all that had happened and been said in their eventful afternoon. Finally, Vadom ended their quiet contemplation.

"Lily, if you are ready, I would have us perform the ceremony. After that, I think we should tend to your arm, see that you are fed, and then rest. Though we have much to discuss, the day appears to be waning, and I know you have probably already traveled far today."

Lily nodded, wondering what the ceremony would require of her. She came close to Vadom and faced him squarely, ready for him to tell her the steps of the ritual.

Vadom looked into her eyes for a moment, then said, "When I have declared my part, I will speak your words, which you will need to repeat. Are you ready, Lily?"

When she had nodded again in affirmation, Vadom spoke quietly, yet in a voice full of authority and confidence.

"I, Vadom, vampire of the Cave Kingdom and otherwing to Vabiri, take Lily of the Fae as my *vipina*. I will protect and provide for her body and spirit; teach her of the warrior's life of my race; and help her become a strong, wise, and mature adult. I vow to do this to the best of my abilities, and hereby place the mark of my name upon Lily as a sign of my commitment."

Vadom stepped forward and gently placed his hands on either side of Lily's face, the heels of his palms lightly resting against the pulse points just under her jaw. He then brought his lips to Lily's forehead, giving her a feather-light kiss that sent tendrils of magic swirling about her face.

Vadom released her and stepped back once more, waiting until Lily had gotten over her surprise before intoning Lily's part in his quiet, steady voice. Lily repeated the words slowly, allowing their meaning to wash over her as she felt an unfamiliar magic come awake in an unknown place within herself.

"I, Lily, lady of the Fae, accept as my *vapa* Vadom the vampire. I will give him my respect, attention, and best effort as he teaches me an honorable warrior's way of life, as well as concede to his judgment and experience in matters of my safety and maturity. I vow to do this to the fullest extent of my abilities, and hereby show my commitment to and seal this pact with Vadom by placing a mark of affection upon him."

Lily gave Vadom a questioning look, and he responded by simply inclining his head within her reach. Imitating the placement of his gentle hands, Lily pulled Vadom a bit closer and softly kissed the center of his forehead. She let go of his face and watched in wonder as a number of golden lines moved straight out from the place where her lips had been a moment before, creating a sun-like marking on Vadom's alabaster skin. He looked slightly surprised, as though he hadn't been entirely certain of what to expect. Vadom studied Lily's forehead for a moment longer, then stepped back.

"It is done. From now on, I will ask you to call me *Vapa,* as a sign of respect, and I will call you *Vipina,* for the same reason."

"Yes, *Vapa,*" Lily replied, absentmindedly touching her face, which still tingled slightly from whatever magic they had just invoked. It was then that Lily finally looked around and really noticed her surroundings, which she had ceased to heed since finding Vadom. She was a bit startled to discover that the evening had nearly faded into nighttime, and some of the stars were already out. Lily worried a little at her lack of attention and felt concerned for Bepo. She had left him unattended for some time. Lily walked to the edge of the stone structure, looking for her mount. Her steadfast amadel was right where she had left him, at the base of the tower. He was nudging the haversack, which Lily had hastily removed from her back to begin her climb. Realizing that the poor creature was probably thirsty, Lily began her careful descent.

As she carefully found her first footholds, Lily noticed Alder's feelings and realized she didn't completely understand them. Was he . . . disgruntled about something?

Alder, is something wrong? I don't quite get what you're . . . upset about.

"Oh, I just would have liked to have known that there was kissing *involved in that ceremony,"* he said, sounding irritated.

Lily was surprised, and not entirely sure how to respond.

Did it bother you? My mother kissed me like that all the time.

For reasons beyond Lily, this seemed to pacify Alder. She decided to ask him about it later, after she had finished climbing back down the tower. Lily's wounded arm was already beginning to sting, and she needed to concentrate on finding places for her hands and feet on her slow descent.

Lily hadn't gotten much farther, however, before her injured forearm gave a throb of pain, causing her to release her precarious handhold on the weathered surface of the monolith's side. When she also failed to support her weight quickly enough with adequate footholds, Lily began a free-fall toward the solid ground a good distance below. Just as Lily registered Alder's surge of surprise and fear, she caught a glimpse of black beside her. A gentle pair of arms caught her securely and seemed to place her, almost instantaneously, onto the ground beside Bepo.

"Was it your arm?" Vadom asked quietly.

Embarrassed now, Lily managed a nod, blushing deeply. Vadom had to think she was completely incapable of keeping herself alive by now. Would he regret taking on the task of training her?

"I'm sorry, *Vipina*. I should have offered to help you down. The Pillar of Sun and Ashes was hardly designed for convenience, and certainly not for beings who cannot fly."

Lily sighed, beginning to feel as though she was the only being in Lamoranth who was earth-bound. Well, perhaps not the mermaids, if they really did exist. Before Lily could bemoan her wingless state further, however, Vadom silently handed her the haversack. She then removed the medical pack and sat down to bandage her arm. The cut wasn't deep, although the punctures from Vadom's teeth had done a bit more than just break through her skin. Lily worked methodically, first cleaning the area with water and soap, then applying an ointment she had helped her mother make from plantain root and mustard seed, at a time when almond oil, lard, and beeswax had all been available to them. Finally, Lily wrapped her forearm with a strip of clean cotton from the pack and tied it off. After tidying the medical kit and rearranging the many bracelets on her arm, Lily gave Bepo some much-needed water, then eagerly dug out some fruit and bread for herself. She was more hungry than she'd realized.

As she chewed her supper, Lily turned over some of the more extraordinary events of the day, but soon found herself too tired to think. Lily laid her head down on her haversack and looked up sleepily at Vadom, who was carefully examining a slightly skittish Bepo. Suddenly, Lily sat up, remembering her manners.

"*Vapa,* you are welcome to any of the food or water in my haversack. Please help yourself."

He smiled softly at her earnest expression.

"Thank you for your generosity, *Vipina,* but I am not able to ingest what you offer. Now that I quite possibly do not require the blood of others to sustain me, I will attempt to hunt and eat only *vu chiroptera,* or in my bat form, which allows me to partake of insects and water."

Lily was so taken aback by this casual pronouncement that it was several moments before she caught herself staring at her new teacher.

Alder, did you hear that?

"Somehow I think that is only the first of many astonishing things Vadom will be saying. To be able to transform one's body at will . . . what strange and amazing magic vampires must possess."

Do you think they might have inner magic after all?

"At this point, I feel my ignorance of their race acutely, and I hesitate to voice any more assumptions that could be easily overturned. Anything seems possible to me now that I am out in the world and with you, Lily."

Lily smiled, even as her eyes closed tiredly.

Sweet dreams, Alder.

"Sweet dreams, Lily."

As Lily laid back down to sleep, she had just enough time to give a thought to what her training might be like in the weeks to come before falling into a deep slumber.

Getting Acquainted

When Alder woke her at dawn the next morning, Lily's iron pain was worse than ever. The Fear had gotten further into her mind than before, several rings farther into her desert consciousness, and Lily felt her normal grogginess vanish amidst the onslaught of panic and confusion. Lily was shocked by how close the Fear had come to her power wells, and she fought strenuously against it, slowly forcing it into submission. Focusing her entire mind on her mother, Lily held fast to her promise to keep the iron on her body, her promise to deliver the scroll. Eventually, Lily felt it was safe enough to divide her attention and speak to Alder.

Alder, I know you like to stay near my senses when I sleep, but I really need you to watch the Fear from now on when I'm unconscious. It snuck far too close to my inner magic for comfort last night.

Lily felt Alder float nearer to the pain and Fear she had just battled, and she felt his spike of concern at how far in it had insinuated itself, past her circle of cherished memories and nearly infiltrating her ring of strongest emotions.

"Are you all right now, Lily? It's never gotten this deep before. I suppose it's because we're well out of the desert, and you've been wearing the iron for an increasingly long time . . . I'll stay closer to the periphery of your mind as you sleep from now on. With Vadom guarding you at all times from outside danger, I can relax on that front and help you more within."

Thank you, Alder. Just wake me up sooner when it starts creeping in again.

"Of course. Why don't you eat some breakfast? It might make you feel better."

Lily sent him the soul-equivalent of a brave smile, then woke herself up completely and opened her eyes. She saw Vadom observing her from several feet away, a look of concern on his refined face.

"Good morning," Lily said, surprising even herself with her cheerfulness.

Vadom smiled slightly, though the concern didn't leave his eyes.

"I confess, it is very strange for me to hear such a greeting to begin rather than to end my waking hours, though that is nothing compared to sitting out in the open just now, knowing the sun was about to break past the horizon, and simply waiting for it without seeking cover. I had no idea the sun creates such colors when it rises," Vadom added, motioning with his hand to the glorious sunrise in the east, then to the spectacular view of the canyon just to the south. "However, I'm sure I tire you with the familiar. Let us focus our attention on you, *Vipina*. There is much I would ask you in order to discover how best to help you and teach you on this journey. Why don't you eat, if you need to, and then I will pose questions once we have set out."

Lily nodded in agreement, then got some bread and water from her haversack and slowly began to attempt a meal. She didn't have much of an appetite, but Lily knew she wouldn't be able to ride on Bepo's back all day on an empty stomach. Feeling a bit better after getting some food down, Lily then offered a portion to her amadel as well. Lily made sure everything was back in her haversack, then put it in Bepo's bowl and climbed up herself. Once she had steered him toward the early morning sun and he had worked up to his cantering stride, Lily began to think about all that had happened the previous day.

One of the things that had piqued her curiosity was her understanding of the words Vadom had been using in the language of the vampires. When he had called her "*Vipina*," the word seemed to mean a combination of things, but Vadom didn't actually mean all of the implications of the word. He intended to call her his student, who was female, young, full of potential, and important to him. There was another shade of meaning, however, that didn't fully translate for Lily, even with her well of language magic. It was the same with "*Vapa*." Vadom had asked her to call him this, and he wanted her to think of him as her teacher, mentor, model warrior, and protector. Yet there was more, Lily was sure. Perhaps her inner magic wasn't picking up on it because it was not Vadom's intention to use the words in their fullest sense, and so they came out in a sort of garbled original form instead.

Lily asked Alder what he thought about this inconsistency as she flexed her arm experimentally, wincing slightly at the dull pain in her left forearm.

"I'm not sure why those words aren't translating normally for you, Lily. It's probably just something else we can blame on the iron, although it could be your youth, too. So you think you're only comprehending what he means specifically, but not the full meaning of the words? And they're not coming across because Vadom's usage is somehow insincere?"

Not insincere . . . it's more like he hasn't fully accepted or realized what the words, or the relationship, imply. Remember how he said Vabiri was supposed to help choose? Maybe that's why he's hesitating . . .

"That could be. Vadom seems to really care for his 'otherwing'. It sounds as though that essentially means the same as 'truemate' does for fairies . . . I wish we could speak Fae sometimes. I'd love to talk to you in the language of our people . . ."

Lily was surprised by the wistfulness Alder was feeling. Did he think the language of souls was inadequate? Or was he just missing the freedom and convenience of being in his own body? Lily felt unsure of how to respond, but was saved from doing so by Vadom's gentle, cultivated voice.

"*Vipina*, now that we are underway, I'd like to discuss some important topics with you."

Lily was surprised to see Vadom sort of floating beside her elevated place on Bepo's back. It took her several moments to realize that he was easily keeping pace with her amadel's canter.

"Are you sure you don't want to ride with me? I wouldn't want you to get tired . . . hovering all day."

Vadom smiled a little. "Levitation requires very little magic of me. Please do not concern yourself. I am more concerned about your domesticated beast, now that it is out of the desert, or the fatigue you yourself seem to suffer. It is, in fact, the first thing I would like to converse with you about. Alder mentioned yesterday that you wear iron that incapacitates you. Could you explain this? I am aware that the Fae do not willingly touch iron, that it is one of your people's few weaknesses, but that is all."

Lily pondered how best to explain.

"You should know that, at least for me, iron hasn't always been such a problem. My mother . . . used to give me iron jewelry to wear every year for my birthday, and I wore it happily, without any discomfort. Lately, I've found out that this is because there was no outer magic to augment the effects of the iron on me. It was just suppressing my inner magic, keeping it dormant, which is pretty ordinary for young Fae anyway. My mother believed my keeping it on would protect me from detection as we journeyed through Ropaz, and she asked for my word that I wouldn't remove it until I reached safety. She thought that it would be dangerous to know about magic and being a fairy, so I only found out about all of that as we were riding to Japeta. Once we entered the city, before the attack, she had me don pieces of iron armor as well, and that's what has really been making me miserable."

"So the pain is entirely physical? Do you feel that you need to be specially trained to endure it mentally?"

Lily thought that over, then shook her head.

"It doesn't just affect my body. I feel . . . panic and confusion with the pain. I've been trying to keep it on the outskirts of my mind, pushing it back when it penetrates too far inside my head. It seems to be focusing almost exclusively on the part of my mind that I'm most familiar with, though I don't know why. Alder's been calling it the Fear since he arrived."

"And how do you push back the Fear, *Vipina*?"

"By reminding myself of pain that was, is, and will always be, far worse," Lily said, very quietly. After several moments of silence, she spoke up again.

"I wouldn't know, but maybe it's something like the Thirst you mentioned. It was causing you to suffer immensely. So was the sun. You weren't yourself, and it affected you terribly. But what tortured you the most yesterday: those painful outside forces or your concern for Vabiri? What was really causing your soul to scream in agony? Sunlight, the need for blood, or the fate of your otherwing now that you have been separated? Physical pain can be controlled, dealt with, and overpowered. I doubt, though, that there are many vampires, however old or powerful, who could try to survive the conditions you suffered for almost two days, at least not without a truly imperative reason to stay alive. Where love is concerned, perhaps most people are both at their weakest and their strongest . . . I can think of nothing worse than losing a loved one who is precious to me. It is the worst of all fears. Does that make sense?"

After a moment, Vadom slowly nodded.

"Perfectly," he answered solemnly.

They traveled for a time without speaking. Eventually, however, Vadom seemed to pull himself from his line of thought and continued to ask Lily questions. He wanted to know how well Lily understood her power. Lily explained the nine wells of inner magic, telling Vadom that her mother had thought she had elemental wings as well as linguistic magic, also called her wings of elucidation. She explained why, briefly summarizing the events of her life since leaving Nather's tribe. Lily told him about the possibility of wings of prophecy that Alder had explained some, and how her mother had also mentioned healer's and warrior's wings, though not in relation to Lily. She concluded by telling Vadom that she didn't understand outer magic at all, except how it seemed to be making the iron she wore gradually heavier and increasing the Fear.

At noon, Vadom insisted on a short break, and Lily gladly dismounted and began digging in her haversack for lunch. She noticed that her food supply was a bit low, as was the amount of water in her container.

"*Vapa*, will there be a safe place to get food and water soon? If I'm careful with what I have, it will probably last about three more days, but it would be nice to find more supplies before then."

"I thought that might be the case, seeing as you must eat enough to continue growing, young as you are. If we continue at this pace, we should reach the witch city of Wikkenod in another two days. It is the westernmost concentration of air magicians in Ropaz. Over time, more and more witches and wizards have moved to their more eastern lands, in order to avoid becoming subject to the nutritional requirements of vampires. I would like to suggest that I enter the city at night, gather sustenance for you, and trade your mount for one more suitable and less conspicuous in the grasslands. Once past Wikkenod, we will need to travel east and slightly south for three weeks, as well as I am able to approximate, in order to reach Ford-upon-Ward."

Lily absorbed this new information, and she felt a pang at the thought of giving up Bepo. It would be like losing another small link to her mother, and Lily wished it wasn't necessary. She was also a bit surprised that it would be taking less than a month to arrive at the bridge city of the River Ward. Her mother had made it seem as though it would take much longer. Perhaps she had been calculating under the assumption that they would be traveling on foot? Vadom seemed confident about procuring a new animal for her to ride. Lily knew she should be grateful that he would enable her to travel all the faster, but she still felt dispirited at the thought of giving up her faithful desert amadel.

"Do I really have to leave Bepo behind? My mother said he would be strong enough for a long journey . . ." Lily trailed off at the stern, penetrating gaze Vadom pinned on her. Lily maintained eye contact, however, and after several seconds, Vadom's eyes softened almost imperceptibly.

"I don't think the beast will remain healthy for much longer unless he is returned to the desert, *Vipina,*" he said softly. "I'm sure your mother didn't mean to take him farther than Wikkenod, for he would attract too much attention. He will probably suffer in the more temperate, not to mention humid, climate of the grasslands. I am sorry you must sever this small tie to your former home, but it is truly what is best."

Vadom hesitated a moment. Then he asked, "Have you nothing else but your memories of her? You said just a short while ago that the sword was hers . . . Do you have anything she gave you before your escape?"

Lily nodded, eyes prickling. When would she be able to keep from crying at the mere mention of her mother? Perhaps if she lived for centuries or possibly millennia . . .

"She gave me a mirror for a birthday once, and I brought it with me. I also have her . . . ashes. I didn't want to scatter them in the desert, especially after I had just found out that the Fae Wood was her real home. I used some of them to make a small statue of her . . . Would you like to see it?" Lily asked quietly, unsure of his response.

"I would be honored if you showed me," Vadom said gently, his face very grave.

Lily slowly dug through her haversack until she found the statuette, still wrapped, and brought it out. She unwound the clothing from her artwork and held it out for Vadom to see. He did the slightest double-take, then his eyes widened, as though he was a bit mesmerized by what he was seeing. Vadom stared at the glass piece for several minutes, lingering the longest on her mother's face, eventually reading the epitaph carefully at the base. Finally, Vadom looked away from the statuette, though he did not immediately meet Lily's gaze.

"She is beautiful, Lily. You humble me. For centuries, I have thought no beings in Lamoranth loved as vampires do. For millennia, I have believed the Cave Kingdom held the only race capable of soul-deep emotions and bonds. How wrong I have been, and for so long, too . . . Your love is magnificent, *Vipina*. I realize now that I have not begun to fully comprehend the depths of your suffering, or your loss. Forgive me for this."

Lily shrugged, feeling suddenly shy.

"My mother used to say when I was little that no matter how old we get, we can always learn new things, as long as our minds are open. Of course, at the time, I had no idea I was going to live more than a century, for the desert dwellers very rarely do, and I didn't take her that seriously. I should have known that it was the truth, though, because my mother was always right, even when I didn't want her to be."

Lily smiled just a little, and Vadom did as well.

"Vabiri has proven herself consistently correct for most of our two millennia together, and I've all but given up trying to demonstrate otherwise. She would be happy, I think, that I am already learning from my *vipina*."

Lily was a bit surprised that Vadom had brought up his otherwing, but she was even more startled by the fact that Vadom expected to learn things from her, the student and the child. She continued to ponder this, even after she had climbed back onto Bepo and they were traveling east once again. Lily's musings were interrupted, however, by a growing curiosity emanating from Alder. Finally, Lily's own inquisitive thoughts got the better of her, and she decided to ask him about it.

Alder, what are you wondering about? Something about Vadom? I keep thinking about Vabiri, what kind of lady she is. I bet she's really worried about Vadom. It must be so hard for her, not knowing where he is or if he's even alive . . .

Lily trailed off, realizing that Alder hadn't spoken up yet. She reproved herself for not even giving him a chance to speak, then conveyed her intrigue and concentration in his direction. His ensuing hesitation only sharpened her interest in his thoughts. Finally, Alder spoke up, although it seemed for another moment as though he would demur.

"I was just wondering what you look like, Lily. I guess I've been curious since we met, but then yesterday, when Vadom said he was going to mark you, I was a little upset by that. I haven't even seen your face, and he was quite possibly changing it. I wanted to know if the mark was visible, but you haven't checked, and I thought it was because you didn't have a way to look at your face at all. But you have a mirror . . . and I've been trying to decide if I could ask you to look at yourself, so I could see you, too."

Lily felt her cheeks heat a little at Alder's words. It was true that she hadn't given a thought to Vadom's kiss-mark, or how it might have altered her appearance. Her mother had always put an emphasis on inner beauty, and Lily had always thought that was because of how unusual her features were among the desert dwellers.

"It's all right if you don't want me to see you just yet. I mean, you can't see my body either, so I suppose it would only be fair if you asked me to wait until

you reach the Fae Wood. It really doesn't matter all that much; I do enjoy the suspense in strange sort of way . . ."

Lily felt her heart warm slightly as Alder retreated, thinking he had overstepped himself.

Alder, I'll hold up the mirror when we're done traveling for the day. How does that sound?

Lily felt a surge of happiness from Alder, and she smiled, pleased to have made him feel such excitement and anticipation.

Alder, haven't you seen me in any of my memories? I've looked in that mirror before, just not that often. My mother told me when she gave it to me that she hoped it would lead me to reflect more on my mind and soul, rather than my exterior. She was always more focused on things like that . . . I guess I just don't think about my appearance very much. I was always made fun of for my pale skin and golden eyes. They're so much lighter than anyone else's in the Joquobon . . . It just wasn't something I liked dwelling on, being so different, being so disliked for it . . .

Lily trailed off as she recalled the malignant stares and whispers that had followed after her all of her life, feeling a vague sense of dread at the remembrance. What if Alder didn't like the way she looked either? Lily felt dismayed at the thought, but Alder interrupted her thoughts before they could get any more out of hand.

"Lily, if your fright or misery have anything to do with showing me your face, then it can wait," he said, very gently. *"Although I'd love to see you, it's not worth you feeling so distressed, what with everything else you're dealing with right now. If you'd rather, and don't mind, I can just float around your circle of long-term memory until I find one, maybe of that birthday when you received the mirror. Is that all right with you?"*

Alder, I already told you I would look in the mirror, and I will. Those bad feelings were just a result of me remembering all the cruel things people said . . . and did. But that's behind me now. You've made me curious, though. What do you look like?

Lily was surprised by the evasive turn his feelings took.

"Well, I have silver eyes, and sort of silvery-blond hair that I like to keep a bit long, almost shoulder-length, to cover my ears. Pale skin, like all fairies. Average height, typical muscles from all the warrior training, but still kind of lean, especially compared to the Fae who bulk up over the centuries . . ."

Lily felt him shy away from something again, and she wondered how to encourage him to keep going.

Do you have some sort of birthmark or scar, Alder? You seem hesitant about something, but I wouldn't mind that in the least. You had me at silver eyes, to be honest . . .

Lily felt Alder's surprise, then his relief. His feelings became rather sheepish.

"No, it's not any unusual marking . . . It's just that, ever since I was born, my mother, and a lot of the Fae of my acquaintance, have called me . . . pretty."

Lily started to laugh at the utter consternation in Alder's voice.

"Oh, you laugh, but it can undermine your confidence after a few decades. I am an adult male Fae and a warrior, and I'd rather be thought of as masculine, or striking, or something other than 'lovely'."

Lily couldn't help but chuckle a bit more. Thank goodness she hadn't told Alder she thought he was sweet! She could only imagine his chagrin if she had vocalized that particular thought. She also felt reassured by Alder sharing his own insecurities about his appearance. Lily wasn't at all confident about her own looks, and it was a bit of a relief to know that he felt uncertain, too. Before she could commiserate with him, however, Alder continued speaking, as though to himself.

"All these years, I've secretly hoped to have a beautiful partner, a lady who would draw attention from me and my looks . . . But the Captain and even my father have been right all along. Her soul is so incredibly radiant, no exterior, however dazzling, could compare. I see now how physical appearances aren't as big a part of the truemate bond compared to personality and common ground and a lot of other things. She is beautiful where it matters most, and I see how fortunate I am in this. I will have to reassure her that I find her attractive in every way, but not yet . . ."

Lily was absolutely stunned. Alder thought he was her truemate? He had mentioned the term before, in comparison to otherwings, but she had only been curious about its meaning in a general way. Certainly her mother had never mentioned this kind of bond. And yet . . . he had heard her, come to her, when her need was greater than ever before. His soul had left his body and traveled a vast distance to save her from her despair. Even Vadom had sought Alder's permission to train her as a warrior, as though Alder had the right to help make such decisions on her behalf. But why had he not spoken of it to her? Why had he let her think they were simply friends and traveling companions? Would it be dangerous for her enemies to know? Lily struggled with her tumultuous emotions, knowing they would cause Alder confusion and possibly worry.

She would examine her feelings about the overwhelming possibility of being Alder's truemate later. What had they been discussing? Physical appearances, and marks . . . Lily felt herself blush fiercely. Alder had been upset about Vadom kissing her! Did that mean that *he* wanted to . . . no, surely not! He had never even seen her . . . but he had asked to see her, hadn't he? And then, when he had assumed that she couldn't hear him, Alder had called her soul beautiful . . . How had she been able to hear his thoughts?

"Lily, is everything all right? Did I say something wrong?"

Lily marshaled her scattered wits with considerable effort before she responded. She was definitely not ready to have such an important discussion with Alder. Lily groped for something she felt she could say that was at least obliquely related to what they'd been speaking about.

Fine, everything is fine. Oh, and I don't think you need to worry about Vadom's mark, because mine sort of sank into his skin, almost right away, and now I can't see it. His is probably the same on me, don't you think?

Though Lily could sense Alder's uncertainty, he didn't press her. Her relief must have been obvious, for he reluctantly answered her question despite his perceptible misgivings.

"I suppose so. I guess it bothered me more to think that he had a claim on you, that he can see you and protect you and . . . and I can't."

And kiss me, Lily thought. She could hardly believe that, after being shunned as undesirable her entire life, there was suddenly someone who was actually envious of any who showed her affection.

Vadom has claimed me as a pupil, true, but I think it's very lucky that being his student means being protected by him, at least until we enter the Fae Wood. I'll consider myself incredibly fortunate if I can learn the essentials of being a warrior during this journey as well. Once I've been taught how to use weapons and magic, I'll be protecting you as well as myself, as much as I can. I'll be a warrior, too. I won't lose you out of ignorance like I did my mother, Alder.

Lily tried to express the strength of her conviction about this to Alder. Even if he wasn't her truemate, he was without doubt her first and only friend, and he had risked his life to save hers, without even knowing her. She thought he understood. He seemed a bit worried about it, however.

"Lily, I know exactly why you feel this way, but I want you to be aware that some of the older Fae might have a bit of a problem with it, at least at first. Warrior Fae are most content when their loved ones are happy and

carefree, and the typical warrior's training is too intense for gentle-hearted Fae. They will see you as a child, too innocent to withstand the rigors of testing your battle wings. Frankly, I'm interested to see how Vadom handles your new education, especially since he believes female vampires are treated much the same as peaceful Fae."

While Lily wanted to ask Alder if *he* was going to have a problem with her warrior training, she realized, at the mention of her new *vapa,* that she had been completely ignoring her surroundings since lunch. Lily quickly surfaced from her internal conversation and peered about her. To her right, the basin of the canyon had gotten quite shallow. It looked as though they would be leaving it behind by the end of the day, and Lily felt a bit of apprehension at the thought of entering Ropaz so soon. Then she scolded herself. Wasn't she lucky to have Alder and Vadom escorting her? Wasn't she fortunate to have gotten past the Magentay Canyons without any mishaps, or without even being required to hike in and back out of this strange rock valley? Lily reminded herself that she was that much closer to the Fae Wood, to Golden Court, and to fulfilled promises. She had to stay focused, even with her accidental revelation about Alder. Her next set of obtainable goals would be commencing her warrior training and reaching Wikkenod. Satisfied with her new objectives, Lily checked on the Fear in her mind, and, upon finding it about the outer rings and more or less under control, she turned her attention to Vadom. He was levitating effortlessly a few feet away, intently scanning the area around them.

"I'm sorry for my inattention just now, *Vapa*. Do you have another question for me?"

Vadom turned toward her and floated a little closer. A faint smile curved his mouth upward.

"I considered scolding you, for I attempted to speak with you and you did not respond. However, I realized I was going to have to make allowances for a *vipina* who isn't just talking to herself when she appears to be concentrating on her thoughts. From now on, when your face takes on that expression, I'll attempt to be patient. I imagine it is difficult for Alder to be without a body at this time, when his new companion is vulnerable. Communication will help ease that frustration, as well as strengthen the new bond between you."

Lily could feel Alder's embarrassment at distracting her, though it was nothing to her own at the mention of a 'bond' between them. She had to smile, however, when she sensed that Alder was feeling a grudging respect for Vadom as well, perhaps because he was being so accommodating of their unique circumstances.

"Thank you, *Vapa,* for being so understanding. I apologize for being rude, it was unintentional," she added earnestly.

"All is well, *Vipina,*" Vadom said softly. "Now, before we discuss your training, I wanted to ask you about the beings who attacked your mother in Japeta. You called those creatures the xydolem, and this is a great cause for concern if that is what they really were. Why did you call them that?"

"Because that's what my mother called them, when she said that she pitied them," Lily responded, feeling certain of her answer. The events of that night were permanently emblazoned on her memory, and she knew that she wasn't relating the facts incorrectly.

"Your mother seems to have been remarkable in numerous ways, but this is certainly exceptional as well. No one feels pity for xydolem. They are a despicable race, avenging themselves in horrible, unforgivable ways. Whatever wrongs they have suffered, real or imagined, nothing can justify the punishments they have inflicted on females and children of the Cave Kingdom throughout the ages."

Vadom's voice had become utterly without emotion or inflection, and Lily felt a small thread of real fear for only the second time in relation to the vampire. He seemed to have momentarily effaced his more gentle, polished personality, leaving behind a completely focused, absolutely lethal being. Lily could suddenly see how Vadom had endured five centuries of warrior training, and she uneasily began to realize the implications of having him for her *vapa.* When she noticed that Alder was quietly affected by Vadom's baleful intensity as well, Lily felt a bit better. At least she wasn't the only one reacting carefully to this new aspect of Vadom. Lily tried to remind herself that she had asked for instruction willingly, and she felt the return of her resolve when she also remembered why she had requested it. She spoke softly into the silence.

"I am sorry for what they have done to the innocent vampires of your home, *Vapa,* but my mother was certain the twelve beings who ambushed her were xydolem. I can describe how they looked if you need more evidence than this."

Vadom seemed to bestir himself, and he visibly relaxed.

"No, that is unnecessary, *Vipina.* Xydolem can hardly be mistaken for anything else. I was simply hoping that there were not so many working together in one place. You also said they mentioned the Misruler?"

"Yes. They wanted to know where my mother had been, and why she was in the desert. That's how I found out about Chieftain Nather's betrayal," Lily said, and she couldn't keep the anger and pain out of her voice. Vadom noticed, but he didn't comment on it.

"So the Misruler has garnered the allegiance of at least a dozen xydolem," he said softly. "These are ominous tidings indeed."

Lily was still struggling with her anger at Nather and would have let this statement pass, but Alder's marked interest in Vadom's words caused Lily to cage her anger and attempt to pay attention.

"What do you suppose he knows about the Misruler that we don't, Lily? This person must be more of a threat than the Fae are aware of, I think."

I loathe the Misruler on principle, seeing as this being is ultimately responsible for my mother's death. I wonder why they didn't look for me at all though?

This temporarily stymied Alder.

"Perhaps Nather never mentioned you? If they only asked for information on your mother, he might have thought that you were beneath their notice."

"What is Alder saying about all this, *Vipina*?" Vadom asked.

"Oh, he's worried about the Misruler. I guess this being is not common knowledge among the Fae, when it sounds as if the exact opposite should be the case. Then we were just trying to figure out why Nather didn't tell the xydolem about me. I think he might have accidentally saved my life," Lily said grudgingly.

Vadom was silent for a moment.

"True accidents occur very rarely, *Vipina*. Did this Nather ever express interest in you or your mother personally?"

Lily thought uneasily of the day they had absconded from the tribe, when Nather had looked at her in such a frightening way, grabbed her arm, threatened her . . . She unconsciously rubbed her upper arm and looked over at Vadom from the top of her amadel.

"The last words he said to me before we escaped were that he wondered what would become of me once my mother had been killed for using the Anathema," she said quietly.

"He threatened you?" Vadom asked, very quietly, and he scrutinized Lily for her reaction, watching as she shivered involuntarily.

"His eyes, his face . . . were so cruel. I felt threatened, and I knew he was dangerous. It was common knowledge that he abused his wife, and anyone near him when he was in a rage. I was afraid of him, and my mother tried to keep me away from Nather as much as possible. That last day, just before we ran away, he grabbed my arm, pulled me way too close . . . but then the baby arrived, so I pulled my arm out of his grip while he was distracted."

Lily stopped talking when she felt a surge of fury from Alder's soul. The immensity of it surprised her, then worried her.

"Alder?" she said out loud, forgetting to speak in her mind, she was so taken aback by his uncharacteristic anger.

"Alder, you need to control yourself. Lily is upset enough as it is," Vadom said steadily, though Lily saw banked anger smoldering in his eyes as well.

Lily felt Alder attempt to suppress his emotions.

"Sorry, Lily. I didn't mean to make you feel worse. It's just the thought of some beastly desert dweller laying a hand on you, wanting you . . . I can hardly stand it."

"Wanting me?" Lily repeated aloud, confused. "For his new wife, you mean? I would never have agreed to that!" she exclaimed vehemently.

"If he had made certain that your mother wasn't there to protect you, you may not have had the choice to deny him what he wanted of you," Vadom said, and Lily heard the adamantine anger twining through his voice as he spoke. "It seems that, as of seven days ago, the xydolem, and hence the Misruler, did not know of your existence. I fear, however, that Nather may reveal you out of vengeance, now that you are otherwise out of his realm of influence. We will have to be extremely careful, for the xydolem could be searching for you even now. I see why your mother thought iron so necessary. Avoiding detection is the best chance we have of crossing such a great distance without encountering formidable opponents. I'm only sorry that suppressing your considerable inner magic will cause you so much suffering, *Vipina*. It would appear, however, that the Misruler suspected your mother of planning some form of resistance, and that something was protecting you and your abilities. Let us proceed cautiously and take no unnecessary risks, for anyone capable of defying the Misruler should be kept safe in any way possible."

Lily was afraid of and upset by Vadom's words, and she couldn't bring herself to speak for some time. Lily struggled with the realities of her situation, to accept them, but she ultimately felt tired and inadequate, hurt and hunted. The afternoon was growing late, the sun well behind them, before Lily finally reached a few conclusions. A selfish, violent desert dweller had betrayed her mother. A group of nightmarish xydolem killed at the whim of one who was known only as the Misruler, a being who was more dangerous than perhaps anyone knew. And finally, Lily had been kept alive and safe, all of her life, quite possibly because she herself had magic powerful enough to threaten the machinations of the Misruler.

Blades, Bows, and Throwing Stars

It was with relief that Lily dismounted from the faithful Bepo that evening, about an hour earlier than usual, at Vadom's indication. Her mind was only going in circles at that point, and Lily felt ready for even a modest dinner. She dove into her haversack and collected some bread, a couple of vegetables, and the water container, then sat down and tucked in.

Vadom eyed her in amusement, though he also seemed a bit baffled.

"Are three such small meals a day enough for you, *Vipina?* Do young Fae need to eat more? I think they must, for you are perhaps thinner than you should be, and seem hungrier than your rations allow."

Lily was mortified, but then realized that her *vapa* meant no offense.

"My mother always made sure I was never hungry," Lily said, then admitted, "and that entailed more food than I've been consuming on this journey."

"When we reach Wikkenod in a couple of days, I will make sure you have enough supplies to eat properly," Vadom said quietly.

Lily felt a rush of gratitude toward her calm and considerate teacher.

"Thank you, *Vapa,*" she said, smiling sincerely.

Vadom seemed slightly taken aback as he gazed upon Lily's face, but then he returned her smile, though in his more gently subdued manner. Lily thought she saw just a trace of fondness in his eyes, and it seemed to soothe some of the cracks in her soul ever so minutely.

When she had finished eating, Vadom stood up and gestured for Lily to do so as well.

"I halted our traveling for the day in order to begin your warrior instruction this evening."

Lily tried to mask her surprise, but she didn't know if she completely succeeded. What with all of the conversations and revelations of the day, she had not remembered that she was to start her training. She looked at Vadom expectantly, her fatigue momentarily forgotten. Inside of her, Lily also felt Alder's excitement stir and anticipation rise.

Vadom took in her change in demeanor and smiled faintly, then he became very serious.

"It is customary for the student to formally request a portion of his, or her, teacher's time before each lesson begins. I would like to keep with this tradition."

He paused and waited expectantly. Lily straightened her shoulders and met Vadom's eyes fully.

"*Vapa,* may I have some of your time this evening to begin my warrior training?"

"You may have one hour. Please sit, then listen and watch me carefully."

Lily complied, focusing intently on Vadom. He paused, then began to speak.

"I have determined that, due to the potential hazard we face by accessing your inner magic, I will primarily be instructing you in the competent usage of weaponry. There are a set of weapons, universal to many of the races of Lamoranth, that you need to be aware of, because the majority of your possible enemies will be able to use them against you. These classic tools of conflict fall into five broad categories. Each contains weapons that serve different purposes and have their own strengths and weaknesses, depending on the style of combat you develop, as well as the style of your opponent. Those categories are as follows: blades, blunt weapons, spears and polearms, ranged weapons, and magical weapons. While different races throughout Lamoranth will often specialize in certain categories, most warriors of any people will know how to counter the attacks of an enemy with knowledge of all five of the categories.

"Over the next few weeks, I think that I will first explain and then test you with all of the weapons of which I am aware. Due to our unique circumstances, I believe it would be best to then select two weapons for which you show some propensity, then commence your training with a focus on just these. By instructing you on the basics of both a long-range and a short-range weapon, you will be able to defend yourself in a larger number of situations, should the necessity arise.

"Now, I want to introduce you to the weapons I possess. Vampires use night magic, which I believe the Fae call Void element, and we must fashion all of our own fighting tools out of this magic. Though you may need to check with Alder later, I can store these weapons in my body, as undiluted night magic, in a similar manner to the concentration of power stored in your fairy mind.

"The following are weapons from the blade family. Over the centuries, I have come to favor these tools for a variety of reasons, among which are their durability, versatility, precision, and close-range lethality."

Lily then watched in amazement as Vadom made a loose fist of his right hand, then touched it to the left side of his chest by his thumb and index finger. She saw a smoky black handle slowly form, and when Vadom began to pull his fist away from his heart, he was unsheathing a shiny, onyx-colored sword from his very body. Lily gasped, but quickly slapped her hands over her mouth, not wanting to break Vadom's concentration. Alder, too, seemly slightly surprised. Lily could tell that, though he was definitely professionally interested, he was also almost boyishly excited for a display of skill from a very old vampire.

"Greatsword, one of the largest blades that exist," Vadom said, and cut the air with a big, heavy-looking blade several times, with the ease and familiarity that Lily felt when she wound her hair in a cloth head wrap. Vadom put the dark sword away a few moments later by adjusting his grip on the hilt, using the slightest flick of his wrist, and, putting his fist to his chest once more, sent the blade handle-first back inside of himself.

Without moving his arm, Vadom began forming another weapon handle, and almost immediately, he was unsheathing a smaller, lighter-looking sword, also midnight-hued.

"Shortsword, most common among the desert people," he said. Lily recognized this as a very similar weapon to her mother's, which now hung sheathed on her own back.

Vadom proceeded to show Lily a dizzying variety of blades, sheathing and unsheathing them all with graceful agility and blurring speed. The swords were short and long, from daggers and knives to shortswords, eventually becoming so large that they had to be wielded with two hands, like the greatsword. Many were curved rather than straight, and still others differed only because they were single-edged instead of double-edged. Vadom called each one by name, and Lily worried that she wouldn't be able to remember them all.

Among the shortest were the dirk and poniard, which Lily's iron-belted blade strongly resembled. Vadom explained that they were good weapons to wield in accompaniment with most types of one-handed shortswords. The blades grew a bit longer as Vadom illustrated the use of a gladius and a pair of anelaces. Then came noticeably larger swords, closer to the first that her *vapa* had shown her. These Vadom called a falchion, scimitar, flamberge, cutlass, claymore, and broadsword. Finally the weapons became so large that they required two hands, causing Vadom to wield them differently in a way even Lily could distinguish. The greatsword appeared once more, as well as a hand-and-a-half sword, among others with names that sounded exotic and foreign to Lily.

"All of the previous blades were swords. The following is a rapier," and here Vadom pulled out a startlingly thin, long blade. "It is also technically a sword, though more commonly called a foil. It is utilized in a style of combat called fencing, which is comprised almost entirely of thrusting gestures, without the cutting movements of the other blades."

Lily observed her teacher's change in stance and altered arm movements.

"This is often a good weapon for warriors of a slighter build. When used correctly, it can compensate for the smaller size of the wielder."

Though this information reassured Lily somewhat, she couldn't help but think that a bigger blade would feel more secure in the heat of a battle. She pictured herself facing a half-dozen xydolem, holding some of the weapons Vadom had just shown her. Lily couldn't really see herself inflicting much damage with a rapier, which probably required more precision and skill than she would be able to acquire in her weeks of training with Vadom.

Vadom sheathed his Void foil, then placed his other fisted hand to the opposite side of his chest. When he removed six blades at once, Lily's eyes widened.

"Throwing knives, the most useful blades that can be used in multiple numbers, due to being both short and light," Vadom said. Before Lily's eyes, his arms straightened out in front of him with such speed and force that it took her a moment to realize that he had only let fly one knife from each hand. As Vadom launched the next two, she managed to notice that he held them by the blade rather than the handle when he aimed. As he threw the final two, Lily tried to follow their progress in the air, and just saw them as they became embedded in a smallish rock a good distance away. They formed a perfectly straight line with the other four throwing knives down the exact center of the rock.

Lily had hardly blinked by the time Vadom had retrieved his six knives and replaced them in his chest. He stood in his original place once more, then crossed his arms and put just his fingertips to his chest. Out came eight black metal discs, four in each hand, with multiple sharp points protruding from the rounded edges of each. Lily only just kept her jaw from dropping.

"Throwing stars," Vadom intoned.

He proceeded to aim and throw them one at a time, alternating hands, at a new rock, a bit larger but farther away than the rock sporting six new knife holes.

When Vadom had returned from gathering his throwing stars, he spoke again.

"Though the last two I have shown you could also technically belong to the ranged weapons category, they are generally acknowledged as blades due to their method of inflicting harm by cutting or slicing. The next set of weapons I will show you are more firmly members of the ranged category. This first is a bow and arrows."

Lily felt a shiver of unease travel down her spine upon hearing the weapon's name. She couldn't help but recall Phepin, Nather's guard, shooting arrows at her and her mother the day of their escape. Even though he had not meant to harm them, Lily would never forget how they had been more worried about that one bow and quiver of arrows than the six shortswords their pursuers had kept at the ready. Lily watched her *vapa*'s demonstration with her full attention.

Vadom proceeded to remove a completely black bow from the right side of his torso with his left hand. He held it straight out in front of him, holding it perfectly vertical, just as he stood. Vadom then reached his right hand to his right shoulder, removing a sharply pointed arrow by its feathered end, and fitted the arrow to the middle of the bow, just above his grip. Vadom used the tips of his fingers to maintain his hold of the arrow's feathered end and pull back on the cord, tautening the bow enough to unleash the arrow. A split-second later, the arrow had struck yet another rock. Vadom fired a half-dozen more arrows in quick succession, forming a perfect triangle around the first arrow.

Vadom gathered his arrows as quickly as he had the throwing knives and stars, but he paused when he had restored the bow and arrows to his torso and shoulder and came to stand near Lily once more.

"*Vipina?*" he said softly.

Only then did Lily realize that she had instinctively covered the back of her head and her neck with her hands and arms. She slowly lowered them, noting almost distantly that her hands were shaking. Lily forced herself to meet Vadom's steady gaze.

"What's the next ranged category weapon, *Vapa?*"

"The crossbow, a more mechanical version of the bow and arrows," Vadom said smoothly, though he still watched Lily carefully. He demonstrated after removing the black weapon from his body, pulling arrows from a point lower than his shoulder this time, and fitting the arrows on the portion of the weapon he named the crosspiece. Lily noticed that this weapon couldn't fire as many arrows as the bow, at least not in such a quick succession, because the cord had to be reset after each use. However, it did seem as though it would be easier, as a novice, to aim accurately and achieve a decent distance.

"Longbow, the largest of the bow family, capable of reaching the farthest targets. Although you are too petite to wield it effectively at this time, I'd like you to be able to recognize it, for it is the favored weapon of the elves. Although those elves who go on to be warriors often come to utilize other weapons, every elf in the Forest of Ancients is competent with a longbow."

Lily was surprised by how far Vadom's arrows were able to travel, and she hoped she would be able to keep a healthy distance from unfriendly elves in the future.

"Sling," Vadom said, and he removed from his chest a weapon somewhat similar to one that Lily had seen in action before, always in unpleasant circumstances. She remembered, all too clearly, when a group of desert boys had purchased slingshots from a merchant in Japeta during a festival several years ago. Lily had been one of their favorite targets after Ignis had chased them away from his amadels. She had sported welts from their stones all over her body for a full moon cycle, until her mother had noticed the bruises and apparently told the boys off.

Lily couldn't help but wince as Vadom unleashed a volley of smooth, black Void stones. His observant eyes didn't miss the movement, and Lily wondered if her teacher was beginning to think her a complete coward.

She willed herself to give away none of her apprehension for the rest of the weapons introduction.

"The sling is a smaller model of the most commonly used weapon of the giants. They can shoot small boulders accurately with their slings, though they more often use large chunks of ice for ammunition, seeing as they live in the Evertundra and there is a never-ending supply at their disposal."

Lily attempted to picture giants, based on her mother's fairy tale descriptions, wielding enormous slings full of ice, but her imagination failed her.

"What does ice look like?" she asked.

At Vadom's slightly surprised look, she added hastily, "My mother told me a couple of bedtime stories about giants when I was little, but she only mentioned that their home was covered in snow. Is ice like snow?"

"Both snow and ice are forms of frozen water. Snow is a variety of precipitation, coming from clouds in the sky, and it is essentially tiny pieces of ice. Ice is often clear, like water, and looks like solid water in appearance. It accumulates over time in a cold enough climate, and often has a smooth surface that is difficult to walk on."

So ice looked like glass? Lily shook her head in puzzlement. She had never really understood the concept of 'cold', at least not beyond the chill of some desert nights.

"Will Ropaz feel cold?"

Vadom seemed amused.

"I imagine that, in comparison to the desert, the rest of Lamoranth will feel cooler to you, *Vipina*. Ropaz will not be cold, but it will be less hot than the Joquobon. Now, I'd like to show you two more weapons, also of the ranged category, before the sun is finished setting."

"Sorry for interrupting you, *Vapa*," Lily said, slightly chastened.

"There is nothing wrong with curiosity or asking questions, *Vipina*," Vadom said readily. "Knowing when and how to ask for information is what is important. Feel free to question me whenever I'm not speaking or demonstrating, and I will either answer immediately or at the end of the lesson. We can adapt this strategy as I see what allows you to learn most effectively."

"Thank you, *Vapa*. What are the last two ranged weapons?"

"One is the stockwhip."

Vadom brought out a coiled length of braided black rope from the center of his chest. Lily watched, slightly ill at ease, as Vadom flicked the stockwhip and caused it to make a loud, resounding crack. Lily was sure, if they had still been at the rim of the canyon, that the sound would have echoed louder than Bepo's noisy gait occasionally had.

"There are variations on the whip, especially with its end, which can be braided into multiple tips, occasionally with barbed objects woven into the material. Length can vary, although the whip begins to lose its effectiveness if it is too long. Though perhaps not a ranged weapon in the truest sense, the whip definitely does not fit into any other category; however, if used properly, it can almost entirely eliminate hand-to-hand combat and the use of most short-range weapons."

After re-coiling the stockwhip and allowing it to sink back into his chest, Vadom summoned the final weapon for the evening from his body. It had a handle the length of her forearm that looked like an amadel-bone pole of a tent, complete with a large bladed head attached to the end.

"Throwing ax."

After demonstrating, Vadom retrieved it from another unlucky rock, which had been cloven into two perfect halves.

"This is the only type of ax that is not generally considered a part of the spears and polearms category. It is meant to be used as a ranged weapon, while the rest remain in hand for close combat. I will go over that category, as well as blunt and magical weapons, tomorrow, time permitting. Now that I have told you of the first two groups, are there any that you have a particular interest in learning as we travel?"

Lily thought over what she had been told in the last hour, then answered slowly.

"Of the blades, I thought many of the different types of shortswords would be manageable, or perhaps one of the blades that is considered a very long dagger as well as a very short sword. One practical consideration that occurred to me was that I already possess my mother's shortsword, though I think I'll definitely tire easily using an iron weapon.

"If I could choose any of your shorter Void blades, however, I was most interested in the anelaces. I was attracted to the idea of a pair of blades, and the anelaces would have nearly the light weight of daggers but could fend off the attacks of full-fledged swords. Because they're straight and double-edged, an opponent would have to be wary of two such weapons.

"Something that I noticed and appreciated was that some of the swords have big hand covers, which would make me feel more secure if I were to wield them. One thing I found strange was that I don't feel as though I'd be good with a curved blade, because it sort of seemed difficult or counter-intuitive, though I'm not sure why.

"Ultimately, I'd like to learn the dagger and the throwing weapons someday, especially the throwing stars, though if I could only pick two of the weapons you just showed me, I'd like to choose two that stay in my hands, that don't have the disadvantage of leaving me potentially unarmed.

"The rapier seemed a bit . . . impractical, like it wouldn't be a good weapon to have in a lot of situations, because you were only stabbing, and never slicing, with it. Though I haven't seen 'blunt' weapons, I wouldn't like to have just a thin, flexible-looking blade going up against one.

"As for ranged, I think the bow and arrows would be my choice. It fires more than the crossbow, it looks like it would inflict more damage than a sling, especially at a greater distance, and . . . it feels less sinister than the stockwhip."

Lily took a deep breath and continued looking at Vadom, whose face had remained completely impassive as she spoke. She clasped her hands in front of her to keep from adjusting her head wrap and waited for her teacher to respond.

"You are an attentive listener and very observant. This pleases me, as an avid pupil will allow me to teach more in the time that we have. I think a type of shortsword or the anelaces would be good choices, though we would start with a single anelace and add the second when you have grasped the basics. I will also have you try both your mother's weapon and my night weapons to see which suit your condition better.

"The hand covering on a sword is called a crossguard or a basket hilt. I'm not certain why you instinctively dislike curved blades, but this could very well be a Fae inclination— you will have to ask Alder.

"Your considerations on the advantages and disadvantages of many of these weapons were largely correct, and I would like you to continue utilizing that analytical mentality as I introduce more weapons to you. I agree that throwing weapons would not be ideal for you at this time, and that rapiers are useful in some situations, but not others. I also would have selected the bow and arrows for your ranged weapon, for the reasons you gave, with the exception of your feeling about the stockwhip.

"All weapons are tools, designed to maim and kill, *Vipina*. The whip is no more sinister than any of the other objects of violence, and this is an important fact to bear in mind. The rapier is no less deadly because it is more elegant, and weapons that have been used against you personally are no more frightening than those you saw for the first time this evening. Before we begin actually practicing with the weapons you select, I see that we will have to have a serious discussion about a warrior's mentality. Your attitude, emotions, and objectives going into a battle or single combat are just as critical as the skills, weapons, and magic you possess. That lecture, however, must wait for another day. It is time that you rested, *Vipina.*"

Lily nodded. She had found it harder to remain focused in the semi-darkness, and now that the twilight had ended and night had just begun, she was really starting to feel the fatigue of a long day full of hard traveling. Before turning toward Bepo's warmth and her haversack pillow, however, Lily looked steadily at Vadom and spoke from her heart.

"Thank you so much, *Vapa*, for your instruction. I am very glad to have begun."

Vadom relaxed his strict demeanor and smiled slightly.

"You're welcome, *Vipina*. You have preempted my last words of the lesson. It is customary to thank your teacher for his time. There is an accompanying gesture, which I would appreciate if you would use, that denotes sincerity of words that all vampires recognize and perform quite often. It is called the *valoriad*, and it underscores thanks, as well as greetings and farewells, to all inhabitants of the Cave Kingdom."

Vadom then demonstrated the gesture for Lily. She watched carefully, wanting to get it just right when it was her turn. He moved his right forearm up and across his body from its natural position at his side, moving only at the elbow, and keeping his palm and fingers perfectly straight and flat. With his lower arm and entire hand in a flawlessly straight line, he brought the tips of his two outermost fingers to rest on his left collarbone, in the hollow of his shoulder. His palm was facing up toward his neck, and his thumb, on the outside and farthest from his body, was parallel to his jawline. Lily imitated the gesture, eyes on Vadom.

"Good, just don't break the line by allowing your thumb to touch your palm, *Vipina*," he said softly. "It is intended as a peaceful gesture, for no weapon can be pulled from one's body easily when held in this way, with the wrist rotated and the fingers so straight."

Lily tried again, this time earning a small nod of approval.

"Good night, *Vapa*," she said, arm still in place.

"Good night, *Vipina*," Vadom said, smiling slightly, and performing the gesture so naturally and gracefully that Lily knew he had done it innumerable times before.

Only when he had slowly dropped his hand to his side once more did Lily turn and head in the direction of her makeshift pillow, stumbling on a rock in the darkness that was now complete. Only when she had laid down her head did Lily realize that she had told Alder she would hold up the mirror to her face. He hadn't spoken a word for the full duration of her lesson, and he continued that silence now.

Alder? Still there?

"Yes, Lily. I was just thinking, that's all."

Would you like me to look in the mirror, or wait for some light tomorrow?

"I'd like to be able to see you clearly; let's wait just a bit longer. What did you think of your first warrior lesson?"

There's so much to know! I see now why it must have taken him five hundred years to learn everything. Vadom was so comfortable with all of those weapons, I feel like I'm going to be totally awkward by comparison. Do you think I should go for one of the true shortswords or the anelaces?

"That will depend on whether or not you can wield his Void weapons. If you can, you'll have that choice. If not, there may be a problem, because I just can't imagine the pain involved in fighting with an iron sword. Still, if you can decide, I would go with the anelaces. Usually, warriors end up being the most skilled with weapons they take a liking to right away. Vadom's also right about training you with a longer range weapon. A bow and arrows could really be useful. I like the idea of you taking down danger before it gets too close . . . Would you tell me why you felt so afraid when he demonstrated with the bow and arrows? And with the sling, too, you were upset. Was Vadom right? Did the desert people hurt you?"

Alder's sadness and anger were palpable, and Lily was surprised by the strength of his feelings. Though she didn't really want to discuss it, Lily did want to be honest with Alder, even if he couldn't always safely share things with her in return.

Some of the desert boys got ahold of slingshots at one point a few years ago, and they liked aiming for me, at least until my mother castigated them. I know the sling is different from a slingshot, but they were similar enough to evoke painful memories. As for the bow and arrows, when Nather and his men chased after us as we fled the tribe's camp, they all had swords. One man, though, Nather's guard, Phepin, had a bow as well, and he shot at us when we came within range. I think I only showed you the sandstorm that I brewed up for them when we met. Anyway, we didn't think he was actually going to hurt us, because my mother had recently saved his life, but he still put on a good show. I remember being afraid that my black hair wrap was a perfect target against the white sands. All of that is behind me now though, Alder. Please don't concern yourself with things of the past. They can't be changed, only learned from.

"You sound so wise, Lily. I just wish I could have prevented your hardships, protected you from harmful people. If only your mother hadn't seen fit to remove you from the Fae Wood, we might have met sooner, and under better circumstances . . . But we many never know Rose's reasons . . . although the Misruler must be behind this somehow. I will finally be able to relax when you come to Silver Court and I can use my body again, that is certain."

Lily was struggling to stay awake and pay attention to Alder, but she could feel exhaustion tugging on her consciousness. Hadn't she wanted to ask Alder something? Vadom had recommended him twice during the lesson as a reference to Fae power and weapons . . .

Alder, I have . . . questions for you . . . tomorrow.

"Anytime, Lily. Sweet dreams."

Sweet dreams, Alder.

And with those last words echoing in her mind, Lily fell fast asleep.

Mirror, Mirror

Lily was forcefully woken by Alder just before sunrise.

"Lily, you need to wake up. The Fear is coming in too far, and you need to push it back. Lily!"

She noticed that breathing was slightly difficult, as though she was laying under several heavy blankets. Lily also noted, as her grogginess quickly burned away, that the Fear was definitely greater than it had been yesterday as they'd been leaving the Magentay Canyons. The pain had never been quite this intense either. Lily summoned her determination and consciously moved to defend the power wells in her mind. She felt a bit dismayed that the effects of the iron seemed to be specifically targeting that place, there in the most prominent part of her oft-used consciousness. Just like her breathing, Lily was certain that the Fear had somehow gained weight and mass as she had slept, proving heavier and more difficult to endure than before.

After struggling and ultimately succeeding against the worsening effects of the Bane of the Fae, Lily surfaced to see with her eyes and attempted to walk some of the slowly receding pain out of her body. Vadom had been watching over her, scanning their surroundings intently and occasionally sniffing the air delicately. He looked slightly surprised that Lily was awake before the sun had risen, and he regarded her carefully before speaking.

"Is the iron becoming more difficult to bear, *Vipina?*"

Lily only nodded miserably, afraid that she would start complaining if she opened her mouth to speak just then. If she had been with her mother, Lily would have been more vocal about the armor and jewelry. She had always been able to tell her mother everything. Lily had only kept her glass artwork to herself to have a secret, something wholly her own. She felt sure that she would have shared that with Rose eventually if they hadn't been forced to flee for their lives, and Lily felt a pang that her mother had never seen anything that Lily had made with the elements. Her mother would never see any of the magic that Lily would perhaps be able to wield when she got older, assuming she made it to the Fae Wood alive. Lily tried to focus on the sandstorm her mother had seen her conjure, and Lily's perfect understanding of the first Fae words she'd ever heard. That would have to be enough. Lily would have to allow those memories to be enough . . .

"Are you feeling steadier now, Lily? That was a rough way to start your day . . . I hate to impart more bad news, but seeing as we will be crossing into Ropaz today, I think you should know that there may be a noticeable increase in the amount of Fear you feel from the iron in the grasslands due to the greater level of outer magic in that part of Lamoranth. You may have to make adjustments in the number of iron pieces you're wearing."

Though a part of Lily rejoiced at the thought of removing some of the armor she wore, that happiness was almost immediately followed by a sense of guilt. She had promised her mother that she wouldn't remove the iron until she was safe, and she had given her word sincerely. It was for her own good, to ensure her own survival . . . Lily's thoughts whirled with her conflicted emotions until Vadom broke in on her inner commotion.

"Would you like to eat a meal and make an early start, *Vipina?* If it becomes necessary, we can begin taking a short break in the afternoons, perhaps after your midday repast, so that you will remain strong enough to continue traveling. The only alternative I see is to remove iron, but that would endanger your word to your mother, which I think you are loath to do."

Lily looked at Vadom and felt her respect for him grow, even as her confusion cleared and fresh resolve to honor her mother filled her heart.

"I would only take off a piece of iron outside of the Fae Wood if death was the only other option," Lily said quietly, staring solemnly into his dark-eyed face.

Vadom returned her gaze, nodding slowly with something like acceptance, though it was still difficult for Lily to decipher his subtle facial expressions.

Lily stretched her sore muscles, though whether they had come from so much amadel riding or as another effect of the iron, she wasn't certain. She dug in her haversack for a quick meal, and they set off soon after, the freshly risen sun directly in their faces.

After riding for a time, Lily felt some of her equilibrium return, and she decided to ask Alder the questions she'd had last night after her first warrior lesson.

Alder? Can I ask you those questions now?

"Sure, Lily. You'll have to remind me what they were about, though."

Lily thought he sounded upset, but Alder seemed to be resisting whatever emotions he was truly feeling, and Lily only understood how confused he was. She wondered if they really were truemates, and if partners so close talked about every little thing, or if some problems still had to be worked out alone. After a brief hesitation, Lily decided not to pester Alder about his feelings. She hoped he would just bring up whatever was bothering him when he was ready.

Alder, Vadom suggested last night that I ask you about Fae reactions to curved blades. Is it just me who sort of dislikes them, or do most Fae feel that way?

"Strangely, many Fae warriors are disinclined to utilize curved blades, such as the scimitar, falchion, and cutlass your teacher showed you yesterday evening. Though all of us are still instructed thoroughly in their use, very few Fae warriors favor blades that seem to symbolize crooked or dishonest intentions. Fae warriors are taught to walk the straight path of life, to act with the best reasons at heart, to commit the fewest possible wrongs, and to respect all those around them. I think this is a small proof that you do have the soul of a warrior, with inherent honor."

What about the whip? Do Fae dislike that weapon? I really had a bad feeling about it.

"I don't know why you had a negative sense about the whip. That must simply be indicative of your personal preferences. Like I said last night, I'd rather you learned the bow and arrows in any case, despite your dangerous past experiences with it. Strange, that you are less opposed to the sling than the whip . . . But there was a second question, wasn't there?"

Oh, yes. Earlier in the lesson, Vadom said that he thought he stored pure night magic in his body like I keep sun magic in mine, but he wasn't completely certain. How do fairies store and access their inner magic? Can we just pull it in and out of our power wells at will? I haven't ever really given a thought to how I use my elemental wings, because it's such an unconscious effort at this point. I don't think all of my inner magic is going to be that easy for me to use, though.

"Well, the inner magic of the Fae is always present, but usually dormant until near the age of maturity. Most fairies practice basic skills with outer magic until their inner power begins to manifest. The general process for fairies and their inner magic is gradual. You discover what pairs of wings you have, and you take the time to learn about each ability. Then you practice each one and determine how deep each well is, how strong and extensive each pair of wings has the potential to become. Finally, fairies hone their gifts over time, slowly mastering their crafts. A fairy who is asked to instruct others with the same abilities is acknowledged to have achieved mastery in at least one aspect of their power."

So when Vadom asked about storing magic, if it turns out that I have warrior's wings, then we are both holding magical weapons within ourselves, just different kinds of magic?

"Yes, exactly. Fairies don't have to make their own weapons out of love element. It appears that vampires have to start from the very beginning and create their tools, while Fae warriors are born with wings that gradually manifest abilities as they grow into their inner magic. If you have warrior wings, then you have weapons stored in your mind, in one of your wells of power. It will take training for you to access them, become comfortable with them, and really learn to fight effectively with them."

Did you notice anything else that would make a vampire warrior different from a Fae warrior?

"Well, it's kind of a small thing, but it appears that Vadom pulls his weapons from his chest. Fae warriors actually channel their power through their arms and out of their hands, almost as if their weapons are an extension of their limbs. I'm also not sure yet if a vampire can wield more than one tool at a time. I know older Fae who can keep some weapons at the ready a small distance from their physical selves, and when they have all of their weapons out, like for inspection, all of the blades and polearms and bows and blunt weapons hover in rings around them, sort of in their orbit, if you will. With the most powerful of our race, the full expression of a warrior's wings can be an incredible sight."

Lily could tell that Alder was recalling someone in particular. The respect in his voice was unmistakable. It occurred to her that she didn't know if Alder had a special teacher, too, or if he was trained by multiple instructors. Lily realized that there was much she didn't know about Alder, and she decided to try to find out more about him in the following weeks while they had such an amazing connection to each other.

Does your vapa *have a great deal of inner magic, Alder?*

Lily felt his surprise at the question.

"Fae don't have quite the exclusive relationship that vampires apparently do. Most young warriors are tutored by their fathers initially. Then they are often assigned to an old or very skilled Fae who can take them through greater and higher levels of magic weaponry and tactical training. My father has a time-consuming profession, and so he asked the Captain of the Court Guard to oversee and participate in my warrior's education. I was extremely lucky to gain such a warrior as my primary instructor. Over the years, he has asked Fae specializing in every type of weapon to spar with me and help me learn the finer points of each tool. I progressed through the different color levels fairly quickly, and I am considered talented for my age."

Lily felt his quiet pride and shared it. She knew that Alder wouldn't boast without being fully justified in his words. Lily wondered if he had been upset a short while ago because he was frustrated with being so confined when he was regularly so active.

I'm not setting you back in your training, am I? I hate to think that you might, well, change color levels because of me. Is that what might happen? Is that bad?

Alder hastened to reassure her.

"No, Lily. Once you have achieved a new and higher level of magic, it cannot be taken away. You will always know how to access it, what it feels like, the amount of focus it requires. There are many levels of magic available to the Fae, depending on the number of wells of inner magic they possess, as well as the amount of outer magic they learn to channel into their minds and control. Those are designated by color, which often correspond to the shade of a fairy's hair or eyes. I won't fall from silver level, and after one month, the only thing I'll have to contend with when I'm back in my body will be muscle tone and endurance. Such physical strength can be regained quickly with discipline. I don't want you to worry about that at all. Just concentrate on making it to the Fae Wood. Please, Lily?"

I will, Alder. Thank you for explaining everything.

"Well, I'd love to tell you more, especially now that Vadom is protecting you, but I still think it would be safer to wait on some things until you arrive. There's so much you need to know, but you already have a lot to handle as it is, and I don't want to add to that unnecessarily. I feel fortunate to have a

companion and friend who endures hardship so gracefully. You haven't uttered a word of complaint, have you? I think everyone will be impressed with how mature you are, especially for your brief number of years."

Lily clearly sensed Alder's pride and affection for her, and worry as well. She felt happy that he cared for her, and that he accepted her as she was. Alder was a huge part of the reason that she was able to go on with her journey at all. Lily wanted to tell him these things, to attempt to express what he was slowly coming to mean to her, but she didn't know how.

After a few minutes, Lily summoned her feelings of growing regard for Alder and softly projected them in his direction within her mind. She immediately sensed his surprise and delight, then he conveyed feelings that were much the same, though they had an edge that was simultaneously protective and frustrated. Lily thought she might understand what he had been upset about. After the slingshot explanation, as well as the bow and arrows story, Alder had probably realized how vulnerable Lily had been to danger for most of her life. Though Lily had rarely considered herself in need of a defender, she had to admit that she felt much safer in the presence of Vadom's solid reliability. Perhaps Alder didn't think he was doing his duty by her, as a warrior, a friend... and possibly as a mate. She decided to correct him on that score.

Alder, I wanted to thank you for waking me up this morning. I don't know what I would do if you weren't here to aid me with the Fear. I don't think I could make it without your presence in my mind. Will you help me stay strong enough until we reach the Fae Wood?

Lily felt his surge of emotion and heard the complete sincerity in his response.

"Of course, Lily. It is an honor to help a Fae lady and friend when she is in need of me."

Lily's heart warmed at Alder's chivalry, something that she had never experienced before. She felt a tiny crack slowly heal in her golden soul, and she smiled at the thought of taking another little step on her path with Alder.

Thank you, Alder.

"You're welcome. Now, perhaps you should take a look around you and make sure you haven't fallen off the amadel or some other such calamity?"

Lily gave a small soul-chuckle at Alder's teasing, then fully surfaced to her surroundings. She immediately gave a start of alarm and gasped aloud.

Vadom was beside her in a flash, his stance defensive, even as Alder anxiously questioned her.

"Lily? Lily! What is it? What's wrong?"

"What happened to the ground? It's *green!* And . . . it's . . ."

Lily lapsed into stunned silence, unable to express how very strange she found the spiky covering of this new landscape. Vadom relaxed, smiling ever so slightly, though attempting to maintain a straight face.

"This terrain is not just rock, *Vipina,* but also earth, which allows vegetation to grow. It is the grass that is green. It will be much taller once we cross the border into Ropaz later today."

"Grass," Lily repeated, eyes still wide and a bit apprehensive. "That's what people refer to when they say 'grasslands'?"

"Yes," Alder said, exasperated. *"Don't scare me like that! I thought you were about to be attacked by a coven of witches!"*

Doesn't all of that green kind of bother you though?

"Lily," Alder said, more thoughtfully. *"Do you know what trees look like? Did your mother ever describe the Fae Wood to you?"*

She told me that the trees in the Forest of Ancients are older than those in the Fae Wood, because the sprites and dryads and nymphs have been living there and watching over them even longer than the fairies in their wood. She also told me that our firewood came from whole, tall trees that had been chopped up into small pieces, without their branches or leaves. Firewood is the most-traded commodity in the Joquobon. You know the place in my mind where my soul resides? It's in the midst of a number of trees such as I have always dreamt them to be.

Lily felt a little defensive, not to mention embarrassed. Her mother hadn't really explained precisely what a tree looked like, but she had her imagination, didn't she? She felt slightly annoyed when Alder seemed at a loss for words. Though she was hard pressed to acknowledge it, the truth was that it was easier to feel thusly than to face what felt like yet another shortcoming. When Alder picked up on the tenor of her emotions, however, he hastened to explain.

"Please don't take my astonishment the wrong way, Lily. It's just that I have been surrounded by trees and grass my entire life, and I've just taken it for granted. You have lived in a place almost completely devoid of non-sentient life, and it's just such a drastically different perspective from my own that I was caught off guard. This is probably not the last time I'll be directly confronted by the unique circumstances of your childhood, but I'll try to handle it better next time. I meant no offense."

Pacified, and feeling a bit remorseful for her pique as well, Lily apologized for startling her two companions.

"All is well, *Vipina*. You will be seeing many new things now that you have left your home. I would just ask that you don't express fear in response to the unknown. We all must learn to face the unfamiliar with bravery and poise, and I believe this journey to the Fae Wood will be an excellent opportunity for you to try to learn such a challenging lesson."

"Well, at least grass means we're approaching Ropaz. I suppose I should be glad that this wasn't a real emergency. I think I'm going to feel completely powerless when something does go wrong . . ."

Alder, I just don't understand why you're speaking this way. Things have already gone wrong! You saved me when I was . . . alone. I rushed into the situation with Vadom, and we brazened that out together, too. I sleep easier knowing that I have a warrior in my mind who has successfully passed through I-don't-know-how-many levels of Fae training, someone who can tell me exactly what to do when I'm in danger. If I can't stay calm, I know you'll help me keep from panicking. If I'm afraid, I know I can count on you to help me be brave. Maybe you could even help me defend myself with a weapon, give me instructions until I can escape. I don't think it will come to that with Vadom escorting us, but nothing is certain. The point is, Alder, that I think you really are underestimating your value as a being just because your soul isn't in your body at the moment. Male Fae see themselves as more than just weapon wielders, don't they?

Lily carefully gauged Alder's emotional reaction to her words. She had thought her last question had been rhetorical, yet Alder was thinking it over intently. He was uncertain and thoughtful for the remainder of the morning, and Lily let him be. Some part of her instinctively felt that Alder needed to work out what she'd said, and Lily knew it would be wrong to interrupt him just now.

When the sun was almost directly overhead, Alder finally spoke again.

"Did you ever consider what you wanted in a mate when you lived in the desert, Lily?"

Lily felt uncomfortable with the question. This was the most direct Alder had been yet about what might exist between them, but she still considered it carefully before answering.

Not much. My mother just told me that I was too young to think about such things on the rare occasions I brought it up. I suppose I did want a protector at times, someone to shield me from the people who were cruel, someone who would stand up for me instead of letting me be ridiculed by everyone. But I suppose, when I was out in the desert alone, making my glass statues, I dreamed about . . .

having a friend. Someone to talk to, to laugh with, to share . . . everything. I wished for an equal.

Alder was quiet.

"Some of the oldest Fae truemates are like that. They say it takes time, and a perfect knowledge and acceptance of one another, to achieve such a relationship. It's certainly never easy to achieve . . . I've always wanted to be more than just a protector. It's just that . . . that's all I understand. I hope— well, I have always hoped that when I meet my mate, she will be patient with me in all things, but especially in this regard. I think that finding my equal is what I've always wanted, too . . . I've just never put it in words like you have. Truly, it must be wise to wish for this for ourselves when we are still so young . . ."

Lily and Alder didn't speak again until Vadom called a halt for Lily to rest. For her part, Lily was preoccupied with Alder's words and what they might mean for her. She was beginning to feel just a bit excited, and it gave her a measure of strength she'd never possessed before.

"*Vipina,* we are making good time. I think perhaps you should eat again."

Lily laughed, and both of her companions were startled by the sound.

"*Vapa,* if anyone should be hungry, it's you. You haven't eaten since we met you!"

Vadom smiled softly.

"Adult vampires need to feed less and less frequently as they grow older, *Vipina.* Before partaking of your blood, I required sustenance only once a month to remain healthy. When we supplement our diet with insects and water in bat form, we can drink blood even less frequently. That is why your hunger multiple times in one day is a bit disconcerting for me. It has been a very long time since I needed blood on a daily basis. Even as young bat pups, we didn't have names for our meals, as I think wizards and witches do."

Lily smiled, and she could feel Alder's amusement as well.

"We name our meals, too, *Vapa,*" she said, grinning.

When Vadom seemed nonplussed, as well as curious, Lily grinned.

"Breakfast is first thing in the morning, when you wake up hungry and need energy to start the day. Right now, around midday, is for lunch. In the evening, the last meal of the day is called dinner or supper. If you're lucky, and there's extra food, you can have snacks in between meals. Those are smaller than meals, but they keep you from getting too hungry, like in the middle of the afternoon. When your snacks are special or unhealthy, they're called treats. I miss those," Lily said, grinning wistfully. "My mother used to buy me bellinnatee on trading fair days," she added sadly, though she didn't stop smiling entirely.

"What's bellinnatee?" Alder asked.

"It's a drink, the only one I've had aside from water. Bellinnatee is bright orange like a sunrise and even sweeter than fruit. My mother would always take me to get a cup of it after she had traded or purchased her herbs, roots, and other medical supplies. Then we would walk around and look at the other things for sale as we shared it."

Lily fell silent, wishing for her mother. Then she tried to distract herself, not wanting to let her emotions get the better of her in front of Vadom. Lily focused on just taking a breath, then on the taste of bellinnatee, the memory of its smooth texture, cool temperature, and sweet aftertaste.

Can you taste that with my senses, Alder?

"It's good!" he said, sounding surprised. *"Bellinnatee,"* Alder repeated softly.

"Can Alder taste your memories, *Vipina?*" Vadom asked, sounding intrigued.

"Apparently he can, at least when he's in the part of my mind that accesses my senses," Lily explained. "He found my eyes and ears fairly quickly, but I didn't know about taste, or smell and touch, for that matter."

"Sometimes I can sort of feel the amadel's ears in your hands, but I haven't really tasted any of your food, and I haven't smelled anything at all. I think if I try to engage your senses any more than I am, I'll start to feel the iron. I want to avoid that so that I can keep a level head in here, so to speak."

"He's limiting his use of my senses to avoid the iron and help me stay focused," Lily said aloud, for her *vapa*'s benefit.

Vadom nodded in approval.

"That is probably for the best. Now why don't you eat 'lunch', *Vipina?* You need to remain as strong as possible, especially today."

Lily felt tendrils of concern from Alder clinging to her mind, and she wondered, a tad apprehensively, what they thought might happen in the next few hours. Surely the iron effects couldn't get that much worse? Though Lily certainly hoped not, she slowly recalled Alder's warning first thing that morning, which she had barely heard through the haze of pain she'd been battling. He had said something about an increase in outer magic, that it might affect her Fear . . .

Lily finished her bread and drank some of her water before giving Bepo a drink as well, filling his wide scooped tongue three times in succession.

She had just decided that she wasn't going to worry about potentially bigger iron problems in Ropaz when she remembered her promise to Alder from the previous day. She returned the water container to her haversack, then dug around until she found her well-wrapped mirror. Lily paused, tracing the rose design on the back of its wooden casing.

Alder, are you looking right now?

She felt his attention sharpen, and Alder's large preoccupation with her well-being was distracted by a thrill of excitement. Lily then felt his surprise, and wondered at the cause.

"I have seen this mirror before. I was present when it was gifted to your mother," Alder explained, in response to Lily's curiosity.

Lily was surprised and then excited in turn.

Who gave it to her, Alder?

She became uneasy when Alder didn't answer right away.

"Her truemate gave it to her, to celebrate the anniversary of their meeting. That Fae warrior is also your father, Lily."

Lily was speechless for several moments. Finally, she asked the question weighing heavily on her mind, the one she had to ask.

And you can't tell me his name because it might be too dangerous?

"Yes, Lily. I'm sorry, I wish it was safe to tell you all about him, for he has a unique place among the Fae, and he is considered all that is honorable, intelligent, and strong. I think you will be a great comfort to him when you arrive, for many reasons. The greatest is because you are a living symbol of your parents' incredible love for each other, as all Fae children are. Another reason is because it is extremely difficult for mated Fae to live after their one beloved has died. Most quickly lose their magic and fade into death, their souls journeying to the Peaceful Realm where all is light and love, to be reunited in spirit. The only exceptions occur when a mate's last request involves continuing to live, and only then for the most important of reasons. The fairies who survive the longest without their truemate are those who live for their child. Let us hope that Rose's beloved can endure, at least until you are able to arrive at Golden Court, as she wished."

Lily felt a terrible panic sweep through her. She had always assumed that her father would be somewhere in the castle city of Golden Court, as her mother had told her, and that she would find him after she had delivered the scroll there and returned Alder to his body. What if she didn't make it to him in time? Alder might know more exactly where he lived . . . perhaps she could look for him first, before her other obligations.

Alder would understand if it was a matter of life and death . . .

Alder, will he already be aware that my mother has died before I come and tell him? Should I try to find him immediately once I've crossed the bridge at Ford-upon-Ward if he is dying?

"He will know," Alder said, very solemnly, with great sadness in his voice. *"Every Fae knows the moment of their truemate's death, no matter where either of them are at that time. I think we should wait to make the decision about finding him until we are in the Fae Wood. Will you trust me on this matter, Lily?"*

Lily knew she would worry about her father until she saw him for herself, if for no other reason than because her mother had loved him. However, she also believed that Alder would best know how to deal with anything related to the Fae Wood, and that included their priorities once they arrived.

I will trust you, Alder. Does this make it urgent that we arrive in the Fae Wood as quickly as possible?

"As far as I'm concerned, it already was. Your safety is paramount, Lily. I also think that news of the xydolem and their concentrated numbers is information that should reach our people as soon as it can. Our monarchs need to know of the potential threat the Misruler poses, for they do not know now. Your mother's scroll may shed light on that as well, which makes the need for you to arrive at Golden Court all the greater . . . I hate to put such pressure on you, Lily, but I will do all I can to alleviate what you will endure. Your trust will not be misplaced in me."

Alder's words calmed the escalating turmoil erupting in Lily's heart and mind. The situation was serious, very much so, but she didn't have to cope with it alone. She had Alder in her mind, and Vadom by her side. If her father really was strong and honorable, surely he would be able to remain alive for a matter of weeks, until Lily could get to him. Her mother would have wanted her to find and comfort her own father, Lily was certain. It was another reason to live, to fight the iron, and to persevere.

"I can sense the strength of your new resolve, Lily. I rejoice in your bravery, for you are going to need it in the weeks, and months, to come. Now . . . why don't you turn that mirror over? A curious soul would like to see a certain face, if you recall. That vampire had better not have marked you permanently . . ."

Though Alder's tone had become deliberately playful, Lily couldn't stop thinking about her mysterious father right away. If he died before she could get to the Fae Wood . . . but Lily knew she couldn't think like that. Everything was hard enough without focusing on failure. She made an effort to control her feelings and turned her attention to Alder and the mirror, to something lighthearted and fun. Lily wanted to do something that would make Alder happy, and she wouldn't pass up this perfect chance to do just that. Perhaps she might even tease him, just a little . . .

What's this you're saying, Alder? You will still like me, even if I have a Void mark on my forehead, won't you? Perhaps I shouldn't show you, just in case it is still visible . . .

When Lily slowly reached for the special-occasions head wrap that had previously swaddled the mirror as she spoke, Alder immediately began to protest, though he didn't sound truly worried. The somber tenor of his emotions had given way to a great excitement.

"Well, I couldn't possibly decide about liking you based on your forehead alone. There are your eyes and nose and cheeks to consider as well. I promise to give all of your features due consideration, Lily. Please, show me!"

When Alder's emotions had reached a fever pitch, Lily slowly flipped the mirror over and looked at the perfectly smooth reflective side. As she carefully examined her face, Lily felt Alder's excitement give way to absolute awe. After a few moments, both of them were blindsided by the force of Alder's reaction.

He was utterly overwhelmed. Lily floundered in his joy, his pride, and his near disbelief. She worried about his small amount of insecurity, but was soon overtaken by his fierce possessiveness and his deepening affection. Alder was somehow fascinated by her as well, as if he wished to be closer to her. Though Lily didn't entirely understand Alder's tumultuous feelings, she felt her uncertainty melting away beneath the intensity of his gaze. None of the desert boys had ever looked at her like *this* . . . Alder looked at her as if she had redefined feminine beauty for him, as though there wasn't even any other female in existence.

Lily didn't know how long she sat by the side of her amadel, upon the strange, prickly green grass, staring into her mirror. She was too caught up in Alder's emotions, and in her own relief that he wasn't disgusted, disappointed, or otherwise let down by her appearance. Lily looked at each of her facial features carefully, affording Alder an unimpeded view. When she had finished, Lily was a little uncertain of what to do next. She looked into her own eyes and read the curiosity there. Lily immediately felt Alder's renewed awe.

"Lily," he whispered. He seemed to feel too much to speak.

Lily wondered if she should try to lighten him up a bit. Alder seemed almost as if he were in shock . . .

Well, no visible Void mark on my forehead. It must have sunk in like my mine did on Vadom. I suppose that means you're free to like me, right?

Alder soul-chuckled weakly, but seemed to gather himself together at Lily's comment.

"*Right. Although 'like' doesn't seem a strong enough term for what I just experienced. I didn't think seeing your face for the first time would be so intense. I thought that, having seen your soul first, your body might not have the huge impact everyone always tells you to prepare for, but I was obviously mistaken. I can understand why some Fae come close to losing consciousness . . . If I had been in my body, with access to my power wells, and I'd seen your entire self, it would have been that much more . . . incredible. You look a lot like your mother, but you have some of your father's features as well. In the end, though, your face is as uniquely beautiful as your soul . . . I really should have known better, with a soul like* that."

Lily felt her cheeks heating at Alder's words. She wished she could return his compliments, and she suddenly wished she could see Alder's face, too. Lily smiled shyly.

I can hardly wait to see your face, then. I can't imagine a more perfect, silvery soul than yours. I bet 'pretty' doesn't even come close.

"*You're blushing, AND smiling,*" Alder said, completely losing the thread of the conversation. "*Tell me, what color is your hair?*"

Lily carefully set the mirror in her lap, then slowly pushed back the black hair wrap so that a bit of her blond tresses were showing on the top of her head. When she had picked up her mother's mirror again and made sure she could see that portion of her hair, just above her forehead, Lily felt Alder's amazement revive.

"*Your hair is the same tawny, honey-golden color as your eyes! How long has it been that shade, Lily?*"

Lily was a little confused by the question. Did fairies' hair regularly change color?

It's always been just this color, Alder; it's never changed. It does grow quickly, though, she added, hoping that this, at least, was a normal Fae occurrence. Judging by Alder's reaction, however, Lily doubted it.

"*How much does it grow, Lily? How long is it now?*"

Past my waist by a bit. Why? Does that matter?

Alder was silent for a moment, causing Lily to stir uneasily.

"Most young ladies your age only have hair about a finger's length long. Only Fae ladies older than two centuries have lived long enough to grow hair as long as yours, Lily. I'm concerned, because this means your inner magic hasn't been fully suppressed by the iron you wear."

Well, yes, but I've been using my elemental wings for years. We already knew that my abilities weren't being completely shut down. My hair probably hasn't grown since I put all of that armor on.

"That's true, but your power might not be fully hidden now if it has been continually active to this extent. Your inner magic might still be seeking an outlet, and that likelihood will increase as the outer magic available to you increases. Iron is supposed to incapacitate fairies utterly and completely, quickly draining them of strength, and killing them painfully and without mercy. I expected you to look unhealthy or haggard somehow, or at least be miserable in appearance, but you are none of those things, Lily. You look tired, maybe a bit thin, but amazing considering the circumstances. The iron certainly affects you internally, with the Fear, and you physically feel a great deal of pain, yet the iron is not making you any weaker. You would have to be at the gold level of power, just measuring your inner magic, to be capable of renewing your wells of power quickly enough to outpace the negative effects of this much iron . . . If it cannot deplete your inner magic as fast or faster than you generate it, then you will be creating a magical signature that many beings in Lamoranth will be able to detect and follow. This puts you in greater danger than I realized, though perhaps your mother knew . . . that might be why she added so much to your burden in Japeta, hoping to avoid exactly this predicament . . . What can we do about this?"

And with that, Alder's feelings took on a worried, distracted air.

Alder, my mother told me that witches and wizards would only be able to detect me if I actually used magic. She was concerned that I would invoke it accidentally and bring enemies upon us. My mother never mentioned danger simply from traveling across Lamoranth. The iron was only supposed to prevent me from those unintentional usages. Are you sure I can be creating a magical signature simply from existing?

Alder still seemed confused and uncertain, and in his preoccupation he did not answer her. After a few minutes, Lily grew impatient, but she still attempted to be calm when she gently cut in on his perturbed thoughts.

What do you think of asking Vadom about it? I'm sure he would be sensing my inner magic if I'm somehow expressing it. Perhaps he will know measures we can take to hide me more effectively.

Lily felt Alder's relief, though it was tinged with envy.

"If he can do anything to protect you that I can't, then we should definitely ask him," Alder said, though it was slightly begrudging.

Lily was a little surprised by his attitude. She had thought Alder would be completely relieved that her *vapa* was right there and willing to help her, quite possibly able to solve her potential problem. Then she recalled how possessive Alder had just felt about her as he had looked upon her face for the first time, especially when he had thought that she might be visibly marked by another . . . Lily felt a bit more certain that they were truemates. He found her so beautiful after all . . .

Are you worried he's going to kiss me again, Alder? I'm pretty sure that was a one-time only kind of ceremony.

Alder hastened to reassure her, sounding rather abashed as he responded.

"I'm sorry to add to your concerns, Lily. Just ignore me when I'm irritated by Vadom. I know rationally that he's not a threat, but all of my feelings are so new and I just don't have a grip on all that it means to . . . know you yet . . . Please ask him if he can sense your Fae magic, and if he thinks wizards or those xydolem will be able to find you by tracking it. If so, see what he can do to hide you more completely. If that involves more kissing . . . then I'll just deal with it. Keeping you safe is our preeminent concern right now."

Though he was clearly very unhappy at the thought, Lily could feel that Alder's sincerity concerning her safety was entirely genuine. Reassured by this, she sought to console him in turn.

I bet he'll have other ways to use Void magic besides another Mother-kiss, Alder. Don't worry. Anyway, I'm glad you know my face now. I only wish I knew yours, too.

Lily felt Alder's happiness warm up again considerably.

"You are so unbelievably beautiful, Lily, inside and out. I am the luckiest Fae who has ever lived. Thank you for sharing another part of yourself with me."

Lily smiled and conveyed her gratitude for his words, then surfaced from their internal conversation and looked about her, wanting to speak with Vadom as quickly as possible. He was slowly circling around her, looking intently from her to the lands around them. Vadom was scanning the solid rock some way behind them as closely as the grasslands before them.

Lily realized, quite uneasily, that countless witches and wizards desirous of making her a slave for her magic lived to the east; vampires who thirsted for her blood and were ruthless enough to try to kill Vadom lived to the north; trolls, who were the neighbors and enemies of the Fae, were roughly to the south; and xydolem, capable of murdering her mother and innocent Cave Kingdom inhabitants, were quite possibly on her trail from the west. Add a mysterious and potentially malignant being called the Misruler, and Lily felt completely surrounded by danger.

She took a deep breath and counted her impressive number of reasons for staying alive. One, she had promised her mother she would deliver the scroll to the King of Golden Court. Two, her mother would have wanted Lily alive, happy, and accepted by her real people, the Fae. Three, she could remove the iron in the Fae Wood. Four, she would be able to meet Alder and return his soul to his body. Five, she could try to find and save her father. Six, she might even have valuable information for the Fae monarchs about conditions in Lamoranth that could prove useful, seeing as she would be moving through a good deal of it in the next few weeks. And seven, Lily would be able to learn how to use her Fae magic. What if she was at a golden level of power, which was apparently rather a lot? She did have nine wells of inner magic, and more than one pair of wings. It would take a lot of training to learn to control all of that potential, and Lily was eager to learn. Perhaps it would be Alder who would teach her how to fly . . .

Lily realized how important it was to make sure she was completely hidden magically, if indeed she wasn't already, and she resolved to ask Vadom immediately.

"*Vapa,* Alder and I were just discussing something, and we wanted to ask you about it."

Vadom ceased his vigilant guarding and indicated his full attention with a nod.

"Alder thinks that I might be detectable by my enemies, because the iron isn't causing me to become any weaker. We were wondering if you could somehow sense my inner magic, even though I'm not using it, or if you would know how to hide it more completely if needed."

"I have noticed very small magical pulses coming from your person, *Vipina,* but it only seems to occur when you are feeling strong emotions. Whenever you speak of your mother, for example, or during some of your discussions with Alder. Though xydolem are very skilled trackers, I think it unlikely that they could detect such slight expressions of magic unless they were very close to your physical location. I will know if they are near well before they will be aware of us, at least if you maintain your greatly suppressed level of magic. I have methods of invoking night magic that can entirely mask one's power, but I hesitate to utilize them because I have no way of knowing how they will affect a fairy. Perhaps we should experiment, as safely as possible, before a dangerous situation arises. What are your opinions?"

Lily could feel Alder's uncertainty and hesitation. She had no idea what might happen if Void element was used to try to mask her love-element-based power wells, but she was willing to try anything that would keep her safer in Ropaz.

"Alder is hesitant, but I'm willing to investigate anything that will make us more secure over the course of our journey. If only I had night magic myself, then you could just teach me how to hide under my own power . . . That would be safe, and incredibly useful. Do fairies have any Void element in their inner magic, Alder?"

"There have been a few Fae in our recorded history who have possessed gold-level elemental wings who had limited access to Void element from within themselves, in addition to water, earth, love, fire, and air. Most Fae with any color of elemental wings can detect the Void element in their surroundings, just as they can sense all the other varieties of outer magic in their proximity, though they cannot actually wield it because it is so foreign to fairy nature. To the Fae, it is considered . . . a malignant form of magic, because it occasionally causes madness in the fairies who attempt to wield it."

Lily was startled by this. She couldn't imagine Vadom using a sinister magic for any reason, but certainly not for her protection. There was no way her *vapa* could naturally store a large amount of negative power inside himself. Lily was certain that Vadom would not have remained such an honorable being over the course of his very long life if this fairy belief was true. She recalled what her mother had said about Void users, as well as her doubts about night magic from a discussion with Alder just the other day. Rose had told Lily that the few witches and wizards who could use Void element were all greedy and corrupt, and that they needed to be avoided.

Whenever Lily had bothered to consider night magic, however, she had wondered if it could really be utterly bad. It felt instinctively wrong to Lily to assume that Void was evil and hateful, just the exact opposite of love element, simply because it was different. Though she obviously had much to learn about the world, Lily was sure that very little was as clear as it seemed on the surface, and the issue of Void magic was probably very complex. Disturbing as it was to consider going mad from wielding a certain type of magic, Lily couldn't find it in herself to make a hasty assumption about the night element.

Don't you agree, though, that if I can learn to use Void element safely, especially from a vampire like Vadom, that it will probably be to my benefit? I don't think we can reasonably rule out any possible method of protection at this point, Alder.

"I have to agree with that. Nothing bad has happened since the Void ceremony yesterday, and Vadom has to be a complete master of that element if his huge array of weapons is any indication. If you are sending out any kind of magical pulse, you are vulnerable, and we need to take steps to eliminate that potential danger. Just proceed with all possible caution, Lily. The iron is already trying its hardest to unsettle your mind, and if wielding the night magic will make that worse, it must be avoided at all costs."

Happy that she and Alder were in concurrence on this point, if not about the nature of Void element in general, Lily relayed their combined opinions to Vadom.

"Alder agrees that I should learn to use Void magic if I am able, *Vapa*. We have to be really careful though, because he says that only a few Fae in history have ever been able to invoke Void element, and some of them went mad from wielding it."

Vadom looked incredibly solemn upon hearing this, and Lily paused. When he did not speak, however, she continued.

"Alder did say that many Fae are able to detect Void element in the outer magic around them. I am willing to learn whatever you think will be most helpful for my protection. If that isn't possible, I think we should experiment with the protective night magic that you wield. Your capabilities might be critical, especially if the larger amount of outer magic in Ropaz increases my chances of accidentally using any kind of magic and drawing unwanted attention."

Vadom seemed to consider her words with great deliberation.

"I know that the Fae believe night magic to be evil and harmful, *Vipina*, but I hope to alter that opinion, at least for the two of you. Perhaps after I have introduced the subject as it is taught to all vampires when they begin their training, you might judge for yourselves. I suggest that both of you think it over more carefully this afternoon, to make sure you are in agreement. I would also like to recommend that we wait until witnessing the full impact of Ropaz and its natural magic on Lily and her iron condition before making a final decision."

Lily shifted uneasily at Vadom's last words. As she clambered onto Bepo, Lily knew she would be watching the height of the grass carefully for the remainder of the day, and the thought made her unhappy. While she never quite got used to the Fear or the pain it induced, Lily did know that she was successfully keeping it all more or less under control within the current circumstances. It apparently wasn't something a fairy ever got accustomed to, but merely endured for as long as possible before some weak moment gave the iron a chance to exploit. Entering the official grasslands of Ropaz was obviously just such an opportunity, and Lily wished she felt more confident as she faced yet another obstacle on this strange journey.

Into the Grasslands of Ropaz

As they reached their regular speed and fell into a collectively thoughtful silence, Lily continued to fret about entering Ropaz proper. Would the outer magic come upon her senses gradually, as it had when she had left the Joquobon and begun traveling through the Magentay Canyons? Or would it be abrupt, intense, and overwhelming?

Alder was also agitated, and it grew worse as the sun began its western descent behind them. Lily didn't try to speak to him. They had already agreed on the Void element situation as far as she was concerned. If he wanted to open the discussion again, Alder would have to bring it up himself. She was getting too nervous to attempt to comfort him, and she rather wished that he would say something reassuring. They were both still too accustomed to looking after themselves, Lily supposed, for Alder to try to soothe her apprehensions right away. They may have possessed a special access to each other's feelings, but neither of them always knew how to respond to those emotions without then communicating about the causes of those feelings. That was probably a truemate ability that took time to understand . . .

It was then, in the midst of her musings about her new relationship with Alder, that Lily felt the impact of the outer magic of Ropaz. Lily supposed that flying into solid rock at a high speed would have a similar feeling. Before she knew it, the ears of her amadel were slipping out of her hands, and she was falling . . .

Lily felt as though she was being punched by dozens of huge fists, all over her body. She knew, on an instinctive level, that her wells of power were drawing on the outer magic she could sense around her. What Lily didn't know, unfortunately, was how to stop pulling that magic inside of herself. She began to panic, even as a wave of pain washed intensely over her. The Fear was nearly to her diamond of gold already . . . and with that thought, Lily remembered that Alder was somewhere inside of her mind. He could help, if only she could summon the concentration to speak . . .

"Lily? Lily! Come on faelani, *speak to me! Tell me what's going on with your body, with your magic. You need to get this under control, now!"*

Lily focused her entire being on speaking to Alder.

I'm drawing it in, don't know how . . . have to STOP!

Lily went to her wells of power, whether to protect them or cease their natural reaction, she didn't know. Alder arrived seconds later, and they both paused a moment in shock.

All nine wells were glowing brilliantly, and the central well was actually roaring with frustration. Lily could see the outer magic channeling into her wells. It was a variety of colors, but much of it was yellow and purple, with smaller and more equal amounts of white, green and brown, black, orange and red, and blue. After just a few moments, the wells began to overflow, and there was magic of every color, though predominantly the gold of Lily's inner fairy magic, spreading out into her mind.

It was agonizing. The pain caused by the outer magic passing through the iron on her body was excruciating, but now that the nine wells were too full, the iron was creating an even more unbearable pain because of the excess. The torment was growing and spreading, becoming more unmanageable by the second.

"Lily, you have got to stop drawing on the outer magic immediately!"

How? I've never even felt it before— how do I keep it OUT?

"Picture a wall around the periphery of your tribal consciousness, where you've been keeping all of the pain and Fear. Nothing comes in, nothing goes out. Build it up, another ring surrounding the whole, and keep it strong. Set boundaries for your magic and force it all to obey your decisions. You have to mentally take charge or it's going to overrun you very quickly. Focus, Lily. I know it's incredibly difficult, but I am begging you to do your best right now."

Lily could just detect Alder's tightly leashed emotions, though determination was certainly his most dominant feeling. She tried to mirror his resolve, but there was just so much magic in her mind, and the iron was making it all hurt her so very much . . .

Lily forced herself to start erecting a wall around the widest ring of her desert mind. Strangely, she recalled the walls of the blacksmith's shop in

Japeta, which had been so odd to her less than a week ago. Now she knew it had been constructed of rock, probably from the Canyons, but she thought about how sturdy it had seemed, how impenetrable it had appeared before her mother had mysteriously unlocked the heavily shuttered window. There had been rectangular blocks of that rock, stacked one on top of another, but without the edges of each row lining up. The Pillar of Sun and Ashes had been much the same, but the blocks had been larger. What was she supposed to use to make her wall? Lily randomly focused on a large portion of her own golden magic, attempting to shape it in a similar manner to the stone structures she had so recently seen. Instantaneously, her magic obeyed her, and she set down that first piece with a huge sense of accomplishment.

After that, Lily focused solely on forming and setting down blocks of magic. She lost all sense of time. The pain was so horrific that she refused to acknowledge it. The Fear she also attempted to ignore. Though it was so very close to her wells of power, and practically touching all of the excess magic, Lily did try to parcel it up as well. When she was able to do so, she threw the Fear as hard as she could over the beginnings of her wall. Despite her efforts, however, it continued to pummel her relentlessly.

Lily set down block after block of golden power, following the curve of her tribal mind's edge. She concentrated on building around her desert settlement, determined to protect the oldest and most familiar part of her mind from the ravages of the Bane of the Fae. Lily knew she was in no way capable of building around the entirety of her mind at the moment, all of those vast and unexplored places that she had not yet grown into or ventured to discover. As those areas weren't in dire jeopardy, Lily made a peremptory decision to let those places await a more opportune time. Through all of her struggles, Alder was speaking constant encouragement.

"That's it, Lily, keep it up. Those blocks look really solid, excellent, you're a complete natural with magical use, nothing is going to get past this wall when it's done. Keep going, just as you are, and use only the golden power. It's yours, and it will be the best material for your mental defenses. Come on, if you can just make one complete ring around the concentric circles of your inner Joquobon, you should be able to take a bit of a break. You're incredible, faelani, *nearly there, I can't believe how quickly you're getting this done."*

Lily let his words flow around her, soothe her, and boost her resolve. She began to notice that the excess power was less and less, probably because she was using it for the wall. The different colors of outer magic seemed to be turning into gold wherever they came into contact with Lily's inner power, and whenever they did, she used them for her mental defenses. Only the black and white outer magic remained as they were, even in the midst of her golden wells. As the fight wore on, Lily gradually became aware that there was only gold and a small amount of black magic inside of her mind. The white-colored magic seemed to naturally disperse over time, both inside and back outside of Lily's head, smoothing out snarls and lumps of elemental magic as it went, easing Lily's suffering just a little.

When all of the golden power was contained by her nine wells once more, Lily paused, wondering about the black-colored magic. It seemed to be resisting entrance to any of her wells of power, preferring not the desert of her mind, but a place fairly close by where Lily had never traversed. It stayed in a concentrated cloud, twisting into itself in constant motion, yet doing nothing Lily did not wish it to do. It was then that she was made forcefully aware of the extra iron pain that was now pounding against both sides of her new wall, attempting to dislodge the blocks she had just set down. Lily feverishly continued to work on her defenses, now consciously drawing from her wells of power to construct the blocks and lay them most effectively.

At long last, Lily realized that her very first block was back in sight. She had nearly created a full circle around her tribal mind. Should she force all of the pain out that had run rampantly into her mind unchecked earlier before she finished the first row of her wall? Lily hesitated, and in her moment of indecision, the Fear lashed out at her, almost as maliciously as the night after her mother's death. Then Lily was screaming, and she couldn't hear Alder's voice, couldn't think, couldn't manage to protect herself in any way from the surge of dreadful, incapacitating Fear that began to take over. There was so much to be afraid of . . . the xydolem, other potential enemies, failure, losing Vadom, losing Alder . . . other things she wasn't even aware of yet. So much was still unknown to her . . .

Just as Lily was certain the pain and the Fear were going to overthrow her, they became less, inexplicably but very noticeably. Lily realized that she had stopped breathing, and she began gasping for air. After she had managed to make her breath even out, she opened her eyes and found herself face to face with Vadom.

Though his features were set into a calm expression, the depths of his eyes betrayed great anxiousness. Lily realized that he was holding her in his arms, and they were shaking, ever so slightly. Vadom was normally so reserved, always maintaining a respectful distance from her, that Lily was startled by this new situation.

"*Vapa?*" she whispered, and she knew that she sounded like a frightened child seeking reassurance. Lily was surprised that her voice was a bit hoarse, and she looked inquisitively at Vadom, hoping that some kind of explanation would be forthcoming.

"Are you stable now, *Vipina?* Is this a threshold of pain that you can tolerate once again?"

He sounded like he needed to be reassured as well, and Lily became aware of the wonderful gentleness of his arms around her.

"Yes, *Vapa*. Alder was trying to help me build a wall with the excess magic as a mental defense around the most beleaguered part of my mind. Then I would be able to control what elements could come in and out, as well as give the Fear a boundary it hopefully couldn't cross. It hurt so much, and then the Fear hit me so hard. I was losing my grip on it all, and right when I had nearly made a full circle around my desert tribe, too . . . And then the pain was less, and the Fear was less, and I realized I needed to breathe . . ."

She looked curiously at Vadom again, and he nodded.

"You slid off of the amadel, and I was worried that it was going to step on you with one of its many cloven feet. You have been writhing in pain for all of the hours since. Then you began to scream, and I truly feared for you. I had been debating about removing some of your iron burden, but I knew it was not what you wished. When you ceased your cries and started to turn blue, however, I knew you would die unless at least one piece of iron was removed. Forgive me for doing that without your permission, *Vipina*, but death really was the only other alternative."

He paused, as though he desired her absolution, and Lily nodded slowly.

"I trust your judgment, *Vapa*. If I wasn't breathing, then clearly the amount of iron I was wearing required serious adjustment. My goal is in fact to arrive at the Fae Wood alive, after all."

Vadom relaxed slightly, and Lily realized that Alder was still extremely upset inside her mind.

"I think I need to reassure Alder right now, *Vapa*. We've had a really difficult time, and he needs to know both that I'm alright and what you did to help. I'll be back."

Lily soon located Alder's silvery soul, which was a hovering sphere of barely leashed horror near her wells of power.

"Lily, what happened? Did you talk to Vadom? What did he say? I didn't want to go to your sensory area in case something changed here. Are you alright?"

Lily took stock of her mind and body carefully, so that she would be able to answer honestly.

We must have officially entered Ropaz, because it felt like the Bepo cantered straight into solid rock. I just couldn't stop my mind's automatic draw on all the outer magic that I was suddenly in the midst of, and it was generating an enormous amount of pain and Fear as it passed through all of the iron I'm wearing. Then you were telling me to build a wall, so I started using the extra magic, because it was handy . . . and you were encouraging me all that time, and then the first ring of my defenses was almost up. The Fear hit me so hard though that I didn't think I was going to make it, but Vadom removed some of my iron, and it was enough for me to get back in control of everything in my mind. He said we were working on that wall for hours, and that I was screaming, and then that I stopped breathing. I can't believe you helped me fight for so long. I wouldn't have even known to start building a wall if you hadn't been here. Thank goodness you were, Alder.

Lily stopped abruptly, realizing the truth of her words. She was extremely lucky that Alder was with her, and Vadom as well. She wouldn't have lived if they hadn't helped her. Lily shivered at the thought, then pushed herself to finish telling Alder of their situation.

I think I'm fine for now, but it would probably be best if I sort everything out inside myself before I get the rest of Vadom's side of the story, don't you think?

"Yes, force as much of the pain and Fear out as possible. I don't know if either can be ejected permanently, not without the removal of all of the iron; but finishing the first ring of the wall couldn't hurt at this point, not if you're up for it. Oh, Lily, I was so afraid for you. That was absolutely awful."

Alder sounded as though he was confessing cowardice, or some other emotion he was ashamed of feeling. Judging from the sentiments she could sense Alder was experiencing, Lily could tell he was really shaken by what had just occurred. She immediately sought to comfort him, though she was as careful as she knew how to be of his pride.

Alder, that was a terrifying situation, and what you felt was completely normal. You stayed calm the entire time, you encouraged me, and you didn't give up. Even though you were afraid, you still did everything you possibly could for me. You shouldn't feel shame for anything, because you helped save my life today. What's more, this isn't even the first time you've rescued me, and we've only known each other for a matter of days. Honestly, sometimes it seems like you're being rather hard on yourself.

Lily tried to convey her opinion seriously and earnestly, but she was completely and utterly exhausted, and that fact didn't escape Alder's notice. He seemed to give himself a shake before responding, feeling slightly chagrined as he did so.

"Thank you, Lily, for putting things in perspective for me. I can't believe you even have the energy to reassure me, especially as you are the one who has endured such a harrowing ordeal. Why don't you finish that wall, then find out more about what happened outside while we were preoccupied? Oh, and when you are nearly finished with your defenses, leave a very small gap in the wall. A fully fortified mind still always has a door, and you'll need to leave a space for one. You might have to force this Void element out of your mind soon, or bring more in if Vadom can safely teach you how to wield it. I will also need an exit eventually as well, and even one completed ring will be somewhat difficult to cross for me."

Focused on the sound of Alder's voice, Lily returned to her task, carefully forming golden blocks and laying them end to end. When she reached her starting point, Lily left a gap about two blocks wide, setting those couple of pieces a bit farther inside her mind as the beginnings of a door. She then set about rounding up all of the pain and Fear that had gotten completely out of control earlier. Though Lily wasn't able to force all of it over the wall, she did notice that those iron effects seemed to stay in close proximity to her newly formed golden ring, as though they were somehow magnetized to her inner magic. She was amazed by how much less pain there was with just some of her iron removed, despite having officially entered the grasslands of Ropaz. Even with all of the outer magic she could sense on the other side of her mental defense, Lily wasn't hurting nearly as much as she had been lately.

Finally, Lily returned to her wells of power, where the black-colored element still hovered like a cloud over her golden inner magic. So this was Void? It certainly didn't feel evil. None of the different colors of magic had felt either good or bad earlier, now that she had time to reflect. No, magic wouldn't really be capable of being malignant or benign, because it just existed. Lily realized that it was up to the wielder of magic to determine its intent, for better or worse. Some part of her recognized the importance of this information, and she stored it carefully away in her memories, resolving to think it over in greater depth some other time.

Turning to Alder, Lily spoke to him once again.

I think everything is under control here, Alder. Why don't you go back to my sensory awareness and listen to the conversation Vadom and I are going to have? I want you to know everything that's happened, but I'm definitely going to need to sleep in the very near future, so it would probably be best if you hear what he says firsthand.

Lily was also unsure how long she was going to last before she had a good cry, both a delayed reaction to the pain and in relief, though she didn't want to tell Alder that and upset him again. Lily double-checked the peripheries and her power wells once more, then surfaced. Vadom's face came back into view, more patient and less anxious than before.

"Is everything settled within you, *Vipina*?"

"Alder suggested that I finish the first ring of my defenses, so I did, then I pushed all the pain and Fear around it. My power wells seem to be fine. They changed all the new colors to gold, except the black and the white. The night magic is just hovering in a place fairly near my inner magic. It doesn't seem to add to the negative effects of the iron, which is potentially very good news. Alder's a bit shaken, but then, so am I. It was so frightening, not having control in my own mind . . . and I think I'm going to sleep for an indefinite amount of time in the very immediate future, so don't be alarmed unless I stop breathing again."

Lily ceased speaking, worried that she was being a bit too cavalier about her near-death experience, but Vadom seemed, if anything, to find further relief in her attitude.

"You are a very resilient young lady, *Vipina*, that is certain. Though the shock may catch up with you a bit later, I should warn you of a couple of things before you deal emotionally with what you've just experienced. The first is that I felt compelled to remove the cuirass and attached plackart and coulet from your torso, so you are now entirely without a breastplate. As a result, you sent out an enormous magical pulse. I am not certain how far it projected, but it was probably upwards of one hundred miles in every direction of this location. Though I sent a Void pulse immediately after, which would indicate to any vampires who sensed you that another of their kind had already laid claim to your blood, that is not a complete guarantee against witches or wizards, some of whom most certainly reside in Wikkenod. Then there are the xydolem who may or may not be tracking you, who would, without doubt, be attracted to your magical signature, as Alder aptly referred to it.

"Because of the imminent danger this posed, and because you seemed to easily absorb the night magic around us along with all of the other elements present, I took a calculated risk and projected a Void sphere about us. Despite the magnitude of your power, I believe that our enemies could fly right over us at this time and fail to detect you. Such is the nature of the Void, which does not appear to harm you, or even trigger the effects of iron upon you. This, at least, is indeed welcome news, *Vipina*."

"So this means I could make my own anelaces and bow to train with? And it won't cause me any mental instability?"

Though Lily was definitely feeling unrelenting exhaustion, she wanted to make sure she was getting the full scope of their inadvertent discovery.

"Yes, I will be able to teach you in much the same way I would begin the training of a vampire warrior. That will include the creation of your weapons of choice, and practicing with them, when I feel you are ready. As for the madness some past Fae have experienced, I believe that has much more to do with a lack of proper training than a fairy's predisposition of mind or body. We will certainly be addressing this concern in greater depth in your warrior lessons. Perhaps it would be best now, however, for you to rest, *Vipina*. I will watch over you and observe any who come near our Void sphere."

"Thank you, *Vapa*. Good night," and Lily made the *valoriad*, just as sincerely as the previous day, though without the same sharp precision.

He smiled slightly, as he had the night before, when Lily had offered this valediction. Then Vadom's face betrayed the faintest uncertainty.

"Would you like to sleep as you usually do, *Vipina*?"

It was only then that she even realized her *vapa* was still gently holding her. Surprised, Lily hesitated. While she wanted to stay in his arms, which felt wonderfully safe, she realized that it might be a difficult position for him to patrol about as he was always doing. Lily gave his waist a slight squeeze, then looked up at him regretfully. Vadom looked a bit surprised at her wistfulness, but returned her hug softly, kindly, and released her.

Lily made her way over to her haversack, collapsing against Bepo's side when the pain wracking her body made coping with movement entirely too much. Luckily, her tired amadel hardly stirred, despite the disturbance, and Lily realized the poor thing really did need to return to his true home.

As do I, she thought sleepily.

"What's that, Lily?"

Oh nothing, just talking to myself. Amazing about the Void sphere, don't you think?

"Oh, you have no idea. I can tell you the Fae had no notion whatsoever that vampires could move about Lamoranth virtually undetectable! At least you won't be susceptible to attack from invisible Void-wielding Cave Kingdom blood drinkers . . ."

Lily felt Alder shudder with a mixture of unease and relief. It was then that she remembered what he had called her in the midst of her iron crisis. Though she thought she knew what it meant, Lily wanted to hear it directly from Alder, without using her well of elucidating magic to second-guess him.

Alder, what does "faelani" *mean?*

Lily felt Alder's soul go completely still inside her mind. After a long moment, he answered her.

"It means 'truemate' in the language of fairies, Lily. It means you are my lady, my one beloved, my ideal and fated life partner. It means you are mine to protect and cherish, and that you are the only fairy with whom I can soul-bond. In finding you, I have become a fully adult Fae, capable of fulfilling my destiny."

Lily felt the impact of his words as they slowly sank into her tired mind. She had thought they might very well be truemates, but for that relationship to mean so much . . . it was obviously a great deal more serious than she had thought. Fairies had much deeper, more meaningful partners than the desert people. With so much magic involved, she supposed that it was not only more necessary, but more desirable as well. When Lily thought about how their souls were now connected . . . that clearly wasn't something that happened to people every day, even very magical beings like fairies. They would have to have a very special relationship to nurture such a magical connection.

Lily's thoughts strayed to her mother, and she wondered how Rose had managed to live so many years without her father, being bonded as they must have been. It made her mother's generally melancholic moods much more understandable. A tiny part of Lily's mind had always wondered if she had somehow been inadequate, that she wasn't ever able to make her mother truly happy and content. She found herself deeply relieved that she had never been the reason for her mother's persistent sadness.

Lily felt disheartened to realize that her mother would never know of her bond with Alder. They had never really discussed life-partners, which was the marital custom of the desert dwellers. Lily had actually avoided the subject, because she had known that none of the men of her tribe liked, or even respected her, and hence would never have asked her mother for her hand. Though Lily had once brought this up with her mother, Rose had been dismissive. She had said only that Lily was far too young to be thinking about it, and that she needed to wait until she was older. Lily had thought at the time that her mother had wanted Lily to know her own mind better, so that she could make her own choice as an adult, perhaps expressing interest in a man of another tribe. Certainly, Lily had assumed that she would be making the decision about her life-partner, based on her own wants and needs. She wasn't quite sure what to think about that choice apparently being taken away from her. Just how much freedom did she have now that her soul was bound to another? Had Lily escaped the tyranny of Nather only to be irrevocably tied to Alder for her eternal fairy life?

And yet, Rose had known that Lily would have a truemate in the Fae Wood. She had never worried, as Lily increasingly had for the last few years, about her daughter finding a supposedly perfect life-partner. Lily thought she would have to be content with the fact that her mother had known Lily would eventually meet Alder, the Fae apparently destined to be hers. Rose hadn't been concerned about Lily's acceptance of a soul-bond either, or that it was in Lily's best interests to do so.

Still, Lily wished, not for the first time since meeting Alder, that her mother was here now so that she could ask her all the questions about masculine beings she had never spoken aloud, along with a slew of fresh queries regarding the new males in her life. Why were some so gentle, while others, like Nather, were so cruel? Why did Vadom make her feel so relaxed and comfortable, while Alder often made her heart pound with excitement, happiness, and something more?

Lily's thoughts turned fully to Alder, and everything he had said and done since they'd met took on greater clarity and significance for Lily. It was why he'd cared so much for her, so immediately. Why he was protective, even possessive of her at times. How he had been able to hear her despair from a thousand miles away and save her with his very soul. Lily was intimidated by the enormity of what Alder was telling her, and she was reluctant to give up the choice she felt was rightfully hers to make, independent of fate or magic. Yet she also felt, deep down, that what they had begun the night they had met was right. She felt a measure of peace wash over her at this realization.

I am honored, Lily said simply, but sincerely.

It was the truth, even if she had her doubts. Now didn't seem like the time to give full voice to her uncertainty though. Even having just met him, and even not taking their fairy bond into account, Lily didn't want to hurt Alder by disregarding their fledgling friendship.

Within her mind, Alder's soul burst into vibrantly silver light. The depth of his relief and joy astounded Lily, just as it had when their souls had first bonded.

"I am honored too, faelani, *more than words can express."*

After a few moments, Lily bestirred herself to ask Alder the question persisting in her mind. Perhaps it would be wise after all to at least hint at her apprehensions . . .

So we are truemates, just like that? It feels very sudden, for something so important. I feel like I haven't been given the time to choose this for myself.

"I can understand why you feel that way, Lily. Really though, the process is very gradual, and we have only just begun. We have made our first bond, but we will make a total of nine soul-bonds before becoming complete truemates. Until that occurs, we are in the state of courtship, called faelanzania. *We must choose to get to know one another and consciously work toward making more bonds. In doing so, we will create ties of respect and trust that will last for the rest of our long lives."*

Alder hesitated, then continued, even as his emotions grew just a bit more solemn.

"I think I owe you an apology, Lily," he said, softly and formally.

Lily was a little surprised at this turn in their extraordinary conversation. Was he sorry for not telling her about being truemates sooner? Though she didn't like it in the least that he had withheld that from her, she could also understand the potential risk it created in their situation. There was so much her own mother hadn't felt safe enough to tell her . . . Lily waited, wondering what Alder would say.

"This morning, I was upset with you. I didn't understand how Vadom could comprehend your feelings and motives concerning your iron skin more clearly than me. I was jealous, and also angry, because once Fae truemates discover one another, a threat to one is an equal threat to the other. Warriors must seriously adjust the risks they take from the point of bonding on, and life is never the same again. It was unreasonable of me to be frustrated with you when you weren't informed enough to acknowledge the full implications of our connection. I am beginning to realize why courtship can be such a lengthy process; for how can you trust me when I do not tell you everything?

"I see now, though, that I was being short-sighted. When you said you would wear your iron to the point of death, you meant it literally, with absolute

seriousness. You kept your word completely, though your honor cost you immensely. I underestimated you, the strength of your resolve and your very soul, and for this I apologize. It was a huge oversight on my part, and I will endeavor not to be such a stranger to your heart in the future, faelani."

Lily slowly pondered Alder's words. After several moments, she responded with equal gravity.

I accept your apology. I'm happy that you've found out about how stubborn I can be, how seriously I take my promises. This is something that I don't think any bond could alter, just as many of the admirable aspects of your character remain unchanged, though we are connected in a special way. I would like to apologize to you in turn, for misunderstanding your feelings and then deciding not to ask you about them. I keep hesitating to communicate with you, and the results are usually less than ideal. I also regret not taking the well-being of your soul into proper account on this journey. We are traveling together now, and I shouldn't have risked your life when I had been told that entering Ropaz could very well be dangerous to me, and hence, to you. I have many excuses, but none would console me if something were to happen to you. I'm sorry, Alder.

Lily felt Alder's soul warm with unspoken acceptance of her apology. Though she had countless questions for him, Lily could feel herself slowly succumbing to her exhaustion. It would all have to wait until she had gotten some rest.

Can we talk about this some more tomorrow? I don't think I can stay awake any longer . . . even though this is important . . .

"*Of course, Lily. It's been a very long day, and you are infinitely deserving of rest. Sweet dreams,* faelani."

And with that, Lily fell into a deep slumber, though her last fleeting thought was that, perhaps, she was more fortunate than she had recently supposed.

15

HONESTY

THE FIRST THING LILY REALIZED, UPON WAKING, was that she was crying. The tears were making shiny tracks along her cheeks, then curving earthward because of her sleeping position. As she tasted the salty drops that had made it to her lips, Lily gave an involuntary sob, then opened her eyes. She hardly noticed that the sun was high in the sky, or that a swirling black smoke largely obscured her view of all above and around her. All Lily knew was that she wanted her mother, in a way that she hadn't felt since she was a very little girl.

She forced herself onto her elbow, only to realize that her body felt as though she had endured the most accurate slingshot rocks of every desert boy in the Joquobon. All night. Even her hands felt bruised, though she only vaguely registered that fact as she opened the haversack and removed the medical pack from within. Soon, Lily was carefully holding her mother's ashes in her pain-ridden arms.

She couldn't seem to stop crying. Lily rocked back and forth, clinging to her mother's remains, completely unaware of anything but the jar she was clutching. Eventually, Lily became more cognizant of her surroundings, and the first thing she noticed was Alder's great concern for her.

"Lily? Lily, I'm right here if you need me . . . just let it all out, you'll feel a bit better afterward."

He continued to convey gentle feelings and deep sympathy to Lily. As her crying slowly began to taper off, she attempted to speak to him.

Thank you, Alder. I can't believe I woke up like that . . . I never cry in front of other people.

"Don't worry, Lily. You don't have to hide your feelings from me, ever. We're always supposed to be there for each other, and that definitely includes the difficult times. I would have been more concerned if you hadn't gotten visibly upset after what happened last night. Why don't you eat something, drink some water? That might help."

Lily gave a watery chuckle, even as she began to recall the events of the previous day.

I find it somewhat amusing that both you and Vadom always want me to eat. It's a bit odd, seeing as you don't need food just now, and apparently Vadom doesn't really either. I guess I'll just have to enjoy it by myself for now.

Lily felt Alder grow a little bashful.

"I only suggested it because I like to eat unhealthy food sometimes, especially when I'm upset about something. When I was really young, I used to sneak into the kitchens at night and hunt through the biggest pantry for my favorite desserts. It was always after my father said something careless in front of me, or I hadn't trained up to the Captain's standards, or more recently, when I was under increasing amounts of pressure for not finding my truemate when everyone else had long since settled down with theirs. I know it isn't exactly the best routine, but then again, it made me feel a bit better, and I never let it get too out of hand. It's too bad there isn't any bellinnatee in your haversack, that's what I would want just now . . ."

Lily was still trying to picture a pretty, silvered-eyed little boy sneaking sweets in the middle of the night when Vadom gently spoke to her.

"*Vipina*, has Alder helped you work through last night's events? You appear to be less distressed now."

Slightly startled, Lily looked up at her teacher and met his steady, concerned gaze. She became aware of the jar she still held tightly to her chest, and Lily consciously loosened her grip before she responded.

"I was upset when I woke up, but I'm better now. Sorry I just broke down like that. Normally I don't like other people to see me when I'm . . . emotional."

Lily smiled up at Vadom uncertainly, feeling embarrassed. She recalled all of the times, as a girl, when the other tribe children had said or done cruel things and caused her to shed tears. They had only increased their unkind words when she cried in front of them, and so Lily had begun holding in her emotions until she was out in the desert, alone, where no one could make her feel worse than she already did. It had become such an ingrained habit that Lily hadn't even always let her feelings out in front of her mother as she got older. Lily remembered all of that sadly, even as she watched her *vapa*'s expression soften and his stance relax.

"I have been patrolling about outside of your protective Void sphere periodically since you began sleeping. When you woke, I thought it best to give you some privacy. Vabiri never likes crying in front of me either. She always says it adds to her sorrow when I'm upset as well."

Vadom's eyes took on a pained expression, and it jarred Lily out of her own unhappy recollections. She wasn't the only person here who had to deal with obstacles and sadness. Both Alder and Vadom were sharing their own hardships with her, and all she was doing was pulling everyone down. Lily wondered what she could do for her new teacher to make him feel any better. With Alder, she knew that arriving safely at the Fae Wood was what he most wanted. But what about Vadom?

"I wish we could get my *vama* from the Cave Kingdom on our way to the Fae Wood, *Vapa*. I'm sorry you have to leave her behind now. Perhaps the other fairies will know how to help her? I would be happy to ask, if anything could be done to make sure she is well . . ."

Lily trailed off, realizing that this might not be improving matters. She continued to watch his face carefully, and she was relieved when one of his small smiles emerged.

"Thank you for your kind words, *Vipina*. As much as I would like to remove Vabiri from the Cave Kingdom, I still believe it is not the safest decision for her at this time. I will wait, and trust that she will disbelieve those who inform her of my death. We have been together for a very long time, and both of us reached a point, many years ago, at which we knew that we would be aware of each other's death, when that time came. Vabiri will have the presence of mind to play the part of a broken otherwing until I find a way to either make contact with her safely or remove her from our dwelling without risk. For now, we both must endure the separation and the uncertainty. In the meantime, I will have to be happy on her behalf that you already consider her your *vama*, for she has wanted to be such for well over a millennium."

Lily could feel her awe mirroring the respect and admiration that Alder was experiencing. To want to adopt a child for so long . . . Lily clearly realized, for the first time, what it meant to be a nearly immortal being, to have the patience to wait for something so desired, the endurance to be apart from one so cherished. Did she want that? Eventually, yes, she did. With Alder . . ? Lily searched her feelings, trying to be completely honest with herself. Her mind hesitated, wanting to know what other options she had, what choices could be made. Her instincts, however, said . . . eventually, yes, she did.

"No one's made me feel so young in a while. You'll meet the occasional fairy truemates who have been together for ages, literally, but they tend to keep to themselves, most often within their family grove or copse. And Vadom is so open about his concern and affection for his otherwing, and also so certain of how she will act in any given situation . . . I hope we to grow to be like them, Lily. They are an excellent example of what lifelong mates should be like."

All three of them lived with their thoughts for a while after that. Soon, however, Lily noticed that she had gotten rather hungry, and she quietly replaced her mother's ashes in the medical pack before pulling the last loaf of bread and a couple vegetables from her haversack. Though the fruit was gone, Lily still ate what she had gratefully, then finished it off with some water. After giving Bepo a tongue-full to drink, Lily packed up the container and continued sitting. She was in no hurry to start riding her amadel with her body as miserably iron-sore as it was.

Not that I'm complaining, but your talk of pantries got me excited for a larger variety of food. Is a pantry just a room with shelves where extra food is stored? My mother and I just had one shelf for our food supply . . . I think there's going to be a lot of changes in my life once we reach the Fae Wood, aren't there, Alder?

Lily could feel Alder's happiness at her words.

"Oh yes, you're going to be permanently safe and well-fed, for starters. Then you'll also be able to learn all about your inner magic, and how to use it. No more iron, ever. We also get to perform several public ceremonies together, so that we are recognized by all Fae as truemates . . . I'm kind of excited to finally be a part of that whole aspect of fairy life . . . it gets a bit lonely, after a while, for unmated Fae in the Wood. Some are faced with a very difficult decision . . . but that is not something you will ever need to worry about, Lily. Most of the changes you will experience will be positive, of that I can assure you. Sneaking into a pantry in the middle of the night for a slice of dribble-berry pie with me, for example, will be nice for a change."

Lily could clearly sense how content these thoughts made Alder, but she couldn't help but feel uncertainty twist painfully through her once more. Public ceremonies? Acknowledging a life-partner she had just met? Lily had never enjoyed being the center of attention, unless it was just her mother's focus on her. And it felt too fast, too soon, to let Alder claim her, even just between the two of them. In front of other people, and complete strangers at that, was enough to make Lily feel tendrils of doubt and panic wrap themselves around her. She tried to force her unsettling thoughts from her mind.

Lily hadn't really had the chance to consider the potentially idyllic conditions her life might have if she managed to succeed in keeping her word. Her mother had assured her that she would be accepted by the Fae, and Lily knew she might have a father in addition to Alder in the Wood, but those possibilities still seemed far off and unreal, a halcyon existence belonging to some other girl. She felt anchored to her present, in the grasslands, with iron and enemies and many miles to go.

On that dreary note, Lily decided she would rather cope with her physical troubles than those that pursued her mind, and she began to surface to her surroundings. She hesitated, however, when she sensed Alder's feelings of unease and hurt. Of all the things Lily had learned yesterday, one of the most truly important had been the need to be more open and honest with Alder . . .

Alder? What's wrong?

"Oh, you just seemed . . . nervous and unsure just now. That wasn't exactly my objective when I was telling you positive things . . . I guess I was just wondering why."

Lily hesitated, uncertain about how much she ought to share with him. Alder seemed so ready to be a truemate, but she didn't feel the same way, at least not yet. Given time, Lily thought she could easily open herself up to a fairy as kind and generous as Alder. If she was honest with herself, a part of her was fighting the inclination to do so even now . . . But did Lily want him to know that? She didn't want to be hurt, but she didn't want to hurt him, either. Lily struggled with what to say, but in the end, she decided to be brave, and to have faith in what she had learned of Alder from their bonding: that he was trustworthy through and through.

Alder . . . I am not ready for truemate ceremonies, public or otherwise. Acknowledging you as my life-partner means that I have someone else to lose, and if that were to happen, I don't think my soul could endure it. I feel as if I am damaged, and I am afraid of so many things. Fighting through all of that to fulfill my promises is taking all that I have to give. But I have seen your kindness, your generosity, and especially your patience, and I must ask you for all of that now. Let me get to know you, and let's make it safely home. If I know you can be my closest friend now, I'll know someday you can be everything else, too.

Lily could feel Alder's soul and the absolute turmoil she had caused, and it made her feel smaller than a single grain of sand being blown about in the wind. Slowly, though, she could feel him calming down, thinking hard, reaching for . . . understanding and courage. Finally, something like peace came over the silver soul inside of her, and Lily felt relief resound through her.

"I don't think I have been fair to you, Lily. I didn't tell you what our bond meant right away, and when I did, I expected you to feel the same way that I do about it. I have been thinking of a faelani *in general terms for a long time, and in keeping with that mentality, I have not been thinking of you, Lily, as I should. I found you in the midst of a nearly soul-breaking experience. It was all the more painful for you because your soul is young and has not been hardened by anything. I understood, when we formed our bond, that you are . . . both innocent and wise, gentle and fierce, powerfully talented and completely modest; you are also empathetic, inquisitive, capable of immense self-sacrifice, and unconditionally loving. Knowing all of this, I should have expected you to wish to proceed with caution, and respected you for it. I understand that you will commit only when you are ready, for it will then be forever. You say I am patient, and you are not wrong. Time is something we have, to take all of the small steps that lead up to a deep, abiding relationship. I think . . . that although I am most anxious to be your truemate in every way, it will be best for me to take this slowly as well. You may have to keep reminding me of that, but if you are as honest with me in the future as you have been now, I think we will come to form a truly beautiful soul-bond."*

Lily felt indescribably reassured by Alder's words. He understood, he really did! She had shown him more of herself, her thoughts and feelings, and he had not gotten frustrated or turned away. She had not discouraged him, but apparently strengthened his resolve to have her. Lily didn't feel so uncertain now. It was much easier to start feeling excited instead. Wanting to share her happiness with Alder, Lily sought a way to say so that he would appreciate in a personal way.

Although surviving is my top priority for now . . . I wouldn't say no to something that sounds as delicious as dribble-berry pie when all is said and done, especially if it's just the two of us . . .

Alder relaxed a bit, clearly amused by Lily's attempt at humor. They had enough to be concerned with as it was, so Lily decided to try to feel more enthusiasm for the Fae Wood whenever Alder brought it up again. Really, it couldn't hurt to let herself get just a little more excited about her new home. Now that Vadom was traveling with them, their chances of reaching the Wood had gone up exponentially. It would hardly be detrimental to her journey to imagine herself doing little things after her promises had been kept, like trying some furtively tasted dessert . . .

"That's more like it," Alder said, and there was a hint of laughter in his silvery voice. He seemed to accept the more light-hearted turn their discussion had taken with some relief.

Lily was more than willing to try leading them into the safer emotional territory that banter provided. She tried to convey the soul equivalent of rolling her eyes at Alder, then spoke up in a slightly saucy tone.

Well, if we're done imagining *the Fae Wood for now, I think I'll surface and try to actually make some progress toward our lovely green home today.*

"I can appreciate a lady who shows practicality in the face of difficult obstacles. Don't think I've forgotten about your glass artwork, though. I know you're a dreamer as well. Fortunately, you seem to balance those qualities remarkably well. That is something, perhaps, you can teach me to do better. Well . . . I'm sure Vadom is wanting to speak with you about the plans for today. Perhaps you had better go check in with him . . ."

Lily heard the slight wistfulness in his words. She rather shared his reluctance to part after the conversation they had just had. It seemed a little too abrupt after the words they had spoken.

I'll come chat with you later, when I'm trying really hard to ignore how Bepo's gait is making my body ache everywhere. I'll need you and your optimism then, definitely.

"Now you're just teasing me . . . but you should tell Vadom if your body really can't handle large distances for the next few days. I'm sure he'll understand, Lily."

I'm actually quite interested to hear from him on how the Void sphere is working. How much iron will it be necessary for me to wear if we're certain we can mask the entirety of my power? I promised my mother I'd wear the iron until it was safe to remove, and technically, a Void sphere might allow me to keep my word to her and travel faster to deliver the scroll as well. After risking your soul last night, I guess I'm more open to iron alternatives than before. As long as I'm keeping the spirit of my promise, my own safety, I feel more willing to take the iron off. It's extremely dangerous to me in its own way, obviously . . . Am I maintaining my honor if I'm thinking this way though, Alder?

Lily was relieved when Alder hastened to reassure her.

"I think you're in the right place with the iron situation. Your safety is the greatest concern for us, just as it was for your mother. She didn't have the Void

option that we do now, with a vampire who really knows how to wield it. If that turns out not to be a guarantee, however, you'll need to think this over more carefully, Lily. Loath as I am to encourage wearing such a massive amount of iron . . . if that's the only way to make sure you aren't detected by anyone, we'll have to see what amount you can bear without collapsing again. I can't believe I'm actually hoping the use of Void element will work out . . . but it wasn't harming you in the slightest yesterday, and it looked even more benign than I ever could have imagined, especially compared to what the iron was doing to you . . ."

Glad that they were in agreement on the safety measures available to them, Lily surfaced to find out what Vadom would say to sway the decision. Within her, Lily could feel Alder's hope, perhaps for more than just the iron situation, and it gave her a sense of peace as she really focused on the grasslands once again.

"*Vapa?* Alder and I were talking just now, and we were wondering how your Void sphere will affect our travel plans. Do I still need to wear the armor and jewelry if you can hide me better than all of the iron can?"

Lily tried to keep the hopefulness out of her voice, but it must have shown on her face, for Vadom looked a bit sad when he responded to her query.

"I am glad that the two of you have been considering some of the Void's useful manifestations, but I must be completely honest with you both in that regard. Normally, I utilize a Void sphere to protect Vabiri whenever she must leave the Cave Kingdom for nourishment. In this way, I am able to guarantee her safety at all times. The difference between you and my otherwing, *Vipina,* is the enormity of your power. Our females are mostly healers, but overall they can wield very little Void element, or hold only the smallest amount of magical power inside themselves. Thus, Vabiri is a being I can shield from the detection of others with little effort. In contrast, I have struggled considerably to hide you, *Vipina,* since we arrived in Ropaz late yesterday afternoon. Even a small amount of your sun magic would be difficult to conceal, and as such I have exhausted an enormous amount of my available night magic in masking you. I regret to tell you that I will not be able to continue much longer today, and in the future, we will have to limit the time that we spend hiding your inner sun magic in this way."

Even as she felt her anticipation plummet, Lily looked carefully into her *vapa*'s face. Though it was barely discernible, Lily thought there was a little weariness in his eyes. She felt guilty for making him so tired. Though her innate sense of self-preservation made her highly reluctant to put the iron breastplate back on, Lily didn't feel right about placing her burden upon her teacher. Without a word, she walked slowly toward the armor, which was exactly as Vadom had left it the day before. Lily hesitated briefly, wondering if she should remove her tunic and wear it the way she had been, or if it would be alright to put it back on over her shirt instead. It occurred to her that Vadom had to have taken her tunic off last night, and that he must have put it right back on once he'd removed the cuirass, plackart, and coulet. She blushed at the thought, and fervently hoped that Alder would never realize that Vadom had seen her, however briefly, in her undertop.

She picked up the armor with deliberation, then began putting it on over her tunic. Lily hoped that keeping this iron from direct contact with her skin would be the adjustment she needed to balance the increase of its effect in Ropaz, with all the grasslands' available outer magic. Then, if she needed more cover from potential enemies, she could hide more of her inner magic by putting the breastplate and its attachments back under her tunic. Lily struggled a bit with the leather straps and buckles, for her mother had taken care of that the first time she'd donned this armor, but she had it all back on soon enough. The increase in pain was intense, but Lily was prepared this time. When the Fear attempted to distract her and make her despair, she resisted weakness, and focused instead on her new mental defenses. Lily thought about her mother too, and how she had promised not to give up. She had Alder to consider now as well. She quickly noticed that the iron effects were attacking her primarily from the gap in her golden wall, where a door would eventually be. It was as if the nomadic tribe of her mind had become a permanent settlement, one with a protective wall as the outermost circle. The Fear seemed to know that the town's gate was the weakest place and hence the most easily importuned. Lily pushed against it there, and after a time, she began to grow accustomed to the new and higher level of pain and Fear. When she felt in control of that small, critical space within her mind once more, Lily opened her eyes and looked immediately for Vadom.

"Does this hide all of my power, *Vapa*, or should I put it under my tunic?"

Lily intentionally avoided mentioning that she would actually be putting it *back* under her tunic and waited for his reply.

"You are not hidden quite as well as before, but I will be able to cover the small magical signature that you are still conveying easily. I hope to teach you how to create a Void sphere on your own eventually, so that you will be able to protect yourself with night magic in the future. This won't be for some time, though, as Void spheres are complex pieces of magic. Once you do have that knowledge, however, perhaps we could first experiment with a combination of our spheres, should the need arise for you to venture forth from the Fae Wood again. We could then progress to a Void sphere entirely your own. Both of these options would allow you to wear less armor for longer amounts of time, or perhaps none at all, depending on the level of skill you develop with night magic. As for now, I think it would be both manageable and wise to give you an hour every few days without your iron on, so that you can rest, both mentally and physically. Might I suggest that this hour coincide with your warrior training? It would certainly allow you greater focus, and I will be able to teach you more effectively if you are unimpeded."

Lily thought it over quickly, then nodded her agreement.

"This sounds like a good plan to me, *Vapa*. I'm sorry if hiding my magic has made you tired."

Vadom's demeanor grew stern.

"*Vipina*, you should never apologize for something essential to who and what you are, especially if it is something positive. You are magically powerful, and that is not something for which you should be sorry. Let us work to teach you control over your sun magic, for that is necessary of one with your abilities. I do not want you to cower every time you inconvenience me. We will be pushing your limits and testing your resolve with great frequency, and you cannot be soft with me, for I will not be easy on you. Do you understand me, *Vipina*?"

Lily, who had frozen with surprise, became slightly indignant. She did not *cower*. She had only apologized because he had seemed a bit weary—

"Lily, you need to consider his words one of your first lessons in becoming a warrior. You will need to be tough, in a way that you have not been before. Remember what he said the other day about a warrior's mentality? Vadom begins to teach you this. Do not take it the wrong way now."

Lily felt relieved at Alder's explanation, and her determination revived. She stood as tall and straight as she could, then looked Vadom straight in the eyes.

"I understand you, *Vapa*," she said solemnly, and then Lily performed the *valoriad*. The bangles on her forearm clanked dully against the exposed armor on her chest.

Vadom made the gesture in turn, then relaxed a little.

"I see that Alder's presence will save me some explanations. I would ask that you reflect on all that I say, however, and make sure that you personally comprehend all that I would teach you, *Vipina*."

Lily nodded, though she was still a bit wary of this sterner Vadom. She realized just how ignorant she was, from the use of weapons to how a warrior was even supposed to think when training and fighting. Lily felt humbled, but she was also curious and a bit excited. This was something new and important, and she really wanted to get it right. If she could learn to be a warrior from one such as Vadom, perhaps, one day, her enemies would think twice before taking someone precious to her . . . Lily felt a flare of ferocity from her central power well, and for the first time in her life, she welcomed it. She knew she would need that part of herself to learn what she must, and Lily was, for once, relieved that she just might have what it would take to face the danger of combat with bravery.

As she climbed onto Bepo, Lily watched as Vadom considerably thinned the smoky black sphere around her. When the Void element had become mere wisps of darkness circling around her, Lily cast a furtive look at Vadom. She couldn't fail to notice how much more comfortable he seemed, as though he had ceased to concentrate upon some considerable difficulty. Lily didn't dare comment on this, however, and they were soon heading in the direction of Wikkenod once more.

Inner Magic

Despite their late start, the witch city came into view that evening. Lily's first impression, still at some distance from Wikkenod, was a haze of purple and yellow in and around the town. It was almost as if clouds had taken on color and descended to that particular place on the ground. When Lily asked Alder about this, he seemed a bit surprised.

"I think you are actually seeing the air element around Wikkenod, Lily. While all fairies can sense the outer magic around them, relatively few can see it with their eyes and determine which element they are near by color. It must be one of the skills you possess as a fairy with gold-level elemental wings. I suppose this shouldn't surprise us, seeing as you can hold Void element inside your mind. When I'm in my body, I can see element colors once I have absorbed them into my power wells, but it would be useful to see which ones you are getting before that point . . . Lily, this is definitely a good thing. If you can see strong concentrations of the elements around you, then you can avoid them on this journey and save yourself the extra iron pain you would have felt had you ridden right into them."

Lily could feel Alder's happiness at this discovery, and she shared it. Any advantage she could use at this point would be welcome. Then she wondered about riding into Ropaz the day before. Why hadn't she seen the outer magic then? It would have been nice not to have cantered straight into that.

Alder, why do you think I didn't see all the outer magic yesterday?

"Well, when it was in your mind, it was a fairly even combination of the elements, wasn't it? That was a normal, balanced amount of outer magic, common to most of Lamoranth. Perhaps you didn't see it because you didn't know how to look for it, or because you were wearing so much iron. Now that

you've seen it in your mind, your perspective has changed a bit. Besides, you don't see all the colors around you just now, right? That's in part because they aren't in a higher, more concentrated amount in nature. If you were to enter Wikkenod, where air element has been magically gathered and condensed, it would feel many times more intense than yesterday."

They both shivered a bit at the thought.

"It's a good thing Vadom is here to collect the supplies you need, isn't it? You can just take a little break from riding, and he'll be back with food and a new mount in no time."

Lily agreed, though she still felt rather sad at the thought of giving up her faithful Bepo. They rode on in silence as Wikkenod grew steadily larger.

When they were only about an hour from the witch city, Vadom signaled for her attention. As Lily turned to look at him, she was surprised to see thick black threads of Void element being drawn into her *vapa*'s chest from the area around them. She was relieved that he was able to make up for some of the night magic he had expended earlier to hide her, though she didn't want to mention it due to her recently denied apology. Just as she began to wonder what it looked like when outer magic entered her own mind, Lily realized that she needed to listen closely to what Vadom was about to say, and she focused her attention on him.

"I have recovered my night magic sufficiently enough to provide you with a very thick Void sphere in my absence, *Vipina*. I will take as little time as possible, for I am reluctant to have you out of my sight at all, however necessary. After considering where to have you wait, I decided it would be best if you were just north of Wikkenod, for you will be able to collect water from the Ancient River, and bathe there if you wish, in the interim. I shouldn't be gone for more than a couple of hours, but I don't want you to enter the city if I should take longer than that. Remember, I will be taking the amadel with me and bringing a new animal back, with food for you, and this will take time to do without attracting anyone's notice."

Lily nodded, but she couldn't help but worry about Vadom anyway.

"How long should I wait before I come after you, *Vapa*?" she asked anxiously.

"You are not to come after me at all, *Vipina*," Vadom said, with gentle finality.

Some of Lily's panic must have shown, for Vadom went on to give her a little reassurance.

"This should not take much time or be very difficult, *Vipina*. Long have I moved invisibly amongst the witches and wizards of Ropaz, without ever coming close to serious injury at their hands."

Lily remained silent, recalling the day before she and her mother had entered Japeta. The last time she had entered a city, she had lost her traveling companion. As she struggled to hide her disquiet from Vadom, Alder began to speak softly to her.

"Lily, would it make you feel better to check your well of prophetic magic? Perhaps it will tell you something helpful or reassuring. You haven't had any really negative feelings about Wikkenod, have you?"

Lily realized, with relief, that she hadn't. She quickly went to her wells of power, listening carefully and focusing on her present concerns. Though it caused an increase in the pain she felt all over her body, after several minutes, Lily had heard one word repeated twice.

Alder, it's just saying 'hide'. But it sort of feels like we're supposed to hide . . . everything.

"Is that because 'everything' isn't hidden yet? It could just be because Vadom hasn't cast his really dense Void sphere around you."

"Could you tell me what the two of you are thinking, *Vipina*? You aren't still worried about me being discovered, are you?"

Lily's prophetic well flared at his words.

"Alder was trying to reassure me, too, *Vapa*, by telling me to check my well of prophecy. It's true that I haven't had any bad feelings, like before Japeta. What I felt just now is more along the lines of a suggestion, like when I found you. It says 'hide', as in to conceal everything."

"When we reach the Ancient River, I will be entirely disguising you with night magic. Not only will your power be undetectable, but no witch, wizard, or vampire will be able to see your physical form either. I do not think even the xydolem will be able to sense you with this level of protection, *Vipina*."

Lily could sense that Alder was greatly reassured by this, but her feelings did not change.

"But what about your protection, *Vapa*? You're sure you can hide yourself completely as well when you are investing so much magic in a Void sphere for me?"

"I will exercise extreme caution on my own behalf, *Vipina*, if this will put you at your ease," Vadom said patiently. He watched Lily's face carefully, and he seemed to relax when she finally did.

"Thank you, *Vapa,*" she said quietly.

Vadom simply nodded in acknowledgment, then pointed at an area to the left of Wikkenod.

"We will need to head in a more northerly direction until we encounter a portion of the river that is seldom used by anyone who lives nearby," he said, by way of explanation.

After another hour of riding, Lily began to grow excited, despite the relative seriousness of their situation. Her mother had told her about the enchantments on the River Ward, and how it ran from the Ocean of Fintilles until it reached Molten Mirror Lake, but Lily had always had difficulty imagining a river. Water was so scarce in the desert that she simply had trouble picturing so much of it in one place, let alone moving along in a certain direction. She found herself hoping they would reach it before night fell, so that she could see it more clearly.

"What are you excited about, Lily? Not that I regret the fact that you're less worried than before . . ."

Oh, I'm just excited to see a river, that's all.

Lily grinned as her statement sunk in and Alder's astonishment grew. What she didn't expect was for him to start to worry.

Alder? Rivers aren't a cause for concern, are they?

"You can't swim!" he exclaimed miserably. "Vadom won't be there to help you if the current is strong, or if you slip on a rock, or if something else goes wrong. Lily, ask him how deep the Ancient River is in this area, please?"

I will, Alder. Don't worry.

"*Vapa?* Can I ask you something?"

When Vadom had nodded and begun to hover a bit closer to her cross-legged position in Bepo's scooped back, she continued.

"Alder would like to know how deep the Ancient River is in this area, *Vapa.*"

"Is he worried because you are not able to swim, *Vipina?*"

Lily nodded, even as she felt Alder's surprise mirroring her own. He was also feeling other emotions, among them both a greater respect for Vadom and a hint of frustration. Before she could question him about his mixed response, however, her *vapa* continued to speak.

"I assumed, after your reaction to grass, that this would be the case. At that point, I began to foresee other potential dangers to you in Ropaz similar to this, simply by virtue of the fact that the desert has limited your exposure to certain aspects of life characteristic to the rest of Lamoranth. In this instance, I have selected a portion of the river that is both very shallow and narrow, so you should not have any trouble. I know the Ancient very well. It is not as great a river as it once was, and there are few places where its current is dangerously strong anymore."

Alder's relief was much in evidence, and Lily allowed her excitement to grow again.

"Thank you, *Vapa,*" she said sincerely, smiling at the imminence of her new experience.

"We should arrive soon. If you listen closely, you will hear the river before you see it."

Lily listened carefully for the sound of moving water after that, though that didn't entirely keep her from considering Alder's small amount of frustration. With her recent decision to communicate better with her truemate in mind, along with the very reassuring results she had gotten already, Lily took a deep breath and asked Alder about it.

Alder, are you frustrated with me for not being able to swim?

She could tell that her question momentarily confused him, though his emotions soon took on a pensive tenor. At length, Alder responded.

"I was not frustrated by you, Lily. Not even with Vadom, really, but more with myself. I do not anticipate your needs as Vadom does. As your truemate, it is my privilege to keep you safe and bring you happiness. Yet there is another who does these things better than me. We may be taking a longer path through faelanzania, *but I think a friend would know how to keep you from danger just the same, and I am disappointed in myself."*

Lily gave herself a moment to absorb his words. Though she wanted Alder to know that she took his concerns seriously, she thought that levity might soothe his disappointment best.

Well, Alder, if you are not as thoughtful as my vapa *two millennia from now, I give you complete permission to berate yourself. If we do decide to complete* faelanzania *and manage to attain the same number of years that Vadom has been otherwing to Vabiri, and you haven't been able to keep me content most of that time, then I suppose we'll need to re-open this conversation.*

Alder seemed temporarily speechless. When he spoke, he sounded faintly incredulous.

"You are teasing me. About my life's most important duty. You . . . think I am being too hard on myself?"

Yes! Goodness, Alder, we formed our first bond less than a week ago. Not only that, you've saved my life multiple times, comforted me whenever I've needed you, and accepted all of my uncertainties without turning away from me. Do I even need to mention the fact that you are doing all of this without your own body? I doubt a single other male Fae could do better than you have in this situation.

Her words and loyalty caused Alder to glow with a brilliant silver radiance in Lily's mind. After a moment, he spoke to her quietly.

"Thank you for giving me the perspective I am missing, Lily. I will be a better Fae for it. I want you to know that, though so much of late has been frightening, or new, or overwhelming, this has undoubtedly been the best week of my life."

Lily felt tears start in her eyes. No one had ever spoken such words to her, in a voice so sincere that there was no room for disbelief. How would she ever be able to keep her distance from him, to be careful of her heart, when he said things like this? Lily had to gather her wayward feelings before she was able to respond as generously as she knew how to be.

I think I'm going to make it my personal goal to make you happy enough to say that every week.

Without voicing anything more, Alder's soul drifted through the vastness of her bright mind, until he reached the special, tree-sheltered place where Lily's own soul always resided in sun-dappled splendor. He was so close, she imagined she could almost feel his shimmering essence. For a time, they simply existed together, finding a few rare moments of peace in each other's presence.

Lily was lulled back to a sense of herself by a gently persistent, almost playful sound. Unlike the soft whispering that came from the wind moving through the tall grasses all around her, the noise of the river, which Lily felt certain it must be, seemed somehow more cheerful. While the grass and wind seemed mournful to her at times, whispering the secrets that had started on a breath, the sound of the river seemed almost to chuckle, as if sharing the laughter of others as it passed by them. She recalled what Alder had said in the Canyons about an ancient river and its origin in the Grandfather Mountains. Lily wondered if the river she was about to see was the remainder of the same watercourse that passed through the Forest of Ancients, that Magentay himself had lived by as he predicted things that had not yet occurred, back when the canyons had barely begun to form.

Vadom hovered to the ground a few minutes later, and Lily climbed down from Bepo's back for the last time. She walked to his head, which turned to watch her movements. Lily patted his forehead, then gently rubbed the soft hair between his calm amadel eyes.

"Thank you so much for taking me so far, my friend. It was difficult, but you never gave up on me, never stumbled or slowed. Vadom is going to find a good place for you, with someone who will make sure you return to the desert where you belong. Fare you well, Bepo."

Lily hugged the amadel's head to her heart for a moment, then forced herself to let him go. When she looked at Vadom, a little misty-eyed, he took hold of Bepo's ears very gently.

"I will find an animal trader whose stock is all in excellent condition and well-tended, *Vipina*. This strange, steady-hearted beast certainly deserves it after the lengths to which he has gone. Do not worry for him."

With that, Vadom carefully began casting a denser Void sphere around Lily. Soon, the smoky black element was so thick about her that Lily could hardly see farther than a few steps in any direction. She still heard her *vapa*'s voice with perfect clarity, however, as he spoke some more words of reassurance.

"I will be back soon, *Vipina*. Please do not leave this place. Remain aware of your surroundings, but try to relax a bit as well. Perhaps some elvish magic has wended its way here from the Forest of Ancients and will ease the pain of your body for a time."

He turned to go, then paused and spoke over his shoulder.

"I hope, Alder, that you will do what is honorable in this situation," and with that, Vadom and Bepo the faithful amadel vanished completely.

Lily was temporarily inundated by Alder's emotions, but he quickly got himself back under control. When he remained silent, as though he was unsure of what to say, Lily grew slightly uneasy. They had been so open with each other today, yet here was still another facet of having a . . . friend of the male persuasion that Lily just wasn't sure how to handle. She hadn't really thought about the ramifications of bathing while Alder was inside her mind. They had formed a special bond, yes, but their courtship had only just begun . . . After casting about for something to delay the bath, Lily quickly decided to fill her water container first, the better to buy time to think of the right thing to say.

As she began to walk toward the sound of the chuckling river, parting the tall grasses about her as she went, Lily was surprised by the Void sphere. She had only taken two steps when it seemed to become invisible, blending into the twilight and deepening shadows around her. Hesitating,

Lily grew concerned that her temporary protection had vanished entirely, but after another minute had passed, she calmed. She could still sense the night magic thickly concentrated around her with her own inner power. Vadom must have simply manipulated it to become clear, so that Lily could see but not be seen. She continued on toward the river.

Lily hadn't gone more than five steps, however, before the grass came to an abrupt end, and a rocky bank began. Her eyes widened as she took in the view before her. The ground was covered with stones for several feet before the steady flow of water could be seen, passing briskly by her. Lily estimated that the Ancient was about three times as wide as her height, while it was shallow enough that she could see clearly to the bottom, except in the very center. She looked both upstream and down, observing the water's southern route until a slight bend in the river's course took it out of sight.

Lily paused a moment more, then slowly approached the water's edge, careful of her steps on the shifty rocks beneath her feet. She took the haversack from her back, then pulled out the water container, which was nearly empty. Lily knelt beside the Ancient, then dipped the container into the water on its side, with its mouth open to the north. When it was full, she put the stopper back in place and carefully set the container back in her haversack. She paused.

Alder—

"I'll just check your peripheral defenses for a while, shall I?"

Lily smiled in relief at Alder's hastily spoken words. Was this the first time he had ever interrupted her when she was trying to speak? She rather thought so, and the reason for his abrupt question made Lily both blush and smile a little more.

Thank you, Alder.

Excited to cast off her iron, even for a short time, Lily quickly undressed now, carefully removing every piece of armor and jewelry in addition to her tunic and leggings, slippers and hair wrap. As the Fear receded and the pain gradually ebbed to mere aches and soreness, Lily felt her contentment spread its wings and fly into joy. As she watched, her very skin began to glow with a soft golden light, even the parts of her body still covered by her underthings. Despite the residual discomfort, Lily couldn't remember ever feeling so unencumbered, so free.

With feelings of happiness growing more profound by the moment, Lily turned back to her haversack and extracted her mother's medical pack, which always had a supply of soap. Rose had always insisted on having the cleanest possible hands when she was called upon for her healing skills . . . Lily shied away from that thought and its many attendant memories, choosing instead to focus on her inner magic, which was bubbling up to the brim of many of her wells of power. She was thrilled to find that it didn't hurt at all, even as they seemed to be trying to pull in more outer magic from the grasslands. Lily found that the beginnings of her circular mental wall seemed to give her a small measure of control over the untamed magic of her surroundings. That was definitely a pleasant surprise!

Curious about her wells of power and how they worked, Lily concentrated on determining which well was enabling her to sense the Void sphere around her. When she was fairly certain she had picked the right one, Lily called just a bit of golden power forth from that well, just as she had when she had summoned the sandstorm in the desert. Lily opened her eyes, and she was amazed to see dozens of rocks within the Void sphere hovering above the ground. A few handfuls of water were also poised above the surface of the river at her feet, forming small globules that were constantly reshaping.

Lily concentrated on lowering the stones back to the riverbank, surprised by the focus it required of her. She could just make out the brown and green colors of her magic after all the rocks were back in place. Next, she tested the water with the toes of her right foot, uttering a small exclamation at the cool temperature. Desert water was always warm from the sun, unless you were lucky enough to drink some straight from one of the three wells in the Joquobon. Summoning a bit of courage, Lily took several steps into the river, past the water that was magically hovering around her elbows, and pausing when the river reached her knees. She hesitated briefly, wondering if it was admissible to bathe in a river that might be part of the drinking water in Wikkenod. After ultimately deciding that Vadom would not have suggested a bath if it wasn't an acceptable thing to do, Lily began washing her hair.

A part of her could hardly believe that she was performing such a normal ritual in such a strange new way, even as she thoroughly cleaned the rest of her body. Her mother had always been very careful to avoid having any of the other members of Nather's tribe know when the two of them took baths in their modestly-sized tent, though Lily supposed Ignis could probably have guessed based on when they took an extra ration of water. Lily had never been able to bathe as often as she would have liked in the desert, where water was so scarce, and she felt happy at the thought of being completely clean with greater regularity from now on.

Lily had a bit of trouble rinsing the soap out of her hair, for she had difficulty maneuvering the water globules over her head. Though the haze of blue water magic became more distinct as her efforts continued, Lily still felt it was taking too long. She ventured farther out in the river, closer to the center, where the gentle current washed the suds from her skin. Lily cautiously submerged her head, carefully holding her breath, as she rinsed the last of the soap from her now shiny blond hair. Lily found her thoughts wandering. She had never really noticed how many shades of gold there were in her hair . . . Some locks were a rich honey color, while streaks so light that they appeared nearly white were present as well, with many shades of tawny blond in between.

Eventually, Lily attempted to end her musings as she returned to the riverbank and searched through her haversack for a spare pair of clothing. Though some of her clothes were acting as wrapping for her breakable items, Lily still managed to locate a fresh tunic and pair of leggings. While she was grateful that she'd decided to pack two sets of extra clothes instead of just one, Lily realized that she was still too wet to wear them. After a brief hesitation, she opened her palms and carefully summoned fire, just as she had done countless times alone in the desert, making figures out of glass.

Lily closed her eyes, concentrating, calling forth air to spread the fire evenly around her. After a few moments, she opened her eyes again, and she saw that the elements were doing just as she wanted. The fire was coming out of her palms in long, thin ropes, then wrapping around her body in a spherical shape, mimicking the Void sphere she knew was still invisibly surrounding her. As a haze of red and orange elemental magic began to blend with the purple and yellow cloud of air power, Lily became absolutely exhilarated by her control.

She experimented a bit more with her ability, attempting to shape some of the river water into ropes and wind them about herself as well, alternating with the two strands of fire already warming and drying her. Occasionally, Lily's hold on the water slipped, and the sizzling sound of water meeting fire and the resultant steam all about her caused Lily to chuckle blissfully. Dawdling a bit more, Lily washed and dried the clothes and hair wrap she had been wearing, arguing that she had no idea when she would next have the opportunity to do so. She noticed as she did that the unknown white magic had drawn near her and the concentration of elements she had invoked, and Lily wondered about this strange new element. Why had no one mentioned it to her yet?

When she thought both she and her clothing were dry enough, Lily very carefully pulled the fire back into her palms and slowly released her hold on the air around her. After making sure that no rocks or water were in midair, rather than where they should be, Lily pulled all of her magic back inside her elemental well of power. With great reluctance, Lily began donning her armor and jewelry once again. Though she would have liked to wait a while longer, she knew that every moment she spent unencumbered meant a large amount of Void magic was being drained from Vadom. This was something she didn't want, especially when he was risking himself in Wikkenod on her behalf.

After she had pulled on the fresh pair of leggings and a long-sleeved tunic, Lily replaced the cuirass and its attached plackart and coulet over her shirt and sat down heavily, hardly aware of the rocks anymore. She struggled with the renewed pain that immediately seeped into her every muscle, down to her very bones. The Fear was as bad as before, perhaps worse, now that Lily knew how wonderful it felt to be completely free of it, for the first time in her life. Could some of her insecurities growing up have been caused by the iron she had always worn? Or had it merely exacerbated her feelings of inadequacy? Lily didn't have long to ponder such questions, however, as the internal struggle grew more intense about her new mental wall. She vigorously and valiantly defended the well-trod circles of her mind at the open doorway, largely succeeding at keeping the Fear either just outside or at the periphery if it made its way inside.

When Lily felt she had the iron situation more or less under control, she wasted no time in calling out to Alder.

Alder? Still there?

"Yes, Lily. I thought you might have put the iron back on, because you were so very happy until all of this Fear started trying to force its way through your door just a short while ago . . . I can scarcely comprehend how you fight it, and sort of . . . organize it the way you do. I've been taking a good look at the first ring of your mental wall, and Lily, it's essentially flawless. The doorway is your only weakness. I was thinking, you know those two blocks you set aside? Well, perhaps if you slid them closer, so that they were almost touching the rest of your wall, but not actually a part of it, you might be able to keep even more of the Fear out. I'd like to suggest you keep adding layers to your defenses, but you need to be careful to maintain a slightly larger amount of inner magic than the

total effect of the iron on your mind and body. Keeping that balance, staying just a little stronger than the Fear that you face, will be challenging enough without working on your mental wall."

Well, how about I make defensive blocks out of a painful amount of excess inner magic, if I ever happen to generate too much. Otherwise, I'll just concentrate on using the doorway to battle the Fear.

"That sounds prudent to me. I also had time to ponder how interesting it is that you still think primarily in desert terms, and that your mental defenses are reflective of those concentric tribal circles that comprise your inner sanctum. I'm rather fascinated by how close together your wells of power are, and that none of them are close to your soul. To my knowledge, this is quite unique. I've been ruminating on whether or not your thoughts will expand to encompass more of your unexplored mind as you travel through Lamoranth and absorb more of other cultures and beings. I feel so privileged to know such things about you and your beautiful mind, Lily. Truly, sun and rain are both upon me as we journey to our home in the Wood."

Goodness, Lily thought faintly, feeling her cheeks getting rosy. She wondered if all fairies were this complimentary, or just the one currently residing in her mind. Her beautiful, unique mind. Lily decided that a slight turn in subject matter would be a bit more comfortable for the time being.

Alder, it was absolutely amazing to use some of my elemental magic without feeling any pain at all. I'm sure you're probably used to it, but it was just so . . . wonderful. I can't wait until we're in the Fae Wood, and I can feel like that all the time. Once we're home, I won't have to worry about blasting a hole in my Void sphere, or draining Vadom, or attracting the attention of enemies.

"Which elements did you summon? Did you use them like you did when you made the statue?"

Lily proceeded to tell him all about it, growing excited once again as she explained. Even as the haze of magical colors finished dispersing around her, she could sense Alder's range of emotions as she relived her bath. His dominant feeling, however, seemed to be pride in her.

"You're concerned that your water control is inadequate, Lily? It sounds like you did quite well, considering you've lived in a desert your entire life! We'll have to walk along the beaches by the Fintilles after you've settled down in the Fae Wood. I'd love to see what you can do with an unlimited amount of water to command. Overall, though, feeling a bit better? Your body probably needed the break from all this iron a great deal, and your mind perhaps even more so.

You'll have to thank Vadom for both of us when he returns."

Oh, definitely. It's as though he knew exactly what would make me feel better after yesterday's incident. Do you think he'll be back soon?

"Probably not for another hour or so. You really didn't take very long. Perhaps you could check on the Void sphere, make sure it didn't sustain any damage when your inner magic came out? It can't hurt to start familiarizing yourself with Void element now. Just be careful not to interfere with the spells he cast."

Lily wasn't quite sure what Alder meant by that, but she did tentatively reach out with her elemental senses to make sure the Void sphere was still whole. She noticed that it had thinned in a couple of places, but otherwise remained intact. When the pain from using her inner magic became too great to ignore, Lily pulled all of her power back inside her elemental well.

I think the Void sphere isn't as dense in a couple of places, Alder. It's still completely covering me, and the spell that keeps it from being visibly black and smoky is obviously still working, but I think I did weaken it.

"Good thing you put all of the armor back on then, Lily. You won't wear the sphere out so quickly with such a faint magical signature. Perhaps you could rest for a while? We traveled quite a bit today, despite leaving a little later. You must be tired."

Lily could feel Alder's concern, but she was too keyed up to try and sleep. Without Vadom's presence, Lily didn't want to make herself any more vulnerable than she was already.

Why don't we just talk for a while? Honestly, I don't like the idea of sleeping without Vadom here . . . Alder, how will we know if something happens to him?

"Well, I'm pretty sure this Void sphere would disappear, or at least thin out a lot more. That is likely to happen if he needs the magic to fight, or conceal himself more effectively, or if . . . he's injured."

Lily and Alder settled into an uneasy silence, both waiting as patiently as they could for Vadom to return. Lily stowed the soap, the medical pack, and her freshly laundered tunic and leggings back in her haversack, then pulled out the remainder of her bread and nibbled it restlessly. When she had finished the loaf, she rewrapped her hair, carefully placing the smooth iron discs back in as she wound the cloth about her head. Completely ready to go now at a moment's notice, Lily sat back down to continue waiting for her *vapa*.

Plight of the Shepitan Coven

Less than a quarter of an hour later, Lily sensed something with her inner power. Some form of magic had bounced against the outside of the Void sphere, then returned in the direction from which it had come.

Alder, I just felt something.

"What? Magic? Inside your mind, or outside the sphere? Describe it for me."

Lily told him what she had sensed, but knew her explanation was lacking when Alder began to feel frustrated.

"Did it damage the Void sphere in any way, Lily?"

No, the sphere hasn't changed at all.

"Do you have any idea what type of magic hit the sphere? Could you detect the element the spellcaster used?"

I wasn't facing that direction, so I didn't see the color of the magic. I can't tell by feel, at least not yet. I think the iron sort of numbs my senses when it comes to finer distinctions . . .

"Could you tell how far away the magician was when he or she sent out that signal?"

Lily felt a bit panicked, but she tried to remain calm. Alder's questions made her feel so ignorant, and Lily wondered how she would be able to defend herself with all of her iron on if she couldn't just hide from whoever was nearby.

Alder, I have no idea how to figure that out! Please, tell me what you think I should do now. That signal bounced back to whoever sent it. They might know where I am. Should I try to hide, or should I start moving and hope that the spellcaster will be thrown off course if I keep changing my location? We need to make a decision, quickly.

Lily immediately sensed Alder reaching a level of composure that she could only envy at the moment. The iron made her mind work too slowly at times like this, when a split-second choice needed to be made. Lily recalled the agony of making the decision to hide from the xydolem, rather than remove her iron and fight them somehow with her inner magic. She quickly shut those thoughts away, before she remembered her mother's final moments, and listened for Alder's instructions. He would know best how to handle this situation, and she was willing to trust his judgment, whatever it was.

"Get your haversack, and let's go. You said you weren't facing the direction it came from. Was it from behind you?"

Lily responded as she stood and slung the strap of the haversack over her head.

I was facing the river, watching it run by, and it bounced from my right.

"So it came from the south, and thus quite possibly from Wikkenod. I say we head north then. Maybe we'll come across a bridge where you can cross the Ancient. If not, we'll just have to figure something else out. Perhaps we can circle back, get past Wikkenod from its southern side . . . For now, though, let's just get you away from this spot. Whoever sent out that pulse, they picked up on Vadom's Void sphere. I don't want you right here if that person comes to investigate."

Alder, what if it is Vadom?

"What if it isn't? We don't know for sure, and that's a risk I don't want to take with your safety. Vadom probably has more than one way to find you, like through your vipina-vapa *connection. He won't give up looking for you, either, but our enemies will if we're patient and cunning enough. Please, Lily, let's just be extra cautious about this."*

Lily couldn't argue with his logic, not with the weight of the iron, the scroll, and her promises resting on her shoulders. She began walking briskly upstream, soon losing sight of her bathing spot with a curve in the river. After only ten minutes, however, Lily felt the magic bounce off of her Void sphere once again. It was much stronger this time, however.

Alder, I felt it again, from behind us. I think whoever it is has gotten closer.

Lily felt Alder strongly check his emotions before he responded.

"I think you should stop walking and hide in the tall grass to our left. We don't know if they can hear your steps, but perhaps it would be better to make as little sound as possible, just in case."

Lily immediately complied, crouching down in the grass despite her invisibility. She wondered if it would be entirely too dangerous to attempt dissembling the Void sphere, so that whoever kept sending those small magical signals would have nothing to find. Would her pursuer discover a very small love element signature, especially if he or she was looking for a much larger concentration of Void? Before she could ask Alder, however, he spoke to her.

"Lily, I just realized that we didn't try consulting your prophetic magic. Would it hurt you too much to listen to what it might say now?"

Lily was instantly frustrated with herself. Why hadn't she thought to check her inner power in a situation like this? It was still so new, and she wasn't used to relying on magic, but still . . . Lily wasted no more time, going immediately to her diamond of golden inner magic and listening intently. Her answer came quickly and clearly.

It says 'Wait', Alder. Do you think that means Vadom?

"Possibly, Lily. Let us hope so. My concern now, however, is that he estimated that it would take him two hours, and it hasn't been that long yet. We weren't expecting him for at least another half an hour, yet your senses indicate that the spellcaster is already rapidly approaching. Would he be able to travel that quickly when he is leading an animal for you to ride? I suppose we should just wait and see, then . . ."

Though Lily could tell Alder chafed at sitting inactively, she was at a loss for alternatives. It seemed too dangerous to tamper with Vadom's Void sphere when she knew so little about that element and how it worked. It was a sort of nothingness . . . an absence of the other elements, yet still something, still tangible enough to be magically manipulated . . . Lily decided to simply go with her instincts and quietly anticipate whatever events were about to unfold.

Mere minutes later, a shadowy form moved soundlessly past their hiding place from the direction they had come from, at an incredibly fast pace. Lily held her breath, unable to identify the being who had sped right by them. Lily consulted her well of prophecy again. Once more, it told her to wait. Lily focused on being utterly silent, and Alder ceased his squirming and held completely still as well. Lily thought he might be accessing more of her senses than usual, for she detected some discomfort from Alder that she never had before.

Suddenly, another figure came into Lily's sight, also from the direction of Wikkenod. This being was slower, and Lily was just able to catch sight of his face in the moonlight. The man was classically handsome, though his forehead was larger and more pronounced than Lily had ever seen on a desert dweller. The magical colors around him were hard to see in the dark, but Lily was fairly sure, after a quick scrutiny, that he was projecting a combination of purple and yellow, red and orange. As she watched, he slowed and came to a stop, struggling to catch his breath.

Is he a wizard, Alder? He has both air and fire element colors around him.

"I think so, just as I believe the first being was a vampire. No one else can move so quickly and so quietly in the darkness of night, not like those who hail from the Cave Kingdom. Are we still to wait?"

Yes. Do you think he's given up on chasing the vampire?

Before Alder could respond, however, the vampire returned. He was a darker shadow amidst the night's shifting shapes, a being completely as one with his surroundings. When Lily looked at his face, she recognized him at once, even before he began to speak. She could feel Alder's astonishment as clearly as she felt her own. Upon Vadom's forehead, shining faintly, was her golden sun-shaped mark, its rays glimmering as much as the slightly oval center.

"Why do you pursue me, wizard?" Vadom said in a voice that chilled Lily with its stern power and commanding authority. He put his fist to his chest, clearly ready to draw a weapon at the least provocation from his pursuer.

Though he was still trying to regulate his breathing, the wizard spoke up at once.

"Vampire, please forgive me for the manner of our meeting. I sensed you as you moved through Wikkenod, but what I wish to ask you is not safe to say in the midst of such a concentration of covens. I am Feron, of the Shepitan coven."

Lily watched as he paused and nodded his head to the right in an automatic gesture. Vadom inclined his head ever so slightly to the right as well, never taking his eyes off of the wizard Feron. Lily could see the Void element around Vadom channeling into his chest, and she knew he was preparing for an attack, despite the wizard's anxious but otherwise relaxed stance.

"What did you wish to ask me, Feron of the Shepitan coven? I have an important matter to see to this night, and I must be on my way. I will hear you out, however, if you will first tell me how you sensed me in your city and gave chase."

The wizard seemed to gather his courage, then spoke again.

"Vampire, I am no expert with the Void magic of your race, but all the members of my coven are taught how to detect the spirit element of the Fae. Even one such being is of inestimable value to a coven, and increases its prestige considerably. I sensed fairy magic upon you, and I followed you carefully, in the hopes that you really were, somehow, a friend of the beings who reside in the Fae Wood. I thought that if you were, perhaps you would be better than the vampire who hunts the members of my coven so relentlessly.

"For many months now, a vampire called Vheneir has stalked the witches and wizards of the Shepitan coven, draining men, women, and children alike of their blood. Just last week, he sent our magister a written proclamation, stating that if our coven failed to assist the Cave Kingdom with our magic, we would face eradication. Our leader has not yet responded, though he fears denying this Vheneir what he has demanded. Vampire, what is your advice? Must we succumb to Vheneir's commands, even if they are against the Ethic?"

Vadom paused, as though weighing his words deliberately.

"Feron, I hesitate to advise you in this matter. Vheneir is on the Supreme Council of Vampires, and he has many supporters on the Council of Warriors as well. These two groups rule absolutely over the Cave Kingdom, and he has been gaining power within our governing ranks for some time. While I cannot safely give you my name, I will say that Vheneir recently tried to turn me to ash for disagreeing with some of his decisions, and I am now in essence an outcast. Let this sway you as it may.

"You, as a wizard, will be hard pressed to find an ally strong enough to aid you against so formidable an enemy. If your magister wishes to resist, your coven's only option would be to flee, by air, in the daylight. If you make it as far as Six Cities, the sheer number of your race in that location would give Vheneir pause, though you would be forever in danger of his retribution. If this is your coven's choice, then perhaps, as members of the Shepitan, a judicious use of fire element, in the presence of Vheneir's officers, who will undoubtedly come for you, would not go amiss. Should you succeed in reaching the High Priestess's stronghold, you would do well to inform her of such aberrant behavior from the Cave Kingdom. She should be informed that vampires are breaking a number of their most strictly enforced laws within her jurisdiction."

There was silence as Feron considered Vadom's words.

"Thank you, sun-marked outcast of the vampires, for all of the words you have spoken. I will take your advice to the others of the Shepitan, knowing exactly the risk we take in our refusal, as well as our greatest chance for survival. You had the courage to resist a tyrant, and you escaped with your life. Perhaps my coven will be as fortunate. I will now bid you farewell, unless you wish to ask me something in return."

Vadom paused, deciding.

"Are there still wizards or witches in Ropaz who would negotiate an alliance with the Fae, rather than imprison them on sight?"

Feron looked startled, then glanced fleetingly at Vadom's forehead, before responding.

"Honestly, very few. While any coven would pay the steepest prices for a chance to obtain Fae magic, very few will do so properly, with respect for both the Ethic and the fairy in question. If, however, you think the Fae would desire open communication with the many covens of Ropaz on a larger scale, to combine forces against this Vheneir and his followers in the Supreme Council, for example, then their best chance would be going to the High Priestess of Ropaz in the Six Cities. If that were to occur," and here Feron paused before squaring his shoulders, "I would be willing to speak to the High Priestess on any fairy's behalf, and to ensure his safety while in Six Cities . . . should I make it there alive in the coming days."

Feron and Vadom seemed to take each other's measure after this, but if they came to any kind of conclusion about one another, it escaped Lily's observation.

"Thank you for your time, sun-marked vampire. May the one who wrongly cast you out of your home meet a fiery demise as soon as may be."

Feron nodded his head to the right once again. Then he took a deep breath, turned, and began his return to Wikkenod.

Vadom did not move until Feron had been out of sight for several minutes. When he seemed satisfied that the wizard had truly gone, however, Vadom finally lowered his fist from his chest and turned toward the grass, scanning it intently. Lily checked her prophetic well once more, but it remained silent.

Do you think it's all right to come out now? My inner magic isn't telling me to wait anymore.

"Yes, I think it's safe. What an unusual wizard, to first chase after a vampire in the night, then to turn his back on one after a civil conversation! And what an interesting talk that was . . ."

As Alder trailed off into his own thoughts, Lily decided to reveal their hiding place.

"*Vapa,*" she said, barely above a whisper.

Vadom's head immediately swiveled toward the sound of her voice, and his eyes seemed to pick her out amidst the tall grass, even with her Void sphere still firmly in place.

"It is safe to come out now, *Vipina.*"

Lily carefully walked back onto the rocky riverbank until she was just a few steps away from Vadom. She couldn't tell for sure, but Lily thought he might be a little angry. He certainly looked serious, and his eyes were scrutinizing Lily acutely. She found herself hoping that if he was upset, it wasn't directed at her. This, unfortunately, was not the case.

"*Vipina,* I thought I made it clear to you that I wanted you to remain in the place where I left you until I was able to return. Why didn't you heed my instructions? It is not safe for you to wander."

Lily straightened her shoulders and looked Vadom directly in the eye.

"*Vapa,* I felt small amounts of magic bouncing off of the Void sphere, but I didn't know whether it was you or an enemy. Alder and I decided to hide in the event that it was the latter. When I consulted my inner magic, it told me to wait in my concealed place in the grass, and so I did. I apologize for giving you cause to worry, *Vapa,* for that was not my intent."

Lily could feel Alder's glowing indignation, but she focused on Vadom, trying to determine how he was taking her explanation and apology. He seemed mildly surprised.

"You sensed the Void pulses I sent to check on you? I did not think you would be able to feel them, and so I failed to mention my use of them to you. Similar to the process in which bats emit sounds that provide them with informative echoes, vampires can also locate concentrations of their night magic by emitting small pulses of Void element toward the last known place where they left a sphere, a weapon, or any other manifestation of their power. From the first echo, I knew that you had accessed some of your power, for the sphere was less dense than when I had made it. From the second pulse, I knew that you had moved from your original location. This was, as I think you understand, a cause for concern to me. And then your sun magic told you to 'wait'? I assume this was after you had already moved?"

Lily nodded sheepishly.

"I didn't think to consult it first, *Vapa*. I was scared, and it was too soon for you to be returning. Alder said an enemy would give up looking for us, but you wouldn't, and that's how we would eventually know you'd returned. We just did what we thought we had to do to be as safe as possible."

Vadom sighed, seeming to lose some of his tension then.

"Though vampires have always spurned the scrying of witches and wizards, I think I am convinced of the reliability and specificity of your oracular tendencies, *Vipina*. When you told me to 'hide everything' before I left, I was sure that I had. I used my usual methods of protection and concealment, without taking into account that I had changed in a very important way. Not only have I adopted a *vipina* since last I walked among the covens of Ropaz, but I have drunk the blood of a fairy and been marked by her. To be a vampire, and detected on account of sun magic . . . it is unheard of, among the rarest of all life's possibilities. I did not think of it, and hence did not prepare for it. While I had already found an acceptable stable for the amadel, I had barely gathered you food before I became aware of Feron. I did not know that his intent was benign, and I was anxious to leave rather than risk further detection. It was due to my haste, what with you in my care and vulnerable, that I did not take the time to procure a new mount for you. I think that is just as well, however, for I heard whispers that bode ill for our journey, and it will be to your benefit that no particular animal will be missed and searched for after this night."

Here Vadom paused, as though gauging Lily's readiness for what he was about to impart.

"The town was abuzz with theories on the origin of the burst of magic on their border with the Canyons last night. Though nothing was confirmed, they are usually inclined to blame vampires for any abnormal magical activity, and a few of their witches sensed my Void pulse right afterward, which would tend to uphold their assumptions. What was of greater concern to me, however, was a single wizard who claimed that a member of his coven had just returned from a trading venture in Japeta."

Lily felt her whole body tense, and she looked up at Vadom with growing dread. What could that wizard or witch have seen? Had he been one of the few who had entered the circular commons around the well in the middle of the night? Had he heard the screeching and wailing of the xydolem and known them for what they were, unlike the regular inhabitants of Japeta? Inside her mind, Lily could feel Alder's agitation reflecting her own concern. They waited together for Vadom to continue.

"He was telling a few of his friends that the other member of his coven had been in Japeta the night a number of merchants awoke to find varying amounts of their merchandise missing. Theft is rare in the Joquobon, and that, apparently, was more noteworthy to him than the animal wailing other Japetans swore they heard that same night."

Lily felt all of the air leave her lungs in one large gust, and before she knew how it had happened, she found herself sitting on the stone-covered bank of the Ancient River. Alder was sending her soothing feelings, and she held on to them, trying to keep a handle on both her sadness and her relief. At least that wizard's coven member hadn't really seen anything, didn't truly know what had happened that night a week ago . . .

"Though it sounds as if no one knows of the true circumstances at this moment, it may only be a matter of time before people put things together and come up with a more or less accurate account of events. When that happens, I want you to be as close to the Fae Wood as possible, *Vipina*. If Nather hears any of the rumors in circulation and decides to speak up about you, if he hasn't already, it will be dangerous for you to be anywhere but within your rightful home."

Lily nodded, still unable to speak past the tightness of her throat, or to see beyond the blurring moisture in her eyes. She wondered how far she would have to journey now on foot, and Lily vaguely despaired at the thought of walking every step of the hundreds of miles she still had left to go to arrive at Ford-upon-Ward.

"I'm sorry for all you have to deal with, Lily. I wish, more than anything, that I could summon my body to fly you straight home."

It's alright, Alder. I'll just be getting a lot more exercise now, won't I?

Lily tried to sound positive, but knew she was missing the mark entirely. She felt so tired, and that made everything else that much more difficult to handle . . .

"*Vipina*, I know you must be greatly fatigued by now, but I would like to put some distance between us and Wikkenod tonight. There is no way of knowing if other wizards or witches detected me in their city, and I highly doubt any others will approach as peacefully as Feron. I think it unwise to remain where we are and chance discovery by those who would ensnare you. There is a way we can travel with speed that will not tire you in the least."

Here, Vadom paused, as though hesitating over some internal uncertainty. Lily wondered how they could possibly continue their journey that night without making her feel more exhausted than she was already.

Alder, what do you think he means? Something to do with Void element, maybe?

"I don't know, Lily. What I would like to find out, however, is why Vadom didn't utilize such a method of travel previously. If he knew of a way to continue east that was faster than having you ride the amadel, why hasn't he suggested it before now?"

Lily could tell that Alder was upset about this, and a bit suspicious as well. She herself already trusted Vadom to such a degree that she simply sat and waited for her *vapa* to continue speaking. Lily watched as his face cleared of its uncharacteristic hesitation.

"While I could attempt to fly you, *Vipina,* as my wings are similar in structure to a bat or a dragon and quite strong, they would not support both of us and your pack for the greater part of our travel each day for a number of days. I would normally have to drink a considerable amount of blood to sustain such activity, and I am not certain how I will be affected now that you have quenched my Thirst. Furthermore, it is always unwise to journey in the air of Ropaz if you do not belong to a coven. The witches and wizards have come up with many ingenious ways of protecting the skies of their grasslands, and a vampire flying by day will attract someone's notice long before we reach the Fae Wood. What I would suggest instead, at least until we procure a new mount for you to ride, is that I run on the ground with you in my arms."

When Vadom still seemed uneasy about this, Lily decided to ask him about it.

"*Vapa,* this alternative is causing you to hesitate, which isn't like you. I don't mind being held by you until the next witch city, not if you can carry me and my haversack at a run."

"My equivocation is not in any way a reflection on you, *Vipina.* It is simply that, among vampires, it is completely taboo to hold, carry, or otherwise embrace any female except one's otherwing. I cannot recall ever wrapping my arms about my own mother, my *vama,* or any of my female relations. It is exceptional that I have both caught you from a dangerous fall and held you as you very nearly died. I did not have time to consider those instances, for they occurred very abruptly, and your life was in jeopardy. Moreover, you are my *vipina,* and with the responsibility that I have to you, I believe such occurrences are to be treated in the same manner as with a *vipin,* without reserve.

"In deliberately carrying you some distance through Ropaz, however, I feel that I am trespassing into that which is forbidden in the Cave Kingdom. Though I do not think Vabiri would feel disrespected or shamed if I protected your well-being in this way, I suppose millennia of custom still have the power to give me pause."

Lily was at a loss for words. Yet again, she felt very young compared to the mature being before her. Unsure of what to say to Vadom, Lily turned to Alder.

Are the Fae like this as well, Alder?

"We are allowed to express affection to close female relations, but being in any way familiar with other ladies, especially those who are unmated, is greatly discouraged. With ladies who have found their truemates, they are too loyal to be comfortable with physical contact to any other warrior, unless it is in a healer's capacity. With unmated Fae ladies, you quickly know, once you have spent a bit of time with a lady, that she is not your truemate. After that point, it only makes the disappointment greater if you linger and wish for what cannot be. Why do you ask? Does this tradition differ in the desert?"

Lily thought over what Alder and Vadom had just said. There was no tradition of this nature regarding women and life-partners in the Joquobon, aside from the expectation of fidelity respected within the wedded state. She didn't know if it was because Ropazians didn't mind casual intimacies, and hence their outcasts did not, or if it had something to do with magic, which the desert dwellers despised enough to declare the Anathema. Love was a kind of magic, was it not? Perhaps those who lived in the Joquobon could not even bring themselves to treat that sort of magic with the reverence it deserved. Whatever the cause, Lily felt slightly intimidated by the way in which other beings in Lamoranth apparently honored and esteemed their significant other. In a way, it seemed restrictive to Lily, yet they both seemed to speak about it as though it set them free . . . and if Lily was honest with herself, the thought of being so treasured by another held a nearly irresistible appeal. How much better would it be if she cherished her life-partner in return? It was not so very difficult to imagine such a thing, lately . . .

"Are you ready to go now, *Vipina*? If you give me your haversack, I will carry it on my back, after I've put your new rations inside it."

Lily handed it over without comment, still digesting the information she'd just heard and her more personal thoughts about it. Vadom pulled a small, pouch-like bag off of his back. Lily had failed to notice it before, in part because of the darkness, but also because of her *vapa*'s lightweight black cloak. He gently placed the pouch bag in the haversack, then immediately slung the strap over his own head, shouldering all of Lily's worldly possessions in one smooth movement. With a look that was still slightly tentative, Vadom held out his arms.

Lily felt a bit unsure. Ordinarily, Vadom was so quietly certain, so confidently steadfast, that she had grown accustomed to following his lead. Now, however, with his hesitation, she felt herself vacillating as well. If this was taboo to him, should she be allowing it? Was she disrespecting Vabiri, the *vama* she had not yet met, in permitting herself to be carried? Lily sensed Alder's mixed feelings as well. Was she hurting Alder, her own mate, in accepting this alternative mode of travel? As Lily looked into Vadom's eyes, which displayed his confusion at her pause, she made her decision.

"I think, *Vapa*, that I can walk for a while."

His eyes widened a little in surprise, and Lily could feel Alder's combination of concern, satisfaction, and disbelief.

"*Vipina*, we need to cover as much ground as possible while it is still night. That will not be easy with your iron encumbrance. Please, allow me to carry you."

Again, Vadom held out his arms, and again, Lily hesitated.

"What about my *vama*? What about Alder? I will not dishonor them, *Vapa*."

Lily unconsciously crossed her arms and straightened her back. Though she didn't want to argue, she did want to do what was right by the new people in her life. If both Vadom and Alder had reservations about something, she believed it was her responsibility to heed both their words and their feelings, then choose the most honorable course.

"I have already said that I do not think Vabiri would mind my holding you as I run you to a more secure location. Though I will not speak for Alder, I think his feelings are probably similar."

"That is true, Lily. I don't want you any closer to Wikkenod than you have to be. Let Vadom carry you to Six Cities. He should be able to procure a new mount for you there easily, and then you will have an animal to ride the rest of the way. Please, I don't mind."

Lily turned resolutely east, determined to start walking despite what either of them said. She found herself staring straight at the Ancient River. She began to wonder, a bit uneasily, if it was much deeper here than it had been where she'd bathed. Within her mind, Lily could feel Alder's mixture of amusement and worry.

"Lily, you can't swim here. It isn't safe for you. Let's just be grateful that you can get to the Fae Wood this much faster."

Neither of you are very comfortable with this new plan, Alder. Do you honestly prefer that Vadom carry me what is probably a considerable distance?

Lily could feel Alder struggle with himself a moment, and that was all she needed to harden her resolve.

"What is Alder saying, *Vipina*? Does he find this arrangement acceptable?"

Lily turned away from the river to face her *vapa* once more.

"He is telling me with words that it's fine, but his true feelings are quite different. I think it would be best for all of us if I walk now, *Vapa*."

Vadom looked at Lily steadily for a time, but she didn't look away. Finally, he spoke again.

"I will respect your decision, *Vipina*. Know this, however: if I think your safety is compromised at any time, I will not hesitate to pick you up and run with you if fighting would prove too great a risk. I also reserve the right to carry you as you sleep, to save time as necessary. I consider tonight one such occasion."

Lily stifled a sigh, realizing that this was the best compromise she was likely to get. It wasn't that she wanted to be difficult, she just wanted to try to do the right thing . . .

"Yes, *Vapa*."

Vadom held out his arms to her a third time, but without a trace of ambivalence.

"Please let me carry you across the river, *Vipina*. After that, you may walk if you wish."

Lily went to him in a few short steps, and Vadom wasted no time in carefully picking her up and allowing her to wrap her arms loosely around his neck.

"About time," Alder said, his tone gruff but relieved.

How fast do you think vampires can run, Alder?

"I believe we're about to find out, Lily."

Suddenly, something occurred to Lily that made her slightly uneasy.

Alder, how do you think Vadom is going to swim with me in his arms?

Before he could respond, however, Vadom turned to face the Ancient, took a few measured steps, and jumped right over the entire width of the river. When he had easily cleared the distance and landed neatly on the opposite bank, Vadom glanced down at Lily. He paused at her stunned expression.

"*Vipina*? Did I startle you?"

As Lily attempted to slow down her pulse, which was hammering from the huge leap they had taken, she felt an excited smile light up her face as she looked at Vadom.

"I'm fine, *Vapa*. We just practically flew over the river! A little warning would probably be a good idea next time, though."

"Then perhaps now would be an appropriate time to tell you that I run twice as fast as I am capable of levitating, as I have been so far. If, in an emergency, I must fly with you, then know that I can fly, even carrying weight, about twice as quickly as I run. Let us hope, however, that it never becomes necessary for you to discover this firsthand."

Lily was attempting to imagine flying with such speed through the sky when Vadom gently broke into her thoughts.

"Would you like to sleep at this time, *Vipina*?"

Lily realized that he was asking, in so many words, if she wanted to be put down and allowed to walk, rather than being carried. Both of them had insisted upon it, and she was so very tired . . . Lily felt that if she continued to protest now, it would be unreasonable, and even unwise, given how close they still were to Wikkenod. She smiled sleepily at Vadom.

"Good night, *Vapa*."

He smiled softly in return.

"A pleasant morning to you, *Vipina*. Rest well."

Without further delay, Vadom began to run east, which was just beginning to fade into the deep blue hues of earliest morning. Lily watched briefly as the pre-dawn landscape sped by her, happy that she would be making so much progress toward the Fae Wood in slumber. Though she wanted to sleep, Lily thought she'd speak with Alder for a few minutes first.

Alder, did you see how far we jumped? And how fast we're running! And he's carrying the haversack and me . . . Does flying feel like that?

"Yes, a bit, only even more exhilarating. Once you start flying, you have a powerful way of being in total control of yourself, and that feeling is most liberating."

Lily thought about her mother, and how she had told Lily she would teach her how to use her wings in the Fae Wood. It made her ache inside, in her desert places, and in her dappled wood too. She felt empty when she noticed the lack of her mother's presence, in those places that had yet to fill again with her peaceful memories. Perhaps, Lily thought, she could try to put new people there as well. Special people, trustworthy people . . .

Will you teach me how to fly, Alder?

The seriousness of her tone made Alder reply quietly.

"I would love to, Lily."

Lily wavered for a moment.

Is it asking too much for you to promise me, Alder?

She could feel his surprise. Lily worried that she'd overstepped, or that she might seem capricious, with her request. Why was she being so silly about it anyway?

"I promise you, Lily, that I will teach you to fly in the Fae Wood. May I ask why you want my word on this?"

It's just that . . . my mother promised, too. It made me so excited to be a fairy, and it was so encouraging to have something wonderful at the end of such a formidable journey. To be able to soar . . . my mother didn't fly from the xydolem. She stayed on the ground, she stayed for me. What if we could have just flown away? I try not to think about what could have been different . . . but to fly, in a way, I think, will feel like shedding the iron does, at least for me.

"Then I will help free you, Lily."

They were both silent for a time, absorbed with their own thoughts. At length, just when Lily was beginning to fall into sleep, Alder posed a question.

"Why do you think Vadom's mark was showing earlier, when we haven't seen it otherwise since the ceremony on the Pillar?"

Though she was incredibly tired, Lily did try to sort it out.

Perhaps because he was searching for me? Worried about me? Feeling really responsible for me? Maybe Feron's detection spells illuminated it? Do you have any theories?

"Well, I suppose when you use Fae magic in a vampire ceremony, there's bound to be some strange, powerful results. I guess consistency would be asking a lot when it's so unique."

The day was breaking as Lily, securely held in the arms of her *vapa*, posed a question of her own.

Alder?

"Yes?"

Vadom, is he acting like . . . well, is this what having a father feels like?

Lily felt Alder's emotions, from sadness to uncertainty, before he settled into a calm, contented resolution.

"You feel for Vadom what I have long felt for Captain Pine. He is a respected elder, a capable teacher, a firm disciplinarian, a trustworthy confidant, and one you will probably grow to love. Yes, Lily, I think, given your situation, that Vadom will be like a father to you now and in the years to come. You are fortunate, indeed."

Both of their souls were glowing as Lily drifted off into unconsciousness.

18

Maturity

Though she was abruptly awoken by the Fear, in what was quickly becoming routine, late in the afternoon, Lily handled it with greater aplomb than she had previously. Perhaps it was due to the fact that she was growing more sure of Vadom and Alder, or maybe the beginnings of her circular golden mental defenses were easing the strain, but Lily pushed much of the pain back in less time than it usually took after sleeping.

When she opened her eyes, the grasslands were blurring past her, and she could just make out the swirling Void sphere that hid them from so many possible dangers. Lily looked up at Vadom in surprise.

"Have you stopped at all yet, *Vapa?*"

Vadom looked down at her, smiling in his gentle way before replying.

"No, I have not yet felt the need to rest, *Vipina*. If you would like to stop briefly and eat, however, a short respite would not be taken amiss."

Lily simply nodded her agreement, and then she was being carefully lowered to the ground. Her haversack appeared almost instantaneously beside her, along with the pouch of victuals Vadom had found for her the night before. Lily was thrilled to find fresh fruit amongst the new supplies, in addition to more bread and vegetables. There was also a medium-sized, white, round food that Lily had never seen before. She held it up excitedly.

"How do I eat this, *Vapa?* I've never had it before."

Vadom's brow creased ever so slightly.

"I'm not entirely certain, *Vipina*. It was on the same shelf as the bread, so I procured one. Perhaps Alder knows what it is and how it is consumed?"

From within her mind, Lily could feel Alder's amusement.

"Honestly, the two of you. It's a wheel of cheese. You put slices of the inside on pieces of bread. Just don't eat the rind— it's a wax that is really only meant to preserve the flavor and moisture of the actual cheese."

Lily repeated the information to Vadom, then ate it as Alder had suggested.

"Oh, this is delicious! It's sort of sharp . . ."

Lily ate several more pieces before regretfully tucking the rest back in the food pouch. Then she stood up, stretched, and took a closer look at their surroundings. She thought the grass was perhaps taller, and a lighter green, than she had seen thus far. Other than that, the landscape looked somewhat similar to the Joquobon, with its vast expanse of gently rolling hills. As the grass waved in the wind, the hills even seemed to shift slightly, just like the sands of the desert. There were the occasional outcroppings of rock, however, that reminded Lily she was putting an increasing number of miles between herself and her birthplace. Just as her thoughts began to turn, as they so often did, to her mother, Vadom spoke into the silence.

"I have been considering the options available to us for traveling the remaining distance of our journey, *Vipina*. Now that we have put some space between ourselves and Wikkenod, I think it prudent to find a new mount for you to ride. Witches and wizards, when they do not avail themselves of air magic to travel, use horses. The nearest establishments of Ropazians from our current location are Six Cities and the moderately-sized town of Wizulaan. I would like to make for the latter. Six Cities, which is actually only comprised of five cities in the configuration of a pentacle, surrounds a crumbling, ancient structure called the Wizzen Peak. Due to the Peak's significance in their culture, this area has always been home to a great many witching families. The six most powerful covens in Ropaz, and indeed the whole of Lamoranth, also reside there. It is the ultimate stronghold of witch magic, where they have long kept the secrets of their people. Vampires do not enter it singly or unprepared, let alone with an iron-bound fairy in their care. I would be much more comfortable stopping in Wizulaan, due to its relative isolation, as well as the fact that it is more directly in our path, being farther south than Six Cities. Do you find this plan acceptable?"

Lily thought for a moment.

"Will we be getting very close to the trolls of the Volcano Crescent, *Vapa*? Would you say they are a more manageable adversary than the witches or wizards of Six Cities?"

"I think it unlikely that we will encounter any trolls. They generally stay within the shelter of the Crescent, and only enter Ropaz occasionally as scavengers and raiders. Even if we do meet with any, they are, at least by common conception, believed to be enemies of lesser intelligence, and are only really dangerous in large numbers. Even taking them into consideration, I feel that Wizulaan is the wiser course."

Alder, do you agree? I think the magic levels near Six Cities might be more than I can handle, and Wizulaan sounds faster and safer to me.

"I agree. Vadom knows this area much better than we do. Even if we do come across a raiding party of trolls, I don't think Vadom would have trouble dispatching them if you were threatened. They have earth magic, but Vadom's on a whole other level with his Void magic. I only mentioned Six Cities before because it's one of the only coven establishments I know of, though I haven't actually been there myself. I just want the easiest, safest route home for you, Lily."

"Alder and I accept your plan, *Vapa,* and we're grateful for your knowledge and strength."

Vadom inclined his head in acknowledgement, then spoke again.

"I thought, *Vipina,* that we might have a warrior lesson now, while you are rested. If you would keep your iron on, for the sake of expedience, I will demonstrate more weapons for you. I would then like to continue toward Wizulaan this evening."

Lily faced her teacher squarely, made him the *valoriad,* and filled her voice with determination.

"Then may I have some of your time to learn weapons this afternoon, *Vapa?*"

"You may have one hour before we progress eastward. Today I will be showing you weapons from the spears and polearms category and the blunt category, as a continuation of your lesson on blades and ranged weapons. The simplest, and perhaps oldest, weapon in the former is the spear itself."

After enlarging the Void sphere around them, Vadom proceeded to pull a long, thin, sturdy stick with one very sharply pointed end from his torso and left leg with his right hand. He made several precise jabbing motions before replacing it in his chest. Though Lily thought it a rather glorified tent pole, she kept her opinion to herself. Perhaps the simplest weapons were at times the most effective.

"The following weapons are derivatives of agricultural tools. There were times when farmers were forced to defend their crops with whatever implements they had at hand, which were most often the tools of their livelihood and trade."

Vadom proceeded to show Lily a war scythe, a military fork, and a billhook. All three had long poles to grip and either a blade, tines, or a combination of both at one end. Lily had only the vaguest notions about agriculture, though she knew that bread was made in part from a grain that grew in abundance in Ropaz. She decided to ask Alder more about it later, focusing her whole attention once more on her graceful, and obviously powerful, teacher.

Vadom then showed her a 'halberd', a 'glaive', and a 'partisan', which all appeared to Lily to be similar to the adapted farming implements, though a bit more elaborate and deliberately menacing. The polearms seemed to her primarily good for keeping enemies at a bit of a distance, and certainly lethal if one had the strength and precision to use them.

"Swordstaff," Vadom said, and removed the weapon from his body. Lily noticed that the pole portion had a greater diameter than any of the previous weapons, and that the blade was truly of short-sword length. "Though occasionally disputed as belonging to the blade category, it nonetheless is accepted most widely as a polearm. It is still used primarily for stabbing, though it retains some of the functions of a sword when properly handled. This is a weapon often used by less magically skilled wizards and witches. It is useful in aerial combat, as well as when they ride horses in ground battle. It is my opinion that young, unskilled, or unscrupulous wizards also use swordstaffs because they mimic in appearance the magical staffs of their more powerfully talented brethren. It is easy for them to detach the sword and bluff more magic then they can really wield, causing more powerful opponents to approach them with unnecessary caution. It is an oft-used strategy and weapon that suits the cunning of their race."

Lily was still mulling that information over as Vadom replaced his swordstaff with a weapon she recognized from their first lesson.

"It's an ax," she said, without thinking. Lily immediately worried that she had spoken out of turn, but Vadom merely nodded.

"I am glad that you recognize it, though it is obviously larger than the throwing axes I showed you previously. This weapon is meant to remain in your hands, and is used most effectively with swinging or chopping motions. The ax can do significant damage at close range."

After demonstrating, Vadom put the ax back in his chest and created from his Void magic another polearmed weapon. It looked something like the ax, except that instead of the broad, two-sided head with blades designed to wedge and cut, there were two long, sharp, curved spikes.

"Pick," Vadom informed her. "Favored weapon of the dwarves. It is also the tool they use to mine for precious stones in their mountains, and this makes them very comfortable with wielding it. Though I have encountered few dwarves in my lifetime, and most of those in recent centuries, all used their picks with incredible skill. The effect on an enemy is similar to a war hammer, which will begin your instruction in blunt weapons."

After a short and dizzying display with the pick, which included arcing strikes, high and low swings, and an exchange of the weapon from one hand to the other that made Lily's eyes widen with awe, Vadom replaced the pitch-black pick in his torso and immediately formed what Lily assumed was the war hammer. It was similar to the tool the desert men used to erect the tents everyone lived in, though those were called mallets. The motions Vadom employed were somewhat familiar, at any rate.

The next weapon Vadom showed her was thicker and longer than a spear, and taller even than Vadom, who was head and shoulders taller than Lily herself. It was unsharpened, however, and Lily wondered if that made it a bit less lethal than many of the weapons she had seen so far.

"Quarterstaff," Vadom intoned. After demonstrating some of its basic maneuvers, he allowed the quarterstaff to liquefy into an undulating mass of Void, which he then reformed into a shorter, though more dangerous-looking, weapon. The medium-sized handle widened slightly at the end, with evenly spaced knobs all the way around the head.

"Mace: a more developed version of the club, which is essentially a shorter and thicker quarterstaff, due to the small pointed protrusions at the end of its handle. Because of the radial symmetry of the head, it can be used to strike from a greater number of angles than weapons like the war hammer, a useful advantage. The mace is one of the war tools favored by goblins and trolls, as are the next and last two weapons I will show you now."

Vadom focused his attention on the head of the mace, and Lily watched with growing trepidation as the knobs sharpened, lengthened, and increased in number.

"Morningstar," her teacher explained. "Different from the mace in that the large number of spikes allow the bearer to combine blunt force with puncture strikes to maim and kill. A reliable weapon well-suited for warriors with strength but somewhat lacking in finesse or strategy." Lily felt herself swallow hard as her *vapa* swung the morningstar with the absolute assurance of long familiarity. Vadom then allowed the morningstar to sink into his chest, even as he pulled out a weapon that made the hair on the back of Lily's neck stand up.

"Flail," Vadom announced. The Void-black weapon consisted of a fairly short pole handle, with a chain attached to the end. The chain connected to a ball as big as Lily's head, which was covered in long, sharply-pointed spikes. It was like a morningstar, only the chain gave it a longer and more flexible range. As Lily watched Vadom twirl and strike with the flail, she felt her courage falter slightly as she imagined a troll or goblin swinging such a weapon in her vicinity. Vadom saw the look in her eyes and paused, allowing the spiked ball to thud into the ground.

"*Vipina,* I am teaching you about weapons so that you will fear your enemies less, not more. As I mentioned to you previously, the knowledge that you are forearmed with is just as important as the physical weapons you wield in any battle. For example, based on what you already know, what would a fighter of your size be able to do to subdue an opponent with a flail?"

Lily hesitated, still feeling intimidated by the flail. She responded uncertainly.

"Approach them with a polearm? A *really* long one, like the swordstaff, to keep out of range . . . or use another weapon with an even longer range," Lily said, her fear receding with the possibilities. "A bow and arrows would be safer, even a sling would be effective if you could hit their head. Or the throwing stars! If your aim was good enough, you could slice your enemy's forearms or wrists, and then they couldn't even swing the flail. Then there's magic too— I could probably sustain a flame that would burn up a flail, or bury the enemy with earth, or blow them away from me with air. It would really hurt with this iron on, but I'm sure I could do it once I'm not wearing it. If there weren't too many opponents, and I learned how to gauge and control the amount of magic I needed first . . ."

Lily trailed off, realizing that Vadom was regarding her solemnly, yet she was certain she could detect a glint of amusement in his eyes as well. She looked at him uncertainly, wondering what he thought of her ideas.

"You are creative, *Vipina,* and that trait will serve you well against the foes in your future. All of your tactics would probably have some measure of success, depending on a variety of other factors, and of course your own amount of training at the time. What I would also like to impress upon you now, however, before we continue any further, is this: whenever it is possible, you should avoid conflict entirely. You should never willingly engage an enemy you do not stand at least a reasonable chance of subduing, if not completely defeating."

Lily was sure her surprise was showing on her face, even as she felt Alder's disgruntlement in her mind. Obviously, he had been taught this lesson as well, and he didn't appreciate it. Vadom looked into Lily's face and seemed almost as though he could read Alder's thoughts.

"Though it hurts the pride of many warriors, the wisest will always realize that there is almost always a choice between risky combat and the more prudent concealment or flight. You will eventually learn that there are more important things than victory and glory, though this is often difficult for the young to see."

Lily felt a dull ache begin to grow in her chest, and it sharpened with every word Vadom spoke and every stubbornly resistant emotion Alder felt in response. She thought of her mother, and the xydolem, and how soft Bepo's ears had felt in her hand, even as she had watched Rose bleed to death far from her home and her mate.

"I understand this choice, *Vapa,*" she whispered.

Vadom went utterly still before her. Alder, too, seemed suspended in time for many long moments, his mortification absolute. Lily wanted to break the silence, but couldn't speak past the painful lump in her throat. After another long pause, Vadom replaced the flail in his chest. Then he slowly bent his elbow, and, holding the *valoriad,* spoke.

"Please forgive me, *Vipina.* I should not have spoken those words to you, not with such arrogance and lack of compassion. I should not have lost sight of what you have endured, and hurt your spirit. In doing so, I have failed to fulfill my *vapa*'s oath to you. For this I apologize, and I will make the greatest effort to protect your spirit better in the future."

"Lily, I'm sorry, too. He was really chastising me, because he could tell I was influencing you, even when I said I wouldn't during your training. I feel terrible for this, faelani. *I didn't consider your feelings but my own, and it has caused you even more pain than you suffer already. Please forgive me."*

The depth of Alder's remorse, and the anxiousness she could see in Vadom's dark eyes, brought Lily back from the dangerous direction of her thoughts. She told herself it wouldn't do to dwell on her painful memories, or to take offense where none was meant. That wasn't how she'd been raised, and Lily realized that she could honor her mother now by honoring her upbringing. Straightening her spine and pushing back her shoulders, Lily spoke into the silence.

"I accept both of your apologies. I know neither of you had any unkind intentions. It's not your fault that my thoughts stray so easily to that battle, and how it might have gone differently. It is useless to consider now if I had done this or that, or if my mother had done one thing or another, or how anything else could have possibly changed the outcome. Why don't we just put this behind us and look forward instead," she finished gently.

Vadom gazed into Lily's face, his own pensive.

"You are so uncommonly gracious, *Vipina.* Your mother lives on beautifully through you."

"He speaks truly, Lily. I feel more honored than ever to be your faelan."

Lily felt a little embarrassed by their praise, but she wanted to live up to their words, to prove them true, and to be worthy of their regard.

"My thanks, both of you. *Vapa,* I believe you said that the flail was the last of the blunt weapons you wished to show me. Was there anything else you wanted to impart before the end of the lesson?"

Vadom paused a moment longer before answering, his expression still thoughtful.

"I think I have said more than enough for today. Do you have any questions for me on the polearms or blunt weapons before we make for Wizulaan, *Vipina?*"

Lily gratefully focused her attention back on the lesson, mentally reviewing all of the new information.

"Do you think I should begin learning any of today's weapons during our journey to the Fae Wood, *Vapa?*"

Vadom considered this briefly before answering.

"I believe the anelaces and the bow and arrows would serve you better in the immediate future, *Vipina.* Both are more suited to your size and natural inclination. I think, after lectures on magical weapons, which you will recall is the fifth and final category of weaponry, as well as on warrior mentality, we can begin your practical instruction with those two in particular."

Lily nodded in agreement. She found it a relief, even a little exciting, to know that soon she would be able to wield such weapons. Watching Vadom as he shrank the protective Void sphere once more, Lily noticed that Alder was still unusually quiet. She waited until her *vapa* had picked her up and resumed running eastward for a time before she spoke to him.

Alder, I was wanting to ask you about agriculture earlier in my warrior lesson, but it can wait if there's something you'd like to talk about first.

Alder seemed to hesitate, but then slowly began to speak.

"I don't want to worry you, faelani, *but I feel a little . . . different today."*

At Lily's immediate and considerable concern, Alder hastened to reassure her.

"Not weaker, just a bit . . . I don't know, stretched out. I suppose that makes sense, seeing as my body is still some distance from here. Though really, if Vadom keeps to this pace, we'll get to Wizulaan in the next few days, I would think. After that, with you on horseback, it should only take another week or so to reach Ford-upon-Ward. I'm sure I'll be fine waiting that long, especially since travel will be completely safe and swift inside the Wood— and that means you can remove your iron. What a great day that will be . . ."

Lily was not entirely convinced that all was well with Alder, but that only strengthened her resolve to make it to the Fae Wood as quickly as possible. They really were making good time with Vadom's help. Lily decided that she would pay closer attention to Alder's condition from now on, and do anything she could to help him endure the remainder of their journey. Feeling the slight unease between them, Lily wracked her mind for another topic of conversation. A detail from her warrior lesson randomly presented itself.

So I am your faelani, *and you are my* 'faelan', *Alder? You haven't used that word before.* Lily hesitated a moment, but decided to continue. *Would you like it if I called you that sometimes?*

Lily knew his answer before he spoke, so great was the happiness she felt from him. Alder's response was just a little shy, but completely certain.

"I would love for you to call me faelan, *Lily. Though I feel unworthy of such a gift, I will strive always to be the Fae you deserve."*

Lily was quiet once more, as amazed and unsure as she had been the other day when Alder had spoken so sincerely about being truemates. She had been meaning to speak to him more about it, privately hoping to discover how long she could cling to the comfort and pretense of friendship once they were among other fairies. What might she expect of their bonding and its significance once they were in the Fae Wood? A part of Lily could still hardly believe any of it was real. Perhaps asking for knowledge would make it more tangible . . .

Please tell me more about truemates, faelan. *How do they usually meet?*

"Well, first, there is usually a great deal of preparation before most

truemates find one another. For every fairy's first century of life, they are encouraged to fully explore their own personalities. Even before the search begins at the age of one hundred years, you should be familiar with your own strengths and weaknesses. That is supposed to help you once you've bonded, because they say problems in the truemate relationship often arise from individual insecurities or small character flaws. Self-awareness takes time, though most Fae know themselves well enough to begin the search after those first ten decades have elapsed.

"What marks the beginning of the search is a ceremony on one's coming of age birthday, during which one of the Fae seers searches your future, insomuch as they can see, for some clue about an undiscovered mate. Most Fae put this intimation to good use and find their mates within the next few decades, though a fair few take the better part of a century to make their discovery. Truemates are often, though not always, relatively close in age, and it is often that a fairy finds his or her mate before that mate has reached their majority. In those cases, the younger mate does not require the aid of the seers. So, in answer to your question, the coming-of-age search is how most Fae meet their truemates."

Lily digested this new information, though it only created more questions in her mind. She wondered how many years Alder had already lived, to have reached the point at which he felt ready for his truemate. He was obviously at least a bit older than one hundred years, and Lily marveled at his age. She wondered just how old exactly the Fae could live to be. Her mother hadn't ever been specific when she'd told Lily fairy tales, snuggling side by side in Lily's nest of blankets, or when she had sung very quietly to Lily in the evenings, tracing designs only she seemed able to see on Lily's face and arms all the while . . . Lily hesitated to ask Alder how old he was outright, however, and decided to find out more about the Fae seers instead, seeing as that was apparently one of her own gifts.

You've mentioned before that there are only two Fae seers in the Wood at the moment. Would you tell me more about them, please?

"Of course. As I think I mentioned before, their names are Quince and Eustoma. Wings of prophecy are the rarest ability of the Fae, so they have had a good deal of work for some time now. Though neither the eccentric Quince, nor his equally unique faelani, *Eustoma, are extraordinarily far-sighted, they have managed to continue the tradition of helping Fae begin their search. They've been good about spending equal amounts of time between Silver Court and Golden Court, to try to help fairies on both sides of the Wood find their mates. For example, Quince told me, at the beginning of my second century, that my*

truemate would be a 'diamond of gold'. As much as I've pondered that, it made no sense to me until I was in your mind."

So I won't have to go to Quince or Eustoma, because you've already found me? Yet you waited at least one hundred years . . . I'm sorry that you've been alone so long, Alder.

Alder hastened to reassure her.

"Oh, you needn't worry about me, Lily. It's not as though either of us could affect when we were born. I myself came into the world at a most inconvenient time for my parents, right in the midst of the most recent war with the trolls of the Volcano Crescent. Your mother briefly mentioned to you that they nearly took Molten Mirror Lake about three hundred years ago, when she told you about the dragons' broken pact. That was when I made my rather untimely appearance. In any case, Lily, I think you were more than worth the wait."

Lily was a little stunned to finally find out how old Alder was, but he seemed to be a bit reluctant to discuss it, so Lily didn't push the subject. Most of her surprise stemmed from the fact that, had she met Alder in the Joquobon, she would have assumed he was in his early twenties. This, of course, would have made him a very good candidate for a life-partner, at least as far as Lily was concerned. A little older could mean a great deal more mature as well, and Lily certainly would have been attracted to that in a young Desert man, given how she was mistreated continually by her peers. Lily wasn't entirely surprised, then, that her difference in age from Alder's didn't bother her as it might have many other girls still in their teenage years. Lily didn't feel as if she needed to change her attitude toward Alder, and she was positive he wouldn't like that in the slightest anyway.

Really, Lily couldn't help but see a number of advantages to having a truemate who had lived longer than she had. Alder obviously possessed a great deal of knowledge about the Fae, magic, the Wood, and indeed the world of Lamoranth at large. In the event that she actually made it to the Fae Wood, a place she hoped to call home in the truest sense, Lily knew she would be able to count on Alder to help her find her place and start a new life, just as her mother would have done. She believed that, whether as her friend or her *faelan,* Alder would answer any of her questions freely, and always offer good advice and unwavering support. Would she need to complete any kind of prescribed education? Could they delay truemate ceremonies until Lily felt ready to participate in them? Lily was sure Alder would know the answers to these and probably a host of other things Lily didn't have any notions about yet . . .

Lily then noticed, despite her preoccupation with her thoughts, the tenor of Alder's emotions, and she realized she wasn't holding up her end of the conversation.

Thank you, Alder. I was just starting to really think about what my life might be like in the Fae Wood, at least after I deliver my mother's scroll, return you to your body, and help my father. When I think of all that I need to learn, all there is to discover about my life as a fairy, I feel grateful that I'll have you there with me. What do you think one of the most difficult aspects of this next phase of my life will be? I have to admit, I'm worried about bonding properly when I'm so far from the fairy age of maturity. I think that might be a part of why I'm having trouble accepting being a truemate. I don't want my hesitation to hurt you, though, Alder.

Lily sensed a melange of emotions from Alder in response to her words, but she wasn't sure she would wish them back, even if she could. Feeling uneasy at Alder's silence, Lily waited as patiently as she could for him to speak. Finally, he responded, his tone very somber.

"I think, faelani, *that the beginning of your life as a lady of our people will be full of challenges. I must say, in all seriousness, that I am just as concerned about bonding properly as you are, just for different reasons. Your words have been forthright, and I must admit, in turn, that bonding with me will not be easy. For most Fae truemates, courtship takes a number of years, and I do not think we will be an exception. The length of* faelanzania *will definitely work in our favor, and most Fae would never dream of rushing us through such an important time in our lives. I do worry that being nearly three hundred years older than you will be an obstacle for us, but I confess that it is one of my lesser concerns."*

Alder lapsed into an abstracted silence, then seemed to give himself a shake. He spoke again, in an obvious attempt to lighten the mood and reverse the serious turn their talk had taken.

"There is something that I do find humorous in all of this, Lily. I had always found it hard to believe, until now, that the search is the easiest step in the path to being fully bonded with one's truemate. Though all of my elders asserted this to be true, that the real difficulties begin once you've met and started your lives together, I found the patience required of searching and waiting to be most trying. I simply wasn't able to believe that decades, which for me became centuries, of self-examination and solitary fortitude could possibly be easier than actively trying to win over my mate. I thought that any difficulty of bonding would be outweighed by the relief that comes with knowing one has a faelani, *and that she*

will be with you always. Though I had long thought myself more than prepared for the challenges of courtship and bonding, nothing could have prepared me for the life I have led since I first heard your voice, Lily."

Lily thought about both the serious and the supposedly more lighthearted things Alder had just told her. That their bonding would be slow and challenging, but not just because of her. That Alder had been lonely for a very long time, just as Lily had felt all of her life in the desert. She thought too about how Alder had been living without his body, physically unable to help her travel to the Wood. How he had to allow her to suffer from the iron, because it was, perversely, her protection from numerous enemies. How he had to watch while Vadom taught her things that he would readily have imparted, had the situation been different. Alder had borne all of this with good grace, despite his great fear for her vulnerabilities. Lily felt her respect for him grow as she considered all of those things, and she clearly projected it in Alder's direction. She was certain he needed that from her, whether as a friend or *faelani*. Lily felt his surprise, as well as his happiness.

"Here I thought you would be laughing at my youthful folly, faelani, *and instead I feel your esteem. Perhaps I should tell you more of my shortcomings, if you will always react so favorably."*

Lily wondered if Alder truly had any serious deficiencies of character. Was she really the truemate of such a Fae? She knew Alder wasn't perfect, but her own inadequacies seemed larger and more numerous by comparison. Could she live up to his long-held expectations about courtship and bonding, given enough time and effort? Though he seemed to be tempering his wishes to suit Lily, that made her feel rather guilty. Didn't he deserve to have the *faelani* he had been awaiting for so long?

"Lily, did I say something to cause you this worry? That was certainly not my intent."

Lily was slow to respond.

I guess it's just that I don't always feel . . . worthy of you. What you were saying about introspection, and on a journey like this no less, has made me realize that there is so much I don't know or understand about myself yet. I don't feel like your equal in that regard, and it bothers me, because it doesn't seem fair to you. Then there are difficulties for our bonding that I don't even know about yet, and it just makes me doubt myself more. I want to grow into myself, to explore all of my magical possibilities, to find my way in the world. I'm worried, though, about how taking the time to achieve the maturity that you already have is going to affect our bonding.

Lily stopped, hoping to guess Alder's thoughts by the turn of his feelings. He was concerned, then understanding, before settling on being deliberately reassuring.

"Lily, never disbelieve that we are fully worthy of each other, even if one or the other of us doubts it at times. All fairies are told, from their earliest years, that the desire of any truemates should ultimately be total acceptance and mutual love. All of that takes time, though. I realize you haven't had the years that I've had to consider all of this, or even begin to want it for yourself. Despite how mature you already are, whether you realize it or not, you still have plenty of growing up to do. There is nothing wrong with that. Know that we can take as long as we need to in order to complete faelanzania, *even if it means waiting until you reach your own majority. I know it is a very new concept for you, but remember that we are fairies, and that means we are immortal. Time is something we have in abundance, and there is no need to rush. I want you to feel as though you have all the time in the world to grow from an astonishing girl to a wondrous lady. All I ask is for you to keep your soul open to me, so we can continue to grow in our understanding of each other. Being your best friend and confidant for the next eight decades would be no less blissful for me than residing in the bright peace of the Afterlight. We are in a unique situation at the moment, and I think that this is probably indicative of how we will ultimately become a very special pair. As such, I refuse to concern myself with convention if it is not in your best interests. Let's not worry ourselves about the length of our courtship. There's really quite enough to think about and deal with in the present as it is."*

Lily felt her vision blur and her chest ache as she listened to Alder speak. She felt more prized than the most brilliant diamond ever mined by the dwarves in the Grandfather Mountains. Alder would never have to steal her heart, she suddenly realized. Lily knew that his patience would softly beckon to her, his many kindnesses would lure her further in, and his generosity would eventually have her giving her heart to him just as freely as he offered his own. All she needed was time, and he had already granted her as much as she required. No amount of iron could ever make her fear their bond now.

Faelan, Lily whispered, hardly able to speak even within her own mind.

"Lily," Alder whispered back.

Without any other words, their souls convened under the trees in Lily's mind.

It was peaceful there, and Lily urged Alder's soul to rest. They were a little more in tune with each other's feelings than they had been before, and so Lily didn't need to voice her concern about Alder feeling stretched too far, at least not just then. He understood that she was worried about his welfare, and he tried to rest for both of them.

Lily watched over him for a time. When she was sure he was in a relaxed state, she silently left him to his sun-dappled respite. She could only hope it would help him recover from the events of the last week, as well as endure the separation from his body with just a little more ease. Though Lily spent the remainder of the day watching the grasslands around her and conferring on their location and relative safety with her *vapa*, nothing untoward had occurred by nightfall. Lily allowed herself to fall asleep after a small meal, knowing that her body, her mind, and a little piece of her heart were all in good hands.

Iron-Bound

She awoke at first light the following morning, feeling both refreshed and terribly weary. When she opened her eyes, done prevailing in her post-sleep battle with the Fear, Lily found herself surrounded by glorious purple. Was this more wizard magic?

"*Vapa*, what is all this purple around us? Did the witches make it? Are we approaching Wizulaan?"

Vadom slowed to a walk, then stopped, the corners of his mouth tilting slightly upward even as he set Lily gently on her feet.

"We are passing through fields of heather, a flower common throughout Ropaz, *Vipina*. I must admit, I have hardly given such things a passing thought in many centuries. You are helping me see with new eyes, and to remember what it is like to be young again. It is a marvel, for me, how unexpectedly the reciprocal nature of a *vapa* and his *vipina* occurs. I will have to tell Vabiri all about it when I can."

Lily decided not to disturb the wistful turn of Vadom's thoughts. She understood all too well what it was like to wish someone near when it was not possible. Lily ate a quick breakfast, indulging in some of the fruits her *vapa* had found in Wikkenod, then focused on finding Alder in her mind.

Good morning, faelan, she said. Though she was a little shy after their conversation the previous evening, Lily tried to speak with Alder as she usually did. *Feeling any better today?*

"Good morning, faelani. *Certainly not any worse, which is as good as can be expected, I suppose. It was quite wonderful to awake to your excitement for*

flowers. All Fae love and care for the flora of the Wood, but ladies are the most fond of flowers, especially the blossom of their namesake."

Lily wasn't entirely sure she understood what Alder was saying.

Are all Fae ladies named after flowers, Alder? I know my mother was, but is a lily a flower as well?

Lily could feel Alder's surprise.

"Yes, the lily is a most beautiful flower. All ladies have been named for flowers since the Wood became the exclusive home of the Fae, a very long time ago. It is part of the magic of the place. All male Fae are named after trees."

Lily immediately tried to imagine what an alder tree must look like. Then she wondered how many different types of flowers and trees there must be. The only ones she knew of were those that had medicinal properties, which her mother had taught her about in their healing lessons. How could mothers and fathers ever decide on the right name for their child when there must be so very many to choose from? When she asked this of Alder, however, she could feel his hesitation.

"Lily, as much as I wish to tell you, this is one of the greatest secrets of the Fae, and it would not be wise to impart this knowledge lightly. Do you think we are safe enough with Vadom for me to divulge the answer to your question?"

Lily hesitated, torn between wanting to know and wanting to keep such an important fairy secret safe. Alder had told her other things about the Fae, yet they apparently didn't rival the mystery of the flowers and trees in importance. At her prolonged inner conflict, Alder began to speak, but was interrupted by a flare of premonition from one of Lily's magical wells. It was immediately followed by a painful encroachment of the Fear into some of her inner circles, and it was many long minutes before Lily was able to focus her mind on the source of her prophetic power.

"Lily, are you alright? Was that from your well of prophecy?"

I've got it under control . . . let me really concentrate on what it's trying to tell us . . .

Alder remained quiet, though he floated close to Lily's nine wells to hear better.

After listening for a short time, Lily relayed the portent to Alder, in case he hadn't been able to hear it, trying as she did not to let too much disappointment color her voice.

It is saying 'iron on', faelan. *I get the sense that it means for a while, maybe the rest of our journey. We must be about to encounter someone or something that makes it imperative for me to remain undetectable, beyond even the protection of my* vapa's *Void sphere.*

Lily immediately felt Alder's sympathy, as well as his banked frustration. She knew he didn't want her wearing her iron accouterments any more than necessary, and both of them had been looking forward to her next short break from bearing all of it. Lily knew, though, just as Alder did, that it would not be wise to ignore her prophetic instincts, such as they were.

I had better tell Vapa *about this. Would you say, based on the timing of the other warnings and advice, that we should be extra careful as we approach Wizulaan tomorrow evening?*

"I definitely think you should tell him, and I agree that we should skirt this wizard city with the utmost caution. Do you suppose it will still be safe for Vadom to take a horse for you to ride? In the event that he must do battle, I think it most prudent for you to have an escape plan that includes a mount."

Though Lily was upset by this pronouncement, as it echoed painfully of recent events, she turned her mind outward to speak with Vadom.

"*Vapa*, I've just had another flash of my prophetic power. It repeated the words 'iron on' several times. I got the feeling that it meant for the remainder of our journey, though it might coincide more directly with our arrival at Wizulaan. What do you think of this?"

Vadom paused in his scan of their heather-covered surroundings to face Lily fully.

"I had planned to have you remove your iron for a short time tomorrow before we reached Wizulaan, after which I would proceed to enter the city for a horse and some provisions at nightfall. We may have to make adjustments to this course, however."

All three of them briefly considered what should or perhaps should not be done during the following day. Finally, Vadom spoke again.

"I think that your warrior lesson for tomorrow will still be a lecture on warrior mentality, though without any attempts at night magic usage that I had been considering. I do not think, however, that we should avoid Wizulaan altogether. The advice of your oracle power is not always negative or indicative of harm, as my very continuing existence attests. Perhaps I will learn something of value from the inhabitants of the wizard city as I gather what you need, *Vipina*. Though it is possible that the sun magic you have imparted to me may bring me to the wizards' attention again, I cannot help but think that the potential danger is worth obtaining a horse and the local news circulating the covens of the city. Perhaps if I take extra precautions to make myself undetectable, just as you will keep your iron fully upon your person, nothing untoward will occur."

Her *vapa*'s words inadvertently gave Lily an idea.

"*Vapa*, perhaps I could give you a piece of my iron to wear. Do you think that it would affect you and hide you as it does me?"

Though he looked a bit startled, Vadom considered her words and replied promptly.

"I had been considering another method involving night magic use. However, seeing as Void and iron seem perfectly compatible, and that sun magic is not easily concealed by the night element alone, this might be a wiser course. Can you spare any of the iron you wear now, *Vipina*? Will this clash with the most recent words of your inner oracle?"

Lily and Alder returned to her wells of power, but nothing more was forthcoming.

"I think it will be all right. I have a number of rings, but I think they may all be too small for your fingers, *Vapa*. Maybe I'll just give you one of my necklaces. I don't think that will make too much of a difference. You may just have to make the Void sphere around me a little bit thicker before you go into Wizulaan. That ought to compensate enough to keep me fully hidden, as it seems I must be from now on."

Vadom nodded, accepting this as a good plan.

"Perhaps Vadom should put the necklace on now, faelani. *We don't know if the Fear will affect him or not. He is still a vampire, but he does contain love element and have a promise of kinship with you. He might need today to learn how to wage the battle you fight, even though it will be on a much smaller scale."*

I didn't think about that . . . He so clearly has a warrior's mental discipline, I hadn't considered that it might really bother him. Do you think it will, Alder?

"The Fear is not something one can rationalize or endure easily, Lily. We cannot anticipate how it will affect him until he puts it on, and I would rather he go into Wizulaan prepared. Better that he remain focused and able to detect anyone following him to your location, especially with a horse in tow."

Lily couldn't fault Alder's logic, and she was about to relay her *faelan*'s concern to Vadom when he spoke up.

"Is Alder concerned about you removing any of your iron, *Vipina*? Given the content of your latest fairy-scrying, I would understand if he disagreed with this plan. I'm sure we can come up with a viable alternative."

Lily felt Alder's respect for Vadom increase, even as she told her *vapa* what Alder had really been worried about. It gave Vadom pause.

"While I do have a very high threshold for pain, this 'fear' is an unknown quantity. I do not think it is quite like normal apprehension, not based on your description of it. Will it cause me to worry for my otherwing more strongly? Or your safety? Or the future of the Cave Kingdom?"

Lily wasn't sure how to answer. Her response was slow.

"It definitely heightens my other concerns, but for the most part it constantly preys on the most familiar, well-used parts of my mind, making me doubt myself and causing pain that never leaves or grows weak. It pounces on even a second of dropped vigilance, and the battle I fight with it every morning never gets any easier. If there is any concentration of Void in your mind, or you have an idea where that bit of sun magic is, keep the Fear well away from those places. Don't give it anything that will make it grow stronger or debilitate you. Do you have any kind of wall to shield your mind?"

"My mind is fully fortified with Void. There is but one small door by which anything could enter."

Lily could feel Alder's awe and admiration.

"It takes a very, very long time, and a great deal of strength, to build up that kind of protection for your mind, Lily. You know the wall you started? You will eventually do the same for the perimeter of your entire mind. You will add to it, bit by bit, until it is actually a dome that fully covers your mind from invasion. I bet his door is probably even hidden somehow . . ."

"Then maybe the Fear will not even be able to affect you as it does me, *Vapa*. I am always pushing it to the peripheries of my innermost mind, near that first circle of my mental wall, but if it can't even get that far with you, perhaps it won't be a problem. Would you like to experiment now, while there aren't any enemies near? I think that would make Alder feel better . . ."

Vadom nodded decisively.

"Yes, I think that would be prudent. I dislike uncertainty of any kind when the safety of the vulnerable is concerned."

Lily reached for her neck, selecting one of her plainer, less feminine necklaces for her *vapa* to wear. It was shorter, one of her mother's gifts from a very early birthday. Lily felt a pang as she realized that she would be seventeen soon, and her mother would not be there.

"Faelani? *What's wrong? If that piece of jewelry is special, perhaps you could give him another one to wear instead?"*

Lily shook off her sadness at the concern in Alder's voice. The loss of this one necklace was not worth making him worry like this. The greatest gifts her mother had given her were not the ones she wore on the outside.

It's fine, faelan. *No need to worry.*

Lily made an effort to smooth her emotions and reassure him before holding the necklace out to her *vapa* without further qualms. Vadom eyed her carefully, then focused his attention on the jewelry hanging from her hand.

One instant the necklace was dangling from her fingers, and the next, her *vapa* had placed it around his neck in an undetectably quick motion. Lily stared at her empty hand a moment, registering a slight decrease in her Fear, then took a deep breath and looked up into Vadom's face. Lily and Alder both watched him closely, wondering what to expect. Vadom seemed to be concentrating, and so they waited silently for him to speak again.

Several minutes passed. Just as he seemed about to relax, Vadom's entire body went rigid. He fell to his knees slowly, as though he was being pulled to them against his will. Her *vapa*'s face began to show pain, and Fear that was growing far too quickly . . . Lily realized that he needed her help. She took his face in her hands and began to speak to him, slowly and clearly. Lily knew what she would have to say to him.

"Vadom, you must push it to the edges of your mind, and out the door. Vabiri needs you to win, to find the strength to come back for her. Vabiri is waiting, and nothing would be worse than failing Vabiri when she needs you, nothing, not even this little bit of pain, right? Your love is stronger, reach for it, fight for it— NOW."

With each use of his otherwing's name, Vadom's struggle increased. He seemed to be gaining the upper hand. Lily hesitated, then spoke again, very softly.

"Please, *Vapa*. I need you, too. *Vama* would want you with me, I think, before it's safe enough for you to return for her."

Vadom shuddered violently, then went completely still. His slightly unfocused eyes clearly showed Lily how stunned he was. Lily could feel Alder's roiling emotions.

"Is he stable now? Should we take the necklace off? I didn't seriously think it would bother him! His love element is tiny compared to yours, and it's just the one piece of jewelry! He's ancient, with a complete Void dome around his mind. Lily, your protector cannot be this incapacitated. I cannot stand it. We are still much too far from the Fae Wood for a crisis like this . . ."

While Lily was sorry that Alder was so upset, and she hated that her *vapa* was suffering, she knew this had been necessary. Vadom would agree with her as soon as he was able, as would Alder, once he calmed down a little. It was unlike him to lose his composure, but then he was usually actively helping her through a serious problem, not helplessly watching Vadom struggle. However, it had just occurred to her that when her prophetic power had said 'iron on', it very well could be interpreted to mean that Vadom was the one who needed to wear iron. She waited for Alder to run out of words, as well as for her *vapa* to recover. Her *faelan* went silent when Vadom's eyes focused once more.

"*Vipina*," he said, as if to reassure himself that she was still there.

"I am here, *Vapa*," Lily responded, keeping her voice completely level and soothing.

"It found the door to my mind," he said, sounding shocked. "Only Vabiri knows where it is, only she has been able to enter for thousands of years. And then it found the sun magic . . . so easily. I didn't even know its exact location, yet it was attacking before I could mount any defenses. And to think what the Fae must endure—"

Vadom's eyes widened as he really looked into Lily's face. She saw the flicker of horror in his eyes before his customary reserved countenance reasserted itself.

"Oh, *Vipina*," he said softly.

They were all silent for a long moment. Lily could tell that her *vapa* needed a little more time to adjust to the iron necklace, and she wondered how she could stall their departure from this particular field of heather for a bit. The answer became clear to her as her stomach gave a bit of a grumble, and Lily realized that she had yet to eat any breakfast. She slowly lowered her hands from Vadom's face and reached for the haversack, pulling the food pouch from it as she sat down.

It was not until she was quietly slicing some cheese for her bread and selecting a piece of fruit that Vadom slowly and carefully moved from his knees to sit as well. Alder chose that moment to speak into the silence.

"I'm sorry I panicked, Lily. That didn't help matters at all, especially when you must have been really worried about him, too. I'll keep my head next time."

Lily could tell that Alder was a bit embarrassed about his lack of composure, and frustrated with himself as well. She realized then that, as patient and generous as he was with her, Alder wasn't like that with himself at all. His ready apology and quick assurances that his misstep wouldn't be repeated seemed to hint at consistent remonstrances from some source or other. This wasn't the first time that Alder had expected Lily to be far harsher with him than she felt the occasion warranted, or that she had any right to be. She decided to try to reassure him now, but give some thought to why he responded this way sometime soon.

I know you will, Alder. We're all going to have weak moments on this journey, given what is at stake, and what we're up against. I don't expect you to be perfect. I'm certainly not, either.

Lily felt Alder's emotions soften and mellow out.

"I am so very lucky," he said, almost to himself. Alder's contentment was great. Then he seemed to bestir himself.

"But what's this about you being imperfect? I have yet to see evidence to the contrary," he said playfully. *"Indeed, I think the longer a Fae must wait, the more extraordinary the mate with which he is rewarded."*

That can hardly be true, seeing as I already have you, Lily replied, keeping up their bantering. She loved it when Alder was happy, especially if she was the reason.

She must have had a blissful look on her face, for eventually, Vadom asked her about it.

"You feel felicity in the midst of hardship, *Vipina*. I would very much like to know what has caused such a smile."

"Oh, just Alder," Lily said softly, and found herself smiling again at Alder's quiet delight in her words. Lily savored the feeling, holding it close to her heart for the difficult days and weeks ahead. She found herself standing, reaching for the haversack, into which she had just replaced the food pouch, and turning toward the sun. The sooner they got going, the sooner they would reach the Fae Wood, and Alder . . .

It was then that Lily realized her *vapa* might not yet be able to move on. She turned back to him casually and looked him over, searching for signs of fatigue. His eyes were knowing and slightly amused, despite her attempt at nonchalance.

"I have pushed the Fear back outside the door of my mind and relocated the entrance, *Vipina*. I will be ready to continue momentarily. Your concern and consideration are appreciated, however. It may become necessary for me to rest more frequently than I have previously."

Lily was still stuck on "relocated the entrance."

Alder, did you hear that? He moved the door . . . Do you think it's because of the night magic he used?

"I don't know, faelani. *How amazing . . . and incredibly useful. For the 'empty' element to both stand strong and allow for transience, to be more than*

vacuous, but less than immovable, is certainly something to ponder."

Maybe I should put blocks of Void in my own small circle of mental defenses . . . just here and there, at random. It might throw enemies off. Then I could fill in the door, but still be able to let you in or out as needed . . .

Lily's plotting was interrupted by the sight of Vadom slowly rising from his seated position on the ground. Though he was as graceful as usual, she thought he moved just the tiniest bit gingerly. That made up her mind.

Faelan, *how do you feel about walking for a bit this morning?*

"I think that's the right idea. We shouldn't push our good fortune too far. You're going to carry the haversack too, aren't you?"

Lily grinned at his playfully forbearing tone. He really was getting to know her. Lily noticed then that Vadom had winced the minutest degree as he carefully scanned their surroundings for enemies. She decided to focus on making some eastward progress for now.

"*Vapa,* I think I'd like to walk a bit this morning, if you don't mind. My body could use some exercise."

Vadom gave her a look that said she was fooling no one, then he deliberately observed the rolling green and purple plains around them again, finally nodding his head.

"If you insist, *Vipina.* There is no immediate danger. There are few stray witches or wizards about in the western part of Ropaz, due to the feeding habits of my race. Fortunately, we need not concern ourselves with other vampires during the day. We will have to be increasingly vigilant, however, once we have passed Wizulaan, for the majority of this land's population lies to the east and the north of Six Cities."

"Which are actually only five cities," Lily said, just to show that she always paid attention.

"Just so," her *vapa* replied, smiling softly.

Without further delay, Lily shouldered the haversack, turned back to the sun, which had now begun its trip across the sky, and started to walk.

20

MARTIAL MAGIC

SEVERAL HOURS LATER, LILY GROUND TO A halt, her stubbornness very much worn out. Water would be good, she decided. Perhaps some more cheese on bread wouldn't go amiss either. She had to keep her strength up, after all. As soon as she let the haversack, and then herself, flop onto the grassy ground, Lily heard Alder's grumbling in her mind.

"About time you took a break. Vadom's been itching to take that big, lumpy bag from you all morning. I could sense it, which means you could, too. Please enlighten me as to why you are making this journey any more difficult than it needs to be?"

Lily couldn't resist trying to tease Alder out of his grumpiness.

And here I was thinking a certain truemate thought me perfect . . . I believe I did warn you about my stubborn streak, but apparently that went unheeded.

Lily knew a moment of triumph when Alder's emotions swayed into grudging amusement.

"Will you at least let him carry you the rest of the day? The plan was to reach Wizulaan by nightfall tomorrow so that Vadom could get the horse for you under cover of darkness. I like that plan," he finished plaintively.

Lily glanced furtively at her *vapa*, who really did seem to be fine now. She was slightly envious of his ability to keep the Fear beating helplessly against the outside of his mind, rather than waging a concentrated and much more heated battle within, but she supposed that was one of the privileges of being an ancient vampire. She was doing well enough, really. The Fear hadn't yet made it to her power wells, or even into the vast majority of her mind's uncharted territory. Alder had plenty of safe room to float around, particularly near her soul, as well. Lily decided she needed to focus on those positive things, rather than dwelling on all of the ways in which this trip could be easier. A list that long would keep her mind occupied, certainly . . .

"*Vipina*, if you are ready to continue, I would ask that you let me carry you. I am sufficiently recovered from this morning to resume our previous method of travel. I think perhaps that Alder will agree with me?"

At Alder's enthusiastic concurrence, Lily decided to give in while she could still do so gracefully. She would be no use to anyone if she collapsed from exhaustion before even making Ford-upon-Ward.

"I would appreciate the assistance, *Vapa*," Lily said quietly.

Vadom nodded, accepting her concession silently. He waited until Lily had eaten a modest lunch and repacked her haversack before hefting it over his head and settling it on one shoulder. Then he turned to Lily and waited, as composed as always. Satisfied that her *vapa* was ready to run with her again, Lily allowed herself to be picked up and whisked to the east.

A little later that afternoon, Lily decided to take the initiative and ask Vadom for her next warrior lesson. She got the feeling that she was supposed to be doing this, but what with the somewhat irregular nature of their daily routine, her *vapa* had always remembered the lessons first.

"*Vapa*, could I have some of your time today for the lecture on magical weapons you mentioned at the end of our last lesson?"

Lily looked up at his face in time to see the approval that briefly lit his eyes.

"You may. I will speak as we travel, in order to time our arrival at Wizulaan for tomorrow evening."

Vadom paused, as though to gather his thoughts, even as Lily gave him her full attention.

"There are many magical races in the world of Lamoranth, as I believe you know. Each has their own unique magic, which is normally kept a secret, but for the wars of the past that have made certain techniques known to some extent. The following information is either the intelligence my *vapa* gave to me during the course of my training, the first-hand observations of vampires whom I trust, or my own personal encounters with the magic weapons that can be found in this world. Bear in mind that even though this knowledge comes from a variety of sources, it is still incomplete. There are few, if any, beings who know all of the magical secrets of Lamoranth. I would like you to be prepared for as many as possible, however, and so I will impart what is considered largely certain.

"All of the beings in our world possess abilities with elemental magic, to drastically varying degrees. I believe you are already aware of the elements of earth, fire, air, and water. You have also confirmed for me the inner power of the Fae, which vampires call sun magic, but which is also called love or spirit element. You must be taught the fundamentals of night magic as well, which you usually call Void. It is important that you understand that the Void is both a magic and a place from which the magic comes. The most significant fact about all of these forms of magic is that they are neither inherently good or evil, but simply exist in nature. As I know you comprehend, *Vipina,* it is up to the being who wields elemental magic whether or not it is a tool for peaceful activities, such as artwork, or as a weapon, meant for defense and attack. Most of the races of Lamoranth use elemental magic for both, as their situation requires.

"What is perhaps most critical to remember, before I speak of which magical people use what, is that all of us must keep in mind that the elements, for whatever purpose, must remain in balance. The greatest disasters in history have occurred at least in part because someone or something tipped the scales too far, and they caused terrible destruction as a result. These dangerous imbalances, whose violent restabilizations have cost this world countless lives and damage, have almost always been caused by magical weapons of great power. Whether it was the inadvertent misuse of a magical weapon, or the extremely malevolent intent of a magical weapon wielder, the magicians who use those elements and tools must always exercise great caution, lest they set cataclysmic events in motion."

Vadom paused and, seeing the look on Lily's face, carefully measured his next words.

"I do not mean to alarm you, *Vipina,* but only intend to impress upon you the consequences of elemental misuse, which is most easily done with weapons. Though few are strong enough to cause the enormous imbalance of which I speak all at once, it can also take place over very long periods of time. It is not entirely improbable that the Ancient River suffers from the imbalance. In ages past, the very desert in which you have lived did not exist, but was much like Ropaz still is today. One must never use magic lightly, for the consequences are complex, far-reaching, and unpredictable."

Lily swallowed and slowly nodded. She had never thought of her abilities, her magic, as a responsibility before, but she definitely did now. To think that so much could be at stake . . .

"How do you know you are putting the world out of balance, *Vapa?* How can I keep it safe when I use magic?"

Vadom regarded Lily with his fathomless dark eyes, then responded softly.

"That is a discussion for another time, *Vipina*. Suffice it to say that, at least for vampires, it is largely instinctive. Most beings cannot disrupt the natural way of things without a magical tool to augment their power. That is why a large amount of training is necessary for any and all such implements that come into your hands. The more you use them, the more you will get a sense for the limitations that exist for them, and hence for you. To force any magical tool or weapon to exceed its natural boundaries is to invite danger to yourself and those near you. That is why highly powerful magical objects are so often coveted, by the weak and powerful alike, because a great number of other beings are in peril and at the wielder's mercy. This is the reason why all vampires are always expected to maintain a rigid code of honor and conduct, to discipline their very spirits to think of others before themselves. Such a mentality makes one's mind less susceptible to greed and corruption, and the evil that inevitably results. This, in turn, spares those who are innocent of wrong-doing."

Her *vapa* paused to let this sink in a moment, then continued in his previous vein.

"I would like to proceed with a brief description of each race's elemental weapons, as well as any other special magic they might possess and use for martial purposes. Among the earth element users in this world are the trolls, the goblins, and the dwarves. As their dwellings indicate, these beings are most comfortable surrounded by large concentrations of their strongest element. It is a well-known fact that both the dwarves and the goblins have used earth magic to carve their cities and homes from the Grandfather Mountain range. Though the trolls are thought to have less skill with the earth element, the Volcano Crescent has long been their rock-hewn stronghold.

"As you can most likely envision, these three races can lift and throw rocks, cause landslides, instantaneously provide defensive trenches or high earthen perimeter walls, and create any number of useful advantages with earth element in combat. The goblins are especially notorious for their 'living graves', which essentially involves burying their opponents alive under a mound of earth. Their over-use of this particular strategy in the last major Lamoranthian war, a couple of ages ago, is a large part of the reason for the condition of the land known now only as the Waste, on the eastern border of the Forest of Ancients.

"Dwarves are also able to detect, call forth, and channel the special properties of virtually any precious or semi-precious stone. Much like the Fear within iron, these gems naturally contain magic to fight you psychologically as well as physically. For example, I myself have been on the receiving end of an incredibly potent sapphire-wielder, and I can say with conviction that gemstones can seriously undermine your mental defenses. The sapphire is the stone of loyalty and faithfulness. The dwarf was talented enough to use the gem to draw out my loyalty to the Cave Kingdom, as well as my faithfulness to Vabiri, and wield it against me . . . it was one of my narrowest victories.

"The trolls are only able to wield obsidian to this effect, which is logical, as that stone is quickly cooled volcanic lava. While they most often use obsidian for its enhancement of vigor and tenacity, more skilled trolls can wield this stone for personal protection and greater insight. You can imagine how this would be to their benefit when confronting a formidable enemy, especially as they are not a naturally calculating race.

"Keep in mind, *Vipina,* that there are other earth magic users in this world. I have been told that elves are amply capable of controlling earth, for their talent lies in growing trees and plants. Witches and wizards have long trained themselves to utilize the power of gemstones, though they are not a fraction as skilled as the dwarves. Vampires can wield earth in a moderate capacity, and it is obvious to me now that fairies are in tune with this element as well. There will be much of this overlap as I continue, and so I encourage you to focus on remembering the strongest element of each race and committing to memory the most potentially threatening weapons that result.

"Next, there are those who specialize in the use of water element. Those races are primarily the giants and the sea-folk, and secondarily the elves and wood nymphs of the Forest, as well as vampires and fairies. As I've mentioned previously, the giants have honed their use of slings to a masterful degree, with pieces of ice as their main type of ammunition. Legends have long told that if one can cross the Arraldo Ice Plain, they will enter the Evertundra and behold ice castles of incredible beauty. The giants, however, have successfully kept outsiders at a distance for time untold with not only their slings, but with ice-needle storms, hail volleys, and coordinated blizzard offensives.

"While these water element weapons are all but common knowledge, there are no reliable sources I am aware of that can vouch with certainty how the giants live their otherwise peaceable lives. What they eat, their recreational activities, and how they are governed are just a few of the things that remain shrouded in mystery. I tell you this because the more information you have about an opponent, the greater your chances of success. Knowing how they think, what they consider important, or sacred, or inviolable, will often reveal weaknesses to your own advantage. Giants are a secretive race of which very little is known, and that gives them an edge over their enemies. Indeed, if not for the continuance of their defenses in the Arraldo, one would have to wonder if the giants had ceased to exist altogether, so seldom have they been seen. As unlikely as that is, one should never fight a giant, or any largely unknown opponent, without extreme caution.

"I know less than I would like about the sea-folk as well, for though I have done the majority of my hunting in the north and eastern parts of Ropaz, I have rarely ventured as far as the Ocean of Fintilles. They are known to the elves as mermen and mermaids, and they are said to take some of their nourishment from the salt water in which they live. Sea-folk are not purported to specialize in any particular weapon, such as I have shown you, though they do command all the creatures in the ocean, some of which are quite lethal. Sea-ladies are also rumored to be able to wield pearls in a manner loosely comparable to the dwarves and their stones. Pearls evoke wisdom, purity, and integrity, all of which, more often than not, will lessen a foe's desire to do battle. If those fail to stir the more pacifistic inclinations of ship-bound assailants, one would assume the sea-folk would utilize a collaborative hurricane assault, or perhaps a series of rain barrages, anything to enhance and weaponize naturally occurring water phenomena.

"As for the other beings who are able to wield the water element, I can say that vampires are largely reactive, rarely using it except to counter or slow an opponent who can use it well. Elves are highly skilled in finessing water element to supplement their earth element usage, particularly in the growing of all living things. Water nymphs, which are a type of wood nymph, use it purely in mischievous ways, to my knowledge. As for fairies, I think we may just wait and see, for I believe your race may command the water element quite masterfully.

"I'd now like to tell you more about the magic of the elves. As I've just mentioned, they are very talented with the earth and water elements. I believe they have cultivated their use of these elements over time because of their affinity with the Forest of Ancients. Long have they been the keepers and protectors of that place, and as such, they have developed their dexterity with earth and water out of necessity. I do not think the Forest of Ancients would have lasted so long without them. Other races have coveted that magic-laden land, including vampires, yet none have ever wrested it from the care of the elves," Vadom said ruefully.

"This, however, is not solely due to elemental power. It is not only trees and plants that flourish in the Forest of Ancients. Elves have a love of knowledge, and study much, for to be thought wise among the elves is the greatest honor they can seek. In this sense, they wish for their minds to grow, for their lives to be ever in progress. It is through their intelligence as well as their magic that the elves keep the Forest of Ancients secure. This thirst for knowledge is not without its consequences, however. Once, when I was very young, I witnessed another pup my age call an elf emissary to the Cave Kingdom 'stupid'. The elf, previously a model of decorum and composure, flew into an absolute rage. The child was punished severely for so blatantly insulting the visiting elf. Always speak carefully in the presence of elves, lest they interpret your meaning as you do not intend and their hot-tempered natures get the better of them.

"Additionally, the elves have a magic all their own, which they call heartsong. With their voices do they wield a power unique unto their race. By singing do they indulge their love of making things grow. Elves even find their mates by recognizing the harmony of their mate's heartsong to their own. I am certain that the heartsong allows elves to wield other abilities, quite possibly for martial purposes, yet if this is so, vampires have not been made privy to it. Though we try to coexist peacefully with the elves, the relationship has never been without varying degrees of tension and uneasiness on both sides. Despite this, I have always thought the elves both an exuberant and generally dependable race, and they have long held my respect for the way they have chosen to live their lives.

"At this point, have you any pressing questions for me, *Vipina?*"

Lily hardly knew where to begin, such was the whirl of ideas in her mind. While some of the information her *vapa* had revealed echoed the fairy tales her mother had told her, the majority of it was new and exciting. It opened up so much of the world, showed her so many possibilities . . . Lily felt a little in awe of all of the races of the world: how they lived, what they were capable of, how they were different from her, but also how she was similar to them. Lily thought about how she had not only been living in a desert literally until now, but figuratively as well. She couldn't help but believe, despite how much it had hurt to leave, that it had ultimately been for the best. To think of all she had been missing out on . . .

"It's all so amazing, isn't it, *Vapa?*"

Vadom smiled at the earnestness in Lily's voice and on her face.

"Indeed it is, *Vipina*. Even to me, the world seems quite large at times, so full of mysteries that no one being could ever unravel them all. There is something humbling about seeing one's place in the midst of such a world."

Lily had to agree. She also knew, in that moment, that she wanted to meet everyone, go everywhere, see and do and discover everything, that she could. She had her whole life before her, and Lily wasn't about to waste it. She knew her existence was a gift, and she wanted to live it to the fullest. As her ideas settled into conviction, Lily felt Alder stir. He was a bit uneasy, but there was more to it that Lily didn't understand.

What is it, faelan*?*

"Oh, I suppose I have mixed feelings about having such an adventurous faelani *to protect, that's all. I can sense how excited you are by all of this, and a large part of me is glad. I have always relished the experience of traveling, too. Still, there will also always be another small part of me that wishes to keep you safely ensconced in the Fae Wood for the rest of our lives. I suppose we'll just have to find a way to reconcile safety with travel on our next trek through Lamoranth."*

Lily felt herself grinning. She didn't think they were doing so badly on this trip, what with Vadom and his Void magic protecting them. Still, she couldn't help but consider Alder's words for a moment, testing herself by attempting to determine how she would feel if Alder ever had to leave the safety of the Wood after they'd arrived. She found that she felt much the same as Alder. Most of her wanted someone to explore the world with her, but there was another small piece that wanted her . . . friend all to herself, safe amidst the trees and shade of the Fae Wood . . .

Perhaps we could agree to stay in the Fae Wood for a while first, Alder. It will take me time to settle in and find my place, I'm sure. I want to see the world, but I want to know all the comforts of home first. I may very well have to remain in the Wood to look after my father, too. Maybe we could wait until after we've completely bonded before we explore Lamoranth together. As long as we plan on going eventually, I don't see the need to rush.

Lily could tell by the upswing of Alder's emotions, and the alleviation of his concern, that Alder was both comfortable and happy with what Lily had said. Lily privately thought that being able to show Alder some of his own remarkable patience was very satisfying.

"I think tempering our eagerness is probably the wiser course, Lily. I'll feel better waiting until we both have more warrior training, if nothing else, before facing the perils for our kind outside the Fae Wood again."

Just as Lily was about to ask Alder more about that, she realized that she was in the middle of warrior training already, and she gave Vadom her undivided attention once more.

"I have thousands of questions for you, *Vapa*, but I think I'd just like you to tell me more about magic and weapons first."

After carefully taking in every detail of Lily's face, Vadom nodded and continued.

"Then I'd like to tell you about those beings who excel in the manipulation of the air element next. The most dominant users are, as you already know, witches and wizards. The winds that blow through the world are theirs to command. This element can be incredibly forceful, or lethally subtle. It is highly useful in enhancing the precision and effectiveness of the other elements. It can feed flames, increase the crushing force of earth, and give water shape and direction. Command of the air element allows witches and wizards to fly, even though they do not have wings. Air cannot easily be seen with the eyes, and hence requires more acute magical senses to defend against and to wield.

"Witches command air element most dangerously with the aid of magical wands, while wizards conjure air very powerfully with magic-imbued staffs. Wands and staffs, especially in the hands of Ropazians, are among the most deadly magical weapons you will ever encounter. There are legends that have been told for time immemorial in the grasslands of wands with almost unimaginable air summoning capabilities. Those same myths particularly idolize a wizard who, so the story goes, fashioned a staff so powerful that it could command air to retrieve recently departed souls from their journey to the afterlife. While there is no evidence that has ever supported the actual existence of such wands or staffs, it is important to realize that witches and wizards believe in these tales with unswerving conviction. They are as integral a part of Ropazian culture as the Goddess they worship and the Ethic by which many of them prescribe their daily lives. It would be unwise to discount any of these beliefs, no matter your own personal ideology, when fighting any witch, wizard, or coven.

"As you well know, *Vipina,* the inhabitants of Ropaz set such store by their magical power that they banish those of their race who are born without the ability to manipulate the air element. That is why the people forced to live in the Joquobon Desert are so unhappy, and so bitter. They do not have magic, and as such, they have been deemed unworthy to live with their families in the grasslands. Though I know your experience in the desert was often a struggle, I would encourage you to try to temper your thinking in relation to the outcasts, for life without magic is full of vulnerability, lacking in joy, and sadly short. Also bear in mind what the Desert of Outcasts says about the people of Ropaz: how ruthless they are in culling out the weak, how great is their determination to be magically powerful. Remember that those who seek magical dominance should be carefully watched, their motives clearly understood, and their desires never underestimated. Those who are willing to lose much also stand to gain much, though they may lose more than they bargained for, and they seldom find satisfaction in what they do achieve. Such beings have proven dangerous time and again throughout history, and it would behoove you to be wary of the overly ambitious.

"In addition to witches and wizards, vampires and dragons are able to summon air as well, though to a lesser extent than the inhabitants of Ropaz. My race has the most success with air element when our wings are out, and I know this to be true of dragons as well, for I have seen them conjure air to aid in flying, particularly with difficult aerial maneuvers. I imagine this might be true for fairies as well, though I don't wish to speak prematurely regarding your people.

"The fourth element I wish to tell you about is fire. The masters of this element in Lamoranth are, almost certainly, the dragons, for they can breathe fire from their very mouths. Though their numbers have dwindled this past age, they are still a formidable enemy to anyone foolish enough to approach Mount Brimstone, or the grazing lands of their prey in the mountain's vicinity, too closely. Dragons are as ancient as elves and vampires, and not all of their abilities are known for certain.

"What is crucial to remember, if ever you meet one, is that they are able to penetrate the mind of virtually any opponent. No matter your mental defenses, a dragon can always read your thoughts and intentions, and they can make their own known to you by placing their words and emotions inside of your mind. This, more than their natural propensity for fire or their incredible physical strength, is their most dangerous weapon.

When an enemy is able to breach your mind, *Vipina,* your peril is at its greatest, for your enemy could control your actions if they possess a greater will than your own. It is fortunate that dragons have never taken advantage of their natural ability, as so many others would have. They wish to rule no one, not even each other, and instead prefer, perhaps even require, wild and unfettered freedom.

"If vampires have a magical weakness, it is fire. It is one of the few things that destroys us quickly and absolutely, and many of my race cannot help but fear it. Fire element is akin to the sun, which all, but myself, cannot endure for long, and even that brevity with the utmost agony. Though we are taught many ways to counter fire attacks, it is still the element of which we are most wary, for vampires cannot control fire in the slightest degree.

"In contrast, I know with certainty that fairies can manipulate fire element with great dexterity. The one and only Fae I have seen in my life, aside from you, *Vipina,* was a male warrior who could do impressive things with fire."

Here Vadom paused, almost as though he could detect the shock Alder was radiating from inside Lily's mind.

Alder, how could my vapa *have encountered just one lone warrior Fae? I was under the impression that you traveled outside the Wood sparingly, and only then in safe numbers.*

"I don't know, faelani. *Perhaps he was caught and imprisoned by a coven, and then met Vadom while escaping somehow. Unlikely, but the alternative . . ."*

When Alder trailed off into troubled thoughts, Lily turned to Vadom and waited for him to continue speaking.

"I was in Ropaz, hunting with Vabiri, when we smelled the blood of the Fae. I hid my otherwing as completely as possible, then went to see if I could overtake him. At the time, I thought only of procuring for Vabiri and myself the considerable advantages of fairy blood. I was still ambitious, some eight hundred years ago, of becoming a senior member of the Supreme Council, and the opportunity to become a day-walker, without the Thirst, was too great to resist.

"It did not take me long to encounter the warrior, for he was making no effort to conceal himself. I came upon him in the middle of a very clear night, when the moon was at its fullest. He stood in the midst of a flat stretch of land, a plain in which the grass was short and hardly swayed, for the wind was perfectly calm. He looked, to my eyes, very peculiar, for his hair was orange, but his eyes were violet. He seemed young, arrogant, and foolhardy, and I thought an easy victory was at hand.

"This, however, was not the case. The Fae warrior detected me, despite my Void concealment, and spoke to me directly: 'I wish to do battle with a vampire of great strength. Are you such a one, blood drinker?' I hesitated, for if he had sensed me, he could have sensed Vabiri as well. This I absolutely could not endure even the thought of, and I knew I would have to kill him. Only in this way could I be completely assured of my otherwing's safety. Even as I dissipated my Void sphere and stepped out of the tall grasses that surrounded the plain, I began to wish that I had a preconceived plan of action for obtaining a fairy's blood. Though the Fae had been all but myth to me until that moment, much like the giants, I wished I had not been caught less than fully prepared for the opportunity that had just presented itself to me. I set my regrets aside, however, and then made certain that I was entirely in control of the Thirst growing ever stronger in my body. I proceeded to respond to his words by saying: 'You shall find out soon enough, fairy.' He looked, in that moment, startled, and a little afraid. I thought him the basest coward, for one of the first things any vampire warrior is taught is that one must never show any emotion to an enemy, and that feelings are naught but weakness in battle.

"My confidence inwardly growing, I approached him with measured steps. I thought to frighten him further, to give myself a greater advantage over him. 'By what weapons do you wish to die, fairy?' Conversely, this seemed to put the Fae on familiar ground. He straightened his spine and spoke with confidence: 'Swords, whips, and fire should be more than enough to finish you, night-walker.'

"I knew a moment of unease, for I had never before encountered a truly competent fire element wielder. Still, I knew he would have no use of night magic, and I also knew from his modest age that he could not have the level of skill I possessed with either swords or whips. I stepped forward and faced him without hesitation, assuming a ready stance for combat. He seemed slightly surprised, then ever so slightly relieved. After a prolonged moment, though, he spoke again: 'Are we not to speak the Exchange of Names?'

"I assumed this was a Fae ritual, for vampires do no such thing. To give an enemy any knowledge of you is to give them a potential advantage. What if I was defeated, and the victor, knowing who I was, went in search of my otherwing? Vabiri is considered a great beauty in the Cave Kingdom, and many a vampire warrior have fought me for the privilege of becoming her new life-partner. Some of our females do choose, on rare occasions, to accept another otherwing if their first becomes ashes. Though Vabiri would never take another, particularly the one responsible for my demise, that has not stopped many from the attempt. I hesitated, therefore, to give my name, though I knew this fairy could have no knowledge of my beauteous otherwing.

"As I watched him and considered the wisdom of this exchange, the Fae warrior seemed to resolve an inner conflict. He raised his chin defiantly, looked me directly in the eye, and said: 'My name is Monkshood of the Fae Wood, and I will be the end of you.' He dropped still further in my esteem in so saying, for I didn't think any amount of skill or power could compensate for such cockiness. It seemed to me that he had gone to a lot of trouble to put himself in a great amount of danger. I responded simply: 'I am a warrior of the Cave Kingdom.' I attacked him immediately and forcefully.

"I nearly beheaded him with my opening strike, yet he blocked me with a great-sword composed of sun magic, orange-hued but also silver-sheened. We exchanged a series of blows, testing each other, seeking weaknesses in one another's guard, attempting to gauge endurance both physical and magical. I began to switch my swords out every couple of minutes, to keep this Monkshood off-balance and to see if there was one with which he was unfamiliar, so that I might press my advantage.

"It wasn't long before my Void-black scimitar caused him to hesitate. I pressed him aggressively, though I didn't think this would yet be the end for him. Monkshood's sword-work was above average for a warrior of just two or three centuries, neither elaborate nor sloppy, but certainly well-versed and thoroughly drilled into him by an exacting teacher. Sure enough, he produced a bright orange, faintly silver whip just as I successfully disabled his sword arm. His counterstrike forced me into a defensive position before I could attack his injured and sword-less arm. I could tell with certainty, though, that the whip was his favorite weapon, and by cultivating his skills with just this one tool, he had grown overconfident when fighting with it. I knew I could seriously shake his composure with a well-executed counter maneuver. Before Monkshood could get a good crack in, I caught a portion of the whip in hand and brought my scimitar singing down, slicing the whip clean through. Vampires cannot easily or quickly repair their Void weapons in the midst of battle, and I was testing to see if the same held true for fairy warriors.

"Judging by the shock on his face, I believed this to be the case for the Fae as well. Monkshood's dismay soon transmuted into fury, however, and he recovered quickly. Out of his other palm he produced another whip, though this one was thicker, longer, and had many sharp barbs on its end. While cracking this new whip in my direction, he coiled the broken whip and replaced it inside himself. With his newly open hand, Monkshood shot a burst of fire directly at me. I was quick to dodge both offensives, though I was already calculating how to bring our battle into the endgame.

"His next offensive truly surprised me. This Fae warrior caught his barbed whip on fire with his elemental ability, yet the weapon did not disintegrate in the flames. When he cracked his flaming whip at me, I dodged again, being all the while extremely careful of my footing. Fortunately, he was holding the fiery barbed whip with the arm I had injured, and his aim was probably not what it could have been. Monkshood's confidence began to build, however, and he smirked at me with an overweening arrogance.

"I knew I couldn't allow him to realize the potential of his fire strikes any further, and so I deduced that I needed to incapacitate his hands as quickly as possible. I brought out my own stockwhip with a sharp crack near his head, causing him to flinch and close his eyes for one critical moment. I moved with all my speed to kick his legs out from underneath him. He lost his grip on the whip as he struggled first to regain his balance, then to break his fall. By the time Monkshood opened his eyes, I had the blade of my scimitar at his throat, with my knee in his sternum so that I would be able to detect any of his attempts at movement.

"It took him several seconds to realize what had happened, and that he had been defeated. I watched as shock, then fear and cowardice, paraded openly across his countenance. 'If you make any attempt to break free, I will behead you,' I told him, looking directly into his eyes. I felt sure he would make an attempt with fire element, I just assumed it hadn't yet occurred to him. I brought out my night magic hoop with my left hand and held it behind my back in readiness. If necessary, I was prepared to use this tool as a portal to summon physical manifestations of the Void element from the plane of eternal night and darkness. They appear as twisted black ropes, which is convenient for temporarily tying up vanquished opponents.

"I was trying to decide how best to proceed. Normally, I procure blood for Vabiri and myself by singing my chosen witch or wizard into a trance. The hum of a vampire is easily able to pass through the meager mental walls that witches and wizards erect around their minds. I suppose, compared to mental defenses comprised of sun or night magic, their more elemental, less eternal protections cannot compare. It is one of the reasons fairy prisoners are so highly valued in Ropaz, for only with a fairy can a witch or wizard obtain true lasting protection for their mind. After entrancing a Ropazian, we then drink what we need, being careful not to drain the being, then put both a temporary Void mark and a simple protection spell on the man or woman. The former warns other vampires that the Ropazian has recently provided blood to another of our race, and the latter is payment for the sustenance provided for my otherwing and myself.

"While witches and wizards are completely absorbed by the stunning song, and must sleep many hours to break free of its hold, I realized that I had no idea if the fairy would be entranced, or if he would be able to resist. If he could, and I thought this likely, especially given his sensitivity to my night magic from the beginning, I did not feel that I could risk Vabiri's safety by leading her into his presence, let alone encouraging her to drink from him. I could not kill him either, for vampires cannot derive the nutrients they need from a dead being. The entire endeavor would be wasted if I had to end his life prematurely. Furthermore, killing a Ropazian is only allowed by the Supreme Council in emergency situations, and even then it does not go entirely unpunished. I had no idea what the repercussions of killing a fairy would be, when so many could partake of the legendary benefits of even this lone warrior's blood, but I knew they would be severe. Still, I would forsake both the magical qualities of the blood, and accept any punishment dealt out by the Council, if it was the best choice to make for Vabiri.

"Another idea occurred to me, and it caused me to hesitate just as much, if not more, than my other reasons. Always I had chosen for my otherwing witches and wizards of the highest moral character I could find. I did not want Vabiri to drink from any Ropazians who were cruel, selfish, or evil. I did not wish for her to sense these vices in the blood she drank, for her to be troubled by those who were not as pure and vibrant as she. Clearly, this fairy warrior was foolish and cowardly. I expected underhandedness from him, and I didn't want my otherwing to be exposed to what his blood would undoubtedly reveal to her.

"Before I could ponder further, however, Monkshood began to plead with me. 'Please don't drain me. Please don't kill me. I only sought to fight a vampire, a formidable opponent, to prove myself strong to the other warriors in the Fae Wood. I only wanted to earn a reputation for courage and strength.'

"I came to a firm decision in that moment. I could never let Vabiri drink of this pathetic, irresponsible male. I found that my own reluctance outweighed even the driving need of the Thirst coursing through my body, which I had been steadfast in ignoring since first entering the clearing. Before I could determine what to do with him, however, he lashed out at me with a ball of flame, as I had been anticipating. I brought my Void hoop forward in defense. Just as the flame passed through the hoop, I gave a sharp twist of my wrist, and the flame disappeared through the portal I had opened into the Void plane. In the next instant, I closed the door to the night magic world, where all is made of tangible Void element and no light or other elements can exist. Monkshood's disbelief was palpable, for he clearly knew nothing of night magic or the quintessential Void weapon. He began to struggle against my foot and scimitar in a complete panic.

"'Please, I am newly mated, and it will kill her if I perish. Spare me, I beg of you.'

"His words caused a chill in my heart. Did he speak the truth? In killing this pathetic warrior, would I be killing an innocent young fairy lady as well? I looked deeply into his eyes, and there I saw the truth of his words. I was disgusted. How could he be so irresponsible? How could he endanger his life-partner in such a way? Any lingering doubts I had about drinking his blood or bringing Vabiri to drink from him vanished completely. To do so would be a pollution that any honorable vampire would eschew.

"'If this is so, you have failed your mate abysmally, to your everlasting shame. Your blood is tainted by this disgrace and useless to me. I free you now only because of the innocent female who would otherwise suffer. Go back to your Wood, and endeavor to do better by her in the future.'

"With those words, I stepped back from the weak-minded, weak-willed Monkshood, and, still holding my Void hoop in readiness with my left hand, I sheathed my scimitar and pointed south with my right. The fairy staggered to his feet, clutching his damaged arm, then looked at me with relief, confusion, and perhaps an inkling of his dishonor. He seemed to waver, then retrieved his barbed whip, which still smoked from his flames, and his great-sword, making it clear all the while that he did not intend to wield them against me again. Monkshood hesitated another moment, then said, 'I will.' With that, he turned to the south and slunk off into the night."

Vadom was then silent for a few moments, allowing Lily, and Alder, to absorb the shocking story he had told them. Lily had a myriad of questions, and she could tell that Alder was overwhelmed as well. She hardly knew what to think . . . a cowardly Fae warrior? A place where only Void existed?

"Tell me some of the things you have learned from this story, *Vipina*. Ask me some of the questions you have about it," Vadom said, his eyes conveying patience and encouragement.

"There was so much information, both about vampires and about fairies, *Vapa*," Lily began slowly. "Vampires can sing through elemental mind defenses, and they pay for the blood they take with magical protection. You can use Void in incredible ways— the Void hoop opens to an entirely Void-filled place, where Void is actually a tangible thing, not just a magic one senses with the mind in Lamoranth! The hoop is a magical tool unlike any of the others, because it's a doorway, where you can pull out physical Void as a weapon, or make attacks on you disappear, like a shield . . . But what about the magical balance you talked about before? How is that not disturbed by the Void realm?"

"That is an insightful observation, *Vipina*. The theory most vampires hold to, though without the benefit of conclusive evidence, is that there must be yet another plane, in which only a magic exactly opposite of the Void element exists. Only in this way could there be true balance. I am also glad that you see the benefits of the Void hoop both offensively and defensively. What else did you learn?"

Though Alder had stirred within her mind as Vadom spoke, Lily decided to question him about it after her lesson had come to an end.

"That fairies are just as fallible as any other being," Lily replied, thinking of Monkshood. "I suppose I'd built them up in my mind, thinking they would all be like my mother and Alder . . . but I see that this isn't true. I've known Alder for such a short time, yet I know I couldn't bring myself to do what that Fae warrior did to his mate. It was terribly selfish," she finished softly.

"So the lesson in that, perhaps, is that you should never limit your views on what other beings can and cannot do. It is good that you recognize this dynamic potential in everyone you encounter, *Vipina*. You may overlook something either very amazing, or very sinister. You are young, and you still have the open mind of your tender years. This will help you see things that others might miss. In terms of a fairy's magical weapons, what did you hear in my account of the battle?"

"Monkshood had warrior wings and elemental wings at the orange level, and he had been trained to wield them both creditably. He was comfortable with his love element magic, which was a part of all of his weapons, but he was at a huge disadvantage because he knew nothing about Void element. He also let his emotions show a great deal, even as you hid yours entirely. That made things more difficult for him as well."

"I think you must be correct regarding that Fae's sets of wings, *Vipina*. His skills certainly seem to coincide with what we know about those fairy abilities. His disadvantages, and how he failed to compensate for them, are also as you have stated. In your lesson on warrior mentality tomorrow, I will be addressing how to deal with emotions in the midst of opponents or enemies in greater detail.

"For now, we have covered all of the magical weapons used by all of the magical races that I am aware of in Lamoranth. This completes my formal introduction of weaponry to you. Do you have any other questions, *Vipina?*"

Lily thought it would probably be best if she took some time to think over everything her *vapa* had just told her. At this point, she was still just trying to absorb it all . . . and then something did occur to Lily, something that probably should have intruded on her thoughts before now. For there was, in fact, one magical race that her *vapa* had not mentioned, yet it was the one set of beings Lily was the most anxious, and the most determined, to know how to fight. She looked solemnly into Vadom's eyes and answered him.

"Do the xydolem have magical weapons I did not see, *Vapa?*"

She watched as a shadow of anger flitted across her *vapa*'s features, which had hardened even as she had spoken. Lily realized Vadom really did feel quite strongly about the xydolem, and she wondered, almost against her will, what havoc they had wreaked in the Cave Kingdom to merit such emotion from her *vapa*.

"It was remiss of me to neglect mention of these beings in your lesson, *Vipina*. You are right both to include them and to arm yourself with all possible knowledge of them. I will tell you what I know of their magical weaponry. The xydolem, as Void-bound creatures, can Void-bind others. It is a terrible thing, one of the most evil ways to abuse the night element. It involves the use of both magical Void element and the physical night ropes from the Void world. They infiltrate the minds of their victims with minuscule threads of the rope, which are imbued with Void element spun into a complicated and sinister obedience spell. It is difficult to detect in most minds, for most beings have both good and bad in the complexity of their minds and spirits. The minion does the bidding of the xydolem until their mind and body sickens, and even then they are forced to do as the xydolem wish until it kills them. Void-binding is an enslavement that no being I know of has ever survived."

Lily took a deep breath. Then let it out slowly. She tried to expel her horror in the same way, but fell far short in her attempt. It was no wonder her *vapa* loathed the xydolem . . . and all the more extraordinary that her mother had pitied her own murderers. They did terrible things . . . yet it was because they had lost everything, and had chosen their own ultimate destruction as a result. That is, if her mother's myth was actually founded from a seed of truth. Lily felt too conflicted about the xydolem to come to any decision about them. They had taken her mother from her, and a part of Lily would never be able to forgive them for this. Yet nothing, Lily thought, could be as simple as hating another. Would such a strong, ugly emotion not weaken her, destroy her, just as thoroughly as it did these creatures? She wanted no part of the emotions of beings bound up and consumed in their own revenge and despair.

Though her thoughts were still full of all she had heard and the questions that had occurred to her as a result, Lily sensed that all three of them had reached their limit for the day. Her *vapa* could hardly speak of the xydolem calmly, while Alder had been projecting something akin to distress ever since Vadom had spoken of Monkshood's betrayal of his mate. Lily herself felt . . . tired. And more than a bit scared.

"*Vapa.*"

"Yes, *Vipina?*"

Lily allowed herself to snuggle into the inviting strength of her vapa's arms. She was suddenly very grateful that this particular lesson had occurred where she could feel a real measure of safety.

"Thank you."

After a few moments, the arms wrapped around her gave a slight squeeze, then held Lily just a little more securely.

Lily felt her mind begin to drift. Then, just before sleep claimed her, she realized that Alder was still very much preoccupied. She summoned some of her love element, despite the pain, and wrapped it about him. Then Lily directed him from the vast sunlit expanse he floated in to her own golden soul in the shade of her imaginary trees, so that she could bask in his silvery light, and he could feel free to do the same with her golden glow.

Rest, faelan. *We can think and worry later.*

"But the xydolem, the Void-binding, and the Misruler's part in their

terrible existence, what does this mean for our people in the Fae Wood, Lily? They act with organization, coordination, and deliberation. This cannot bode well for anyone in Lamoranth. And this Monkshood . . . I can hardly stand the thought of him. To endanger the greatest gift he would ever receive, then act with such cowardice, is sickening to me."

Lily tried to send him what comfort she could muster along their first truemate bond, thinking that might help Alder find some peace. She wasn't quite sure how to reach him directly through their connection yet, however, and the effort and concentration needed was far beyond her. Though she hadn't succeeded, her attempt alone seemed to jar Alder temporarily out of his concerns and disturbed thoughts.

"You are weary, faelani. *It is evening now, perhaps you should eat something?"*

Lily wanted nothing as much as she needed to sleep.

Please rest with me, Alder. I don't want you to weaken yourself by worrying so much.

Alder's soul came a little closer to her own.

"If I'm not allowed to worry, then neither are you. Sleep, Lily, and I will rest, too."

And very soon thereafter, both of them did just that.

21

Dreams and Nightmares

That night, when the moon had made much of its journey across the night sky, Lily had an extraordinary dream. She was wandering through a cool, shady world of green. All was peaceful, and it seemed to her that the breeze whispered knowingly about the green canopy above her head. Lily felt the strangest contentment, greater than anything she had felt even when her mother had lived. Here was safety, here was a place where true and complete happiness resided. There were many other feelings, shared by many other beings, in that place, yet Lily was certain that real hardship rarely found solid footing in this strange world.

She wandered, without goal or direction, past countless thick brown columns, which seemed to support the waving green shadiness above her. Lily gradually felt compelled to follow a much-worn path, which meandered around in a way that seemed almost carefree. Though there were impediments to the path, rocks and bits of firewood and pieces of the canopy, she realized it was important to follow, for it prevented her from stepping on any of the riotous colors that surrounded the canopy pillars.

Soon, however, Lily was certain she needed to leave the well-defined way. When she saw a column with a covering of green needles, surrounded at its base by a profusion of delicate triangles the color of clouds bruised purple by a storm, Lily was certain she needed to begin traveling to the left, perpendicular to the time-worn path.

After a time, the length of which Lily couldn't really determine, she came upon a clearing. At first all she felt was relief, for the way, though somehow familiar, had not been easy. Always she'd had to be careful of the colors, *flowers*, at her feet, and the pillars, which must be trees, real trees, all around her. Then she really took stock of her new environment. There was a great swath of grass, which frolicked with the gentle, playful wind. The sunlight was strong here, at least it seemed so to Lily's eyes, which had grown accustomed to the dappled shade. She stepped out, feeling suddenly close to a wish, a desire, that she hadn't realized was in her heart. Just a little closer . . . and then she looked across the grassy expanse and beheld the most breath-taking sight her eyes had ever seen. There was a body of water, not like a river, but roughly circular, which reflected the brilliant light of the sun and fractured it in every direction. And there, on the opposite side, at the water's edge and standing alone in solitary majesty, was . . . a *beautiful silver tree.*

Even as Lily realized what it must be, despite the discrepancies provided by her imagination, and even as she began to run toward it with every crashing beat of her heart, she felt her mind start to awaken. Lily clung to the wonderful dream for as long as possible, but soon the Fear had crept impossibly close, spreading from her well-known tribe across the vast sunlit lands and pursuing her to her spirit's most sacred place amidst the trees.

You will never live to see that tree.

Lily froze, completely terrified. Where was that voice coming from? It was impossible to separate it from the horrible iron pain she was now fiercely battling. She felt her resolve waver. What if she never found that tree? Lily felt despair threaten to choke her. What a failure she was. That beautiful tree would wait in that oasis of peace forever, for a weak, immature girl who would never show up.

Immature, weak. To think that one such as you could go so far, pathetic. How far you overreach yourself, Fae infant.

Lily felt an overpowering anguish sweep through her. The voice was right. There was so much to do, so much resting on her shoulders. How would she ever accomplish it all? How would she live with herself if she didn't?

Your father will die, your mate will die, and in the bleakness of your lonely life, you will have no one to blame but yourself.

Lily felt pain knife through her at the words, uttered so quietly, a whisper of despair voicing her greatest fears.

"Lily! LILY! Faelani, *listen to me! Why do you shut me out? Tell me what is wrong!"*

And then Alder was there, in all his silver radiance. Lily felt, rather than heard, his gasp of shock. It brought her back to herself, just enough to realize that the Fear had breached her tribe's mental wall, reached her wells of power, and was beginning to enter her well of prophecy. The pain was worse than when they had entered Ropaz, and Lily felt completely incapacitated, utterly without defense. She felt her grip on consciousness slipping, but Lily clung to it, knowing instinctively that if she let go, all would be lost.

Alder began to battle the Fear for her. Lily watched in growing horror as he threw himself at it, again and again, slowly gaining ground and forcing its retreat from her wells of power. But she saw the toll it took on him, she saw how his silver glow began to diminish, and that frightened her more than anything. She had to *do something*. Lily summoned strength she had never before used, had never truly been aware of prior to that very moment, the instant she realized her closest friend, her *truemate*, was in terrible danger. A great roaring, snarling challenge bellowed from her central well of power, and a heartbeat later, the most shocking being Lily had ever beheld burst forth in the wake of its battle cry.

The being was essentially a concentration of golden magic, yet her ferocity was a tangible thing. She was constantly shifting shape, as though she couldn't decide which form would be the most deadly to her enemy, the Fear. She began as an animal almost feline, with sharp claws and sharper teeth. As she prowled closer to her opponent, the being transformed into an immense scaly creature, with enormous webbed wings, that breathed golden fire at the Fear in great bursts from her maw. As the Fear retreated all the way to the tribal peripheries of Lily's mind, up to the beginnings of her circular wall and out the narrow door, the fierce being gave chase, morphing into a feather-covered bird that screeched, plunged, and pecked, using her talons to slash and cut the Fear as it finally departed Lily's mind entirely. At the Fear's final disappearance, the being screeched again in frustration, clearly wishing to give chase. She seemed incapable of doing so, though Lily was somewhat relieved that this ferocious magic being of hers couldn't seem to leave at the moment. Her protection was most welcome, and Lily had no idea how to recall the magical creature to her mind if she left.

A little stunned, Lily hardly registered when the golden being changed yet again, into a creature she had no name for or knowledge of, and used incredible strength to push her mental door closed. When she finished her task, the magic being raced back to Lily's wells of power and came to a halt near Alder's hovering soul. She nudged him, tenderly solicitous, impossibly so, and yet . . . Lily forgot to dwell on this amazing change in demeanor when she took a closer look at her truemate.

Alder's silvery light had diminished, frighteningly so. Lily felt guilty and helpless. What could she do to restore him? He would never make it back to the Fae Wood in this condition, she was certain. Just when she thought panic would overwhelm her, however, Lily caught sight of her bond to Alder, that single shimmering strand that formed the first step of their *faelanzania*. It gave her an idea.

She focused on their bond, then traced it back to her own golden soul, the origination of all her feelings, thoughts, hopes, fears, and strength. When she had a good grasp on this most essential part of herself, the part she was so seldom consciously aware of, except when Alder was concerned, Lily slowly channeled a small part of herself through the bond to the Fae at the other end.

She knew the moment it reached him, could feel his awe and joy at her giving. Alder accepted it hesitantly at first, then couldn't seem to help himself as he opened himself to her completely and absorbed all that Lily offered. She didn't stop until his glow was fully restored.

When her *faelan* was well once more, Lily pulled back, feeling an unprecedented exhaustion. She settled near him, suddenly not sure of what to say or do next. They were both quiet for a while. Finally, Alder gently broke the silence.

"What happened, faelani? *How did it get so far? Usually you wake up much sooner."*

Lily abruptly remembered the wonderful dream she'd been having. She couldn't find the words to describe it, or her feelings about it. Instead, she went to the part of her mind that held her memories, a place she had not been since her mother's death. Alder followed her to that tribal circle. Lily summoned up the dream, and she showed it to him. She felt how profoundly it shook him. When she came to the end, as she had been running toward the silver tree, and then woken up to that terrible voice, Lily spoke into the stunned silence between them.

I didn't want to wake up, because I was dreaming of you.

Alder didn't speak right away. It seemed to Lily, given the veritable tumult of his emotions, that speech was entirely beyond him just now. So, she patiently waited, even as she wondered if any kind of explanation would be possible. At length, Alder seemed to bestir himself.

"Is this the first time you have dreamed of my tree, Lily?"

Yes.

Lily didn't elaborate. She wanted to know more about the mystery of the trees and flowers, but only if Alder told her willingly. Why, for example, did the forest and circle of water in her dream look so much like the sun-dappled wood and clearing in her mind?

The silence stretched again, and Lily had lost all hope of being told anything when Alder finally spoke up again.

"You have foreseen the tree of your truemate, as only the most powerful Fae ladies do, Lily. I would like nothing more than to tell you everything that this amazing portent entails. However, I think that a full explanation must wait, as so much already does, for your arrival in the Fae Wood. I will say this, for you already seem to know it instinctively: that the tree you have seen is indeed a part of me, the tree of my naming, which began to grow from the ground on the day of my birth. May the flowers of your own naming one day grow in that clearing about me."

He spoke the last so fervently that Lily remained silent, unsure of how to respond, if there was really anything to be said after such a statement.

Alder, once we've gotten to the Fae Wood, and taken care of all the urgent things, can we sit down together and have a really long talk?

"Yes, Lily, and I can honestly say I look forward to it. Once we arrive, there are things you will need to know immediately, but everything else I will explain soon thereafter before . . . life and all its duties intrude."

Lily mulled this over before agreeing. There was one thing, however, that she felt she needed to know right now. Despite her desire to understand, though, she still felt uncertain and a little afraid.

Faelan, *what was that changing creature inside me?*

Alder's response was instant.

"It is the magical manifestation of your soul's ferocity, faelani. *You should feel very, very proud that it is a part of you. There is no need to fear it, or your control over it. Though it will always be a very independent part of you, its strength, adaptability, intensity, and protectiveness are all just as they should be. When you are safely in the Wood, I will tell you the name such beings go by, and all the other things you need to know about them. For now, I hope it suffices to say that your magical beast is an enforcer of sorts, and it will make you a much-respected member of Fae society."*

He hesitated briefly, then added one thing more.

"If it is any consolation, Lily, I have such a being inside my physical body,

as part of my inner magic, as well, though he didn't come out of his well of power inside me until I was quite a bit older than you."

Lily sighed, wondering just how different she was from the average Fae. Still, it was a great comfort to her to know that Alder had this bewildering magical ferocity as well. He would tell her all about it when the time was right. That is to say, the first opportunity Lily had inside the Fae Wood to corner and interrogate him. In the meantime, she didn't think the shape-shifting magic would surface again unless her need was dire. Lily felt unbelievably weary from her "enforcer's" brief appearance just now, and it had seemed completely impossible for her fierce being to break free from her iron-bound body. Though she had certainly wished to chase the Fear beyond Lily's mental defenses, she hadn't been able to do so.

When Lily thought about it a bit more, however, this made sense. Lily was certain that, if she could have, that being would most definitely have come to her mother's rescue. And in so doing, Lily thought miserably, she would have shown all of those xydolem exactly who and what Lily was. She turned her mind away from that line of thinking and struggled to find some other focus for her thoughts. Perhaps she should surface to her surroundings and make sure her *vapa* wasn't worried about her. It was very likely that she had thrashed about or cried out in her sleep earlier during the battle with the Fear.

Lily opened her eyes and looked at once into the concerned countenance of Vadom. She distantly noted that the sky was just beginning to lighten, though there was still a bit of time before dawn. Lily focused on her *vapa* once more and used what little energy she possessed to explain what had transpired inside her mind during the night.

Vadom listened intently throughout her explanation, never once interrupting. When Lily had finished recounting the night's events, her *vapa* simply gazed absently into her eyes for a time, apparently deep in thought. Though it often made her feel like squirming, Lily found it more difficult than usual to hold Vadom's gaze after explaining things. What would he think of the changing beast? Lily realized how important her *vapa*'s opinion was to her now, and how much she wished to remain high in his esteem. Surely he must think her completely bizarre . . .

"*Vipina.*"

Lily forced herself to look up into her *vapa*'s face.

"From the very beginning of our acquaintance, you have always looked me in the eye, without flinching or glancing away. It was one of the first ways I knew that you were very brave, and very strong. Even if you are not sure what another being will say to you, perhaps especially then, always look them in the eye. This is a measure of courage the world over, and I would always have you reading another's eyes as they read the strength of spirit in yours."

"Yes, *Vapa*," Lily said, and she made sure that she was meeting his gaze steadily when she spoke. Vadom nodded, then smiled slightly when he saw her add the *valoriad*.

"Then let me say, *Vipina*, that your dream, and what happened after, is incredible to me. My awe of the Fae grows greater by the day. How truly amazing it is that the Fae Wood is so literally named, and that such a powerful race resides there. Though I do not wish to speak overmuch of your shape-shifting creature, as that seems best left to Alder to explain, I will simply say that vampires call beings with this ability, and often the magical manifestation itself, a therianthrope. That your magic acts in such a way, in addition to your possession of so many other abilities, makes you entirely unique in all my experience. What a challenge my *vipina* is proving to be," he concluded with a small smile, full of both reassurance and pride.

Lily couldn't help but smile back. He didn't mind her rather exotic magic, and neither did Alder. When she thought of how completely the Desert people would have shunned her, Lily felt buoyant at the thought of their total acceptance. They were like a family to her now, caring for her just as her mother had. Lily resolved to care for and accept them fully in return.

Resolute

After a brief breakfast for Lily, they continued east, anticipating Wizulaan in the late afternoon or early evening. Lily was content to simply be carried by her *vapa*. It was hard for her to believe that this very evening she would be learning to ride a horse. A small part of her wished Vadom would carry her all the way to the Fae Wood, though the rest of her knew that an alternative form of travel was necessary, both for safety and the honor of her *vama*. Lily wondered when she would meet Vabiri, what she would look and act like. She was beginning to envision a quiet, beautiful lady vampire, with perfect manners and an inherent gentleness and grace. Certainly, Vabiri would be special, for she was the otherwing of her *vapa*—

"Faelani, *have you noticed that smoke in the sky, to the south? Would you look more closely, please?*"

Even as Lily focused her sight over her right shoulder, she felt a small pulse of premonition from her well of prophecy, enough to make her body give a small jerk in the arms of her *vapa*.

"*Vipina*, are you well?"

"Alder is asking about smoke to the south, *Vapa*. Do you see it? I think it's serious," she added with concern, even as she tried to get a better sense of what her magic was telling her. Lily went to her wells of power and listened intently. The portent was garbled by the iron she wore, and it was more painful to access that magic than it had been before. What she did manage to comprehend filled her with apprehension.

"I do see the black smudges on the southern horizon, *Vipina*. I was not entirely certain what it was, for my senses are trained to smell smoke rather than see it, and the wind is still blowing from the west. This has served me well up until now, for I have always lived in the night when the smoke of fire is not easily visible. What does Alder say about this? I think he must be more experienced in this matter than I am."

"It's coming from the Volcano Crescent, and that is never good. It is said that the volcanoes are in tune with the emotions of their inhabitants and that smoke usually precludes an eruption, of either lava and ash, or of trolls, but most often of both. Our people in the Wood may be in danger from an attack. I normally help in the surveillance of Molten Mirror Lake, and as such I'm usually the first to know what is happening with our neighbors to the west . . . but I can tell nothing from here," Alder finished in frustration.

Lily repeated her *faelan*'s words aloud, then added what she had felt from her magic.

"My well of prophecy was difficult to understand. I did clearly hear 'Trolls', 'Deception', and 'Beware'. I think Alder's already figured that much out, though," Lily concluded, a little disappointed. It had really hurt to get even those three words, and they more or less stated the obvious.

"Not necessarily, *Vipina*. The trolls are certainly not known for their deception. They are a simple, straight-forward race. I would think an attack from them would be quite clear."

"I agree, faelani. *Fairies have been able to keep the trolls out of the Wood for so long in part because they rarely change tactics. They always sail a very large contingent of warriors directly for us over Molten Mirror, alerting us to their approach as they near the protective dome. We can then fly out to meet them long before they are able to inflict damage on the dome or reach our shores, and where we also have a huge advantage with our elemental magic and other abilities. They are practically defenseless without their earth magic and with only their blunt weapons for close-range protection. Most of the time there are very few casualties. We choose instead to blow their boats back to the Crescent with air element, and when they scramble to shore, we burn their ships with fire element, then fly home. It has always seemed most peculiar that they choose to engage us where they do not have any hope of utilizing their strengths, but we have all just assumed that they aren't very bright. Then again, the Fae are not aware of the magical properties of obsidian, which every troll does wear on their person. It is fortunate for us that even the power of the black stones could not give them any advantages over our warriors in these large-scale skirmishes."*

"If they are such predictable opponents, then how did they nearly defeat the Fae three hundred years ago, Alder?" Lily challenged, speaking aloud in her agitation. She was hardly going to take the blatant 'Beware' from her prophetic magic lightly. Then she felt Alder's embarrassment and wished she'd tempered her words.

"That happened, from all that I've heard of the whole ordeal, for several reasons. The first was because the King and Queen of Silver Court failed to deal with the potential threat of attack in a timely manner. The second was because the King and Queen of Golden Court had just taken up the throne, and they were living clear on the opposite end of the Wood as well. Normally, one set of royalty or the other are able to sense and counter threats to the Fae Wood through their connection with the dome of protective spells, with plenty of time to spare. The circumstances, however, were not in their favor. The trolls, for the first time in memory, attacked from both Molten Mirror and the southern border of the Wood in enormous numbers. In the end, I think the only reason the Fae were victorious was because the trolls were not able to coördinate their split offensive with enough precision to press the advantage they had created. The Fae, on the other hand, had two brilliant captains to develop a strategy to best use their smaller numbers and deploy their forces to the greatest possible effect. Even then, there might not have been victory, except that the elves came to our aid in the final hour, even though the dragons did not.

"If this is a serious attempt of the trolls to attack us once more, we need to handle things much better than last time. A battle council needs to be held at court. The Guards, Wardens, and unmated warriors need to be given warning to prepare, and perhaps the mated warriors as well. A course of action needs to be carefully plotted by Silver Court, and Golden Court needs to be kept informed of all decisions and actions, especially if their help will be needed . . ."

As Alder trailed off, clearly caught up in his train of thought, Lily repeated his words to her *vapa*. Vadom did not speak right away, obviously deliberating carefully as well. He seemed thoughtful in a way Lily was beginning to recognize.

"What are you seeing that I am still blind to, *Vapa?*" she asked quietly.

Vadom seemed slightly startled, then amused.

"You have eyes like an otherwing, *Vipina,* who sees much and cares deeply. I have come to no definite conclusions, for there are many possibilities for us to consider. One thing seems clear to me, however, and that is that Alder, and you as well, are needed in the Fae Wood as quickly as can be managed."

Lily paused, sensing that she wasn't getting the real answer to her question. Remembering what her *vapa* had said earlier about eye contact, she gazed up at Vadom steadily with another question in her eyes. When he looked back down at her from scanning the southern sky again, he seemed to go completely still, even as he continued his run to the east. After several long moments, he spoke softly, never looking away from her.

"As for the answers you seek, *Vipina,* I think they are for your mate to give you. If he does not just now, I think it is because he has his reasons. Though I imagine it must be difficult for you to wait, you will need to be patient with Alder for the time being."

Lily held his eyes for a moment longer, then nodded slowly. Vadom actually chuckled quietly in response, causing Lily to glance back up in surprise.

"I think you will lead Alder a merry chase, *Vipina.* He had better prepare himself."

Lily mock-humphed, then put her nose in the air in exaggerated pique.

"Well, he certainly gets credit for finding me all the way in the desert. If he can perform that feat and still keep up with me in this chase you speak of, I don't foresee a problem," she replied in her sauciest tone, then ruined her pose by snickering.

"Faelani, *what have I been missing? What are you amused about?"*

With the return of Alder, Lily chortled at his questions, then gave her *vapa* a mischievous wink.

"Alder is asking what we've been discussing, *Vapa.* He wants answers to his questions. He wants pertinent information. Should we tell him?"

"I really must encourage you to pay more attention to your otherwing, Alder. You wouldn't want to miss anything important," Vadom replied, his eyes still lit with amusement.

Lily could hear Alder grumble indistinctly at this pronouncement, and she decided to turn the conversation to a more productive topic.

"When do you think we'll reach Wizulaan today, *Vapa?*"

Vadom gazed ahead intently, and Lily watched as he sent those strange pulses of Void out before them. They returned before much time had elapsed.

"If we travel steadily through the afternoon, we should reach the wizard town in the early evening. Before long, perhaps we should consider the best possible place to hide the two of you during my sojourn into Wizulaan. I had originally planned to skirt its southern periphery, to avoid being any closer to Six Cities than necessary, but given the smoke and Lily's portent regarding the trolls, perhaps passing Wizulaan from the north would be wiser. Regardless, I think finding a place for you to the east of the town would be best, in the event that we must leave in haste. What are your opinions on the matter?"

Lily and Alder debated the issue, but Lily found herself worn out before much had been said. She didn't . . . feel well. Then she realized that the Fear's encroachment into one of her wells of power, not to mention the debut of her magical ferocity, was bound to catch up with her eventually. Lily came to the conclusion that the time for the pain to bounce back must be nearly upon her. Deciding that she should rest and shore up what strength she could before the iron storm blew through her, Lily told Alder as much.

"Of course, faelani. *If you need a chance to recover, we should stop for a bit. Perhaps you could try to eat something and then lay down. Vadom probably won't want to enter Wizulaan until the cover of darkness anyway."*

Lily smiled a little at Alder's solicitous tone. It was moments like this that made it hard to think of Alder as a friend only.

"*Vapa,* could we take a short break, please? I'd like to eat and rest. I think that the pain from this morning might be about to catch up with me."

Vadom came to an immediate stop, his expression becoming solemn.

"Of course, *Vipina.* I should have suggested it myself, for I know you missed your meal yesterday evening and hardly ate this morning. Let me know if you need to remove some of your iron for a time. That might make what is about to come a little easier on you."

Lily nodded, then straightened her legs as Vadom set her down. Without the support of his arms, however, Lily slowly sank to the ground. She only managed to keep from falling limply onto her back by bracing her arms against the grassy ground. Vadom set the haversack directly in front of her, only his eyes betraying concern in his otherwise calm demeanor. Determined not to worry her *vapa* more than necessary, Lily reached for the sack and dug for the pouch of food. After successfully eating some bread and cheese, then polishing it off with water, Lily replaced the victuals. Then she hesitated. After a moment, however, she reached into the haversack once more, this time pulling out the medical pack. Lily carefully removed her mother's ashes, then laid down on the earth, using the sack as her pillow and cradling her mother's remains in her arms.

Soon after closing her eyes, Lily felt the iron pain begin to grow throughout her body. Nowhere was it worse, however, than in her mind, where the Fear rebounded proportionately. Even as she began her arduous battle, Lily was conscious of Alder's reassuring presence. He seemed ready to attack the Fear at a moment's notice, and he guarded her wells of power zealously. Knowing Alder would alert her to any iron effects in that critical location, Lily pushed, pulled, and otherwise forced the Fear back beyond her mental wall. Without a door to expel it directly, Lily simply started throwing it with all her mental might over the first ring of her defenses.

Later, when Lily thought she had things more or less back under control, she allowed herself to slump from her exhaustion and disquiet. At one point, she had felt so rattled by the Fear that the very ground beneath her had seemed to shake. Lily checked on Alder, and, upon seeing his soul unharmed, she surfaced to reassure her *vapa* and inform him of her success. What she saw when she opened her eyes and sat up, however, prompted Vadom to comfort her instead.

"Something like an earthquake occurred while you were preoccupied, *Vipina*. I think one of the volcanoes of the Crescent must have erupted, just as Alder predicted. There were fairly large tremors even here, though we must be about a two day journey from the closest volcano. The overturned earth about us is simply a result of the Crescent's upheaval relatively nearby."

Even as Lily took in the uprooted grass and mounds of dirt that had been disturbed so recently about them, her eyes were drawn, almost against her will, to the south. The sky in that direction was roiling with inky, greasy-looking black smoke. Debris, from chunks of rock to amorphous globs of lava, slowly made their way back down to the earth in aborted attempts at flight. It was incredible, even as it was unsettling. Lily found herself grateful that they hadn't been any closer. She imagined that it would be hard to breathe the air with so much ash and other solid matter in it that normally wasn't present. It was then that Lily felt Alder's unease.

What is it that's troubling you, Alder? Is this a very unusual occurrence? I thought you said the volcanoes echo the feelings of the trolls . . .

"That is true, Lily, and I have seen much smoking and many very small eruptions from the Crescent as a result. However, I have never seen anything even remotely this severe. That smoke is . . . unnatural. There is something about it that worries me greatly."

Lily understood perfectly the potent sway of instinctive feelings, and she relayed Alder's words to her *vapa*.

"This is serious indeed, then. It is more important than ever to get the two of you into the Fae Wood with all possible haste. With any luck, the volcano's unusual eruption will distract those around us, and we might use this diversion to our advantage. If you are well enough, I think we should continue on, *Vipina*."

Lily caught herself sighing. She looked down at the glass jar in her hands, then gave it one last squeeze before replacing it in the medical pack. When she had the haversack tied shut once more, Vadom plucked it off of the ground and had it slung across his back a moment later. Lily attempted to stand, but simply could not summon the strength on her first try. Or her second. Or her third. She just hurt *everywhere*. When she felt tears stinging her eyes, Lily got angry with herself. Why did she have to be so weak? Why couldn't she even manage to stand up? What was she going to do if they were attacked? She wasn't going to be able to do *anything*, that's what. Lily wished her *vapa* would just pick her up and spare her the humiliation she felt now from her utter helplessness.

When she looked up at Vadom from her sitting position on the ground, however, Lily knew she would have to stand up on her own. His eyes were telling her in no uncertain terms. Lily felt a surge of rebellion. Her mother would have picked her up. Alder definitely would have, if he had his body here just now—

"Vadom is teaching you a warrior lesson, faelani. *You must rise unassisted, no matter how many attempts it takes. Show him how strong you really are, Lily. Show him you can overcome any obstacle, no matter how great or small. Show that vampire you are Fae, and the Fae never give up. Do it,* faelani, *I know you can— nothing is more certain."*

Yes.

Lily was filled with determination. Alder believed she could do it, even though she had never been more exhausted than she felt right now. Lily looked about her and saw a rock she could use to hoist herself up. When she had a good grip on it, she pulled herself up until she stood on her own two feet at last. She flashed her *vapa* a look full of defiance, then she turned to the east and began a lurching walk toward the Fae Wood.

"Lily? Faelani, *what are you doing? I think Vadom just wanted you to stand. I really don't think he expects you to start walking."*

Lily ignored Alder and continued her wobbly forward progress. Where did he draw the line? Where did her *vapa* draw the line? Would they treat her like a warrior? Like a Fae lady? Or like a child? Would they be forever changing their attitudes on a whim? If Vadom was trying to make a point, and if Alder was, then she was determined to make one of her own.

Lily continued her slow and painful march, even when Vadom began walking with measured steps beside her. She would show them. She would show them that she was the daughter of Rose the healer, one of the bravest Fae ladies to have ever lived. She would show them that she was strong, even when her magic was iron-bound. She would show them that she always kept her promises. *Nothing is more certain.*

When she stumbled, or tripped, or all-out fell down, Lily picked herself up and started walking again every time. And she did it without help. After a while, the amount of which Lily was never able later to recall, she tripped on a stone and fell in a sprawling heap in the grass. Lily knew that this time, she would not be able to stand again. She got to her hands and knees, and began to crawl.

"*Vipina.*"

Lily couldn't decide what the tone of his voice was trying to say. Then she decided she didn't care. She had a message of her own, and she didn't need her voice to make it clear. Lily kept on doggedly, refusing to cease her forward motion.

"Faelani, *I am sorry that you are upset, but he was just trying to teach you—*"

"I am not upset," Lily said. She really wanted to be on her feet for this . . . She crawled to a rock and pulled herself up, one last time. When she was looking her *vapa* straight in the eye, clinging to the rock as she did so, she continued.

"But I want you both to know, that I will do whatever it takes to keep my word to my mother. If I have to walk the rest of the way to Golden Court, I will do it. If I have to *crawl* the rest of the way there, I will do that too, even if I have to leave my pride behind in Ropaz. And if you think I need to be toughened up, if you think that I am not strong enough, in body or in mind, then *think again.* Because *nothing is more certain* than my arrival in the golden fairy city by the sea. *Do you hear me?*"

Lily was vaguely aware that she had begun to shout, and that tears were trailing haphazardly down her cheeks. She hardly cared. At that moment, her central well of power gave an almighty bellowing roar, one so loud and so defiant that she was certain, as she looked unflinchingly into the deep, dark brown eyes of her *vapa,* that he heard it, too.

"I hear you, *Vipina,* with great pride in my heart," Vadom said, his words accompanied by the *valoriad.* Her *vapa*'s eyes were just a little wider than usual, and his mouth was curved ever so slightly upward.

"Oh I hear you, alright. I will, without a doubt, have the most strong-willed truemate in the Wood, not to mention the bravest and strongest faelani *as well."*

"Might I suggest, now that we have all learned a valuable lesson, that I take us to the eastern side of Wizulaan? Though I fully believe you when you say your feet will take you home, I would rather provide you with a proper mount to get you there with all haste, *Vipina*."

Lily, in her exhaustion, absently moved her hand in a gesture her mother had frequently made. Whenever one of the desert dwellers in Nather's tribe had said or done something irritating, she would wave her hand in an elegant little triangle, as though to say, 'I haven't all day'. Lily had always wanted to do this to someone, but had never had the nerve before. The last thought that occurred to Lily before she lost consciousness was that she had made her *vapa* smile yet again that day.

23 The Philosophy of Night Magic

WHEN LILY WOKE UP, SHE FOUND THAT night was completely upon them. The next thing she realized was that Alder was protecting her wells of power from a considerable amount of pain and Fear. She realized, with reluctant resignation, that the iron effects were worsening, and there would be no relief until she was safe enough to remove it all. Her next thoughts were tinged with panic. Alder would continue to protect her when she needed to sleep, and that almost certainly meant that he would be hurt and weakened by the iron in her mind again. Lily rebuked herself for endangering the generous soul inside herself before working hard to remove the Fear from the tribal circles of her mind. Its whispers were just a shade too quiet for her to make out, and for that, Lily was grateful. Perhaps if she could keep it out of her wells of power, she would never again understand the sinister voice of iron Fear in her mind.

After a concentrated mental struggle, Lily decided Alder was safe enough for her to relax a bit. She hadn't pushed all of it as far out as usual, but she just didn't have the strength to throw any Fear over the beginnings of her small golden mental wall. Perhaps later . . .

"How are you feeling, Lily? Are you still worn out from earlier today? Normally, you are able to fight the iron effects with more . . . strength of purpose."

Well enough, and you? Do you know if anything has happened while I slept?

"I don't think so, nothing drastic enough to rouse you from your slumber at least. Perhaps we should check with Vadom. I'd like to know if we passed Wizulaan by the north or the south. He may have observed something of significance if he took the route closer to the trolls."

Without further delay, Lily surfaced to the night and her *vapa*'s reassuring presence.

"Good evening, *Vapa*. Did we miss anything?"

Vadom looked down from his careful vigilance of their nearly blurred surroundings. Lily could hardly see anything at first, yet when she looked to the south, she saw the sky was still faintly glowing with the orange-red illumination of lava. It was closer than when she had last looked this way.

"And a good night to you, *Vipina*. Several groups of witches and wizards flew overhead before the sun set. I think news of the eruption has traveled quickly, and many wish to know more of this unusual occurrence. Because of all the coven movement about us, I opted to run to the south of Wizulaan. It seemed unwise to pass between that town and Six Cities, what with the flurry of activity that has taken place among the Ropazians today. I have seen no trolls at all, though I was not necessarily expecting such a sighting. They must be concerned with their internal affairs just now."

Lily mulled this over briefly, then asked another question.

"Do you have a place in mind to hide us now that we are east of Wizulaan, *Vapa*?"

"I must say in all honesty that I do not. This next portion of Ropaz will be unfamiliar to me, and we will have to make calculated improvisations at times. I hope to get a more precise sense of our remaining distance, and any other towns or villages we may encounter, from the inhabitants of Wizulaan while I am procuring a horse and more food for you. News of the trolls and their eruption would be welcome as well. Now that I have had time to adjust to this iron necklace, I believe I will remain undetected for the duration of this foray. I think it will prove fortunate that the two of you thought of and accustomed me to this method of concealment when you did. We will need to use the utmost caution to reach Ford-upon-Ward without incident."

All three lapsed into a brief silence, each focused on different aspects of the night's activity for their small traveling party. Just when Lily was about to ask Alder a question, however, she caught sight of something in her peripheral vision that caused her to gasp, for it was not something she had seen to either side of her, but rather something almost directly above her. Tilting her head back sharply, Lily tried to make out the shapes high above her in the darkness. Though her heart pounded with fear that the xydolem had found out about her and chased her down, Lily didn't make another sound as she struggled to stay calm and think clearly.

"Lily, what did you see up there? Could you look up again? Ask Vadom if they are Ropazians or members of his own kind."

Lily relaxed a little at Alder's controlled tone and logical conclusions. Weren't the chances much greater that some coven members were out later than they meant to be after scouting the Crescent eruption? Or that a vampire or two were here and taking advantage of that fact? Lily braced herself and looked up again. The shapes had nearly blended into the inky darkness of the night sky over Vadom's left shoulder, moving with great speed toward Wizulaan. When her *vapa* noticed the direction of her gaze and lingering tension, he softly reassured her.

"Five witches and three wizards, all much more focused on getting back to the safety of their homes than the ground below them here. They could not detect us through my Void sphere regardless, *Vipina*. As a warrior in training, situations like this are an opportunity for you to methodically assess the situation for danger and react accordingly for your own safety. I would prefer you remain calm, rather than feel fear at the presence of potential enemies. Until you learn to maintain your equanimity, please always remember that I am watching over you."

"I will, *Vapa*," Lily replied quietly, relaxing into his arms once again.

After a short time, Vadom slowed to a walk, veering slightly to the right. When he had climbed most of the way up one of the rock-strewn slopes about them, he parted some of the tall grass on the incline and revealed a tiny cave in the side of the hill. Lily's eyes widened in surprise.

"I thought you didn't know any hiding places in this area, *Vapa*!"

The very ends of Vadom's mouth turned up slightly.

"I did not, *Vipina*. However, finding caves is second nature to a vampire. This will be a snug place for you to be while I am in Wizulaan."

Lily looked into her small and temporary resting space, noting a few scattered animal bones on the smooth rock floor. Though they were proof that something had been here at one time, it also felt as though nothing had been in this tiny place for a while. Satisfied that she wouldn't be meeting with a new creature when she certainly would rather not, Lily nodded her approval of the little cave.

Vadom set Lily down gently, holding her arm to steady her when she wobbled precariously on her own feet. It was then that Lily noticed a hint of light at the back of the cave. She looked up at the roof of her hiding place and saw a small, naturally formed aperture that let in a measure of moonlight. That soft white glow was reflecting off of a portion of water that had gathered in a shallow indention in the stone floor. Lily wondered how the water had gotten to such an unlikely place, but was prevented from asking due to the knot that had formed in her throat. This roughly circular gathering of water reminded her of Alder's special silver place in the Wood . . .

"I will leave you here for the shortest possible amount of time, *Vipina*. Wizulaan is less than an hour back to the west, which I will traverse with all speed. Though procuring nourishment and a horse for you will take a bit of time to accomplish without detection, you should expect me back in roughly two hours, during which time I would ask you not to leave this cave. I will be sending Void pulses to check on you periodically, so please do not become unsettled by them. I would also like to predetermine a signal between us, so that you may contact me if you feel you are in danger. What do you feel you can manage that will reach me, *Vipina*?"

Lily was startled by her *vapa*'s question, but quickly applied her mind to it. Using her inner magic would be miserably painful and was definitely not feasible at present. Lily also had qualms about attempting to manipulate the unfamiliar outer magic of Ropaz. At the very least, it would cause her a great deal of iron pain as well. The obvious answer, then, appeared to be Void use. That element, however, like so much else, was still largely unknown to her. It seemed to be an unnecessary risk, unless . . .

"*Vapa*, may I have some of your time for a quick Void lesson?"

Vadom gave Lily a measured look.

"After everything that I told you about night magic yesterday, you are willing to apply yourself to learning how to wield it?"

Lily deliberated before she spoke. She knew her *vapa* wouldn't have asked if the answer wasn't important to him. Though she had reservations, Lily felt certain that turning her back on Void element was the wrong choice to make. She had to understand it if she was to understand vampires, xydolem, and who knew what other beings in Lamoranth. Remaining entirely ignorant would only put her at a disadvantage . . . and she thought that if she began avoiding night magic now, she'd never work up the courage to face it later.

"You have been using Void for a very long time without corrupting your magic or your heart, *Vapa*. I choose to use Void element for protection and defense only— never to bind others. I choose to be careful, like you. I know you will not lead me astray, *Vapa*."

Vadom gazed into Lily's solemn eyes and nodded after a few contemplative moments.

"I know that your spirit is a little intimidated by night magic just now, *Vipina,* but you are wiser than you know to come to terms with it willingly at this time. It will not be as frightening when it is not so foreign to you. I will be very careful as I enlighten you on this subject.

"The first thing I need to know, *Vipina,* is whether or not you have any night magic in your mind at this moment. You have mentioned in the past that it hovers some small distance from the concentration of sun magic in your mind. Is there any present at this time?"

Lily focused on her wells of power, trying to determine if there was any Void element near her inner magic. Sure enough, it floated in a loose conglomeration nearby, at the edge of the vast plains of her mind. How had she failed to notice it? This was probably the same portion of Void element that had entered her mind when they had crossed into the grasslands days ago. It was certainly a subtle magic . . .

"The Void element from our entrance into Ropaz is still in my mind, *Vapa.* Can you teach me with that?"

Vadom was already nodding.

"Yes, I was hoping this was the case. Night magic will generally do nothing without direction, but I didn't know whether or not you had cast it out with the Fear you endure. That will be adequate for this evening. I can teach you how to draw night magic into your mind at another time. For now, let us concentrate your energies on sending out Void pulses.

"I know that you can detect these when they bounce off of your Void sphere, but wielding them is another matter. First, you must gather a small portion of the night magic and give it form. As you know, it is a magic that easily binds, and this holds true of it even when you are binding it into the shape best suited to your purposes. Void binds itself more easily than anything else, making it a malleable magic, open to your every suggestion.

"After you have given it a roughly spherical shape, think clearly of what you wish the pulse to seek out. In this instance, focus on me, or my night magic, or our avowed connection as *vapa* and *vipina.* After this is firmly fixed in your pulse, you can send it in the general direction of what you seek, and it should go readily for as long as it is able. With practice, you will learn how to judge distances and make your pulse of adequate size. With more iteration, you will be able to embed a few words into your pulse, effectively sending brief messages to the individual you seek.

"Why don't you try just forming a Void pulse now, *Vipina*. I will be able to determine how best to help you once I have seen your first few attempts."

Lily nodded, ready to try her hand at Void use. She did have a couple of questions first, though.

"Should I try to form the Void pulse inside my mind, or outside, first, *Vapa*?"

"Why don't you try outside your mind to start with, *Vipina*. It is easier to gauge the amount of night magic you are using when you can see it with your eyes, as you are able to do."

"That makes sense. And how is a pulse different from the Void sphere that you've been using to hide me? Can I eventually learn to make that, too?"

"Yes, I can teach you that in time, though you already know that a Void sphere is a more complex use of night magic. It is dissimilar primarily because it is imbued with an entirely different intent. Rather than finding, seeking, and communicating, a Void sphere is designed to hide, shield, and protect. It is much larger, and, by necessity, a shell, and encouraging that hollow space to remain just the same as one's normal surroundings is actually rather difficult. Add to that complication its relative density, and whether or not it is hiding the beings within or allowing them to be visible, and a Void sphere can require a good deal of concentration to form correctly. If not created with a clear purpose and some degree of skill, a Void sphere can very easily become a prison, caging the occupants until the magic runs out. Always remember, *Vipina*, that night magic most naturally binds, and most often in the negative sense at that."

"Why is that, *Vapa*? Why does it lean toward evil? I don't understand how it works."

Vadom gave Lily another of his measured looks.

"Vampires throughout the ages have asked these same profound questions, *Vipina*. What I am about to tell you is what the wisest of my kind can best determine about night magic. As I have just said, Void element is open to a user's every suggestion. Is any night magic wielder completely without evil? Is any sentient being so simply good, or bad? You are young, but I think you already know that the world is never so obviously black and white. We live in a world with many kinds of gray, and night magic does not discriminate. If it is gathered and used by an honorable vampire who is intent on killing an enemy, who can say whether the outcome is good or bad? Void will take the shape of a sharp and well-balanced sword, for the vampire wishes to kill. But what if the vampire hesitates, knowing as he does that killing is never without immense repercussions, and is very seldom imperative? Perhaps the blade will go dull, or the hilt will become overly heavy. Void will reflect both the good and the bad in the wielder. Even the most focused and determined of my race have fallen victim to the complexities of night magic. Few can know their hearts absolutely, all of the time, and live with perfect clarity of purpose. Void element reveals any and all steps off of the path of honor, any uncertainty with decisions, just as clearly as it can show the good in a wielder, often by manifesting exactly as one intends. Do you comprehend what I am telling you, *Vipina?*"

Lily swallowed hard. Then she tried to clear her mind. It was obvious that one's purpose in using Void had to be as transparent as glass, or the night magic would misconstrue her intent. No, that wasn't quite right. It wasn't malevolent, it was just . . . able to detect and portray all of a wielder's wishes, for good or ill.

"So, Void will do exactly as a magician wants, only if that person is completely good or utterly bad? So it's really rare for it to be entirely obedient?"

"Yes. Also, night magic tends to do exactly as instructed if the user is absolutely solid in his or her convictions. If a warrior encases his otherwing in a Void sphere when danger approaches, and he desires to hide her, no matter what becomes of him, the Void sphere will keep her from all detection, even for a short time after his death. But is this not, in a way, a prison for the otherwing? Is she not powerless to go to him and offer healing, even if the enemy departs? Even then, Void reflects the bad side of something good."

"Void is like a mirror," Lily said slowly, thinking it all over. "It is a magic that shows us who we really are. It makes us see our true nature, entirely, and shows us, *binds* us, to the consequences of our choices. No wonder it's a bit frightening."

Vadom was quiet for a moment before he replied.

"I know six thousand year old vampires who could not have come up with a more apt analogy. Your understanding is to be commended, *Vipina.*"

Lily looked up at Vadom, startled by his praise. Then she smiled hesitantly.

"Well, I've seen the xydolem all bound up, and then I've traveled with you, *Vapa*. I've seen Void at its extremes, and I think I'd probably fall somewhere in between. Using Void is sort of like magically measuring the rightness of any decision you make, and being able to cope with what comes after that. I can see that much, at least. It's a place to start."

Vadom inclined his head in acknowledgement.

"It is a very good beginning for you, my *vipina,* though you honor me in placing me so high in your spectrum. I am as prone to uncertainty and its magical results as any Void wielder, and hence, I belong in the middle, with the vast majority of Lamoranth."

Lily seriously doubted that, but she kept such thoughts to herself. She'd be lucky if she could remain as self-aware and as steadfast in her convictions as her *vapa* by the time she reached his age.

"And now, *Vipina,* that you have truly begun to comprehend the Void, please attempt to form a pulse."

Lily nodded, feeling slightly nervous. Still, there was no going back now. She went to the small area of her mind where the portion of Void floated, not too far from her inner magic. Lily concentrated on separating a small circle of it, not sure how much she needed. It took her a few moments, but eventually she managed to separate a chunk of Void from the rest. What now? It simply hovered, twisting in on itself over and over. How was she supposed to get it outside her mind?

Faelan, *how do you think I should move it outside?*

Alder responded eagerly, as though he had been desirous of speaking.

"You might just have to try different methods until you find one that works for you, faelani. *Vadom has been pulling Void into and out of his chest, but as a fairy, you may have better luck channeling the night magic through your arms and out of your hands. This is all so fascinating, isn't it? Vadom's entirely overturned everything I've ever thought about the Void in such a short period of time!"*

Lily grinned, then deliberately turned her thoughts back to the task at hand and decided to try moving the Void out of her chest first. Did she need to say something specific? Or should she sort of direct her thoughts at the magic? Lily got a firm mental grip on the Void element she had pulled aside, then visualized it going down to her chest and outside her body. It moved, but sluggishly, before coming to a twisting halt.

Lily frowned. She reminded herself that Void was supposed to be malleable, open to her purpose if she was clear on it herself. Perhaps channeling it through her hands would have a better result. Lily firmly clasped the night magic with her mind once more, then loudly pierced the bit of roiling blackness with her order, condensed into two words: HANDS. OUT!

The Void shot straight down Lily's neck and spread out at her shoulders before streaking down the length of her arms. Before she could so much as blink, the Void pooled momentarily in her hands before blasting out of Lily's body entirely. The two small, twisting pulses ricocheted off of the floor, walls, and ceiling of the little cave before Vadom calmly reached out and grabbed first one, then the other, with his own hands. Surprise lightly crossed his features before he met Lily's astonished eyes.

"'Hands'. 'Out'. Did you place these words in your pulse intentionally, *Vipina?*"

Lily shook her head.

"No. I was trying to figure out how to communicate with the magic. I tried picturing what I wanted it to do, but that didn't really work. Then I sort of stabbed the piece I'd pulled from the bulk of it with those words, and hoped it would follow directions that way. Did I do it correctly?"

Vadom nodded.

"This was well done for a first attempt. Let me explain further, and perhaps that will help you. Generally speaking, every race in Lamoranth handles magic in their own way. Some groups, like the trolls and the goblins, primarily and often solely use words, though they are widely considered weaker beings as a result. The Ropazians need wands and staffs, the elves utilize song, and the dwarves require stones. With these tools, often in conjunction with the use of magical words, they are thought to be moderately powerful races. The beings who can wield magic with neither words nor a tool of some kind, however, are acknowledged to be the most powerful beings in Lamoranth."

Vadom paused and looked at Lily expectantly, as though waiting for her to provide an answer. Lily quickly reviewed the magical races her *vapa* hadn't yet mentioned.

"Vampires," she said first. She'd never heard Vadom speak to the night magic, yet it obeyed him.

"Dragons," Lily quickly added. Surely they couldn't carry any tools about with them, and hadn't her *vapa* told her that they couldn't speak words aloud, but instead put thoughts directly into the minds of others? Who else? Lily didn't know about the giants, and perhaps Vadom didn't either. Mermaids couldn't speak aloud under water, but hadn't her *vapa* said the ladies wielded pearls? Just then, Alder gave the slightest wiggle near her wells of power. Lily laughed aloud, then met the arching brow of her *vapa* with her final answer.

"And fairies!"

Vadom's countenance softened for just a moment before displaying his amusement.

"And fairies," he agreed with a slight smile.

Thank you, Alder, Lily thought with a grin.

"Hmm, what?" he replied innocently. His bright silver glow gave him away, though.

"As we know, vampires, dragons, and fairies can put their minds to the task of wielding magic with remarkable results. Whether it be a masterpiece of glass, or a perfectly clear and hollow Void sphere, our races are best able to shape magic with proper mental concentration. Perhaps you are wondering, then, why you were successful with the Void pulse only after you injected words into a designated portion of night magic?"

Lily's felt her eyes go wide. That was exactly what she had just been puzzling over as he spoke. If she didn't know firsthand how difficult it was to read the mind of another, she would have begun to wonder about her *vapa*. Lily nodded to encourage him to continue.

"What you succeeded in doing, *Vipina,* was implanting a message into your pulse. You accidentally bypassed giving the pulse instructions. Try again, but do this: use your thoughts. Wrap specific directions around the pulse, giving it a more defined shape. Tell the night magic you select that it must find Vadom the vampire, your *vapa,* who is in or around the wizard town of Wizulaan, less than an hour to the west. Gently impress it with what you want to know about me: where I am precisely, or my state of physical health and mental well-being. If you pay attention, you will feel the subtlest click when the pulse is adequately informed. Then, whether it is inside your mind or out, release it. If you have formed and instructed the proper amount of night magic, it will eventually find what you seek and bounce back to you with an answer, doing what you have shaped it to do."

Lily thought back to the earlier part of their conversation and tilted her head to one side.

"More or less, right, *Vapa?*"

Vadom nodded solemnly.

"Just so, *Vipina,* in correlation to your intent. I am glad to hear you are taking the most important aspect of this lesson and applying it to all the rest. It would be wise of you to habituate yourself to such a mode of thinking. Now, why don't you try again, unless you have any questions for me first?"

Lily began to turn her attention inward, but stopped as something disturbing occurred to her.

"*Vapa,* I wouldn't hurt you if I sent a pulse to find you, would I? Not even if I was angry with you, or upset about something else?"

"This is a good question, *Vipina.* No, a pulse of this size, imbued primarily with the intent of finding or communicating, would not cause the recipient harm. If you were upset, the night magic might convey that to the being you seek, even if you do not directly put your feelings in the message. However, if you were angry with me, the pulse might feel like a glancing blow or a light slap when it reaches me and bounces back to you. Such are the workings of Void element."

Vadom hesitated, giving Lily one of his searching looks. After a moment, he spoke further.

"I said that this is a good question, my *vipina,* because skilled night magicians can in fact create pulses designed to maim or kill. I would rather not speak of this in detail now, however, for I feel it is premature. At a later time, when you know more and have attained a certain level of competence with night magic, I can teach you of this technique if you wish it. For now, suffice it to say, if you see a pulse in your vicinity that looks as though it has a distinctly oily or greasy texture, do not let it bounce off of you directly, and only let it bounce off of your Void sphere if you cannot dodge it entirely. It looks as it does because it was formed with deliberately malevolent intent, and it is dangerous."

Lily felt slightly ill at her *vapa*'s words, and quickly turned her mind to forming another Void pulse. She siphoned a portion of Void, finding success when she sort of twisted some out of the rest, rather than allowing it to twist into itself. With her thoughts, Lily carefully wrapped her intent around the forming pulse . . . Find Vadom the vampire, my *vapa,* who stands before me in this cave, watching patiently. Discover what he feels behind that calm facade . . . *snick.* Lily almost missed it, yet she knew she would not have missed the sudden stillness of her pulse. It twisted no longer, but waited only for her order to leave. Lily hesitated a moment, then clearly spoke the words 'Be safe' in her mind, deliberately piercing them into the center of her Void pulse. With that done, she pictured the pulse leaving her mind through her right hand and going on its way.

In the next instant, it had shot down her right arm and used her hand as a platform to take off, making straight for Vadom. Lily watched in surprise as it bounced forcefully from her vapa's chest and directly back to her, making contact with her head before she could so much as blink. Then she felt emotions not her own: a flicker of sadness and the name Vabiri, followed by a hint of happiness and an image of her own smiling face. Lily felt stunned by it.

"Goodness, faelani. *I'd say you're taking quickly to the use of Void element. Are you alright?*"

Yes, I guess I just wasn't expecting the response I received. He misses his otherwing, but I make him happy, don't I?

"*Of course you do, Lily. You are becoming the child of his heart, just as he is becoming the father of yours. In the Fae language, there are endearments for this relationship. You would call Vadom* 'praetam', *and he would call you* 'praetii'. *I have called Captain Pine* praetam *for over two hundred fifty years, and Iris I have called my* 'praetuu' *for nearly as long. They call me their* 'praetoh'."

Lily could feel how Alder cherished the connections he was teaching her. Her wings of elucidation picked out the meaning of the words, and Lily understood them clearly, though the Fear didn't let this inner magical use go unpunished. Though she heard the Fae words as though listening for them through a sandstorm, her heart swelled at what they truly meant. Alder called Captain Pine 'branches that shelter and trunk that supports, father of my heart'. He called the healer Iris 'petals that whisper of honor and love, mother of my heart'. And to think that Pine and Iris called her *faelan* 'sapling I cherish for reaching the sky, son of my heart', . . . Lily decided they must be special fairies indeed.

I can't wait to meet your praetam *and* praetuu, *Alder. They obviously know who deserves a place in their hearts.*

She felt his shy reaction to her words, but there was something more . . . it was as though Alder didn't quite believe her. He was modest, yes, but he was also partially diffident. Lily worried about this lack of confidence in her friend. She realized that it might very well be tied into other things about him that she had already noticed, like the impatience with himself, and the occasional self-castigation. Lily decided, right then and there, that she would try to bolster Alder's soul, to make him believe more strongly in his worth as a person. Even as newly bonded as they were, surely she was within her rights as his truemate to do some—

"*Vipina?* Is everything all right within you?"

Lily was pulled from her concerns as she distantly perceived the words of her *vapa*. Still, she would have to think about this newest revelation about . . . her *faelan* soon.

"Yes, *Vapa*, I'm fine. I've been learning important things, from you and from Alder, today, and I was just thinking them all over."

Vadom gave a slow tilt of his head.

"That is good. Why don't you tell me how the Void pulse worked, before I leave for Wizulaan."

Wizulaan? Wizulaan! Lily had forgotten all about it.

"Do you still have enough night time to make the trip, *Vapa*?"

"Yes. There are many hours of darkness left, more than enough for me to journey to the wizard town and back. I will do all that I can to 'Be safe', as you have requested."

Vadom then lowered his chin as he raised his brows, waiting attentively for Lily to elaborate. She hastened to explain, suddenly aware of time passing. When she had relived the whole attempt aloud to her *vapa*, he gave a nod of approval.

"I am pleased to hear that the night magic obeyed you so readily. It is also notable that you heard the click, and that you observed the stillness of the Void element when the spell was truly complete. The stillness is indicative of a well-made pulse. I take it then that the pulse informed you as instructed? I know only that it delivered your message clearly, which was also well done of you."

Lily hesitated, having already omitted her exact inquiry in favor of a very vague and brief explanation. She should have known her *vapa* wouldn't let her get away with that.

"I told the pulse to discover . . . the state of your mental well-being," Lily said, rather too casually, borrowing one of Vadom's own earlier phrases.

"And are you reassured, *Vipina*?"

He asked without a hint of censure in his tone or his gaze, which he held steadily to her own. It was that patience that gave Lily the courage to speak honestly, from her heart.

"I am glad that I can bring you a measure of happiness, even though my *vama* cannot be here," Lily said, very softly. In an even quieter voice, she added, "You make me happy too, *Vapa*."

Vadom's eyes widened as she spoke, and he looked away for just a moment when Lily finished speaking. It was the first time Lily could remember her *vapa* ever breaking eye contact with her. She knew a heartbeat of uncertainty before Vadom looked into her eyes once more. Then it was her turn for rounded eyes. There was a wealth of emotion in his face, much more than she had yet seen. Her *vapa* was letting her see it.

Slowly, he made her the *valoriad,* and held it for several moments. Then, without a word, Vadom turned and left the cave.

Lily wasn't able to move right away, still a bit stunned by what she had just seen.

"Your praetam *is really opening up to you,* faelani. *I'll admit that wasn't quite the reaction I was expecting. You were brave, to speak first, and truly. He has, however, repaid you in kind."*

It was almost strange, to see him so animated! Normally I'm looking for little clues in his eyes, on his face . . . but that was quite different.

"Indeed. It seems a vampire is raised to be like . . . a frozen river. Though the surface gives little away, much runs just beneath the ice unseen."

Lily thought this might be an accurate description of a certain silver Fae as well, but she kept that to herself for now. She wanted to consider carefully how best to strengthen Alder's confidence, if that really was something he needed, and if she was the best person to do it. Lily found that she was more than willing to take on the task on Alder's behalf. It made Lily a bit nervous that she was getting so invested in her truemate so quickly and so easily, as though she hadn't given herself enough time to just be his friend before wading into deeper and unfamiliar territory. And yet, even as it unsettled her, Lily could admit to herself that she was a little excited, too. After losing her mother in such a terrifying way, Lily was fairly certain she would have closed her broken heart to all others for a very long time without Alder's presence when she needed someone most. It was a relief to know she had avoided at least one negative consequence of that night in Japeta. With that thought, Lily took a breath and turned her mind fully to Alder, who seemed unsure of her contemplative state.

I think you are right about vampires, Alder, at least if the rest are like my vapa. *And to discover that in the midst of my first Void lesson . . . I'm learning so much, about so many things.*

"I believe it's becoming a really eye-opening trip for everyone concerned, Lily. Still, I think you should take this opportunity to clear your mind and rest a bit. It might be nice to wash up with that natural basin of water. And then . . . well, I would like to propose some alternatives to your iron situation, faelani. *I think it's becoming too much of a burden, more than it needs to be to remain effective. Would you please talk with me about it?"*

Lily was a little startled by Alder's words, but she could hardly deny the reality of their situation: the iron was really starting to take its toll on her. She could barely walk due to the pain, and the Fear was growing at a much faster rate than she could now get rid of, which endangered Alder, her inner magic, and her mind. Despite all of that, he had still asked, not demanded, that she make adjustments, and for that consideration of her independence, Lily was both relieved and grateful.

I can't really argue with that, Alder. I hope you've come up with some good ideas, because I haven't given it any proper thought, though I guess I should have been considering possibilities. What are you thinking?

Lily carefully knelt down at the edge of the little pool of water as she waited for Alder to answer. He remained silent, as though gathering his thoughts, so Lily carefully cupped the cool water and splashed it on her face and neck. She belatedly opened the haversack and dug for the medical pack, extracting the bar of soap upon completing a quick search. After giving her face, neck, and hands a quick but thorough wash, Lily hesitated. Alder was hovering pensively near her wells of power, as he had been for some time. Nowhere near the ring of her sensory awareness. Before she could talk herself out of it, Lily carefully unbuckled the straps of her cuirass and lifted the whole thing over her head, carefully checking her inner magic as it tried to escape the confines of her wells of power. Without pause, she took off her damp long-sleeved tunic and scrubbed under her arms, blushing a bit as she did. Just as Lily was rinsing off, Alder finally spoke up, his tone very serious.

"I was just thinking, Lily, that perhaps you could put some clothing on—"

Lily burst into laughter, unable to contain her mirth. She rolled onto her side, the better to catch her breath as she slowly subsided into chuckling.

"—underneath some of your iron," Alder finished uncertainly. *"You find this a cause for joy,* faelani? *I am confused, though I am glad your heart is light."*

Still fighting the occasional small paroxysm of snickering, Lily managed to reply.

No, Alder, I'm just being silly. What were you saying?

Perplexed, Alder repeated himself. Lily avoided a relapse by focusing on him intently.

I think this may be a good compromise, Alder. It will tone down the effects of the iron, but I'll still be firmly bound. I'll just have to be careful as I make the switch, so that I don't give off a love element signature like the day we entered Ropaz and Vapa *had to remove my breastplate.*

"Good thinking. I'll stay by your inner magic and keep an eye on things. I'll let you know if the Fear acts up. Be careful, faelani.*"*

Over the next half an hour, Lily proceeded to remove portions of armor and jewelry a little at a time, quickly washing and rinsing her body as she went. She was disturbed to find that her greaves and cuisses had dug deeply into her skin, causing both angry redness and terribly discolored bruises all over her legs. Lily was relieved to slip on a clean pair of leggings before replacing the armor and pulling a second pair of leggings over top. She decided to wear her sleeveless tunic once more, then buckled the cuirass with its riveted plackart and coulet back on over it. Lily cinched her large belt, sheath and dagger still attached, around her hips with a grimace. Her arm bands and bangles, necklaces and earrings she replaced as they had been on her skin. Lily was accustomed to wearing the jewelry, and she could already sense her inner magic pushing against her diminished iron pain. It wouldn't do to tip the delicate balance she was attempting. Lily jumped in surprise when a Void pulse bounced off of her protective sphere without warning. She realized her *vapa* was checking up on her, as he had said he would, and she concluded her efforts feeling reassured by his vigilance.

Lily finished by pulling on her jacket, which she had yet to wear. The clean garment, made of woven and dyed amadel hair, reminded Lily of cool desert nights, when her mother would sing forbidden songs in her quietest voice. Only laments, after all, could be sung in the Joquobon. Yet her mother had often flouted that rule. She had taught Lily her numbers and letters as a small child, and then history and healing as a young girl, with memorable little melodies. Lily found herself humming the tune she'd been taught to help her memorize a long list of uncommon herbs and roots when she felt a surge from one of her wells of power.

"Lily! What did you just do? I think you've taken too much iron off— your magic is reacting too strongly. There was a lot less Fear near here until a moment ago as well. What's going on?"

Nothing, Alder. I was very careful, and the only thing that has changed is the pair of leggings layered under my greaves and cuisses. I guess my belt is on the outside of my tunic now as well. But honestly, I didn't even bother taking down my hair. I was just humming to myself because my jacket reminded me of my mother.

"Well, that sounds about right, seeing as the armor has been bothering you so much more than the jewelry— wait. You were thinking of your mother . . . and humming? Would I know the song?"

Lily could tell by Alder's forced nonchalance that he was not asking idle questions.

I know a lot of songs, Alder, Lily said, feeling just a touch defensive. *The one I was humming just now wasn't really a song, though. It's just a melody to help me remember a bunch of lesser-known roots and herbs with unusual healing properties. My mother taught it to me in secret.*

"*Music,*" Alder said, sounding a bit dazed. "Faelani, *I think one of your wells of power, the one that just surged, contains your musical wings. The barest hint of a song, of your singing voice, set it off. This is another of your inner magic gifts, Lily.*"

Lily felt as stunned as Alder sounded. It seemed as though they had figured out what another of her nine wells of power held. She was a bit surprised they hadn't discovered this one before now . . . and yet, she hadn't felt at all like singing since before . . . since before. Lily wondered if they should test this new inner magic a little more, or if that would be pushing their luck too far. The Fear had definitely wanted a piece of that music-related magic, after all.

Should I try humming again, just to make sure? It really didn't hurt all that much, Alder. I'm in better shape with my extra leggings on, honestly.

"*Well, if you're certain it won't bother you, perhaps you could hum the first dozen herbs or so. We'll need to let Vadom know about this, just so he's informed on your sensitivity to music. Not that it's come up much so far in our journey, but it won't hurt to make him aware of this accidental discovery.*"

Not needing further encouragement, Lily cautiously began humming the start of the list, mentally reciting the words for Alder's benefit.

'Good to know each healing herb,
Odd though helpful for pain to curb.
Many the deeply earthen root,
Will often aid to make hurts moot.
Know you acorus, agar agar, anise—'

"Don't forget 'sherdios', young fairy. Good for achy joints if you don't have beggars' buttons handy, even if it is a bit slimy," said a cheerful voice.

The Gongoozler

LILY FROZE, THEN SLOWLY OPENED HER EYES, hardly daring to find out who had just spoken aloud in her little cave. Her hand slowly crept toward the dagger on her belt, even as she pushed back against the painful twinge of inner magic the stranger's words caused her. Lily didn't dare reach for the sword in her haversack until she knew more about who she was dealing with. She only vaguely registered Alder's spike of alarm.

"Lily, what is it? Why are you so upset all of a sudden? You can handle the Fear at this level, faelani, *I know you can. It's less now than it has been recently—"*

Alder. There's a man at the cave's opening. He just spoke to me.

"WHAT? Give me his race, age, weapons, and intent, Lily. Assess him as a threat, quickly."

Lily could hardly believe how immediately Alder responded to her panic. She could feel him racing to her sensory awareness even now. Determined to answer him, Lily took a good look at the male standing, apparently without a care in the world, at the mouth of her hiding place. The only exit.

I can't tell much with the moon back-lighting him, but his voice sounded deep and mature, like a middle-aged man maybe. Unarmed, I think. At least, his hands are free, for what that's worth. And I don't think he means me harm at the moment. He already gave away the element of surprise, after all.

"He might just be waiting for you to move. He may have heard you, but he can't see you, not with a Void sphere like this one. Stay still, faelani, *and try not to make a sound. What did he say to you before?"*

He told me not to forget sherdios, for aching joints. He called me a young fairy as well.

Lily held her breath as Alder's tension built. She knew the moment he reached her eyes and beheld their unexpected visitor, for his hesitant relief was palpable to her.

"I think I know him. He is an elf, a very old one."

Lily felt a measure of her own relief, mixed in with sheer surprise.

Who do you think he is, then?

"I fully respect your healthy sense of self-preservation, young Fae lady, but I will not harm you. I just thought to swing by and offer my greetings when I heard your laughter. One can never resist the unpretentious and unrestrained joy of youth, and fairies really do have the best laughter in all of Lamoranth."

"Oh, that settles it. He is definitely the Gongoozler."

"The Gongoozler?"

Lily accidentally spoke aloud, then froze once more.

The man at the entrance, however, was clearly delighted.

"Ah, my reputation precedes me! That is the title I've claimed this age, just a little inside joke. No need to go into particulars, but it amuses the Elf Lord a great deal, and one never ought to give up the opportunity to entertain the leader of an entire race. But enough about me. What quest brings you so far from home, young fairy lady, hmmm?"

Unsure of how to best to answer this strange being, Lily countered with a question of her own.

"Could I not ask the same of you, Gongoozler? We are a very long way from the Forest of Ancients, after all."

The elf clapped his hands together in apparent excitement. A shower of stars burst out of his ears simultaneously. Lily gasped in surprise in spite of herself.

"Ah, she possesses a sharp wit, wonderful, wonderful! You will certainly need it out in the wide world, my new Fae acquaintance. Now, can you see my unassuming self a bit more clearly? Feel a little more comfortable, perhaps?"

Lily readily studied the Gongoozler's features in the new starry glow of the cave. Only a little taller than herself, his body was slender, but not without strength. His long, pale green hair was shot through with strands of gray, and it hung loose just past his shoulders. The occasional braid twisted random green locks from his face. His skin was a soft shade of light brown, and finely lined, as if his mouth turned up and eyes crinkled into a smile often. The Gongoozler's clothing was unassuming, but Lily could see that it was very well made, the stitches tiny and perfectly straight, with subtly embroidered designs. He had a bow, a quiver of arrows, and a little pack upon his back. Lily wondered what it held.

Is it safe to speak with this elf, Alder? I don't want to tell him anything if he is not.

"He'll try to get information out of you anyway, Lily. That's what he excels at: meddling in the business of every being in Lamoranth. Goodness knows he's had a lot of practice. I've seen him at Silver Court several times, checking up on all the notable Fae present, getting a sense of the court's favor on certain issues, seeing how well the magical balance is being upheld. He knows everything about everyone, but he's not one to share what he knows, not even to Elf Lord, or so they say. My theory is that he just likes knowing things, for the sake of knowing them. Or being the only person to know something, or simply being the first person to know something. Anyway, the Gongoozler is considered a nomad, and rather an oddity. Any being you meet who's lived more than an age, though, is bound to be at least a little eccentric. If you want to speak with him, I think it's alright, but if you say very much, he'll put it all together very quickly. It's uncanny, the way he extrapolates . . . then again, he's just about seen it all. I think that's part of why he's always full of surprises."

Lily regarded the visitor with renewed interest. What wonders had he seen?

"Have you really seen it all, Gongoozler? Have you seen a giant?"

The elf chuckled.

"Not in a very, very long time, young Fae. And I certainly hope I have not seen everything, for what could I seek to discover then? No, there is much to keep me busy these days, even putting the recent troll disturbance aside. At the moment, I look to confirm a mere whisper of a rumor, about some very nasty creatures working together, and off I go, into the great white desert. Have you heard of the Joquobon, my little Fae petal? It is a hot, dry place, with little water and no magic at all. Sand is of exquisite quality, though. A jar of it makes quite the birthday gift, I can tell you."

Lily felt sick at the thought of word spreading about the xydolem attack, however insubstantial. Should she ask him to remain silent about it? Would he listen to her, or pry for more information than she could safely give?

"Lily, if I was in the Fae Wood, and I had heard your story, I would have paid the Gongoozler to relate it to the Elf Lord as soon as the opportunity

presented itself. I think you should tell him, if you can bear it. The sooner the elves know, the better. They are much closer to the Misruler if that being is in the north, after all. They need to know what is happening beyond the borders of their forest."

Lily took a deep breath and gathered her courage. She felt Alder's silent support as she began to speak.

"Gongoozler, I will tell you about the xydolem attack, if you give me your word you will tell the Elf Lord about it as soon as you can."

She watched as the elf went completely still. His gaze went from observant to acutely focused in an instant.

"I will give you my word if you speak truly, Fae lady. First, however, I would ask you if we have time before your vampire guardian returns, or if he will mind my conversation with you should he come back in the midst of your tale."

Lily hesitated again, not sure of what her *vapa* would think of this.

"He is guardian, not master, for you have not asked for my help to escape, you keep your own counsel, and you laugh without reserve. He is a vampire, an old and powerful one, for he has so perfected the making of a Void sphere that even I cannot see it or you, even after several minutes of effort. If he's gathering food for you, or drinking for himself, it would have to be from Wizulaan, which doesn't give us much time, especially if he's been gone long enough for you to lower your vigilance. What do you think, fairy petal?"

Oh my.

"I know, and that was nothing. You haven't even actually told him anything yet. Wait until you really hear him get going."

Lily thought the elf's words over briefly, then made her decision. Slowly, she began to form a Void pulse, twisting a piece away, shaping it with her intent, and piercing it with a message. When it froze, she was certain it would find her *vapa* and give her his relative location, as well as whether or not he had a horse in tow. He would also know about her unexpected visitor. Without delay, Lily firmly directed it out of her right hand, and off it sped, much to the Gongoozler's surprise.

"Goodness, what an impressive Void pulse! So he's in Wizulaan for your sustenance, not his own, I take it. He must be repaying a blood debt to you with Void instruction like that. I haven't seen a sun-magicked vampire in ages, literally, yet here is one now, and at such a crossroads in time . . . quite possibly fortuitous, certainly interesting. Worth pondering for a bit, for where is his otherwing? Not here, or she'd be doing the talking. Left behind in the Cave Kingdom? Most likely, for he wouldn't be able to bear leaving her anywhere else, even if that Vheneir is causing trouble . . . Is your night magic pulse back yet? He must still be in Wizulaan then. We'll have time for your story, I believe. This is sure to be unique, an increasingly amazing prospect. A very young Fae girl in the Joquobon Desert? When did she get there? Why does she speak fluent Ropazian? How is she connected to a coordinated xydolem attack? So many unknowns, and her astute silence offers little in the way of answers. The vampire has clearly begun teaching her the value of maintaining one's composure. Puzzling, very mysterious indeed. Oh, and there's your pulse returned. All is well?"

Lily nodded, then realized the Gongoozler couldn't see the movement. The pulse had confirmed that Vadom was in Wizulaan, in the process of leading a peculiarly docile and very strange-looking beast out of a stable. He had somehow managed to implant his own message into her Void pulse: 'Be careful what you say. Ask Alder'. That settled it. Her *vapa* must know of the Gongoozler, and he believed she was safe enough in the elf's presence.

"All is well, as long as I speak carefully," Lily responded with a small smile. Then, abruptly remembering her manners, she added, "Please feel free to sit. Can I offer you any food or water?"

The Gongoozler shook his head as he fluidly sat down.

"Thank you for your offer, but I eat as little of Ropazian food as possible. So utilitarian and plain, utterly uninspired cuisine. Once you've had a few meals in the Wood, I expect you'll know what I mean. The Fae certainly know how to make magic in the kitchen."

Lily wanted to ask him if he had ever tried cheese, but he nodded benignly and began to speak again.

"As for the words of your vampire guardian, I think that speaking carefully goes, conversely, without saying, no matter who you are talking to, really. Now, I confess, though I do not normally, to a measure of excitement. This tale is still unfolding, after all. Those are the best kind, in my experience. Would you mind telling me if you are starting at the beginning, or somewhere in the middle?"

Lily thought that over, but she wasn't entirely certain she knew it all herself. It did seem a pretty sure thing that her mother had withheld pertinent knowledge, and that the scroll might contain part of it. Where to start with this Gongoozler, though?

"I think it depends on who you ask. This may be the middle, but it is my beginning in it."

The elf's face took on a look of bliss.

"She sees beyond herself, to what makes the past and future of her present. A little prophetess, perhaps? Not that the Fae will let me know, stubborn saplings. As if the gryffyns haven't been grumbling about Magentay for the last few eons. Now though, time to listen."

He focused the whole of his intensity on Lily once more, and she took a deep breath. Pushing aside his incredible words, she began to speak without further delay. Lily told the Gongoozler nearly everything, except her mother's name and her own. She explained their precipitous flight from Nather's tribe, and, skipping the stop for iron armor, she haltingly related the terrible night in Japeta. Lily tried with all her will to keep her emotions in check, yet she couldn't help shedding a few tears. One muted sob escaped, though Lily was more or less able to keep herself together. She omitted Alder entirely, and skimmed her meeting with Vadom, concluding merely by telling the Gongoozler that she sought to reach the Fae Wood to fulfill her mother's last wishes. It was all she could do to take a few measured breaths after saying her piece. The elf looked very serious, and very sad, for many long minutes. Finally, when Lily was feeling a little calmer, he looked up from his folded hands and spoke.

"My deepest condolences, little Fae lady, on the loss of your mother. I grieve with you, for I think she must have been quite exceptional, especially for you."

"Thank you, Gongoozler."

Lily didn't know what else to say, so she didn't try to find more words.

"Are you going to be alright, Lily? If I had my body, I would send this nosy elf on his way. At least we know that the elves will soon be aware of the threat this Misruler poses in Lamoranth. You are so strong, to be telling this painful story yet again."

Lily sent thankful feelings in Alder's direction, but didn't say anything more. She felt exhausted. She wanted to sleep, but she knew it wasn't wise with Vadom still out. Realizing he should be returning soon, Lily wondered if he would wish to speak with the Gongoozler.

"Would you like to wait for my *vapa* to get back, Gongoozler?"

The elf looked up from his folded hands again, as though pulled from his thoughts.

"Yes, I think I would, if you don't mind extending the hospitality of your cave for a little longer. So he is your *'vapa'*, hmmm? Extraordinary! I've never heard of such a thing occurring—does that make you a *vipin ... -i*? An adopted female fairy child, going through the extreme rigors of a vampire warrior's education, imagine! But I think you must have left out some of your story, little petal, for no blood debt would compel an honest vampire to make such an enormous decision, and without his otherwing, too. This blood must have saved his life, yes, and it is life debt that has started you down such an unusual path. Fascinating . . ."

Lily was rather relieved when the Gongoozler lapsed into contemplative silence once more. The next thing she said would probably give Alder away, and that was one thing she truly did not wish for this elf to know. It was just too much of a risk for her friend. Lily resolved to be silent until her *vapa* returned. Deciding another Void pulse would be excellent practice, Lily carefully formed one, waited for the stillness, and sent it. She was startled when it immediately bounced back, rather forcefully colliding with her stomach.

"Oof," she wheezed on impact.

Both Alder and the Gongoozler found this entertaining, much to her chagrin.

After a few little soul-chuckles, Alder made sure she hadn't done herself an injury, amusement still in his voice. Lily might have been a tad peeved, but unreserved amusement from him was still rare enough that she just let it go, allowing his happiness to dissolve her pique. Somehow, Lily could already detect a pattern in the making.

"Are you quite all right in there, little Fae lady? I take it your vampire has returned?"

"Yes to both, Gongoozler."

"Why don't we go out and greet him? The quieting spell he used to calm that horse isn't going to last much longer, and the poor thing is going to be terrified upon realizing she has a vampire keeper. Let's see if we can help, hmmm?"

Lily didn't ask how the elf knew her *vapa* had procured a horse. She didn't think she really wanted to know what mental feats of agility the Gongoozler had performed to reach the correct conclusion, or what magic he possessed that had accurately assessed the situation. Either way, it was time to learn how to ride a horse. Lily felt a mixture of nerves and excitement at the prospect. She found herself eagerly following the elf out of the cave, then stopped herself. Vadom had asked her to wait in the cave until he got back, and even if the Gongoozler had heard him, she had not. Lily hovered indecisively at the cave's entrance. Though she strained her eyes for a glimpse of her *vapa*, the landscape was illuminated only by the light of a half-moon tonight, and she couldn't see him.

The Gongoozler stood about a dozen steps from the mouth of the cave, facing west expectantly. Suddenly, Vadom and an odd, sleepy-looking beast appeared a little in front of the elf, as though her *vapa* had abruptly taken down a Void sphere. Though neither of them moved or spoke for many long moments, Lily was completely diverted by the horse. The Void pulse had given her the slightest glimpse, but it was nothing to seeing such an animal in the flesh. The most unusual thing to her eyes what that the horse had only four legs. That probably made its gait entirely different from what she was used to sitting. The hair was very short, and a rich brown color. Its ears where tiny, and Lily wondered how she was to direct it once she was riding. Before she could speculate further, however, her *vapa* spoke up at last.

"Gongoozler."

"Yes, that's me. I believe I recognize you, though some time has passed... Vadom, isn't it? Yes, I never forget a face, even the most impassive ones. You are otherwing to the bold and beautiful Vabiri, as I recall. Good evening. I've just had the pleasure of meeting your delightful little fairy lady. I believe you are making for the Fae Wood? Most intelligent of you, as I doubt she will be very safe anywhere else. Now, to the task at hand: would you like me to calm this mare and teach the lady the basics of riding a horse? Not that I think the two of you couldn't figure it out, but it might save you some time."

Vadom gave the Gongoozler another probing look, but the elf remained perfectly calm and did not shift his gaze.

"Will you first give me your word, Gongoozler, that you will only speak of her physical appearance to the Elf Lord, on pain of death?"

"I swear on the Forest of Ancients that I will reveal the lady's appearance to no one but the Elf Lord, on pain of death. I think I know why you ask this of me, for I already have an idea of who she is— there are only so many fairy ladies known to be outside the Wood who could also be the mother of this child, after all. You need not fear that I will tell any Ropazians. Now, let us see if we can help this horse."

Vadom nodded in agreement and lifted the spell he had cast on the mare. Lily's heart gave a pang when the horse immediately whinnied in fear. Eyes rolling and tiny ears laying all the way back on her head, she stamped her front hooves in obvious terror. Vadom took several steps backward, even as the Gongoozler stepped forward, already speaking a stream of soothing words to the horse. After a few moments, the mare seemed to calm down a little. The elf spoke to her some more, slowly approaching, gently coaxing, his voice so musical it was nearly a song. Vadom walked over to Lily, who stood watching, eyes wide, as the Gongoozler tamed the horse.

"He bewitches her without magic, *Vapa*," Lily said, tearing her gaze away to look at him directly. He seemed perfectly calm, as always, yet she had not forgotten his shockingly open countenance from before. *Frozen river once more*, Lily thought.

"So it would seem, faelani. *Are you excited to learn to ride a horse? Once she's completely gentled, of course. It should be fine if Vadom keeps his distance."*

Lily smiled a little at the concern in Alder's voice. Apparently he was a bit nervous, too.

"How was your rest in the cave, *Vipina*? Obviously not entirely uneventful, but you have energy enough for the day ahead? It would be best to continue east for a time after sunrise, I think."

Just as Lily was about to reassure him, Alder gave her a mental nudge.

"Don't forget, we need to tell him about your musical wings, Lily. Best to keep him current on what we know of your inner magic."

Lily started in surprise. She'd totally forgotten about their inadvertent discovery in the excitement of the Gongoozler's arrival. Lily quickly thanked Alder, then told her *vapa* what they'd found out in her quietest whisper. Vadom took a moment to absorb the news.

"What a pleasant revelation for you, *Vipina*. It shouldn't be too difficult to limit your exposure to singing or instrumentation until reaching the Fae Wood. Thank you for letting me know."

Instrumentation? Like a hand drum, Alder?

"Fairies have and play a large number of instruments, Lily. The hand drum is just one option available to musically inclined Fae. I'll make sure you are introduced to all of them, and then you can learn to play whichever ones you get excited about."

Sort of like the weapons lessons I've gotten from Vapa?

"Yes, only music is largely for fun, a form of art designed to help Fae explore their emotions and express their inner selves. Most fairies learn how to dance to music as well."

Dance?

"Perhaps I should leave you in suspense, faelani. *It would be a wonderful surprise for you."*

Lily heard the excitement in Alder's voice and decided not to ask him about dancing again until they were home. Clearly, he thought it would be the most fun for her to find out about this firsthand, and it did give her something else to anticipate at the end of their journey. She was just about to tell him so when Vadom spoke to her softly.

"I think we have encountered a bit of good fortune, *Vipina.* I was only going to be able to instruct you to ride the horse based on my observations of Ropazians riding them. I had hoped that your familiarity with amadels would be foundation enough for you to make adjustments as necessary. I find it infinitely preferable, however, that you learn to ride from someone with a great deal of experience doing so. An elf is better still, for no one understands beasts and wild things as the elves do. Are you ready for him to see you?"

Lily nodded, then began walking slowly toward the Gongoozler and her new mount. She could sense Vadom altering the Void sphere so that she would be visible. The elf looked up just then from his hands, which had been making soothing paths up and down the horse's neck. When he caught sight of Lily, he froze. Lily did, too. He had looked at her with horror in his eyes. In the next moment, however, the Gongoozler was absolutely livid.

"What is the meaning of this, Vadom? Explain yourself! How could you do something so vile to a fairy child? It is beyond shame!"

Before Lily could blink, Vadom was standing in front of her, his stance unmistakably defensive.

"Explain about the armor, faelani, *and quickly, before they come to blows. The elves are hot-tempered, but they listen to reason. Make him see why it is necessary— tell him of your promise."*

"Wait! Gongoozler, please do not blame my *vapa,* for the iron I wear is not his doing. I promised my mother I would wear it until I reached the Fae Wood. It was the only way she knew how to give me a real chance to make it across the south of Lamoranth without being detected. So far, it has worked well, especially in conjunction with Void spheres. Please don't be angry."

After another heated moment, Lily saw Vadom relax his stance. He stepped aside so that Lily and the Gongoozler could see each other once more. The elf looked at her again, no longer with fury, but with his face full of a look Lily barely recognized. Pity. She found that her heart could not accept it. Staring the elf straight in the eye, Lily decided to take control of the situation.

"With all due respect, Gongoozler, dawn is approaching, and I would like to be riding this horse into the sunrise. Would you please be so kind as to begin your instruction?"

The elf gazed into her eyes for a time, and Lily watched with secret satisfaction as the pity disappeared. He was thinking again, but those thoughts were obviously chaotic. In the next moment, though, the Gongoozler shook his head, clearly attempting to focus on the task at hand.

"Whatever is the world coming to?" he mumbled softly to himself, sounding very old.

Lily walked the rest of the way to him. When she reached him, she tried to answer, even though he hadn't really asked her.

"Perhaps it is what it has always been, and we are the ones who are changing. And if things are difficult, isn't it good that we begin to see the world for what it really is? And isn't it thrilling to find ourselves more capable of living than we'd ever imagined? Do not lose heart or hope, for you will surely have need of both, Gongoozler."

Lily felt Alder stir inside her mind.

"Ah, faelani, *only you could manage to deliver the wisdom of youth to an ancient elf without giving offense. I think you've really made an impression on him."*

I think I'll settle for not insulting him. I didn't mean to lecture, he just seemed to need comforting words, so I offered what came to mind.

"Then I think you must have inherited some of your mother's healing instincts, Lily, for that is just what the best healers do: they see pain or distress, and they find a way to soothe, no matter who it is, no matter what the circumstances. You have shown him that you are proud, strong, and wise, a lady of the Fae, and he will not forget it."

Lily looked into the face of the Gongoozler once more, and, upon seeing him apparently mulling over her words, she approached the horse cautiously. She glanced back at her *vapa,* who was watching both the horse and her carefully. Lily smiled bravely at him and turned intently to the horse. She came close, allowing the beast to get used to her presence. The mare didn't seem troubled by her. Lily began to speak softly to her. In her most soothing voice, she told the horse of her great need to reach the Fae

Wood, of her promises, and of the danger too. Lily whispered about her *vapa,* and how good and honorable his heart was, how much she cared for him. In an even quieter whisper, Lily informed her that this particular vampire teacher didn't need blood anymore, especially not the blood of beautiful horses. She told the mare that her mount now must be as noble as Bepo, the imperturbable amadel she had ridden before. Then she absently asked the horse for her name.

WHIRLWIND

Lily was down on her knees in the next instant as iron pain slammed forcefully through her entire body.

"Lily! Hang on, get control of it. You can do this. I am a fool for not thinking of this sooner— your wings of elucidation must be powerful enough to allow you to communicate with beasts and beings who do not use their mouths to speak. That takes powerful magic. How are we going to keep the horse from talking to you? Where is Vadom? Where is the Gongoozler? One of them needs to get you away from the horse, or you need to back away yourself. Keep fighting, Lily, that's it."

Lily fought the pain and Fear from her wells of magic, then opened her eyes with an effort. Her *vapa* and the Gongoozler where both looking at her with a great deal of concern just a few feet away.

"*Vipina,* are you well? What happened?"

"I found out that her name is Whirlwind, *Vapa.*"

Vadom's eyes widened slightly, but he said nothing. His gaze slid to the elf beside him, then back to her in question. Lily shrugged. The Gongoozler probably knew more about her inner magic than she did by now. Still, no need to elaborate at this point. Lily stood on shaky feet and concentrated on the mare once more. She rubbed her hands up and down Whirlwind's neck as she had seen the elf do, complimenting her lovely name all the while.

When Lily reached Whirlwind's back, she hesitated. The mare was narrow and barrel-chested, not like an amadel's wide, scooped proportions at all. There was something buckled to her back that must be meant for sitting, but Lily wasn't sure how to get up. She glanced down and saw a loop hanging down from Whirlwind's side. For her foot, apparently. Looking back up and seeing a handle of sorts just at the base of the mare's neck, Lily grabbed ahold of it, put her toes carefully into the loop, and gave a bit of a hop to propel herself upward. She nearly failed at getting her other leg over, for her iron aches certainly hadn't diminished. Lily was almost surprised, then, when she realized she was successfully sitting atop Whirlwind. She put her other toes in the other loop, then looked over at Vadom and the Gongoozler and grinned at them, feeling a thrill from doing something new. A short laugh escaped her as the feeling shot through her.

"Well done, *Vipina,*" Vadom solemnly said with pride in his eyes. Lily knew it wasn't just for her success with the horse so far.

When she turned to measure the Gongoozler's reaction, she received a bit of a surprise. Her laughter appeared to have jarred him out of his thoughts like nothing else could have. He was shaking his head, as though to clear it, even as he looked at her upon the horse. He began walking smoothly toward her, his gaze more assessing now.

"If you have the strength of will to learn with an iron breastplate and belt on, I must at least be ready to teach you what you wish to know, Fae lady. First, however, let me have a word with this Whirlwind of yours."

He went to the mare's head and spoke to her gently. Lily missed some of it, although she thought she caught 'her special ears hear you' and 'listening hurts like spurs'. After another soothing sentence or two, Whirlwind nickered. Lily could have sworn the noise sounded almost deliberately reassuring. The Gongoozler rubbed the mare's nose, then turned back to Lily.

"She understands that she shouldn't try to talk to you, fairy petal. Now, let's make some adjustments to the way you're sitting the horse."

Lily listened carefully as the elf named and pointed out all the parts of the horse and the saddle. He proceeded to describe the ideal posture, how to handle the reins, and how to use the stirrups. She saw his shoulders tense when he noticed the armor on her calves and thighs. He had been explaining how she could steer her horse with her legs only, in the event that she lost her grip on the reins or ever had to ride without a saddle. No mention of her hidden iron was made, however. He patiently watched and helped as Lily practiced riding in loose circles near the cave. Lily felt herself growing warm, both from the exertion and from the heat of the rising sun, and took off her jacket. The Gongoozler's eyes went wide at the sight of her jewelry, but again he remained silent. Lily listened to all he said about riding at different speeds, on varying terrain, and how to watch for Whirlwind's nonverbal communication. Finally, after telling Lily what she needed to know about taking care of her horse, the Gongoozler pronounced her informed enough to travel safely.

"May this help to speed you to your rightful place, young Fae lady.

It seems your *vapa* has chosen a very good mount for you, a mare who is spirited but steady too. Why don't you take a break while I help Whirlwind, ah, acclimate to his presence? Then I'll feel better as we part ways."

Lily nodded her agreement and slipped rather clumsily from Whirlwind's back. Her legs ached more than ever. She wobbled uncertainly for a moment before steadying herself against her new mare. Before she made for the cave and some breakfast, however, Lily spoke once more into Whirlwind's ear, reminding her of what she'd said about her *vapa* earlier. "I trust him, and so can you," she finished in a whisper.

It only took Lily a moment to retrieve her haversack from the little cave, and Vadom was still standing several feet away from Whirlwind when she exited with her burden. The Gongoozler was speaking to him intently. Lily felt a little uneasy, and she hoped they hadn't begun to argue.

"I can see why you are concerned, Lily, but I have a good idea of their topics of discussion. You don't need to worry."

If it concerns me, why can't I be a part of the conversation? What can't they say in front of me?

Lily felt Alder's uncertainty and indecision, and it bothered her.

"It may have to do with you, but it could also be about the vampire trouble too. This would be a good opportunity for Vadom to let the Elf Lord know about Vheneir and his blatant threats to Ropazians. The Gongoozler may have asked him for more information about it, which would make sense. I think Vadom may very well have been a member of the Supreme Council, and his take on matters would be of import to other rulers. The elves and vampires are neighbors after all, and I know they've always kept a wary eye on each other."

Lily mulled this over, and she had to admit it was a possibility. That didn't mean she had to accept it without a murmur, however. She straightened her spine, folded her hands over her chest, and kicked a small rock in their general direction. It made a satisfying amount of noise as it ricocheted off of other stones littered about the mouth of the cave. Both Vadom and the Gongoozler immediately looked her way. Lily raised a brow and gave them a look that she hoped conveyed something to the effect of: Might I walk within earshot now? The Gongoozler looked like he wanted to laugh, but didn't quite dare, so he smiled widely instead. Vadom, however, raised an eyebrow right back at her. Lily knew that look. She stood no chance against it. Better to give in as gracefully as possible now and ask questions later.

"Has Whirlwind gotten used to your proximity, *Vapa?*" she asked in her most innocent voice.

Alder started laughing inside her mind, even as she dropped her stance and started walking toward the others.

"So impertinent, faelani. *I can't wait to see you in action when we finally make it home."*

Lily smiled but didn't reply, for she had stopped walking and fixed her attention on the pair before her, still a short distance away. Vadom had turned his gaze toward Whirlwind, who regarded him nervously. She didn't lose her head, though. Slowly, he approached her. The mare's skin flickered, and she tossed her mane a bit fractiously, but she stood her ground. Vadom looked her in the eye, and he seemed surprised by what he saw. Then, before he made another deliberate move, Whirlwind stretched out her neck and touched her velvety nose to his chest, directly over his heart. Vadom, as still as he normally was, seemed frozen in place. After a long moment, Whirlwind moved away and nickered. She didn't seem frightened at all. Instead, she moved on to the Gongoozler and nudged his hand hopefully.

"Did you hear what she said to you, Vadom?" the elf asked softly.

When Vadom shook his head, the Gongoozler translated, though Lily, much to her relief, hadn't been standing close enough to hear the words.

"She said, 'The golden girl trusts your good heart, and so do I.'"

Lily casually sat down and began digging in the haversack for food, her heart beating a little fast. She hadn't thought Whirlwind would repeat what she'd said! Still, if it meant that her *vapa* could levitate or run near her as she rode, it was for the best. Out of the corner of her eye, Lily tried to gauge her *vapa*'s reaction. He was gently petting Whirlwind's long neck, and his face showed a totally uncharacteristic absentmindedness. Lily had never seen Vadom quite so unaware. She found herself thinking she ought to scan their surroundings, just in case . . .

"I think Vadom might be attempting to speak to Whirlwind, Lily. He's never really had the opportunity to try communicating with a horse before. After the number of quieting spells he's worked on such animals, it might take him a bit to start listening, and then to hear them, if he as a vampire is able. I do not believe, though, that he would ever lack enough vigilance to allow enemies near you. Please, don't worry."

Lily, however, couldn't quite shake her feeling of uneasiness as she consumed a modest meal from the remainder of the Wikkenod supplies. She shared that feeling with Alder, who seemed troubled by it.

"We must let Vadom know about this, and the Gongoozler as well. From here, his journey will be about as lengthy as the remainder of ours, and he is much more likely to encounter Ropazians and vampires on his route. Does your well of prophecy shed any light on this? Will it hurt you too much to check?"

Lily honestly wasn't sure. She cautiously approached her wells of power and listened for anything her prophetic magic might reveal, but she couldn't make anything out clearly. When the pain grew to the point at which Lily had to back away, the only thing she felt relatively certain about was that her feeling of worry was somehow connected to the trolls.

I don't know why my well of prophecy is less distinct than before, Alder, but I think the uneasy feeling is due to something that will happen with the trolls.

"After that unusual eruption and smoke, I can believe there will be trouble with the trolls, Lily. As for your prophetic power, I think there are plenty of reasons for it to be acting as it does. Even at the best of times, most Fae seers have difficulty comprehending the portents of their magic. You are very new to the effort, and you are fighting the effects of a great deal of iron, which would render any type of fairy magic unreliable. Except the Void element you can wield, apparently. But the most likely reason for your struggles, I think, is because the Fear actually made it inside your prophetic well of power. I don't know of any Fae who has survived such an ordeal . . . but I imagine it will take a while for you to heal the damage it wrought. You might not prophesy at full strength for some time, faelani*."*

Lily was stunned by this, and not a little upset. Had the Fear, that terribly sinister voice, harmed this part of her inner magic beyond repair? Was there anyone who was going to know how to help her heal it?

"I'm sorry to cause you distress, Lily. I just didn't want you to be continually frustrated and puzzled by your well of prophecy's lack of cooperation. We will find a way to repair it, that just might take some time to figure out. I will help you. We can't risk allowing the damage to remain if there is a chance it could worsen with time. It will certainly be a priority when we are settled in the Fae Wood. For now, though, why don't we attend to the Gongoozler and his departure?"

Though Lily was still worried, she had to admit Alder's distraction was a valid one. She decided to give this more thought at a better time, then surfaced to the increasingly warm and sunny day around her. Vadom was still gently petting Whirlwind, and the Gongoozler was offering the mare a carrot. Lily watched as her new mount eagerly lipped the vegetable off the elf's extended hand. She would have to remember that Whirlwind liked carrots. They had never been Lily's favorite, and as such, there were a couple at the bottom of her haversack still. That led her to wonder if her *vapa* had also managed to collect some food and water while in Wizulaan, or if securing her new horse had entirely occupied him. Before she could ask, however, the Gongoozler broke their easy silence.

"I think I have taken another step toward seeing nearly everything there is to see in the world this morning— a vampire befriending a horse after sunrise! It could very well be a first, and I do so love being the first to witness something remarkable or rare. On this harmonious note, perhaps I should wish you both a safe conclusion to your odyssey and make my own way home. Be assured that I will keep my word to both of you."

With that parting affirmation, the Gongoozler turned to the northwest, and seemed on the verge of setting out. He hesitated, though, and slowly turned back toward Lily, his mien very solemn.

"May I ask you a question, young Fae lady, before I go?"

"Yes, Gongoozler, though I may not have the answer," Lily replied, curious about what the old elf so wanted to know that he delayed his sojourn back to the Forest of Ancients. Within her mind, Alder stirred.

"How are you able to cope with so much iron upon you? I have been told many times by fairies much older than you that the combination of pain and 'the Fear' make it well and truly the Bane of the Fae. How do you resist it?"

Lily considered her words, though she already knew the answer. Finally, she replied.

"My worst fear has already been realized. I lost the only person in all the world who I loved and who loved me, and yet I survived, because there is love and hope in the world still. What can the Fear taunt me with now that I could not endure, knowing this?"

The Gongoozler absorbed Lily's words, and it seemed to her in that moment that he could have been a part of the tall grasses all around him as they swayed in the wind, or the solid ground beneath their feet, so in tune with their surroundings was he. At last, the elf seemed to pull himself from his deep contemplation. With a wide smile that belied his solemnity, the Gongoozler gave Lily and Vadom a small bow from the waist.

"It is a pleasure to have met you, Fae lady, and I wish you safe traveling and a bright new life at the end of your journey. Vadom, it has been good to see you again, and to become better acquainted. I hope that happiness can be wrung from this turbulent time in your life, and that all who matter to you will soon be secure. Fare thee both well."

Lily automatically made him the *valoriad*.

"Thank you, Gongoozler. I hope that you travel swiftly and safely as well. Be wary of trolls, should you encounter any, for I feel uneasy about them, and farewell until we meet again."

"May the darkness of night hide you from your foes and the brilliance of the moon light your way, Gongoozler," Vadom said formally, making the customary gesture of sincerity as well.

Without further delay, the elf turned north and gracefully loped away. Lily watched him until he disappeared in the windblown grasses in the distance. Though the weariness she felt fell a little short of exhaustion, she knew it was going to be a long day in her new saddle upon Whirlwind. Despite her fatigue, however, Lily couldn't help but feel a bit triumphant. The elves would soon know about the threat the xydolem posed, and that might mean some small measure of inconvenience to the Misruler, if he was indeed responsible for those terrible red creatures. That might mean fewer unwary victims like her mother, and for that, Lily was almost fiercely glad. With her thoughts buoying her strength and resolve, Lily mounted Whirlwind and looked expectantly at Vadom.

"Ready to go now, *Vapa*?"

25

CONCERNS AND CONFIDENCE

VADOM, WHO HAD STILL BEEN GAZING INTO the distance from which the Gongoozler had vanished, turned to Lily and met her gaze as he replied.

"Yes, I am able to continue, though a short rest when the sun is brightest later today would be welcome. At that point, I think you will also need to eat and sleep, *Vipina,* for you were awake all night and will most likely have sore muscles from learning to ride. Is this agreeable to you?"

Neither Lily nor Alder had any objections, so Lily hefted her haversack onto her back and attempted to climb up into Whirlwind's saddle. The weight, combined with her fatigue, however, proved more than Lily's body could handle. Before she got too frustrated, Vadom silently glided to her side and easily lifted Lily, sack and all, onto the horse's back. Lily gave her *vapa* a grateful look, then turned expectantly to the east. Soon, soon she would be in the Fae Wood, the home of her father and her truemate. How quickly could they reach the safety of Ford-upon-Ward and the sanctuary beyond? Lily realized, as Whirlwind began to trot, then gradually broke into a canter, that Vadom may have found out how close they were during his trip into Wizulaan.

"*Vapa,* did you happen to find out how far we are from Ford-upon-Ward? It would be nice to know how much of our journey still remains."

"Yes, *Vipina,* I was able to obtain that information, both from listening to a few conversations and with a small stroke of luck. I listened to several of the grocers speaking with their customers as I gathered some food for you, and I discovered that there is just one coven that maintains a settlement called Goddess's Retreat. This small town is only two or three days' steady riding to the east of Wizulaan. As I was determining which was the best kept stable, I happened across a mapmaker's shop. Right in the window was a very well done, elaborately illuminated map of Ropaz. It was highly accurate to my knowledge, and so it seems we can rely upon its creator for a determination of our own route. The artist depicted Ford-upon-Ward as almost directly south and a little farther east of Goddess's Retreat. Even better, he measured the distance from Goddess's Retreat to Ford-upon-Ward as two days of steady riding, perhaps only one long day of hard riding."

Lily's heart pounded with excitement. The Fae city on the River Ward was only five days away, perhaps as little as three days if they avoided entanglement in any trouble! Though they still had hundreds of miles to go, and still further to travel within the Fae Wood, Lily felt hope truly blossom in her heart. Never had she yet felt as though the end of her immense trek was drawing near, but her *vapa* was saying just that now.

"It is wonderful to feel such joy and anticipation from you, Lily. Vadom has certainly brought us good news. I hadn't realized we would be able to make such good time on a horse, yet Whirlwind seems strong enough to persevere in the pace we'll be setting on this next leg of our adventure. Excellent! Do you think he found out anything about the Volcano Crescent situation? Gossip must be flying among the witches and wizards about the eruption and the trolls. Could you ask him for me?"

Of course, Alder. The more information we have to take to the Fae courts the better.

Lily looked over at her levitating *vapa* to find him steadily and patiently regarding her.

"Alder and I are excited about how much closer Ford-upon-Ward feels now, *Vapa*, and Alder would like to know if you heard anything about the Volcano Crescent."

Vadom nodded, though a shadow of concern flitted across his features.

"Your otherwing anticipates the second part of my reconnaissance. The covens of Wizulaan spoke of little else, and speculation was rampant regarding nearly every aspect of the eruption. Everyone seemed certain that the northernmost volcano of the Crescent has been razed, and little but its foundation and a great deal of lava and rubble remains of it. Some were concerned that the lava would damage the southern borderlands of Ropaz, though most believed the lava would more naturally flow into the great lake of legend. What seemed much less obvious was why the eruption occurred at all, especially with such great force. Some wizards thought the trolls, in their stupidity, had become self-destructive, for no one knew of any coven that had provoked or attacked the home of the trolls. The majority of witches, however, thought the most likely culprits for the demolition were the Fae of the Wood."

Lily was jolted immediately by Alder's considerable shock.

"No! The Fae would never initiate conflict with the trolls. Never has it been done, never has it been considered with any seriousness! We do not know which of the volcanoes is home to the females, children, and elderly of the troll race, or if each peak holds trolls of all ages. Without knowing where the warriors reside, such a drastic step would not be given credence, let alone allowed and executed, by the monarchs or advisors of either Fae court. What's more, such an unprovoked act of war would have to be given years of planning and preparation, and I knew nothing of any such designs mere weeks ago. It is impossible, and the Fae are being unjustly maligned by any accusations of culpability. What would we gain by antagonizing our neighbors to the west? In reality we would have everything to lose by such a dishonorable act."

Lily conveyed Alder's words to Vadom, even as the Fae in question fumed at the Ropazian accusations. She found herself naturally trusting her friend's assertions, especially as they were logically sound and fit what she did know about her people. Lily found herself hoping her *vapa* would also be in concurrence.

"What Alder says seems informed and pragmatic," Vadom replied. "Rarely do any races in Lamoranth commit unprecedented actions on such a large scale, especially ones that have so little apparent benefit and such high risk. And for such a blatant martial act to occur with virtually no planning or any obvious allies? The likelihood is all but non-existent, based on the information we currently possess."

"It will be non-existent no matter what other information we gather, because it could not, would not have been the Fae. We must discover the real culprit and report our findings to Silver and Golden Courts as soon as possible. We cannot afford to be dragged into conflict again so soon after the last battles. The Fae have not yet entirely recovered from the losses three centuries ago. Neither are the elves likely to contribute more of their own warriors to our defense after the casualties from that time. Diplomatic solutions must be fully explored and the best option performed with all speed. I can only hope the right Fae are assessing the situation at home . . ."

Lily felt herself growing uneasy as Alder continued to analyze the Fae Wood's precarious situation. Was he serious about taking the time to gather more information? She had promises to keep, and Lily didn't think she would be able to handle this additional burden, on top of all the other pressures and pain in her life right now. With Alder completely preoccupied, Lily turned to Vadom for advice.

"I think Alder wants to try to find out who is really responsible for the Volcano Crescent upset, *Vapa*. Is it selfish of me to feel overwhelmed by that? Couldn't we just push for Ford-upon-Ward as quickly as we can and tell the Wardens there in three or four days' time? Will that make a significant difference to the outcome of this situation, do you think?"

Vadom considered Lily's questions before answering with care.

"I think you are always entitled to your own feelings about any given issue, *Vipina*. You have oaths to fulfill and pain to endure, dangers to avoid and distances to cross. Now is not the time to test the extreme limits of your endurance, if you are not at them already. I believe Alder speaks as a result of the heat of this moment, out of a longstanding sense of responsibility and honor. When he has a little more time to think things through, I am almost certain your well-being will reassert itself as his greatest priority once more. You are learning a lesson in being mated just now. Remember always to be patient and to consider what is best for both of you before you speak or act. I will be silent for a time to allow the two of you to work this out, though I'd like to tell you one other thing first."

Feeling much calmer after Vadom's reassuring words, Lily nodded attentively.

"Though I was listening carefully to all the Ropazians in my vicinity, and even probed the minds of a couple of the most well-informed individuals, I heard not even the barest hint about the xydolem or their activities. It would seem, at least for now, that we are out-distancing any rumors, or that they are being silenced deliberately before becoming well known. This seems in keeping with the xydolem's ostensible desire to remain undetected, which works in our favor just now. Perhaps those creatures are one of our lesser concerns at the moment."

Though Lily hoped that was the case, it seemed too good to be true after what had transpired in her last days in the desert. Would Nather really just admit defeat and say nothing of her? Had the xydolem simply vanished without a trace, like a nightmare forgotten upon waking that left only a vague sense of unease in the light of day? Troubled once more, Lily thanked Vadom for all he had done during his foray into Wizulaan, then turned her thoughts inward to speak with Alder as their morning of travel wore on.

He was much as she had left him, though if anything, he had worked himself into a greater state of agitation. Cautiously, with Vadom's words still echoing in her ears, Lily began a conversation she wasn't sure she wanted to have, though she knew it was necessary.

Alder, did you happen to hear what my vapa *said about the xydolem?*

That certainly got his attention. Alder's focus turned sharply back to her, though he still seemed to remain unaware of Lily's emotional tension.

"No, I didn't hear that part. What did he say?"

That he listened for any word of them thoroughly, but to no avail. He thought it could be nothing, or it could be deliberately nothing, in which case we should still be wary. I think I will always be vigilant of the danger they pose, but . . . perhaps they aren't our biggest problem just now. What do you think our greatest concern is right now, Alder? I'd like to know what your thoughts are at the moment.

"I am seriously concerned about the Crescent situation, Lily. The Ropazians think the Fae are responsible, but more importantly, do the trolls think that? Will they retaliate? The Fae will not know that the volcano was destroyed. From across the vast distance of Molten Mirror, they will think it is an eruption of epic proportions, and think themselves under threat from livid, unreasoning trolls. The Fae leaders will not know the cause, and an attack of the trolls will not be understood or dealt with as it should be. There hasn't been a disaster like this since the time of my birth, and I am very worried for our people."

Lily could feel Alder's deep worry for the Fae Wood, and she found herself admiring both his intelligent analytical ability and his dedication to find some sort of feasible solution. His words, however, were not what Lily had hoped and needed them to be, and she knew she had to voice her own greatest concern now and hope that Alder would understand.

Alder, I'm inspired by your feelings about the safety and well-being of the Fae Wood. I hope that when I reach the Wood myself, I will have similar convictions. However, I am not there yet. The Wood may very well be in impending danger, but I am in constant danger in multiple ways right now, and I am so, so weary. When I think about what is best for the two of us, and Vadom, I honestly believe that making straight for Ford-upon-Ward is the safest and best option.

I can only wear this iron skin so much longer before it catches me in a weak moment and drags me into that overwhelming despair. We are so incredibly fortunate to have encountered only one good vampire, one good wizard, and one good elf since we left the Joquobon. The longer we stay in Ropaz, though, the more likely we are to meet with Vheneir's vampires, or a coven keen on fairy mind protection, or trolls out for revenge, or even xydolem searching for me on Nather's say-so.

I must make it to the Wood, Alder, so that I can keep my word to my mother and deliver the scroll to Golden Court. Your soul is in danger with every moment it is not put back in your body, and my father is suffering severely because of the irretrievable loss of his truemate. What if your body sickens and suffers some permanent damage? What if my father succumbs to his loneliness and pain before I can meet him, tell him of my mother's last years, and offer what comfort I can? The longer we delay, the greater the risks that I cannot countenance. I'm sorry to bring up all of our obstacles, dangers, and responsibilities when I know you are already aware of them, but Alder, will it not be sufficient to tell the Wardens what we know and have them send warriors to scout out the gaps in our knowledge in a few days' time? For I cannot take any more burdens now, my friend. I hope you can understand.

Lily felt shaky and miserable even after she had said all that she felt she'd needed to say. She had always avoided conflict, accepting her mother's words as wise and usually indisputable, and taking the mistreatment from Nather's tribe in her stride. It had gone on her whole life, and a part of her had always wondered if she deserved it somehow, for it had been prevalent and unremitting. Always in the desert, Lily had found solace in her glass-making and her imagination, never in fighting or standing up for herself. It was terribly difficult for her to do so now, but if Alder was truly her mate, she knew she had to be his equal, in her convictions as well as everything else. With turbulent feelings, Lily waited for Alder to say something.

As the silence drew taut, she tried to sound out Alder's sensibilities. He was in a state of chaos, and even as Lily nervously awaited his reply, she sensed his emotions coalescing into panic, misery, fear, and anger. When Lily's trepidation quickly began to escalate in response, though, Alder broke the silence.

"Faelani," he started, then paused. "Faelani," he repeated, savoring the word as he hadn't since his first few uses of it over a week before. After another long moment, Alder continued.

"I am so sorry that I have put you in a position where you had to choose yourself over what amounts to the Fae of the Wood. I knew this would be difficult for me when I found my mate and began faelanzania. *Yet even*

knowing beforehand the trouble my sense of responsibility would cause, still I have failed you in my very first test of loyalty. You should not have had to remind me of the considerable and myriad adversities we face, nor that my first thought should always be of you. I am ashamed of my thoughts, and what my actions would have been, had my soul been in my body today. Let us make our way directly and as quickly as possible to Ford-upon-Ward, Lily. You are right in all respects, even regarding the trolls. We know enough to put the Wardens on the right trails, and they will serve to confirm and further detail what we will tell the courts with all haste. I hope you can forgive me for putting you in such an untenable position, and I fervently hope you will speak up if it happens again. I am afraid it will, and that you will be the one to suffer for it."

Alder's feelings were so downcast and upset that Lily didn't know what to say right away. She had rather expected conflict, not for Alder to entirely agree. She had anticipated anger and defensiveness, and instead her friend, her truemate, had been worried and miserable, as if his worst fears about himself were materializing. What anger he had felt hadn't been directed at her, of that Lily felt strangely certain. What was becoming clear was that there was much Lily still needed to learn about Alder and his obligations in the Wood. Lily resignedly added those things to the list of other questions she would be asking upon entering the unassailable safety of the Fae Wood. Although how impenetrable was the Wood with the possibility of another martial engagement with the trolls? Lily decided she didn't even want to consider such a thing, even as she became aware of her own crushing headache.

Summoning her last existing reserves of strength, Lily sought to put Alder a little at ease.

Alder, I accept your apology, and I hope you'll take my own as well. We've only just met, after all, but we're in a situation where we have to try to understand each other as newly mated Fae probably rarely do. It's fine if we have to talk things through like we did just now. I can't tell you how relieved I am that you listened to me. It's alright to make mistakes, remember? Neither of us are perfect, and our abysmal circumstances only serve to challenge our every strength and plague our every weakness. I'm sorry for throwing it all in your face just now. If there was a better way to handle this predicament, I hope you'll tell me so that we can deal with the problems in our future with more aplomb.

Alder didn't say anything, but Lily could feel a slow but definite shift in his emotions. The negative began to acknowledge the positive, his bleakness fading away to be replaced by unexpected joy. And as this change occurred in Alder's soul, something wonderful came into being in his silvery essence. It was belief and conviction, in strength and possibility and greatness. It was a fragile newborn thing, yet unspeakably beautiful for its brave foray into life. Lily basked for some time in the quiet, steady heartbeat of Alder's infant confidence, and felt something of the pride of a parent upon the birth of their first child. How glorious it was, how marvelous indeed, to have helped create such a thing, and to desire always to nurture it and help it grow into all that it could be. What couldn't Alder do with such a brilliant golden addition to his magnificent soul? Lily thought that he could achieve or overcome anything at all. With an excruciating throb of premonition from her prophetic power, Lily was stunned to realize that they might, one day, have great need of the confidence that now existed within Alder.

Just before Lily began to feel uneasy about the future, Alder softly spoke to her.

"Thank you, faelani, *for this gift. No one else has ever been able to inspire confidence in me as you just have. I don't have words for the gratitude I feel . . . but thank you, for being so patient and generous with me. You could have gotten angry and justly berated me. You could have let your sense of betrayal put distance between us and rescinded the trust that I value so very much. Instead you have shown me my mistakes without censure and put me on the right path without demeaning me in the least. I feel humbled by you, empowered by you, and so, so happy. I had no idea that finding my truemate would be this good. All I really wanted was to feel less alone, but meeting you has given me so much more. I hope I learn soon how to make you feel like this, too."*

Lily felt herself smiling with relief and happiness. She was a little proud of herself as well. Not only had she stood up for herself, but she had still managed to show Alder the generosity and patience that she so appreciated receiving from him. She felt like more of a peer, and an equal, to Alder than she had yet so far, and it was surprisingly satisfying.

Thank you again for listening, faelan. *That is all a desert girl can ask for. Except for the unconditional agreement, of course.*

Alder seemed amused, and his response was lighthearted.

"Desert girl, or lady of the Fae, you will always have my ear, Lily. And agreement whenever I can manage it."

For a while, they simply existed in companionable silence. Before long, though, Lily wasn't able to ignore her body any longer.

I'd better ask Vapa *for a break, Alder. I'm not going to be able to sit in this saddle much more, and some sleep would definitely be welcome.*

"Go ahead, faelani*. I'll just be in here thinking things over if you need me."*

With that, Lily focused her eyes on the grasslands of Ropaz around her. She thought it must be about midday, and for that she was rather relieved. Turning to her left, where Vadom levitated just a few outstretched arms away, Lily spoke up.

"Would this be a good time to eat and rest awhile, *Vapa*? I feel awfully worn out."

When she felt an unexpected throb of guilt emanate from Alder, however, Lily hastily added to her ill-considered words.

"You were right about the sore muscles, *Vapa*. I'm probably going to need help getting off of Whirlwind's back, if you don't mind."

Vadom studied her face for a prolonged moment as Lily carefully reined in her mare. He didn't say a word until he had gently set Lily on her feet beside her horse.

"The two of you have resolved your disparate points of view, *Vipina*?"

"Yes, *Vapa*. We've agreed to make straight for the Fae Wood."

Lily left it at that. Vadom was still looking at her intently, and he seemed . . . a bit angry. What was wrong now?

"Tell him I am listening attentively, faelani," Alder said, sounding both steady and resigned.

Surprised, Lily repeated his words to Vadom, who gave a small nod of what might have been approval before his features took on a very stern cast.

"Judging from Lily's words and expressions, not to mention her obvious relief, it seems you have regained the proper perspective, and none too soon, Alder of the Fae Wood. I know not how involved fairy families become in situations such as these, but as a vampire, I feel I must speak my mind to you now.

"Your otherwing must always come first, Alder. If every warrior constantly maintains this mentality, then it is a serious contribution to the balance and stability of both your own home and the Fae community at large. No one around you should ever have to think twice about whether a mated lady is adequately and indisputably protected. Among vampires, it is a matter of great shame for such a question to ever arise in relation to one's own otherwing. By detracting from your commitment to your mate, you run the risk of pulling other warriors from the protection of their own otherwings, and in so doing, it is almost guaranteed that someone, at some point, will suffer the consequences of your negligence. Most of the time the one to come to harm will be your own mate, and Lily deserves the very best from you at all times, Alder.

"I don't know what obligations you are required to fulfill in the Fae Wood, but believe me when I say that in the end, all comes to naught if your otherwing has not been cared for first and foremost. You are old enough, I think, to have seen this for yourself, and now you are experiencing it as one newly mated. Remain vigilant against allowing any other priority to outweigh your mate from this day forth. Nothing can ultimately be more important to you now than Lily. If this happens again, Alder, you will answer to me."

Lily was stunned. Even as she attempted to comprehend her *vapa*'s censure of her *faelan*, though, Alder responded.

"Lily, please tell Vadom that I have heard his words and take their meaning with all seriousness. Please also thank him for allowing me the opportunity to resolve this with you before involving himself. He has given me an honor that I do not know if I deserve, but I am grateful for it."

Lily spoke Alder's words aloud, still experiencing mixed feelings about this unexpected and rather exclusive conversation. Her *vapa*'s words were a sharp reprimand, even after Alder had fully complied with her needs and wishes. Lily turned back to Whirlwind and uncinched the girth that kept her saddle in place. Once she had more or less tumbled all of the mare's tack to the ground, Lily reached into one of the saddlebags, searching for the brush she needed. Whirlwind deserved a rubdown as she cooled off from the exertions of the night and morning. Even as she began caring for the mare, Alder's surprise registered with her senses.

"Are your indignant feelings on my behalf, faelani?*"*

Yes, Alder. I thought Vapa *was rather harsh with you, considering you heard me out and immediately agreed with me.*

Alder didn't speak for a moment, though Lily could feel the tenderness of his emotions.

"Lily, your protectiveness of me, especially in the wake of my egregious lack of judgment, warms my soul. But I must tell you, in all fairness, that Vadom was easy on me just now. Perhaps it is the way of vampires to allow new mates to work disputes out on their own, but the Fae get much more involved during faelanzania*. Everyone wants to see truemates become fully bonded, and they are often quick to offer both advice and criticism. This usually comes from immediate family members and close friends, though many will speak up if*

the mistake on the part of either truemate is great. Any lapse in a Fae lady's protection is considered a serious misstep, and that's just inside the Wood. Here in Ropaz, it should have been unthinkable. The vampires are in the land of witches and wizards much more often, and have developed satisfactory methods of protection, so perhaps that is why Vadom was not more harsh with me. However, I have jeopardized our courtship and your very well-being with the direction of my thoughts, and I have shamed myself in so doing. I shudder to think of what your mother would have said, or what your father might say when we tell the tale of our journey home . . ."

Lily wasn't sure what she ought to say as Alder trailed off into obviously miserable thoughts. It was becoming clearer to her what a mated warrior's duty was to his truemate, and the expectations were apparently high. But what of a mated lady? What could she be rebuked for once in the Wood? What actions would be perceived as failures to her *faelan?* Lily pondered those and similar questions as she finished brushing Whirlwind and set her to graze in the tall grasses all around them. After thinking carefully, and partaking of the fresh food and water that Vadom had stored in the saddlebags, Lily finally spoke up as she laid down to rest.

Alder?

"Yes, Lily?"

Could you tell me what will be expected of me as your truemate in the Wood? Will everyone be as hard on me as they are on you?

Alder seemed startled by the question.

"What will they expect? Well, probably that you have some healing abilities, as most ladies do. This naturally makes Fae females nurturers and peacemakers. They contribute to improving the health and well-being of all the Wood's inhabitants, based on their levels of magic. They seem always and easily to smooth their truemates' way, both in their faelans' *professional duties and personally, with more private pursuits and problems. Ladies bolster their warriors with an instinctive grasp of their partners' needs, and hopes. I've observed that Fae ladies usually adjust more easily to truemated life than their counterparts, perhaps because they are more accustomed to thinking of others before themselves.*

"As for whether or not they will be harsh with you . . . I will make sure that it is not so. You are young, have been through a terrible ordeal, and have a lot of magic that you will need to learn to cope with very quickly. We have more than enough valid reasons for lenience, at least enough to ensure that you have the time to settle in to life in the Wood and adjust to a future you never anticipated."

Lily mulled Alder's words over. What it all seemed to boil down to was that she needed to be Alder's support, just as he protected and supported her. Giving and taking was a part of all solid relationships, wasn't it? And *faelanzania* ensured that everyone bonded at their own pace, and that everyone else knew where a couple was in their courtship. As for knowing with her instincts what Alder most needed, she had recognized his lack of confidence and helped him begin to feel it, hadn't she? Perhaps she wouldn't be found wanting as Alder's truemate after all. No use worrying about it just yet in any case.

Thank you, faelan.

"Of course. And Lily . . . I want to thank you, once more, for your patience with me. I can only say I am immensely relieved that I didn't hurt your feelings today. Any other Fae lady would probably have lamented her fate for having such a thoughtless truemate, yet you have proven to be exceptional yet again with your acceptance of who I am and how I think. In a way, I am a little relieved that this happened now. This was an incredibly important lesson for me to learn, and it was best for me to hear it directly from you, and from Vadom, who truly has your best interests at heart, rather than a host of Fae attempting to mediate at some later date."

Lily hesitated, then decided Alder valued her honesty too much for her to let what she wanted to say now pass unspoken.

My feelings were a bit hurt today, Alder, I won't deny that. But I'm also aware that I don't know as much about our situation as you, or even Vadom, at this point. That has been bothering me as well, though I keep reminding myself that there is a lot of risk in my knowing too much prematurely. Even with those limitations, I am learning a great deal, but Alder . . . I am still just as capable of making mistakes as you. Sometimes I feel as though you make too much of me, and make too little out of yourself. I've noticed repeatedly since we met that you are quick to find yourself wanting. I've been concerned about it, and I want to help your confidence grow now that you know how it feels to truly believe in yourself. I will do what I can for you, but I think it should be you who builds yourself up, instead of relying solely on me. I am starting to realize, after being with you and Vadom, that living in the Joquobon has left me with doubts about myself, too. I think we both need to work on being confident, not just you, Alder. I don't want my limitations to become yours as well.

Lily held her breath for Alder's response, half afraid of what he would say. Was it too soon to bring this up with him? She could feel from him more surprise, and concern as well. Finally, he became very thoughtful and determined.

"Lily, even being as objective as I can, I don't think I have ever made too much of you: not your bravery, not your intelligence, not your powerful magic, not your kindness. What mistakes you have made are fully justified by your age and this situation. I could give you a lengthy list of reasons why any fairy in the Wood would find you an extraordinary being. I'm not sure, though, that it would convince you. Perhaps only time will do that. I see that the desert dwellers undermined your sense of self-worth more than I thought, and I am warning you now that it has just become my personal mission to build you up in your own estimation. If we are both trying to do this for each other, maybe we can also try to think of it for ourselves as well. That way, we may reach the point, someday, at which neither of us feel limited by other peoples' opinions of our supposed shortcomings."

Lily felt strengthened and encouraged by Alder's words. She was secretly pleased that her friend and truemate thought so highly of her, and that he was determined to make her think that way about herself. She was more than willing to do that for Alder in return. They were both like glass being worked, still hot enough to mold themselves into whatever they wished. Lily thought both of them deserved to be the people they truly wanted to become by the time their glass cooled.

I think that sounds perfect, faelan.

Though Lily wanted to stay up the rest of the day talking more with Alder, she could feel the heavy blanket of sleep covering and warming her, lulling her into much-needed rest.

Thank you for the things you said this morning, Alder. I want to think it all over after I've gotten some sleep.

"Of course. And don't worry, I shall rest too. We both need to keep up our strength for this last push to the Wood."

Lily smiled, happy that Alder had anticipated her request. The last thing she recalled doing before succumbing to slumber was sending her happy feelings toward Alder's soul, and sensing the same from him in return.

26

Travelers' Travails

Lily woke a very short time later to the gentle hand of Vadom on her shoulder, coaxing her to wakefulness. He was speaking, and Lily realized she needed to concentrate on what he was saying.

"*Vapa?*"

Lily frowned slightly at her slurring voice, still thick with sleep.

"*Vipina,* I am sorry to wake you when you have gotten so little rest, but it is not safe to linger here. Are you alert now?"

Lily sat up slowly, taking in her surroundings as she attempted to focus her mind. Judging from the sun, it was perhaps late afternoon. No wonder she was groggy, for she couldn't have gotten more than a few hours of sleep. Whirlwind was saddled and ready nearby, not to mention pawing the ground a bit anxiously. Lily's attention finally honed in on Vadom, whose face was calm but whose eyes revealed an urgency she couldn't ignore. Lily began wondering uneasily what was going on.

"I'm awake now, *Vapa*. What's happened?"

"I have been monitoring our surroundings as usual, *Vipina,* and what I saw just a few minutes ago to the south is a cause for concern. There is a large contingent of trolls, marching in loose formation, making almost directly for our current location. We need to move out of their way, quickly."

Lily scrambled to her feet, her mind racing. She slung her haversack across her back and moved to grab Whirlwind's reins. Vadom lifted her up into the saddle and she was soon galloping east, Vadom levitating closely by her side. It was only after they were well under way again that Lily spoke up.

"*Vapa*, it doesn't seem likely that the trolls are coming this way because of us. Why then do you think they are? Are they making for Six Cities? Are they hoping to secure Ropazian allies for an attack on the Fae Wood?"

"I do not think so. At least, that is not my first guess. How do the trolls know that the witches and wizards of Ropaz didn't attack them? We know better, but I doubt they are so well-informed. With the Fae as their target for revenge, it seems most likely that they are marching just far enough north to avoid being seen from the Wood. The immense golden dome that covers the entire fairy forest and protects the Fae from all outsiders is probably only just out of sight from here.

"Furthermore, most beings in Lamoranth know that the High Priestess of Ropaz is very slow to make martial pacts, regardless of race. She wouldn't make a move to form an alliance unless there was a clear advantage for the covens of the grasslands. I think it most likely she will wait to see how successful the trolls are in their preliminary attack of the Fae, who will be the trolls' immediate scapegoat, guilty or not."

At this, Lily expected some sort of reaction from Alder. She was surprised when he remained silent. She couldn't feel any of his emotions on this sensitive topic, either. Where was he?

Alder?

Lily felt escalating panic when she received no reply whatsoever. She forced herself to remain calm. She looked over at Vadom, who was still speaking.

"*Vapa*, I don't feel Alder, and he's not answering me."

Some of her alarm must have shown on her face, for Vadom's countenance tightened slightly in response.

"Search for him, *Vipina*. I will make sure that Whirlwind stays the proper course, and that we keep a safe distance from the trolls."

Lily nodded in a jerky motion and then concentrated on locating Alder inside her mind, keeping only the barest awareness on remaining astride her mare.

Alder? Alder, are you still here? Faelan*!*

Lily checked by her wells of power, then the circle of her sensory input several rings out from that central location, where Alder most frequently observed their outer surroundings. He wasn't in either place. Lily could feel, in an almost detached sort of way, the iron-induced Fear seizing on her growing despair, feasting on how scared she felt. Not even magic seemed to encourage it as her swelling dread did now. How had she ever survived her mother's death? The effects of the iron had seemed such a distant thing at that time, too. She had to keep looking. And even if he wasn't here, perhaps he was simply close enough to his body now that it had recalled him? Lily told herself, repeatedly, not to give up hope. It was too premature to suspect the worst, wasn't it?

Lily flitted through her ring of memories, thinking it unlikely that Alder would pry. Then she realized the one place he most enjoyed that she had not yet checked, and sped across the grasslands of her mind to the tree-filled wood beyond. She was heading for her innermost soul now. He often gravitated toward her there, sometimes without realizing he had done it. That seemed her best prospect now. Lily burst into that place moments later, and felt inexpressible relief when Alder's beautiful silver soul floated very near her own golden spirit. Did he seem just a little dim? Lily hoped it was only her frantic nerves telling her that. Cautiously, softly now, she spoke to him.

Alder? Faelan? *Are you well?*

No answer. Well, perhaps he had stirred the slightest bit, but Lily hardly trusted herself to be objective about his well-being at the moment. Searching for a calm she didn't feel, Lily reached for their special truemate bond. Maybe she could communicate with him in their own unique way. With infinite care, Lily channeled some of her golden essence through their first *faelanzania* bond, just as she had once before. It was only several agonizing moments later that she felt Alder stir to awareness.

"Faelani?"

His silvery voice sounded disoriented and tired and incomparably wonderful.

Faelan, *I was so worried! Are you all right now?*

Alder must have begun picking up on the tenor of Lily's emotions at that point, for he sounded fully alert when he responded.

"Yes, Lily, I'm fine. When you sleep, I have been practicing my meditation. Part of my early warrior training required being able to relax without fully sleeping, as it is a necessary skill for prolonged battle or sieges. I've been able to hold my meditative state for longer and longer amounts of time as our journey has progressed, but I still always return to full vigilance well before you. I'm actually surprised your wakefulness didn't communicate itself to me. You feel your emotions keenly, as I well know by now. Did something disturb your sleep?"

Yes. I'd only slept a few hours of the afternoon when my vapa *woke me up. He said that there were a large number of trolls marching our way, and that we needed to move farther from their vicinity without delay.*

"*Trolls? Marching? In Ropaz? This cannot be happening! Did he have any idea why?*"

When I asked him if he thought they were looking for an alliance with the witches and wizards, he didn't think that was the case, because of the cautious policies of the High Priestess. Before we discussed anything more, though, I realized you hadn't spoken or felt anything that I could sense, and I went looking for you. I'm so glad you're still here and that you were just meditating, Alder.

As Lily's relief swamped her, causing a small retreat of the Fear toward the outer ring of her mental defenses, it apparently crashed over Alder as well. He was surprised, then concerned.

"Faelani, *I'm so sorry to have worried you. I always assumed that if you woke up first, I would sense your thoughts and feelings and return to full alertness. If it would ease your mind, I can simply forgo meditating for the remainder of our travels. Barring any more unforeseen circumstances, I'll probably be back in my body in about a week, perhaps even less. I should be able to last that long without much difficulty.*"

Lily struggled briefly with her more selfish concerns before responding.

No, Alder, I think you should meditate whenever you can to keep up your strength, especially in light of the trolls' movements. We don't know yet how they will affect our plans. Now that I know where to find you, I won't panic again.

"*Well, if you're sure, Lily. Why don't you surface and make certain you're safe with Vadom. I'll feel better once I know you're riding Whirlwind without too much difficulty, too. How do your muscles feel?*"

Lily hadn't given her body a thought since this morning. It was mentally easier to just ignore it. Now that he mentioned it though, her legs were a strange combination of fiery aches and partial numbness. That couldn't be good. She was also a bit hungry . . .

Sore, especially my legs. A meal would be welcome as well. Do you think we can afford to stop though?

"*Let me get to your sensory awareness, then I'll have a better idea. Chances are that a short break will be fine. Could you actually see any trolls to the south, or did Vadom tell you? He might have used his Void pulses, and that might mean they're a more comfortable distance away. Not to mention you've been riding for what, another hour or so? Let's get some more information and then reassess.*"

Alright, Alder.

Lily sent her feelings of care and affection in Alder's direction, making sure that they wrapped him up and cushioned him from everything else.

She could sense his surprise, and then his great happiness, as he steadily made his way to her sensory perception. Lily surfaced to waving grasses, a sun well behind her, and an almost unbearably tired and pain-ridden body. Yes, a short rest would be most welcome at this juncture. Lily turned to look at Vadom, who was levitating beside her as usual. What was rather out of the norm was that he was traveling backwards, staring intently at the grasslands behind them. Vadom felt her gaze almost immediately and slowly turned to face her as he spoke, his voice belying his concern.

"How is Alder, *Vipina?*"

Lily felt Alder's pang of guilt, touched with surprise, at the question, even as she hastened to answer. After she had explained his meditation, Vadom nodded in approval.

"It is good that he learned how to meditate at a young age, for it has certainly been useful for him on this journey. I had not planned on teaching you the art of meditation for a time, but perhaps it would be wise to make it more of a priority. Obviously it can be put to good use in times of peace as well as times of war and imminent battle."

As her *vapa* mused on that topic, Lily found herself gritting her teeth against the agony in her legs. She gripped her pommel with one hand in concentration, even as she managed to keep the reins steady in the other. After a moment, she risked a good look behind her. Lily didn't see any trolls, much to her relief. For now, they were outpacing the enemy. Lily could feel Alder's tension decrease considerably inside her mind.

"It looks as though we are relatively safe for now, faelani. *Vadom will certainly maintain a high level of vigilance as long as we are in Ropaz and react to all threats promptly. I can still hardly believe how fortunate I am that he safeguards my truemate in these circumstances. There can hardly be a more perfectly suited individual in all of Lamoranth for your protection on this immense trek than he."*

Lily sent feelings of agreement in Alder's direction, though she didn't break her concentration on riding with any speech. Her vision was blurring slightly on the edges . . . how odd . . .

"Faelani, *what is happening to your eyesight? Lily? Lily, tell Vadom you need to stop . . ."*

Lily concentrated the last of her will on turning toward Vadom.

"Vapa . . ."

Lily saw his eyes widen and his arms reach for her before the world went black.

When next Lily was cognizant of her own mind, she knew that she was deep in the realm of her own magical imagination. Lily dreamed of many things. The images flashed through her mind at random, as varied and incredible as could be. Though much was blurry to her sight, each picture seemed tinged with emotions that Lily could feel with total clarity. There was a ruinous rocky rubble, where a fiery and viscous substance smothered everything in its path. Though Lily could not see anyone, there was an overwhelming sense of fear and uncertainty. She saw a beautiful lady and a handsome Fae warrior, both with pale purple features, whose faces were etched with worry and impending sorrow as they kept watch over a bed in a private room. Lily saw several girls her own age, laughing and smiling together, their short hair and large eyes all the startlingly bright colors of fairy magic. She didn't think she had ever seen anyone so carefree. Just then, they all stood on their feet, joined hands, and began to sing. The sound they made together caused Lily to feel light of heart, if only for a few moments. It was then that she glimpsed a few other young Fae, watching longingly from an unobtrusive doorway to the room, faces full of pain and envy. Just as she focused on one of those other girls, head heavy and blue eyes carrying an unjust burden, Lily heard Alder's voice, and knew her time for dreaming was over for now.

"Faelani, *Lily, you need to wake up! Please, I know you are tired and hurting, but you must come back now. The Fear is encroaching upon your wells of power. It is far too dangerous to risk it making contact with your magic ever again, Lily. Come on, awake,* faelani, *and make me more proud than ever.*"

Lily struggled into wakefulness at the sound of Alder's entreaty. She doubted anything less could have recalled her from such fascinating dreams. Why was she so disoriented? Shaking off deep sleep wasn't normally quite so difficult. It was obvious that Alder had been trying to reach her for quite a while, though, for he was keeping his panic in check only with rigorous control. Focusing her mind with an effort, Lily managed to speak up.

Alder?

"Lily! Oh, faelani, *at last! You were unconscious for a time, and you felt beyond my reach. Not too long ago, though, you began to sleep a healthy slumber. The Fear retreated, so I think Vadom must have done something to heal some of the pain in your body. You had better go talk to him; he is probably very concerned for you."*

Lily pushed through to her physical surroundings and immediately beheld a vast expanse of starry sky. The moon was waxing there in the firmament, and Lily took a moment to enjoy its soft white light before slowly sitting up from her prone position on the ground. Vadom was in the act of replacing her mother's medical pack into Lily's haversack just to her right. Whirlwind was grazing directly in front of her, though a few paces away, still saddled. She could see traces of a fire a little to her left, with a half-empty cup on the ground beside it. As she inventoried her physical aches and pains, Lily realized that there was a bit of cool relief internally where a short time ago, the pain had reached a feverish intensity. How had her *vapa* helped her this time?

"*Vapa*, I'm awake. Thank you for catching me earlier," Lily said, feeling embarrassed as she recalled those last darkening moments before waking to Alder's voice once more. She had never fainted before, and she hoped to never do so again. Lily did not like feeling weak.

Vadom immediately turned and surveyed her carefully, relief lighting his eyes. He walked toward her and gracefully knelt down beside her.

"How are you feeling, *Vipina*? I found a good supply of willow leaves in your healer's bag and took the liberty of brewing the leaves in a tea for you to drink. I wasn't able to get you to swallow much in your unconscious state. Why don't you drink the rest now? And then, though I wish it were not the case, I'm afraid we must be on the move once more."

Lily's heart sank at the mere thought of mounting Whirlwind in the immediate future, and Alder's alarm and spike of defensiveness let her know that she wasn't the only one to harbor doubts about her ability to press on without a good night's rest. Vadom seemed to understand, for he continued with an explanation.

"The situation with the trolls is worse than we feared, young Fae. They are not acting under their own leadership or direction. The trolls are following a group of xydolem on this eastern march."

Vadom gave Lily and Alder a moment for this earthshaking news to sink in. Alder's concern deepened into dread before transmuting into anger, while Lily could hardly think about it calmly at all. She was still torn between fear and a terrible anger of her own when her *vapa* gently covered her hand with his own.

"I said previously that if I ever thought you were in imminent danger, I would carry you as far as I deemed necessary to remove you to safety. I consider tonight such an occasion. Whirlwind does not have sufficient night vision to carry you at speed by naught more than the moon's light. We will place your haversack on her back and I will hold her reins to help guide her as I run. She should be able to keep up with my moderate pace if she holds to a gallop. You will need to sleep for as long as you can to maintain your strength, *Vipina*. Our travel will be grueling now that we must stay ahead of some highly motivated xydolem. Our biggest advantage is that the trolls are wholly unaccustomed to travel, and the xydolem will not push them so hard that they will not be able to fight in battle at their journey's end. Now, before we set out, can you tell me what you think brought about your collapse earlier this evening? Was it the iron you wear?"

Lily almost responded automatically in the affirmative, but then she stopped to consider. The iron pain hadn't been quite so bad since last night, when she had put clothing between her skin and quite a bit of the armor she wore. It had been more a case of already being weary, then failing to get more than a nap after learning to ride a horse and proceeding to speed through Ropaz on Whirlwind for a good portion of the day. And then there had been Alder's need of her soul's strength, when he hadn't easily come out of his meditative state . . . When Lily told Vadom her thoughts, a little of his tension seemed to leave him.

"I had hoped it was from causes other than your iron, *Vipina*, for we cannot risk you removing any portion of it now that the xydolem are no more than a few miles away. These other circumstances can be accommodated and mitigated. Let us go now, and gain some distance from the trolls as they bivouac for the night."

Without further delay, Vadom scooped Lily up off of the ground, made sure that all traces of their fire were erased, and began leading Whirlwind toward the east, curving slightly toward the south as well. Lily looked over his shoulder into the night, and she thought she could just make out the light of cooking fires on a distant swell of grassy land. She shivered at the thought of the xydolem being so close. To distract herself, Lily asked the first question that came into her mind.

"What did you brew the tea in, *Vapa*? I don't have a kettle in my haversack."

"I formed one out of night magic, *Vipina*. Remember that I usually travel with Vabiri, and she is forever concocting tisanes, ointments, healing potions and the like. She often leaves them in witch and wizard houses with sick or elderly members to ease suffering and discomfort. It is her way," he concluded with a fond, proud look in his eyes.

As Lily hesitated over asking questions to find out more about her *vama,* Alder softly spoke.

"Faelani, *I think it might be best not to speak too much about Vadom's otherwing. Though he is all that is disciplined, it may still divide his focus, and we just can't have that right now. I think, if I were in his position, it would be very difficult for me to rescue someone else if you were very far away and I wasn't certain you were safe."*

Lily realized Alder was right. She remembered how her mother couldn't even speak of her father in all the years they had been parted. It probably wouldn't be kind to try to satisfy her curiosity about Vabiri when she was still in the Cave Kingdom, not to mention while they were in the midst of a mad dash to the Fae Wood.

I think you're right, Alder. Perhaps I should ask him how he thinks the xydolem became involved with the trolls, instead? Or what, precisely, they plan to have the trolls do?

"I would certainly like to have those answers as well, though I don't know how Vadom would be aware of that information."

Perhaps with Void pulses?

"True! And yet . . . if the xydolem are highly skilled with the Void element, he may not risk using pulses that such beings could detect. Our complete obscurity is paramount now."

Lily couldn't help but agree. Still, it wouldn't hurt to ask Vadom his thoughts about their situation. When she voiced her curiosity, her *vapa* nodded as though he approved of her train of thought.

"The xydolem's involvement in these events, though very unwelcome, does make more sense of the troll upheaval. It is a serious possibility that the xydolem razed that volcano with their malignant night magic, and the trolls obey them out of fear of that power. Now they march at the command of the xydolem, who can utilize their vast numbers to stage a multi-pronged assault on the Fae Wood. The fairies will not be expecting anything approaching this level of military complexity, and they will be dangerously unprepared. If we arrive much before the trolls, perhaps we can spare the Fae a considerable number of casualties with the information we possess."

"Where do you think they plan to initiate battles, *Vapa*? How can you tell this is what they plan to do?"

"As Alder has said before, the only time in history the trolls seriously threatened the Fae was when they attacked on two fronts. I'm sure they will sail a force across Molten Mirror Lake as usual, even as this regiment behind us moves to strike Ford-upon-Ward. They could also be making for the Ocean of Fintilles, to launch a nautical assault on the opposite end of the Wood. Perhaps to encroach upon Golden Court? Yet the location of Fae cities is certainly not common knowledge, and how would they have discovered such things? There is also a small possibility that there is a third battalion, heading for a destination on the southern border of the Fae Wood, though there is no way for us to determine this. The Fae will need to scout that perimeter thoroughly to assess any threat from that direction. This is more experienced, lethal maneuvering, clearly on the orders of the xydolem, or perhaps the one who commands them."

Lily felt the stirrings of her inner ferocity, that therianthropic being who couldn't abide threats of any kind, even as the rest of Lily felt fear and uncertainty. Was the Misruler at work again? What did that being have against fairies? What justification could there be for a seemingly unprovoked act of war, and through a coerced third party, no less? Lily felt grateful, then, that Vadom was running her to the Wood, that she was getting ever closer to her goal and ultimate destination, even though her own body couldn't take her any farther just now. They simply had to make it to relative safety, to protect the home where Alder and her father resided . . .

Lily's last thoughts before falling into a deep sleep were filled with potential plans for thwarting this serious enemy of her people.

27

A Warrior's Mind

When Lily woke to the sun's early rays the following morning, it was as though her mind had continued plotting how best to prepare herself for the imminent troll and xydolem attacks while she slumbered. Lily impatiently shoved the iron Fear to the peripheries of her concentrically circled mind, then surfaced to Vadom's vigilant countenance.

"Good morning, *Vapa*. Do you think I could have some of your time for a warrior lesson today?"

Vadom looked down with a little surprise in his eyes, even as Lily felt Alder's mixed feelings about her request. She remained quietly firm, steadily holding her *vapa*'s gaze to show her unspoken resolve. She may have learned about Void pulses the night before last, and how to ride a horse just yesterday, but Lily had yet to actually wield a weapon. That, she decided, would not be the case by nightfall. If battle was nearly upon her, she refused to be completely helpless anymore. Even if she had only the most elementary knowledge, it still might save her life, and thus Alder's as well. She couldn't afford to neglect this training now.

Vadom slowed, then came to a complete stop.

"Why don't we discuss this over your breakfast, *Vipina*. Whirlwind will benefit from a longer stop after such a full night of travel, and I wouldn't mind allowing the sun to rise a bit higher, so that I need not look directly into its bright light."

Lily nodded, though she was uncertain, for the first time, about whether or not Vadom would agree to teach her when she asked. She pulled her haversack from Whirlwind's back, only to realize how winded the poor horse was. Lily quickly removed the saddle as well, then took the bit out of the mare's mouth. She thoroughly brushed the horse and set her to graze before turning back to her own haversack and the saddlebags for food and water. Thanks to her *vapa,* there was plenty for her to eat, and Lily tucked in with gusto. As she drank a measure of water, however, Whirlwind approached her and nudged her hopefully. It took Lily a few moments to realize that her mount was thirsty.

After a minute or so of giving her mare water, Lily worried about whether or not they would have enough for the remainder of their journey. She could feel Alder's concern as well.

"Whirlwind certainly requires more water than Bepo, the amadel, doesn't she? Will we have enough, do you think?"

I'm not sure. I've been wondering if we could forgo stopping at Goddess's Retreat in favor of heading directly for Ford-upon-Ward, but I think my vapa *realized that it would be necessary.*

"He must have. That, and the fact that Goddess's Retreat is the only landmark we have to ensure that we don't overshoot our destination. Short of getting within sight of the Bubble, encountering that town is the only way we really know to start heading south."

The Bubble?

"Remember when Vadom mentioned the golden dome that protects the Fae Wood from the other inhabitants of Lamoranth? It has been affectionately nicknamed the Bubble, since it sort of looks like one. It is an ancient, highly complex, and incredibly powerful piece of fairy magic. The spells that created and maintained it have been lost over time, but it is still the Fae's primary fortification against those who wish our people harm. It is the Bubble that will seriously hinder the trolls and even the xydolem from entering the Wood. It has kept out Fae enemies for a very long time, and it hopefully will for more countless years to come. My main concern about it now, however, is how it will affect you while you wear so much iron. Vadom must be keeping us at a distance from it for that reason."

Even as she worried over this new concern, Lily felt grateful that her *vapa* seemed to think of everything. She surfaced to her surroundings and packed up the saddlebags, wondering about Vadom's silence so far. Lily glanced at him, his expression pensive, as she replaced her nearly empty water container into her haversack. Her eyes lit upon her mother's iron sword, and she felt another swell of determination. She would insist on, argue for, even plead her case for more warrior lessons if she had to in order to convince Vadom—

"*Vipina,* are you speaking with Alder now?"

Lily started out of her thoughts, realizing her *vapa* had noticed her glance and now watched her patiently. She shook her head, even as she closed up the haversack and moved to sit near Vadom. When he saw that he had her undivided attention, Vadom spoke.

"Before we discuss the practicalities of your next warrior lessons, I'd like to obtain some information from Alder, if he possesses it. Is he listening, *Vipina?*"

Lily felt Alder startle in surprise, then sensed his hopeful resolve. He wanted to be more useful, Lily realized, as though he wasn't already an invaluable asset in their unlikely trio. She was glad that he felt no wariness about what Vadom might ask, or hesitant about giving answers that might very well pertain to the Fae Wood. It was important to her that these two trust each other as much as she trusted both of them.

"I am listening, faelani, *and I will answer if I can."*

Lily repeated his words, then sat still to hear what Vadom would ask.

"I would appreciate it if you would share whatever you know about Goddess's Retreat, Alder. If we continue at this pace, we should arrive there sometime during the night, and I'd like to be as prepared as possible."

"I don't have a great deal of knowledge about Goddess's Retreat, but I do know that it is one of the two closest witch towns to Ford-upon-Ward, along with the coastal town of Wizamoor, and that it is considered one of the most sacred places in Ropaz. There is a legend in the witches' beliefs that their Goddess became weary with her people's misuse of nature and magic, and that she cried many tears in that place. It is said she created a large pool in her sorrow, and that it remains there to this day to remind all the covens of Ropaz to refrain from abusing their magical abilities or their home in the grasslands."

Lily repeated Alder's words, fascinated by the tale. Even a goddess, it seemed, could grow sad and weary with the wrong-doing around her. Vadom looked thoughtful.

"Do you think the coven there will be peaceful then, Alder? Or perhaps more complacent, as they are accustomed to living in a location considered holy by their people?"

Alder replied after a thoughtful moment.

"I think they are probably a bit more of both of those traits than most other Ropazians at present. However, I know that, at least in the past, they were ever hopeful that a fairy would wander out of the Wood so that they could utilize that Fae's magic. In ages past, when the Fae still moved about Lamoranth,

Goddess's Retreat was known for capturing and enslaving more fairies than any other witch habitation, even Six Cities. I would not consider it any safer than the other wizard cities of Ropaz. Perhaps even less so, as they must have passed down very effective detection spells for sensing fairy magic. The good news is that the Coven of Retreat has never, ever attacked Ford-upon-Ward. They may covet fairy power as much as all the other Ropazians, but they fear, or at least are cautious of, the Fae themselves, and will not strike out except in retaliation. We will have to be as vigilant as ever until we are inside the Bubble, but then we will be safe from witches and wizards."

Lily conveyed her *faelan*'s words to Vadom, mulling them over as she did so. She wasn't feeling quite so in awe of the legend now that she was acquainted with more of the reality. Surely their Goddess wouldn't approve of enslaving others, a huge misuse of magic, both witch and Fae? Perhaps Goddess's Retreat was not the reminder it was supposed to be for the Ropazians. As if on cue, Lily's well of prophecy seemed to lurch and sputter inside her mind, affirming Lily's thoughts and sending garbled messages she couldn't make out.

"*Vipina*, are you all right? What is it?"

"Faelani, *get control, push that Fear back. What set off your prophetic power?"*

A little short of breath, Lily explained what she had been thinking of, and the apprehension she'd felt about Goddess's Retreat. Both of her companions were troubled by it.

"It seems we may need to reassess our route to Ford-upon-Ward after all. Surely we can find small streams or a rivulet for Whirlwind to drink from so that you can have the remaining water on a straight path to the Wood, faelani."

"Does this feel like your premonition about Japeta, *Vipina*, or more like Wikkenod? Would our lives be in danger, or do we need to exercise great caution?"

Lily tried to sort it out, but her prophetic magic wouldn't cooperate.

"I can't tell. I don't think there would be death, it didn't feel that awful . . . but there might be serious consequences. Maybe trouble we could do without."

Lily heard Alder sigh inside her mind, and she found herself grinning.

What's this, Alder? Would you rather avoid trouble in such intriguing circumstances? Where is your sense of adventure and daring?

She started to laugh at his moment of incredulity, and kept laughing when he soul-chuckled.

"Your sense of humor always takes me a little by surprise, Lily. Here I am, fretting about my faelani *like a proper newly mated Fae, and you tease me, as if we were attending some pleasant garden party at Silver Court."*

Before Lily could ask about gardens and parties, Vadom spoke up, effectively refocusing her attention.

"I do not wish to disrupt your happiness, *Vipina,* Alder, but we need to make some important decisions and then continue toward our destination."

When Lily nodded, feeling a little guilty, Vadom went on, unperturbed by the interruption.

"I would like to continue to Goddess's Retreat as planned, so that you will be fully provisioned no matter how events unfold. While I think you have enough food, water is another matter. Even with your uneasy foretelling, I believe having the necessities is of great concern. What route would each of you choose at this point?"

"We were actually discussing this a little while ago, *Vapa.* Alder would rather head straight for Ford-upon-Ward, watering Whirlwind when we can. I'm not certain which route would be better. There are obviously positives and negatives with either choice, and I'd just as soon choose the path with less potential danger and the quickest possible arrival."

Vadom paused to absorb their opinions, and Alder spoke up.

"I might actually prefer to stop at Goddess's Retreat, Lily. Vadom is right—we have to keep your mount healthy, and water is an essential. While we all hope to make Ford-upon-Ward in a matter of days, we may very well have to take evasive action if anyone dangerous gets too close. We need to supply ourselves accordingly, in the event that we end up staying in Ropaz longer than expected. I trust Vadom's judgment, and he has made his thoughts on this clear."

Lily mulled that over a moment, then decided she agreed. While she hardly wanted to think about getting stranded in Ropaz, it certainly wasn't outside the realm of possibility. Being caught unprepared was a problem they didn't need to add to their burdens.

"*Vapa,* Alder and I want to be fully supplied and ready for anything. We agree that a stop at Goddess's Retreat would be best."

Vadom nodded slowly, studying Lily's face as he did so.

"Very well. When we arrive at this town sometime tonight, we will exercise all possible caution and stealth. Barring unforeseen circumstances, we should be turning to the southeast by dawn tomorrow for the last leg to Ford-upon-Ward."

"Well, not actually wholly unforeseen," Alder grumbled. *"I suppose I'll*

just have to start getting used to that now. Potential disaster imminent, brace for future obstacles."

Lily felt herself smiling, at both her *vapa* and her *faelan*'s words. Vadom's next topic of discussion, though, found her very solemn once more.

"Now that we are in agreement on our route, I would like to address your request for the continuance of your warrior training, *Vipina*. I believe that we have reached the point where practical application would be best. I think your mind is both informed and strong enough to begin the more physical aspect of a warrior's education, though we will have to accommodate your body's current limitations with care and vigilance. As such, I will need to create night magic weapons suitable for you to use. I will dedicate my morning to that endeavor as we continue east, if you feel you are able to ride your mare until we break for lunch. At that point, we can dedicate an hour, perhaps two, toward your training, and then I would like to travel on. We gained a night's distance from the trolls, but I think it would be unwise to relinquish much of that lead."

Lily completely agreed. Staying well ahead of their enemies was obviously of great importance. She honestly didn't think she would be able to train for very long regardless of time constraints, what with all of her iron on. She made him the *valoriad* and gave Vadom a smile full of determination.

"Sounds good, *Vapa*."

With a nod of acknowledgement more serious than usual, Vadom helped Lily saddle and mount Whirlwind. Lily was slightly surprised when he passed up the haversack for her to transport, but she accepted it demurely. She realized that he must need the fewest possible hindrances while simultaneously levitating, making magical weapons, and remaining vigilant of their surroundings. Honestly, that was rather impressive—

"It sounds good in theory, but I am rather hoping Vadom eases you into things on your first day. I remember the aches and pains from starting my own warrior training, and I wouldn't wish that on a prattling courtier, let alone my truemate in our present circumstances."

Lily had mixed feelings about Vadom holding back. On one hand, it would be more practical in their given situation, as Alder suggested. She hardly wanted to be in more pain than she already was now. On the other hand, however, Lily didn't want to enter into real warrior training half-hearted.

I will try not to overtax my strength, Alder, but I do want to give it my all for the hour or two my vapa *has planned for me. I don't think he'll let me overdo it on my first attempt. I think we just need to trust him to know how best to proceed.*

Lily could tell Alder was wrestling a bit with her answer, but she remained silent, hoping he would come around. She could feel his conflicting emotions, from concern to pride. Finally, he responded.

"You are independent by fairy standards, Lily, just as your mother was known to be. I think your unconventional upbringing has made you strong enough to adapt and thrive in the Fae Wood, and for that, I am grateful. Still, I suppose I will have to learn how to be a good truemate for one so autonomous as you. I hope you will let me know if you don't feel like you have enough space to be yourself once we are inside the Wood and have gotten past the troll crisis, especially if I am the reason."

Lily wasn't quite sure what to make of Alder's response, and she nearly decided to leave him with his thoughts. Still . . .

I'm sorry if this isn't what you wanted to hear, Alder . . . I just don't want to really start my warrior training with less than my best effort. What I learn could make all the difference in the next few days, and in the future as well. What if my vapa *teaches me something with a sword this afternoon that keeps the xydolem at bay for just one or two critical moments? What if a decent shot from my bow makes a troll think twice about approaching me? If I have the opportunity to learn something that could keep us safe, I don't want to enter a lesson for such information with deliberate timidity.*

Lily sighed with relief when Alder came to understand her rationale. His pride in her grew, though his worry remained, an omnipresent though muted feeling that wouldn't be disappearing, she felt certain, until Lily was inside the Bubble.

"I see now why you are so insistent this morning, faelani, *and I can hardly fault your reasoning. The more you know, the better you can protect yourself if it becomes necessary. I think you should do your best and trust in Vadom to test your skill and endurance. I'll try not to interfere, but I'm not making any promises, either."*

Lily smiled at the protectiveness bound up in Alder's final words and decided not to remind him of his initial promise to Vadom at the Pillar of Sun and Ashes. It wasn't as if she had ever needed to remind Alder to act honorably. It was an inherent part of him, one that had won her trust much more swiftly than she would have thought possible.

Feeling a welling sense of anticipation, Lily attempted to focus her mind on her impending warrior lesson. After a time, as if his thoughts were in accord with hers, Vadom spoke into the companionable, though concentrated, silence that their morning of travel had created.

"*Vipina*, can you hear me?"

"Yes, *Vapa*. Alder and I have both been absorbed by our own thoughts this morning."

Vadom nodded, then continued speaking, though he did not cease his levitation over the beautiful waving grasses in their path. Lily kept pace with him on Whirlwind accordingly, assuming that some verbal instruction was forthcoming. What extraordinary things would she learn about the world of Lamoranth today?

"I have finished the creation of your pair of anelaces, as well as your bow and a quiver with arrows. I'd like to say a few words about a warrior's mentality, now, before you attempt to wield your weapons for the first time. I will tell you what my *vapa* told me, for they are words I have never forgotten, and never will, no matter how many years may pass, or how many good vampires become ashes in the winds of the world."

Vadom paused, then slowly came to a halt and landed soundlessly on his feet. Lily gently reined in her mare, then dismounted. In silent accord, they cared for Whirlwind, then drew a little ways away, to a level portion of land in the midst of all those rolling, sloping Ropazian hills. Lily faced Vadom squarely, back straight, tired arms and legs ready to move. She wondered what had made her *vapa* so solemn, more even than usual. Inside her mind, Alder was quiet and acutely focused. Vadom seemed to gather himself, then met Lily's eyes as he spoke.

"You have demonstrated great physical and mental fortitude, *Vipina*, from the moment we met. You are young, but your courage is that of a much older being, steady and deliberate, ever mindful of the consequences of your actions. Knowing of these attributes, I now wish to impart to you one of the most important lessons I ever received in the course of my warrior training.

"Whenever you train, and especially whenever you engage in combat, you must fully assume the mentality of a warrior. You have shown glimmers of this before now, but from this moment forward, I want you to deliberately set aside all of you that is soft, gentle, caring, and merciful. When you hold a weapon in your hand, you must forevermore mute all of your emotions and focus all of your intellect and cunning on your opponent. You must *never* lose your ability to reason while you fight another being. Emotions will only hinder you: pity and fear will cripple your resolve, concern will lead to hesitation, anger and retribution will make you sloppy, and happiness has no place on a battlefield. Distractions can be fatal, and emotions are nearly always distractions. Cease to acknowledge your feelings when you engage in combat, for you must be the impartial judge of every enemy you face.

"Only then, when you can calmly decide the fate of another being, are you ready to take arms against them if your mind determines it must be so. Without the disadvantage of emotion, you will be able to focus only on the task at hand, without hesitation or eagerness. Always analyze the strengths and weaknesses of your opponent. Always be aware of your own abilities and limitations. Note in the greatest possible detail your surroundings, and whether or not they are conducive to battle. This includes not just the terrain, but other enemies, other allies, and the factor of time. You must think ahead to likely outcomes and consequences, and whether or not they are acceptable. This most often entails whether or not you can afford to be injured, even if victory is certain.

"In short, you must take into account absolutely anything that is capable of affecting combat and its outcome. For once you engage in a fight or battle, you must be prepared to maim or kill your opponent without losing your total and unshakable composure. You must be equally and unflappably ready to be maimed or killed as well. That is the reality of martial acts, the reality of victory or defeat. The fact is that battle is only ever glorious in retrospect, and oftentimes not even then. Fighting is dirty, gruesome, painful, wearying, and soul-depleting. To make it your life is to make your life nothing. Engage in combat when it is necessary, and be grateful that you can indulge in the emotions and feelings that make you who you truly are and what you most wish to be at all other times."

When Vadom finished speaking, Lily was still, perfectly still. She knew an important decision was upon her. Though, as she reflected, she realized she'd already set her course. Learning how to survive threats, how to protect others, and how to control the turbulent therianthrope inside herself was absolutely essential. Taking this next critical step in her warrior training would enable her to do what she knew she must. Armed with this certainty, Lily began an attempt to set her emotions aside.

At first, she failed utterly. Lily had never needed to separate herself, detach what she felt inside from the reasons for those feelings affecting her on the outside. She kept trying.

"You might try visualizing your emotions as controlled by an element of your choice," Alder suggested softly. *"After a time, I found that burying my feelings with my inner earth element made me a more effective fighter. Then, when my training was over, I could dig them up again."*

Lily immediately abandoned her attempts to shove her emotions behind a hastily constructed, mentally locked golden door. She considered, then discarded the idea of using night magic. Lily knew it would nullify her feelings forever if she sent them through a Void hoop, which she wasn't sure she had yet in any case. So would fire, burning up the emotions that made her who she was. Air was too capricious, as likely to blow her feelings to the fore of her mind as to sweep them away in great gusts of power. Earth, like Alder, then . . . and yet, Lily realized she needed an element that was as foreign to her as the dislocation of her feelings. The sands of the desert were hers to command, but her weakest element, the one she least understood, was water. Should she visualize her emotions at the bottom of the Sea of Fintilles, amidst the merpeople's dwellings? But what if such attempts drowned her feelings, beyond hope of recovery? It would be better to just numb her emotions, then allow them to thaw when each lesson was over . . . and in that, Lily knew she had found a solution. She would encase her feelings in ice.

Focusing on the circle of her emotions once more, Lily began channeling her inner elemental magic into an overlaying icy ring, making sure that it covered her fear, inadequacy, and excitement. The circle of ice was not big or thick enough. What now? So many more feelings, woven into every memory, affecting all she saw and did, emanating from her very soul . . . Her soul. Of course! What if she built a wall of ice around her golden soul, keeping the most fundamental part of herself separated from her warrior lessons, her warrior life? Surely that would make her cold enough for violence, cold enough for the pain and death that would inevitably follow in the wake of her decision to train as a vampire warrior.

Lily immediately crossed the grasslands of her mind and built the shell of ice. She blocked the emotions of her soul with her own transparent inner magic, there in the shady woodland of her spirit. Her feelings grew fainter and fainter, until she did not experience them at all. Lily had never felt so numb. Through the icy encasement, she caught golden glimmers of her true self. She could almost detect the fear that was bouncing determinedly against her new warrior wall, fear of this terrifying lack, this deafeningly calm state of readiness.

Lily opened her eyes to the pale waving grasses and the endless blue sky of Ropaz and tried to look as a true warrior would. This land was no longer strange and beautiful, but a place with few good hiding places or strategic vantage points. The sun was directly overhead, bright but not shining into her eyes or her *vapa*'s. She was facing an ancient and incredibly powerful opponent, unarmed.

Lily looked directly into the eyes of her *vapa*, showing him her absolute icy commitment. For many long moments, Vadom said nothing. It seemed that he might speak, but some minute hesitation maintained their mutual silence. Lily decided it might be best to speak her own mind.

"This is dangerous."

Vadom relaxed infinitesimally.

"Extremely."

"It must always be like this?"

Again the slightest, critical diffidence.

"Yes, at least for the time being. It will cost you, however, and you must always be able to pay that price."

Lily thought she might know what that price would be. Could she afford it? To freeze her emotions and deal with them in the aftermath of a lesson or battle? To go against her truemate, who wanted her to be a half-hearted warrior? To be different from all of the gentle, nurturing Fae ladies and become a killer instead? To find a quiet strength of purpose that would make her as a vampire in the Fae Wood?

Lily nodded.

Vadom studied her acutely, but she did not waver. Not now.

"Only when you must be a warrior, *Vipina*. Only then."

Lily nodded again. She didn't think she wanted to be without her feelings for long. She was but an empty husk of her true self without them— unreasonable or excessive or overly sensitive though they might be at times. Having only her thoughts made her incomplete, and even her intellect alone saw the benefit of being whole whenever it was safely possible.

Vadom gave a curt nod in reply, his blankest and most solemn expression firmly in place. His ambivalence was gone as though it had never been. Slowly, he performed the *valoriad*.

Lily returned it. Her unfeeling calm brought an incredible patience. She waited.

Vadom next brought his fists to his chest and brought out a small set of swords: her anelaces. They were the deep black of night magic, perfectly balanced, and unadorned but for two marks at the base of each blade. One was a beaming sun inside a diamond, the other was a crescent moon with four stars wrapped around its outer curve and two more stars tucked inside its inner curve.

Vadom approached Lily with steady steps, swinging the swords so that his grip moved from the hilts to the blades without breaking stride. He presented them to Lily, and she grasped them firmly. She felt her inner magic stir, the wild shape-changer— and something more. Lily stood silently, awaiting instructions.

Vadom stepped back several paces, then brought out his own anelaces. They were slightly larger and displayed only the moon and stars insignia, but were otherwise similar in their lethal elegance.

"Practice sheathing and drawing them. Carefully, hilts first."

Lily did so, noting that they went to hover with the rest of her night magic, in that place that was neither blindingly austere nor vastly rolling, but somewhere in between. They didn't get any smaller, precisely, yet they fit easily over that bumpy, uneven place inside her mind. Drawing them back out was similar, and a little simpler, than calling forth Void element for a pulse, as they were already formed. Lily repeated the procedure until Vadom nodded.

"Good. Sheath just one, then mirror my movements with your single anelace."

Vadom then led Lily through a series of stances and positions, all of his movements perfectly fluid and sure. He spoke as Lily tried to imitate him.

"When wielding this or any blade, you must first do a number of things naturally and unthinkingly. Keep your muscles relaxed and at the ready. Keep your posture straight. Keep your breathing regular. Balance and footing are critical. Your feet should be shoulder-width apart with your weight evenly distributed. Keep your feet on the ground whenever possible, and slide them about near the ground as you move. Ground them more for attacks, while blocks, also called parries, require less weight on the soles of your feet. Make yourself as small of a target as possible: keep your body perpendicular to your opponent, with your shoulder and sword arm pointed at them. This will protect your chest and torso with their vital organs and allow you to move more smoothly from the defensive to the offensive."

Lily absorbed his words as she moved, making adjustments as she went. There seemed to be a rhythm to this, a beat as certain as that of her heart, and she began to let it have its way as she experimented with her balance and sought out the surest footing in each stance. She never took her eyes off of her *vapa,* and she listened intently as he named each position and indicated whether it was for attacking or a type of block. The offensive moves were all variations of cutting or thrusting, it seemed. The blocks were different ways of deflecting an opponent's blows. Lily began to visualize how flaws in these rudiments could be exploited and made a few more changes to her movements. Her mind then started rearranging the stances, altering movements so that there were combinations of attacking positions, then parries that could become counter-strikes. Would that series of movements tire her opponent faster than herself? Would those stances save her from blows but put her on the defensive?

"Do you have questions, *Vipina?*"

Lily blinked. Had he seen them in her eyes? She repeated her train of thought.

Vadom nodded in approval.

"You anticipate what I will eventually teach you. I encourage you to continue thinking of these positions in terms of their variety of ultimate uses. Watch me and I will show you some useful combinations and counter-strikes."

He proceeded to demonstrate, naming each stance and position as he performed them again, in a new order. Lily thought she had most of the names and their corresponding actions committed to memory by the time Vadom came to a halt once more. She felt a mounting tension inside herself and wondered if she ought to mention it to her *vapa,* or if it was a natural part of her combat-ready state.

"Though in other circumstances I would wait to spar with you, *Vipina,* I think I'd like to go ahead and do so now. I can sense your fairy magic stirring, and I believe it would be better if we knew how those forces within you react to engagement with an opponent. Use what you have just been taught, at a speed that is comfortable for you. I will adapt and guide you through both offensive and defensive practice."

Lily nodded, and her magical tension mounted. She took up an on point position, her body at a right angle to Vadom's, her weapon ready and pointing toward her *vapa*'s throat. When Lily felt sure of her balance, her footing, her readily adaptable series of movements, all open to change based on her opponent's actions, she opened with a simple attacking maneuver.

The instant her blade met Vadom's, Lily felt her inner warrior well of power respond emphatically. It was not a surge of inner Fae magic, an uncontrollable pulse of power, like her prophecies. Nor was it the readily manipulated elemental magic. It wasn't even like the involuntary glimpses she'd experienced with her musical and linguistic abilities. This was a slow, steady, unstoppable force. This was a warrior's strength and endurance. This was control of a martial conflict. This was victory or death in combat.

Though her iron pain escalated rapidly, Lily instinctively knew better than to try to curb the new-found magic of her warrior wings. She channeled it into every stance, imbued every movement with her Fae fighter's lethal grace. Lily followed her original plan of combinations, trying offensive, then defensive. Her *vapa* was giving her at least a semblance of control, and her warrior spirit seized it readily. When he masterfully took charge of their sparring session, Lily felt her warrior magic reach new heights of intensity, automatically attempting to alter the flow of their simulated battle in her favor.

Lily wasn't certain how long she lasted before the pain brought her to her knees. All she knew was that she couldn't go on with any true balance or purity of form. She realized that she was breathing heavily and attempted to regulate it, taking air into her nose and slowly out of her mouth for several long moments. Lily met Vadom's eyes and wasn't sure what he was thinking. She waited, grateful that her warrior magic was slowly subsiding with the cessation of hostilities.

"That was very good, *Vipina*," he said quietly.

Lily wondered if she would feel happiness for his words later. Or would it be resignation, or dismay? Was this something she wanted to do well? No . . . it was something she *needed* to do well. Lily was completely certain that she would need to use her warrior magic for protection. Hence, it was a necessity. She tried to rise to her feet. When she managed it, her *vapa* spoke once more.

"This was a well-executed practical introduction to the sword for you. Let me show you basic blade maintenance, and then we will proceed with a short application on the care and use of a bow and arrows. Out of consideration for your iron restrictions, it will be brief. I do not think your fairy magic will be quite as stirred by the bow, but we will adapt the lesson as needed."

Though Lily was acutely aware of her finite strength, she knew she had enough for the remainder of her lesson. The bow and arrows wouldn't be the same as a sword. As if having a target farther away would lessen the intensity of her Fae warrior's magic. Still, she would need to stay completely focused and totally dedicated, even if the threat was a short distance away. Lily deliberately, though very carefully, tested her endurance against the effects of her iron skin. She knew that the pain and Fear were not going to overcome the strength of her will, not yet. Lily held tightly to this conviction and gave her full attention to her *vapa*.

Vadom showed her how to concentrate night magic in her palm and polish her entire sword in a continuous, circular motion, searching for and smoothing out any nicks or scratches. Lily knew this might someday be the way she cleaned blood from her weapons, too, and wondered how she would feel about that later. She spared a brief thought for the emotional backlash that seemed imminent, but refocused with grim persistence on the lesson at hand.

"Always make sure your weapons are clean before you store them with your inner magic, *Vipina*. Many a careless warrior have sickened or died from being less than meticulous about maintaining their weapons. I will be strict about this until it is second nature to you," Vadom concluded.

Lily nodded. It made perfect sense to her. She inspected her anelace closely, and, finding nothing amiss, held it up silently for inspection. Once Vadom had carefully looked it over as well, Lily sheathed her new sword hilt first through her chest, then waited expectantly for the bow and arrows portion of her lesson.

Her *vapa* smoothly brought out a small bow, already strung, and a quiver, full of fletched arrows. Unlike her first warrior lesson, Lily felt no fear. This weapon she had seen in the hands of her tribesmen all of her life, and she realized that there was an advantage to having those years of observation. Lily accepted the quiver first, noting both the moon-and-stars and sun-in-diamond crests marking it, then slinging it on her back as she always did with her haversack. She pulled out an arrow and examined it closely, from the needle-sharp arrowhead to the feather-like protrusions on the opposite end of the shaft. So light. So lethal.

Lily accepted the bow from Vadom after replacing the arrow. She tested the string, then the flexibility of the bow itself, as she had seen Nather's guard, Phepin, do countless times. She wasn't certain why this was done, except perhaps that there was an ideal give to each that required some degree of diligent maintenance. How often had she noticed the guard dismantle the bow, then restring it, cursing with all his strength as he bent the weapon with the sweat of perseverance. Lily looked up from her examination to find her *vapa* watching her closely. When Vadom saw that he had her full attention, he continued by naming each part of the bow and arrow, then demonstrating how to aim and shoot an arrow properly several times.

"When using this weapon, adjust your stance so that you are perfectly centered, legs shoulder-width apart for balance and perpendicular to your target. It is your torso that must swivel if your opponent is in motion. Keep the bow parallel with your body, at least as we begin. You must be relaxed but at the ready, with your shoulders back and both your elbows and your knees slightly bent, never locked. When you fit an arrow to your bow, use the tips of your first two fingers and thumb to hold the arrow behind its fletching, while your bow hand steadies the arrow near its head. Now you try, *Vipina*. Once you have a sense of it, I will explain more as needed, particularly on aiming and judging distance."

Lily mimicked Vadom's previous stance, keeping in mind all that he had just said. She took her time fitting her first arrow to her bow, then pulled back experimentally. She nearly fumbled the arrow, so intent was she on applying her strength to tautening the string of her bow. Frowning, she tried again. The string dug into her first two fingers, and Lily realized they would be sore if she fired very many arrows today. Could she afford to have hands that ached for the next few days?

Shrugging that thought aside for the moment, Lily aimed at the thick clump of grass Vadom had just targeted. His motions were so natural, with all the appearance of effortlessness. Lily's arms assured her that this was not the case. How far back should she pull the string of her bow? She tried stretching it as far as her arms were able, and, sighting down the arrow, let it go with a twang.

The arrow shot straight out, heading directly for the clump of grass, but ran deeply into the ground a few feet short of the target. Lily blinked, then looked at her *vapa* questioningly.

"You used enough strength, you simply didn't yet know how to angle your bow to account for distance. Let me show you."

Vadom demonstrated how longer shots required aiming more toward the sky, and Lily watched, a little fascinated, as her *vapa* made arrow after arrow speed through the air in great arcing trajectories. The higher he angled, the farther the arrows traveled before planting themselves amidst the waving grass.

"You might also try loosening your grip on the back of the arrow just a bit. You'll notice the difference that makes once you've been practicing regularly for a time. For now, concentrate on stance, grip, and angle. Eventually we will take into account any wind, and work on lengthening your distance and improving accuracy. Go ahead and fire a few more, *Vipina*."

Lily shot quite a few more arrows, experimenting on the fundamentals, getting a sense of the bow's limitations, as well as the things she needed to work on to improve her proficiency with this particular weapon. All the while, her warrior magic was strangely still, as though waiting for the right moment to become an unstoppable force once more.

Vadom watched Lily's efforts with a critical eye, observing and committing to memory all of his student's movements. Lily was certain he would know exactly how to help her improve whenever they had time for another lesson. When her quiver was nearly empty, Vadom signaled for Lily's attention.

"I'd like to try one more thing, *Vipina*, before concluding this lesson. I'm going to throw moving targets, and I want you to try your best to hit them. Your opponents will very rarely be stationary, and I believe it would be best for you to accustom yourself to constantly adjusting your aim now rather than sometime in the future. Indicate when you are ready to begin."

As Lily resumed her shooting stance, her warrior magic rose up once more, slowly and steadily bringing crystal clarity as she notched another arrow. When her *vapa* threw a palm-sized stone up and to her left, Lily's torso turned without conscious thought. She had taken aim, adjusted for distance, and let the arrow fly before her mind caught up with her instincts. Her arrow just nicked the rock, sending both spiraling crazily off in opposite directions and back to the ground.

Lily spared a quick glance at Vadom and saw him nod just a bit, as though he had confirmed something to himself. Her *vapa* tossed up several more stones, to Lily's right and left, very far away, and one so close that Lily barely got her shot off in time. Her arrows often came close to their targets, but she only actually hit one more. Before she knew it, Lily's quiver was empty.

A moment after Vadom stopped throwing the targets, Lily felt her Fae magic slowly sink back into the warrior well from which it had come. This, she decided, was a good thing, as the iron pain was approaching an intensity she could hardly bear. Lily could only be grateful that the Fear was still a safe distance from her wells of power. Allowing it too close was a risk she couldn't take right now.

"Your skill with the bow is high for a beginner, *Vipina*. It seems you have chosen your initial weapons wisely, as they seem very in tune with your fairy magic. Let us end this lesson now and consider it well done. We will go over the care of this weapon when we are free of time and safety constraints. I will collect your arrows for you today, while you bring forth your emotions once more. Have Alder help you."

Lily allowed her Void bow to sink into her chest and torso, then started for her innermost soul without delay. Alder met up with her as she was passing her recent memories, and they made their way to the dappled wood together.

"After a lesson like that, my praetam *always says, 'Powerful, intelligent, and stubborn, an impressive combination today, Alder'. I think this can be accurately attributed to you at the moment,* faelani*. Even with your feelings so contained, it was still unmistakably you who faced down an ancient vampire with a sword in your hand for the first time. The way you tried to wrest true control of the sparring from him! And then the way two of your arrows hit such small projectiles during your very first training session— that takes strong warrior magic, certainly."*

Lily felt the vaguest unease. She needed to free her emotions, now. It wasn't right that Alder was saying such things, and she was feeling nothing at hearing his words, his silvery voice. She said nothing in reply as they made their way to her frozen soul. Though Lily detected Alder's concern at her lack of response, she was more focused on how she was going to melt all of that ice. Would summoning some of her fire element do the trick? Could she burn her soul accidentally, though?

Then they arrived, and Lily had no more time to plan. She turned to Alder, urgent especially now that she could see her ice-encrusted soul.

Will fire element be safe to use, Alder?

"I think so, but perhaps you should manifest that magic as a bright sun, rather than flames. Do you think you can do that? Just draw a little elemental magic out at a time, and will it to become the beaming rays of the desert sun, heating all they illuminate. That should keep your soul safe from harm."

Thank you, Alder.

Lily very carefully summoned some of her elemental magic, concentrating on making it shine like the intense desert sun, which made all beneath its emanating rays hot and dry. It was working fairly well, slowly but surely melting the ice around her soul, until her magic began summoning something else. Suddenly, there were bursts of color in Lily's mind. Red and orange swirled about her, green and brown buffeted Alder's silvery soul, and even purple and yellow intermingled with overwhelming power. The pain that this colorful magic brought made Lily feel like screaming in agony, particularly when the white magic came to investigate as well. The Fear rose up, as quick and deadly as a sandstorm, ready to annihilate her fairy mind with brutal forcefulness.

"Lily, you must rid yourself of this outer magic— quickly, convert it into your golden inner power. Then go to your desert circle and start adding to your mental wall, using this extra magic to your benefit. Once you do this the pain will diminish, but you must begin immediately before you are overrun. You must, Lily, do it now!"

Lily automatically did as Alder commanded, knowing instinctively that he was able to think far more clearly right now than she. This had worked when they entered Ropaz, hadn't it? Lily had melted her icy warrior resolve enough to feel very frightened. With movements stiff but unceasing, Lily struggled to form blocks worthy of her mental defenses. It was the tiniest bit reassuring to set the altered portions of magic on the foundation she had already struggled to put in place around her inner sanctum. At least she wasn't starting from scratch this time . . .

It took a while, but in the end, Lily succeeded in controlling the extra magic she had accidentally summoned and the resulting ravages of the iron in her mind. As soon as she was certain that Alder, her soul, and her wells of power were secure, Lily rested. Alder, her constant support, hovered nearby.

"Are you quite alright, faelani*? I suppose we should have anticipated trouble from the iron, what with your warrior magic so active during your lesson. If it makes you feel any better, your elemental powers are nothing short of incredible. To be able to summon it about you, despite your temporary limitations . . . but I bet you don't really wish to discuss that right now. Perhaps you ought to speak with Vadom? I have no idea how much time has passed, but if we aren't on the move, we need to get going, Lily. I'm sorry you must press onward when no fairy has probably ever wished so fervently for a restful sleep, but you are getting so close! My excitement grows with every rolling hill you travel,* faelani.*"*

Lily was grateful for Alder's soothing flow of words. He seemed to know that nothing helped her more than his steady encouragement, his silver-smooth voice. Her soul was free of all the ice she had used to numb it, and her affection for Alder seemed all the greater for her brief cessation of feeling. Lily sent her melange of emotions in his direction. She knew he would recognize not just her gratitude, but also her growing regard for him in the tangle. Lily surfaced from her Fear-ridden mind to endure her pain-wracked body, but she rewarded her own endurance by focusing only on Alder's surge of happiness.

"*Vapa?*"

Lily felt disoriented and unspeakably fatigued. She noted that the sun was well past its zenith, and that Vadom was carrying her at a run beneath the endlessly blue Ropazian sky. Lily let her hand brush against the tickling tips of the pale green grass as they sped by, wondering what her *vapa* might have to say about her most recent collapse. Would her warrior lessons have to come to an end? Honestly, Lily wasn't sure how she felt about that. Did she know enough to save Alder, save herself, if it came to it?

"*Vipina,* it is good to see your eyes open and clear once again. Will you tell me what happened this time? Did your warrior magic cause iron repercussions?"

"No, at least not by itself. I accidentally pulled in outside elemental magic when I tried to melt the ice around my soul. It really hurt, *Vapa,*" she added quietly. Lily allowed herself to rest her head against his chest, right over his steadily beating heart. She wondered if her birth father, when she found him in the Fae Wood, would ever comfort her, or make her feel as protected, as her *vapa* did. It was difficult for Lily to imagine.

"Your iron suffering will soon be at an end, *Vipina.* We will arrive at Goddess's Retreat just after nightfall, and after the briefest of halts, we will make for Ford-Upon-Ward. We may arrive there by dusk tomorrow, as I plan on carrying you the rest of the way."

Lily could hear in his voice that Vadom would brook no argument on that. She was far too tired to speak up. No matter how good a horse Whirlwind was, she just could not stay in her saddle right now. That meant she had to accept her *vapa*'s edict, as they had no choice but to keep moving, as far ahead of the trolls and their xydolem masters as possible.

"That's probably for the best, *Vapa.*"

Vadom looked down at her closely for a protracted moment. He seemed to be choosing his words carefully.

"You will always have me, *Vipina,* should you be in need. I know Alder will ever be the same. Do not hesitate to ask for our help if you require it, *vladi.*"

Though Lily felt a sharp ping from her iron as her inner magic translated the new vampiric word, it was nothing to the wonderful felicity she felt about its meaning.

"I take it you like being called a 'vladi'*?"*

Lily could tell that Alder wanted a translation, but it took her a moment before she could reply.

He called me 'precious one', Alder.

"That is fitting, don't you think?" Alder asked gently. *"You have become precious to Vadom, his one and only adopted child. And to me, as well. He is right,* faelani, *that you will always have us, father and truemate, if ever you need help. You have only to ask."*

Lily felt like the most fortunate girl in Lamoranth just then. No amount of iron could take that away from her. She would make it to the Fae Wood, and things would get better. Her life would go on, and she'd make her mother proud, wherever her soul now resided. She would be the best *vipina,* and eventually the best *faelani,* too, for Vadom and Alder deserved no less than her whole heart.

Lily looked up at her *vapa* and waited until he looked down at her. Then she smiled her biggest smile and made the *valoriad.* Vadom's mouth turned up just a bit at the corners, and his eyes softened for a few moments. He pulled her a little closer to his heart for a beat or two, and Lily knew a quiet, special joy as she drifted into sleep.

28

A Meeting of Minds

Lily woke back up before much time had passed to a loudly rumbling stomach. When was the last time she had eaten anything? She hadn't gotten around to lunch earlier . . .

"You didn't rest for very long, Lily. Did you have any dreams?"

No, faelan, Lily said, still sleepy. A little sheepishly, she added, *I'm rather hungry.*

"Then we should definitely stop so that you can eat, faelani. You need to keep your strength up for this final push to the Wood."

Lily could hardly dispute that. She turned her mind out to the rest of the world and asked her vapa if they could take a short break.

"Of course, *Vipina.* I am glad to hear you have an appetite after your exertions this afternoon. We are still well enough ahead of the trolls for you to eat and rest."

Reassured, Lily went straight to the haversack that Whirlwind carried once Vadom had come to a stop and deposited her gently on the ground. After rummaging in the food pack and drinking some water, Lily thought she'd ask Alder what he had thought of her lesson.

So, how did my weapons lesson compare to yours, Alder?

"Well, I was a bit older before I began my warrior training in earnest. The Fae tend to wait until prospective fighters have grown into their bodies, so that they are ready to develop their strength and have decent balance. Male Fae tend to take a while to mature, and the teachers each warrior asks to train him in each type of magic and weapon must agree unanimously that he is physically and mentally prepared to begin instruction. This takes time for some."

How long did you wait before Captain Pine started teaching you?

"I was considered young to begin, as I picked up my first short sword in my third decade. Captain Pine took his time with my lessons, incorporating a lot of elemental magic instruction, as I am able to access all of them to various extents. I had much to learn from an early age, but I do think I am becoming a capable warrior, as well as a reliable leader of other warriors. Captain Pine has unerringly taught me everything I've needed to know, when I had to know it. I am forever offering up my gratitude, though all he ever does in response is to throw an arm around my shoulders and give me a squeeze. He is a fairy of few words, usually."

Lily was growing excited to meet Captain Pine, who Alder held in such high regard. She wondered if he had taught her faelan what she had learned today. How would a Fae warrior prepare a fighter-in-training for the numbness, the emotionless resolve? When Lily asked Alder, he pondered a moment before responding.

"What Captain Pine told me, early on, though not at the commencement of my training, was that a Fae warrior must fight with the heart, but it must be buried deep inside you. He likened it to a tree: that a warrior should keep his heart in his roots, unseen but vital to being complete, and integral to true strength. A warrior who keeps his heart in his leaves and branches may not be able to weather the tough storms of battle, and such vulnerability could bring him crashing into those around him, causing harm to his brothers when he should stand tall and strong."

Lily thought about the wisdom of Captain Pine as she restored her remaining bread and cheese to the food pouch. Was this the same instruction as her vapa's? Or was it what Vadom truly practiced but didn't know quite how to explain to her? Perhaps he had realized that the traditional method taught to male vampires might not be as effective for a lady Fae. She decided to set that line of thought aside for a time when she could truly come to understand the nuances of a warrior's mind.

Lily stood and stretched, every muscle sore, much of her skin bruised, and weary to her very bones. She went still, as she often had after making her glass figures in the desert, a time when she had accepted pain of another kind in her life. Lily felt the constant pull of the earth under her feet, the wind causing ripples in the grass, the gentle heat of the sun warming her face. As she relaxed into her surroundings, she could sense more of the magic in this strange land. It was a place that was both ever rolling into changing hills and a constantly beautiful, uninhabited landscape with a vastly majestic sky.

When she finally turned her back to a sunset resplendent with color and silent grace, Lily sensed something irregular in her surroundings. She looked into the distance and thought she saw a soft white glow in the direction they were traveling. Lily looked at her *vapa* with a question on her tongue, only to realize she wasn't sure of what to ask.

Vadom turned from his concentrated scan of the sun-embracing horizon and took a few gliding steps in Lily's direction.

"Are you ready to continue, *Vipina?*"

Lily nodded, ready to sleep a bit more before reaching their destination after dark. It would be in her best interests if she could rest now, as she would need to be awake and alert for at least part of the night. Vadom gently swept her up and started running. Whirlwind galloped alongside them at the end of her tether, the misshapen haversack tied to her saddle, unperturbed by the vampire who led her.

Not long after night had fallen, and the world had grown quiet and still for a time with the sleep of the sun, Lily was awakened by her vapa. Immediately, she sensed that unidentified white magic once again. Was it somehow a part of Goddess's Retreat? They must be close if Vadom was gently waking her up.

"Do you think Vadom will hide us in another cave? I can't see much in this dark, but I'm sure he will have a plan of action for tonight. He'll go in, get water and food, and get out, while we wait somewhere safe. I can't say I like missing the opportunity to reconnoiter Goddess's Retreat, but considering who I get to be alone with, I'm not going to bemoan my fate."

Lily realized, a little belatedly, that Alder was a bit keyed up about tonight's anticipated action. Or, perhaps, any unanticipated events that might occur. She hadn't forgotten the garbled premonition from her well of prophecy, and she doubted Alder had either. Before Lily could respond, however, she lifted her head from her *vapa*'s shoulder and got her first look at Goddess's Retreat. It took her breath away.

Everything was white, a purer white even than the finest sands of the Joquobon. The dwellings of the coven were strange to Lily's eyes, as they seemed to be made of the very earth around them. Yet how could earth take on these many-sided shapes, and a color so far removed from brown? Even the roofs, which were topped by the tall, waving grass to which she'd become so accustomed to seeing, had gone white. It was as though the brightest of suns had bleached the entire town the color of bones.

Lily's eyes were then drawn up a slight incline, around which the whole coven seemed established. The white magic was strongest there, and suddenly, Lily knew what she would find when she walked up that hill. And walk up it she knew, somehow, that she must. It was not her prophetic power that nudged her, but her cracked heart and soul that sought the peace she sensed just ahead.

Lily didn't even realize that Vadom had set her down on her feet, let alone that she had started walking straight toward Goddess's Retreat, until Alder's voice pulled her from her reverie.

"Faelani! *Where are you going? It is not safe for you to get any closer to this coven settlement. Please, let us wait where Vadom indicates while he gathers water and food."*

But Alder, I must go to the top of the hill. She waits for me there.

Lily could feel Alder's concern and confusion.

"Who is she, Lily? How do you know you can trust this witch? And won't the elemental magic of this town cause you harm? You could not go anywhere near Wikkenod or Wizulaan, remember?"

"She is not a witch, *faelan,* and she won't let me be hurt."

Lily started walking again, but before she had taken three steps, she felt the lightest brush of her *vapa*'s hands on her shoulders. She turned, impatient, yet knowing she'd have to try to explain what she was seeing, and feeling, to her guardians.

"Who is not a witch, *Vipina?* What do you see?"

Lily met Vadom's calm eyes and tried drawing some of the steadiness from his gaze. She turned and pointed to the top of the hill.

"*Her,* above all the rest, whiter than all the rest. Can't you see her, *Vapa?* Can't you tell she is saddened by all the cruelty, all the evil? That she isn't like that in any way?"

Lily swung back to Vadom, willing him with her eyes to understand. He returned her look for several long moments. At last, he responded.

"*Vipina,* it goes against all of my instincts to allow you to enter this or any place where a coven resides. However, if you can convince me that it is safe for you, then I will let you go. There is only one way I know of that will assure me that no harm will come to you in Goddess's Retreat, and that is to enter your mind and see this town as you do. It is highly discouraged, however, for a foster father ever to enter the mind of his vipin or vipina.

The temptation to dictate instead of instruct, to change instead of allow growth, is to be scrupulously avoided. If you are set on this course, though, I ask permission to enter your mind now, so that I am completely certain of your safety."

Is this alright with you, Alder? I trust him, but part of this choice is yours.

"If this is the only way to talk you out of it, then he can come in. Briefly."

"Go ahead, *Vapa*. Alder and I are ready for you."

Vadom nodded, then gave their surroundings a thorough inspection. Once he completed his surveillance, Vadom thickened Lily's Void sphere until the black of the night magic was easily visible. Satisfied, he placed his hands on Lily's neck with infinite gentleness. Lily held very still, not sure what to expect next.

That was when she felt the presence of another mind in the uncharted vastness of her own. Her *vapa* had entered, and he immediately began to search for Lily's desert-like inner sanctum. He soon arrived, and thereafter he tested the beginnings of her circular mental fortifications. After a moment, he vaulted over a spot that only had a single ring of blocks. Though it wasn't without effort, it was far easier for him to enter than Lily would have liked.

And then he was gliding through the oft-used portion of her mind, an immensely old and powerful sentience that all but overwhelmed Lily herself. It made her uneasy, and if it had been anyone other than her *vapa,* Lily would have been utterly terrified. Alder, tense but calm, waited by the ring of Lily's sensory awareness. He had not been able to see what she had seen, and Lily wondered how her *vapa* would be able to see what her truemate could not.

Vadom made his way through the lesser rings of Lily's tribally organized mind, heading unerringly for her wells of power, as though he understood that her outer senses would be nearby. Though she could not recall ever doing so before, Lily floated her soul out of the dappled shade of her inner wood, following Vadom's path across the vastness within her to her desert core. Vadom paused when he first beheld Lily's golden soul, beautiful even though it sported so many cracks.

"Oh, Vipina," he said, a wealth of emotion in his deep, soft voice. Only then did Lily realize that she wasn't the only one who was exposed by the sharing of her mind. Vadom's voice was always so carefully modulated, yet it was not here and now. And then, suddenly, she felt her vapa's swift and potent anger.

"*The xydolem will pay dearly for this,*" he whispered, his voice soft with lethal fury.

Lily was startled, then a bit unsettled, by Vadom's words. He just hadn't ever seemed like the type of being to thirst for vengeance. As though he sensed her uncertain feelings, Vadom tamped down on his simmering rage.

"*Forgive me my outburst, Vipina. Please lead the way to your eyes that I may see as you do.*"

Lily felt the weight of his words as though they were a command. She felt like her will was under siege, though her vapa did not demand anything of her. This was what it meant to allow a being who was not her truemate into her mind. It felt as if she was giving up a great deal of her control and independence. Lily knew she wouldn't forget this sobering experience anytime soon.

Just over there, by Alder, Vapa.

When Vadom turned in the direction she indicated and caught sight of Alder's silvery soul, Lily felt a pang of anxiety. She wasn't the only one at Vadom's mercy right now. A moment later, Lily knew she had been foolish to worry. She could feel Vadom approach Alder slowly and with infinite care, making sure not to disturb her faelan's brilliant silver soul.

"*Well met, Alder of the Fae Wood.*"

"Well met, Vadom of the Cave Kingdom, otherwing to Vabiri."

They seemed to size each other up and reach some sort of accord in an instant, though neither of them spoke another word. Before Lily could begin to understand their strange exchange, however, they turned in unison toward her outer senses and looked out of her eyes together.

"*Where is this woman you saw, Vipina?*"

She felt her companions' intense concentration, but Lily knew that they couldn't see the white lady. She was impossible to miss. Lily drifted closer to them, wondering if that would help. She had never stayed here with Alder and viewed the world from a distance, as if through a window. She always surfaced and fully lived in her surroundings when she was awake. It felt a little strange to look out at the world from here, and not be truly a part of it.

She is at the top of the hill, waiting for me. For us. Do you see her beckoning?

"*I see a witch town shut up tight against the vampires of the night, Vipina. The Ropanians rarely venture out after dark when they would make themselves so vulnerable to my kind.*"

"I don't see anyone either, faelani. *You must be seeing her with your inner magic."*

Vadom seemed a little surprised.

"You cannot see as Lily does?"

"I am here without my wells of power, and I did not want to harm her by attempting to summon outer magic. The iron would punish her for it severely."

Vadom's mind seemed to approve of Alder's caution and forbearance.

"Have you tried using her inner magic?"

Alder seemed to hesitate a moment, then responded.

"Among the Fae, that is simply not done, barring a few specific exceptions. Mates should not use each other in that way."

Vadom accepted that respectfully, then sank into thought for a moment.

"Vipina, could you summon that magic which enables you to see the elements? The smallest amount would be sufficient."

Lily indicated the affirmative, though she tried to brace herself for the pain without her visitors noticing. She went to her well of elemental magic and called for the tiniest possible portion. And, as she expected, more than just a bit gushed out before she sent it to Vadom and Alder and clamped down on the rest. The iron pain came, swiftly and without mercy, while the Fear tried to shove past her to get to her inner magic. The familiar struggle ensued, though Lily wasn't about to lose to the iron now, with the Fae Wood tantalizingly close. She held on to that knowledge dearly until she'd beaten the Fear out near her circular mental wall.

When Lily had things under control, she went back to her wells of power, doggedly prepared to summon more magic if she hadn't yet convinced her vapa about the white lady. She knew with complete certainty that this was important enough to endure the suffering. Lily didn't know how she knew, but—

"Wait, Vipina. Rest a moment, please."

Lily subsided, hoping against hope that Vadom had seen what he needed to see. She could feel Alder valiantly subduing his worry and concern, while her vapa seemed infinitesimally shaken by what she'd just had to do. That seemed a little odd to Lily, though she was admittedly a bit dazed at the moment. Didn't Vadom battle a portion of iron from her necklace because of her sun magic bond with him? He had known she fought the same thing on a larger scale, hadn't he? And yet, it was one thing to know something, and quite another to watch it unfolding up close . . .

Lily's thoughts were interrupted by a rush of realization from Alder. She and Vadom both turned from their thoughts toward him, waiting for an explanation.

"Faelani, *I still didn't see anything out of the ordinary when you sent us that inner elemental magic. But I think I know why we didn't: it isn't your inner elemental power that is sensing this unknown entity. I believe you must have wings of enhancement, and they are picking up on a magic that isn't precisely considered one of the elements at all.*"

As Lily struggled to process this new information, Vadom spoke up thoughtfully.

"*You said that the female is 'whiter than all the rest,' Vipina? The High Priestess and her coven all wear white to symbolize the purity of the goddess they worship. Many Ropazians wear white clothing, to honor and respect their goddess, as well.*"

But Vapa, *she isn't just wearing white. She IS white.*

They all fell silent. It took Lily a few protracted moments to allow what Alder and Vadom were saying, as well as her own observations, to make sense in her pain-ridden mind. She and Alder gasped in realization almost simultaneously, just a second behind Vadom's small surge of surprise.

"Faelani, *the Goddess of Ropaz is summoning you,*" Alder said, stunned.

29

Goddess's Retreat

Lily entered her first coven town ever in the arms of her *vapa*. It hadn't taken much longer to convince Vadom and Alder to allow her to enter Goddess's Retreat. Lily had gone to one of the wells in her mind that had never appeared to give her any trouble and very carefully summoned a bit of the magic within. To her surprise, it had obeyed her much more readily than some of her other magic did. Her *vapa* had taken the pain from her, without explanation. She hoped it hadn't hurt him too much.

With that enhancing power, Vadom and Alder had been able to see all of the white magic, and the Goddess as well. Alder had seemed totally shocked, but Vadom had taken it a bit more in stride. Lily assumed that Vadom had been around people who believed in her for so long that proof of her existence was just another step on a winding road. Alder's exposure to Ropaz, though, had been very limited, and he had little reason to give any credence to the deity of the witches and wizards. Both had been completely convinced that the white lady would never harm Lily, and so Vadom had left Lily's mind as carefully as he had entered it, pulled Lily's body back into his arms, and begun to make his way into the quiet little town of Goddess's Retreat.

When they had passed a number of dwellings and made it most of the way up the hill where the Goddess waited, Vadom stopped and carefully set Lily on Whirlwind's back. When Lily looked down at him in question, he gave her that familiar hint of a smile.

"It will save us some time if I get water and food while the Goddess watches over the two of you. I will rejoin you shortly, *Vipina*."

Lily nodded, then urged her horse up the last of the steep incline. It leveled abruptly, and Lily could only stare a moment at the natural beauty before her. The top of the hill was shaped, rather unexpectedly, like a bowl, with a lip that dipped steeply down to form a hollow space. It was rather comfortingly like an amadel's back. The depression was full of water, but not like any water Lily had ever seen. This liquid shimmered and shone, as if something about it was profoundly magical. There were white benches set at regular intervals around the pool, and Lily dismounted so that she could walk to one of them. She passed two benches before settling on the southernmost seat. The one that was just a tiny bit closer to the Fae Wood than the others.

The Goddess was nowhere to be seen, but Lily knew, perhaps because of her wings of enhancement, that she was there. Lily contented herself with just sitting and taking in the serenity of her surroundings. After a few quiet moments, she spoke to Alder.

Do you think she'll talk to us, or do you think she just wanted to have us rest here for a bit?

"I don't know, faelani. *I'm still trying to grasp the fact that the Goddess is a true entity! The Fae do not pay her homage, though we try to respect all living things and uphold the natural balance of the world of Lamoranth. I suppose our largely peaceful way of life would meet with her approval, though we fall under her purview only in a very broad sense. If ever I meet with witches in amicable circumstances, I will make my respect for their deity quite clear."*

They lapsed into silence, and Lily found herself allowing the tranquility of the pool to permeate her battered senses.

"Good evening, Lily, Alder."

Lily turned to see the Goddess, sitting right beside her on the bench. She couldn't make out the white lady's features clearly, but she did see kindness and beauty in the ethereal face next to her. The Goddess was draped modestly in an unadorned white robe, but she was somehow anything other than plain. Lily didn't think that any being so full of love could be ordinary.

"Good evening, Goddess."

"I apologize for not making myself known to Alder and Vadom just now, my dear, but I thought it would be best if your *vapa* saw the inside of your mind and realized the depth of your trust in him. His knowledge of your mind, magic, and soul will be invaluable when he teaches you all of the lessons you must learn."

Lily shrugged in acceptance, and the Goddess smiled at her.

"You were made from the strongest magic and the strongest love, Lily Silverhall Gildenthrone. Never forget this, even in the difficult years ahead of you."

Lily nodded, unable to speak past the lump in her throat. She knew her mother had loved her deeply.

"I have a few words to say to you as well, Alder Waterfield Silvergrove."

Lily felt Alder's surprise as he quickly snapped out of his worry-tinged thoughts.

"I am listening, Goddess."

The white lady smiled again, and Lily knew that she didn't need to repeat Alder's words aloud.

"I say this to you, Alder, with the certainty of one who has watched the ages roll by, full of those who were weak and those who were strong; those who felt affection and those who loved profoundly; those who crumbled with cowardice and those who were brave beyond measure. I know, young *faelan*, that you will never disappoint your truemate. You will always, always be enough for Lily. As great as she may come to be, you will ever be her equal in all things. Release your doubts and let no one resurrect them, for you and Lily are just as truemates should be."

Lily could feel the impact the Goddess's words had on Alder, and she sent all the gentleness and care she could spare to wrap his shocked silver soul. When several moments had passed, the Goddess took Lily by the hand and stood. Together, they walked to the edge of the pool and gazed down into its shimmering depths.

"So much sorrow I felt that night," the Goddess said softly, as though to herself. Turning to Lily, she said more clearly, "I shed these tears when I first realized my people were divided, and that many had willingly forsaken the Ethic in pursuit of magical domination. Now, I rarely allow anyone other than my priestesses to view this pool, and fewer still are permitted to touch the water within. I want you to be one of those few, however. Come, lay down by the edge, and I will wash your hair."

Lily, feeling very honored and a bit shy, sat down near the edge of the pool and began taking down her hair from its wrap. When she had carefully set aside the cloth and the thin iron plates, Lily laid down on her back and looked to the Goddess kneeling beside her. Smiling softly, the white lady gently tilted Lily's head and submerged the back of her head in the pool. As the Goddess gently massaged her scalp, Lily felt all the pain and Fear leave her body, as though it had never existed. She felt tears of gratitude well up and spill out of her eyes. The Goddess tsked softly, then carefully wiped Lily's eyes with her fingers, starting at the bridge of Lily's nose and sweeping across her cheekbones to her ears. Lily felt her eyes widen in surprise, for they were somehow completely dry.

"Dear fairy petal, you have cried so much, and you will cry still more, I think, amidst the toil on the difficult path ahead of you. Let this moment be peaceful."

Lily nodded, and the Goddess resumed her care of Lily's hair.

"The tears of a lady can be a powerful thing, Lily," the Goddess said musingly. "Sometimes they bring relief, other times they perpetuate sorrow. From the eyes of the compassionate, they can even give healing in unexpected ways. I think I see what kind of tears you shed, my dear, and I think your mother must be smiling at you from the Peaceful Realm of mine that she has entered."

Lily's eyes popped open.

"Is she all right? Is her soul happy there?"

"She is fine, although she waits for her truemate to join her. When they are reunited, she will be content to exist until your time comes to go there as well."

Lily closed her eyes again and reached for Alder. He softly glowed for her until the Goddess gently sat Lily back up. When Lily reached up to touch her hair, it was completely dry.

"That ought to get you to Golden Court in one piece, Lily dear."

"Thank you, Goddess," Lily replied, with all the sincerity she felt in that moment.

"Good luck, golden ones," the Goddess said. Then she smiled at them one more time and vanished as suddenly as she had arrived.

Lily sat, lost in thought, until Vadom arrived a few minutes later. He approached silently, looking lighter of heart than Lily had yet seen him.

"Did the Goddess talk to you as well, *Vapa?*"

Vadom's mouth turned up at the corners, but he didn't elaborate. When his gaze focused on Lily, he stopped, eyes widening slightly in surprise.

"Did the Goddess take away your pain, *Vipina?*"

Lily nodded, then briefly recounted what the white lady had said to her and to Alder. Vadom approached them and sat down nearby, absorbing Lily's words with his full attention. They were all quiet for a brief time, soaking up the comforting atmosphere of the Goddess's retreat.

"This is the first time I have seen your hair, *Vipina*. It is lovely."

Lily turned to Vadom, a little surprised. That was nothing to how she felt, however, when she brought a lock within her own sight and saw that it shimmered and shone, just like the Goddess's pool.

"Is it all like that?" Alder asked, sounding slightly dazed.

Lily, a bit overwhelmed herself, wandered over to where Whirlwind calmly stood, waiting for the journey to continue. Lily distantly noticed that the mare's muzzle was wet. Reaching for the haversack, Lily set it gently on the ground and then proceeded to dig through its contents for her circular hand mirror. She would have tried looking in the pool, but Lily wasn't sure of what her reflection would look like from that particular surface. She wasn't entirely certain she wanted to find out just now. Finding the mirror, still wrapped in a piece of her desert clothing, near the bottom, Lily gently unwound it. Then, taking a deep breath, Lily held it at an angle that would allow her to see a portion of the back of her head.

It was all shimmery. From the crown of her head to the end of every strand at her waist, Lily's hair shone like the twinkling stars far above her. Alder was mesmerized. Lily found herself wondering if she had her father's hair, though with a goddess's extra shimmer.

At that very instant, Lily felt some of her inner magic rise up, fill the mirror, and speed unswervingly toward the Fae Wood. The pain and Fear crept forcefully back into her mind in response, and Lily was trying to keep it from regaining its hold on her when she felt the mirror being pried from her fingers. Lily opened her eyes to see Vadom trying to take the mirror from her without causing her harm. She didn't know, though, if the magic would allow her to release her grip.

"Faelani, *you must let go! Your wings of enhancement will stop trying to send the message if you unhand the mirror. Vadom will help you, but you must release it now!"*

Just as Lily was trying to regain control of her hands, a face appeared in the mirror. A face that wasn't hers, but had shocking similarities. Their eyes met for just an instant, and Lily was so surprised by that face and those eyes that she dropped the mirror from nerveless fingers.

With the contact broken, Vadom snatched up the mirror, wrapped it in her rumpled garment, and shoved it back in her haversack. Lily's hair wrap and the iron plates, as well as the small bundle of food and water he had just obtained, quickly followed. Once the haversack was closed and strapped to Whirlwind's saddle, Vadom picked Lily up and began to run. Lily, still stunned by the surge of magic and that face in the mirror, distantly noted that her *vapa* hastened down the hill and out of the little white coven town, Whirlwind following easily in his wake. Once he was past the outskirts of Goddess's Retreat, Vadom put on a burst of speed and began to sprint.

Lily, still struggling through a haze of pain and confusion, tried to sort out what was happening.

Alder, what's going on?

"Faelani, *were you thinking of your father when you looked in the mirror?"*

Alder's voice was gentle, but Lily could tell he was shaken.

No . . . well, maybe in passing. I just wondered if I have the same hair that he does, and then my inner magic came out of nowhere . . .

"You do have his hair, faelani. *And some of his other features as well. Did he get a good look at you, too?"*

We just made eye contact for a second, Alder. I could see, in his eyes, that he is . . . broken.

Lily felt miserable even as she forced herself to tell Alder what she had seen. The peace she had felt by the Goddess's pool was fading, to be replaced by iron-induced Fear and the weariness of her travels, not to mention the important things she would have to do once she got through Ford-upon-Ward. Lily felt guilty for allowing her father to be last on her urgent list of tasks. She had put delivering her mother's scroll before her father, before Alder even. Her father clearly didn't have much time left before he . . . left the Fae Wood to be with her mother. Lily shouldn't have shunted him aside just because she hadn't known until recently that he might have wanted her for a daughter after all. And Alder! Wasn't the safety of his soul more important than a rolled up piece of paper? He could hardly speak at the moment, and he was usually such a steadfast presence in her mind. He might want to inform the king about the trolls and xydolem first, but as far as Lily was concerned, they could do so from wherever her father or Alder's body were—

"*Vipina,* are you well?"

Startled, Lily looked up at the grave face of her *vapa.*

"I'm alright, I just . . . I saw my birth father's face in my mother's mirror, *Vapa.* And he is . . . broken. And nothing can heal him."

Lily snuggled into the hollow of Vadom's shoulder, needing to feel his strength.

"It was an accident. Alder said my wings of enhancement can send messages through mirrors, but I didn't know that until after, *Vapa.* So when I wondered if I had my father's hair when I was looking at mine . . ."

Lily trailed off, suddenly too tired to keep speaking.

Vadom was quiet a moment, then he let out a small sigh.

"I am sorry the Goddess's peace for you was so short-lived, *Vipina.* I think, however, that it is only her generous removal of your iron pain that allowed you to survive the mishap with the mirror. Your surge of fairy magic was big, enough to push past the iron you wear and my Void sphere. I'm certain it was enough to wake every witch and wizard in Goddess's Retreat. While they will stay indoors until dawn, I am more concerned about other pursuers. There have been several xydolem scouts examining terrain for the trolls, and while I have kept us undetected and a comfortable distance from them so far, they will not have failed to sense you by the pool. We must make for Ford-upon-Ward as fast as may be."

Lily's hazy confusion was burned away by her *vapa*'s words. They were in danger, and it was all her fault. What had possessed her to look in the mirror anyway? How could she have been so careless—

"Faelani, *if you are castigating yourself for this incident, I beg you to stop. It is my fault this happened. We had just found out about your wings of enhancement, and I should have told you about them, at least enough so that you would know the risks while you wear the iron. Even if I hadn't told you then, I should never have let you unwrap that mirror. I just wasn't thinking clearly . . . I was enchanted by that place, and by the Goddess, and most especially by you, and I let you walk right into what could have been a fatal situation. If the Goddess had not just removed the iron pain and Fear you had been feeling up until then . . . I cannot bear to think about it. What was she thinking, saying those things about me?*"

Lily could feel how utterly downcast Alder was, and she wished she knew how to pull him back up. Here was the perfect opportunity to try to bolster Alder's confidence in himself, and Lily searched for the right words to say to help her truemate.

Faelan, *I believe everything she said to you was true. I will always think so, until you do, too.*

Alder seemed to pause, as though he was weighing Lily's words and tone carefully.

"Faelani, *are you alright?*"

It was the total gentleness of his voice that had Lily fighting back tears. Drifting near his silvery soul, Lily tried to explain, but her voice wobbled badly.

It was just so peaceful, and then it really wasn't again. I forgot about the danger for a little while, but it was there all the time. And now I've made things even worse. And I don't know what to do even if we do make it to the Fae Wood before the xydolem catch up to us, because it feels as though I have to choose between my mother, and my father, and my truemate, and the unsuspecting fairies of the Wood who have no idea about the trolls, and how in the world can I make a decision like that?

Lily knew she was losing any semblance of calm, but Alder didn't seem to mind. He just wrapped her more tightly with feelings of reassurance and affection, and Lily gradually regained her composure.

Sorry about that, faelan.

"Lily, you don't have to apologize. Anyone in your situation would be scared, and certainly a little distressed. Maybe we should talk some things out, and then you'll be able to make better decisions. I keep wondering if we are close enough to tell you what you need to know, but with the xydolem in pursuit . . . would you mind waiting a little longer? Just until we are inside the Bubble?"

An hour ago, Lily might have protested. Ford-upon-Ward was, after all, only a hard day of traveling away, and they had been undetected, thanks to the vigilance of her *vapa*. Now, though, Lily had drawn all of the attention they had so hoped to avoid. She couldn't forget, either, how easily Vadom had entered her mind. He could have obtained any information, any magic, if he had wished to do so. If unscrupulous beings captured her . . . Lily knew she had to keep deliberately in ignorance of the Fae Wood for just a bit longer. This didn't even chafe her pride now, as it had begun to in the last week or so. It was simply the wisest course now.

I can wait, Alder. What else would you like to talk about?

"Well, I want to address our list of tasks once inside the Fae Wood. I think it is giving you worry when it is not necessarily a cause for concern. To my knowledge, my body would not have been moved from my rooms at Silver Court. You need to deliver your mother's scroll at Golden Court. You told me yourself that your mother moved to Golden Court to live with her mate, and as far as I know, your father still resides there. Then there is the warning about the Volcano Crescent and xydolem-led trolls, which must be delivered to both courts.

"So, Lily, we really just need to travel to Golden Court, for three reasons, and then to Silver Court, for two reasons. I say Golden Court first, because your father is probably less stable than me, and you need to give the king the scroll and the warning as well. Then we can go to Silver Court to restore me to my self,

and deliver the warning there. That will probably be a mere courtesy, as there are Fae tasked with passing messages back and forth between the Courts with their wings of enhancement, and they will know before we even arrive. Still, in the interest of equality and politeness, we should speak to them personally as well, after we have made me whole once more. Does this make you feel any better, Lily?"

Lily definitely felt better. Alder's calm and accurate logic had that effect on her. Now they had a plan. Things always seemed better, somehow, when there was a plan. Now that she knew what to do after Ford-upon-Ward, getting there seemed simpler too: keep moving south, stay alive. Surely they could manage that, with the immeasurable assistance of her *vapa's* guardianship.

Yes, Alder, thank you. Unless your body or soul is in jeopardy, I think we should make directly for Golden Court first, as you say. Then, when we go to Silver Court right after, we may be able to rest a bit, together.

Lily could sense Alder's wistful longing for just that. They settled into a comfortable silence, and Lily felt herself nodding off after a time. She knew she shouldn't, that she should try to stay alert, but it was dark outside, and she felt safe in her *vapa's* arms . . .

30

Disappointment and Deception

Lily was startled awake sometime later by a loud whinny from Whirlwind. She jerked her eyes open, looking around for her mare in drowsy confusion. It was just before dawn, and the world was still softly tinged in gray and lavender light.

"I was just about to wake you, *Vipina*. I regret the necessity of this, but I believe we need to split up for a time this morning."

That certainly brought Lily wide awake.

"What, *Vapa?*"

Lily knew it was a stupid question, but her panic was dulling her wits. Inside her mind, Alder was grimly staying calm, though his concern was loudly broadcasting itself to her senses as well.

"*Vipina,* two of the xydolem scouts have been pursuing us all night. They weaken with the dawn, however, and I believe they will grow weaker still as the day draws toward noon. I must dispatch them early in the day, when they are at less than full strength, but before we have to concern ourselves with the Coven of Retreat. Those witches will almost certainly catch up to us in the afternoon, for they will be traveling by air. I'm not certain at what precise time we will arrive at Ford-upon-Ward, but I don't think we should depend on the aid of the Wardens with the coven, no matter how close we are. They might not recognize you as one of their own from a distance, and they would have no reason to interfere with a dispute between wizards and a vampire."

Lily digested Vadom's words with growing trepidation. There were just too many ways someone could get hurt or end up in serious trouble today. The danger was near, and closing in fast.

"*Vipina,* I think we should halt, very briefly, so that you can eat something, and then I want you to continue south and east on Whirlwind. I am going to circle back and ambush the scouts, then catch up to you. Whirlwind was allowed to drink of the Goddess's tears, so I believe she will not tire. Certainly she has been galloping all night without slowing. I've never known a horse to keep pace with one of my kind, and as a result I think you will continue to make good time until we reunite."

Vadom made no mention of failing to return to her, and Lily couldn't bring herself to say anything to the contrary. This was totally different from leaving her mother behind to fight. Vadom was at the pinnacle of warriorhood, and taking just two xydolem by surprise. That was nothing like her healer mother being caught unawares by a contingent of monsters. At night. Still, Lily only managed a small breakfast before she could no longer swallow past her mounting tension. She offered Whirlwind some of their fresh water, and the mare readily drank. Lily stalled by rewrapping her hair, complete with the small iron discs, which she hadn't done in their precipitate departure from Goddess's Retreat. With a heavy heart, Lily gripped the edges of her saddle, staring hard at the tooled leather. After a few moments had passed, Vadom put a hand on her shoulder and gently turned her around, so that Lily had to look into his face.

"I will be back soon, *Vipina,* for I know what I am doing. Do not worry that your past will repeat itself. I will see you when the sun is at its zenith, if not a little before. Now, I want you to assure me that you will be at your most alert while I am away."

Lily struggled as her fears collided with her belief in her *vapa*. After a moment, she looked into his eyes and made him the *valoriad*.

"I will continue south, and I will not cease my vigilance for an instant, *Vapa*."

Vadom nodded, satisfied. He thoroughly checked Lily's Void sphere, then added to its density until the smoke-like magic swirled darkly about her. Lily swallowed, knowing she would have to be brave today, though it wasn't what she wanted to have to do.

Without delaying further, Lily mounted Whirlwind and turned the mare so that the rising sun was on her left. She would angle east with Alder's guidance. It was very difficult to keep her back to Vadom as she urged her horse from a trot to a canter, then into a gallop. She did not, however, look back, because she knew it wouldn't be her last glimpse of her *vapa*. She would see him in a matter of hours, and they would all be the safer for it. Except for the scouts. Lily found that she couldn't summon up more than a glimmer of pity for them, as her mother probably would have; but then, Rose had always been the most far-sighted and understanding person Lily knew.

Lily shied away from thinking of her mother further, and instead made a thorough survey of her surroundings, as she had promised she would. Then she turned deliberately toward lighter thoughts of the Fae Wood, and what it would be like inside the Bubble. So many new experiences lay before her, yet Lily hadn't really had a chance to prepare herself for any of that. Would she be able to make friends? Enjoy all of her magic lessons? The one certainty before her was that she would, eventually, complete *faelanzania* with Alder. By the sound of things, and from her *vapa*'s actions recently, Lily was sure they'd have more than enough help to make the strongest possible bond. Then something occurred to her, as she was reviewing everything Alder had ever told her about the Fae Wood. A little nervous, Lily decided to ask Alder about it, while she had the chance.

Alder, will your parents like me?

Lily's worry grew when he didn't answer right away. Finally, he responded.

"Faelani, *it is generally acknowledged that, when two Fae become mates, they lose sight of much of the world around them in their happiness and excitement. As time goes on, they complete their nine bonds, settle into their life together, and refocus on all the other aspects of their existence. Sometimes, though, a pair of truemates will remain entirely devoted to each other, long after* faelanzania *is completed. The bonds for them are such that their mate becomes their entire world, and little else is of much importance to them. Lily . . . my parents have this type of bond.*"

Lily attempted to understand this in the silence that followed. It wasn't surprising, exactly, that such strong and lasting bonds caused such behavior, but . . . what kind of parents did that make them? Lily felt her therianthrope snarl with anger deep inside. Because her truemate was telling her that his own parents didn't think he was important.

"*Lily . . . I stopped blaming my parents for the way they are a long time ago. You'll see, soon enough, that they just can't really help it. Their life together has not been an easy one, and I think they turn to each other because of all the obstacles they've had to face side by side. They've made a lot of mistakes, some of them very costly, but I've come to believe that they've done the best they could in a situation they had no choice but to accept. I hope you won't hold it against them,* faelani, *if they do not accept you into their hearts as most other mate-parents would.*"

Lily wanted to be able to reassure Alder that this was fine, but the words wouldn't come. Someone like Alder deserved so much better than a disinterested, uncaring mother and father. He needed love, and he undoubtedly deserved it. Lily realized, then, that all of Alder's talk of and admiration for Captain Pine was far more significant than she had perceived. After another moment, she spoke into Alder's growing apprehension and embarrassment, for it only angered her further that he felt such things at all.

Your parents, I will try to respect. They brought you into the world, after all, so they aren't completely terrible. But Alder, I'm going to give my affection to your praetam *and* praetuu *instead, just as you do.*

Lily was relieved to sense the happiness that Alder derived from her words. She belatedly comprehended that this must have been weighing on him more than she had known, and Lily could only be grateful they'd cleared the air on this matter now rather than later.

"I could ask for no more than what you offer, Lily. Thank you for understanding. I didn't know if you would have trouble accepting this about me. Your relationship with your mother differs so much from mine . . . Rest assured though, faelani, *that Captain Pine and Iris will come to care for you very deeply."*

They fell into a strange silence, absorbing the new knowledge between them, and the expectations it changed. Lily bestirred herself after a bit, realizing she needed to keep a sharper eye on the land around her, the horse beneath her, and whoever might be in the sky above her. Though she rode as fast as she dared, novice horse rider that she was, it still didn't seem fast enough. Hours crept by, even as they sped through the remaining distance to the Fae Wood. How had such a tense day remained so uneventful? Lily didn't dare hope for nothing to actually happen, except for the return of her *vapa*. Should he have caught back up to them by now? She decided not to even think about it unless Vadom still hadn't returned by early afternoon. Then she would worry. Excessively.

"I don't think you need to grow anxious about Vadom yet, Lily. It is not quite midday. You know, we should be able to see the Bubble anytime now. Certainly we are approaching the vicinity of its northern border. I can hardly believe we are so close to home, can you?"

Lily felt a tingle of excitement. Could they really be so near their destination at last? She strained her eyes, intently scanning the horizon for a tell-tale shimmer of fairy magic.

Will you be able to see the Bubble too, Alder?

"Yes, I will. Everyone in Lamoranth can see the Bubble if they are close enough, faelani. *Its formidable appearance is part of how it deters unwanted visitors. As fairy lore would have it, there are some races in this world who cannot even come close to the golden dome without being pained by it, and so they keep it ever out of sight."*

Lily found that surprising. Was it sort of like how iron was for fairies? That it innately caused harm to some, without any apparent or rational explanation? When she asked Alder, he seemed intrigued by her line of thought.

"I never wondered how or why the Bubble could be so abhorrent to certain others. I cannot even recall which races the legends say cannot endure its magic. And to compare it to the Bane of the Fae . . . it is a solid enough object, I think, to hold up to that comparison. Would that we could replicate the Bubble's substance and turn it into an everyday material to plague our enemies—"

Alder look, look! There it is— the Bubble!

Through her rush of excitement, Lily felt Alder's corresponding joy. It would be a true homecoming for him, entering the Fae Wood once more. Perhaps she would discover a good home beneath the Bubble as well. Would she live with her father, at first, while he was still . . . there? Or would she always be with Alder in this new life? Before she could ask him, however, Lily's well of prophecy gave a sluggish rumble. Pain lanced through her, as surely as her premonition of danger.

Lily gripped the pommel of her saddle tightly with one hand and kept her reins in the other, desperately trying to keep her seat and maintain her speed through the brief but intense battle she waged with her Fear. Alder sped toward her wells of power to safeguard them, then forced himself to wait in taut silence for the iron effects to subside. Lily managed fairly well, but was too troubled to speak about her intuitive magic's warning right away. What had that been about? Her *vapa*? Witches? The Fae Wood? Something she didn't even know about yet? It had been fairly minor, compared to the dread she had felt on previous occasions . . .

Lily decided to shake it off for now, but practice even greater vigilance. She focused fully on the part of Ropaz through which she was passing. Turning carefully, she looked back at the hills she had just traversed. No sign of danger, or her *vapa* either. Looking to her right and left, Lily saw more of the same. Before her, the Bubble was shining in the distance. It was comprised of all the colors of magic, including glints of gold and flashes of silver, which swirled on its iridescent surface. Suddenly, she wondered how they would enter Ford-upon-Ward, precisely. What did a town built on a river look like?

Alder, how will we find Ford-upon-Ward? Is there a hidden entrance, or is it an obvious part of the Bubble?

"*It is only visible to fairies,* faelani, *and elves who have passed through it at least once with peaceful intentions. When you are close enough, you will see that the gateway has a stronger concentration of magical colors than the rest of the Bubble. Then you simply knock, and Wardens will listen to your request for entrance. Those who are expected, such as the diplomatic elves, are allowed into the Antechamber, so that they can verify their identity and specifically state their reasons for visiting the Fae Wood. As you are unexpected, you will have to give them a great deal of information completely outside the Bubble. I don't like that it keeps you in Ropaz longer than necessary, but they are always exceedingly cautious about who they permit inside. The Wardens are tasked with the protection of the Wood along the northern border, and they must exercise extreme caution so that an enemy does not infiltrate our home and jeopardize the safety of the Fae.*"

Lily felt a sinking sensation in the pit of her stomach. Tears threatened, yet she forced herself to ask a question that had not occurred to her before that moment.

Alder, will they let my vapa *enter the Wood?*

His hesitance told her as no words could.

Lily was definitely crying now. How could she leave Vadom behind in Ropaz? He was a part of her new life, and she was growing to love him. How could she bear to lose him like this?

"Faelani, *please, don't distress yourself. I will do all in my power to see that your* vapa *enters the Fae Wood. I've been thinking that we could grant him sanctuary in the Antechamber, given his situation with the other vampires of the Cave Kingdom. That ought to give us enough time to explain Vadom's character and relationship with you, and then he will have a much better chance at gaining admittance into the Fae Wood proper. Do not lose hope yet, Lily, please.*"

Lily felt that paralyzingly stricken feeling loosen its grip on her. Alder had clearly given this matter a good deal of thought and determined the best course already. He knew how things worked, and how best to handle—

THWHACK.

Whirlwind stumbled nearly to a halt as something large collided with the Void sphere around them. Lily looked around frantically, caught completely off guard. She cursed her lack of attention, today of all days, and tried to force her mind to assess the situation calmly. It hadn't been a Void pulse, for Lily had been hoping to sense one from her *vapa* all morning, and would have probably gotten a message from him besides. That hadn't been fairy magic either, because it had felt just like all the rest of the magic in Ropaz had so far. So, if it wasn't a vampire or xydolem with night magic, and wasn't a fairy with inner power . . . it must be Ropazians.

Lily scanned the sky in all directions, straining her eyes to catch any glimpse of an air-borne witch or wizard. After several tense minutes, however, she still hadn't sighted any other beings in her vicinity. Somehow, this was even worse than seeing an enemy nearby. How could she protect herself and Alder against an invisible foe? Spurring Whirlwind on, Lily asked Alder, though she was very careful to remain at the height of watchfulness now.

Alder, what was that? What can we do? Are we in trouble?

"I think and fervently hope that it was the wizard equivalent of a Void pulse, Lily. They are searching in earnest for the fairy who was in Goddess's Retreat last night, and so they are using the air magic they have that detects the Fae. I don't know if they sensed your Void sphere, or if they would much care even if they did. With any luck, Vadom's night magic protection for you will hold until he arrives and renews it as necessary. So, I don't think we're in dire straits just yet, but I think we should travel as hard as we can until we reach the Bubble. It is very dangerous to be directly under the air of a coven of witches on a fairy hunt."

Lily looked straight above her, up into the endlessly blue Ropazian sky. She thought she saw the tiniest of specks at an impossible distance away, like a pebble that didn't know up from down. Was that the witch or wizard? Searching for her? Lily scanned the rest of her surroundings intently, but saw nothing else out of the ordinary. She shivered. Having all of this invisible danger around her was positively maddening.

Do you think we ought to send a Void pulse to find my vapa*? Do you think it's safe, if he hasn't sent one to check on us yet?*

Alder deliberated before answering.

"I think it might be best to send one ourselves first. We don't want to wait until we're in the middle of a crisis to call for help. It is nearly the appointed time to meet back up, and he should be en route now, without any xydolem scouts still around to detect our Void pulse. As long as the enemy can't pick up on our location, I think it's safe. Why don't you go ahead, faelani.*"*

Without further preamble, Lily pulled a portion of night magic apart from the twisting amount fairly close to her wells of power. She wrapped it with her intent and embedded a message for her *vapa* within, telling him of the searching coven above her. When it stilled in readiness, Lily sent it in the direction from which she had just traveled. Once the pulse was on its way, both Lily and Alder remained silent, counting the moments it took for the night magic to return. A reassuringly short time later, the Void pulse bounced back.

"Did he say anything in reply, Lily?"

Yes, to rest a moment and he would rejoin us shortly. It sounds like he is fine. I'm so relieved, Alder. I know he's perfectly capable, but I just didn't like being apart all morning, knowing he was doing something dangerous on my behalf . . .

"He has only done his duty and protected you as he has sworn to do, faelani. *A warrior such as Vadom is more than able to calculate risks and find the best solution in situations like this, where danger lies in all directions. Why don't you rest a moment, as he suggested, and eat something. There may not be time to stop later. The coven is surely patrolling as close to the Bubble as they dare to go, in the hopes of catching the stray fairy before he or she can enter the Wood and escape them. I am glad that Vadom will rejoin us for our traveling this afternoon and evening."*

I'm glad, too, Alder. I wouldn't mind a break and some food. Whirlwind could probably use some more water as well.

Gently reining in her mare, Lily came to a stop in a dip between hills, then dismounted. The day was a little warm, so she shrugged out of her amadel jacket and stored it in her haversack after she had pulled out her food pouch. After eating a little and giving Whirlwind some more water, Lily repacked the haversack, lashed it back to the edge of her saddle, and began to pace restlessly. Her *vapa* should be here any time now. Then they'd push on to Ford-upon-Ward, with the coven, hopefully, none the wiser.

THWACK THWACK THWACK.

Lily looked up anxiously, heart sinking. There were quite a few pebbles above her now. And they were more like rocks in size, actually. It seemed her luck was running out.

Alder, what should we do now? Wait for Vadom, or keep moving? I feel like a target and they're all decent shots. I don't want to stand still.

"I don't know, Lily. I'm not sure that they are really detecting you. It seems more like the Void sphere is absorbing their air detectors. Perhaps the coven can't figure out why their signals aren't coming back to them and have come to investigate, in lieu of finding a fairy easily out in the open. My main

concern is that moving will somehow alert them to your exact location. Like with the Gongoozler, remember? And Vadom did tell us to stop and wait . . . Let's give him a little longer to catch up, and think of alternative action in the meantime."

They waited in tense, anticipatory silence for minutes that stretched into ages. The air detectors went from occasional hits to a near-constant barrage as the coven homed in on Lily's location. The Void sphere began to show signs of strain, thinning on the top and swirling in irregular eddies from the coven's magic. When Lily could make out the forms of the witches and wizards above her, she could take it no longer.

Alder, I think it's time for some of that alternative action. We might be in trouble if we move, but we are definitely in danger if we stay put now. I'm going to send another Void pulse to my vapa, *explaining, and then I'm riding Whirlwind as fast as I can for the Bubble. Are you alright with that?*

"I hate to be without Vadom any longer than necessary, but I have to agree with you. Your Void sphere looks like it's nearly worn through from the strain. When that happens, the danger to you will be immense, as they will be able to track you much more easily than they are now. Go ahead and send that pulse. If Vadom isn't nearly here, I think we must ride on."

Lily hastily tried making a Void pulse, but fumbled it in her rush. She took a deep breath, let it out, and made another attempt, this time with her intentions perfectly clear. The night magic clicked into readiness. Lily sent the urgent message out, to the north and slightly west. Glancing up, she could make out the blue and white cloaks and even the prominent foreheads of more than a dozen witches and wizards. The covetous eagerness on their faces chilled Lily to the bone.

The pulse came back almost immediately, much to Lily's relief.

He is nearly here, Alder, and wants us to wait for him.

"Then we should comply, faelani. *He must have a plan, and we'll just have to hold on."*

THWACK. THWACK. THWUMP.

With that last heart-stopping concussion, the Void sphere began to give way under the Ropazian onslaught. Just when Lily was really starting to feel frightened, Vadom arrived. Lily couldn't remember ever being so happy to see anyone in her life.

"*Vapa*, thank goodness! What do we do now?"

Lily noticed at that point that Vadom was carrying . . . a body. Shocked, she realized that the being, who was at the very least unconscious, had red hair, and features not totally unlike her own. He was certainly not a native of Ropaz . . .

With nearly blurring speed, Vadom set the body down on the ground in the middle of the dissolving Void sphere. A moment later, he had checked that the haversack was secure, grabbed Whirlwind's reins, and picked Lily up. He then began running with all a vampire's haste toward the Bubble, leaving still inside of the large, perfect Void sphere in which he had arrived.

No one spoke for a little while after that. Lily distantly noted that her *vapa* had turned much more to the east than the southerly course she had set for most of the day. Lily was more absorbed with worry that they'd be discovered by a stray air detector, when she wasn't thinking about that body. Who had just taken her place as a captive of that coven? Who would become a magical slave for the witches and wizards of Goddess's Retreat in her stead? She felt terribly uneasy about it, surprised and upset that her *vapa* had done such a thing, and that she was the reason. Deep inside her mind, Lily could tell that Alder was troubled as well.

"*Vipina,*" Vadom said softly. Lily immediately looked up into his face, wondering how to ask about what had just taken place.

"That body was a decoy, *Vipina*. I made a counterfeit being out of night magic, one who looked just like the red-haired Fae warrior I fought many centuries ago. I attempted to put a little of the sun magic you gave to me inside it. It is my hope that the members of that coven will not realize their mistake until it is too close to nightfall for them to risk pursuing us in the dark."

Lily felt herself go weak with relief, and she sensed Alder relax with Vadom's explanation as well. Neither of them had wanted another fairy to suffer in their stead. Now they just might get away from the power-hungry Ropazians, thanks to her *vapa*'s cunning and lightning-fast actions.

"I formed the decoy after investigating the xydolem scouts. As it turned out, they were not actual xydolem, but two fully Void-bound trolls. I incapacitated them, for the xydolem may not react as quickly to scouts who are captured, presumably by a coven, than to scouts who are inexplicably dead. Either way, we may avoid the xydolem's notice if we make it to the river city by nightfall, as planned."

"It sounds as though he has done the best he can to put both the xydolem and the Ropazians off our trail, faelani. *I am feeling much more optimistic about your safety now, and I have your* praetam *to thank, without a doubt. Let us hope our luck holds and no one picks up our trail until we are under the Bubble."*

Lily was, in large part, as relieved and grateful as Alder. However, there had been that rumble of apprehension from her inner magic . . . and Lily was never going to ignore those warnings, however slight this particular one had been.

"*Vapa,* Alder and I are so grateful for what you've done today to protect me, especially since I caused our trouble with the mirror in the first place. Thank you."

Lily accompanied her words with an instinctive gesture of sincerity, and Vadom looked down at her and her heart-felt *valoriad* with a hint of fondness in his dark, direct gaze.

"You need not thank me for protecting you, *Vipina.* I think any vampire *vipin* would be eagerly asking about my skirmish with the troll scouts, or at least how I made a realistic-looking decoy from nothing but night magic. I confess to a measure of pride in you, *vladi,* that you are more concerned about the beings around you, even one that is counterfeit, than in fighting and deception. Though it is not necessarily how a warrior should think, I could never fault a being with a heart as generous as yours."

They all went quiet then, still feeling the gravity of their situation. Though Lily was cautiously optimistic now about their chances of making Ford-upon-Ward, she thought she ought to warn Vadom about her premonition, just in case it meant something beyond the dangerous beings they had just deceived.

"*Vapa,* my well of prophecy . . . sort of rumbled earlier. I'm a little worried about its warning."

Vadom's eyes narrowed a little, in concern and in thought.

"When exactly did your magic do this, *Vipina?* When you first saw the witches?"

"No, *Vapa.* It was when I first saw the Bubble. Alder and I had been talking about it right when it came into sight."

Vadom pondered this, drawing conclusions he didn't seem to like.

"Then I think we will have to remain very vigilant for the remainder of the day, *Vipina,* and ready for more trouble, no matter how close we are to our intended destination."

Revelations

From that point on, Lily didn't know who was more tense, her companions or herself. The afternoon drew on, their shadows gradually lengthened, and all three of them, and even Whirlwind, were in a constant state of suspense. No matter that Vadom sensed neither witches above them nor more scouts behind them. No matter that the Bubble loomed before them, seeming to touch the sky the closer they came to its base and the safety of the Wood. Lily felt as though she would come out of her skin waiting for something bad to happen.

Alder, I don't think I can take much more of this. Do you think my inner magic could have been wrong? Or do you think we'll have trouble with the Wardens, somehow?

"I don't know, faelani. *We seem to have thrown off our pursuers, but your prophetic magic, even damaged by the Fear, has not yet been incorrect. I think we should be prepared for anything. You, in particular, will need to be ready for questioning by the Wardens tonight. Even if nothing goes amiss, it will be a bit of an ordeal to convince them to allow you inside the Wood. I wish, as your mate, that I could speak on your behalf and spare you the interrogation, but it is not possible without my body."*

Lily could clearly sense Alder's feelings about the impending situation, and she wished she could remedy his frustration. She tried by responding with a little teasing.

Well, Alder, I suppose I'll just have to keep speaking for myself, at least until we have you back in your body in a day or two. One wonders how I've managed to communicate without a truemate for nearly seventeen years, but I guess I'll just have to keep muddling through.

Alder's fond exasperation lightened Lily's heart a bit.

"I'm not sure how your strength escaped my notice for even a moment, my independent one. Forgive my presumption for wishing to carry some of your burden, but you may have to let me, a little, once things settle down, or I shall feel quite useless by your side."

Though his tone was teasing, Lily sensed an underlying truth to Alder's words. She responded a little more seriously than he probably anticipated.

Alder, I am always going to want you with me. It's just that I might need you in ways other than what you were told to expect, I think.

Alder was very quiet for a moment.

"You will tell me, Lily, when you need me? Tell me, until I know without you having to ask?"

Lily realized that this was important to him, very much so. Her reply was utterly solemn.

Yes, faelan. *I will always tell you.*

Some of Alder's tension seemed to leave him then, as though a weight neither of them had noticed on his soul had been lifted. Surprised, Lily wasn't quite sure what to say in the silence that fell between them. She wasn't sure there really was anything more to say, at first, and then she realized that there was, quite obviously, one thing more.

And will you, Alder, my friend and my truemate, always tell me when you need me? Whatever I can do, you have only to say, faelan.

Lily could have sworn his soul trembled ever so slightly before he answered.

"Thank you, Lily. I will speak up if I need you, too."

Feeling as though they had just had an unexpectedly important conversation, Lily felt herself smiling a bit. For a newly mated pair, they really were doing pretty well.

"*Vipina. Vipina,* Alder, I need your full attention now, please."

Lily and Alder were pulled, a bit guiltily, back to their dangerous current predicament by the steady words and voice of Vadom. Lily felt the tension of the day return in full force, whisking away her moment with Alder. Regretfully, she surfaced to the highly alert face of her *vapa.*

"Sorry, *Vapa.* Alder and I were just talking about something."

Vadom must have heard the unspoken 'important' Lily had left off at the end, for his face softened just a fraction.

"No need to apologize, *Vipina.* I suspect the two of you will have to seize time for each other when you can, to make the fairy bonds you both require. It is simply that it is evening now, and we should probably be on the lookout for Ford-upon-Ward. Alder has told you what you need to know to find it, I assume?"

"Yes, earlier today, and about what to expect of the Wardens as well. I'll start looking for the entrance to the river city now, *Vapa*."

Lily began scanning the giant Bubble that dominated her entire view. Though all of the colors of magic danced and swirled on its surface, Lily could tell now that the predominant color of this protective barrier was the gold of love element. Did the Fae believe, then, that this was a wall built in love? Or was it just less coincidental than she had realized that vampires called fairy power sun magic? If this golden dome was all the Cave Kingdom's inhabitants had seen of the Fae for time immemorial, Lily understood Vadom's usage of the term a little better now.

Though she watched continually for a denser patch of gold, Lily still hadn't spotted it when Vadom tensed suddenly, his arms curling about her protectively. Lily swung her gaze around and up to his face, but he was looking intently over his shoulder. Lily kept quiet, sensing that he was using Void element to track something she couldn't see or otherwise detect. In her mind, Alder was waiting in a suspense tinged with dread. It seemed as though Lily's premonition was about to manifest.

"*Vipina*, it seems that the xydolem's troll troops have moved faster than I anticipated, or indeed thought possible. They are very near, though the xydolem are cloaking them heavily with night magic. We will be lucky to reach the entrance to the river city before them."

Lily took a moment to absorb this news, then her mind raced to think of something, anything, useful in their predicament.

"But how do they know where Ford-upon-Ward is? Surely none of them are fairies, or elvish friends of the Fae? Don't we have an advantage in being able to pinpoint the location of the entrance?"

"While it seems highly unlikely that the Fae have a traitor to contend with, this is also not the first time we have wondered at this enemy's knowledge of the Fae Wood, *Vipina*. I don't think we can count on the river city's precise whereabouts as an advantage with a potential informant causing such trouble. Let us also not forget that at least some Ropazians know the general vicinity of this fairy establishment, for it was on that map in Wizulaan, after all."

Lily continued to wrack her brain for anything worth suggesting to her *vapa*, but the iron and its attendant fatigue slowed her thinking, no matter how hard she tried to concentrate on a solution.

"Faelani, *I think you should keep looking for the entrance to the Wood. Vadom will devise some way to outmaneuver our enemies, or at least beat them to our mutual destination, and keep you safe. If the worst occurs and it comes to a fight, we still have Whirlwind to ride on if we must.*

"*Do you think he can tell how many trolls there are? Their numbers might be more than he can take on alone, and that does not bode well for the unprepared Wardens. Without being properly mobilized, there will be a much higher number of casualties than if some warning had gotten to them in time.*"

Lily could tell how frustrated, even upset, Alder was by all of this. She concentrated on doing her part to help her companions, looking for the magical density in the Bubble that meant safety. Before she caught a glimpse of that long-awaited sight, however, Lily began to feel the ground vibrating through her *vapa*'s hold on her. She looked over his shoulder, straining to see the force that could shake the earth beneath her, but she saw nothing more than a large smudge of smoky dark gray against the brilliant colors of the setting sun. When Lily glanced up at her *vapa*, his face was grim. Lily snapped her attention back to the Bubble, renewing her efforts to sight Ford-upon-Ward.

It was not until the twilight was deepening into night that Lily saw what she had desperately been seeking. The golden density of the entrance to the river city was in stark contrast to the nearly translucent quality of the rest of the Bubble, especially in the gathering darkness.

"*Vapa*, I see it! I see the opening to the Fae Wood! It's just ahead of us now."

Lily pointed directly at it for emphasis, hardly able to contain her excitement or relief. For a moment, her terror at the feeling of her enemies' feet right behind her, and the fact that the xydolem were spurring the trolls on, was subsumed by an overwhelming need to knock on that door and gain admittance. Vadom's shoulders seemed to loosen minutely, and he made a slight adjustment to their course so that they were making straight for the Wood's entrance.

A mercifully short time later, Vadom had to slow from his sprint to a run, so that they wouldn't overshoot their destination. Beside and slightly behind them, Whirlwind slowed in obvious relief, clearly in need of a respite after their intense journey from Goddess's Retreat. Just before they reached the entrance, Vadom made them visible, though the Void sphere was still reassuringly protective. At last, he came to a complete halt when Lily pointed at the portion of wall she could almost reach out and touch, the golden entrance, where, finally, she could enter her new life as an unfettered fairy.

Gently, Vadom set Lily down on her feet. Lily looked up at him and smiled, suddenly full of nerves, though wonderfully excited as well. His eyes softened just a touch, then encouraged her without words. Lily squared her shoulders, turned to the swirling golden wall, and knocked. Once. Twice. And a third time, just for good measure. Then she stood back a step, and waited.

They didn't have to wait long. Almost instantly, nine very imposing warriors sprang from the seemingly solid golden wall and surrounded Lily, Vadom, and Whirlwind. Their coloring ranged from pale blue to vibrant purple. One Fae warrior was a light green, reminding Lily just a little of the elvish Gongoozler. Every last one of them held a weapon in hand.

Vadom remained utterly still, though Lily felt him close beside her, ready for anything. Alder was vacillating between immense relief at the warriors' presence and indignation over their actions. Lily decided she wanted to be the first to speak.

"I have come to request admittance into the Fae Wood for myself and for my *praetam*, who is in need of sanctuary."

Lily spoke in Ropazian, though she used the fairy word for *vapa* deliberately in the hope that it would gain him entrance into the Antechamber. A burly Fae warrior with pale blue hair and eyes, standing almost directly in front them, responded, also in Ropazian. His gaze raked her intently, though she wondered how well he could see her in the growing gloom of night.

"Your request is noted. Begin by stating your names and your business traveling at such speed and at nightfall."

His gaze flicked to Vadom, and his hold on his mace tightened. Though Lily was nearly squirming with impatience, she knew she had to explain as much as possible and hope they were allowed inside before the trolls and their masters arrived. Inside her mind, Alder was obviously itching to speak, but he kept silent, letting Lily remain fully focused on this critical conversation.

"My *praetam* is Vadom of the Cave Kingdom. I am Lily Silverhall Gildenthrone, truemate of Alder Waterfield Silvergrove, and I have come to return his soul to his body and to deliver a message from my mother Rose to the Golden King. I also have urgent news about the trolls of the Volcano Crescent that the fairy rulers must hear as soon as possible."

Lily could feel the incredulity of the Fae warriors around her. They had been focused almost exclusively on Vadom, who was apparently a much greater threat than herself, yet her words brought her the wide-eyed scrutiny of nine pairs of eyes. Lily made herself meet the gaze of the big, blue-featured leader, steadily refusing to look away. Slowly, he lowered his weapon, as though he couldn't bear to keep it pointed in her direction. He seemed almost unable to look away from Lily's eyes. When he tore his gaze from her face and took in the iron she wore for the first time, Lily was certain his mouth nearly dropped open, though from what emotion, she couldn't tell. It took him only an instant to school his features, however, and to speak again.

"Your claim is a great one, young lady, which can easily be proven false. Will you consent to a test, that we might determine if at least one part of what you say is true?"

Lily felt her impatience begin to get the better of her. Alder stirred, his frustration going from a simmer to a boil.

"I understand Captain Beech's caution, but we do not have time for a test! See if you can impress upon him the urgency of our current situation, faelani."

"I will consent to a test, but it must be done quickly. The trolls are very close behind us. Can you not feel the ground shaking from the pounding of their feet?"

Lily watched three of the five warriors she could easily see divert their attention from herself and Vadom for the first time. She also saw their wary faces grow tight with concern as they looked beyond the circle of their fellow warriors into the moonlit night. Vadom, however, chose that moment to recapture their attention.

"My *vipina* will only undergo a test that I give you leave to administer, Fae. It would also be prudent for you to heed her warning pertaining to the trolls. There is a battalion of them only a mile or two northwest of here, being led, possibly Void-bound, by an organized band of xydolem. It is their night magic which cloaks your enemy from sight. We know not who they answer to, only that the trolls are obeying the xydolem out of fear that they will raze another of their volcanoes in the Crescent."

Though Vadom had always seemed to have a quietly commanding presence, Lily could see that the effect his words had on the Fae warriors would have stunned them regardless of her *vapa*'s softly assured delivery. Though these were obviously well-trained warriors, it was clear that they were reassessing what the bigger threat, and the higher priority, was to them at the moment. Lily thought they must be aware of the smoking volcano, at the very least, and would want to know what they and their fellow warriors faced on the Wood's western border. In front of her, the blue leader, Captain Beech, looked grim. His eyes flicked to a bright purple warrior on his right side.

"Bring the Captain of the Court Guard out here quickly. Apprise him of the situation first."

Lily could tell this was good news from Alder's happy response.

"He is bringing Captain Pine here, faelani! *I know my* praetam *will sense me, and then you will be allowed in the Wood for certain. But . . . he should be either at Silver Court or Golden Court. Perhaps even preparing warriors at Molten Mirror Lake. We do not have time to wait for him to fly from any of those places . . ."*

In mere minutes, however, the bright purple warrior returned, another purple warrior right behind him. The new Fae was more mature, his hair and eyes the light, pure purple of amethyst. Lily thought he looked as though he had recently been worn down by great sadness. She could certainly recognize the signs of such emotion in another now. What suffused his fine features at the moment, however, was a desperate hope, fearful of being for naught. Startled, Lily realized she had seen him somewhere before, as if in a dream, with a lady who was lavender as well . . .

"I have been told of all you claim, young lady, and I would have proof before we allow you to enter the Wood," Captain Pine said, his eyes nearly as direct and discerning as her *vapa*'s.

Lily smiled a little, feeling suddenly nervous about meeting Alder's *praetam*.

"It is a pleasure to meet you at last, Captain Pine," she said, and made the *valoriad* automatically, though she realized belatedly that he might not understand the meaning of her vampiric gesture.

There was a slight stirring in the circle of warriors around her. Some of their faces began to betray traces of hope, and amazement. Captain Pine went perfectly still.

"The test is this: that I enter your mind and speak to Alder myself, if he is indeed with you."

Before Lily could reply, with reluctant agreement, Vadom spoke to Captain Pine, his voice more intimidating than Lily had ever heard it.

"I will not allow this."

Pine and Vadom then seemed, to Lily, to have a contest of wills with their eyes. Captain Pine did not seem as calm or steady as her *vapa*, though. He was too worried about Alder, she thought, to win out against one such as Vadom. His reply, after an agonizingly protracted moment, was increasingly angry.

"I have been told that this fairy child calls you her *praetam*, yet you would bring her all this way and then not allow the test that would gain her admittance into the Wood?"

"Such an ordeal is not necessary for her to endure, and we do not have enough time besides. Ask questions for Alder to answer and Lily to speak aloud, if you wish to be reassured of his presence."

Captain Pine clearly did not like being told what to do, especially by a vampire. He began arguing with Vadom, who parried all his verbal attacks with total calm. Lily could feel Alder growing upset inside her mind. She got the feeling that his *praetam* was normally much more composed than he was at the moment. What else would convince these warriors, and quickly?

Suddenly, the answer became clear to her. Even as she reached for the haversack still securely fastened to Whirlwind's saddle, Lily berated herself for not thinking sooner of the obvious evidence she could easily show these warriors to confirm her identity. As she rummaged for the item she needed, Lily noticed that there was silence now all around her. No one spoke, and it made the shaking ground even more pronounced than before. Lily turned calmly to face her *vapa* and the fairy captains, quickly but carefully choosing her words. Then she held up the mirror, making sure she never looked at its reflective surface.

"Captain Pine, Captain Beech, this mirror belonged to my mother, until she gave it to me as a gift for my fourteenth birthday. She told me then that knowing myself on the inside was far more important than what I would see when I looked at myself in this mirror, and that she hoped it would remind me to reflect on my mind and soul, those parts of me that are of greatest value. When I showed Alder this mirror, he said he was present when my mother received it as a gift. And when I looked into this mirror last night, I accidentally saw the face of my father, a golden fairy, and I saw that he is broken, and cannot be healed by anything other than death."

Lily stopped a moment, needing it to keep her tumultuous feelings in check. She saw that every face before her was very solemn, and very sad.

"Is this proof enough, Fae warriors, that I am who I say, and that my business in the Wood is urgent?"

She was met with absolute silence. Though it was an effort, Lily kept her back straight and her chin up. She had to be brave if she wanted to keep her promises. She'd always known that. Finally, Captain Pine bestirred himself. He took a hesitant, almost deferential step toward her.

"May I see your mirror a moment, young lady?"

It was difficult to hand it over, but Lily placed it in his big, outstretched hands nonetheless. Captain Pine looked at the back first, appearing to recognize the rose and the Fae words carved into the wood. Then he turned it over and seemed to concentrate a moment. The mirror began to glow with soft purple magic, and an instant later, Lily heard her father's voice for the first time.

"Pine? Is she real? Have you found her already?"

"Yes sir, though it is she who found us. My force was about to leave the Ford when I was informed she was knocking on the gate for admittance. It would seem she did not need our aid in escaping any witches or wizards, as her *praetam* appears to be capable. Her vampire *praetam*."

There was a moment of silence as Lily's father apparently absorbed this news.

"Give him conditional entrance to the Antechamber, Captain Pine, and bring my daughter to me immediately."

"Yes, Your Majesty."

Lily's happiness and relief at her father's words were suspended in shock at Captain Pine's response. Your. Majesty. Lily's world seemed to go completely still.

Alder?

"Faelani," he said, very gently, *"your father is Oak, truemate of Rose, and the King of Golden Court."*

Lily felt her chest grow tight, and breathing became something of an effort. Because if her father was a king, then her mother . . .

"That mirror was carved from a branch that fell from his tree in a storm long ago. Then he gave it as a gift to your mother, Queen Rose of Golden Court."

"But *faelan*, if my parents are . . . royalty," Lily choked out, "then . . . what does that make me?"

"You are the Princess of Golden Court, faelani. *And, as things stand now, you are heir to the throne."*

"A princess, Alder? A princess. That was what you couldn't tell me, all those times?"

Lily distantly noted that she was sitting on the ground, rather than standing. How had that happened? The Fae warriors about her all looked stunned, though she was quite sure they weren't as shocked as she was at the moment. Her *vapa*'s face was as calm as ever, but he was obviously concerned about her. Her, Lily, the *princess*. By the Goddess, she'd never suspected. Not once, in her entire life.

"Faelani," Alder said, and Lily could tell, by the softness of his voice, that, somehow, there was more. *"Lily, I am sorry such a secret was kept from you. But the thing I was not telling you,* faelani, *was that I am more than I have told you, as well. I am Prince Alder of Silver Court."*

"Prince Alder of Silver Court? *Prince Alder of Silver Court?"*

No matter how many times Lily spoke it aloud, it was not getting any easier to believe. Lily saw darkness entering the edges of her vision. Strange, as it was already night. Lily felt the arms of her *vapa* around her then. She let herself curl against him, grateful for his nearness. Then something occurred to her, and she looked up at his face.

"*Vapa,* you are not a king, are you?"

He smiled a little, shaking his head.

"Despite its name, the Cave Kingdom has not had a king or queen in many ages. The Supreme Council has written and enforced vampire law for a very long time, in conjunction with the Council of Warriors." Vadom paused, then added, "I have had the honor of serving terms on both councils in my lifetime."

This, at least, Lily had suspected. Not surprising, really, that other vampires would trust her *vapa* to make good decisions and then uphold them.

"Not a prince either, then," Lily said, smiling at him weakly, trying to rally a bit.

Her effort didn't escape the observant eyes of her *vapa*. He lifted a gentle hand and cradled one side of Lily's jaw, and she knew he was offering comfort in his own way.

"No, not a prince. But, *Vipina,* I think it important for you to remember that Alder is not a prince to you, either. He will always be your otherwing, first and foremost. His soul has always been bared to you, *vladi,* and so I think you will realize soon that you know all that is most important about him already."

Lily knew this was true. She also knew Alder would have told her if it had been safe at any point on their journey here. She wasn't seriously angry, really, more like . . . significantly overwhelmed. Thankfully, the Fae Wood was only steps away, and they were all about to enter. She could work out her feelings in a few days, when everything else had been taken care of first. Like how she felt about being a fairy princess. Why hadn't her mother said anything, indicated, even obliquely, that Lily would someday have to leave the desert and take on a role as exalted as this? Before Lily became too absorbed in that and similar thoughts, a volley of arrows rained down on the entire group surrounding her. The enemy had arrived.

32

The Antechamber

Lily scrambled to her feet, staring wide-eyed at the arrows embedded in the ground around her Void sphere. It was so thick, so strong, that the arrows hadn't been able to penetrate the sphere at all, instead glancing off and burying themselves in the earth about her. Not all of the Fae warriors had been so fortunate. Four of the nine had been hit, mostly in their arms or legs. One of them, though, had taken an arrow deep in his back. Lily watched as he fell to his knees, bright purple eyes filled with pain. It reminded her of a different attack, on a different night, and she reached out her arms and ran the steps between them to catch him before he landed face down on the ground.

With Vadom beside her, Lily held the warrior up, even as the other Fae turned around to face an invading force they could not see. Beech and Pine began shouting orders, effectively coordinating those still able to move. In short order, the injured were being pulled into the golden doorway by their unscathed comrades. Beech himself took the gravely hurt purple warrior from Lily, hauling the semi-conscious Fae through the entrance. When everyone else was inside, Pine took both Lily and Vadom firmly by the hand, then, concentrating in silence for several long heartbeats, stepped straight through the swirling golden Bubble and into the Antechamber.

There was organized chaos in the space they entered, but Lily barely noticed. The magic of this place was something altogether different from that of Ropaz, and neither her wells of power nor the iron she wore were unaware of the new atmosphere. Lily could feel it hovering near her, the immensity of sun magic inside the Bubble. If she let any of it into her mind, to become transmuted into inner magic . . . the iron pain would crush her. Lily stood, unmoving, attempting to shore up her mental defenses, trying to maintain an extremely heightened level of focus, so that the Fear would not overtake her. Not now.

Lily was dimly aware of Vadom gently taking her by the shoulders and steering her farther into the Antechamber, away from the immediate proximity of the densely swirling golden entrance. As she cautiously began directing her attention to her surroundings once more, Lily saw that Captain Pine had moved away from them. He was striding quickly after Captain Beech, toward the far end of the enclosed area, just beyond which a river burbled merrily. He glanced back, once, with a preoccupied look at her. Then he passed through a second, smaller golden doorway and over a very old-looking, beautifully crafted stone bridge. It was not until Lily felt the strong and conflicted feelings of Alder in her mind that she realized Captain Pine would want to truly verify his *praetoh*'s presence and well-being, but that he must call his warriors to battle without delay.

Lily then became aware of the warriors who had remained in the Antechamber. Half of them were injured, with three of them cursing in pain and frustration as they attempted to remove arrows from their arms or legs, or were prevented from doing so by their uninjured fellow warriors. With all of her mother's healing instruction, Lily knew that it was the fourth injured Fae, the one lying unmoving with the arrow in his back, who needed assistance as quickly as possible. Before she could look about for Whirlwind and grab the medical pack, however, Lily felt a deep jolt of pain in her mind. It took her a moment to realize that the expletives of the warriors were in the Fae language, and that her magic was trying to translate them. Painfully. She knew, then, that the iron had to come off, and soon, or one well or another of her inner magic was going to cause the Fear and iron pain to overtake her.

"*Vapa*," Lily said, looking up into his alert, concerned face, "could you help me get the iron armor off, please?"

Before Lily could do more than blink, Vadom was unbuckling and removing her cuirass, including the attached plackart and coulet. Lily tried to take off her belt and dagger, but her fingers were clumsy. With dogged patience, she kept at it until it loosened and fell to the ground with a thump, clanking against the breastplate her *vapa* had already discarded. Vadom had moved on to the greaves on her lower legs, so Lily started unfastening the cuisses strapped to her thighs. A few moments more, and all the armor lay on the very short, dark green grass that covered the ground at Lily's feet.

"Lily, are you alright? Is the pain bearable now?"

Lily hastened to answer when she heard the worry in Alder's voice.

It hurts much less, Alder. The jewelry is uncomfortable, but I don't know if I have time both to remove all of it and to give medical help to these warriors before the battle starts. We need to get them out of harm's way as quickly as we can.

Lily was already scanning the Antechamber for Whirlwind as she answered Alder. It seemed to be a very small Bubble within the actual Bubble. With short grass carpeting the ground and a well-worn path leading from the large entrance to the smaller door, it was just big enough to accommodate a modest building a little way off from the path, presumably for a small number of guests. A simple shelter, apparently for horses, was just off to its side. The Fae warriors had gathered on the opposite side of the path to assess those who were injured. Finally, Lily caught sight of Whirlwind, still fairly close to the entrance to Ropaz, industriously grazing on the startlingly green grass about the path. Lily immediately jogged toward her horse.

"We need to do the same with you, Lily. Can you afford to leave the jewelry on any longer?"

The sun magic here . . . it is keeping its distance, like it's being repelled by the iron. It's my inner magic that's the trouble, trying to do things that the iron would pounce on. It would be best, at this point, if it was all—

Lily was interrupted by a shout of pain from one of the injured warriors. Glancing over, she saw that one of them had haphazardly yanked an arrow from his calf, and he now bled profusely. She needed to get over there before any of them did anything else foolish.

Just as she reached Whirlwind's side and pulled the haversack from her saddle, Vadom, who had followed her back over to her mare, quietly caught her attention.

"*Vipina,* Captain Pine handed your mirror to me once he escorted us through the entrance. I believe he didn't want to risk you sending another unintentional message with it, but it should be safer now, with your armor removed. May I ask what you are planning to do at the moment that prevents you from removing your iron jewelry?"

Lily silently accepted the mirror her *vapa* held out to her, still careful not to look at her reflection. She began digging quickly and methodically through the contents of her haversack.

"Those warriors can't afford for me to delay a moment longer, *Vapa*. Having the armor off is enough of a relief from the iron for now," Lily responded, hoping that this was the truth.

After grabbing an extra hair wrap and winding it about her mirror, Lily searched and quickly managed to unearth her mother's medical pack, as well as her water pouch. Without wasting another instant, Lily carried her things to the Fae warrior hurt worst of all.

When she knelt down beside his prone form, she could see that the arrow was still deeply lodged in his back, just below the ends of his purple hair. She had to try and help him. He couldn't wait for assistance to arrive, and he wouldn't make it to wherever the nearest healer was, no matter how close. The arrow had punctured his right lung, and his breath was already coming in irregular gasps. Lily knew all about respiration. Her mother had taught her how the body worked: what could go wrong, what impact different injuries would have in various places, and all of the consequences from the available treatments or lack thereof. She knew, in this instance, that once the gasping became a wet-sounding rattle in the warrior's throat, it would be too late.

Lily pulled out thick cotton padding from her pack, then faced the warrior's back directly, mentally preparing herself for what she was about to do. Looking at the two uninjured warriors who were sitting on either side of their fallen friend, she met their eyes and spoke as calmly as she could.

"Hold him down, by the shoulders."

Somewhat to her surprise, both Fae nodded and immediately did as she said.

"What is his name?"

"He is Poplar, my lady, of the Seaside Stand."

Lily nodded, examining the arrow and its angle in Poplar's back, trying to determine how much it would bleed when she removed it. Did she have time to make a poultice to bind it? She had to do what she could to keep his lung from collapsing, immediately. The trick would be to pull the arrow out without doing any damage to the ribs it was lodged between. Perhaps, she could try using some of her magic . . . maybe channeling just a little into his back would stop the bleeding, at least? Lily calmed her churning thoughts and made a quick plan, hoping against hope it would be enough to save this warrior.

Turning to Vadom, she said, "*Vapa*, could you make a poultice for me if I tell you what to mix, and how much?"

She had decided that she had to do her best without magic, at least at first, and a poultice could make a critical difference for Poplar by reducing inflammation and pain. It would be particularly helpful if the arrow had been coated with poison, for the herbs would draw out any toxic agents.

Nodding, Vadom instantly knelt down beside her, next to her medical pack, and pulled out her mother's mortar and pestle. As Lily concentrated on the arrow, she gave Vadom clear directions, listing slippery elm, flaxseed, lobelia, and goldenseal as the proper herbs needed. When he had ground the herbs into powder, she indicated that it was time to add water to give the mixture a more paste-like consistency. That completed, Lily had her *vapa* spread the paste onto a clean pad of cotton, satisfied with their perfunctory efforts as she eyed the results. Knowing they didn't have any more time to spare, Lily took a deep breath, gave a nod of warning to the two other Fae warriors, and gave her undivided attention to the arrow. It needed a quarter turn before removal, so that it would slip back between Poplar's ribs. She did it, winced at the deeply pained noise the purple Fae made, and, loosely bracing the shaft of the arrow in the crook of her thumb, pulled the arrow out of his back with calculated force from her other arm.

Poplar gave a terrible cry, and Lily was both miserable and relieved to hear it. The pain must be horrible, yet he had still been able to draw breath and utter it, and that was good news. What was quite the opposite, however, was the gush of blood that instantly began to flow from the gaping hole in Poplar's back. Lily knew what she had to do next. Grabbing the cotton bandages she had set right beside her, Lily immediately staunched the wound, applying pressure as the two uninjured warriors kept Poplar from thrashing about.

"*Vapa*, poultice please," Lily said, with a calm she did not feel more than superficially. There was too much blood, and it was getting dangerous for Poplar.

In a coordinated move, as though her *vapa* was not wholly unfamiliar with being an assistant in such situations, Lily lifted the cotton so that Vadom could press the poultice to the wound. Lily grabbed fresh bandages and pressed down on the injury to the wide, muscular fairy back before her. For many long moments she kept up the pressure on both poultice and padding, listening intently to Poplar's breathing. It was still labored and irregular, but hadn't worsened. Considering the arrow was out, that was better than she had expected. Still, Lily wasn't sure their efforts were going to be enough. The bleeding had slowed, but wasn't stopping, and he had already lost too much. Mind racing, Lily assessed her remaining options, and felt sadness grip her. There wasn't much, as stitches wouldn't stop internal bleeding, and she didn't know what could be done for the damaged lung at all. If it collapsed . . .

Alder, is there any way for me to use my inner magic to help him?

Alder, who had been a silently frustrated and highly concerned presence in her mind for many strained minutes, spoke up quietly.

"I believe I know which well of power holds your healer's magic, faelani. *I will show you how to draw from that magic, if you practice the utmost caution. I don't want either you or Poplar to suffer any more than necessary."*

Lily answered him with a solemnity at least as great as his.

I will do just as you say, Alder, if it means I can save him. The wound is too serious, too deep, to be healed with mundane means alone. If his lung collapses, he will die.

"Then let us go to your inner magic without delay. You have done well to slow the bleeding, especially after removing the arrow. That will make it easier to heal him with your inner love element."

After a few more tense moments, Alder arrived at Lily's diamond of gold. He went directly to one of the corner wells, then spoke again.

"I know not exactly how the lady healers wield their magic, but I can guess based on how I use my own abilities, and from speaking to one of my friends, Willow, who also heals many warrior injuries. Try concentrating on what you wish to do. That is the start with all inner Fae magic. Focus both on your desire to heal, to make Poplar whole, as well as what, specifically, must be done to remove the danger to him. The first will activate your healing magic, the second will guide it as you need. With detailed instructions, based on your knowledge, you will be able to direct it accurately, and channel it into his body with the proper intent. Try your best, faelani, *and you will give Poplar a chance at life that he would not otherwise have, for Fae ladies are not allowed in the Antechamber, even to heal Wardens harmed by their guardian duties."*

Lily, spurred by Alder's words and encouragement, gave the whole of her concentration to doing just as he had said.

I wish to heal this Fae. I want to repair the damage done to his body, before it is too late.

Instantly, Lily felt, and saw with her inner eye, her healing magic rise up and out of one of her wells of power. She knew a moment of exhilaration, for she was certain, if she gave just the right directions, in just the right order, with just the right amount of her sun magic, that it would be enough to do as she most wished for Poplar.

With the utmost care, she formed a small ball of her golden healing magic, much as she twisted and shaped Void element for pulses, and imbued it with her intent in a similar way. Lily directed the ball, which she fervently hoped would be enough to heal the arrow wound, down her arms and between her palms, which she had hovering over the bleeding hole in a nearly-clapping pose. She had removed the bandages just an instant before, so that she would have an unimpeded view of Poplar's injury.

Lily took just a moment to visualize what lay beneath Poplar's broken, bleeding skin. Where to start healing? Perhaps going to the deepest part of the injury, and thus the most dangerous to him, would be best. Placing the golden ball directly on top of the poultice-smeared wound, Lily sent her magic deep inside, trying to feel out all that was wrong. She found that the tip of the arrow had just pierced the lung, and so Lily began there, knitting delicate tissues back together, sealing the critical injury done to Poplar's respiratory system.

That done, she followed the path the shaft of the arrow had taken backwards, checking on ribs and muscles, sending her golden magic to repair all that had been in harm's way. Slowly, layer by layer, Lily healed, making sure each was fully functional and no longer bleeding or painful before moving on. When she came at last to Poplar's punctured skin, Lily carefully used her golden ball, which had gone from the diameter of a piece of fruit to the size of a marble, to clean away all of the herbal paste and blood. When she was satisfied that he wouldn't suffer from infection, she visualized a needle and thread in her mind's eye and, with the magic she had remaining, embedded it into the ragged edges of Poplar's skin, encouraging them to come together once again. When only a very small hole remained, Lily released the dregs of her golden ball in a thin, shimmering layer over the top of the gap. Curiously, she told it to make new skin, wondering if it would obey. To her delight and rising triumph, it did.

Lily stared a moment more at Poplar's back, looking at the perfect, unmarred skin visible through the rent in his sleeveless leather warrior's jerkin.

I did it. I saved him!

Even as she thought the words, her mind and body were wracked with pain. Gasping, Lily blindly reached for Vadom as her iron jewelry punished her severely. Clinging to her fierce determination, Lily rode out the waves of Fear crashing inside her mind. It had been worth it. The fear she had felt for Poplar's life had been greater than this, more potentially devastating than what the iron Fear could taunt her with now. She would just keep it away from her wells of power, especially her healing magic, until she had some control over it . . .

"*Lily!* Faelani, *are you alright? I know it feels terrible, but it is so much less Fear than in Ropaz. You'll have it pushed back in no time, I have not a doubt. I am so proud of you, Lily! I went to your sensory awareness and saw most of your first healing, and I must say, it was completely incredible— I have never seen a single healer do so much, in one effort, in all of my years. It was ingenious of you to wield your love element as you do the night magic, and amazingly effective. I think your mother would be bursting with pride if she had seen this just now,* faelani."

Steadied by both Alder's voice and his words, Lily felt herself gain the upper hand in her inner battle with the Fear. Shoving it back, she sent her feelings of triumph his way.

I did it, Alder. I was finally able to do something other than run from those bloodthirsty xydolem! Thank you for your help, faelan. *I don't think I could have used my healing magic without your guidance. We both saved Poplar just now.*

Lily felt the warmth of Alder's happy glow spread through her mind, making the pain retreat a little bit further.

"We are solid partners in critical situations, Lily, that is abundantly clear. Perhaps, though, you should check on your patient, and reassure Vadom that you are well. It probably wasn't easy for him to step back and let you heal, knowing it would harm you. At least you removed your armor first— I shudder to think of what that would have cost you with the Fear, but your quick actions prevented the worst from occurring, for all concerned."

In complete agreement, Lily slowly opened her eyes and focused on what was taking place in the Antechamber. Her *vapa*'s face swam into view, steady and calm, yet the underlying tension in the arms that held her told her far more than Vadom's face ever did. She smiled up at him, letting her happiness with the successful healing break through. Lily's smile became a little brighter when her *vapa*'s arms relaxed about her.

"Your *vama* will be so proud of your great talent for healing, *Vipina*. I cannot wait to tell her all about this remarkable day. No vampire can be both healer and warrior, yet you, *vladi*, will someday achieve greatness in both spheres. Vabiri always said we should wait for a very special young person to come our way, and she was as wise in her patience as she is in so many other things. Congratulations on a well-performed healing, *Vipina*."

Lily couldn't help but give Vadom a hug before climbing out of his lap and turning to look at Poplar and the other warriors again. The two who had assisted her were alternately looking from their comrade's uninjured back to Lily, both looking a little in awe of what they had witnessed. Poplar himself seemed to be sleeping peacefully. Lily decided it would be best to let him wake up on his own, rather than disturbing him.

"I think we ought to let him rest a bit," she said softly to the others. They nodded instantly, giving silent agreement.

Lily then wondered if she ought to help the other three injured Fae. Glancing at them, she took in their wounds and quickly assessed the danger to each. Two of them had taken arrows in the arm, and, while a lot of cursing was taking place, their faces told her that they were feeling a level of pain they could tolerate. The third warrior, with vivid blue hair and purple eyes, seemed to be slightly worse off. He was the Fae who had pulled the arrow from his calf, and while the bleeding had slowed, there had probably been too much blood loss already. Lily was certain he wouldn't be able to walk unaided.

The other three will be alright if they receive healing soon, Alder. Do you think I should offer to help them?

Lily felt Alder hesitate, sensed his reluctance and concern.

"Lily, while your offer is generosity itself, I think we should allow them to pass into the Wood and be healed by the Fae ladies who volunteer to stay in Ford-upon-Ward to care for the Wardens. Those injuries are of a less serious nature, and the steady and competent healers currently living in the Ford will be able to tend them once they are helped across the bridge. I would rather you not risk the iron pain when their lives are not in jeopardy, faelani."

Lily could tell that Alder was worried, and rightly so. She decided that while she might not be in the best position to heal the injured three, she could make sure that they got to Ford-upon-Ward with all haste. At least then their wounds would be seen to before the impending battle began just outside of the Bubble. Getting to her feet, she glanced about to see if either of the Fae captains had returned. It appeared that neither had come back over the bridge yet. With both of them in the Fae Wood proper, who was in charge in the Antechamber? Turning to the two Fae on either side of the slumbering Poplar, Lily quietly asked them.

One of them quickly stood and gave Lily a small bow from the waist. "You are, Your Highness."

Lily paused in the moment following this pronouncement to take a deep, calming breath. She could do this. She had to help in whatever way she could . . .

"Very well. In that case, I would like for the three others injured here to be helped into the Ford immediately. If you would help one, and inform those two unscathed warriors over there to see to the Fae with the leg injury, I believe they will be able to receive healing before their wounds become truly serious."

Turning to the unharmed warrior still sitting next to Poplar, Lily looked into his worried face and softened the order she had been about to issue.

"I would ask that you assist the other Fae with an injured arm over the bridge to Ford-upon-Ward. I will watch over your friend and make sure that he is resting and recovering as he should."

Rising gracefully, face easing into greater relief, the second warrior bowed to Lily as well.

"Thank you, Your Highness. I am Yew, also of the Seaside Stand, and my tree is not so far from Poplar's. We have always been close, and I am deeply grateful that he will not need to be burned this day. Command me as you will."

Lily inclined her head to acknowledge his thanks, then silently watched as the two Fae walked briskly to the others, conveyed her instructions, and carried them out efficiently and without hesitation. When all seven warriors had passed through the door and over the stone bridge, out of Lily's sight through the swirling walls of the Antechamber, she turned in concern to Vadom.

"*Vapa*, where are the captains? The trolls have arrived at their door, and the enemy must be driven back! I don't know if the xydolem can pass through the Bubble's entrance, but it's not a risk they should take any longer. Is there anything we can do?"

Vadom seemed to consider her words, looking over her head at the gateway in question as he weighed their options. Through the golden iridescence of the Bubble, the large smudge of Void magic was just visible in the star-lit night beyond. It hovered, casting a pall on a great deal of their view of Ropaz. It was clearly out of place and obviously a serious threat. Would the Wardens, in addition to Captain Pine's Court Guards, be enough to repel an entire battalion of trolls, and their xydolem masters as well? Could Lily do anything else to help without endangering Alder or her promises to her mother?

At the thought of her mother and her promises, Lily realized that one of the promises she had made had specifically been to keep her iron on until she was safely in the Fae Wood. The problem was, Lily wasn't all the way inside, and she definitely didn't feel safe yet. Hesitating, looking at the iron bracelets on her arms, Lily wondered if she could take this brief lull in the action to remove her jewelry. Would she be honoring her word if she took it off now? Was it safe? If Lily wanted to use her magic, it would be safer to be free of the pain and the Fear . . . and yet, as Lily considered it, she realized that having unfettered access to her inner wells of power might not be the best idea. How much control would she have over her magic without the iron effects keeping it in check? What would Lily's therianthrope do once she could leave Lily's mind? With a sinking heart, Lily realized her wild one would go straight to the battle, and Lily had no idea how to prevent that from happening. If this was the case, Lily would have to keep some of her iron on, for her own good. She couldn't risk the xydolem just on the other side of the Antechamber door sensing her or damaging any of her magic, not now.

"Lily? I can feel your emotions becoming resigned and sad, but what Vadom is saying is meant to be reassuring. Is something else wrong?"

Lily had been so wrapped up in her own thoughts, she hadn't even heard her *vapa* speaking. She quickly and quietly told Alder what she had been thinking. He was soon as resigned as she was.

"I hadn't even thought of that, Lily, but you're right. Your magic, in all likelihood, is going to create quite the spectacle. You're going to need the help of strong, mature Fae to regain control of it all. Now is definitely not the time or place for that. I'm sorry you have to suffer still, faelani, *even inside the very entrance to the Wood."*

It's alright, Alder. Only a little bit longer, and I will be upholding my word to my mother and keeping both of us safe. Don't worry. Now, I think I need to speak to my vapa, *and pay attention to what is going on around me.*

"Of course, Lily. I'll be right here."

Lily focused on her surroundings once more, and looked into the patient face of Vadom.

"I'm sorry I wasn't listening, *Vapa*. I just realized that I'm going to have to keep my iron on, and I was explaining why to Alder."

When Vadom's eyebrows furrowed slightly, Lily gave him her reasons as well. He gave a small sigh when she finished speaking.

"I cannot fault your reasoning, *Vipina,* but please, if you will be healing, do so with the utmost caution if the jewelry will be remaining on your person."

Lily nodded, then thought it would be best to try to change the subject.

"I didn't hear your answer to my question, *Vapa*. Would you please repeat it?"

"Of course. I was simply stating my opinion that Captain Pine must be mobilizing the Court Guard, while Captain Beech is readying the Wardens. The former were prepared to leave for Ropaz already, and the latter are always attentive to threats to Ford-upon-Ward. Between those two combined forces, they should be able to take on a battalion of trolls without too much trouble. I think, however, that they will require my assistance in fighting the xydolem, should those creatures choose to engage in this conflict."

Lily's heart began to pound painfully at her *vapa*'s words. She knew she wouldn't be participating in the battle directly, complete novice warrior that she was, but did Vadom really have to leave the hard-won safety of the Antechamber to seek out the xydolem? Was she going to have to wait here, caring for the injured and wondering what was happening to her *vapa* outside all the while?

"I think we should each do our part to ensure victory in this battle, *Vipina*," Vadom said quietly. "For me, that means making sure the xydolem are distracted from controlling their minions. For you, that entails tending to the fallen who make it back into the Antechamber. You will also be able to direct Poplar, and perhaps a few others left behind to assist you, in getting the injured to Ford-upon-Ward. You have ably demonstrated your capacity for leadership, *vladi*, and it will be needed in this space once the battle has begun."

As Lily absorbed and tried to accept her *vapa*'s words, she caught a flicker of movement in her peripheral vision. Turning toward the swirling gold wall of the Bubble and the gateway, Lily realized she could see the trolls now, for the first time ever. She felt her eyes go wide. There were *hundreds* of them, all armed with flails, morningstars, hammers, maces, or quarterstaffs. A small group of trolls, off to one side, had the bows and arrows that had already proven so dangerous. Every one of them possessed the shiny black volcanic rocks as well, their obsidian woven into necklaces or armbands to keep their hands free to wield their weapon of choice.

Aside from their battle-ready dispositions, Lily couldn't help but note that the trolls vaguely resembled the volcanoes they inhabited:

their jagged features displayed their molten tempers, their stocky frames were clearly filled with explosive force, and their inky black hair, lips, fingernails, and eyes seemed as inherently powerful in them as obsidian was to the Crescent. Though they had nowhere near the ancient sophistication or powerful night magic of her *vapa,* Lily couldn't believe that such beings, attacking in such large numbers, were anything less than a serious threat to the Fae Wood.

"*Vapa?*"

"Yes?"

"How many warriors are in a battalion?"

"Approximately one thousand, *Vipina.*"

Lily nodded, not entirely surprised when a contingent of that size was forcibly demonstrating their numbers before her very eyes.

Faelan, *do you feel the same way about what my* vapa *was saying?*

"Lily, if my wishes on this matter were uncontested, you would have all of your iron off and be in Ford-upon-Ward with the other healers by now, if not on your way to Golden Court with a full escort. Unfortunately, neither of the captains will be able to administer an Antechamber test or perform the time-consuming passing spell until the battle is over, so you must remain here until given permission to enter and then led through. I can hardly believe we have come so far, only to be delayed in receiving the full protection of the Wood now, just before one of the biggest battles the Ford has ever had to win.

"While I don't like the idea of you being separated from Vadom, I also think it is generous of him to help the Fae in such a critical way, especially after his cool reception. I have complete faith that he will thwart this battalion's leaders and swing the fighting in our favor. I also think that his belief in you, and your ability to both heal and direct the Fae warriors within the Antechamber, is an indication of his high regard for you. If he didn't think you so capable, he would have you hide in the guest quarters, and perhaps even stay by your side. I know you are worried for him, Lily, but you must believe in him and his capabilities as well."

Lily took in Alder's words, as well as his feelings. She could tell he was upset about all that was happening so quickly, worried about her, and frustrated that he couldn't do what he saw as best for her himself. Lily couldn't help but notice the subtly imperious tone of his voice at first, even as it gave way to the gentler, more concerned tone he usually used when he spoke to her. She supposed that the brief change was probably just his *princely* mode of dealing with something that was, on this rare occasion, beyond his ability to manage. Lily chose not to comment on that, however, and instead asked a question that Alder's response had caused her to wonder about.

I have to pass another test? I thought my father said I should come to Golden Court immediately?

"He did, but it is Captain Beech, and then Captain Pine, who are tasked with ensuring that all who enter the Fae Wood either belong here, or have come for a peaceable reason. They will make absolutely certain you pose no threat, because it is their sworn duty to do so. They are primarily concerned with keeping all the Fae in the Wood safe, while your father, as one of the Wood's kings, has both overlapping and separate duties from the Captain of the Waters and the Captain of the Court Guard.

"King Oak sits on the Gildenthrone, and so he is one of the Wood's primary protectors, for he supplies much of the magic that supports the Bubble. However, his other aims are more diplomatic, as he maintains relations with Silver Court, the various Fae families, the mer-people of the Ocean, and the elves of the Forest. One of his most important goals, after keeping the balance of magic in the Wood, is to find his successors and train them to be the next rulers of Golden Court. He has been thorough, since your mother vanished from the Wood, in his search for golden level Fae, or at least fairies with the potential for golden power who could be strong enough to replace him and sit the Gildenthrone. Until today, and your arrival, however, none were known to exist under the Bubble except your father. We have all lived in dread for years of the day that just came to pass, when King Oak sensed the death of his mate. If he diminishes quickly, following her and passing on to the Afterlight, the Bubble will collapse, unless another golden truemate pair are alive and able to ascend the throne."

Lily felt such pain and shock that she was speechless. She couldn't allow herself to think about her mother at all right now, or about the fact that she would be losing her father all too soon. She thought she might burst from all of the questions she couldn't give voice to, though she knew there was nothing she could ask that would shake her sense of . . . destiny? Responsibility? She felt as though she were being slowly weighed down by . . . the immensity of her future. Was she really understanding what Alder was telling her? Was he warning her as to the nature of the welcome she would be receiving in Golden Court? That she would be embraced with relief, but never, subsequently, let go? If Alder was a prince, with matters this weighty resting, at least partially, on his shoulders, then it was no wonder he was so serious so much of the time; that he was constantly self-critiquing, and found praise so surprising. The troubles of the fairy kingdom seemed largely his to solve, and had been for some time, despite his relative youth. If what he had previously told her about his parents was true, and her own father was not the king he should be without her mother's presence . . . the Wood could not possibly be as safe as it needed to be. And, as the Princess of the Fae, Lily would have to help, would have to *do something* about it.

Faelan, she whispered, investing in that one word all she felt, all she feared, and all her stubborn soul wished to conquer in this new world she had entered and wished to protect.

She waited, quietly and hopefully, for Alder's reply. His response was just as soft, just as uncertain, and just as determined.

"Faelani, *I think anything is possible now that I have you, and that you are here at last. I won't let them take advantage of you. I will protect you and guide you through Court life, and together, perhaps, we can keep our people safe, even from the likes of this Misruler.*"

It was just the reassurance Lily needed to choose, and to accept, where her life's path was leading her. In a way, it made her mother's loss easier to bear— to see, at least in part, why her mother had made the ultimate sacrifice for her. Rose had known what she was doing when she left the Wood, even if no one else did. She had known what was necessary, and Lily's survival had been paramount. The xydolem, somehow, must have known that with Rose's death, the Wood was incredibly vulnerable to attack. What they might not yet know, however, was that Lily existed, that she lived and breathed and, most importantly, had the power to take her mother's place. It was an advantage the Fae Wood could not afford to lose.

Feeling a little older, and feeling a little wiser, Lily turned quietly to Vadom and took in the features of his face again, drawing comfort from his steadiness. He turned from his scrutiny of the trolls, who were now pounding the wall of the Bubble with their variety of blunt weapons, and, meeting her gaze, went completely still. After a moment, he slid a few words into the silence between them.

"Alder is telling you more of what you need to know, *Vipina?*"

"Yes, *Vapa.*"

Is he ever, Lily added, trying to tease loudly enough for Alder to hear. She knew a moment of triumph when she startled Alder yet again with her attempt at lightheartedness. Lily thought she could almost picture him shaking his silver-haired head in bemusement when he replied.

"Your levity stuns me, Lily . . . I just want you to be prepared going into Golden Court. Everyone has their own agenda, and everyone will want your help to further their goals. You are strong enough to take them all on, if you go into it aware of the plays for power and knowing your own mind. I wanted to give you as much notice as possible, because we aren't going to have much time to talk during or after this battle. I know how hard it is to shoulder being 'Your Highness' when you are young and less than fully informed. I have no doubt, though, Lily, that you are up to the task, especially with me and with Vadom watching over you. We'll get through this, just like we've already made it through so many other things since we met."

Lily sent Alder her feelings of agreement, trying to focus on the fact that, whatever happened next, she wouldn't have to face anything alone. Resolved to help the Fae warriors however she could in the Antechamber now, then deal with Court matters later, Lily gave her full attention to the rapidly escalating tension in the small space she was currently occupying. What to do first?

Catching sight of Whirlwind, who had gotten a little skittish upon sensing the danger so close, Lily decided the horse would be safer in the animal shelter off to the side of the path. Medical pack in hand, she walked over to the mare and stuffed the pack into her haversack before slinging it over one shoulder. Lily then caught up the reins, which were dragging on the ground, so that she could lead Whirlwind to the simple construction. Once there, she dropped her haversack and tied her horse's reins to one of the hitching rails that circled the building at about waist height. Looking over Whirlwind for any injuries or more minor problems, Lily spoke softly to her as she did.

"You have been an incredible horse, Whirlwind, and so very brave. Thank you for staying with us and helping us when we needed you. Why don't you rest here until things settle down?"

After getting a knicker of agreement, Lily left the semi-enclosed animal shelter and walked toward her *vapa,* who had moved a little away from Poplar's prone form in order to keep an eye on Lily and both of the doorways. When Lily reached Vadom, she first checked on Poplar. He was still sleeping a healthy slumber, his breathing perfectly even, his temperature and color normal. Just as she was standing back up and about to ask her *vapa* when the fighting would start, a deafening BOOM resounded from the gateway leading to Ropaz. Jerking her head in that direction, Lily could see through the thick golden door that dozens of trolls were working together to bring a horizontal column of night magic crashing into the Bubble. Lily tried to temper her rising unease at this latest assault, but some of it still must have shown on her face. When he saw Lily's expression, Vadom spoke calmly into the unnatural stillness following the offensive crash of their enemy.

"The captains must mobilize their warriors on the other side of the river, *Vipina,* where they have an adequate amount of space to organize, and where the warriors will receive their orders and necessary intelligence without being distracted by the close proximity of the—"

BOOM.

"—enemy. I know not how long the golden dome will hold, but I am sure that every one of those Fae warriors do, and they will not wait too long to repel this invasion. Better to take a few extra minutes for preparation that may save many of their lives, rather than rushing rashly into a battle and exposing their desperation to protect those within their home."

Lily took a moment to absorb this, then attempted to remain relaxed but at the ready.

BOOM.

It was then that Lily heard a sound that sent chills racing down her spine. From inside the Wood, the assembled warriors had begun to chant. Their strong, deep voices joined together in a harsh melody that seemed to promise destruction and defeat to their enemies with every note. She thought the Wardens and the Court Guards must be ready to attack the long-time assailants of the Wood who now dared to test their northern border.

BOOM.

Sure enough, both Captain Beech and Captain Pine passed over the bridge and through the door mere moments later. Behind them followed only eight Fae warriors, each with a face set in lines of deadly intent. Lily gazed at them in surprise, taking in their amazing range of colors. One was red-eyed, another orange-haired, and the third through the door had pale yellow features. After them came a green warrior, the same Lily had seen just a few moments ago. The next Fae to pass into sight had both brown hair and brown eyes, and he was the biggest warrior she had yet seen. The last three Fae across the bridge were all purple featured, though there were differences among them as well. One had hair that seemed almost blue, while another had hair the exact same vivid purple as his eyes. The last warrior had hair and eyes so pale they were a gentle lavender, a color completely at odds with his fiercely lethal expression. Lily sensed that he was the steadiest of them all, and the oldest too.

BOOM.

As Lily watched, Captain Beech led the eight Fae warriors along the well-worn path to the entrance to Ropaz. They arranged themselves in what was clearly a predetermined configuration, then all went completely still, concentrating deeply despite the aggression of the trolls only steps away outside the golden dome.

Alder, what are they doing?

"They are working magic, Lily. If I were to guess, I would say they are each gathering their strongest element, at their respective power levels, to form a very strong repelling spell."

What do you mean by their power levels?

BOOM.

"Do you see how they are different colors? That is the easiest way to determine what level of inner magic a fairy possesses. Though it is a long and complex process, every Fae eventually discovers how many wells of power exist within their mind, and how much magic each well can hold. Most Fae are born with eyes the color of their greatest potential of magic, and as they grow and learn, they pass through the various levels of inner power, discovering more magic and how to—"

BOOM.

"— wield it. A fairy's hair usually shows how much inner magic they can competently use at any given time. Younger Fae have shorter, brighter colored hair, while the older Fae have longer and paler hair, particularly when they have trained for a great deal of time with the full extent of their inner magic. And, though I hope this doesn't muddy the waters too much for you, so to speak, each magic level tends to lend itself to certain abilities, though that varies a little more from Fae to Fae."

Fascinated, Lily studied the warriors at the gateway with new eyes.

BOOM.

With only the iron jewelry to contain her, Lily tried letting her mental guard down enough to view the magic swirling around each fairy. Though it gave her a bit of a headache, her inner eye confirmed what Alder said: each warrior attracted outer magic of the same color as his features, and hence his inner magic. At the core of each warrior, too, was either silver or gold inner power, the magical love element unique to the Fae.

So the red and orange Fae warriors are strongest with fire element? And Captain Beech is the best of this group with water element?

A little surprised, Alder answered in the affirmative.

"That is—"

BOOM.

"*— just so,* faelani. *The orange Fae will be a stronger fire wielder than the red warrior, though, just as all three of the purple Fae will be considerably more accomplished with air magic than the yellow warrior. Remember all of the inner gifts you possess as well: you do not have just elemental power, and so too do each of these Fae have other abilities. Some will be almost unbelievably skilled with a particular weapon, yet no more than basically competent with another. One of them may have wings of elucidation, capable of interpreting every word the trolls in his hearing utter, even as the rest of them hear only gibberish. At least one—"*

BOOM.

"— of the purple warriors probably has wings of enhancement, and he will not only send and receive messages via mirror to and from other spectra, but that well of power often gives the Fae in question incredible speed, both in combat and in flight."

Feeling a strange and mounting excitement, Lily asked one of the countless questions Alder's information stirred in her mind. She was thrilled to finally be safe enough to have her queries completely and unhesitatingly answered.

What are spectra, Alder?

"A spectrum is a group of nine Fae warriors, put together because their combination of skills complement each other and cover the widest possible range of fairy gifts. Nine is the number of greatest power among our people, encompassing the full spectrum of colors, power levels, and magical abilities. The most enthralling of warriors' tales describe the feats and glory of a few perfect spectra, of sets of nine who, collectively, had every power known to Faerie. This last age—"

BOOM.

"— and more, kings and queens have not been able to leave the obligations of their thrones to fight in a spectrum, and few Fae today can remember witnessing the incredible inner magic wielded by such powerfully grouped warriors. Still, the spectrum before you is most impressive, about as strong a nine as you will see in the Fae Wood now. The captains have taken their strongest and created a new spectrum, the better to spell their initial sally against this invading force of trolls. It seems about half are Wardens and half are Court Guards, as you can tell—"

BOOM.

"— by the emblems on their jerkins . . . I am surprised that the Wardens are sharing this honor, but the situation is most serious, and Captain Pine does attract some of the Wood's finest warriors . . . Though your enhancing wings didn't seem like a gift in Goddess's Retreat, Lily, I can hardly tell you how fortunate that communication has proven to be, to bring these two separate branches of warriors together in the Ford on this exact night . . ."

Alder trailed off, apparently inspecting the spectrum before them with a knowledgeable and critically assessing eye. Lily took the chance to observe them too, even as the regular pounding of the trolls continued. She noted this time how five of the Fae had golden domes sewn in gleaming thread on their cured leather tops, with what she thought must be a stylized River Ward closing the large half-circle at the bottom. A smaller half-circle was also present along the river thread, most likely symbolizing the entrance right in front of them. The other four warriors had a glittering golden castle emblazoned on their jerkins. Lily thought that Golden Court must be even more fantastic than she had ever been able to envision with her considerable imagination. Unexpectedly, Lily felt her therianthrope stir, in excitement and anticipation, or from some other nameless emotion, she wasn't sure. Alder's attention abruptly veered from the spectrum of warriors and turned inward. Lily felt a gust of his concern even as he spoke to her.

"Lily, you are sure the iron jewelry is enough to keep her inside your mind? It is definitely not safe enough for her to make her appearance yet. One wrong move, and you could be in danger of abduction or worse by xydolem. You have come too far to risk falling into their clutches, faelani."

Lily checked the activity of the Fear in her mind, then tested her mental defenses. Grimacing, she answered Alder's tense question.

It is enough, Alder. Don't worry, there is still too much in her way for her to break free.

Before Lily could respond to her true-friend's relief, however, she became aware of a small shift in Vadom's stance beside her. Focusing fully on the Antechamber, Lily saw that her *vapa* was paying close attention to Captain Pine. He was coming out of the animal shelter now, having apparently inspected Whirlwind, the saddlebags, and her haversack. On his way toward them, the captain's eyes seemed to take in everything, missing nothing. When Pine's eyes rested briefly on the small pile of iron armor haphazardly piled between the guest building and the path, Lily squirmed just a little at his disapproving look. Before she, or Alder, who shared her moment of chagrin, could speak, even to each other, the captain focused a moment on Poplar behind them, then a longer and more wary sizing up of Vadom, before finally resting on Lily, giving her a thorough, impersonal perusal. Lily held still, meeting his eyes when his gaze landed at last on her face. Captain Pine stood on the path, not saying anything, never taking his eyes from hers.

"Lily," Alder said, very quietly.

Yes?

"I think Captain Pine is going to give you the Antechamber test, or at least ascertain whether or not what you have said about me is true. I ask you to submit to his requests, so that his mind is clear when he goes into battle. I can't bear the thought of him being distracted by a personal matter and . . . getting injured or worse because of me."

Of course, Alder. I trust him if you do. It is my vapa *who will not be so readily persuaded, depending on the test. Do you think Captain Pine will still wish to enter my mind?*

Though Lily still felt rather uneasy about that possibility, she would endure the invasion if it meant both putting her *faelan*'s *praetam* at ease and gaining her admittance into the Fae Wood proper. She could only hope that Vadom didn't find Captain Pine's requests too demanding.

"That is what he will most wish to do, but if I know him, he will have thought of a way to be certain of both of us without incurring the wrath of your guardian. Let us wait for him to speak first."

They didn't have to wait much longer.

"You still wear iron. Why is this so, young Gildenthrone?"

Caught a little off guard by the question, Lily answered honestly.

"I have always worn this jewelry. Each piece was a gift from my mother over the years . . . and I'm not quite ready to remove it all. I have no idea how my inner magic will respond to such freedom, and now did not seem the best time to find out."

Captain Pine nodded, accepting her response. There was another short pause before he spoke again, amethyst eyes boring into hers.

"You claimed to be the truemate of Alder Silvergrove before, yet you did not appear to know that he is the current prince of all Fae. How do you explain this? The Alder I know would not have withheld such an important thing from his mate."

Lily felt Alder wince in her mind. She wasn't unaffected by Pine's words herself. She could still hardly credit the fact that she, an outcast among the desert Outcasts, was soul-bonded to a lofty fairy prince. While she knew she would be reeling at the realization of her mate's full identity for a while, Lily also knew she didn't have the luxury of being overwhelmed just now. She had to convince the Captain that all was well before he left for the battle, and, judging by the magic she could sense from the Fae warriors at the entrance, Lily didn't think that was much time at all.

"Alder told me he was keeping important knowledge from me, in the event that I was captured by any number of beings in Ropaz who would have used it against the Fae Wood and the two of us. Bad enough that I was a young golden fairy alone in witch and vampire territory, keeping just ahead of trolls and xydolem, but if they could have pulled from my mind the fact that I was a princess? And carried with me the soul of a prince? Alder was safeguarding valuable information and trying to keep us out of more danger than we were in already. Even I can understand and accept his decision on that matter, though it frustrated me at the time."

Though Lily didn't like being unaware of pertinent details, she felt defensive of Alder now that he was being questioned on his choices. The entire journey had seemed nearly impossible when they'd first met, and without finding her *vapa* soon after, they never would have made it. With those odds, Alder had been right to tell her as little as possible. Surely Captain Pine could see the rationale? Apparently he did, for he let the matter drop in favor of a new, if related, subject.

"I still want to hear what Alder has to say about this entire situation, and how he came to join you, if what you claim about him is indeed true. As your *praetam* refuses me entrance to your mind, however, I will settle for an alternative: I will open my mind to the two of you, and we will speak mind to mind from me instead of from you."

Lily felt her eyes widen, then glanced up at Vadom in question. Her *vapa* looked her in the eye a moment, reading the acceptance of this new plan in her gaze. Then he turned and gave Captain Pine a glare so intimidating, so full of unspoken threat, that Lily was completely certain it would have cowed absolutely every last one of the trolls raging in a frenzy on just the other side of the golden dome, had they been on the receiving end of it. Captain Pine, though clearly realizing what lay in wait for him should he try harming Lily's mind in any way, did not back down. It was only then, really, that Lily understood just how desperate Pine was to find out for himself whether Alder still lived, that his soul was still in Lamoranth, and unharmed.

We had better go to his mind quickly, Alder. He will not be able to fight with a clear head until he knows you are safe and well. How do we accomplish this?

"Thank you for agreeing to this so readily, Lily. I can hardly believe how he acts— my praetam *is not at all himself right now. He is never normally so forceful, so ready to disregard tact and safety. I cannot believe he meets such a look from the likes of Vadom, as though the ire of such a warrior is of no consequence to him. My* praetuu *Iris must be in great distress about the condition of my body. That is the only reason I can think of for him to be so visibly disturbed."*

Lily could tell that Alder was only getting more worried with each passing moment, and there was no need for that now. They had a way to set Captain Pine's mind at ease that was acceptable to everyone. Lily focused on the two warriors beside and in front of her, still staring intently and with barely veiled hostility at each other. Not knowing what else to do, Lily stepped forward and reached for Captain Pine's head, putting her hands on either side of his face and gently pulling him down to her shorter height. That certainly got his attention. His gaze snapped to her in surprise at the liberty she'd just taken.

"Ready?" she asked.

33

The Battle Begins

"Yes," Captain Pine replied, with no hesitation whatsoever. He then, very gently, set his forehead to hers.

Lily focused her inner eye on what was about to occur, noting that Alder was steadily moving to the periphery of her mind, near the circular tribe with which they were both now so familiar. A little nervous that her remaining iron Fear would be a threat to Alder and the captain as it lingered about the beginnings of her mental defenses, Lily resolved to keep both Alder's soul and his *praetam*'s mind safe while they talked.

When Alder, as well as a part of her own consciousness, were at the very edge of her mind, leaning against a two-tiered portion of her curving mental wall and looking out for Captain Pine, they both suddenly sensed him, very close. The brush of his mind, obviously familiar to Alder, caused both of them to perk up in anticipation.

Alder? Are you there?

"Praetam! *Yes, I am here!*"

The surge of intense emotions that came from Captain Pine brought tears to Lily's eyes. He had been so worried, so afraid he had lost the fairy boy, now all but grown, who had always been as a son to him. Lily observed with amazement as his impending grief and fearful hope faded into transparent relief and joy.

Oh Alder, my silver sapling, my praetob, where have you been? Your praetuu and I have been out of our minds with worry! What happened, that you left without a word? Are you all right?

"I am so sorry to have caused you such concern, praetam, *but I heard my mate crying out for help, and I had to go to her immediately. Queen Rose gave birth to Lily in the Joquobon Desert sixteen years ago, and they had just set out for the Wood from the great white desert when the xydolem attacked Her Majesty and took her life. My* faelani *was devastated,* praetam, *and all alone. My soul seemed to know what to do, so I let that part of myself fly all the distance that separated us, to keep my truemate's soul from breaking. There was no time for me to spare a thought to the body I had to leave behind. I was nearly too late to save my Lily as it was."*

Alder's soul gave a miserable shudder then, as if he was thinking of things too terrible to put into words. After a moment, though, he collected himself and continued.

"I have been fine within her mind ever since, praetam. *She has taken good care of me, and I have tried to do the same for her, though I have wished for my body desperately many times. Crossing Ropaz with my* faelani *was both completely wonderful and utterly terrifying, depending on how close all the dangers to us were at the time."*

Well then, Alder, let me be the first to congratulate you on finding your truemate. What a memorable Discovery Bond the two of you must have forged! You can make up your absence to your praetam by relating every instant of your meeting to her, and allowing her to plan your Recognition Ceremony, I would think. If those fail, I would simply relate the whole of your journey until she calms, or is distracted by some part of it or another.

Lily sensed Alder give the soul equivalent of a sigh, and she thought it imparted both fondness and exasperation. She herself was relieved that Captain Pine was so happy, so entirely convinced of Alder's presence. Lily knew her story must have been hard for the Wardens to believe, and Alder's direct verification could only smooth their way. That put her in mind of some of the other things Alder perhaps needed to bring to Captain Pine's attention. Not wanting to interrupt them, but feeling the pressure of time weighing against them, Lily quietly interjected a comment into their conversation.

Faelan, *Captain Pine, I am sorry to disturb the two of you, but I think we ought to share what we know of the troll situation now, before battle is engaged. Alder?*

Lily left the telling of their information to Alder. Though Vadom had summarized the immediate problem outside the Bubble, Alder proceeded to tell Captain Pine, succinctly, all that they had heard, sensed, and surmised about the happenings in and around the Volcano Crescent. When Alder fell silent a few minutes later, his *praetam* was fully concentrating on the critical situation unfolding before them.

This changes our outlook on things considerably. If the xydolem are the true enemy, and the trolls only pawns, we do not want to exhaust our forces on the lesser evil. You say you are not certain whether or not any trolls, here or at other potential attacking points, are Void-bound?

"Vadom may be able to tell once he has gotten close enough to detect any night magic the xydolem may be exerting on the trolls. He told us a little while ago that he planned to fight the xydolem alongside the Fae, because he has a much better idea of what is in store with our more dangerous enemy this night. Praetam, *I would like to request that Vadom be granted sanctuary in the Wood after this battle, just as Lily has asked. I owe him a great deal, and I know my* faelani *will need him as she begins her new life here. Certainly he is the perfect* praetam *for her. We have traveled far with him, and I am convinced that there are few beings in Lamoranth as worthy of trust and as noble as Vadom the vampire."*

Captain Pine took in Alder's words solemnly and with obviously serious consideration. Lily sent her feelings of thankfulness toward Alder, letting him know what his intercession on Vadom's behalf meant to her. She knew she would be much braver with both Alder and Vadom helping her gain her footing in the Fae Wood. Alder accepted her grateful emotions and softly sent her reassurance.

Their interaction was interrupted, though unintentionally, by Captain Pine. He was feeling a good deal of surprise, and Lily wondered what had caused it. Alder, too, turned back to his *praetam,* not entirely sure how to interpret his mentor's unspoken emotion.

"Praetam, *what is it? Is something wrong? Aside from the obvious, that is?"*

Captain Pine seemed to give himself a shake.

No, nothing beyond the troll situation, now. I suppose I just haven't had time to consider what these early days of soul speaking will mean for the beginning of your faelanzanta. I'm sure that Iris will speak with you both about this, and she'll know how to help the two of you once Alder is back in his body.

Captain Pine sounded relieved to be able to put that part of their future in Alder's *praetuu*'s capable hands. Lily felt a stirring of uneasiness, at not knowing what Pine was speaking of, and she felt an echo of that feeling in Alder. She whispered to him, hoping the Captain wouldn't overhear her.

Faelan?

"I'm not sure, Lily. We might have to pick a good time to bring this subject up with him again, preferably before I get back in my body. I don't want to be unprepared for anything, especially in Silver Court, on your first day there."

Alder subsided, and Lily decided that she would rather concentrate on the difficult night remaining to them, rather than another new problem. She and Alder were becoming rather accomplished at undertaking and overcoming challenges as they came. However, with a hinted concern that wouldn't materialize for a day or two, Lily mentally placed the soul-speaking consequences problem in the same part of her mind that was currently storing her shock with being a princess, the implications of having a king for a father, and her disbelief at being the truemate of a prince. Leaving her impending difficulties for later consideration, Lily thought she ought to refocus on the Antechamber. It would probably be nice for Alder to speak with Pine more or less privately for a moment anyway.

Going to the ring of her sensory awareness, Lily listened to the sounds around her, as she couldn't see with her eyes half-closed and so near Captain Pine's face. She could still hear the Bubble-muted roar of a thousand battle-ready trolls and the booming of their weapon, spurred on by beings she really didn't want to think about. On the other side of the Antechamber dome, Lily could also hear the chilling battle chant of a reassuring number of Fae warriors. With their myriad abilities and extensive training in combat and magic, surely they could prevail against the intensely primitive contingent of trolls? Especially with her *vapa* there to help them contend with the xydolem—

"Faelani, *ready to go?"*

Lily started just a bit, surprised Alder hadn't lingered to speak with his *praetam,* but quickly acquiesced. She was glad that his soul was a little brighter. Turning outward, Lily opened her eyes just in time to see Captain Pine straighten and take a small step back from her. She let her hands release him and fall to her sides, though she kept her eyes on his face. When he had focused on his surroundings once more as well, Lily offered him a smile, feeling a little shy after their meeting of minds.

"So nice to make your acquaintance, Captain Pine," she said, belatedly recalling her mother's unrelenting insistence on polite behavior. She received in response an unrestrained smile and happily flashing amethyst eyes.

"Oh young lady, the pleasure is entirely mine, I assure you. I am very happy to welcome you to the Fae Wood at last, Lily Gildenthrone."

Lily smiled at his words, more naturally this time.

"Thank you. Perhaps we ought to steel ourselves against a welcome of any kind for the neighbors currently knocking on our door though, Captain?"

Amusement glinted in Pine's eyes as he turned to look at the entrance to Ropaz, his curving lips forming a positively lethal warrior's grin.

"Depend upon it, little petal," he said before jogging over to the gateway surrounded by Captain Beech's spectrum. Lily and Vadom watched as he slowed, cautiously set a hand on Beech's shoulder, and spoke directly into the other captain's ear. The spectrum all seemed able to hear his words, for all of them appeared to divide their attention between the information he was imparting and the spell they were working. After a few moments, all of them nodded, as though to confirm their understanding of Captain Pine's words.

Alder's *praetam* then took off at a run down the path, speeding right past Lily, Vadom, and the lightly sleeping Poplar. He passed unimpeded through the door and over the stone bridge, crossing the River Ward and out of their sight. The warriors' chanting instantly fell silent, and Lily assumed the Captain was now imparting their news to the combined forces of the Wardens and Court Guard standing at the ready in the Ford.

She felt her senses winding uncomfortably tight in anticipation of battle. It occurred to her only then that Pine had not confirmed whether or not she, let alone Vadom, could pass into the Fae Wood proper. Would Alder ask her to wait with the healers there if she had passed her Antechamber test, as Lily assumed she just had? Once she crossed that bridge, Lily didn't think she would be allowed to return to the Antechamber any time soon, and she didn't want to wait patiently in safety when she could be helping, making herself useful, closer to the action. Lily decided to keep quiet and stay put. The warriors would all be focused on the battle, not her, and she would then do what she could for the injured after the fighting start—

"*Vipina*, I take it Captain Pine is convinced of Alder's presence, and of your identity?"

Lily gave an internal sigh. She should have known that every Fae warrior in the Wood may pass her by in favor of a battle, but her *vapa* would definitely have different priorities.

"Yes, *Vapa*. We have made him very happy with our safe arrival."

"Did he say that you could pass into the Wood, or when you would be taken over the river?"

"No," Lily paused, "at least, not to me. Alder?"

"We spoke only briefly after you gave us some space, Lily, but he said that either he or Captain Beech have to escort you through the bridge door. The passing spell required takes more than half an hour, and the door often holds

on to newcomers for longer than that to determine whether or not they may pass through. What with the repelling spell nearly complete, the warriors will need the door unimpeded to get to the battle. There just wasn't enough time to introduce you, let alone Vadom, to the second door. I'm not happy about it, but if I am realistic, I know that you will be safe enough in the Antechamber. No enemy to the Fae has ever gotten in even here— it is a matter of great pride to the Wardens that this is so."

Lily quickly relayed Alder's words to Vadom, who nodded in acceptance, if not in approval.

"The battle will start any moment," Vadom agreed, "and he is needed elsewhere. I cannot be happy, however, that you are not farther away from the violence and the danger."

Lily merely raised her eyebrows at that comment, refraining from responding. Her journey wasn't over, so why would the danger simply vanish? That seemed entirely too convenient to conform with the reality in which she usually found herself. Vadom, returning his eyes to her after checking the bridge door, smiled faintly upon catching her expression.

"Ah, my brave *Vipina,* ready to do whatever is necessary in any situation," he said fondly.

Lily was a little startled by this comment, and by Alder's ready feelings of agreement.

"Lily, you have yet to shy away from anything difficult or daunting for the whole of our quest. You can hardly blame us for thinking such things about you."

I'm feeling a little daunted about being a princess, Alder, Lily confessed. It was a relief to tell him, even if it was couched in a major understatement. Alder sent her soft, silvery comfort in her mind.

"Of course you are, faelani. *Any lady who understands responsibility and duty would be intimidated. Believe me, I sympathize completely. However, you must trust me when I say that you can do it— you have not just the magic needed, but the heart and the mind as well. Time and experience will provide everything else you will require to be a most excellent princess. Try not to worry about that just now, though, Lily?"*

Lily accepted Alder's reassurances, at least for the time being. At the moment, she needed to make sure that she was as ready as possible for the battle. With any luck, Vadom wouldn't change his mind about her participation and relegate her to the guest building to watch from a window after all. Lily gave a mental snort— as if she'd fall in with such a plan.

"Lily, I think you should wake Poplar now, if you think he will be in good

enough shape to walk about. Captain Pine has described the invasion procedure to me in the past, and the warriors about to cross the bridge will be filling the Antechamber completely any second now. We will be in the way, and, with all of the noise in here, Poplar will never hear the end of it if he is seen sleeping by everyone."

Lily, a little amused, thought this was a good suggestion, and she turned and knelt by the purple Fae without delay. Gently, she put a hand to his shoulder and gave him a little shake, bringing her face close enough to his ear to make herself heard in the growing din. The warriors across the bridge were chanting again, and it was giving Lily the occasional shiver down her spine even now. She could hardly imagine a more intimidating sound. It almost, though not quite, made her pity the wild, undisciplined trolls who had incurred the wrath of these Fae.

"Poplar. Poplar, you must wake up now."

Lily moved a strand of his shoulder-length purple hair back from his face and watched as his lids slowly opened. For a moment, his eyes retained the forgetful oblivion of sleep. In the next instant, however, he seemed to recall the events directly preceding his loss of consciousness, and he shot up to a kneeling position before suddenly going still. He rolled his shoulders experimentally, then actually tried looking over his right side, as though searching for the arrow that was no longer there.

"I have removed the arrow and done my best to heal you, Poplar," Lily said in a calm, hopefully soothing voice.

His head quickly pivoted about, and he looked at her in surprise.

"Your best must be quite impressive then, my lady, for I feel no pain at all. I offer you my deepest thanks. Command me as you will."

His words reminded her of his friend and family member, Yew, who hadn't returned after helping the other wounded Fae across the bridge and into Ford-upon-Ward. She had rather been hoping he would, so that she could enlist his help in addition to Poplar's in caring for the injured.

"I am going to be in need of assistance very shortly with the wounded Fae who are brought back to the Antechamber from the battle, Poplar. I would appreciate your help if they need to be kept still or carried to the Ford."

Though he looked disappointed, Poplar gracefully inclined his head to her.

"Yes, my lady."

"It might be nice to have a few others to help us, warriors who could still act as reinforcements if the battle runs long. Do you think Yew would forgo the fight to aid us?"

Poplar perked up again, then looked worried.

"He and I have trained together for the last one hundred fifty years, but neither of us were alive when the last hostilities with the trolls took place. I don't like the idea of him going into his first real battle without me. We are brothers-in-arms, and I feel responsible for him, as he does for me."

He stood, as though to find Yew immediately, but paused, obviously a little dizzy. Lily jumped up and put a steadying hand under his elbow. Poplar blinked in surprise, then nodded his thanks, a bit embarrassed.

"I'll be right back with Yew, my lady. I don't know that we will be able to talk anyone out of such a promising fight, except perhaps for any Willows who are here— most of them would rather heal than harm. I will return in a moment."

Poplar took off for the bridge door at a run, and Lily watched him go for part of the short distance before turning to Vadom, satisfied that her Warden helper was hale and whole.

"According to Alder, *Vapa*, we need to move to the side so that the Fae warriors have room to pass through in formation. Maybe we ought to go over to the buildings for now?"

Vadom inclined his head and fell in step with her as she started walking in Whirlwind's direction. Lily paused, however, when she caught sight of her pile of iron armor. Remembering the look Captain Pine had given that pile, Lily winced again and detoured to pick it all up and move it out of the way. She had only just reached down for her belt and dagger, though, when Vadom put a staying hand on her shoulder, then scooped it all up himself and walked the remaining distance to the guest building. He deposited all of the pieces in a small cascade of clanks on the porch that fronted the structure, then remained standing there, presumably to wait for the rest of the Fae to come into sight.

Lily reached his side not a moment too soon. Captain Pine re-entered the Antechamber with three Fae warriors at his back, and they were followed by three more. Lily squinted at the bridge beyond the door, and realized that both the bridge and the door were only wide enough to accommodate three abreast at a time. It was currently filled with orderly rows of warriors, as far as she was able to see. She watched as another row of three filed into the Antechamber, then fluidly moved to flank the first three behind Captain Pine, even as the second row of three moved to the opposite flank. Now a single row of nine Fae warriors was striding purposefully behind the Captain, obviously primed for the fight. Lily watched this new spectrum approach Captain Beech and his spell-workers, even as another trio of warriors entered the Antechamber, and the spectrum-forming process began again in concerted, efficient concentration.

Lily could feel Alder's excitement at the spectacle. She supposed that nothing like this had happened in his lifetime, and as the prince, he might not be allowed so close to danger, regardless. She focused again on the warriors before her, noting that the first few spectra to arrive each had a red, orange, yellow, brown, and green warrior, then usually two blue and two purple warriors to complete the nine. Lily was a bit surprised, then, when the next spectrum to cross the bridge into the Antechamber had three red, three orange, and three yellow warriors. The spectrum after that had all green and brown Fae.

"Those are specialized spectra, faelani. *The fire spectrum will focus primarily on setting things ablaze: the red and orange warriors will start and direct the fires, while the yellow warriors will sustain and increase their efforts with air. The earth spectrum behind them will probably shake the ground to get the trolls off balance and counter any of this particular enemy's magical offensives. Most of the Fae will take to the air to fight with the advantage of height, leaving those spectra to give the trolls trouble below them."*

Lily was impressed. She then remembered something her *vapa* had taught her, though, that made her a little uneasy for the warriors before her.

"What is it, Lily? Every warrior before you is more than up to a fight with trolls, and those who are hurt in this conflict will come directly to you. The Wardens are ever ready to protect the Ford. The Court Guards were prepared, too, for a mission into Ropaz, and it shows."

I just hope they remember that fighting the trolls on land will not be as easy as engaging the trolls on Molten Mirror Lake, and that they assess the threat of this battalion with all seriousness. Have you noticed that every single one of the trolls has a piece of obsidian? That will give them extra protection, and make them more tenacious besides. Didn't you tell me before that the Fae don't fully understand the magic of the trolls' black stones? And what exactly will it mean for tonight's combat if the xydolem really have Void-bound all of these trolls? I guess I just don't like all of the unknown variables and misinformation that could tip the scales in our enemies' favor, Alder.

Lily knew her concerns were valid when Alder grew a bit uneasy. What could they do to warn the Fae warriors? The Antechamber was completely full now, with perhaps eleven spectra poised to exit the Wood and begin the battle in the wake of the repelling spell. Including Captain Pine, that made one hundred warriors, comprised of both Wardens and Court Guards, the first wave of resistance against the invading battalion.

"Lily, would you please voice your concerns to Vadom? Perhaps he will have the opportunity to say something, or at least warn the others through example when the fighting begins."

"Vapa?"

Vadom turned to Lily in question.

"I was just thinking that these Fae might not be accounting for the trolls as earth element beings who are actually on land, and that they're definitely not aware of how the trolls can wield obsidian to their own advantage. Is there any way we can let them know about those things and what it means to fight a potentially Void-bound enemy?"

Vadom held very still for a moment, thinking quickly. Then his eye was caught on something over Lily's shoulder, back at the bridge door. Lily turned and saw Poplar and Yew making their way toward her by going around the precise formation of assembled warriors. After skirting the periphery of the Antechamber and passing Whirlwind's temporary shelter, they took the shallow steps to the guest porch and made small bows to Lily.

"Captain Pine agreed that we should stay and assist you with the injured, Your Highness, given that Poplar still hasn't learned how to keep his back from being an enemy target," Yew said, giving her a small grin. That grin became a grimace when Poplar punched him in the arm.

"He did not say that! The Captain didn't think I should be fighting when I just about needed my tree torched earlier. And I had my back to empty grasslands anyway— like you weren't facing the vampire at sunset yourself, Blue Yew!"

Lily didn't know whether she should be amused by the cousins' antics, or a bit dismayed that her helpers were razzing each other in the final moments before the biggest battle the Fae Wood had seen in three hundred years.

"*Saplings,*" Alder sighed, appearing to share Lily's divided response to the pair before them.

Lily found his comment a little comical.

Alder, these two can't be that much younger than you.

Alder gave a small start at her amused response.

"You will find that, as near-immortal beings, most of our people mature rather slowly, Lily. Any Fae under the age of five centuries will readily be called

a sapling or a petal by older fairies, especially when their behavior betrays their relative youth. Hence, my own name-calling, as it were. I suppose that indicates my own lack of years, doesn't it?"

Before Lily could respond, Vadom cut through the levity.

"Poplar. Yew."

The two snapped to attention, all playfulness vanishing instantly. Lily couldn't blame them when her *vapa* had used that particular tone of voice with them.

"I will be participating in the battle about to commence. The two of you have been tasked with helping Lily tend to the wounded. However, I am sure I hardly need to tell you that you are her Wardens, charged with preserving her safety while she must stay within the Antechamber, and that you are the only protection she will have once I must leave her side. If any harm befalls her, I am holding the pair of you personally responsible. Have I made myself perfectly clear?"

Expressions solemn, postures rigid, Poplar and Yew both responded promptly in the affirmative.

"Yes, sir."

"We will guard her most carefully, *piurteth*."

Lily kept her own face serious as well, even as she learned the Fae word for 'respected elder'. Though it didn't sound as if she would need to be defended, it couldn't hurt to have these two alert for trouble. She watched as Vadom nodded, satisfied, then turned to her, his gaze gentling just a fraction.

"Be careful, *Vipina*, and try not to overexert yourself. I will see you in a few hours' time, when the battle has ended."

Lily knew he was reassuring her, all but guaranteeing his safe return, but she suffered no delusions that the intervening time from now until then would be pleasant. She didn't want to see needless pain, let alone death by violence.

"You be careful too, *Vapa*. See you soon."

Lily accompanied her words with the *valoriad*, which her *vapa* returned before turning and walking briskly around the spectra toward the captains by the gateway. Lily watched him until he reached Captain Pine and began speaking to him. Then she switched her gaze to her Wardens, who were still looking quite serious.

"Will it just be the three of us in the Antechamber, then?" she asked.

"To start, yes. Captain Pine wants the three Willows to be outside in the beginning, so that they can help those who need immediate healing.

Then their main task will be to assist or carry the injured in here. We take charge of the wounded from there, only keeping one of the Willows if the damage is severe. The Captain also ordered all spectra to look out for their own. That means that if one of your nine falls, you are responsible for hailing a Willow or bringing your brother-in-arms to the Antechamber personally. That ought to ensure that everyone is taken care of as needed."

Lily thought this sounded like a good plan. She tried to think of any problems that might arise, but nothing immediately came to mind. She was curious about something though . . .

"How close is Ford-upon-Ward and the healers there? Will you have to carry the injured very far, or do the ladies have a system that allows them to help the wounded right away?"

Poplar and Yew exchanged startled glances.

"Just on the other side of the bridge, Your Highness," Yew answered.

Poplar elaborated, giving Lily an idea of how the healers took part in the battle.

"The warriors' living quarters are on the main road through the town, and the ladies will be preparing beds for the injured in the other buildings on either side of that road. Once all of the warriors have passed through the Antechamber, the ladies will wait mere steps from the bridge, with carts, probably, ready to do all they can the moment any warriors are brought across the river to them."

Reassured by this information, Lily nodded, then turned back to face the gateway to Ropaz, wondering when the storm would finally break. The tension nearly crackling in the air was enough to make her skin prickle in wary anticipation. She watched as the magic swirling about Captain Beech's spectrum seemed to coalesce before them, taking on a shape roughly similar to the entrance itself. Lily could sense that it was a destructive magic, a spell woven with the intent, in this case, to do harm. These Fae were not going to allow the trolls to go unpunished for bringing battle to their door.

When Captain Beech gave a curt nod to Captain Pine, the latter turned to the spectra filling the Antechamber and spoke with the resounding voice of command.

"The repelling spell is ready, and so are every one of you! We will charge the enemy in the wake of the repulsing magic, and we will show them what happens when the ire of the Fae is roused. Take heed, however: the black rocks they wield are obsidian, stones formed from a volcano's molten heart.

Be as wary of these trollish weapons as you would any dwarf with his gem. You have already been told of the earth maneuvers this enemy is capable of, and those of you who fought three centuries ago know better how to counter those tactics tonight. Now, it is time to protect our people and our home against these Void-bound attackers with every weapon at our disposal! Fight for honor, fight for glory, and fight for the Fae Wood!"

"Honor, Glory, and the Fae!"

The warriors took up the chant, seeming almost to imbue it with a magical power. A moment later, Captain Beech and his spectrum unleashed the repelling spell. Lily watched, even through the painful discomfort of her magical translation of the Fae language. She was shocked as the entrance-sized spell shot with incredible force through the gateway. It hit the thick body of trolls directly outside and kept right on going. Going and going, silencing the booming column of dark magic, cleaving the enemy force in two. It left only unmoving bodies where a great many frenzied trolls had been just seconds before.

Lily felt a species of horror at the instantaneous destruction, of so many deaths wrought without the chance for defense, without mercy. The scene etched itself on her mind, the harsh, unforgettable reality of combat utterly undeniable.

"Lily, faelani *. . . look away if you need to. What will follow now won't be any easier for you to witness."*

Lily wanted to look away. She did. But . . . she wasn't just any Fae lady. She was a princess. Normal ladies waited patiently for the aftermath of battle, on the other side of the River Ward, where they were absolutely safe. She, however, was in the Antechamber. And that wasn't just because there hadn't been time to take her across the bridge. It was because Captain Pine had taken her measure, seen all the iron she wore, and read in her face the determination that had gotten her all the way across Ropaz. He had known she could handle being here, close enough to actually see the fighting. Close enough to bear witness, and to help. And so Lily, for the first time, intentionally called for her therianthrope, that wild part of her that was strong enough, fierce enough, to endure the carnage and still do what needed to be done.

That magical being gave a roar from her central well of power, sending Lily into a peculiar state akin to battle-readiness. She didn't feel ready to kill, yet her emotions were muted beneath a wave of fierce determination and a portion of wildness that shot about untrammeled through her mind.

That muffling of her feelings brought Lily a clarity she knew she would have to hold on to with all of her will throughout this long night.

No, Alder, I can't. To turn away from the bravery of these warriors is to dishonor them, and their reasons for fighting. I will acknowledge the risk every one of them is taking by helping with my eyes wide open.

Lily felt from Alder the fiercest pride she could imagine in response to her words, and she knew that she was doing the right thing. She could still feel his underlying concern and worry, but she was his *faelani*. Those were probably feelings he would always have for her, no matter where she was or what she was doing. She accepted them, even as first one, then another of the spectra charged out of the gateway and took to the air. Lily could just make out the shape of the wings coming out of their upper backs, glowing faintly with the color of each warrior's inner magic. She watched as the fire spectrum sent fiery balls of magic swinging into the writhing mass of trolls, listened to the howls of pain and fury that their elemental magic evoked. Lily observed, faintly incredulous, as Captain Beech's air-borne spectrum redirected their rolling repelling spell, reversing its course so that it created a new path of destruction in the right half of the bisected troll battalion. It was only then that she noticed as, to her surprise, the earth spectrum took to the air and flew over the repelling spell's original trail. The earth directly below them seemed to rise up and meet them, and Lily didn't know if they were causing the earthen wall to form up, or if the trolls were controlling the huge upheaval of the ground there.

"Divide and destroy," Poplar said grimly, his face intense as he watched the battle unfolding.

Lily nearly jumped. She had completely forgotten about the two Wardens standing beside her. Recalling her own objective for this fight, Lily swept her gaze over the Antechamber. She marveled at how quickly the Fae spectra were passing through, forming up and approaching the entrance at a run, and proceeding into Ropaz with weapons in hand and battle cries on their lips. She wasn't sure how they would get wounded warriors back into the Antechamber when there were still fresh Fae fighters entering the fray, but she decided to trust in both the speed and the eagerness of the last warriors to engage with the trolls and clear the space. That, and hope the injuries wouldn't be too great in number right away, what with so many spectra in the air and out of reach of the blunt weapons swinging uselessly at them from the ground.

Turning back to the action, Lily's eyes were drawn to the left side of the battlefield, and particularly to the shadowy form of her *vapa*. Her eyes widened in amazement at the sight of his large, leathery black bat wings, and at the lethal grace of his flying. He seemed almost at one with the cloaking darkness of the night. Only the faint glow of the golden dome and the light of the moon illuminated his black-clad figure, swooping, diving, constantly in motion and unceasingly stilling the trolls below him with the weapons in his hands. It seemed to Lily, though, that he was searching, focused on finding the xydolem in his midst and giving them the fight they had orchestrated.

"Looks like we've got our first wounded coming in now," Yew said at her left.

Lily immediately concentrated on the Antechamber, and found that the last three spectra were pausing just before the gateway as a couple of uninjured warriors were bringing in Fae who had sustained damage from the battle raging just outside. With Poplar and Yew right behind her, Lily quickly made her way to them, only vaguely aware of the surprised looks she was getting as she gave her full attention to the injuries each Fae sported. One of them, an orange warrior, had what Lily thought must be a morningstar blow to his calf. There was a great deal of blood coming from the gash. He had probably gotten hit after pulling up from a diving attack. The other Fae, of green level, had taken a hit to the shoulder, and it was definitely dislocated. There was very little bleeding, though, and Lily thought it must have been a club or quarterstaff that had done the damage. Lily took a deep breath and then wasted no time before attempting to control the situation.

"Poplar, Yew, please help these two over to the side, so that the rest of these warriors can join the battle."

Her Wardens obeyed, quickly clearing the way for the thirty or so unwounded Fae itching to exit the Antechamber.

"Poplar, please take this green Fae to the Ford. I've never reset a shoulder, and now is not the time to learn, especially as the broken bones and injured muscles will need to be healed first anyway."

As Poplar briskly headed for the bridge door with his slightly dazed charge, she turned to Yew and the orange Fae. Lily thought she ought to slow or stop the bleeding from his calf before sending him on to the healers in the Ford. Kneeling down at his side and slightly behind him, Lily set her hands on the gash as gently as she could. She formed a very small golden ball of her healer's magic and summoned it to her fingertips. Lily then tried to visualize the little ball flattening and spreading, covering the entire superficial portion of the injury. The magic did as she wished, clinging to the Fae's lower leg and stopping the bleeding almost entirely. Satisfied, Lily stood, stringently controlling the iron pain and Fear in her mind as she did.

"Yew, please assist him across the bridge. Make sure he puts no pressure on that leg."

He nodded and started off for the door, taking most of the orange Fae's weight as he did. Lily watched their careful progress a moment before turning to face the gateway to Ropaz once more. She was striding in that direction in the next instant when a green Fae, tall and gracefully thin, appeared with a gravely wounded red warrior. Lily felt a start of recognition from Alder.

"If you could please carry him about halfway in and lay him down, I will do what I can until my Wardens return to get him across the bridge," she said, eyes already on the gaping rent in the red fairy's side. Lily forcefully pushed aside a bit of squeamishness at the sight of the nearly disemboweled warrior. It was a truly awful, not to mention dangerous, wound. The tall green Fae, though a little surprised, calmly did as she requested.

Lily put her hands to the red Fae's side the instant he was on his back in the center of the Antechamber. She called the healing power as before, but she made the golden ball bigger, thinking this injury would need more magic to heal, for it was both wide and deep. Lily gave all of her concentration to sending the magic down her arms, through her cupped hands, and into the prone body below. She spread the ball of magic out over all the torn skin and muscle, then sent it far enough within to keep the Fae's insides where they belonged. When the golden magic was clinging securely, Lily gently pulled her hands away and took a deep breath, controlling the iron effects once more.

"What an excellent bandage, young lady," the green Fae said softly. Lily turned to him, surprised at the gentleness of his voice, especially coming from a face splattered with blood. Black blood, Lily thought, feeling her stomach churn slightly. That was something about the trolls she would rather *not* have known.

"Thank you. I'm just trying to go with my instincts and hoping it's enough to get them to the healers in the Ford," she replied. Then she added, looking at him with the worry she felt, "I hadn't ever healed anyone with magic before tonight, you see, and I just want them all to make it."

The green Fae blinked, looked at the unconscious warrior between them, and then back to Lily's earnest face.

"You are doing an incredible job, young lady, and certainly expediting the care of the injured. Would a few suggestions set your mind a little at ease?"

When Lily nodded eagerly, he gave her a serene smile and pointed at her hands.

"It is best for each patient if your hands are completely clean when you begin. This is easily done with magic, if soap and water are not available. Simply rub your hands together, as though chafing them for warmth, and think of your healer's magic. Picture it cleansing your hands. I believe, at your level, that will sanitize your hands sufficiently."

Embarrassed, Lily quickly experimented, and found her hands free of blood moments later. Holding them up happily for him to see, she said with chagrin, "I can assure you that my mother taught me the importance of cleanliness when healing. I don't know how something so ingrained slipped my mind."

His serene smile returned for a moment before giving way to a very solemn look. He glanced down at the Fae between them again, then over to the gateway and fully engaged battle just beyond.

"I can think of a few good reasons, child-from-the-queen's-mirror. If you maintain your calm during this storm, every warrior to pass by you will have a much better chance of seeing the dawn. Now, I will teach you one thing more, and then I must return to the battle to do my part."

When he saw that Lily's gaze was completely fixed on him, he swept a hand over the torso of the wounded red Fae, indicating that her attention should fall on her golden binding.

"This exemplary bandage is doing exactly as you directed it to do: hold in the intestines, slow the bleeding, and keep the injury from worsening in any way, regardless of whether or not he is moved from this spot. It is so tangible that any competent healer will even be able to use it when they work their own healing magic, and believe me when I say that golden power goes a long way. Efforts from you such as this will allow the ladies in the Ford to heal many injuries in their entirety.

"My suggestion then is simply that you imbue this magic with another directive. If you tell a bandage such as this to begin healing the wound it covers, then I believe it will do so. The only thing you must be careful of is being adequately specific. Tell it to begin healing at the deepest part of the injury, and to work its way to the surface slowly. Most of the ladies across the bridge will sense such a spell on a binding and then be aware of the need to check what it has been able to do. Better, they will be able to continue a healing rather than begin one, and that is definitely in the patient's favor. Why don't you try this on our fallen warrior now, and I will observe you."

Lily, eager and determined, put her hands to the binding again and reconnected with her magic. Taking a moment to settle back in, Lily waited until she felt in tune with the warrior's body as well before carefully sending her desire to heal into the golden power clinging to his side. She was explicit in her instructions, telling the magic to go to the deepest reaches of the wound, to slowly knit and heal, to restore all that was broken and restart all regular functions of what was hurt. It was much the same as what Alder had taught her about healing, except that she wouldn't be seeing it through to the end, but telling the binding what to do in her stead. When she felt certain the magic was doing as she wished, Lily delicately removed her hands and looked up at the calm green Fae.

After a moment, he looked up from the warrior's side as well.

"Perfect," he said simply. Then he added, "I think he is out of serious danger now. Just make sure that he is taken across the bridge fairly soon, so that he can be closely monitored by the healers there. As more wounded come in, try your best to prioritize who is in greatest need of you, and the healers in the Ford, and see to them first. If you have trouble deciding, the warriors grumbling about returning to battle are usually the ones who can afford to wait," he concluded, a twinkle in his eyes.

Lily smiled at him, grateful for all he had told her.

"Thank you so much for the lesson, *piurteth*. I will follow your teachings most carefully."

He inclined his head, looking just a little pleased, before rising gracefully to his full slender height.

"I do not know that I am as venerable as some, but I am happy to impart knowledge to one so ready to learn, and so naturally talented. It has been a pleasure to meet you, golden petal, despite the circumstances."

With a final bow, the green Fae smoothly made for the gateway, where several warriors with injured brothers-in-arms were just entering the Antechamber. Lily quickly stood, even as she noticed Poplar coming up beside her, looking to her for directions.

"We need to get those three over here, and then it would be best to get this red Fae across the bridge as soon as Yew returns to help you."

He nodded, and both of them headed for the new arrivals. Lily fell into a rhythm, directing the placement of the injured who came in, mentally making a list of who needed tending first, caring for them as best she could, and finally making certain that all of the wounded made it through the bridge door in a timely manner, bandaged as needed. She was proud of Poplar and Yew, who rose to the occasion and did all she asked of them with admirable efficiency. If not for the iron pain, spreading slowly but surely through her body, and the Fear, causing her unending mental strife, Lily thought she could have kept up her efforts all night. As it was, she had to take short breaks occasionally, beating the iron effects into submission when they got to be a bit too much.

It was during those brief respites that she looked to the gateway, trying to see how the battle was going through the swirling magic dome. She had noticed that the Fae warriors had fought hard to surround the dwindling troll battalion, and that they had recently begun an aggressive aerial assault that had forced the remaining trolls to put their backs to the golden wall of the dome. She couldn't be sure, but it seemed that, after a number of hours, the battle was going more definitely in favor of the Fae. Certainly the alternating walls and trenches formed by the earth spectra as they gained ground on their enemy were keeping the frenzied trolls hemmed in. Though individual trolls made attempts to disrupt that earth magic with their own, they were not able to counteract singly what the Fae warriors did with such a skilled and coordinated effort.

Lily was allowing herself a small amount of relief when her eyes swept back to the entrance, as had quickly become a habit as she looked for the new wounded to appear. What she noticed in this glance, however, made her go completely still. The gateway, which had swirled so densely with magic when she had first arrived, had thinned. It was now almost completely transparent, and easier to see through than the rest of the dome on either side and above. Lily didn't know whether this was due to the weapon the trolls had wielded against it for many critical minutes, or if the repelling spell had damaged the entrance somehow earlier that night. Certainly the number of Fae warriors who had been passing in and out continually for hours wasn't helping, either. Before she could decide on the most probable cause, Lily felt a painful jolt of magic from her prophetic well of power. Already sitting, Lily doubled over from the brief flare of agony. As soon as she was able, though, Lily stood on shaky feet and began walking unsteadily for the guest building.

"Lily, what was that? Did you just get a prophecy? Were you able to understand it this time?"

Lily forced her legs to move faster, taking the stairs to the porch without pause.

'Armor On'.

She repeated the words grimly for a tensely waiting Alder.

It told me this the instant I realized that the gateway has been worn down to nearly nothing.

Lily reached for her armor, still in a pile just where Vadom had left it, as Alder gave in to a moment of shock. She had buckled on her greaves and cuisses before he recovered and forced himself to begin calmly planning what they should do next.

"You are going to get all of your armor on, as quickly and carefully as possible, and then you are going to tell Poplar and Yew what you think is about to happen."

Lily stood, cinched her belt, checked her dagger, and then fought a horrible deluge of pain. If the situation had been any less dire, she wasn't sure she would have been able to overcome it. As it was, it took all of Lily's courage to reach for her breastplate, lift it over her head, and fasten the buckles under her arms. More pain, intensely battering her mind, her will, and her soul. Lily fought, knowing that time was against her, and that if she didn't win this internal battle, the injured Fae warriors laid out right in the middle of the Antechamber would be completely vulnerable to any trolls who got inside. Finally, after an eternity had passed in the space of a minute, Lily opened her eyes and searched for her Wardens.

She didn't see either of them. What she did see were the six unconscious warriors she had bandaged just before her rest. They had come in a little while ago after that aggressive maneuver by the Fae outside. None had been brought in since then, and that was why Lily had taken the opportunity for a short break. She had assumed the battle was waning, and that there might be fewer fairy injuries with victory close at hand. Lily didn't know what to do, but she wasn't going to allow those six Fae to be killed in cold blood, not when she had worked so hard to keep them alive.

What should we do, Alder? It may be a few minutes before Poplar and Yew return, and we need a plan in case the trolls break through during that time.

"Would you be willing to climb up on the roof of this building and try cutting the trolls down with your bow and arrows, Lily? That would be the safest option for you at this point."

Lily hesitated. She didn't think she was a good enough shot to injure more than a few trolls. If a greater number than that got inside, with the Antechamber being so relatively small, they would be upon the injured in a matter of seconds. Lily just couldn't stand the thought of it.

Please, Alder, I've got to at least try to rouse these six warriors first. Three of them may be able to move on their own and make it through the bridge door, out of danger.

"*Would that they knew the spell to take you with them,* faelani," Alder said tightly.

Lily didn't waste another moment, but ran flat out to the fallen and made straight for the enormous brown warrior, the biggest Fae she had yet seen. While his upper left arm had sustained a huge mace blow, Lily thought such a sturdy warrior would still be able to walk, at least a short distance. Kneeling beside his head, Lily gave his right shoulder a gentle but firm shake.

"Fae, you must wake up now. Awaken Fae!"

He stirred, slowly blinking his eyes open and focusing on her face. Lily could tell his mind wasn't very clear, but he was listening to her.

"Sit up. I will help you."

Lily shuffled behind him and heaved him into a sitting position. To her relief, he immediately began trying to stand. She scurried to his front and lent him a hand, helping him lumber to his feet. Glancing at his uninjured arm, she took it and positioned it so that he was cradling his other arm just so.

"Walk to the bridge door and cross to the Ford, Fae. Go now."

Still obviously a bit hazy, he started for the door, his large strides steadily covering the distance. Lily turned and chose another less severely wounded Fae to try to wake. She looked up incessantly at the gateway, now to all appearances an open entrance. How much time did she have? When she got the yellow warrior, also with an arm injury, but to the elbow in a particularly gruesome manner, awake and to his feet, she turned to point him in the right direction and saw, to her immense relief, Poplar and Yew heading her way.

"We just helped the earth warrior across the bridge, Your Highness."

"Rather a relief that you woke him up, my lady. I honestly had no idea how we were going to move him to the Ford without his participation."

"Poplar, Yew, I think the trolls are going to be able to pass through the gateway any minute now," Lily said urgently. "We have to try to get these five out of the Antechamber before that happens."

Both of her Wardens went rigid and whipped about to inspect the entrance to Ropaz, where a considerable number of trolls were now being maneuvered by the Fae warriors outside. Her Wardens let out several virulent curses in response to this unprecedented danger.

"They are using the dome to trap the enemy and prevent them from fleeing, but there are still enough trolls that they cannot see beyond them to the entrance— which is definitely compromised," Yew said grimly.

"Do you have a plan, Your Highness?" Poplar asked intently.

"I want these five out of harm's way. Three of them have head injuries, and we cannot wake them. Both of you need to take one each, and lead this yellow Fae as you go. Get back here absolutely as quickly as possible. I will rouse this Fae with the leg wound and try to get him up while you make this trip. We'll rescript the plan from there."

They had already moved to follow her instructions, slinging two of the Fae with head injuries over their shoulders. Poplar got in the face of the yellow warrior and said just enough to harden the fairy's face with determination. The five of them made straight for the bridge door at a decent clip, leaving Lily to kneel beside the leg-wounded Fae. She managed to wake him after several interminable moments, and had just gotten him to a sitting position when Poplar and Yew burst back into the Antechamber, running back to her at full speed. Poplar picked up the third and final unconscious Fae, slowing just enough to mind his well-bound head. Yew did the same for the sitting warrior, who was clearly in too much pain to argue being carried. They took off again, moving as quickly as their burdens allowed.

"Faelani, *please, I am asking you to get out of the open now. Get into the guest quarters until your Wardens return, and then the three of you can devise a strategy for defending yourselves here in the Antechamber."*

Lily sprinted for the concealing safety of the guest building porch, more than willing to comply at that point. Before she had made it even halfway, however, nine weapon-bearing trolls fell through the entrance as the last of its magic gave way. Looking about themselves in amazement, their eyes locked on her with desperate, battle-frenzied vengefulness. Then they came straight at her.

Crossing the River Ward

Lily reacted entirely with her instincts. She knew that allowing her warrior's magic full sway was her best hope for survival now. She called for her night magic anelaces, even though she knew they were the wrong weapons to wield against very strong trolls with a deadly array of maces, morningstars, and flails. Still, her *vapa* had given her one lesson with the anelaces, and she knew that little bit of experience might save her, or at least keep her from a more serious injury.

With her small swords at the ready, Lily turned and quickly assessed the nine trolls, who were trying to form a circle and surround her. One of the bigger trolls, however, quickly lost patience with that tactic and took a menacing step forward, swinging his club at her with brutal force. Lily ducked low, maintaining her fighting stance and her balance, grateful his height had made the attack just high enough for her to dodge entirely. Moving almost without thinking, Lily took advantage of the careless opening he had given her and deliberately performed a lunge, keeping her elbow straight but unlocked as her small sword went deep into the troll's thigh, striking the bone. The face of her opponent went slack with shock as his leg gave out and he fell to the ground with a howl of pain and rage.

Lily didn't have the chance to see whether or not he dropped his weapon, for his fellow fighters were clearly furious about what she had managed to do, and they were closing in on her for retribution. Lily found that unfair, considering she could have struck higher, through his torso, and made the blow a potentially fatal one. When the opportunity to strike had appeared, though, Lily hadn't been able to do it. She thought at first that it was because she hadn't had the time to ice her emotions, and couldn't look at dealing death with the assessing detachment her *vapa* had taught her. However, Lily realized her reluctance most likely stemmed from the simple truth that she had so loved the healing she had been working most of the night that she didn't want to be the one causing such harm to others. Whatever the reason, Lily knew it would be foolish to believe that the trolls would show her any mercy in return. She would have to fight to win.

Turning a little so that all of the remaining trolls were still in sight, Lily got into her battle-ready stance again, more excruciatingly aware of her surroundings than she could ever remember being before. The slightest shift of weight or weapon from any of the eight opponents before her did not escape her notice. For a few critical moments, they seemed to regroup, obviously at a temporary loss as to how to deal with a female who wasn't completely helpless. Lily fervently hoped they wouldn't find out just how little she actually knew about the weapons in her hands, but thought that was probably too much to wish for given the circumstances.

One of the trolls lashed out at her suddenly with his mace, and Lily only just managed to step back in time. She knew she stood no chance of deflecting attacks like that directly, not against a very physically strong enemy with a very large blunt weapon in his black-nailed hands. His reach was much longer than hers, and his guard was up after watching her incapacitate his comrade. Emboldened by her small retreat, the others pressed in, apparently assuming she had simply gotten lucky moments ago.

Their mistake, Lily couldn't help but think grimly. When the second troll on her right brandished his morningstar in a threatening but negligent gesture, Lily gathered her courage and went on the offensive. As the only part of the troll she could reach with any kind of dependable self-preservation was his outstretched, upraised arm, she tried one of the techniques her *vapa* had taught her, hoping to inflict an injury and lessen the odds against her. Lily concentrated on the footwork, the angle of her blade, the direction of it at exactly the right moment, and could still hardly believe it when she managed to cut him deeply in the crook of his elbow. Blood spurted from severed veins, and the morningstar fell from his nerveless fingers only seconds later.

Lily tried to keep him in her peripheral vision as two of his war-brothers attacked her simultaneously from her left. Apparently they'd had enough of fighting a pesky fairy girl, for their faces showed their clear desire to finish her off and move on to greater things. Lily couldn't help but think that it was a very good thing they had no idea who they were really fighting, for she knew it would probably either make them determined to capture her, or gleeful to take the life of their enemy's princess. Lily supposed it depended on whether they were thinking for themselves, or if they were Void-bound and therefore slaves to the commands and motives of the xydolem. She didn't know the critical answer to that question, what with the iron so painfully blocking her inner power from being in tune with what was magical around her. She had hoped that she would sense some distortion in the trolls by the xydolem, as Void element didn't actually cause her pain. If there was a way to tell, though, her *vapa* had not yet taught her how to discern the malignant form of night magic in living beings.

Facing the encroaching trolls more directly, Lily tried to determine how she could possibly go up against two of them at once without incurring a serious wound. Just as she was readying herself to duck, sidestep, or retreat, Lily heard furious shouts from behind her. Not daring to look, Lily stayed completely focused on her opponents. She was momentarily stunned, however, when the two attacking trolls suddenly seemed to sprout arrows from their necks. She watched as their eyes went almost instantly blank with death, even as they collapsed to the ground.

Then Poplar was there, swinging a broadsword with enough focused strength to fell several of the remaining trolls before they could recover from the surprise attack. More arrows were shot from behind her, and Lily realized it must be Yew with the incredibly fatal accuracy with a bow. Lily surveyed the carnage with both relief and sadness, only to freeze at what she saw beyond Poplar's imposing frame. More trolls. The sprinkling of enemies had become a deluge, and Lily knew they didn't have a chance of keeping so many away from the bridge door for any length of time. Not that this secondary door had thinned in the slightest. It was as thick as it had been when Lily had first set eyes on it, and she realized it had to have even more protective magic than the gateway, to require a passing spell so much more complex than the entrance. What she should be worried about was their own survival. They needed a plan. They needed help.

Suddenly realizing there were two beings she could always reach out to, Lily sought the advice of her *faelan*, never dropping her defensive stance.

Alder, do you think I should try sending a pulse to my vapa*? We need help, but the trolls are cutting us off from the Fae outside.*

Lily was hit with a tempest of emotions before Alder firmly battened them back down in his silvery soul. She realized then that he had been suppressing his presence so that she could focus fully on her skirmish with the trolls. Lily felt grateful that he had been protecting her in the only way he could— by preventing himself from becoming a distraction.

"Yes, try sending him a pulse as soon as you safely can. Wait for Yew to come up and fight alongside Poplar, so that you have enough cover to concentrate. If possible, see if they can fly you to the roof of the guest quarters, where you'll be safe a little longer."

Lily had to give ground as a new troll gave Poplar a wide berth and came directly for her. There were trolls everywhere, and Lily wondered how the Fae warriors outside could possibly fail to notice their enemy passing through the gateway in droves. Did they mistake, in the dark, the dwindling troll battalion as an increasing death count? Lily eyed the troll's flail warily, trying to decide how to stave him off and implement Alder's plan at the same time. Then, with an impossibly quick flick of his wrist, the troll sent the sharply spiked ball straight for her chest. Even with her sword up, Lily's tired legs and exhausted arms could not move fast enough to evade the blow entirely. She despaired just a moment, wishing her strength hadn't chosen this exact moment to falter. Though she managed to deflect the intended direct hit, the terrible metal sphere of the flail still screeched across a portion of her breastplate before tearing the skin of her shoulder, pulling free of her flesh when it encountered the snugly fitted iron armband she still wore.

Feeling her own horror as well as Alder's, Lily tried to push it aside and focus enough to stay away from another clout from her opponent. She tried to find a weakness, anything about him that she could exploit for her own survival, but only saw a string of huge obsidian pieces tied around his neck and a look of vengeful fury in his eyes.

Eyes that, in the next instant, had an arrow directly between them. Lily was only able to stare at the lifeless form on the ground at her feet for several long moments after it fell there with a loud clatter from the flail's chain. She tried to bestir herself— the battle wasn't over, her part wasn't finished. She had to pulse her *vapa* for help, before Yew or Poplar got hurt or worse. Still, the effort to push that death from her mind and focus on calling to her Wardens was an immense one.

Turning, she saw that Yew was running toward her, allowing his inner magic to recall his bow and arrows within as he approached. His gaze lit on her bloody shoulder in a combination of helpless rage and self-recrimination.

"Yew, I need you to fly me to the roof of the guest building so that I can call for my *vapa* with night magic."

Though he looked a bit confused, he barely slowed as his wings sprang out of his back and his arms reached out to catch her up. Then he launched into the air and flew the short distance to the guest quarters, landing lightly and depositing her with care upon its roof. He hesitated, then pulled out his bow and arrows again and started firing them furiously, picking off the trolls around Poplar as quickly as he could.

Without waiting to see if Poplar would join them, trusting that he knew what he could and could not handle in this situation, Lily went to the place near her wells of power in her mind. She focused on twisting apart some of the night magic writhing close by, and, wrapping it with her intent, she formed her pulse knowing exactly with what it would be imbued. When it stilled in readiness, containing her message and awaiting departure, Lily released it, hoping it would reach Vadom in time. She watched as it shot out of her hand and straight for the portion of the Antechamber fronting Ropaz. Her heart gave a lurch when it came up against the golden dome and was deflected completely. She watched as it bounced against the Bubble repeatedly, hitting lower and lower each time. Lily's relief knew no bounds when it bounced down as low as the gateway, then passed immediately through it and out over the heads of the trolls milling in thick disorder about the entrance.

Though she wanted to keep sitting where she was on the slightly sloping roof, Lily doggedly rose to her feet once more. Carefully cleaning her anelaces as her *vapa* had taught her, Lily made sure not a drop of black blood remained on her blades. She couldn't bear the thought of any of it going back into her mind, this terrible evidence of pain and violence and death—

"Lily, your anelaces are completely clean. It will be safe to sheath them again now, faelani*."*

Alder's voice was gentleness itself, and Lily shook off the tumult of panicked feelings that had crept up on her unawares. She was so tired of the iron preying on her mind, making her susceptible to fears and weaknesses she could not afford to have, now more than ever. She stored her blades and called forth her bow and arrows, wrapping Alder in feelings as she did. It made this night easier to bear, knowing that Alder was enduring it with her. He took all that she offered, the good and the bad, freeing Lily to concentrate more acutely on survival.

Lifting her bow, Lily winced as the flail wound shot hot spikes of pain down her arm and into her chest. Grimly determined now, Lily pulled an arrow from her quiver and set it to her bow, just as her *vapa* had instructed. She kept in mind all he had said about this weapon and then picked her target carefully. Lily wanted to practice on trolls nowhere near Poplar for the moment, fearing, in her inexperience, that she might hit him instead. Yew was doing an excellent job of covering for his friend, so Lily decided to try to prevent the trolls who had skirted widely around Poplar from getting any closer to the bridge door. She suddenly remembered, too, that Whirlwind was still in the animal shelter, tied to the railing inside and very vulnerable. Lily was determined to do her best until help arrived.

Shifting her stance, relaxing her shoulders, taking in the conditions and terrain about her with an archer's eye, Lily selected a target, trying to remain unemotional about the fact that she aimed for a being who lived and breathed. She made one last adjustment, trying to anticipate the troll's movement on the ground below, then let her arrow fly.

Lily felt an impossible melange of emotions when her arrow lodged in the troll's upper arm. There was relief, that she had missed the unguarded back she had been aiming for, yet she was not unhappy that he had dropped his weapon and fallen to his knees, trying to see the arrow from an awkward angle. And, quiet as a whisper, Lily felt a small measure of pride, that her first arrow in an actual battle had found its mark and taken an enemy out of the fight, at least temporarily.

"Nice shot, faelani."

Lily felt the ghost of a smile on her lips, knowing Alder had sensed her inner conflict and was letting her know that it was alright. Her tiny victory was short-lived, however. The trolls below had, of course, noticed the arrows raining down on them, and the more astute of their number were attempting to scale the guest building to put an end to the two archers picking them off from above.

"Poplar!"

Lily, who had been trying to decide where to aim her bow next, looked for the Fae warrior below anxiously, worried that Yew had called to him because he had been injured by the dozens of trolls running about. Her eyes soon found him, a spot of purple in an area swelling with black, as though all of the unprecedented fighting had bruised the Antechamber. Lily was relieved to find him unharmed and turning as soon as he could toward their lofty vantage point. She saw when Poplar's eyes locked on the trolls trying to climb up the guest quarters, for his fierce expression became fiercer still, and he rushed to help them with the latest threat.

Lily returned to finding targets, aiming for trolls with large amounts of obsidian around their necks or upper arms. Better to try to take those opponents out at a distance, she reasoned. She hadn't attempted to maim more than a few, however, before the clamorous din of battle concussively spiked just outside the gateway. Lily spared the entrance a glance in between arrows and froze just an instant upon seeing the mass of smoky black warriors fighting where, a brief time ago, there had been no sign of them at all. She felt a stab of fear for the Fae outside. What if this was some terrible magic of the xydolem, turning the tide of battle? After a few long moments of trying to keep one eye on the trolls in the Antechamber and the other eye on the happenings just outside, Lily watched the night magic warriors pass through the gateway en masse, stalking a scattering of horror-struck trolls.

The Void fighters came in staggering numbers, but not one of them showed the trolls the slightest mercy. They fought with lethal precision, in groups and singly, taking on every troll who stood and resisted and every troll who ran in circles about the Antechamber, too frightened to escape the trap that space had inadvertently become. Lily wanted to take her eyes away from the packed confines of the ground below, to avert her gaze from the carnage. She did not do it, however. Lily knew, now, that it was not the xydolem who had made warriors such as these with night magic, but her *vapa*. And she would never do him the dishonor of looking away when he fought like this for her, in response to her plea for help. So Lily watched, from the safety of the roof, until every troll from the invading battalion was dead. In a very short time, silence descended, for the battle was finished.

When the last remaining troll had taken his final breath, the Void warriors all began stepping toward the vampire near the gateway, cleaning their various weapons as they went. Her *vapa* became the center of a swirling cloud of night magic, and for several seconds, he was entirely obscured from Lily's sight. When he reappeared, she saw that his stance was rigid, and his eyes were scanning the fallen trolls . . . anxiously.

Without thought, Lily formed a little pulse, telling it to reassure her *vapa* and convey where and how she was right away. Sending it, she watched it zoom to Vadom, who snapped about and appeared to catch it midair, before it could bounce off of him. She saw the flash of relief that crossed his face when he heard her message and found her with his eyes, standing on the roof of the guest building. In the next instant, he vanished, only to reappear on the roof right next to her, moving faster than her eyes could follow. Though the Fae warriors were beginning to re-enter the Antechamber, Lily was completely focused on her *vapa*, checking him over for any injuries. To her relief, he didn't appear to have so much as a scratch. She saw the moment his eyes came to rest on her shoulder, however.

"You are hurt."

His voice was calm, but Lily looked in his eyes and caught a glimpse of fire and fury.

"It's not so bad, *Vapa*, really. My armor took the worst of it," she said, trying to reassure him.

Honestly, the physical pain was only an echo of the unrelenting battering her mind took from the Fear. Lily knew that she could tolerate much worse than what that troll had managed to inflict.

"We will find you a healer immediately," Vadom said, still in that calm, furious voice. Lily didn't think he was angry with her, but she really didn't want to ask.

"My guess is that he is angry with himself, faelani. *He has adopted you as his child, and he considers your safety his greatest priority. As your mate, I feel responsible as well, and I can understand if he is berating himself for leaving your side. Probably he is thinking of the ways he could have handled this situation differently, ways that would have spared you danger, pain, and fear. A warrior such as Vadom will castigate himself in silence, then renew his determination to keep you from all harm."*

Lily didn't like the sound of this. It was hardly her *vapa*'s fault that the Antechamber had been infiltrated for the first time in history. He had been hunting the xydolem, as no one else could, and had probably kept those beings on the defensive, changing the course of the battle before ever letting loose those night magic warriors. The trolls had obviously lacked proper leadership for the majority of the battle. And Alder, too, felt self-recrimination when he didn't even have a body to protect her with? Lily thought they were both being unreasonable.

I hope, faelan, *that you are not feeling any guilt for how this night has turned out. There is only so much either you or my* vapa *could have done tonight.*

"Lily, you are as generous as always. But . . . I could have confirmed my existence and your identity for Captain Pine much faster, and perhaps left him enough time to escort you through the bridge door. I talked with him instead,

doing what I wished for myself instead of putting you first. I am not blameless for what has happened to you since sunset."

Lily didn't really think there had been enough time, no matter what Alder was saying, but before she could think of a reply, a series of exclamations drew her attention back to the gateway. It appeared that many of the Fae warriors had been completely unaware of the trolls who had passed through the entrance, and the extensive carnage that they witnessed upon re-entering themselves was causing quite a stir. Lily was still looking in that direction when Captain Pine returned. She saw the look of utter horror on his face, and heard him when he began shouting in alarm.

"Where is the Princess? *Where is she?"*

"Captain, up here," she called hastily, not wanting Alder's *praetam* to remain so upset.

Pine's head snapped around, just as her *vapa*'s had done, and the relief was much the same as well. He took to the air and was on the roof with them in a matter of moments. His gaze quickly traveled over her. And froze on her shoulder.

"You are injured."

Lily suppressed a sigh. Before she could say anything, however, Captain Pine turned around and bellowed, "Willow! Willow by the Lake, to me!"

She watched as several heads turned, and many others looked up in curiosity. Lily caught sight of the tall, gracefully thin green warrior who had given her the healing lesson and waved to him with a smile. He waved back, then flew up to them.

"It would seem that you are a lady of many talents, golden petal."

She followed his gaze to the bow she still held in her left hand. When she looked back up to his face, a reply on the tip of her tongue, she paused at the deep concern that had marred his calm countenance. He had noticed that she wore even more iron than the last time he had seen her, and he was clearly very worried about it.

Another series of shouts had them all turning to look again, this time to the little bridge door. A spectrum of warriors had just entered the Antechamber from the Ford, and they were clearly shocked by the sight that greeted them. Captain Pine immediately made to go to them, but paused, speaking over his shoulder to Willow.

"Heal her shoulder and then bring her to the bridge door."

Then he took flight, winging the short distance to the newcomers. Lily thought, based on their jerkins, that they were more of the Court Guard. Why were they here, if they hadn't known about the battle?

"May I, young lady?"

"Yes, please, Willow," Lily said, pulling together her wayward thoughts and giving him a tentative smile. She tried relaxing her muscles as he stepped toward her, knowing that made it a little easier to heal such wounds. He smiled reassuringly.

"As you know, this injury is fairly minor. It will take me but a minute to restore."

Lily nodded, ignoring the sting of her torn skin as Willow placed his hands on her shoulder, carefully not touching any of the iron Lily wore. Then she stilled, feeling warmth spread over and through the damaged spot, as though a part of Willow's serenity had connected to her and soothed that which was disturbed. It lapped around her shoulder in gentle waves, soon ebbing and taking the pain away with it. When the warmth was gone entirely, Lily opened eyes she hadn't realized that she had closed, and then looked up into Willow's calm face.

"Does it feel like that when I heal, too?" she asked curiously.

"Every healer's touch is a little different, and unique to them. It is generally believed that a healer's abilities are similar to their overall temperament," Willow explained quietly. He hesitated, then asked her a question of his own.

"I know that Captain Pine is not at all himself tonight, or he would have noticed your iron and realized the implications of bearing so much of it. May I ask why you wear it, aside from even how you can possibly endure so much on your person?"

"I wear it because I promised my mother I would keep it on until it was completely safe to remove it," Lily replied immediately. "It hasn't yet been safe to take it all off. There always seems to be some danger lurking that I must hide from, or protect myself against. Then we realized that my inner magic would be out of control once I was entirely free of the iron, and that I would need the help of older Fae to help me learn to manage it initially. Even now, I still don't think it's safe," Lily finished, trying to sound out why that was so. With the battle over, she should have been able to shed her iron skin, yet her inner magic . . . was uneasy.

Alder, do you feel this?

"I can feel your uneasiness. I must ask you not to consult your prophetic well of power, though, faelani. *With this much iron on within the Bubble, you*

will be overcome too quickly for either of us to counter."

Lily knew that was true, but even this vague sense of something was enough to have her keep her iron where it was. Looking over at the bridge door, Lily felt the uneasiness sharpen and become more definite. Yes, she thought with a sigh, it would seem she would have to endure the iron just a little longer. She would have to trust that she would know when the time had come to remove it all for good, even the jewelry her mother had given her as gifts for so many years.

"*Vipina.*"

Lily turned upon hearing her *vapa*'s voice. She looked at him in question. He leveled his gaze on her, seeming much more himself as he did so.

"If I think your mind is in jeopardy, I will be taking off as much of your iron burden as I deem necessary," he stated in no uncertain terms.

Lily, however, was only reassured by this. While every inhabitant under the Bubble would suffer immensely trying to help her with that particular task, it would scarcely bother her *vapa* at all. This, too, meant that someone she trusted would help her, not a complete stranger, should she need it.

"That is a relief for me to hear, *Vapa*. I am grateful that I will have your help when the time comes for the iron's removal. It isn't going to be easy for me," she finished quietly.

Her *vapa*, as usual, seemed to know what had gone unsaid. He nodded, then held out his arms.

"All will be well soon, *Vipina*. For now, let us focus on getting you through that door and on to Golden Court."

Lily hugged him briefly, then allowed herself to be picked up and flown to the bridge door. Once she was within earshot, she could hear Captain Pine explaining to the newly arrived Court Guard spectrum what had happened since sunset. Many of them looked at her incredulously. When Pine turned and saw her, in the arms of Vadom, with Poplar, Yew, and Willow following silently, he encompassed them with a sweeping hand motion while turning back to the Court Guards, switching to the Ropazian language. Lily assumed this was for her benefit, and she was grateful for the courtesy and safety of Alder's *praetam*'s gesture.

"This group will know, much better than I, what occurred inside the Antechamber during the battle. I have told you what I know, and why you did not encounter the princess or me on your flight here."

Lily wondered, even as her *vapa* set her down on her feet, if Captain Pine was in trouble for some reason, and if these warriors had the authority to hold him accountable for some mistake he had made. Before she could figure out who to ask, however, the purple warrior who was apparently in charge of the new spectrum looked at her directly, made her an elegant bow, and then spoke to her, also in Ropazian.

"Are you the young lady who used the Queen's mirror to contact King Oak?"

"Yes. I am Lily, daughter of Rose, and I made that contact accidentally while in Goddess's Retreat," Lily answered, hoping that only a few questions would be asked before she could be on her way. It was the middle of the night, and she was exhausted by recent events. With any luck, she would be able to get a little rest on the way to Golden Court. Amazing, really, to think that she would be there sometime tomorrow, at long last.

"And is it true that you were pursued to the Ford by a large contingent of trolls?"

"I don't know if they were aware of us or not, but they were making for Ford-upon-Ward to attack— we believe at the instigation and perhaps coercion of a group of xydolem."

Many wide eyes regarded her in surprise and disbelief.

"Did you see these xydolem with your own eyes?" he asked with skepticism, almost as though he was humoring her. Lily felt her chin trembling, but she refused to get visibly upset in front of these strangers. Looking him straight in the eye, Lily answered him, fighting to keep her voice steady.

"I saw twelve of them together in the Joquobon Desert, when they attacked and killed my mother."

There was absolute silence for many long moments, before the purple Fae, his face full of shame, bowed low and stepped back from her without another word. One of the other purple warriors in the spectrum stepped forward, presumably to continue questioning her. Lily, however, had had enough. Surely she had some kind of authority, the ability to get herself through this door without further delay? She was, after all, going to have to explain things to the king . . . her father. Once was going to be hard enough, and she didn't want to waste time hashing out every painful and frightening detail in a field full of troll corpses. Perhaps it was time to try taking charge of the situation.

Turning to Poplar and Yew, who were standing at the ready just behind her, Lily tried to do just that.

"Yew, would you please check on my horse, Whirlwind, in the animal shelter, and bring the haversack on the ground near her to me?"

"Yes, Your Highness," he said deferentially, and moved to do as she asked.

Lily watched him go a moment, then began turning back to her interrogators. Her eyes, however, caught on one of the fallen trolls lying so deathly still on the ground nearby. She paused, focusing on the large piece of obsidian set in an ornate armband he still wore. Her inner magic stirred. What did this mean? Why were the bodies important? Or was it their black volcanic stones that were significant? Lily found herself walking to the troll, kneeling down in the blood-soaked black ground, and touching the obsidian of the armband. Her magic flared again, causing her pain, but it was just bearable. She had gotten the smallest hint from that disruption, and it was enough for her to know what needed to be done, even if she didn't yet know why.

Laying a hand over the troll's heart in a respectful moment of contemplation, Lily then gently removed the armband, stood, and walked back to the group of astonished onlookers by the bridge door. Her *vapa* was regarding her steadily, not at all shocked by her behavior. Feeling reassured, Lily turned to her other Warden and gave him her instructions.

"Poplar, it is very important that every piece of obsidian be respectfully gathered from the fallen and brought into the Wood. There will be one thousand obsidian necklaces or armbands, one decoration on every troll. Please tell Captain Beech that not a single one can be left behind or destroyed. Please go now and make sure it is done."

If Poplar thought this was unusual, he gave no outward sign. Taking the armband Lily held out to him, he bowed to her courteously.

"Yes, Your Highness."

He took off in the direction of the gateway, which appeared to be mending itself, very slowly dropping the thinnest of veils over the entrance once more. Lily noticed that many of the warriors who had fought in the battle were collecting the fallen trolls and carrying them out from under the Bubble. Turning back to Captain Pine, Lily looked him in the eye and spoke steadily.

"What is being done in the aftermath of this battle, Captain?"

"Captain Beech is overseeing the search for any of our fallen still outside the Bubble and in need of attention. He will also make certain that all of the trolls are laid out and cremated, to ensure, if they were indeed Void-bound, that they are freed beyond any further control of the xydolem. Then the stronger element wielders will restore and balance the earth, grass, and air damaged by the battle to their former state, so that no one will be able to use those indicators as a marker for the gateway in the morning."

Lily nodded, finding all of this satisfactory. Clearly the Wardens knew exactly what they were doing. Still, she was a little concerned about any potentially injured Fae still outside.

"Willow, would you please personally oversee the care of the wounded outside? My mind would be at ease if I knew you were binding their wounds and making sure that all are taken to the Ford for further healing in my absence. I hate to think any should suffer needlessly now that the battle has ended. Will you do this please?"

Willow bowed.

"Yes, of course. I did not sense any seriously wounded when I realized the fighting was over, but a thorough search is the most prudent course of action. I would ask first, however, if any injured warriors were in the Antechamber when the trolls arrived? They are the reason I returned."

"No, there were none. I had Poplar and Yew carry all of them across the bridge when I realized how thin the gateway had become, and they had only just emptied the Antechamber when the first trolls stumbled inside. No Fae who came to harm are in this space now."

Willow smiled, relieved.

"That is excellent news. How well you have cared for your charges, Your Highness. I think the Fae casualties for this battle will be few, if any, thanks to you. We Willows are not so organized, as the act of going from healer to warrior so frequently takes a great deal of concentration and discipline. We are not always able to be the go-betweens that are most needed in combat on this scale. I should like to be the first to offer you my gratitude for your help tonight, golden petal."

Lily nodded to him, understanding the inner conflict of being both a fighter and a healer. She was only just beginning to truly realize the implications of that internal struggle herself.

"I accept your thanks and offer you my own in return, Willow. Your lesson in the thick of things made me better able to help those who came under my hands. Thank you for sharing your knowledge and your patience with me."

Willow bowed again, looking a little touched by her words. He then turned and flew quickly toward the entrance, passing through in short order. Lily turned back once again to the Fae who had come to collect her, choosing her words carefully before speaking.

"Captain Pine, I would now like you to perform the spell that will allow Alder, my *vapa,* and me to pass through this door. We have passed your Antechamber test, and we cannot afford further delay on this journey. I would then like to be escorted to Golden Court. My mother bid me deliver a scroll to the king, and I want to fulfill my promise to her as soon as possible. Spectrum of the Court Guard, you may act as escort, if those are your orders and reason for coming here."

Lily paused, not certain what to do in the silence that followed.

"Make some small impatient gesture, Lily, then give them an expectant look, as though you can't imagine why you aren't being obeyed immediately. Your words to all have been perfect, by the way. You are, without a doubt, your mother's daughter."

Lily hid her grin behind an expectant look, raising an eyebrow as her *vapa* occasionally did. Then, recalling one of her mother's impatient movements with a pang of both sadness and fondness, Lily deliberately set a hand on her hip and cocked it slightly to one side. This had cowed many a desert dweller, no matter how recalcitrant they started out.

Lily was a little delighted when the Court Guards moved to either side of the door, making a clear path for her to step right up to the thickly swirling second entrance. She did so, able to see a small distance past the old stone bridge, to where a handful of beautiful ladies stood waiting on just the other side of the River Ward. Lily knew a moment of uncertainty.

"What is it, faelani*? I don't think this new feeling is about any of your magic."*

It wasn't.

Alder, look at how lovely they are. And I am not dressed anything like them. What will they think of me?

Lily could feel Alder's consternation before he even spoke.

"Lily, it does not matter what the lady Wardens think, only that they show you the proper respect."

When this failed to reassure Lily at all, Alder tried again, a bit worried now.

"Faelani, *you are without doubt a golden beauty, just as your mother was a famed silver beauty. I know I am your truemate and that I am biased, but I think I can safely say that few ladies will ever outshine you. As for their attire, they are wearing practical healer's half-dresses, and are not trying to impress anyone with such garments. The lady Wardens are famous for being the most level-headed and practical females in the Fae Wood, and as such, I do not think they will be concerned with your foreign clothing so much as how many injured they still need to tend to. Perhaps you can use that as a vehicle for conversation?"*

Lily felt much better this time. Of course Ford-upon-Ward would have the bravest of ladies living there, ready to heal unexpected injuries and be in constant proximity to the entrance that served to keep the dangers of Ropaz and beyond at bay. She would be able to relate to such ladies, just as Alder said.

Thank you, Alder. You have shown me that my worries are needless.

Lily could feel the relief Alder experienced at her words. She wrapped him in her gratefulness for his concern and reassurance, and felt him glow happily in response.

"Excellent. Let us be off to Golden Court! What is holding us up, now?"

Lily surfaced to find out. When she turned back toward the Antechamber, she saw at once that Captain Pine and her *vapa* were staring each other down in a most intimidating fashion. Lily felt a little anxious at their open animosity. Both *praetam*s were important to her and to Alder, and it would be so disappointing if they didn't get along. Catching sight of Yew just to the side with her haversack, Lily decided to give them another minute to sort things out themselves before she intervened. Meanwhile, she would have a quick word with her Warden.

"Your horse is unharmed, Your Highness, though skittish at the smell of so much blood. I did what I could to calm her, then brought your bag as requested," Yew said, holding it up easily with one hand.

Lily nodded, relieved that Whirlwind had gotten through the battle unscathed.

"Would you like me to see that she is stabled in a particular place, Your Highness?"

Lily paused, considering, but she honestly wasn't sure of her answer.

"I am making straight for Golden Court from here, Yew, and then directly to Silver Court after I speak with the king. Alder needs to be put back in his body as soon as possible. I'm not sure where I'll end up ultimately, so perhaps we should leave Whirlwind in Ford-upon-Ward for now?"

Yew nodded in agreement.

"The Ford is roughly equidistant from each court, about four hours of straight flying from each. You could easily wait until you know where you'll want her kept and then send for her. You'd have her the next day, perhaps even the same day, if she is fleet-footed and starts out early enough."

"She's fast," Lily confirmed with a smile. "She was even before she drank some of the Goddess's tears from the sacred pool, and brave, too. I would appreciate it if you would see that she's looked after for me, Yew."

Eyes a little wide, Yew looked back at the animal shelter with growing enthusiasm.

"I'd be happy to, Your Highness. Is there anything else?"

Lily recalled the order she'd given to Poplar and felt the solemnity of the night weigh upon her.

"Actually, Yew, I charged Poplar with a task that will require both delicacy and respect, as well as take a measure of time if done alone. Would you help him do as I have asked?"

Yew was already nodding and bowing. Setting her haversack down at her feet, he answered.

"Yes, I will. He is outside?"

At her confirmation, he turned and took a sort of flying leap that landed him just in front of the gateway. When he turned around to wave at her, Lily smiled a little and returned his wave, watching as he passed out from under the Bubble. She then turned herself back toward the fairy captain and the former vampire councilor still clearly having a contest of wills. Feeling frustrated and a little upset, Lily marched up to the pair, gently took them each by the hand, and began walking toward the bridge door, towing them both in her wake. That certainly got their attention. She could feel their surprised gazes on her back.

When Lily arrived in short order before the door, she spun to face the pair.

"Alright. What is going on," she made a gesture that indicated the space that separated them, "between the two of you? Need I remind either of you of my desire for haste?"

When her *vapa* raised an eyebrow at her tone, Lily gave him a very genuine pleading look.

"*Vapa*, we're only four hours away from Golden Court! Why can't we leave?"

His eyes softened a little at her nervous, excited urgency. Before he could answer, however, Captain Pine spoke up instead.

"This vampire, one who has been personally granted sanctuary by the golden king, responds to this generosity by refusing to give his word that he will not do violence to the Fae of the Wood while he is under the dome."

His words were accompanied by a glare that had Alder cringing in her mind. Lily considered his words, then replied, hoping logic would gain her the result for which she wished.

"Captain, if Alder were in danger, say while he was attending his duties at Silver Court, would you defend him with your sword if it were necessary?"

"Of course," Captain Pine answered, as though this fact was abundantly obvious.

"Yet you would deny my own *praetam* the right to wield a weapon to protect me in the same place, or any other under the Bubble?"

Momentarily stymied, Pine turned slowly toward Vadom.

"Is this why you refuse to give your word on this matter?"

"I must be free to watch over my *vipina* as I see fit. Though I would never harm any female or child in the Fae Wood, if Lily is in need of my protection, I will not hesitate to use force against anyone else if it becomes necessary. In addition to this, I have begun teaching her the knowledge of a warrior, and we will both have need of our weapons during her lessons."

Everyone was silent a moment, waiting to hear Captain Pine's response.

"If this is indeed the case, I will be content with your word that you will only wield weapons to protect or instruct your *praetii* within the Fae Wood. I will accept no less from one who can wreak such utter destruction on his enemies."

Vadom gave his word in solemn tones, causing many of the warriors about her to ease their tense postures. Lily realized that, as old and powerful as many of them must be, few were probably as lethal as her *vapa*. Considering they were willing to fight to the death to keep enemies out of the Wood, they would want to make sure that a being as strong as Vadom would not use his powerful magic against anyone under the golden dome.

Apparently satisfied that the vampire was a reliable ally at last, Captain Pine walked briskly to the little bridge door, seeming to find a calm he obviously hadn't felt in a while. After a moment, he gathered himself, put his hands to the door, and indicated that Lily and Vadom should now do the same. Lily quickly picked up her haversack and slung it onto her back, then placed her hands on the door, as her *vapa* was already doing. As she watched, Captain Pine started to glow with the soft purple light of his inner magic. He said nothing aloud, but Lily had the feeling that he was communicating with the door somehow. She waited patiently in silence, content to be so close to achieving her ultimate goal, to reaching the end of her journey to Golden Court at last.

Perhaps fifteen minutes passed, and Lily was actually beginning to feel rather sleepy, when suddenly, without any warning at all, she felt the door start to suck her in with incredible force. She started to experience another curious sensation as well, beginning in her hands and slowly working up her arms. It was magic, old and defensive. Lily could feel it working through her whole body, weighing and measuring her mind, her magic, even her soul. It passed through her, even as she herself passed through the doorway. Lily felt the exact moment that the spell was complete, that she had been found worthy to enter the homeland of her people. She felt suspended in time for one more protracted moment, and then, before she could process what was happening, Lily found herself flying through the air.

She landed with a bone-jarring jolt on her hands and knees. Opening her eyes, Lily first saw stone, and realized she had landed on the old bridge spanning the Ward. Before she could do more than wonder if she would rather have landed in the river itself and taken her chances in the water, Lily felt Vadom's hand on her shoulder.

"*Vipina*, are you well?"

Lily sighed, wishing her poor *vapa* didn't have to ask her that question quite so often.

"Yes, *Vapa*. Perhaps the magic of the door wasn't certain about letting my pride into the Fae Wood. I suppose I should be grateful it let the rest of me pass through."

Inside her mind, Lily heard what sounded suspiciously like a smothered silvery soul-chuckle.

"That was quite the peculiar experience. I believe it took the better part of an hour for the passing spell to allow us entrance. Given the amount of magic we both possess, perhaps it is not so surprising that the door's inspection of us took so long."

Lily simply nodded in agreement. She climbed wearily to her feet, in a little more pain than before, but as yet still unaided. Lily glanced up then and saw the lady Wardens, all of them with looks of horror dawning on their lovely faces. When all five of them let out cries of shock, Lily sighed again, feeling a little offended on her *vapa*'s behalf. He may be a vampire, but for any lady to consider him a threat was just ludicr—

"Faelani, *I don't think they are shouting because of Vadom.*"

Lily had no opportunity to assess the cause of their distress, however, for Captain Pine was barreling past her, across the remainder of the bridge, and standing in front of the ladies in the next instant. To his credit, he seemed to be trying to reassure them, rather than assuming he needed to defend them against the vampire in their midst. Whatever he said, however, did not ease their horrified looks. Lily began slowly walking toward them, determined to try to calm them down herself if necessary. While she thought her *vapa* would understand their anxiety, she didn't want him to be hurt by the lady Wardens' reactions, either.

"No, not him, *her*! What is she wearing?" one of the ladies all but cried in outrage.

Lily felt an immense amount of Fear rise up and threaten to consume her. Falling to her knees again, Lily clapped her hands to her ears just before the iron pounded her with pain. Through the mental beating that ensued, Lily was only distantly able to realize that the healer must have spoken in the Fae language. After a few interminable minutes, when the worst had passed, Lily managed to summon a bit of indignation. The ladies had thought her attire distressing after all, apparently.

Alder, I thought you said they wouldn't care about my desert clothes?

Lily was still rather fuzzy, but she was sure Alder had put her mind to rest on that matter.

"Faelani," Alder said, very gently, and just the slightest bit amused, *"they are upset because of the iron you wear, not your clothing. They know what it does to you, as healers, and they wish to take such pain from you. That was very bad, just now, Lily. Are you sure it isn't possible for you to take the iron off now?"*

I had the feeling earlier that I needed to keep it all on, but not for much longer, Alder. And while I appreciate their desire to help, perhaps they could begin by speaking in Ropazian, so that my wings of elucidation don't get ruffled.

"They mean well. I think they are mishandling the situation because the magical implications of wearing so much iron are not widely known and thus didn't occur to them. While every Fae in the Wood knows that iron will cause them to experience terror and a horribly painful death if they wear it, due to the Fear, the nuances of the suffering is a topic of hypothetical debate, so little is known for certain."

Lily realized, rather uneasily, that this was most likely because fairies who put iron on were shortly in no condition to speak of what was happening, and the chance of being overwhelmed by the Fear and forever silenced . . . she supposed she shouldn't be surprised by the ladies' reactions then.

Forcing herself to uncover her ears and stand up again, Lily opened her eyes to see a number of anxious gazes pinned to her face. These now included the warriors of the Court Guard spectrum acting as her escort. They had circled around her on the bridge, presumably to try to calm the commotion they'd heard upon passing through the Antechamber door. Offering everyone a tentative smile, Lily tried to set about reassuring them, and then making sure this didn't happen again.

"I'm fine, sorry to worry everyone. The Fear attacks whenever one of my wells of power try to do something magical. I'd appreciate it if everyone spoke in Ropazian until my wings of prophecy indicate that it is safe for me to remove the iron I wear."

Lily watched as every face, from the ladies, to Captain Pine, to the Court Guards, went from worried to completely stunned. That had not set everyone at ease as she had hoped it might. Finally, one of the lady Wardens spoke up, speaking decent Ropazian.

"What else will cause the Fear to attack your mind, little petal, that we all might avoid it?"

Lily paused a moment to consider the question.

"Healing, but I have control of that by keeping my hands away from any other injured Fae; trying to use my warrior weapons, but I can avoid that too by using my night magic; looking in my mirror and thinking of other fairies with mirrors, because of my wings of enhancement; summoning any of the elements or getting too close to a high concentration of them; hearing singing or, most likely, any type of music; hearing or seeing any language that isn't Ropazian, which all of you know about, because of my wings of elucidation; listening to my well of prophecy, although none of us can do anything about that; and getting really upset about something or defensive of Alder can set off my therianthrope, which the Fear does not like *at all*. I think that's everything," Lily concluded. Then she frowned slightly as something occurred to her. She had mentioned eight types of inner magic, but she had nine wells of power. Was she forgetting one, or had she not learned what that one was yet?

What does my ninth well of magic hold, Alder? Do we need to tell them about something else?

"It pretty much has to be a well of facets, Lily."

What?

"You know what those are without realizing it, faelani. *Vadom fought with a large number of night magic facets in the Antechamber just a short time ago. They are magical duplicates of you, powerful puppets in a way, that you must learn to animate and control, one by one. Not very many fairies have them, and if they do, they generally only have a few. Royal Fae tend to have a greater number. I'm not sure how many I have in total yet, but I know your father used to be able to control up to thirty facets of himself at once, on the warriors' training field. Your mother, too, used to be able to perform five healings simultaneously, so great was her concentration and magical strength."*

Lily was somewhat awed by this new information. Pulling herself together before her mind could wander too far exploring all the possibilities this magic presented, she quickly thanked Alder and focused on all of the concerned fairies staring at her on the bridge.

"Alder says my ninth well of power probably contains facets, but that hasn't caused me any trouble so far, so I think we don't have to worry about it for now."

Every face was incredulous now. Did they think the iron had made her delusional? Lily decided to brazen out the situation. She was, at last, only four hours from Golden Court, and she was determined to be there by sunrise. Walking steadily across the rest of the bridge, passing over the River Ward, and finally stepping onto the land of the Fae Wood waiting for her on the other side, Lily smiled brightly.

"*Vapa,* fly me to Golden Court?"

Vadom's eyes thawed a bit, the worry for her giving way to a sharing of her excitement.

"Of course, *Vipina.* I am sure if we continue east, we will be sure to spot it near dawn."

Lily pivoted to the left, to face the direction her *vapa* had indicated with a small tilt of his head. She couldn't wait to see this rather intense adventure all the way through to the end. She would just keep going until she couldn't go any more, and that meant traveling on until the Sea of Fintilles was stretched out before her.

Ready, Alder?

Lily felt him give another one of his little soul-chuckles.

"Ready to fly into Golden Court after a wonderful, nerve-wracking journey through Lamoranth with my faelani? *Yes, I rather think so."*

Lily grinned, feeling momentarily lighthearted, despite everything.

Surviving against all odds and making it to one's destination with both *vapa* and *faelan* unscathed must do that to a young lady, Lily reasoned.

"Alder is ready too, *Vapa*. I say we go now."

As Vadom strode toward her, however, Lily noticed the ladies having an intense whispered conference with Captain Pine. Their eyes were getting wider and wider as he related something to them. Suddenly, one of the lady Wardens looked right at Lily and spoke to her.

"You are the healer who made the bindings for so many who came to us?"

"Yes, that was me," Lily answered, a bit cautiously.

"All of the warriors here in the Ford are either recovering or at least stable. We healers by the river would like to thank you for the magic you gave so generously."

Surprised, Lily gave her a tentative smile.

"Of course. I was happy to be able to help. Let us hope that Willow does not have many injured Fae to bring from outside the Bubble now that the fighting is over. I've put him in charge of binding them and making sure they are brought directly to you here."

"Willow by the Lake?" another lady asked.

When Lily nodded, they all gave her approving looks.

"We will continue to wait for him here, then."

"Safe flying, petal. Don't let your *praetam* go too fast or too high."

"Best of luck at Golden Court, young healer."

Though Lily found the idea of her *vapa* flying unsafely with her laughable, Lily inclined her head to them courteously, then made them the *valoriad* for good measure.

"And good luck to all of you and your patients. May they all continue to mend under your watchful eyes and gentle hands."

The ladies all stood a little straighter, then nodded to her solemnly, as if she were, somehow, one of them.

"Ah, faelani, *they definitely approve of you. You have quite won the lady Wardens over, and they are notoriously difficult to impress or surprise. They are the bravest ladies in the Wood, after all, and they recognize you, no doubt, as one of their own."*

Lily felt immeasurably happy at Alder's words. Already she was gaining the acceptance of the fairies in the Wood, and she couldn't help but think that this boded well for her future here. Nodding once more to the lady Wardens, Lily looked to Captain Pine inquiringly.

"Ready to go now, Captain?"

Though he looked a bit weary, Pine made an affirmative gesture and began walking toward her. Grumbling, the spectrum who had come to escort her began making their way to Lily as well. She didn't catch everything they mumbled under their breath, except for the blue warrior of the group.

"If the blood-drinker can keep going, so can we."

Lily froze, then slowly looked the Fae directly in the eye, crossing her arms across her chest as she did.

"His name," she said clearly, a wealth of warning in her tone, "is Vadom."

The blue Fae, obviously older if his long, sky-colored hair was any indication, met her gaze belligerently. At first. When Lily increased the displeasure in her eyes and made it clear, without words, that she would never, ever look away first, for she had a much more important point to make than he did, the warrior muttered his amendment.

"Va*dom*, then."

Nodding with what she hoped was a regal air, Lily swept the rest of the spectrum with her gaze, silently stating, she was sure, that her demand included all of them. When each one had indicated, in some way, that he understood her, Lily utilized her mother's 'carry-on-then' gesture.

"Please lead the way, then, Captain Pine."

"Yes, Your Highness," he said, sounding a bit bemused.

Vadom then picked her up, haversack and all, and took to the air, great leathery black wings flapping all but soundlessly in the wee hours of the night. In the quiet of that breath-taking leap toward the stars, Lily heard Alder speak very softly in her mind, as though talking to himself in a whisper. She struggled to listen through the blanket of sleep that was covering her, quickly and quietly, in the safety of her *vapa*'s arms.

"Ah, my princess, you are just as spirited as your mother . . . I think perhaps even more so. Let us hope your father is not so shattered that he cannot see this and value you when morning comes."

Though Lily felt troubled by what he had said, she succumbed to sleep before she could form a word to ask Alder what he meant.

35

Sunrise at Golden Court

Lily woke several hours later from a strange but peaceful dream. There had been an extraordinarily beautiful and unmistakably sophisticated lady, with dark black hair and light green eyes, industriously cleaning a very nicely appointed . . . cave. Lily allowed the gentle but insistent voice calling to her from far away to recall her from that other place.

"You need to wake up, *Vipina*. Come now, I do not think you will want to miss your first glimpse of Golden Court, *vladi*."

That certainly caught Lily's drowsy attention. She checked on the Fear first, making sure it hadn't encroached too far. Satisfied that it hadn't had enough time to cause her serious trouble, Lily opened her eyes and looked, still rather blearily, in the direction her *vapa* was flying. There was, in fact, a golden spot of light ahead of them in the slowly diminishing dark. Lily felt a spark of her previous excitement kindle once again.

"Are we nearly there, then, *Vapa?*"

"Yes, perhaps an hour away now, though no more than that. I thought you might want to take the time to wake up and prepare yourself for what awaits you at Golden Court."

Vadom paused, as though he wanted to say just the right thing, but wasn't sure what those words were. Suddenly nervous, Lily wondered if she ought to tell him about her dream. If it really had been Vabiri she had seen, would it make her *vapa* happy to know she was alive and well, or would it hurt him to hear about her doing something so normal, when he was so very far away? Vadom must have caught the indecision on her face.

"Is there something you wish to tell me, *Vipina?*"

"Yes," Lily said hesitantly.

Her *vapa* waited patiently, appearing mildly curious about what she would say.

"I just had a dream about a lady who was cleaning, looking very determined all the while."

Vadom looked puzzled.

"Did you recognize the lady, *Vipina?*"

"I think so. At least, she is as beautiful as I've imagined she would be."

Though his wings never ceased their steady beat, Lily felt her *vapa*'s heart speed up.

"She had long black hair and light green eyes. I thought she looked quite safe in her cave," Lily added softly.

Vadom let out a sigh. Then he smiled wistfully.

"If Vabiri is cleaning, it is either because she is putting off some other task she does not wish to do, or because she is incredibly bored. My dear one hates to clean," he said fondly.

After a silent moment, he spoke again.

"You have given me a great gift, Lily. If my love is in our cave, then she is safe. If she is doing that which is odious to her, then she knows she needs to stay put to remain so, and has only just begun to grow impatient. Though I cannot like that she worries, I am immensely relieved that those who threatened her to force my cooperation have kept their word and left her alone after my compliance. If they were going to harm her, they would have done so right away, perhaps so that her mourning would not garner any notice and draw attention to my disappearance. My heart is easier now. Thank you, *vladi*."

Lily hesitated a moment, then asked the question she had been too afraid to utter before now.

"So you don't mind coming into the Fae Wood with me, *Vapa?* I've wanted you nearby so much, but I feel a little guilty too. I don't want to keep you from returning to the Cave Kingdom for my *vama* if it's time . . ."

Vadom's eyes clouded briefly.

"I have always planned on taking you all the way to Golden Court, and then Silver Court right afterward, *Vipina*. If I had still harbored any doubts about accompanying you into the Fae Wood, however, they were brought to an end during this night. You could have been hurt much more seriously, or even killed, during your time in the Antechamber. Both of us depended upon the Fae to keep you safe, and they very nearly failed completely. I cannot leave you here knowing this could happen to you while I am gone, at least until Alder is made whole again and proves his suitability as your protector to me. After that, we should perhaps discuss this again."

Lily nodded her agreement, allowing herself, briefly, to feel selfishly relieved that her *vapa* would be with her the first time she appeared in each Court. It would be reassuring to have a staunch ally present as she met some of the fairies who would help shape the course of her life, and, hopefully, a few who would love her just a little. Though she was not allowing herself to get her hopes up as far as her father or Alder's parents, she wanted very much to see and get to know the whole Alder and to meet Iris, and perhaps to finally make friends with other girls near her own age. This was her chance to start anew, after all, and Lily wasn't about to waste it.

"I am so glad that Vadom has put your mind at ease on this matter, faelani. *It is good, for both of us, to know his plans and be able to count on his presence in the coming days."*

I agree, Alder. I hadn't realized how anxious I felt about him leaving unexpectedly until he told me his exact intentions, and I could set that worry aside. Now I don't have any excuse not to think about what is likely to happen at Golden Court this morning, do I?

Alder gave the impression of sighing, then.

"I think it might be best to give you some idea of what you're in for, Lily. Though I have not been much at Golden Court, I have spent most of my life in Silver Court, and it was modeled after the magic and rules of the Gildenthrone. The king and his advisors are nearly always in the throne room by first light, and the courtiers come and go throughout the day. During the daylight hours, matters of the realm are discussed, the most urgent having priority. Magic is supplied to the throne by the royals, which in turn powers the Bubble. There is usually a day each week to hear complaints from any Fae of the Wood who come to Court to have problems resolved. There is nearly always a day of healing as well, when those who need the assistance of the Wood's greatest healers can appeal for their aid. Many other activities and amusements are a part of court life, to break up the day-to-day duties of those charged with the running and care of the Fae Wood. I do not think, though, that any of those routines will be in effect today, for the Golden King is awaiting your arrival."

Do you think I will have to say very much? I haven't really given it a lot of thought. I suppose I assumed we would finally get there, I would hand over the scroll to the Golden King and watch him read it, and then I'd answer his questions about my mother. If he's my father though . . . does that change things?

Do I have to tell him the entire story in front of everyone?

"The thrones at both courts have been more of a burden than a responsibility for the royals in recent centuries, Lily. I'm sorry to say that your father, especially without his truemate, will be struggling to supply the Gildenthrone with the magic it requires, even with the court helping as it can, and he will not be able to leave it and have a private conversation with you. However, I think your plan is simple and effective. Let Captain Pine introduce you if you wish, then explain how and why you came to deliver the scroll. At that point, your father will either ask you for the rest of the story, or read the scroll. After that, if you are feeling overwhelmed and need an excuse to leave, we do have a rather pressing reason to leave for Silver Court."

Lily appreciated Alder's attempt at levity as much as his giving voice to what needed to be done when they entered Golden Court at last. They lapsed into thoughtful silence, both hoping for the best, but not fully knowing what to expect. Before she had much time to muse on the events about to unfold, Lily felt warmth on her face. She opened her eyes to the world and beheld the most beautiful sight she could ever have imagined.

It was dawn, the rising sun casting exquisitely soft light on a panoramic vista of leafy green trees. They stretched out before her, all different sizes and shades of green, every one unique from all the rest. Occasionally swaying in a butterfly breeze, their leaves rustled in a sibilant whisper of welcome. The dormant strength of the immense canopy beneath and before her gave way unexpectedly to a sparkling, jewel-colored body of water. The sea went on out of sight, fast friends with both the horizon and the oft-visiting sun, which gave them the gift of light and color each day. It did so now, bringing out the brilliance of a spectacular golden castle that soothed and sang to Lily's previously arid soul. Before her, filling her eyes and her heart, the castle's whimsical towers and spires reached gracefully for the sky, as though to embrace the gentle lavenders and peaceful pinkening of the slowly waking firmament. Lily took in the glittering windows, magically glowing white stones, and great powerful golden doors, and she knew she was home at last.

"Faelani," Alder said, as much in awe of her feelings as she was.

Oh Alder, there cannot be a more beautiful place in all of Lamoranth than this.

Lily thought her heart might burst, it seemed so full of some emotion she had never felt before. She reached out for the golden castle, as though she could touch it as they flew ever closer. Lily watched as the castle began to glow more brightly, the faint golden light of its white stones becoming more pronounced, revealing its need for the sun to share its luminescence. Only the surprised murmuring of her escort diverted Lily's attention from the enthralling view they fast approached.

"*Vapa,* it is so wonderful, is it not?" she asked breathlessly, somehow tearing her riveted gaze from the fairy world to look at his face and read his reaction there. Lily was a little startled to see her *vipina*'s mark on Vadom's forehead, clearly visible in the early morning light.

"I had thought nothing could beam so lovingly as the sun, *Vipina,* yet this Golden Court is as brightly welcoming as the dawn," he said, smiling just a little as he shared her enthusiasm.

"It shines in welcome of you, Princess. The Gildenthrone senses your approach and acknowledges you," Captain Pine said quietly, seeming as surprised as everyone else by the magic of the golden castle.

Lily wondered at his words, statements she would have thought impossible not so long ago. They flew on, getting closer, and the details of the castle by the sea became more and more clearly defined. Lily marveled when she was near enough to see the incredible scenes shallowly etched into many of the walls and towers of the castle. Her artistic sensibilities were momentarily enthralled, hardly believing that the history of the Fae, for that was, surely, what she was viewing, had been carved right into the very stones of one of the Wood's most ancient structures. Though Lily would have loved to fly about the castle all day, watching the legends and true fairy tales unfold before her eyes, she had finally arrived at Golden Court, and her escorts were descending.

Vadom silently followed their lead, though he soon moved his wings differently, angling so that he landed just before the magnificent golden doors of the castle, before any of the Fae warriors had circled all the way to the ground with their more avian wings. Her *vapa* set her down with infinite care, discreetly ensuring that she was steady on her feet before stepping back and taking in the castle that now dominated their vision. If not for the rhythmic lapping sounds of the Fintilles breaking on the shore, Lily would not have recalled the sea just beyond the immensely large fairy stronghold that had momentarily hidden the great waters from her sight. Her whole awareness was now focused on the enormous double doors she would be passing through in mere minutes, for they had in deep relief a masterpiece that stole her very breath.

On the right-hinged, shining golden door, all was fierce and powerful magic. Fairies, elves, Ropazians, trolls, vampires, and others she had never seen except in her imagination, including dwarves, mermaids, dragons, and still more beings she could not name, filled the space. Every one of those depicted were poised, ready for something, waiting with their gazes fixed on that which was on the opposite door. Lily turned to follow their line of sight, and she was filled with an irrational fear. There were nothing but shadows on the left-swinging door. The artist's skill had somehow made some of the shadows deep, others shallow but menacingly close, and all almost indistinguishable from the overall, sinister darkness. The incorporeal shapes inspired uneasiness, whispering of nightmares that ensnared the mind at its most vulnerable. Lily was sure for an instant that she could see xydolem grotesquely winging about in a corner of the foreground, even as the rational part of her mind scorned the possibility that those beings would be allowed on such a spectacular work of art. She focused instead on the power she could feel emanating from the doors. The magic of the ages was indelibly embedded in this great arching passage, and Lily could feel it with every beat of her heart.

"The Portal of Lamoranth," Captain Pine said quietly, sounding a little disturbed. "I have never before seen it closed. Always, it is open to admit the Fae of the Wood into their capital city."

Almost as if they had heard the captain's softly uttered words, the great golden doors swung silently open, of their own accord. Lily found herself walking slowly toward them, straining for a glimpse of what lay beyond. She couldn't see, and she froze, feeling a little afraid.

"It's all right, Lily. I am here, and so is Vadom. There is no need to fear this place, for it is your true home and your destiny."

Lily gave herself a shake, then resumed her deliberate pace, which had faltered to a halt for just a moment. Alder was right, and there was no turning back now. She walked without stopping through the portal, and found herself in a large, airy entryway. There were Court Guards standing at attention around the perimeter of the oval-shaped space, one at each side of every hallway that led off to other parts of the castle. Lily counted nine passages and eighteen of the Court Guard, one of whom stepped forward to meet the arriving group and subject them all to his alert green gaze. Though his eyes passed quickly over her spectrum escort and Captain Pine, his right hand twitched instinctively to release a weapon when he got a good look at Vadom. Before the situation got out of hand, however, Captain Pine sharply held up his hand in a halting gesture.

"This vampire is the *praetam* of Princess Lily, and he is not to be attacked," he said in Ropazian.

When the wide-eyed Court Guard turned and stared at her incredulously, Lily felt a bit uncomfortable. When he made to speak, Captain Pine held up his hand again abruptly. He moved forward, close to the other Fae, and murmured softly to him, more quietly than Lily could make out. She realized that the captain might very well be speaking in the Fae language to his Court Guard, and she was grateful for his consideration. Though she had the iron Fear well in hand at the moment, she knew that could change in an instant if something set off her inner magic. The castle itself was steeped in sun magic, and it would be all too easy to start pulling that power into her mind in a moment of relaxed vigilance. Lily made herself wait patiently as Captain Pine gave his orders.

Another minute had the Court Guard nodding in repressed excitement, turning about, and making a small circle in the air by his head with his index finger. The other seventeen Fae warriors immediately came to him and listened as he spoke very quietly to them. Lily saw most of them look at her in astonishment as their leader relayed their instructions. Finally, the group broke apart, and an orange-haired warrior stepped forward and spoke to Lily and her escort in very slow Ropazian.

"We, the Portal Court Guards, welcome Her Highness, the Princess Lily, to Golden Court, and request her presence in the Throne Room at her earliest convenience. His Majesty, King Oak, has ordered us to direct her ladyship to him there upon her arrival at the castle."

Pausing to give her *vapa* a careful look, the orange Fae continued.

"Having been informed of the vampire Vadom's aid of our brothers-in-arms, the Wardens, this past night, as well as his word of honor given to our own Captain Pine in the Antechamber, we will allow this esteemed *praetam* to our princess royal to enter the castle of Golden Court and continue his protection and instruction of Her Highness therein."

Lily sensed that this acceptance was significant somehow, but before she could ponder their official welcome, she noticed several Fae of her escorting spectrum move forward and pass through one of the open doorways at her left. Then Captain Pine was approaching her, looking as though he had a few things to tell her.

"Princess, now that you have been granted permission to enter Golden Court, some of your escort are going ahead to ensure that one of the longer passageways to the Throne Room is clear of other Fae. I believe this is the safest way of preventing your inner magic from stirring and causing you unnecessary pain, seeing as it will most likely be entirely deserted at this hour. In a few minutes, I will lead you there, and you will be granted an audience with King Oak, his advisors, and the courtiers who are early to rise to their duties. I trust you find this satisfactory?"

Though she was a bit taken aback by his formality, Lily nodded solemnly and responded politely, taking refuge in her deeply ingrained manners.

"Yes, Captain Pine, seeing His Majesty at present is entirely satisfactory. Thank you for smoothing our way with the Portal Court Guards."

The Captain nodded in acknowledgement of her words, then gave her an encouraging look before turning to speak with some of her escort. They waited there in the oblong entryway, and Lily's heart began to pound as she realized how close she was to meeting her father.

Alder, is it going to be all right? What is my father going to say to me? What should I do?

"Lily, faelani, *it is going to be fine, please, don't worry. I do not think your courage will fail you, but if you are still nervous when we reach the Throne Room, I will help you. Though I'm honestly not sure how your father is going to handle your meeting, you must simply be yourself and all will be well."*

Lily allowed Alder's words to permeate her mind, instilling his calm, confident assurances in the place of her uncertainties. In the end, it didn't matter if Oak was her father or just her king. What did matter was that he had been her mother's truemate, and that he needed to read the scroll that Lily carried as soon as possible. Only then would her promise to her mother be fulfilled.

"*Vipina,* would you like me to carry your haversack for you?"

Lily turned to her *vapa* and gave him a grateful look. Lifting the slightly bulging bag off of her shoulder and over her head, Lily handed it over, a little relieved to be free of its weight. The iron was heavy enough. Recalling, though, what she had just been thinking, Lily opened the top of the well-worn haversack and rummaged about for the scroll as Vadom held it steady. She found the precious parchment near the bottom, beneath the medical pack, food pouch, and well-wrapped mirror. Her mother's iron sword gave her a pang of sadness, but she felt a measure of peace when she caught sight of the tightly wound extra tunic that currently swaddled the glass statuette she'd made in Rose's memory. Firmly grasping the scroll, Lily withdrew it, then rearranged everything else and closed the haversack once more. Nodding to Vadom in wordless thanks, Lily squared her shoulders and looked toward the passageway on her left that she would soon be traversing.

I want to go now, Alder. Do you think it's safe enough for me to take charge and start off? I'm ready.

"*Go ahead then,* faelani. *They have been gone long enough to check a fair amount of the halls you'll be walking. There won't be many Fae loitering about at this hour anyway.*"

Lily straightened her spine, lifted her chin, and made for the passage. Her *vapa* glided smoothly and silently into motion at her side, as if he had known she wouldn't wait until directed. Though all the warriors thronging the entryway froze at the sight of her determined strides, none moved to stop her. Hearing a faint sigh somewhere behind her, Lily saw Captain Pine come up along her other side a moment later. As Lily passed out of the airy oval room, she could hear many of the Fae following quietly in her wake.

As Captain Pine led her through a series of modestly sized hallways, Lily allowed the tranquility of the castle to lull her just a bit. When they came to a series of stacked rectangular stones, leading up, and, presumably, to another hallway, however, Lily paused, a little uncertain, to watch Captain Pine and her *vapa* as they ascended.

"*This is a staircase,* faelani. *It is something like a ladder, that will allow you to reach the upper floors of the castle easily. Hold the banister against the wall if you are feeling a little uneasy about them.*"

Relaxing at Alder's explanation, Lily reached for the railing on the wall that stretched up the length of the staircase and began to climb up as the two before her were doing. She felt just a tad winded by the time she reached the top, and rather hoped they were getting close to the Throne Room. The hallway they were traversing now had quite a few doors on either side, and Lily found herself peeking into some of the adjoining rooms out of curiosity, for most of the doors stood open. When her inner magic twinged at some of the objects she saw in the third room she glanced into, however, Lily decided to keep her eyes ahead for the time being.

Another hallway, a second and longer staircase, and yet another hallway later, Lily wondered if they would ever make it to their destination. Just as she was doing a little mental grumbling, Lily realized that the hallway they currently traversed had a great number of doorways, all leading to other fairly large corridors, and that it was widening. There were elaborate works of art on the white stone walls as well, some made of cloth woven with brilliantly colored thread, others out of materials she hadn't ever seen before, all depicting Fae doing a variety of different things. The warriors all looked brave, and the ladies all appeared completely happy. Lily tried not to slow her pace, reassuring herself that she would be able to linger some other time to absorb all of the beautiful pictures in this place.

Finally, a doorway appeared at the end of the hallway that was so marvelously elaborate, Lily was certain she had reached the Throne Room. Taking a deep breath and tightening her grip on the scroll in her hand, Lily continued walking forward, trying to emulate the calm, authoritative posture of her *vapa,* who still walked by her side. Captain Pine had gone a little ahead, and was just now speaking to the Court Guards stationed at both sides of the doorway leading into the Throne Room. As these new warriors listened to their captain, their eyes took in Vadom with wariness, Lily with amazement, and her iron with complete horror.

Lily kept walking until she stood just feet away from them. There was some kind of design on these doors as well, but she was too nervously excited to look properly. Lily's breath was coming quickly and shallowly; her heart was pounding so loudly that she could hear the thumping of her blood in her ears; her mouth was dry, and her whole body was a little shaky. Her mind had gone completely blank. All she could think about was the fact that her father was on the other side of these doors. He was waiting for her to tell him about her mother. Was this going to be awful? Wonderful? Both? Lily didn't think she could stand even one more moment of suspense.

"Take a deep breath, faelani *. . . that's it, now another. It's going to be all right. Every Fae is nervous at his or her court presentation, and everyone else knows it, because they all went through it at some point in their first century, too. I will be right here the entire time, Lily. You will never be alone."*

Lily tried to allow Alder's words, his mellifluous voice, to soothe her, and it worked just enough to keep her panic at bay. She had to hold on to her composure. She didn't want anyone but Alder to know about the absolute tumult her emotions were in right now. She didn't want any of the wide-eyed strangers to see her when she felt weak, uncertain, and scared. Holding tightly to Alder's soul in her mind, Lily silently slipped her hand into her *vapa*'s, needing all the support she could get for these last few steps. Vadom glanced down at her, seeing it all in her eyes as Lily looked up at him. Pausing, apparently searching for words, he maintained their locked gazes for a moment. Then he looked down at their intertwined hands a moment more.

"You were born for this, *Vipina,* and now it is time. It doesn't matter what they say or do, only how you react. You can always be stronger and braver than the company you must keep if your will and your heart are greater. Go into that room knowing that when you leave it, your promises to your mother will be fulfilled, and that you will be able to begin your life as a fairy, as a princess, and as an otherwing to one who is worthy of you."

Lily felt a little calm impose some much-needed order on her chaotic feelings then. She steadied herself as best she could, holding close the truth of her *vapa*'s words, as well as her *faelan*'s brilliant soul. Giving Vadom's hand one more squeeze, Lily released him and turned toward the last pair of doors she had to go through. Making her spine as straight as she could and rolling back her shoulders, Lily took those last steps, passing Captain Pine, passing the Court Guards, and passing over the threshold and into the Throne Room.

36

Gildenthrone

The magic of the place was the first thing Lily noticed. It swirled and danced all around her, beckoning her further. All was white stone and early morning light. The room was a gigantic oval, the long, gently curving sides alternating with slim marching arches that encompassed soaring windows and shallow niches. The windows to her right gave a spectacular view of the deep purple-blue ocean, while the windows to the left provided an unimpeded view of the great green Fae Wood, its uneven leafy canopy stretching out as far as the eye could see. There were beautiful fairies in beautiful clothing mingling near the oblong walls, many of them artlessly framed by the slender columns that separated each niche from each window. The niches all contained a statue of glass incredible enough to arrest Lily's artistic attention, had she permitted it. She did not, however, allow herself to dwell on the priceless masterworks about her, but instead focused her attention on the dais at the far end of the very long room.

At the top of nine stairs, which were rounded enough to appear to be curving toward anyone who approached, was a throne made of gold. It was all pointed edges and neatly squared corners, immediately contrasting with everything else in the room. It was unadorned and very wide, enough to easily accommodate two people. At the moment, however, there was just one fairy sitting there. He was large, obviously a warrior, filling out his simple but elegantly fine garments. His hair was a tawny gold, and his eyes were intensely golden too, though their remarkable color did nothing to hide the shattered depths of his soul as he looked out listlessly over all he commanded.

Though it hurt horribly to see one so fractured, Lily made herself take measured, deliberate steps toward the golden Fae, her king and her father. The magic of the throne continued to move like the wind all around her, almost visibly ruffling Lily's desert tunic, seeming nearly to pick at the bloodstained tear at her shoulder, and swirling down to the black stains on her knees that had witnessed the suffering and death of others. Most of all, the magic seemed to take offense at her iron skin. Lily ignored it, refusing to be distracted by anything now that she stood just an arm's length away from the first step of the dais.

She waited there a moment, vaguely aware of the profound silence of the room about her. King Oak had not yet looked up, and Lily was not willing to wait any longer for his notice. She had traveled more than a thousand miles to meet this Fae, and at least that much further again to cross this room with her head held high, and she refused to stand patiently by while he allowed himself to live with his memories. She knew that was the path to self-destruction, and it was a road she had chosen not to take. Gathering a portion of the potent magic dancing about her, Lily pushed it, hard, directly at the Golden King. It bounced off of him forcefully, and he snapped abruptly to attention, an incredulous glare forming in his eyes and face. He looked down from his throne for the cause, and froze when he beheld Lily. His eyes drank her in, took note of every detail, flickered with shock at the iron jewelry and iron armor, landed on the scroll with a hint of curiosity, and dwelt at length upon her face. Finally, he spoke.

"You look like her."

Lily knew, of course, to whom he referred. Though her soul ached, Lily spoke the words she had come so far to say.

"I am Lily, daughter of Rose. I have come to you, Golden King, to fulfill a promise I made to my mother on the night of her death. I gave her my word that if anything should happen to her, I would deliver this scroll to you, and watch you read its contents. Take it, so that I might grant my mother's final wish."

Then Lily held out the scroll, perhaps a little more imperiously than she had intended, and stood rooted to her spot at the base of the steps. She wasn't going any closer to that throne. She was not. Her mother had once sat on that throne every day, and Lily just could not get any closer to it right now.

From one side of the throne, a small, unobtrusive lavender Fae stepped forward. Lily watched as he made his way efficiently down the steps directly to her, bowing low before speaking to her in a well-modulated voice.

"Your Highness, I am Fig, majordomo to the King at Golden Court. Please permit me to convey this scroll to His Majesty," he said, bowing again.

When he straightened once more, Lily studied him carefully.

"Faelani, *Fig has been the steward of Golden Court for many centuries, and he is completely trustworthy. He offers to take the scroll because the King may not be able to leave the Gildenthrone at this time. I would suggest that you give it to him. He will have it only briefly.*"

Lily held out the scroll to Fig, who took it respectfully with both hands. She watched as he walked carefully up the dais and presented it to the King, who all but snatched it from Fig's outstretched hands. Once in his possession, however, Oak could not seem to bring himself to open it. The entire court held its breath, yet the King made no further move to break the special seal that closed the parchment. The magical seal only he could remove. He traced a line of it here, a character there, then held the scroll tightly against his chest for many long moments.

At length, he looked up, directly at Lily. His golden gaze seemed to pierce her somehow.

"Tell me your story. Tell me why she left and took you so far away from me."

Lily didn't know her mother's reasons for living in the desert, only that the scroll would explain. She didn't bother telling her father this, however, but chose to tell him of her entire life instead. A brief sketch of her early years in the desert was all she could bring herself to relate. She hoped she convinced him that even if neither of them had been very happy, they had been more or less content: Rose with her healing of the desert dwellers, Lily with her secret lessons and songs, her birthdays, her daydreams and glass.

Their amadel escape from Nather was quickly told, and then came Japeta. Lily forced herself to speak every detail she could remember of that horrible night, from the iron armor to the xydolem by the water well. She cried useless tears in front of a room full of strangers, and it was no comfort at all that King Oak grieved just as much as she did. When she had fought to regain her composure, Lily went on, more easily telling of her meeting with Alder. She heard murmurs of astonishment from the fairies around her, and even her father raised his eyes from the scroll in his hands to look at her in surprise.

"Prince Alder has been with you these past weeks? That is a great relief."

Lily felt Alder stir within her mind, a little pleased, but rather uneasy as well. She thought she understood his conflicted emotions.

Lily next told her father and his court about the Magentay Canyons, and her rescue of Vadom. This apparently shocked a large portion of the courtiers, for several of the ladies actually fainted as Lily sketched that part of her tale. She didn't go too in depth, feeling that a meeting so personal should be kept between her and her *vapa*, with Alder being the obvious exception.

She moved on to describe the long trek across Ropaz, from Wikkenod to Wizulaan, mentioning that her *praetam* had given her warrior lessons and that she had met the Gongoozler in between. The razing of the northernmost volcano of the Crescent followed, and Lily took great pains to tell the king what she had felt, what they had discussed, and what the three of them had concluded on that and the following days as they continued east. She didn't know how informed her father or Golden Court's Fae were on the troll situation, but she wanted to make it as clear as she could so that it would soon be delegated properly.

When Lily came to what had transpired at Goddess's Retreat, she had the courtiers buzzing again. Though she chose, once more, to keep some of the details to herself, King Oak looked up sharply when she spoke of what the Goddess had said about her mother's soul. Though he still looked unspeakably sad, there was a very small measure of peace in his eyes now that had not been there even a few moments before.

From there, the telling went quickly. Oak had seen her in the mirror, and that flash of magic had alerted the xydolem and thus, their troll battalion, of her presence in Ropaz. There was the mad dash for Ford-upon-Ward, and the ensuing attack of both a coven and trolls outside the golden dome. Next came the battle waged by the Wardens and the fortuitously deployed Court Guards against the invading force, and finally the infiltration of the Antechamber. This last caused another round of fainting by some of the lady courtiers, and even the male Fae looked disturbed as she spoke. Lily mentioned her healing efforts and personal combat only in passing, though she did say that she was pleased to meet the lady Wardens when she finally managed to cross the bridge over the River Ward.

"And then Captain Pine and my *vapa* flew me straight here," Lily concluded.

She looked up at her father expectantly, though she hardly knew what she was waiting for from the absently gazing golden king. Lily knew he had been listening throughout, absorbing her tale and even intuiting some of the details she had left out, yet he continued to contemplate the scroll in his lap without speaking for many long minutes.

Lily willed herself to have patience. Her *vapa*'s words to her just before she had marched into the Throne Room echoed in her ears, and she knew she had to be strong enough, brave enough, to find out what was in her mother's scroll before she could leave this place. All around her, the courtiers seemed to rustle and whisper in poorly veiled curiosity. Lily willed herself to be as still as her *vapa* could be, and her gaze did not waver from the Golden King or the scroll he clutched in his hands.

At long last, Oak looked down at her from the Gildenthrone. He seemed surprised by her, then terribly saddened by her. Letting his gaze rest once more upon the scroll in his hands, Lily heard him speak, in the softest of voices, as though to himself.

"Ah, *faelani*, what a daughter you have given me."

Lily couldn't seem to breathe. She clutched Alder's soul as tightly as she dared, and she did not let go.

"Oh Lily, I'm deeply sorry this is so painful for you. Hold on to me, and we will make directly for Silver Court when he has finally opened that accursed scroll."

So Lily did hold him closely, for an unknowable length of time, until, at long last, King Oak took the scroll in one hand and slowly, deliberately retraced her mother's seal in its entirety. The scroll began to glow with the faintest silver light, and its impact on her father was like a physical blow. Even more astonishing, though, was the moment when the scroll began to speak, in her mother's heart-breakingly lovely voice. Lily knew a moment of utter fragility before Alder's powerful silver presence recalled her from her loss. Then she forced herself to listen to every word, knowing her mother would have expected no less from her.

"My dearest Oak,

If you are hearing this message, it means that I have passed on to the Peaceful Realm, though I never wished to leave you behind for that journey. It also means that our daughter, Lily, has kept her promise to me, as I knew she would, and arrived safely at Golden Court with this scroll. It is because of our child, *faelan*, that I have made the most difficult choices of my life, and caused you pain that I have felt myself, every day, since we parted. Please allow me to explain now why I believed that this trespass on our love had to be.

The very same night we conceived our Lily, in the early hours just before dawn, I had a dream unlike any I have ever had, before or since. The great seer Magentay summoned me to the canyons, yet a river flowed there, and they were not the deep and cavernous wonders that we know them to be now. He called me by name, and made me welcome in a shallow cave he had fashioned into a home. Magentay told me of a prophecy that he knew, with complete certainty, would someday come to pass. He prophesied that great evil would rise up in the north, and a fairy princess would be born just before the height of the evil being's power. She would be Lamoranth's best chance for survival in the final battle for balance against the destructive one. If this petal failed, the world would be swallowed into the Void, but if she succeeded, Lamoranth and its races would endure and prosper in greater harmony than before.

In my vision of Magentay, he told me that this girl child, the one central to the last of his Great Prophecies, lived inside of me now, the princess of the last hope. He said that my daughter, in order to come of age, must be kept alive and safe by being taken alone to a place without magic. Only then could she fulfill her destiny. The dream ended, and I woke to find you sleeping peacefully beside me, as always. My heart was in pieces, however, for I knew that when you came to, you would know right away of our child, and that you would never let us leave you. I had to decide my course immediately, and be well away before you awoke with the dawn. With Magentay's strange visit still coursing magically in my mind, I knew I had to be a queen to my people before being the truemate of my majestic Oak. I packed a bag with only the essentials and your most precious gifts to me, and I left. I made my way with all of my stealth to the Joquobon Desert, the only place I knew of that was truly and completely without magic of any kind. During all of these years, I have listened carefully to the whispers that have come to me from Ropaz, quietly speaking of one called the Misruler. I believe this being means great harm to Lamoranth, and I would caution you, my love, to find out all you can of this creature and do what must be done to protect the Fae Wood and our allies.

As I lived for nearly eighteen years in the great white desert, I was also raising our daughter the best that I could, giving her all the love I could spare from a heart that longed with every beat to return to your side. Our Lily is so wonderful, my dearest Oak, as you must already see for yourself. I think she is gentler and kinder than me, more stubborn and fierce even than you, and, at times, stronger and wiser than both of us. She knows nearly nothing about magic, but she is incredibly powerful, and will need guidance and love to flower— all that you can find in yourself to give. I ask you, my *faelan,* to live on without me and to delay our reunion in the Afterlight. Our daughter will need your help to succeed in her great ordeal and to weather the difficult days ahead for the Fae and for Lamoranth.

And now, child of mine, a few words for you alone. I have loved you every moment of your existence, and never once regretted the great gift you have been to me. I have marveled at your many strengths, and at the dearth of your weaknesses. I have watched you grow up to become a lady, quiet and sure, who has given me no end of pride. Your sorrows and your joys have always been mine too, and I thank you for sharing yourself with me, in your abundantly generous way.

I knew, when you looked into my eyes and promised to wear an iron skin, if that is what it took to reach the Fae Wood, that our people would have their new queen someday, and that I need fear for them no longer. I think, my darling, that you are probably wearing it still, uneasy of shedding this and other burdens of your past, uncertain of what will be expected of you once you are free. I have never lied to you, Lily, and so I will honestly say that your responsibilities will be great indeed. I do not believe, though, that they will be more than you can handle. Your father, the truemate you will meet, and the friends you will make, will all help you on the difficult path before you. And now, I bid you to remove your iron and your doubts, and to take your place as a Fae lady and the princess royal. Have courage, child of mine, and know that you will always have your mother's boundless love.

Farewell, my beloved mate and darling daughter, at least for now. My soul awaits you both in the world of all light, at peace now that my part is done. I will be here, content to stay until your times come as well, to be united once more and at rest in the brilliance of the sun.

With all my love,

Rose"

Lily was having trouble breathing again. She had sunk to her knees at some point, then sat down completely, her legs too unsteady to support her. In the silence of the Throne Room, her soft, gasping breath and shimmering tears hardly disturbed the grieving quiet. Lily rocked slightly back and forth, her arms wrapped around her middle, trying to hold herself together as she lost her mother all over again.

"Oh, faelani, I am here. Just take one breath at a time. I will help you keep your soul in one piece."

Lily felt Alder go to her innermost soul, there in the dappled fairy wood of her mind, where she was straining to endure this latest trial. She didn't know how he took their single bond and wrapped it once around her, securely holding her together, but she knew a moment of relief when he took a length of their intertwined souls and wrapped it once about himself as well. Lily felt more firmly anchored to him now, and she didn't think, after another few moments, that her resurfacing grief would be able to overwhelm her. She didn't hold back then, knowing she would survive, knowing that, eventually, the pain would be a little less, and she would feel more herself again.

Opening her eyes, Lily looked up at her father, the king. The agony on his face was like a blade through her heart— a sharp, deep pain that would, at best, be an ugly scar for the rest of her days. Lily knew, then, that as much as she hurt, her father would always be hurting worse. She had cracked, but she was holding together, with Alder's help. Her father, though, had lost the very person who was soul-bound to him, and what was left of him were only fragments. Oak would never be whole, never without pain, ever again in the world of Lamoranth. And so Lily wept for him too, grieving for the shattered father she had already lost. She wondered if there was anything she could do for him. If she only knew what would help, even the slightest bit, she would do it.

An idea came to her then, and she immediately gathered her strength to carry it out. Turning to look back at the doors she had passed through to enter the Throne Room, Lily saw right away that both her *vapa* and Captain Pine were hovering, tense and anxious, on the threshold. It was clear they wanted to come to her, and to Alder, but didn't dare do anything that might send the Golden King past the point of no return. Lily tried to call to Vadom, but no sound would come out. She stretched out her hand to him, mouthing '*Vapa*' in silent entreaty. He instantly began crossing the long oval room to her, disregarding the fear he inspired in the courtiers. No one moved to stop him, and he was kneeling beside her, haversack and all, in a matter of moments.

Setting the bag aside, he gathered Lily into the circle of his arms, rested her head on his shoulder, and held her securely, lovingly, as she continued to cry. He placed a very soft kiss on her tightly wrapped hair and whispered soothing words in her ear. Her arms around his neck, Lily let herself be gently rocked, feeling indescribable relief when her sadness receded just a little. Eventually, when her tears were utterly spent, and Lily felt exhaustion in every way that seemed possible, she lifted her head from her *vapa*'s damp shoulder and pressed her wet cheek to his dry one for a moment. Then she pulled back a little, just enough to look fully into Vadom's face. She would need his help for her small plan, both the fulfillment of her promises and the tentative gesture she wished to make to her father.

"I need to shed my iron skin now, *Vapa*."

He looked at her for a moment with immense pride, then slowly released her so that she could sit back and start removing her jewelry and armor. First, Lily reached for the haversack, pulling out her medical pack and her amadel jacket in readiness. Then, she started with her earrings. They seemed as good a place to start as any, and perhaps the smaller pieces ought to be the first to come off, when her fingers weren't clumsy with pain. Lily started in on her necklaces after that, carefully unclasping them and putting them in her jacket pockets one at a time. Her bangles and armbands came next, leaving her arms feeling exposed, but tingly with the promise of freedom.

Lily waited as Vadom finished removing her greaves and cuisses, taking a little break before bending over and taking off her dainty anklets. With her arms and legs free, Lily was starting to magically hum, as though her wells of power were trying to tune themselves with the magic of the Gildenthrone. All of the courtiers seemed to sense it, and she noticed then that Captain Pine had approached and stood nearby, ready for anything. Lily gave Alder a small nudge, just to make sure he wasn't so preoccupied that he missed the reassuring presence of his *praetam*.

"It is good that he is close, Lily. He helped me through much of my own magical growth and taught me how to balance what was inside me with what was in my vicinity. Captain Pine is a good Fae to have with us just now. The court advisors are all present and will be able to help some as well, though I don't think you've really noticed them yet. I am certainly relieved that one so powerful as your vapa *is here to help you, too. It is finally safe for you to release your inner magic,* faelani, *and I have no doubts about how extraordinary an event it will be for the youngest member of the Gildenthrone family to present her magic to the Throne Room of Golden Court. You will need all of your*

strength to reel it back in when it is finished introducing itself . . . Your belt and dagger next, I think."

Moving to uncinch her belt and unwind it from her hips, Lily quietly repeated Alder's warning to Vadom. Nodding, not appearing overly surprised, her *vapa* began unbuckling her cuirass, plackart, and coulet, catching her eye and waiting until she indicated she was ready before carefully lifting her breastplate and its attachments over her head. Even as Lily watched him set it atop the rest of her iron on the jacket, she felt the surge of her inner magic as it tried to break free at last. She gave a sharp gasp of pain as it struggled to surface, however, for the iron was not all off yet.

Reaching with unsteady fingers for her hair wrap, Lily made a conscious effort to unravel the material, trying to catch the rounded lamés as they fell out of place. What iron discs she missed were caught by the quick hands of her *vapa*. At last, she won free, allowing her wrap to float slowly down to the ground. Lily had just an instant to hear the stunned inhalations of the entire court, and to catch a glimpse of her shimmering golden hair, still clean and giving off a faint white glow, before her inner magic rose up, broke through the undefined boundaries of her mind, and burst forth into the Throne Room.

Out it poured, unformed, undirected, dancing with the magic of the Gildenthrone in wild abandon. All nine of her wells of power cut loose, slowly beginning to swirl around her, making Lily the center of a magical vortex. Though she thought she could occasionally pick out a golden weapon here, a twirling facet there, all else seemed to fade into the background of her awareness when her therianthrope gave an immense bellowing roar and entered the magical fray.

She looked just as Lily had always imagined a dragon would be: all glittering scales, bat-like wings, and a greatly-powerful presence. Her magical ferocity launched herself into the air, seeming to steady her fledgling flight once she got caught up in the vortex of the rest of Lily's inner magic. After her wild one had flown the perimeter of the room a number of times, she began to change shape, from the dragon to an enormous feline that prowled about the room, which soon sprouted feathery wings and took to the air again with a wild screech.

Throughout it all, Lily felt indescribably exhilarated. She had never known freedom like this. Her mind had never before been so free of fear and doubt, of nagging pain and discomfort. Wishing it would go on forever, leaving all her cares and sadness far behind, Lily at first ignored the

Fae who were trying to approach her. They were all different colors, though every one of them had features that had paled with age. Assuming they were the advisors Alder had spoken of, Lily paid them little mind, instead focusing on her shape-shifter, encouraging her to try this form, then that.

When Captain Pine, her *vapa,* and even King Oak tried to rein her in, however, Lily was forced to consider bringing her fun to an end, at least for now. The problem at present, though, seemed to be the fuzziness of her mind. Nothing was as clear as it should have been, nothing seemed to be responding in the normal way of things. It was a little scary, actually. It was this fear that jolted Lily out of her magical euphoria, so different from the Fear of iron, yet disturbing in its own way.

She began trying to twist the inner magic back where it belonged, not really attempting to control it so much as redirect it. This very slowly began to work, and the golden power gradually funneled back into her mind. After several of her wells of power were full once more, the Fae trying to help her were actually able to lend her their support, and most of the rest of her magic came to rest in its proper places. Throughout this rigorous endeavor, Lily was comforted by the presence of her *vapa,* who oversaw everyone helping her with keen and protective eyes. He too was able to help channel her golden magic back into its wells of power, though his touch with sun magic was not so practiced as that of the Fae ranged around her.

It was her father who handled the golden magic most assuredly, replacing it in the largest amounts and with the greatest precision. His actions seemed instinctive, and Lily wondered if she would someday come to wield her magic so confidently. When only her therianthrope remained, however, not even her father could get her to obey him. She continued shifting whenever a new shape took her fancy, unceasingly in motion and more inclined to flit about with the Gildenthrone's magic than to return to her well of power, where she had been so very long confined. Lily's exhaustion began to creep back into her awareness, and she knew she didn't have a great deal of time before she was too weary to lift so much as a finger to crook in summons of her magical ferocity.

It was then that the answer to her current dilemma presented itself in her worn out mind. Sucking in a deep breath, Lily called out to her therianthrope the one thing Lily knew she would heed.

"Wild one, our mate needs us! We must take him to Silver Court without delay, and we must not worry him in the meantime. We must save our fun for later, when he can join us."

Her shape-shifter went absolutely still. Caught in the snare of Lily's words, her ferocity seemed to reach out for Alder, as though to check on him now that he wasn't quite so close by. Her *faelan,* after a split second of surprise, obligingly began broadcasting uneasiness and concern. Before Lily could even thank Alder for his quick response, her wild one gave a strange worried pulse of magic, then bounded straight for her. Lily braced herself for impact, and still got knocked flat on her back as her therianthrope surged into her mind as forcefully as she had left a short time ago.

Lily laid still a moment, focusing inside herself as her wild magic made straight for Alder, then nudged his silvery soul in concern, solicitously asking after him in her own way.

"Did you finally get to have a little fun, lovely one? Are you alright now that you got to stretch your wings a little and bother everyone in the Throne Room?"

Lily wanted to laugh at Alder's crooning tone, and still more when her wild shape-shifter preened at his attention.

You shouldn't encourage her, faelan, she said, though her heart felt the lightness of the moment.

"Oh, Lily, she's going to have to run wild to keep up with my own magical enforcer. She is positively tame by comparison," Alder said ruefully.

Lily found this a completely intriguing bit of information about her truemate, but before she could pursue the matter, she heard her *vapa*'s steady voice, recalling her to the Throne Room.

"*Vipina. Vladi,* is all well within you?"

Lily slowly opened her eyes, wincing slightly at the headache she now had, courtesy of her therianthrope.

"Yes, *Vapa.* Alder is fine. I may have exaggerated just a bit to get my wild one's attention."

"I think, in this instance, that was an acceptable method of handling the situation. But what of you, *Vipina?* Now that the iron is entirely gone, do you still feel pain anywhere? We will need to be especially aware of your physical discomfort for a time now, to make certain that the iron you wore did not cause you any lasting harm."

Lily took a moment to inventory anything unusual with her body or mind. While she thought that she was going to be fine physically, given a week or so of rest, it was her mental and magical recovery Lily was fairly certain would take more patience. The Fear had been battering at her mind for so long that she knew she would have to make some adjustments. Her magic, too, hadn't come away unscathed from harboring the Fear so close by. Certainly her prophetic power, if nothing else, was going to have to be carefully checked soon.

"My body is just very tired, *Vapa,* and feeling weak, at least right now. It is my mind that will probably need more than just rest."

Vadom nodded, accepting this. She could tell he was already considering how to address this concern. Slowly sitting up, Lily grimaced slightly at her headache, even though it seemed to be slowly receding. Relieved, Lily looked around for her haversack, spying it just a few feet away. Though someone, probably her *vapa,* had put her amadel jacket full of iron accouterments in the haversack, her mother's medical pack was still right beside it. Lily stood on slightly shaky legs and made her way over to the pack. Kneeling before it, she opened its sturdy flap and reached inside for the very special jar she had carried such a great distance.

Lily stood, the jar in her hands, and took it to the Golden King. He was standing near the dais with a grouping of Fae, presumably the advisors who had helped her just minutes ago. They all stepped back discreetly as she approached, their eyes quizzically regarding the container she was holding. Turning, King Oak looked at her in question.

"Father," she said, very softly. She could still hardly believe it was really him.

"Yes, Lily?" he asked. He couldn't quite seem to believe it, either.

Holding out her mother's remains, Lily looked him in the eye and searched the very depths of her heart for the right words to say.

"These are her ashes. I have been carrying them with me, but I want you to have them now, if you feel like you need her close, sometimes."

Her father's eyes locked on the glass jar in her hands. Slowly, he reached for the container, reverently taking it and holding it close. Lily just looked at it a moment, feeling countless things. She lifted her hand and set it on the jar, right above her father's arm. After a moment, Lily thought the ashes seemed to glow faintly, going from an ordinary gray to a very special silver. Then, to her complete shock, the ashes began swirling within the glass jar. As they moved unaided within the container, they slowly transformed into hundreds of brilliantly red rose petals. Lily was absolutely speechless for many moments, deeply touched by this small remnant of her mother's fairy magic. At last, she was able to speak the final words she needed to utter on this momentous morning.

"Good-bye, Mother. I love you."

Then Lily removed her hand, turned, and began striding for her haversack. Blindly, she shoved the medical pack back inside the larger bag, then swung it up and over her head, hardly slowing as she made for the door at the far end of the room. Vadom followed her without saying a word. When Captain Pine appeared beside her as well, Lily forced herself to speak past the lump in her throat.

"Captain Pine, I would appreciate it if you and Fig would escort me out."

Nodding, Pine turned back to catch the majordomo's attention.

Lily continued for the door, focusing all of her attention on taking even steps, keeping her head high, her back straight, any detail that distracted her heart from her feelings. Somehow, if she could just get out of this room without totally breaking down again, it would be all right. Finally, Lily was crossing the threshold of the Throne Room. Then she was running.

Startling the Court Guards stationed in the hallway, Lily ran flat out all the way down its length, only slowing to take the stairs at a reasonable pace. She was most of the way down the next hallway before her tired body forced her to a walk.

"You did so well in there, Lily, I don't even have the words to tell you how much. You have done all your mother asked of you and more, and now you can move forward. Perhaps just a little more slowly forward on the stairs, though."

Lily choked out a little laugh, her constricted lungs loosening just a bit.

Can we make it to Silver Court today, Alder?

"That will depend on how much magic Vadom has left for flying. It isn't even mid-morning, so if we started out immediately, we would probably arrive around dinner time. There are quite a few family groves and copses where we could stop and rest along the way, if needed. I would love to reach Silver Court by the end of the day, but I understand if you or Vadom would rather set out tomorrow, after you've both had some time to restore yourselves."

Lily appreciated her truemate's willingness to wait another day, but she didn't want Alder outside of his body any longer than necessary. Though her well of prophecy was quiet just now, Lily was fairly sure it would erupt the next time something important was about to happen. She didn't think it at all advisable to wait for some magical sign that Alder needed to be fused back together when that, to her mind, was already abundantly obvious.

Coming to a halt, Lily turned and found her *vapa* a few steps behind her. He was gliding silently in her wake, keeping a watchful eye on her.

"*Vapa*, how do you think we should proceed from here? I would love above all things to make it to Silver Court today, to meet Alder in person, but I will defer to you. I know you have been running, fighting, and flying a great deal. If you need to rest, I can, too, and I can speak with Fig about Golden Court matters in the meantime."

"Though I will need to revert to *vu chiroptera* in the near future, I am still able to fly today, *Vipina*. Your fairy blood sustains me in ways I had never imagined, and I am not so weary as I would have been before our meeting. I think it would be best to take care of Alder as soon as possible, before anything else can go amiss. With your otherwing secure, you will both be able to turn to your royal duties more effectively."

Despite her grief, still so fresh from her introduction at court, Lily's heart lightened as her *vapa* said exactly what she had wanted and needed him to say. To her surprise, her elucidating magic had translated his vampiric words, and she wondered if he would allow her to see his "form of the bat" when he transformed. With something so interesting to think about, Lily failed to notice right away that Captain Pine and the majordomo Fig had caught up to them and stood just behind her *vapa* in the hallway. Turning to them, Lily informed them of the decision she and her companions had made.

"Captain Pine, Majordomo Fig, thank you for coming to walk me out. Alder and I wish to travel on to Silver Court today, and my *vapa* is ready to fly us there. Captain, it would be a great help if you could fly with us, guide us, and smooth our way as you have done this morning. I know, too, that Alder would love to see you right away when he is in his body once more. Would you come with us, please?"

Looking a bit tired, but incredibly happy, too, Captain Pine nodded resolutely.

"I may need to stop briefly when we are about halfway, but I want Alder whole and embracing his *praetuu* and his new *faelani* by sunset. Let us all do our best to make this happen."

Nodding in agreement, Lily then looked to Fig, knowing she needed to get a few things straight before bursting into Silver Court at the end of the day. After requesting that Pine lead them back out of Golden Court, Lily gave the majordomo her undivided attention once they were walking through the castle's maze of halls and stairs again.

"Fig, I would greatly appreciate it if you would apprise me now of what the Fae Wood has or has not done regarding the trolls in the Crescent. I think it would be best for us to be cognizant of what Golden Court knows and has done before arriving at Silver Court. From there, we'll need to see what they know, and what they plan to do, and coordinate efforts as needed. Alder has been concerned since we felt the destruction of the volcano, and he has expressed his desire to see the entire matter properly handled most emphatically."

Looking to the majordomo, she blinked in surprise at the mixture of relief and admiration in his gaze.

"Your Highness, prior to this morning and your personal report of events, Golden Court knew only that there was a sizable eruption in the Volcano Crescent four days ago. I am in regular contact with Plum, the chamberlain of Silver Court, and he told me that Their Majesties were most distraught that such a disaster should occur when they were trying to cope with the illness of their son. His Majesty, King Oak, then summoned Captain Pine to Golden Court to report what he knew, and to discuss whether or not some of our Court Guard spectra might be needed to counter an imminent troll invasion. Before the Captain arrived, however, His Majesty saw your face in His mirror, and so when Captain Pine did arrive, he was promptly ordered to take as many spectra as he saw fit to Ford-upon-Ward so that you could then be retrieved from Ropaz."

"So the Golden Court Guard warriors we may need at Molten Mirror Lake or on our southern border are all still at the Ford, weary from the battle they have already waged with the trolls who attacked there," Lily said uneasily.

"And we don't want to pull any of the Wardens from that location, either. If the door is still dangerously thin, they need to finish restoring the magical balance just outside to conceal its location, and then they need to stay to protect the weak spot in the golden dome."

"So that leaves the Guards at Silver Court where they started— without reinforcements," Lily concluded, after repeating Alder's words aloud.

Everyone was silent a moment, worrying the problem this way and that in their minds.

"We could still draw a portion of the spectra from the Ford on our way to Silver Court," Captain Pine suggested. "Many of the warriors will rise to the challenge if it is asked of them."

"Nearly every male Fae in the Wood, and some of the ladies as well, are competent with one weapon or another," Fig added. "If there was an adequate amount of time before a conflict on the great lake, many capable fighters could be summoned from the general population and sent there to repel an invading force."

"I would like to know how my parents have directed the Silver Court Guards. We assume they are prepared, but with Their Silver Majesties, nothing is certain," Alder said grimly.

Lily took it all in, but something didn't feel right to her.

"We might be mistaken in thinking there is a battle about to break out at all," she said slowly. "If the xydolem destroyed one of the trolls' volcanic homes, then forced a march on one thousand of their best fighters, who does that leave in the Crescent? Displaced, grieving females, children, and elderly trolls? Without any xydolem present to conscript them into battle, there may not actually be a fight coming from that direction. *Vapa,* were you able to detect any of the xydolem outside the Antechamber last night? Is it possible that they all came to the Ford, and didn't leave any of their number behind in the Crescent to organize a multi-pronged offensive?"

"I did sense the full dozen you saw in the desert, *Vipina,* but as soon as they, in turn, became aware of me, they left the battlefield immediately. It would seem that they do not want anyone to know that they are working together, and they are avoiding being seen."

"So they may be going back to the Volcano Crescent right now? Or to one of our other borders?To regroup?" Lily asked, troubled by the thought that more trolls might get caught between the Fae and the xydolem who seemed to despise them.

"If that is the case, we ought to send a diplomatic envoy to the Crescent without delay, so that a peaceful resolution might be reached before the xydolem can instigate another troll attack," Fig said. "And perhaps it would be prudent to scout the southern and eastern limits of the golden dome in the meantime, so that we know more exactly where the remaining threats lie."

"I will see to it that a few spectra of Golden Court Guards take those patrolling duties. There is no need for any of this conflict, none at all, except for the unknown motives of the xydolem," Captain Pine growled in frustration.

The whole group fell silent once more, this time pondering the vengeful warmongering of the Void-bound killers. Finally, Captain Pine spoke up again.

"With Alder gone, little has been done, and none of it as it should be," he admitted, sighing. "When I set out from Silver Court the other day, I told my warriors to stand at the ready and await mirror instructions from me at Golden Court. I should probably contact my second in command, Sycamore, and apprise him of our intelligence, then order him to withhold engaging the trolls until we can at least anticipate the xydolem's next move."

As everyone murmured their agreement with the Captain's course of action, they found themselves in the large, airy entryway for the second time that morning. Lily had hardly noticed where they were going, she had been so absorbed in the conversation. She watched as Captain Pine moved to the front door, mirror in hand, a little away from the Court Guards stationed by the various passageways about the room. Lily then turned to fully face the small lavender Fae beside her.

"Fig, it has been a pleasure to meet you. Thank you for all of your help this morning," she said sincerely, doing her best to smile her gratitude.

Fig immediately made her an elegant bow.

"Your Highness, the pleasure has been all mine. It is my hope that, when all of us are more at leisure, I can get to know you and your requirements well enough to help you transition smoothly into your new life at Golden Court," he replied graciously.

Lily felt a twinge of uneasiness from Alder, and she worried about the cause of it.

"Thank you, Fig. I know I'll need all the help I can get. In the meantime, we'll try to stay in touch with you, so that Golden Court knows what is happening on the other side of the Wood."

Fig bowed to her again with a grateful smile, then made to return to the Throne Room, a slight spring in his step.

Lily turned to her *vapa,* deciding to wait beside him for Captain Pine.

"Do you think we'll be able to fix the troll problem peacefully, *Vapa?*"

"It is not outside the realm of possibility, *Vipina,* but it will take some fortunate timing and careful negotiating. It will be difficult to make contact with the trolls before the xydolem do, if that is their plan. It will be more difficult still to negotiate with beings who are cowed by an enemy who is much stronger than they are. Let us hope we are quick enough to the former that we do not have to cope with the latter."

Lily nodded, feeling herself fill with fresh determination. Free of her iron, she thought she could do so much more than she had ever considered before. She would see to Alder first, then they would both be able to help handle the Crescent situation.

"Lily, Alder, I've news from Sycamore," Captain Pine said grimly, striding quickly toward them. Bracing for the latest news, Lily prepared herself to hear whatever he had to say without flinching.

"King Linden and Queen Hyacinth have ordered every Silver Court Guard in the palace to fly to Molten Mirror and kill any trolls who try to cross the great lake. Silver Court is currently undefended."

At Alder's surge of frustration, Lily knew that it was time to go. They needed to arrive at Silver Court as soon as possible.

"Ready to fly, *Vapa?*"

Sunset at Silver Court

Moments later, Vadom was winging back to the west, Lily in his arms once again. Captain Pine was right beside him, the well-worn haversack's shoulder strap loosened to allow the bag to hang below and beneath his amethyst wings. Lily had debated leaving it in the care of Fig at Golden Court, but had decided it would be better to have the sack and be prepared than to need something or other of its contents and have to make do without. Though she had been a bit concerned about the iron in the bag affecting Captain Pine, he had assured her that it wouldn't be too cumbersome for him during the flight.

"I trained with iron for many years to qualify for the position of Captain of the Court Guard, Your Highness. I slowly built up a small measure of endurance to the pain, though nothing like what you are able to withstand. While my magic isn't too pleased to be so close to your armor, there is only that ache of encroaching physical suffering. The Fear only intrudes when a Fae is actually wearing iron on their person, or it is directly against their skin. I am not truly doing so in this instance, for I know that I would never be able to withstand the mental torment of it."

Though Lily was disturbed by what he said about iron in relation to himself, she was also glad to hear that the contents of her haversack weren't bothering the captain unduly. Soon, she had put that and other worries aside and settled into the rhythm of their flight. The sun seemed to be following them as they passed over the peacefully swaying forest below. Lily watched the trees for a while, then accidentally dozed off.

When she woke back up, the first thing she noticed was . . . night magic. Her sleep-clouded mind had a little trouble with that, especially when she slowly opened her eyes and saw that the sun was just past its zenith. Realizing that they were no longer flying, Lily looked to the face of her *vapa* in confusion.

"*Vapa?*"

Vadom, who was still holding her in his arms, opened his eyes, and the steady flow of night magic around them slowed, then stopped. It was still there, just visible to her inner magic, only now it was an undirected part of the world around her.

"The Captain and I are taking a small break from flying, *Vipina*. Nothing is wrong, our wings simply need to rest for a short time."

"And you are gathering more night magic, too? Do you think you'll need it?"

Though her questions had his eyebrows raising, he answered her as readily as always.

"Yes, I was. It is second nature for a vampire to call to the night magic when at rest. It is to be hoped that this will prepare a warrior adequately for whatever is coming. Though I do not think I will need the magic for Silver Court, we should all be ready to take whatever action is necessary for dealing with the trolls of the Crescent as soon as may be."

Nodding, Lily carefully rose to her feet, her eyes next finding Captain Pine on the high and rocky promontory where they had stopped. He had taken the haversack off of his back and pulled in his wings. The Captain seemed to be calling outer magic into himself as well, though it was colorful elemental magic he summoned. Lily walked over to her bag and removed her food pouch. She had woken up feeling surprisingly hungry. Lily ate and drank her fill of the remaining supplies, knowing they no longer had to conserve food or water. She offered what she had to Pine, and he gratefully ate some bread and cheese as well. Though he hadn't been very excited about the Ropazian fare, he seemed pleasantly surprised by the sharp flavor of the cheese. Lily smiled a little at that.

They continued to make their way to Silver Court shortly thereafter. Once they had settled into their flight again, Lily tried to rest a bit more, but she found that she was too excited, and rather too nervous, to fall back to sleep. What would it be like, seeing Alder for the first time? How, exactly, were they going to get his soul back in his body? Would it change things between them?

Alder, probably picking up on the tenor of her emotions, spoke softly to her.

"Faelani, *there is no need to be nervous now. Everything will be fine. I can already feel the pull of my body calling me back, and it grows stronger the closer we get to Silver Court. Once I am whole again, I will be able to handle the troll situation, with the help of the Advisors and of Captain Pine."*

And there it was, Lily thought, heart sinking a little. He didn't need her help, or at least he wasn't asking for it. She didn't know how to offer her assistance, but surely, with all of her inner magic, she could do something? Shouldn't a princess be involved in matters such as this?

"Lily?"

Though his voice was perfectly even, giving away little, Lily could feel the uncertainty Alder was trying to hide. She realized that he had meant to reassure her, and he didn't understand why his words had done just the opposite. Summoning her courage, Lily decided to speak up.

Alder . . . remember what you said, just before we entered the Antechamber? That you would tell me when you needed me? That promise meant a lot to me, faelan. *Will it still mean something to you, though, when you're back in your body, and back to being a prince? I know some things will be different, but . . . I don't want this closeness of our souls to change.*

Lily's heart was beating so hard, it almost hurt. What was he going to say? How would she accept it if he pulled away from her? Lily had been able to keep Alder all to herself since they had met, yet he was, apparently, a prince with many obligations. This was going to be difficult, and she hadn't been given any time to prepare herself for it. What she was starting to sense from Alder's soul, however, took the edge off of the vulnerability and uncertainty that she was feeling.

"Lily, my faelani, *I don't want to lose what we have, either. I forget, sometimes, that you don't know much about how my life has been before you. I have needed you for centuries. I have waited all my life for you. I didn't even realize how much I was struggling being alone, until these past days and weeks, when I never had to part from you. Being a prince in the Fae Wood is a great burden, and it will take time, I think, for me to broaden the boundaries of my mind to encompass more than my duties, my never-ending, ever-expanding responsibilities. My parents being who they are, the weight of the Silver Throne has nearly crushed me at times. For so long, I've been trying to do everything that everyone asked of me, but it's just never enough for them, and it gets so unbearably frustrating. I still can't quite believe, even now, that I don't have to*

just survive anymore. That really, I have to start standing up for myself and my truemate now, and put us first, before the Throne of Stars. Lily, it is hard for me to say, to admit, even to myself, but . . . I need you by my side. I do. You, no one else. I am usually so very reserved, but I don't want to hold back or hide myself from you. You mustn't let me. I want more than anything to form more bonds and complete faelanzania *with you, but we cannot do that if I go on as I have been."*

For a moment, Lily felt as though she had just survived a sandstorm, and, having been buffeted on all sides by wind and sand so fine it was nearly dust, there was now profound quiet. Alder needed her. He wasn't just saying the words into the quiet between them, but admitting that he would need her more than ever once he was back in his body and back in his very demanding life. And so she would always be there for him, because today would be the day they both started their lives anew, and they would be doing it together. Lily knew what Alder wanted, deep down where he had hardly been able to make himself look. She shouldn't feel so uncertain, and she would try not to be. Much better to trust in him, and in herself, if she could.

Lily sent Alder all that she felt, and wrapped his soul with the indescribable *good* he was making her feel. Wistfully, she wondered if they would find a way to keep sharing like this, soul to soul, where no one else could intrude. Lily tried to soak up every tiny bit of Alder's emotional reply, that which he shared with so few other people. He had been feeling as exposed as she had, was as unaccustomed to sharing like this as she was, and somehow, that made it easier to do.

It was because they were close, and their guard was down, that Lily felt the tug on Alder's soul almost as strongly as he did. Lily was startled by the sensation, but that was only until she felt Alder's own reaction to the pull. Then she was worried. Why was he so uneasy? Hadn't he said that he had been feeling the call of his body, trying to make him whole again?

What's wrong this time, Alder? Are you alright?

"It felt different just now, Lily. Not so much an 'I'm over this way, come back', but more like 'Hurry, something feels wrong'."

Let me go tell my vapa *and Captain Pine. I am sure they will fly as fast as they can for Silver Court, if they aren't already. Best that they have a little warning if there's going to be trouble.*

"Go ahead, faelani. *That is about all we can do just at the moment. I'm going to try to stay still in here— I'd rather not be dislodged by something entirely out of my control."*

Getting increasingly worried now, Lily quickly surfaced and explained what was happening to their *praetams*. Though she had held some small hope that either Vadom or Pine would have a reassuring explanation for what was going on, their troubled looks only heightened Lily's concern.

"It is not good that the beckoning of his physical self has altered, especially from a benign to an agitated summons, *Vipina*."

"We must get to Silver Court as quickly as possible. If there's trouble with Alder, then Iris is surely in the middle of it, just as his parents probably are. Once he has returned and can speak for himself, it will be fine."

Lily couldn't tell if the Captain was speaking for their benefit or his own, but she didn't feel any better about what was happening.

"Vadom, as a vampire, can you magically increase the power of your wings and fly faster?"

"Yes, it is possible to do this with night magic, but it takes a very large amount. I will not be able to maintain that level of magical output for very long."

"I am much the same. I have wings of enhancement, but my inner magic is low from everything that has been happening recently. Do you think you could fly for one hour, then make the last hour's distance in half the time? That is the most I think I can do."

Vadom nodded.

"Yes, that will be manageable. We shouldn't risk more than that if there is conflict at or near our destination. It wouldn't do to reach Silver Court, or have to fly on to the great lake, with severely depleted magic."

Lily sighed in frustration, knowing she had plenty of inner power to spare, but that no one else could use it. While she thought she could manage some of her elemental and healing abilities fairly well, she didn't yet have a true understanding of how to wield her own magic yet. Recalling how she had barely been able to redirect her unencumbered inner wells that morning, it seemed unwise to offer her help when it would more than likely backfire on them all.

Feeling as though she was nothing but dead weight, Lily sighed again.

"Faelani, *we are less than two hours away from Silver Court now. I don't think anything too terrible could happen to me in that amount of time. Let's just try to relax until our arrival.*"

I just wish there was something I could do to help. I have all of this magic, and it isn't doing anyone any good, Alder.

Alder seemed amused by her words.

"Lily, it may be true that you haven't come into your powers yet, but that will not take you long, I think. And, lest you forget, even if Vadom must carry you now, you are the only one who can carry me, *and isn't that the main point of getting to Silver Court?"*

Lily blinked, then felt a small smile pull at her lips.

Well, there is this little matter with the trolls that might require warriors like Captain Pine and Vadom. Perhaps even a young desert fairy princess might be useful in some way. You never know.

"Ah, now there is my faelani, *teasing me without mercy until I cannot possibly take myself too seriously. Well, since my presence is clearly superfluous, I think I am going to leave your senses for now and stay by your lovely soul for a while. I shall miss being so near."*

Once Alder was settled, Lily tried to simply enjoy the remainder of the trip. She was, after all, very close to her truemate, and in the arms of her *vapa*. She wasn't fleeing anyone for her life, had taken care of the weighty promises she had made to her mother at Golden Court, and was, in fact, a fairy princess. She felt rather worn out by it all, but was this new life really so bad? Certainly not.

Alder's soul was tugged several more times by his body, with increasing amounts of force. Though it made them both more tense than they would have liked, there was nothing else that could be done to hasten their arrival at Silver Court. Lily marveled at how self-possessed Alder gradually became, reaching that state of calm he had always managed to find in the crises they'd faced outside the golden dome. She wondered what that said about the atmosphere of Silver Court, and if that was the normal state of things, or if the Crescent situation was exacerbating a very delicately balanced court.

Finally, Captain Pine and Vadom exchanged a look.

"Please hold on tightly to me, *vladi*."

Lily readily complied, and then they were shooting across the sky at a speed she would have thought completely impossible. It seemed as though they were on a collision course with the sun, which had begun falling to the earth before them at a pace that appeared much slower than theirs. Lily, after her initial surprise, found the magically-boosted flying totally exhilarating. She wondered when someone would teach her how to use her own wings of enhancement, and how fast she'd be able to go. How did one use that magic while simultaneously using another, like warrior magic? Could a Fae have more than one pair of wings out at once?

Lily was so absorbed in her questions that she didn't notice when her *vapa* and the Captain slowed their pace right way. She definitely noticed the pull on Alder's soul, however. It was getting worse each time, as though his body was desperate to have his spirit back. The most violent tug yet had Lily fully surfacing to look for Silver Court, anxious for a glimpse of the place where the rest of Alder resided. She nearly gasped aloud when she saw it spread majestically out directly before her. As it was, her *faelan* caught the swift surprise she experienced, and, though obviously reluctant, he left her innermost soul, traversed the vast grasslands of her mind, and returned to her sensory awareness. Then his soul was filled with a sense of homecoming, strong enough that it took them both unawares.

Silver Court had an air of mystery, an ancient allure, and Lily let herself be captivated by its beautiful subtlety. If Golden Court was as glorious and open as a bright summer morning, then Silver Court was a deep, quiet winter's night with the full moon shining. It was not a castle, but an elegantly sprawling palace. Though taller than most of the trees that comfortably surrounded it, Silver Court was more a part of the Fae Wood than its outstanding golden counterpart.

Lily drank in the smooth, unadorned stones that glowed just a little like Alder did within her mind. She took full advantage of her aerial view, able to see Silver Court's true shape as she probably wouldn't be able to do as well from the ground. Eight modestly sized towers, very evenly spaced, surrounded an enormous silver tower, the central heart of the palace. All were the same distance from the large tower as they were from each other, and all were connected to it and to each other through a network of single-level buildings. Though Lily was certain they were of good size once inside, they looked like little more than covered passageways from up in the sky.

What was even more striking than the palace's overall wheel and spoke shape, however, was the fact that all nine towers were shaped rather convincingly like trees. The trunk of each tower was slightly conical, while the tops gave the appearance of branching out, then tapering off, looking like very rotund teardrops. Lily was captivated by the sight, from the nine triangular gardens that the sentinel towers watched over to the tiny teardrop windows she could see dotting every smooth, silver surface. It was an incredible sight, and she couldn't help but feel a strange sense of wonder.

"*Welcome to my home,* faelani," Alder said softly, seeming pleased by her reaction.

It is as if the Wood borrowed moonbeams from the night, faelan, *and fashioned them into the same solid shapes of the trees all around. It seems so substantial that it could outlast time, yet as able of fading away as the moon at dawn. How does it seem capable of both, Alder?*

"You appreciate the true beauty of Silver Court, Lily, just as the Fae who designed and built the palace could have wished. It is said that the towers of Silver Court will only stand for as long as they are needed, and not a night longer. I know that the palace was built by Fae, ages ago, to aid the slowly waning magic of the Gildenthrone and to prevent the Bubble from collapsing. The families of Silver Court pride themselves on their contribution to the protection of the Wood, and they fiercely love this palace that allows their giving to be so grand."

Though Lily wasn't certain, it seemed almost as if Alder did not quite share that enthusiasm.

You love this place, but not for the same reasons, Alder?

Alder seemed to give a sigh, and his beautiful soul was the embodiment of weariness.

"Just so, my insightful one. Silver Court is my home, and the mystery of it calls to me, as though I must unlock its every secret to be the true master of the palace. It is just that only a select few can actually give of their magic to the Throne of Stars, and those few Fae must sacrifice much to give what is required. My parents thought they had the solution to this problem early in their reign, nearly six hundred years ago, but I have always thought it was like they tried to answer a non-existent question. It was from this that I learned that, sometimes, things simply are the way they are, and are best left as is, so that there is balance. I am all for innovation and progress, but not at the expense of other things of equal importance. Traditions, after all, are almost always upheld for a reason, even if we have lost that reason or that need over time."

Lily absorbed Alder's words, certain there was more to what he was saying than was obvious, but didn't feel like it was the right time to probe into his parents' reign, or his part in the workings of Silver Court. No, she thought, heart suddenly racing as she realized that they were descending, now was the time to brace herself for her introduction to the silver palace. And its silver prince.

Following Captain Pine, her *vapa* slowed to a normal flying pace, heading straight for the immense central tree tower, as if being drawn toward the flame of a burning candle. When they were nearly upon it, Lily could see a little inside the windows in the upper portion of the structure that they were apparently about to enter. There were a great many Fae within, and Lily wondered what had caused such a gathering, or if Silver Court always had so many courtiers in attendance.

"Something is going on, and I don't think it's good," Alder said grimly.

Anxious now, Lily held very still as Captain Pine, then Vadom, landed neatly on the wide, deep windowsill of an entrance that looked directly into a huge, rectangular room. Across the long expanse, all backs were turned to them as the Fae watched the drama unfolding directly in front of what had to be the Throne of Stars.

Sitting on the glittering, faintly magical silver bench was a beautiful Fae lady, sobbing and gesticulating with a lack of poise that was clearly unnerving for those who watched from the floor. Her hair was a pale lavender that seemed to turn silver when the late afternoon light touched it. She appeared to be distressed by the heated argument between a light purple male Fae who was standing just in front of the unoccupied half of the throne and an incredible lavender Fae lady. This second lady, clearly a healer worthy of the lady Wardens, was as composed as the other lady was not. Though on her knees, she fiercely fought the old purple Fae warrior with all the verbal ripostes at her disposal, even as she held tightly to . . .

Lily's every racing thought came to a stop. The whole world seemed to still as she beheld the male Fae the lavender healer held tightly to her chest. He was all she could see. Shoulder-length silver hair, fine features, and a long, strong body, clearly discernible even though he was dressed in loose, comfortable clothing. His lax frame rested on a low-slung cot, as though he had been carried in on a sort of litter from another room. Lily was completely and utterly spellbound.

From the depths of her mind, she felt Alder wiggle a little, his feelings a strange mix. He seemed pleased by her reaction, yet . . . embarrassed as well.

"I am wearing my sleeping attire in the Silverhall. My feet are bare . . . this is a great indignity. I wish you were not seeing me for the first time like this, faelani."

You are my perfect, handsome faelan, *and I want to get closer,* Lily said fervently.

Even as her magic seemed on the verge of erupting with joy, however, they watched as King Linden suddenly snatched one of Alder's hands from their folded position on his chest. Even as Iris attempted to take it back, the Silver King tried to set Alder's hand upon the arm of the throne. Lily felt Alder's complete horror. What was his father doing? Was he going to try to use Alder's inner magic to power the throne? But fairies were never supposed to use each others' magic, not even the inner power of their truemates . . . and Alder was comatose, completely vulnerable . . . Lily felt just an instant of terror before her therianthrope burst from her well of power and out into the Silverhall. Without conscious thought, anger exploding, Lily leaped from her *vapa*'s arms and jumped onto her wild one's back before she flew too far away.

Uncaring of the shocked cries below her, Lily held to the base of her dragon's wing joints as she made straight for the Throne of Stars and the prone form just beside it. All she could think of was protecting him. Lily didn't completely understand the danger, but Alder was not safe, and she couldn't bear it another second. She let her wild one have her way, bellowing a wrathful warning to all within hearing, and especially to the king who was, unbelievably, threatening the well-being of his only son.

When they had flown to the thick, ornate glass riser on which the throne was placed, Lily slid off of her therianthrope's back and into a crouch, ready for anything. Her dragon-shaped wild one executed a tight turn and landed next to Alder, clearly intent on defending him. Lily only distantly noted her ferocity's tolerance of Iris before focusing entirely on Their Silver Majesties.

Queen Hyacinth had begun screaming at the sight of Lily's dragon, jumping off of the Throne of Stars to point and wave at it in a complete panic. King Linden was gaping in astonishment and confusion, his face the picture of incomprehension, even as he moved instinctively to protect the queen. Lily decided it was time to get their attention on her. She had never, in her entire life, been as lividly angry as she was right now, and it was *their* fault.

"What do you think you are doing?"

Lily tried as hard as she could with her tiny amount of remaining composure to keep her voice level. When their eyes swung to her, filled with a total lack of understanding, Lily realized that they couldn't speak a word of Ropazian. And that was just the very last grain of sand that pushed her over the edge to an almost unreasoning fury.

"How dare you threaten the safety of my *faelan*? *How dare you*! He is unconscious, in no condition to be near the throne, yet you would risk his magic and his life to fulfill your own needs? It is despicable! You are a shame to the Silverhall, and a shame to the institution of parenthood! Get away from him, *get away from my truemate*! *Now!*"

Lily was hardly aware of how loudly she was shouting, only of the fact that neither the king nor the queen had moved in the slightest. It made her even angrier. But that was nothing compared to how she felt when King Linden took a step forward, as though to return to Alder's side. Lily couldn't have described the sensations she experienced, not knowing if he was moving toward her utterly vulnerable truemate to do him harm or not. So she did the only thing she could think of in that moment: she formed a shell of ice around her soul completely, quickly, mercilessly. Then she drew her night magic anelaces, stepped directly between the approaching king and her mate, and went into a defensive stance.

Staring him in the eyes, letting him see exactly what she intended, Lily caused King Linden to go utterly still mid-step. His eyes widened, as though he finally realized who she must be, and then he paled, as if he had deduced why she was so very angry. Then he put his hands on his hips in apparent irritation, clearly about to try to blunder through the situation.

"Now, young lady," her inner magic translated for him, "you have no idea how things are handled at Silver Court. Alder knows his duty, and he would accept the measures we need to take despite his insensible state, I am sure. I know my son, and there is no Fae more responsible in the whole of the Wood. If the Throne of Stars is low on magic, he is always willing to provide it, regardless of the circumstances. It would be best if you stepped aside and let us get on with providing Silver Court, and thus the Fae Wood, with the magic it requires to remain secure."

Lily didn't move a muscle and had no intention of doing so. This Fae thought like a king, not a father, and there was no way she was going to allow him to endanger Alder. Searching a moment for the correct Fae word in her sparse and rusty vocabulary, Lily held her battle-ready stance.

"*No.*"

King Linden's face hardened in anger. Before he could reply to her blunt refusal, however, Queen Hyacinth renewed her screaming, reaching a greater volume than before. When the king swung around to see what had so upset her, Lily stared for a long moment at his unprotected back. He, the great threat to her mate, was presenting her with a wide, easy target. He would never be a danger to Alder again if she struck now—

"*Vipina*, put away your weapons."

Vadom approached on foot, keeping pace with Captain Pine, who was tensely absorbing the entire scene. Logically, Lily knew she could always trust her *vapa* to tell her the right thing. She just couldn't think of anything but the serious threat Alder was under, couldn't take any chances when her *faelan*'s situation was so very precarious. She tilted her head toward Their Silver Majesties.

"Danger. Danger to my mate."

Vadom spared them not a glance.

"They are no true threat now. Alder is safe. Your magical being protects his body, and you yourself can protect his soul by returning him to his physical self now. You do not need your warrior's weapons for this fight, *Vipina*. Today, you must feel. Let me do battle for you if it becomes necessary. Stand down now, *vladi*."

And, because she trusted him absolutely, Lily sheathed her anelaces and slowly thawed the ice encasing her soul. She immediately felt horror, that she had been so close to cutting down an enemy when his back was turned, and for that being to be Alder's *father* . . . Overwhelmed by her *vapa*'s intervention, Lily looked at him in silent agony. He held her gaze, his eyes very solemn.

"Remember this lesson, *Vipina*, for it is a very hard one to learn the wrong way."

"Yes, *Vapa*," Lily choked out, still trying to find her emotional equilibrium.

"Faelani, *why don't you put me back in my body now, so that we can clear up all of this confusion and worry together*," Alder suggested softly.

Lily felt fathomless gratitude to him, for not being angry with her, for suggesting just the right thing without judgment or censure. She turned and walked slowly to the cot on which her *faelan* lay unmoving, negligently nudging aside her highly alert therianthrope. Lily felt peace come over her then, a quiet joy that grew as she took the final steps to Alder's side. She knelt, hardly noticing that Iris had released her hold on him and stepped back, her face radiant with happiness. Lily looked closely at her truemate's face for the first time, and she knew what she felt in her heart and in her soul were the beginnings of love.

Oh, Alder, she whispered, hoping he knew what feelings she was wrapping around him. He glowed more brightly than ever before, lingering to soak up her strongest emotions, saying not a word. Lily lifted a hand and brushed her fingertips against his cheek, then a strand of his silvery soft hair. Inside her mind, Alder trembled. Lily felt warmth spread up from her fingers, and something else, something new. It was as if her entire body was tingling a little from those small, gentle gestures. Just looking at his handsome face made her heart beat faster, and his eyes weren't even open yet, his features not yet animated with the presence of his soul.

Lily knew it was time to return him, but it was almost painfully difficult to let him go. Slowly, Alder made his way to the periphery of her mind, pausing just inside the beginnings of her mental wall.

"Lily, I will always be nearby. Our bond will always connect us, and we will grow closer as we journey through faelanzania. *It will be all right."*

Hurry and open your eyes, Alder. I want to see them. I want to see you.

Alder was silent a moment, seeming to dwell in his thankfulness of her response.

"Then perhaps it would be best if you set your forehead to mine. I shouldn't have any trouble moving back in that way."

Lily did as he asked, cupping the back of his head with one hand, setting her other over his heart. Its beat reassured and steadied her as Alder gave one final small pulse of emotion, then appeared to hop over her mental wall and directly into his own mind. Lily probed a bit, anxious that he was transitioning smoothly. She encountered a strong silver dome over a good deal of his mind, even as she watched him hover over a specific spot in his impressive defenses. He appeared to sink into and through the dome a moment later. Relieved, Lily pulled back, then surfaced completely, eager for her first glimpse of Alder's eyes.

Patiently, Lily waited, trying to picture what Alder's mind was like, what familiar paths he was traveling to reach his soul's innermost place. Only a few moments later, Alder stirred, much like a dreamer caught in some other reality. Lily thought he must be attempting to test how much control he had over his body. Gradually, he seemed to settle in, and his recumbent form was slowly invested with the slight but telling tension of conscious awareness. Then, very slowly, Alder opened his eyes and looked right at her.

Lily's magic seemed to explode inside her mind, and her entire body felt as though it were sparkling with energy. Joyous music was resounding inside her, a song so sweet and boundlessly happy that she felt tears start in her eyes. All she could do was gaze into his face and take him in. Lily had no words for this moment, none at all.

Not knowing what to say, and suddenly feeling rather shy, Lily became acutely aware of the fact that she still had her hands behind his head and on his chest. Alder was reassuringly warm under her palms. His silky hair feathered her fingertips, and his heart was beating quickly, nearly as rapidly as her own. Those details seemed to fade back out of her awareness, however, as she studied his eyes more carefully. They were silver and gray, like rolling thunderclouds just before a storm, and hinting at the same volatility in their depths. What was most astonishing to Lily, though, were the tiny flecks of gold just around his pupils. Not simply tempestuous eyes, no, but eyes that let sunlight peek through in the midst of the storm. Alder's eyes were like his soul, extraordinary and unique, and Lily thought they suited him perfectly.

"Faelani."

Lily's eyes widened at the sound of his voice, and the joyful melody in her mind quieted so that she could take in every word. The tone was a little deeper than she had imagined it would be, and his voice was a bit gruff, though she thought that might only be from recent disuse.

"Faelan," she said happily, still basking in the soft glow of his eyes. Alder was so *very* handsome, it quite distracted her from the words she should probably be saying. He smiled widely anyway, however, clearly satisfied with the one important word she had been able to utter.

"Lily, thank you. For my safe return, and . . . all the rest, too," he finished softly, his eyes drinking in her every feature. Always, however, his eyes returned to her own, as if they couldn't ever stray far. Lily wondered if he could sense a bit of her own soul through her eyes as well. They lingered in a moment of mutual silence, neither finding further words necessary just then. Lily only hoped he could see how much she cared for him, how she was trying to convey her feelings with her gaze.

Then, very slowly, Alder raised one of his hands and gently, gently let his fingertips trace the side of her face, down to her jaw, where her pulse pounded madly. Lily knew it was little more than what she had done to him a moment ago, yet she felt shivers racing down her neck and through her whole body with the touch. It wasn't at all the same as their souls being close, but . . . this was *quite* nice too, Lily decided.

Before Lily could have another coherent thought, however, she heard a rather incredible bellowing roar, directly from . . . Alder? In a burst of silver magic, an immense gray dragon erupted from her *faelan,* immediately taking to the air and circling, spinning, diving, and ceaselessly, irritably moving. Clearly, her *faelan*'s therianthrope had been detained for far too long. He was almost mindless in his search for a way out of the Silverhall, trying to escape the great teardrop dome by windows that were all too small to accommodate his large, serpentine form. Lily was amazed at his intrinsic wildness, so much greater even than her own fierce one's independent nature. Turning to look at her therianthrope, Lily spoke softly to her with her mind.

Can you help him calm down a little, wild one? I think he needs us, especially you.

Lily watched as her magical ferocity looked up at the restless, agitated being up above them. With a decidedly considering air, Lily watched as her wild one shifted from a dragon to the feline form with the feathery wings. Oddly, though, her therianthrope was much smaller in that form than she had been at Golden Court just that morning. She looked like . . . a cub with little down-covered protrusions sprouting out of her upper back. Lily wished she had chosen a more impressive shape, but decided not to intervene as her therianthrope made her way deliberately off of the glass riser and amongst the courtiers, all of whom stepped back to give her plenty of space. After a few paces, Lily's wild one laid down on the stone floor, tilted back her head, and gave a small, rather plaintive growl.

Alder's therianthrope went totally still up near the ceiling, then spun about, hastily scanning the entire hall below. His eyes soon locked on the tiny golden being in the middle of the floor, and he sinuously swooped down to close the distance between them with breath-taking speed and agility. Alder's therianthrope halted, however, just a few feet from Lily's youthful wild one, appearing to hesitate. Beside her, Lily felt Alder try to sit up. As unobtrusively as possible, Lily slid one arm down to his shoulder and the other around to the middle of his back, quietly trying to help him without being obvious about it. When Alder was in an upright sitting position, and had swung his legs over the side of the cot, Lily sat down on the open space beside him.

Slowly, not taking his eyes from his fierce one, Alder wrapped his arms loosely around Lily's waist. Lily, a bit surprised but definitely pleased by this turn of events, shyly snuggled a little closer. She then watched as Alder's therianthrope turned to look at them for a moment, apparently stymied and in need of a little guidance. He stared first at Alder, then at Lily, then slowly turned back to the tiny therianthrope still lying on the floor. They all watched as she rolled onto her back and swatted playfully at him with one paw, giving another, happier growl. Alder's wild one froze for a long moment, then slowly crept forward, changing into a winged feline as he did.

Ever so carefully, Alder's shape shifter stretched out his forelimbs and loosely encompassed Lily's little therianthrope. He watched, apparently enthralled, as she rolled over, stood up, and began running in little circles, making something of an effort to catch her tail. Quickly tiring of that activity, Lily's wild one stretched up on her hind legs and tried batting at his whiskers. He reared back slightly in surprise, then actually leaned in closer so that she had better access. No sooner had he done this, however, but Lily's fierce one stopped playing and rubbed her face against his, nuzzling affectionately.

Alder's wild one froze yet again, then, very gently, nuzzled back. Lily and Alder both started in surprise, then went completely still themselves at this exchange. They looked at each other in confusion and amazement, both wondering if the other could explain the strange phenomenon they were experiencing. While Lily couldn't feel the nuzzling itself, she could sense how comforted her therianthrope felt as a result of being near Alder's wild one. By the look in Alder's eyes, he was feeling the emotions of his own therianthrope as well. What was going on? Was this normal?

No one moved for many long moments, except for the wild ones as they became acquainted with one another. Then, very slowly, Alder tried to stand up. Lily, as casually as possible, stood as well, surreptitiously giving Alder her arm in such a way that, for all appearances, she didn't want to let him go for even an instant. It wasn't exactly a falsehood, she realized as Alder found his balance. He took a cautious couple of steps to the edge of the raised glass platform, then held more firmly to Lily's arm, threading it with his own, as they carefully made their way down the steps. From there, it was little effort to walk until they stood directly in front of their happy wild ones.

"Fierce one," Alder said, his voice calm and full of an undeniable authority.

Reluctantly, his therianthrope tore his gaze from Lily's little wild one, seemingly irritated by the interruption. Alder gestured to Lily herself with his free arm.

"This is our *faelani,* Lily. We must protect and cherish her always."

Alder's magical fierce one studied her for a moment, then gave a huff of acceptance. Lily found herself impulsively stepping forward, reaching out a hand to this magnificent part of her *faelan*. Though she heard many of the courtiers let out gasps of concern, she ignored them, offering her hand to the silver therianthrope with total trust. If he was a part of Alder, then he would never harm her, of that Lily was completely certain.

Hesitantly, as though he was entirely unaccustomed to being approached with friendly overtures, Alder's ferocity carefully lowered his head so that they were at eye level. Lily held his gaze and smiled at him, letting him see her deep feelings for her truemate, every part of him, in her face. It seemed that he recognized her emotions for what they were, for, in the next instant, he reached out a paw with startling speed and swept Lily carefully into the circle of his forelimbs.

Lily only just suppressed a very un-princess-like squeak of surprise as she found herself snuggled up against the warm silver fur of Alder's fierce one. She kept her body relaxed, though, and began petting him behind an ear after recovering from her initial surprise. Turning to look at Alder, she saw in his face a mixture of faint exasperation and something . . . altogether more profound. Before she could find the right words to say to him in his moment of solemnity, however, his fierce one angled his head to the side, leaned in, and *licked* her bare arm.

"Ugh! *Alder*!"

Jumping out of his fierce one's grasp, Lily bounded back to Alder's side, quivering with damp indignation. Alder looked at her helplessly for a moment, then, upon getting a good look at the expression on her face, started to laugh. Soon, he was almost doubled over with mirth. Lily found her minor pique dissolving at the incredible sound of Alder's laughter. It was barely short of mesmerizing, and she couldn't help but join in after a moment's resistance.

Eventually, their laughter subsided, and Lily became aware of the Fae, and the vampire, watching them avidly a short distance away. Turning, she smiled hugely at her *vapa*, wanting him to share in her happiness. Though his face gave nothing away, Lily saw how his eyes softened in acknowledgement, letting her know that he felt some measure of her joy. She then turned to Captain Pine and the lady Iris just beside him, who were much more obviously thrilled by the morning's events. Feeling a bit nervous, Lily took Alder's hand in hers and gave him a little tug. He glanced down at their joined hands, then up to her face in question. Lily tilted her head slightly toward his special parents, hoping he would understand her wish for a proper introduction. Alder, on catching sight of Pine and Iris, brightened even more and immediately led her to them.

"Captain Pine, you have already met my *faelani*, and even escorted her into the Wood personally. Many thanks to you, *praetam*, for your help with her safe arrival. Lily, this is the Fae warrior who didn't allow any storm to uproot the sapling I was for many years. Please let me properly introduce you to Pine, Captain of the Court Guard, with many purple level talents."

Lily smiled and made him the *valoriad,* as she still didn't know the fairy princess equivalent of that gesture. The captain smiled warmly and made her an elegant bow. Then he quite naturally brought the lovely lavender Iris forward for her introduction.

"*Praetuu,* please allow me to make known to you my *faelani,* Lily Silverhall Gildenthrone," Alder said, in a very quiet but extremely pleased silvery voice. "It was because of her cries in the great white desert that I had to leave so precipitately, *praetuu,* and I am sorry to have caused you worry in my unexplained absence. Thank you for taking such good care of my body while my soul journeyed far away. Lily, this is the mother of my heart, Iris, a Healer and former lady Warden."

Though her eyes had widened considerably at Lily's full name, she smiled in forgiveness at Alder's apology. Dipping into one of the most graceful movements Lily had ever seen, she rose just as elegantly and smiled beamingly at both of them.

"It is wonderful to meet you at last, my dear. Welcome to the Fae Wood."

Pausing to look at Alder, she asked a very quiet question.

"You are her prince then, *praetoh*? She is not your princess?"

Before Alder could respond, however, their conversation suffered an unwanted intrusion.

"Is anyone going to bother to introduce *us* to the fairy who threatened us in our own throne room?" Queen Hyacinth's voiced piped up shrilly.

Taking a deep breath, Alder turned toward the glass riser where both of his parents still stood.

"Mother, Father, this is my truemate, Lily, who lived until recently in the Joquobon Desert. Lily, these are my parents, King Linden and Queen Hyacinth of Silver Court."

Lily simply nodded in acknowledgement of them, not offering the *valoriad.* Their Silver Majesties, however, went from fumingly angry and offended to disconcertingly happy in an instant.

"Welcome to the Wood, and welcome especially to Silver Court, Princess! We are indeed very pleased to have you here after so very long a wait," Linden said effusively.

The Silver King descended from the riser and headed for their little group. All of his earlier desperation had vanished, to be replaced by an ebullience that had him softly glowing with lavender magic. He was closely followed by Queen Hyacinth, who was somehow even more unaccountably enthusiastic than her truemate. Lily was inwardly amazed that they could both act as though their threat to Alder had never taken place. It was not something she was ever going to forget, of that Lily was utterly certain. These fairies were not to be trusted.

"Alder, dear, now that you've taken a nice long break, naughty sapling, you must handle this horrible troll emergency. After that huge eruption, we sent the Silver Guards to the Lake to kill the invaders. The trolls must be levels beyond livid, so we sent all the warriors we had on duty. Do make sure they have specific orders before any fighting. Have Captain Pine help you now that he has returned, and the Advisors, of course. Your father and I are just going to get some rest. It has been exhausting without you, and we need a chance to recover."

Without another patronizing word, Their Silver Majesties began sweeping toward a side exit of the Silverhall. Lily felt her anger at them bubble up again. Was this how Alder was treated by his own parents? Were they really such uncaring rulers, to leave their Court to relax when a quarrelsome neighbor was openly hostile? She was not going to tolerate this kind of treatment of Alder, even if everyone else in the hall said not a word. She was *not*. When Lily moved to pursue the Silver Court monarchs, however, Alder gently kept his hold on her arm. Lily looked up at him in frustration, her anger clearly sparking in her eyes. Her *faelan* just smiled softly at her, though, and gently traced the fine bones of her hand with his fingers.

"I appreciate your response to my parents more than you could possibly know, *faelani*, but now is not the time to confront them, either about their behavior or about certain truths they have not yet realized and will soon need to face. Let us turn our efforts toward the proper handling of the Crescent situation first, Lily, please."

Though Lily wanted to give Their Silver Majesties a piece of her mind, she knew Alder was right to handle their most pressing concern before dealing with anything else. Reluctantly, she nodded.

"We can just talk to them sometime soon, then."

Very soon. This disrespect of her truemate was not going to continue much longer. Lily's therianthrope growled fiercely in agreement, startling everyone in her vicinity. Alder smiled again, more widely this time, then turned them both back toward the riser and the Throne of Stars. He paused, looking carefully at the large silver chair, apparently assessing it with a practiced eye. Alder seemed to lose some of his tension after his brief inspection, though his eyes showed concern at whatever he had concluded. Slowly, they ascended, making for a more modest seat to the immediate right of the throne. Once there, Alder sat, pulling Lily down beside him to his right. After a moment, Alder motioned to a Fae who seemed to materialize out of the air to the left of the throne. This male Fae had coloring so pale a blue, he put Lily in mind of the moon on cold desert nights, when only a barest hint of the sky's daily color showed on the nightly white sphere.

"Plum, have you been in contact with Fig today? Has he had the opportunity to relate recent events to you, such as my *faelani* reported during her introduction to Golden Court this morning?"

The pale blue Fae inclined his head.

"Majordomo Fig mirrored me just before midday, Your Highness. He gave me a thorough recounting of Her Highness's words and actions, which I related to Their Majesties and the Advisors posthaste. It was decided that any further action by Silver Court must needs await your return, and that of Captain Pine."

Lily tried to listen to what the chamberlain was saying, and to what he wasn't. If Alder's parents had heard it all from Fig, then why had they been threatening his body before his imminent return? Why had they not realized right away who she must be? Who exactly had decided to delay any action in anticipation of their arrival, instead of preparing the Silver Guards for what they were truly about to face on Molten Mirror Lake? None of it was making any sense to Lily. She looked to Alder in confusion, but he was looking unsurprised. Catching her look, he smiled resignedly.

"When my mother hears upsetting things, she tends to react volubly, and in the ensuing dramatics, she frequently forgets most of what she hears. This inevitably seems to cause my father to fixate on only one or two details, to the exclusion of all other information, as well. At that point, the Advisors or myself generally make decisions on behalf of the Silver Court, as our judgment has been deemed by the families of our part of the Wood as more sound on such occasions."

Lily could hardly believe her ears. Why in the world would such a couple be allowed to sit the throne when they handled difficult situations so badly? This was hardly a safe or stable state of affairs. At her incredulous look, Alder released a small sigh, as if in agreement with her sentiments.

"When we have some time, I will explain how our current predicament has come to pass, *faelani*. First though, I think we ought to try to solve the troll problem."

Lily nodded firmly. She mustn't get distracted now, or let Alder become unfocused, either. Lily turned back to Chamberlain Plum, deciding to let Alder do the talking for now. He certainly knew how to get the right things done at Silver Court, and she was determined to help as soon as she saw an opportunity. As if sensing her inner resolve, Alder straightened a little on their small throne and began questioning the chamberlain.

"Plum, has any reconnaissance been done over or around the lake, or of the Crescent itself?"

"No, Prince Alder."

"So can we assume no diplomatic alternatives to this predicament have been considered or implemented?"

"You assume correctly, Your Highness."

Lily felt the tension build up in Alder's strong frame. Silently, she put her hand on top of his, where it rested in the center of their seat. He went still a moment, flicking a glance at her out of the corner of his eye. Lily gave him her calmest smile, her most confident look. She knew they could fix this, could make right what the xydolem had wronged. Slowly, Lily felt Alder's tension decrease. Gently, he threaded his fingers through hers, and Lily experienced that tingly feeling again.

"Then I want two spectra scouting immediately, one of the dome's perimeter on the lake and its surrounds, the other flying high over the Volcano Crescent. Captain Pine, please make this possible and oversee their efforts. I want them reporting to you as they complete their surveillance, and I want you mirroring anything relevant to me. No harm is to come to any trolls unless they engage first. Any xydolem that are seen, however, may be destroyed on sight.

"As they complete their first rounds, Plum, I want a diplomatic spectrum carefully assembled. Cool, level-headed green and brown level Fae, with purple level Fae rounding out the group. Most or all of them need to be fluent in the trolls' language. See that a trustworthy spectrum is ready to speak with any peaceful envoys that may come from the Crescent as soon as possible."

Alder paused as Captain Pine and the chamberlain both bowed and moved to do his bidding. Then he turned to a small glass riser to the left of the Throne of Stars, upon which sat nine pale-featured pairs of Fae. Lily could tell they were old, not so much by the pastel shades of their hair, but by the things their eyes seemed to say without them deigning to speak anything aloud at all. As if they approved of Alder, but not as the

Silver Prince. As though they'd only approve of her three hundred years from now, if not later. Like there were Fae somewhere in the Wood who could be handling this entire fiasco better. Lily did not like those eyes, or the Advisors who couldn't seem to help themselves as they sat there in judgment and disapproved of everything they heard and saw.

"The Throne of Stars is low on magic, but not dangerously so," Alder said, addressing them for the first time. "Who should I offer my gratitude for providing power to the throne in my absence?"

Alder asked the question quietly, gaze fixed on the old ones. At length, one purple Fae stood and spoke into the sudden silence of the Silverhall.

"Those of the families who can provide have provided. As they will continue to do after you have left for good, Alder of the Waterfields and Silvergroves."

Lily felt, more than saw, her *faelan* flinch at the Advisor's words, even as urgent whispering swept through the Silverhall. It made her angry. It filled her with the desire to fly back to Golden Court and leave all of these thoughtless, hurtful Fae behind them. For the first time in her life, Lily was entirely free of iron, and it made her feel bold. It made her feel confident rather than doubtful. It made her feel as if she could stand up and do something to protect someone she cared for, instead of hesitating or remaining silent. Her truemate deserved so much more respect than this. Lily asked herself what her mother would do, if she thought King Oak was being chastised. That was what was happening now: Alder was being openly criticized, even though he had been self-sacrificing on behalf of Silver Court for centuries before even being called to his true destiny, with her, at Golden Court. Lily smiled, and she knew it was a dangerous smile. Because her mother would not have tolerated such disrespect of her truemate. Not at all.

Standing, Lily prowled along the glass riser, making directly for the shorter riser full of Advisors. Her wild one sidled up beside her, no longer small or playful. No, her therianthrope was all the ferocity Lily felt in that moment. She was the immense golden dragon once more. Upon reaching the edge of the riser, Lily climbed up onto her wild one's back, nimbly walking amidst the sharply spiked scales along her fierce one's strong, proud neck, until she was crouched on her therianthrope's great head. Lily was just an arm's length from the lavender Advisor now. She stared into his eyes, taking his measure. Arrogant. Angry. Frustrated. Worried. Perhaps he knew exactly how important Alder was after all.

"Fae," she uttered softly, never breaking their locked gazes.

"Your Highness," he returned, his voice giving nothing of his thoughts away. Too bad for him that his eyes told her everything she needed to know.

"My truemate's parents do not treat him as they should. Do you think that gives you leave to do the same?"

"No, Your Highness," he said tightly.

"And do you think, Advisor, that difficult circumstances permit you to denigrate the Fae who steps up and leads you, cares for you, empowers you?"

The purple Fae swallowed, holding back his anger and . . . perhaps his shame, too.

"No, Your Highness."

"Do you really believe, Old One, that a warrior like mine will leave Silver Court without the support it needs as he moves on to fulfill *faelanzania* and his destiny?"

The Advisor was silent a moment. He broke eye contact, turning to look up to where Alder sat, just beyond the Throne of Stars. Slowly, his gaze returned to Lily.

"No, Your Highness," he answered, his voice somehow calmer than before.

Lily gave him a nod. Then, she turned her stare on the other Advisors. One by one, she met their eyes, making sure every one of them understood what she wished them to know. Some gave way quickly, others were stubborn or proud. In the end, however, all wordlessly acknowledged her demand.

Slowly, her wild one pulled back her head, lifting Lily high in the air before turning and lowering her to the space on the riser just before the Prince's chair. Lily slid off of her fierce one's head and stood just before her truemate. Alder was looking at her with a confused expression, grateful but uncertain, vulnerable and strong all at once. Walking up to him, Lily leaned slightly over him, placing her hands at either side of his head against the elaborate silver chair. Alder's eyes never left hers.

"You are my Golden Prince now, *faelan,*" Lily said softly. "I will allow no one to malign you, to give you less than the respect you deserve. If Silver Court has grown too accustomed to treating you badly, then I will insist on moving to Golden Court as soon as possible. There I can make sure you are able to keep growing, to branch out, to become stronger and more yourself. Can you accept this?"

Alder held her gaze a moment longer. Lily felt herself falling into his stormy eyes. She had just enough time to wonder, rather fancifully, if she would be struck by lightning or shaken by thunder while caught in their depths.

"Yes, I can, *faelani*. If, that is, I can protect you as I see fit in return."

Lily cocked her head slightly to one side, considering. This seemed like one of the many ways in which they would need each other, would have to be each other's equal. She nodded in acceptance, then sat back down beside her truemate, feeling as though she had done something truly worthy of her *faelan*.

38

In the Shadow of the Throne of Stars

Several hours later, Lily was struggling with a number of inner problems. One was hunger, dinner having long since passed unnoticed, and night having fallen completely. Another was fatigue. She would have given much for even her lumpy haversack to rest her head upon. And then there was her well of prophecy, doing . . . something. Try as she might to bring some word or picture into clarity, Lily couldn't decide what this premonitory feeling was about. The need to exercise caution, and . . . something specific. She sighed, trying to concentrate on the strategizing that had occupied the entire Court for the majority of the evening.

From what her tired mind could discern, about half the Court wanted to beat back the trolls in the time-honored tradition, while the other half were withholding judgment until Captain Pine mirrored Alder with the results of the Silver Guards' reconnaissance. Though no one came out and said it, everyone seemed disbelieving of a threat from the xydolem. No Fae had seen any of the creatures in Ropaz, after all, and no fairy could be certain that the battalion of trolls who had attacked the Ford had been Void-bound, either. Lily could understand the skepticism, but her absolute faith in Vadom precluded any comforting thoughts of the xydolem being far away. They were probably somewhere in the Crescent right now, dealing out more fear and suffering while she just sat here . . .

Forcing herself to maintain her erect posture on the Highness throne, Lily found herself wishing it wasn't quite so uncomfortable, in more ways than one. While she couldn't do anything about the un-cushioned bench seat or the responsibility it signified, she could take care of her own needs.

Looking over at Vadom, who had stationed himself near the Highness throne beside the glass riser, Lily hopped up from her seat and made her way to him down the glass steps.

"Yes, *Vipina?*" he asked softly when she stood before him.

Lily gestured to her haversack, slumped on the ground by his feet. She had seen Captain Pine hand it over to him hours ago, before he had departed for the great lake.

"I'm just after my food pouch, *Vapa*. I'm hungry, and it doesn't seem like there will be a break for food or sleep anytime soon."

Vadom nodded in agreement.

"I assume that older Fae do not need to eat as often or sleep as much as a fairy your age, *Vipina*. You will have to take both as you need them, so that you are ready to do what is necessary as events unfold."

Pulling out the food pouch from her haversack, Lily nodded at his words. She had begun to assume as much by the behavior of the Advisors and courtiers. Even Alder, weak though his body had to be from its recent ordeal, seemed to be holding up better than her own physical self.

"Thank you, *Vapa*."

Lily bounded back up the stairs and reclaimed her seat with Alder. Only as she was pulling out bread, cheese, and water did she notice that the quiet hum of conversation had died down rather noticeably. Lily tore off a portion of bread and popped the piece into her mouth, then glanced at Alder. He was watching her with a look she couldn't quite interpret. Fondness? Amusement? Not sure what to do, Lily offered him some of her water.

"You should probably eat something too, Alder. Maybe we could ask Iris what's best for you now that her healing magic isn't caring for your body?"

Alder was silent a moment, apparently surprised by her words. Then he took a drink of water before handing it back to her.

"I'd like to try the cheese," he said quietly, giving Lily a small, private smile, as if they were sharing a joke between them as well as the edible sustenance.

Lily grinned and handed it over as she ate more bread. Food just tasted so good when she was this hungry, and sharing what she had with Alder made it even better. When they had polished off most of their victuals, Alder summoned Plum out of nowhere again.

"Lily, if you are ever in need of anything while in the Silverhall, tell Plum and he will provide it for you. As chamberlain of Silver Court, it is one of his duties, and it is a matter of pride for him to do so. Is there anything else you require now? Are you still hungry?"

Lily looked over at Plum. There was a slight flush of red high on his sharp cheekbones, and he did seem to be a bit upset. She gave him her best attempt at a conciliatory smile.

"Some fruit would be lovely. And a pillow and blanket, please," Lily said, before a couple of other things occurred to her. "Also, Plum, could you speak with Vadom and see that he has a comfortable place to rest in the palace? I would appreciate that very much."

When Plum puffed out his chest just a fraction at her request, Lily thought she was back in his good graces enough to ask for one more small thing. She leaned over the side of the throne and whispered in Plum's ear, for he had obligingly bent at the waist to hear her better.

"And Plum, could you bring Alder some slippers? I don't think he likes being so informal when he's sitting the throne."

Plum bowed, a happy glint in his eye, and smoothly departed. Lily's feeling of gratitude that Plum spoke and understood Ropazian was distracted by Alder taking her hand in his own.

"You must be terribly tired, Lily. I'm sorry for not taking care of you better, especially after the journey you've just finished. Perhaps you'd like to get some sleep in a quieter place? I'm sure that Plum has had your rooms prepared by now."

Lily was shaking her head before Alder's words were all out of his mouth. She had never slept alone before in her life. There was no way she was starting now, in a seemingly unfriendly place with the threat of the xydolem and trolls casting a pall over everything.

"I need to be close to you, *faelan*," Lily said softly, squeezing Alder's hand and begging him with her eyes to understand, to let her stay.

Alder's face softened in comprehension.

"That's all right, *faelani*."

They waited quietly until Plum returned. When he did, the chamberlain brought good tidings: Fig had mirrored him to inform Silver Court that two spectra of Golden Court Guards had just completed their reconnaissance of the Wood's southern border. No signs of any trolls or xydolem had been found anywhere near the Bubble. Furthermore, a third spectra, comprised of water and air warriors, had flown up and down the coastal perimeter of the Fae Wood, and there was no indication that an attack would be coming from that direction, either. It seemed, then, that Molten Mirror Lake was the only place remaining for another confrontation of forces.

Plum also had three simply dressed Fae following him soundlessly, an artful image of the palace of Silver Court embroidered in gray thread on their garments. One carried an enormous glass bowl full of fruit, many of which Lily had never seen or tasted before. The second palace fairy held a sumptuous folded blanket and overstuffed pillow in his arms. Lily politely accepted both offerings, even as she watched the third quiet Fae kneel beside Alder and place a pair of soft-looking slippers by his feet.

Lily nibbled a piece of fruit that she actually recognized while she watched Alder out of the corner of her eye. He stared at the slippers for many long moments. Finally, her *faelan* slid each foot into a slipper, obscuring his long and elegant feet from view. When Alder looked up at her at last, Lily smiled their secret-sharing smile for him and offered a piece of fruit. He accepted it, giving her such a happy thank-you smile in return that Lily knew just how touched Alder was by her gesture.

After eating a couple pieces of fruit and making sure that Alder ate some, too, Lily glanced to her right, expecting to see the cot still nearby on the riser. The cot, however, was gone. Lily wondered what she was going to sleep on, now that the stealthy palace fairies had whisked away the temporary bed where she had planned to nap. Before Lily could decide what to do next, Plum appeared at her side. He was holding a rectangular hand mirror.

"Your Highness, there is a Warden named Poplar who has mirrored to speak with you," Plum said, giving a slightly disdainful sniff before adding, "he would not share the nature of his communication with me."

Suppressing a smile, Lily solemnly accepted Plum's mirror.

"Thank you, Plum. He is checking in with me as I asked him to do last night after the battle."

Glancing at Alder and seeing that she had his attention, Lily held up the mirror so that he could see Poplar's bright purple features as well. The Fae warrior smiled when he could see both of their faces.

"Your Highnesses, may sun and rain both ever sustain you," Poplar said in greeting.

"And you as well, Poplar of the Seaside Stand, Warden of the Ford," Alder replied. "Please let me take this opportunity to thank you, Fae, for your protection of my truemate in the Antechamber last night. My gratitude is root deep and sky high."

"It was an honor to wield my sword in protection of the Princess," Poplar said solemnly.

After a short pause, he broke out into another broad smile.

"And also to follow her orders. Princess, Yew and I have done as you asked and retrieved all one thousand obsidian ornaments from the trolls prior to their cremation. They have been placed in a number of large earthenware bowls used by the Wardens for many everyday tasks in Ford-upon-Ward. The lady Wardens helped Yew and I to purify each piece and offer songs of peace and light for the deceased warriors. Do you have further instructions regarding the obsidian, Highness?"

Lily's well of prophecy chose that moment to erupt. She felt her head snap back and crack against the throne, but she was only vaguely aware of her body at that point. Lily's mind had become a mess of golden cords, branching out in all directions, forging random paths to all the places, both familiar and foreign, in her mind. One cord in particular seemed to pulse with magic, and Lily mentally grasped it, needing something to hold on to in the rush of power. She clearly saw a large body of water, misty in an early morning light. The fog all but obscured the volcanoes towering distantly on the far shore. What was of much greater interest, however, were the trolls paddling to the rocky shore in the foreground.

They ground all seven boats against the bank between widespread trees with thin, weeping branches. The trolls stood with their heads held high, seven of whom had crowns set with large, symbol-carved pieces of obsidian. They came forward and addressed Alder, Lily, and the eighteen Fae who flanked them. Though Lily could not hear their words, she thought their eyes were full of both sorrow and anger. The Alder in her vision motioned the trolls to sit on chairs around a large table, upon which sat a number of ordinary bowls filled with shiny black stones. The trolls sat down heavily, and they grieved for a time. Then they began to speak.

Lily felt pain, then, and knew she needed to pull away from the prophecy. She was more than a little unnerved, however, when she could not find the way out. Looking all around, she could not see where she had come from, or how to get to the part of her mind that she understood. Then she heard a voice. A beautiful, silvery voice that she knew she would recognize and follow no matter where life took her.

"*Faelani*! Lily, wake up!"

Then she heard another, equally familiar, wonderfully soothing voice.

"It will be alright, Alder. She is dealing with her prophetic magic. She will open her eyes when the portent has finished manifesting to her."

Lily did open her eyes then, not wanting either her truemate or Vadom to worry another moment.

"I'm fine," she rasped, then winced at the unpleasant pain in the back of her head.

That pain was mitigated, however, when she realized that she was sitting on Alder's lap. With his arms around her. Lily felt the tingliness start up again under her skin, and she let herself snuggle into the safety of Alder's warm, solid chest. She could definitely get used this. Lily looked over at her *vapa* and grinned at him. He seemed to relax at her expression, and the corners of his mouth tilted up ever so slightly.

"*Faelani,* are you sure you're all right?" Alder asked, pulling her attention from her *vapa* to the concerned face of her *faelan.* "Should Iris look at the back of your head?"

Lily told them again that she was fine, then conveyed what she had seen, trying to relate every detail she could recall. Vadom's face grew even more impassive than usual, but Alder's face more obviously gave away some kind of internal struggle. Lily wasn't certain why they were less than happy with the vision. It showed trolls calmly speaking with the Fae, didn't it?

"What's wrong? This is what we've been hoping the trolls would do, isn't it? We just need to ask Poplar to have the obsidian brought to Molten Mirror Lake before dawn. I think we should assume it means this coming morning, rather than a later date, just to be safe. Is Poplar still in the mirror, Alder?"

Lily was looking for Plum's rectangular hand mirror, but she didn't miss the look that passed between Alder and Vadom regardless.

"What is it?" she asked, failing to see why they both looked so wary. These two, of anyone in the whole palace, would believe that what she had just seen could very well be in their near future. Why, then, were they so reluctant to speak?

"*Faelani,* if there are going to be peace negotiations with the trolls, that is excellent news. I just would rather you stayed safely here at Silver Court while they take place, rather than forming part of the welcoming committee," Alder said, shuddering slightly.

Lily felt her mouth falling open. After the journey they had just finished, did Alder seriously think she couldn't handle herself under these circumstances?

"*Vipina,* I must express my concern with your participation as well. Your safety would not be absolute in the situation you have described."

Lily hopped off of Alder's lap and began to pace a portion of the glass riser. She mentally replayed the vision. Though she didn't actually invoke her prophetic magic, she could feel the press of it in her mind, and she knew she needed to be by the lake. Lily carefully ordered her thoughts, then spoke again, looking them in the eye by turn as she did.

"My magic is telling me that I need to be there. I think this is because having a lady Fae present for such a meeting is the clearest possible message of peace we of the Wood could give to the trolls of the Crescent. If it is a matter of my safety, please consider this: in my vision, they come without weapons, either on their bodies or even in their boats. While a few appeared angry, I didn't think any of the trolls looked ready for a fight. The majority of them seemed much more as though they were sad and weary, in search of help. Alder is by my side, and two spectra are ranged about us. We outnumber the trolls, and are all more powerful than they are besides. Can we compromise? Alder, would you be easier if I promised not to enter any conflict that may arise? If I was in a Void sphere of my *vapa*'s making the entire time? For I truly believe my presence is required for the best possible outcome in the morning."

Lily held her breath and waited. She wanted Alder to agree with her and to trust her. She didn't want to have to sneak out of the palace and find her own way to the lake, but Lily knew she would do what she felt she had to do for the sake of the Fae Wood. Her resolve must have shown itself on her face, for both Alder and Vadom seemed to see it. Her *vapa* merely raised his brows, but her truemate tensed, clearly upset.

"And if I won't compromise? Are you going to try to go on your own?"

Lily felt a surge of frustration, but she tried her best to keep it in check.

"I won't wait around the palace when I could be truly useful somewhere else. And I don't want to be afraid of trolls, Alder. If I start avoiding them now, it will only make it harder on me to face them later," Lily admitted, fists clenching.

That definitely had Alder thinking about it. Lily kept quiet, but couldn't help continuing her pacing. Her therianthrope, who had returned to her mind hours ago, made an appearance once more. All of the agitation, restlessness, and frustration that Lily felt seemed amplified and embodied by her wild one. Alder certainly didn't miss that, either. Sighing, he stood and caught her hands in his.

"I agree to your compromise, Lily. Reluctantly," he added at her relieved expression. "And if there is even the slightest hint of danger, I am removing you to a safe location, and you are fully cooperating."

"What about you? Will you stay out of harm's way with me?" Lily asked, realizing that she didn't want Alder at risk, either. Even the idea of it filled her with a species of dread she didn't even want to contemplate.

Alder sighed and nodded his head.

"I will stay with you. Even as the Silver Prince, I was never allowed to take many chances with my safety. The Throne of Stars, the Wood itself, could not afford to lose me and the magic I could provide. Now that I am your Golden Prince, that safety is even more critical than before. No one else is capable of becoming the next golden monarchs, Lily. We must be careful of ourselves in order to protect the future of the Fae Wood and our people."

Though his words rang with sincerity, Lily detected something more in Alder's tone. Like what he was saying was some endless refrain that kept coming back, no matter the preceding verse. The caged behavior of his therianthrope was starting to make sense to Lily now, and she began to wonder if this was one of the reasons Alder had been so unhappy before he met her.

"I hear you, Alder," she said, giving his hands a gentle squeeze. Her reassuring smile had him relaxing a little.

"I begin to truly appreciate the patience of mated warriors, *faelani*. All I want is to sequester you in the palace with a spectrum or three or nine to guard you, yet I must compromise and take you into the presence of trolls instead."

"Well, I think all will be fine and you will not regret it, Alder. Though if I have seen a future that does not come to pass, or one of the trolls produces a flail out of thin air, please feel free to take me right back out of the company of the trolls," Lily said, making an attempt at lightheartedness.

Alder seemed to see right through it, though. His eyes softened at the mention of a flail, and his arms came around her in a reassuring embrace. Lily felt safer right away. And pleasantly tingly. After a few moments, Alder pulled back. His eyes flicked down to her shoulder, then back up to her face.

"No more pain or fear for you, *faelani*," he said softly.

"I trust you, *faelan*," Lily replied, because she did.

They held each other's eyes for another long moment, then Lily turned toward Vadom, giving him a small smile.

"This plan is acceptable to you, too, *Vapa?*"

Vadom inclined his head.

"As I am to accompany you and keep you in a Void sphere at all times, I will not argue against what you and your otherwing have agreed upon. Let us hope all is peaceful in the end."

Nodding, Lily resumed her seat on the Highness throne, and Alder followed suit. Motioning for Plum, he requested a mirror to contact Poplar again. The Warden responded almost immediately.

"Your Highnesses? All is well?"

"Yes, Poplar, we think so. Lily has had a vision and believes the obsidian will be needed at Molten Mirror Lake at dawn tomorrow morning. As you are a good seven hours of flying away, you will need to leave as soon as possible. Enlist the help of as many Court Guards or other Wardens as you deem necessary to transport all of the bowls of obsidian to the Lake. You will find us by the Willows. You know where they are?"

"South of the delta and north of the Cypresses, Highness. I will gather a couple of spectra and we will be there," Poplar said confidently.

"Thank you for your help, Poplar," Lily said.

The purple Warden smiled, bowed his head, and faded from view.

Lily found her inner magic settling down a little now. It felt, somehow, as if they were on the proper course. Before she could feel a measure of relief, however, the Advisors chose that moment to voice their objections. Their spokesperson was the same sharp-tongued lavender Fae from earlier in the evening.

"We hope, Prince Alder, that hasty decisions are not being made at this time. As the Princess has not yet been Tested for any magical gift at any power level, perhaps another course of action might be more prudent?"

Lily sighed. Somehow she doubted that such impertinence would be given voice if they were at Golden Court. Certainly not after her introduction this morning. Since no one at Silver Court had played witness to that rather ostentatious magical display, however, Lily supposed they would have to humor the Advisors. This time, anyway. Glancing over at Alder and discreetly rolling her eyes, she caught the amusement in his before he affixed a polite expression on his face and responded.

"Your suggestion is being taken under consideration, Advisor Larch. Perhaps some additional information should be sought at this time. Plum, could you mirror Captain Pine for me, please?"

The chamberlain glided silently forward, mirror in hand. After focusing a moment on its reflective surface, Pine's voice could be heard.

"Sun and rain on you, Plum. Need I report?"

"Yes, Captain. The Prince wishes to speak with you."

When Plum had handed over the mirror, Alder held it up so that Lily could just see Pine against a night sky full of stars.

"*Praetam*, any intelligence you and your Guards have gathered at this time would be welcome."

"I mirrored Sycamore upon leaving Silver Court, and he had already ordered dome perimeter sweeps to check for incoming trolls. Those spectra, after a full sweep, have reported only seven boats rowing together toward the Fae Wood. They will be reaching the Bubble in a few hours' time. As ordered, we have allowed them to approach uncontested, as they have made no attempt to engage us. They do not appear to be armed."

"And has the spectrum reconnoitering the Crescent itself reported back yet?"

"They haven't yet returned, since they had to wait for me to arrive and let them out, but they have done several mirror check-ins, and the volcanoes appear to be dormant. At least four are not even smoking, and they are surveying the remaining fo— three as we speak. No eruptions seem imminent, or even likely, at this time."

Though the courtiers began murmuring at the Captain's words, Lily was too busy mentally checking that everything Alder's *praetam* was reporting corroborated with her vision to distinguish anything more than the quiet hum of their voices. Glancing at the Advisors, she saw more than one openly surprised face among their number. Finally, Lily took in Alder's expression and posture. He was completely unfazed by Pine's report. Lily found herself more than a little relieved that her truemate trusted both her and her *vapa* and the conclusions they'd reached without the aid of anyone else.

"Thank you, Captain. I believe we will be able to reach a decision on how to proceed now that your Guards have reported. I will give you additional orders shortly."

When the magic faded from the mirror and all that could be seen was its regular reflective surface once more, Alder looked directly over at the eighteen Advisors sitting and whispering on their small glass riser. Lily watched as her *faelan* allowed them to speak amongst themselves, patiently waiting for them to reach the correct conclusion.

At last, their spokesperson, Advisor Larch, stood and looked first at Alder, then at Lily.

"Given this latest information, and its concurrence with the Princess's vision, we, the Advisors, agree that peaceful negotiations should be the next step undertaken with our neighbors to the west. We consent to Captain Pine's further use of the Hatch as necessary. However, should the trolls fail to reach a diplomatic solution with those Fae who meet with them by the Willows, we, the Advisors, insist the trolls vacate the protective dome over our Wood posthaste."

Lily didn't see any problems with this plan or its stipulations, and was glad the Advisors were in accordance with Alder and herself. She just hoped, at this point, that she would have a quiet moment to ask Alder about the Hatch before they actually arrived at the shore of Molten Mirror Lake. Looking to Alder, Lily watched him nod in graceful assent to the Advisors' decision.

"I am glad we are all in agreement. Let us allow Poplar's orders to stand as they have been given, and inform Captain Pine that those Wardens and Court Guards will be arriving with the obsidian. Should the peace talks go awry, we will have a number of spectra on hand to send the trolls back to the Crescent immediately. In that event, Vadom and I will remove Lily from potential danger and return to Silver Court to discuss what will need to be done to ensure the continued safety of the Wood and its inhabitants."

When everyone greeted Alder's words with approval, Lily felt herself relax a bit. Her fatigue returned, more insistent than before, and Lily knew then that she would have to sleep for at least a few hours before she could do anything more tonight. It wouldn't be long before they would need to leave for the Lake, but Lily decided to catch up a little on her rest before it was time to depart. Setting her pillow resolutely on Alder's lap, Lily pulled her blanket around herself and laid down. Though Alder started and then froze a moment, his eyes held nothing but concern when he looked down at her. Levering her feet up onto the throne as well, Lily managed a drowsy smile for her truemate.

"If everything is settled, I think I need some sleep before we fly to the Lake, Alder."

Lily felt some of the tension leave his body then. Tentatively, Alder wrapped an arm around her waist, effectively securing her from rolling off of the Highness throne while she slumbered.

"Go ahead and rest, Lily. I'll wake you in a few hours when it is time to fly out."

Nodding, Lily was about to close her eyes when she caught a glimpse of Plum in her peripheral vision. She had a good idea as to why he was all but wringing his hands, too.

"Plum?"

He glided forward silently with all of his ice-blue dignity and grace.

"Yes, Your Highness?"

"Could you please mirror Fig and fully update him on the events of the evening for me? I'd like Golden Court to be completely informed and aware of what will be happening in the morning."

The last thing Lily registered before succumbing to sleep was that she appeared to have a budding talent for preoccupying Chamberlain Plum.

Mourning by the Willows

Though Lily vaguely recalled being roused when it was time to begin the short flight to Molten Mirror, she didn't truly wake until the first rays of dawn's light slowly rose past the horizon and followed her toward the great lake. She was, as usual, in the strong arms of her *vapa*.

"Good morning, *Vapa*," Lily said softly, yawning as she tried to finish waking up.

"And a good morning to you as well, *Vipina*," Vadom replied, seeming a little amused, as he always did, by this particular greeting.

"Are we close to the Lake yet?"

"Look and see for yourself, *vladi*," Vadom answered, indicating with a nod of his head in the direction they were flying.

Lily looked over and gasped at the vista unfolding before her. With trees of all shapes and sizes directly below them, it was something of a shock to see them come to an abrupt end where the wide expanse of the lake began. The surface looked nothing like the Sea of Fintilles or the Goddess's pool, however, or even like the water running through the channel of the Ancient River. The liquid of Molten Mirror was a pale slate-gray color with just a hint of purple, and it seemed almost too viscous to even be water. Pre-dawn fog still hung thick in the air just above the lake, and, far in the distance beyond the vast body of unusually flat water was a semi-circle of triangular peaks, just as she had seen with her prophetic magic. It was, without any help from fairy or troll, a place of great natural beauty. Lily felt herself expand and accept this new domain, felt it come into being in a dormant part of her mind, as though she had just been waiting for the sight of the actual location to make it come to life in her own head. It was a part of Lamoranth, and a part of her, too.

"What do you think, *faelani?*"

Lily tore her gaze away to look for her truemate. He was flying just ahead and to her *vapa*'s left, a boyish grin on his handsome face. Her breath caught in her throat at the sight of Alder's silvery wings, the magical feathers catching and glinting even the softest pre-dawn light. Lily realized that she hadn't even properly looked at fairy wings yet, and decided now was the time to look her fill.

"Amazing," she responded absently.

Oblivious to the new focus of Lily's attention, Alder spoke again.

"It is an extraordinary sight, isn't it? I've asked the Gongoozler about it, and he says there is nothing else like Molten Mirror Lake in all of Lamoranth. We think it is because of the volcanoes' past eruptions. The ash and lava have mixed with the water running into the lake from the River Ward to create a very unique body of liquid. Consequently, the Fae who can successfully summon portions of the Lake with their magic are only those talented with both water and earth elements. Very interesting, don't you think?"

Lily nodded her agreement, temporarily diverted from her perusal of Alder in flight by the strangeness of the Wood's western border. Her thoughts then strayed to the reason for their trip to this place, and Lily felt herself focus fully on the impending meeting with the trolls. As if sensing the direction of her thoughts, Alder looked ahead, scanning the ground below and ahead of them, before turning back to Lily and Vadom.

"We are nearly there now. I've been in regular contact with Captain Pine and Poplar all night, and we believe all will be ready in time for the arrival of our guests. I've also spoken with our selected diplomats regarding what will be said, what shouldn't be said, and what the Fae would like to achieve through this discussion. I believe that spectrum is prepared for peaceful negotiation. Can you think of anything else that we ought to do before the trolls reach the Willows, *faelani?*"

Lily was thrilled that Alder was asking for her opinion, and she thought hard for a moment before responding.

"Your *praetam* confirmed that all of the volcanoes are inactive? And he let the seven boats in through the Hatch?"

"Yes, the entire Crescent is quiet. The scouts summed up their reconnaissance with the word 'subdued'. And the Captain did create a time-limited Hatch to allow them through the Bubble. They are being escorted, while under the dome, by two spectra of Silver Court Guards. This is both a security measure and to ensure that they make straight for the Willows, as your vision indicated would be best for a peaceful outcome."

Though Lily didn't want to think about a different ending for this meeting, she knew they had to try their best to be prepared for anything. A terrible thought had her stomach turning, but she forced the words past her lips.

"What are we going to do if the trolls are Void-bound? If the xydolem control them?"

Alder and Vadom exchanged a look, and Lily felt her twisted stomach sink painfully.

"*Vipina,* Alder has asked me to determine, as quickly as possible, whether or not the visiting trolls have become slaves to corrupted night magic. If the xydolem have them Void-bound, then they will have to be killed, for the safety of everyone in their vicinity. It is the only freedom we can grant them."

Lily closed her eyes for a moment, clinging tightly to her composure. She had seen Void-bound trolls die, only the night before. It was just so hard to allow the trolls to keep dying when it was the xydolem who were causing the bloodshed, who deserved punishment for terrible wrongdoing. Why? Why were they creating so much unnecessary hardship?

When Lily was certain she could open her eyes without betraying her feelings and speak with a steady voice, she did so.

"I understand."

Alder looked sad, but his underlying strength could not be missed. Lily realized that Alder had been making big, difficult decisions for a long time, and he would make one today, too, if the situation required it. She couldn't help but admire him for it, and decided to take his lead in the hours ahead.

Only a few minutes later, everyone began their descent. All the Fae warriors circled while Vadom winged directly down toward the weeping trees, table and chairs, and waiting Court Guards. Lily was relieved to see all of the bowls full of obsidian carefully arranged on the table, and she was happy, despite the solemnity of the occasion, to see both Poplar and Yew vigilantly keeping watch over the warrior trolls' adornments. Giving them a small wave in greeting, she found herself smiling when they waved enthusiastically back. Vadom, upon seeing their interaction, landed gently only a few arm-lengths away from Lily's Wardens.

"Sun and rain upon you, Poplar, Yew," Lily said in the Fae language. While it was still about all she was able to say in the language of her people,

Lily knew she wouldn't have the luxury of being timid when it came to learning Fae. Best to just jump in, even if she found out later that her accent was in need of polishing.

"And on you, Princess," they both replied, bowing a little as they spoke.

"Thank you both for so carefully gathering the trolls' obsidian and bringing it all the way here," Lily continued, now in Ropazian. "I have a feeling it will mean a great deal to the Crescent visitors who are about to arrive. Have you had a chance to rest yet?"

Both Wardens grinned and shook their heads.

"Sleep now? When things are so exciting? I don't think I could if I tried, Highness," Poplar replied, obviously thrilled to be in the thick of unfolding events.

"We are old enough that we sleep less than we did in our first century, and Wardens are trained to postpone sleep in critical situations if necessary," Yew added, by way of explanation.

Lily tucked that piece of information away to ask Alder about later. Was it like the meditating he had utilized on their journey across Ropaz? Could she learn how to delay her need for sleep, or was she too young to safely do so? If it was possible, that might be a useful skill to try to master . . .

Before Lily could follow that errant train of thought, however, she felt someone gently tugging on her hand. She turned and looked into Alder's very serious, tempest-eyed face.

"*Faelani,* if this meeting becomes dangerous, I will be leaving with you, and Poplar and Yew will be escorting us to a safer location. Vadom will stay and fight if any of the trolls are Void-bound, otherwise he will be accompanying us as well. If, for whatever reason, one or all of us cannot fly you away from this location, then Captain Pine has my permission to retreat with you. Your safety is of great concern to everyone here."

Though Lily didn't like the thought of failed negotiations in the slightest, she knew it was wise to prepare for the worst. She looked her truemate straight in the eye and nodded her understanding and acceptance of Alder's protective plans. The last thing she wanted to do was distract the warriors present from communicating effectively with their besieged guests. That wouldn't do the Fae any good, or the trolls either. There was no way Lily wanted to abet the xydolem even indirectly.

Alder seemed to calm a little at Lily's ready acquiescence. He gave her hand another squeeze, then slid it to the crook of his right elbow, enabling him to escort her to their place in the center of the assembled Fae warriors. Lily felt a steady calm cloak her. With Alder at her left, Vadom at her right, and a large number of spectra spaced around them, behind them, and in the trees nearby, she felt far less imperiled than she ever had outside the Wood. Add to that the tables arranged for discussion with the obsidian peace offering, and Lily knew they were as prepared as they could be for their approaching guests.

They all stood in silence for a few moments, centering themselves for their appointed tasks and watching as the sun at their backs slowly brightened the world around them. It was then, out of the mist slowly being burned off of the glassy surface of Molten Mirror, that the first of the Court Guards escorting the visiting trolls came into view. They were alert, entirely focused, and clearly prepared for the Fae present to greet them by the Willows. The Silver Court Guards landed one by one on the rocky shore of the great lake, nodding to Captain Pine at Alder's left before turning back to face the most recent arrivals to the Fae Wood.

In the minutes following their advent, the trolls paddled into view. Lily had to suppress just a tiny shiver at the sight of the trolls' stocky bodies and jagged features, not to mention their wild black hair, inky lips, sharp ebony fingernails, and obsidian eyes. She focused instead on their leaf-shaped watercraft, trying to determine from what material they were made. Lily tried not to let even a hint of her uneasiness show, knowing it would alert the protective Fae around her and create tension that wouldn't help in the slightest.

Next, Lily observed the number of guests: nine total. There were seven boats, two of which had one young troll paddling and one very old troll concentrating on the shore and the fairies waiting upon it. Those two old trolls, along with the five propelling and directing their own craft, had elaborate, symbol-carved obsidian circlets crowning their heads. They advanced slowly, finally grinding to a halt on the rocky shore amidst the willow trees.

The five mature trolls secured their boats, then half-turned and waited for the elder troll leaders to disembark from their own crafts, aided by the young trolls accompanying them. When the seven crowned trolls, heads high, took a few steps forward, the remaining two stepped back, apparently present only to keep an eye on the boats and the proceedings. After a few steps more, the leaders halted. The eldest among them, standing second to the left, puffed out his chest and began to speak. Though he primarily directed his words to Alder, his sorrowful eyes shifted periodically to include Lily in his wizened gaze.

"Fae of the Wood, we thank you for this opportunity to speak with you about the grave events that have recently befallen the clans of the Volcano Crescent. We who have crossed the lava lake to speak peacefully with you are the seven remaining chieftains of our race."

After introductions were made, they fell silent, apparently waiting for how the Fae would reply. Though Lily had understood every word the chieftain had uttered, she didn't think she could speak the troll language coherently in response. She hoped that the Fae spectrum of ambassadors, with their limited knowledge of the trolls, were up to the task of translating and answering for Alder and herself.

"Chieftains of the Volcano Crescent, I am Alder, the Silver and the Golden Prince of the Fae, here to speak as the voice of the monarchs of the Wood. This is my truemate, Lily, Golden Princess of the Fae Wood. On behalf of both the Silver and Golden Courts, we welcome you to our home today."

After waiting a moment for one of their attending Fae to translate his words, Alder continued.

"It is our hope to learn of your motives for the attack on Ford-upon-Ward last night. I must inform you that your battalion of warriors fought in fierce combat with our Wardens and Court Guard, and there were no troll survivors. We had solid evidence to believe that they were, one and all, Void-bound, and hence thought it unwise and dangerous to allow for prisoners. We were told by one well-versed in night magic that death was the only mercy that could be granted to your enslaved clansmen."

Stepping partially toward the tables behind them, Alder motioned to the earthenware bowls placed there and gestured to the one thousand obsidian adornments they contained.

"Though it was necessary to cremate their remains, our warriors respectfully gathered your brethren's obsidian pieces. Please consider this a peaceful offering from the Fae."

The mixture of grief, anger, and relief on the chieftains' faces told Lily how hard the troll leaders were taking this news, how troubled they were by what had come to pass. Slowly, Lily walked around the table and stood by a chair, waiting for their guests to come forward and sit down in the seven chairs on the lake side of the table. Walking with bowed heads and obviously heavy hearts, the clan leaders stepped up to the bowls of obsidian and sat down, many of them grieving openly. Lily sat quietly, shedding a few silent tears of her own. It was so hard for her to witness the suffering of beings who did not deserve the wrong done to them.

Lily wasn't sure how much time passed, only that Alder gently took her hand and offered her the comfort and support she needed in those moments. She may have had some seriously frightening and painful experiences in the Antechamber, but she had come away ultimately unscathed and safer than she had ever been. None of the trolls who had tried to take her life or storm the entrance to the Fae Wood could say the same. Gathering her composure, Lily looked up at the chieftains sitting opposite the table from her and realized that many of their gazes had come to rest on her. Wiping at her wet cheeks with the sleeve of her well-worn dark tunic, Lily put her hands on the rim of the bowl in front of her and carefully pushed it toward the troll chieftain sitting directly across from her.

The clan leader solemnly rested a hand atop the obsidian in the bowl, staring almost absently at the armbands and necklaces, apparently gathering his thoughts to speak.

"It was the xydolem who forced this losing battle upon our clansmen, and this isn't the first time this has happened, either."

Lily, shocked as she was by the latter half of this pronouncement, still caught a flicker of movement well behind the stocky body of the chieftain directly before her. Tilting slightly to try to pinpoint what had snagged her attention at such a critical moment, she saw nothing but the two young trolls waiting for their leaders by the boats. One was still and quiet, but the other was fidgeting, twitching, and generally unable to conceal his flustered state. Even as Lily tried to refocus her attention where it belonged, her gaze lingered on the disturbed young troll. She watched as he flicked his wild mane of black hair in agitation, momentarily giving her an unobstructed view of his neck. What she saw made her breath catch in her throat in a split second of complete terror: a twisted, oily black rope of Void element was wrapped so tightly about the troll's neck that Lily distantly wondered how he could push breath through his constricted throat. That troll was Void-bound. Inside the Fae Wood. Eavesdropping on a peaceful meeting of trolls and fairies.

Frozen, Lily tried to get her mind to *think*. Not about the other trolls she had encountered who were enslaved by night magic, and especially not about the xydolem she had seen in the desert, their entire bodies wrapped in oily black coils just like the ones she could see on the troll not ten steps away. No, she needed to alert the warriors around her to the danger in their midst. Even if it meant she was effectively sentencing that young troll to death, she realized with pain in her heart.

Slowly, Lily turned her head so that she could make eye contact with Alder. He was intently focused on the chieftain who had just spoken, apparently stunned at what the troll leader had said as it was translated to him. Lily didn't dare give herself and her discovery away by reclaiming her truemate's attention. Where was her *vapa*? He had followed her around the table, but he hadn't sat down. He was probably close behind her, keeping watch over the proceedings. Could she send him a Void pulse? Would a Void-bound troll be able to sense her use of night magic? Lily decided it was an acceptable risk. Once her *vapa* was told, he'd know exactly what to do to keep everyone present safe from a danger they could not see.

Carefully, Lily twisted a piece of night magic and formed a pulse in her mind, clearly shaping it with her intent, to warn Vadom, and filling it with a precisely worded message: Void-bound troll, boats, right one. When it stilled, she sent it to him, trying not to tense as she waited for a reply. Almost instantly, Lily saw the Void sphere around her thicken considerably with unpolluted night magic. There were exclamations all around her, and Lily realized her *vapa* must have made her invisible. Fae and trolls alike were jumping up from the table in alarm, but none moved faster than the vampire among them.

Vadom vaulted over the table and occupied chairs, a lethal blur heading directly for the Void-bound troll. The young, doomed being saw the danger bearing down on him just in time to throw himself to the side, away from his unbound companion and the boats. The troll rolled and then sprang to his feet once more, facing the array of warriors whose attention he now held exclusively. His face went blank, then totally slack, for just an instant before being imbued with utter rage and unadulterated hatred.

In his blind fury, the troll now sprang toward Vadom instead of away. To Lily's shock, a Void weapon, as oily as the rope around his neck, pushed straight out of the troll's chest, blade first. The needle-sharp black rapier, having burst out of the troll's body backwards, caused him to begin bleeding copiously. He paid the injury, and his fast-flowing black blood, no attention whatsoever. Instead, he attacked Vadom with a vengeance, though with no skill at all. Lily realized that, as a troll, he had probably only ever learned to fight with blunt weapons, never with blades. He looked as if he had about as much experience with a rapier as she did. Vadom disarmed him with consummate skill, though he was extremely careful never to allow the rapier to touch his skin.

When Vadom had his weapon pressed to the young troll's throat, just below the oily black rope of magic, he spoke calmly into the noisy, confused, and angry group around the table.

"This troll is Void-bound."

There was more confusion and anger as her *vapa*'s words were translated as needed, and a hint of fear began to show in the eyes of many of the assembled, particularly the trolls. Lily continued to sit silently, unsure of what to do. She could tell by the steely gray of Alder's eyes that he wanted to take her and leave, his role as a prince and representative of Silver Court in second place to his protective instinct. The only thing that prevented him from doing so was the fact that he was the only one who seemed to realize she had never left her chair at the table. Lily spared only a moment to ponder how strange it was that she was safer simply remaining in the trolls' presence, rather than potentially bringing attention to herself by fleeing. What she needed to concentrate on, after all, was how to deal with this latest development. Speaking in her quietest whisper, certain it would reach only her truemate's ears in the melee, Lily posed the dreaded question.

"Must he be killed, *faelan*?"

Though he gave no outward indication that he had heard her, Lily knew that Alder had. His face, so solemn before, looked as though it was hewn from stone now. Still, she knew he was carefully assessing, trying to determine if a peaceful outcome could somehow occur if the Fae were forced to kill one of their visitors. Lily knew she had to help him if she could, even though it made her ache with sadness for the young troll.

"Alder, I can see where that troll is Void-bound. I sent a pulse to my *vapa* as soon as I caught sight of the oily black night magic rope around his neck. That is why Vadom changed my Void sphere and attacked so quickly."

Alder was so surprised that he nearly turned to look at her, but he caught himself before giving away her location. Even with his determination not to expose her, Lily didn't miss the surprise or the questions in his eyes as her truemate stubbornly fastened his gaze on the neck of the troll, where Vadom still held his weapon steadily. Lily had no idea how she could see the corrupted Void magic now when she had been unable to see it just last night, but confusion regarding her magical abilities would have to wait. A decision needed to be made quickly, the fate of a troll sealed.

Alder stood slowly, placing his palms flat on the table before him. When he spoke, her *faelan*'s voice rang with an undeniable, inescapable authority.

"Chieftains, your clan member is Void-bound, a slave to the xydolem until death. He must be killed, for the safety of all present here, and for the security of the Fae Wood. Can you grant him an honorable death, or do you wish one of us Fae to take responsibility?"

In the silence that followed the translation, Lily found herself anxiously scanning the foreign faces across the table. Would they accept Alder's words and execute one of their own? It was horrible, and hurt even to contemplate, but Lily knew she couldn't let her feelings for one endanger the safety of the dozens of beings at this gathering, or of the troll clans of the Crescent and Fae families of the Wood. Whoever had control of that troll right now knew too much, and was threatening them all with bodily harm besides. Lily thought, a little bleakly, that being a princess entailed a much greater amount of responsibility than she had yet been able to consider. When that sobering thought was accompanied by a pulse of her prophetic magic, Lily knew she was beginning to learn an important and very harsh lesson.

"I will take his life and free him from the evil magic of the xydolem."

Lily turned her head to look at the chieftain who had spoken. He appeared to be a bit older than the others, but not as time-worn as the two eldest clan leaders. Though there were a few defining lines about his eyes and mouth, both features were still hardened with quiet determination. Lily slowly reached out her hand and grasped Alder's arm. She was going to need his support to get through this morning with some semblance of composure.

When Alder laid his hand over her own for several long moments, acknowledging her need of him, Lily felt herself calm a little. This was going to be terrible, but at least everyone around her felt the same way about it. There was only a sense of duty, of protection and survival, at this loss of life. Lily knew the chieftain would make this as painless as possible for his kinsman, and she tried to take comfort in that one small fact before she began to grieve for the enslaved young troll.

Lily's sorrow, however, was premature. In a monstrously fast maneuver, the Void-bound troll lashed out at her *vapa*— with a long piece of the oily black night magic. Forced to retreat, Vadom dodged the troll's offensive, leaving the rogue troll uncontained and armed with a piece of corrupted Void element. It was in that moment that Lily realized she might have to help her *vapa* with the enemy troll. As many warriors as there were about her, only she and Vadom could see the true danger this puppet-like being wielded. Lily wracked her mind for a solution that wouldn't put her directly in harm's way. With the number of spectra ranged around her, it would be foolish to take on a warrior who was fighting with a weapon she had no idea how to safely counter. She had also promised Alder that she wouldn't enter into a conflict, and that was exactly what was happening right now. How could she help the others to see the troll's Void bindings?

Lily scanned her surroundings, hoping against hope for a solution to come to her. There were all the Fae warriors and troll chieftains arrayed before her, poised and ready for action, yet holding back because of the intricate and lethal dance in which Vadom and the troll appeared to be engaged. They hesitated only because they had no idea what the enslaved troll was fighting with . . . Lily next caught sight of the other young troll, who had taken refuge behind the watercraft he had rowed across the great lake— the lake!

Without wasting another precious second, Lily stood and summoned the inner magic from her elemental well of power. She focused on the water of Molten Mirror, remembering what Alder had said about needing control of both water and earth elements to wield it. Lily concentrated on only a small portion of the lava lake's contents, lifting it from the rest with surprising ease. It took only a little more effort to fling the viscous water at the Void-bound troll and soak him from head to toe, keeping some of the water clinging to the corrupted rope of night magic in his left hand and the blade in his right simultaneously.

"Faelan, can you see the troll's Void weapons now? Can they safely fight him like this?"

Alder nodded quickly to let Lily know he had heard her whispering, then spoke in a ringing voice to the Fae warriors already closing in on their enemies' slave.

"Fae, this troll must be killed and his body burned immediately. The water shows you the Void bindings and rapier he fights with— do not let these weapons touch you!"

Though Lily was primarily concentrating on keeping water upon the oily black night magic weapons, she did not fail to see how swiftly the Void-bound troll's ending came. Two spectra moved in with perfect coordination, surrounding the troll and thoroughly outnumbering him. Lily watched in relief as her *vapa* stepped back, removing himself from the fight as the Fae warriors took total control of the situation. In the next moment, Vadom appeared at her side, looking Lily over carefully. In the very second she split her attention and glanced at her *vapa,* to make certain he was unharmed as well, Lily heard a sickening crack. She knew then that the troll no longer suffered. When she returned her attention to the skirmish that had just concluded by the shore of the Lake, the remains of the young troll were already being consumed by a substantial, incinerating fire.

"Alder," she said softly, trying to speak past the tightness of her throat, "*faelan,* his obsidian . . ."

Almost instantly, Lily could see silvery wisps of magic flow from her truemate's fingers. The shimmering strands of Alder's inner magic took hold of the armband that as yet withstood the searing flames and pulled the piece away from the purifying fire, directly toward the table before them. When Alder had the obsidian ornament in hand, he softly uttered a few words in Fae and then respectfully placed it on top of the other pieces in the earthenware bowl closest to Lily. She leaned her head against his upper arm, needing to be near her truemate at that moment.

It was only then that she noticed many of the troll chieftains had turned to watch the obsidian armband float through the air and into the hand of the fairy prince. When she noticed that many of their gazes caught upon her as well, Lily realized that she was visible once again. Her *vapa,* standing reassuringly at her side, must have believed that the threat to her safety was over. Lily supposed that it was, at least for now.

Everyone respectfully watched the cremation of the young troll until only ashes were left. When the fire waned and flickered out, a gentle breeze carried the remains out over Molten Mirror Lake, though whether it happened naturally or with a gentle push of Fae magic, Lily couldn't tell. After a long moment of silence, every being present turned and looked at Lily and Alder. Lily realized then that they were leaders, and would someday be rulers, of their people. That meant, even though there were many other beings present who ruled, like the chieftains, or had led, as with Vadom, or even currently commanded others, like Captain Pine, that everyone would defer to Alder and herself in this moment. Lily began to truly comprehend that in the Fae Wood, what she and her truemate said carried a great deal of consequence. With their words alone, either one of them could determine the outcome of this convening of neighboring races.

Lily knew what she wished for in regards to this meeting, and she knew Alder wanted the same: a peaceful resolution, with open communication and solidarity between the trolls and the Fae. Straightening, Lily looked up at her *faelan,* at the same moment that he looked down at her. Seeing that they were of one mind, Lily faced forward and met the eyes of each of the chieftains in turn. She tried to convey both sympathy and strength in her gaze. With an all-encompassing gesture that welcomed them back to the table, Lily finally spoke.

"Please, chieftains of the Volcano Crescent, be seated once more. As you have seen, the warriors who are present will protect us from harm. Let us continue speaking as we were before."

Hoping her words were enough to regain their lost footing, Lily decided to set an example and be the first to sit down. Alder waited until her words had been translated, then took his seat as well. None of the troll chieftains hesitated to return to their places at the table. Trying not to show her obvious relief, Lily looked attentively at their guests. When everyone was settled in their places, Alder spoke into the subdued atmosphere of the meeting.

"Chieftains, you have come to the Fae Wood to represent your clans in the Volcano Crescent, and we appreciate that you have traveled here peacefully to speak with us about recent events between our people and yours. You have told us that the xydolem are responsible for the attack last night. This, at least, we knew. Would you tell us, though, how this came to pass, and when it has happened previously?"

The troll directly across from Alder sighed deeply once the question was translated, but he readily answered, obviously prepared for the inquiry.

"Prince Alder, we believe this is the third time the xydolem have coerced the clans of the Crescent into foolish confrontations with your warriors in the Fae Wood. It was only a few days ago, however, that we even realized this was happening. Let me start by explaining what has occurred to our people in the last week.

"They came in the night. A dozen crimson xydolem stole into the volcano of the Blackstone clan, catching them all unaware. It was not until morning that we of the other clans saw the smoke of their distress calling for help in the sky. What our first group of warriors found when they answered the plea, however, were friends who had become strangers, trolls without lava in their veins. They attacked us with empty eyes, causing much grief and loss of life. By the time the sun was past its zenith and beginning to fade away into the night, the enemy, no longer trying to hide themselves, had complete power over every troll in the Blackstone clan. With that control, the xydolem forced the Blackstones to cause such an eruption as has never been seen before in the history of the Crescent.

"We did not understand at first why the enemy in our midst caused the Blackstone clan to destroy their very home, but it did not take us long to find out. Those of us before you now sent our most gifted obsidian wielders into the usurped volcano, ordering them to use all of their stealth to determine the plans of the xydolem and report back undetected. When the seven returned, they told us that the xydolem hoped to provoke the Fae of the Wood into another conflict in a series of conflicts, in order to deplete the number of Fae warriors able to fight for their home. The xydolem want to weaken you, though we do not know why.

"What we did come to realize, however, was that this enemy has been using us, the clans of the Crescent, to harm our neighbors to the east for some time now. We convened, in the home of the Ashes clan, the southernmost of the volcanoes, and pooled our knowledge. What our elders, as well as our writings, told us was greatly disturbing. The chieftains of the past had twice misinterpreted the signs of xydolem infiltration. Nearly eight hundred years ago, the xydolem were much more insidious, taking control only of the majority of our chieftains: level-headed trolls who, for no discernible reason, set aside the safety of our clans and sailed across the lava lake in a futile effort to engage the Fae. Our records and stories tell us that they were repelled long before reaching the shore we are gathered upon this morning, first due to an invisible barrier and then the fairy fighters' power over the elements. No satisfactory reason for this incursion was ever given, before or after the attack, for the five chieftains who led the boats all died within the following year.

"Just three hundred years ago, the xydolem grew a little bolder. They bound with their dark magic our strongest warriors and made them desire riches and glory. Our scribes at the time were puzzled by the fact that our strongest, who are always the most selfless among us, suddenly wanted wealth and status that they did not need. Not only that, but they fervently believed that the only way to gain power was to attack the Fae of the Wood, conquer them, and sell them to the witches and wizards of Ropaz. But why do this, when we had never successfully engaged the Fae before, and when we have always kept our interactions with the Ropazians at the very minimum? One scroll described a blank-faced obsidian champion speaking at length about the importance of attacking before the fairy prince could be born, though how he knew of the baby's impending birth, no one had any idea."

Alder, who had been listening to the translations attentively, went rigid in his chair. Lily herself could hardly breathe for a moment. Had the xydolem deliberately struck out at the Fae in order to harm Alder? Lily felt her therianthrope seethe within her at the very thought, and she could tell, just by looking at the warriors about her, that she was not the only one angered at the thought of such a scheme. Before anyone could give voice to their outrage, however, the troll chieftain continued.

"And then there are the events of the last week, all of which were orchestrated by the xydolem yet again. They blatantly captured and stole the freedom of an entire clan. It is only because of our seven strongest and bravest warriors that we even know they have been culpable before now, or have any inkling of why. Our obsidian champions also discovered, through their eavesdropping, that the xydolem suspected a plot by the late fairy queen that necessitated an attack on the Fae with all possible haste. They thought a Crescent attack would either distract those involved or foil their enemies' plans entirely.

"It was at that point that we, the chieftains of the Volcano Crescent, truly realized that our race has no contention with the Fae of the Wood, nor have we ever had such a dispute. The xydolem are our enemy, and they are, obviously, your enemy as well. That was when we decided, just yesterday, that we had to try to speak with the rulers of the Fae, if they would hear us. For we have invoked an ancient troll magic, an earth protection spell that has been passed down for countless generations of chieftains, over the remaining seven volcanoes and the clans that they shelter. The xydolem have been unable to penetrate this defense, and as long as we recast the spell at regular intervals of time, we should be able to keep them away from the rest of our people indefinitely. We hoped that you, the Fae, would see this as a mark of our competence with magic, as well as our capability of standing against our foes, and that you would find us a worthy ally against the xydolem as a result."

The chieftain glanced in each direction at the other clan leaders before leaning back in his chair, clearly having said all he had needed to say. A silence fell over the table as translations were finished and everyone present took a few moments to absorb the chieftain's words. Lily was trying to take it all in, but her mind returned continually to the "plot" her mother had apparently gotten the xydolem so incensed about. That had been nothing more than Lily's existence and safety, and perhaps even their precipitous journey back to the Fae Wood. It was bewildering to think that she had, even indirectly and inadvertently, been the catalyst for the events that had recently transpired.

Trying to shake off her thoughts, Lily focused on everyone around her instead. Alder was still tense and clearly mulling everything over from an altered perspective. Her *vapa,* now sitting beside her, was as calm as always, giving nothing of his inner reflections or feelings away. The rest of the Fae looked collectively troubled and angry. It was clear they hadn't realized, or perhaps believed, that the problem was so serious, let alone of such a wide scope. If it was not just the usual problem with the trolls, but a millennium-spanning scheme carried out by the xydolem, then who was the master of those creatures? Suddenly, whispers of the Misruler were sounding a little less far-fetched, even if no solid proof of that being's involvement had yet been uncovered. As for the trolls, they were obviously weighed down by grief, but there was a toughness, a rock-solid determination that emanated from them as well. They seemed to realize, like never before, that they were under threat by a powerful enemy, and their resolution to obtain a trustworthy ally was readily discernible.

Just as Lily was about to bring her attention back to Alder, her eyes once again caught on the boats pulled up on the great lake's shore. She had noticed a small movement, and, given what had happened earlier, allowed her senses to focus on the discrepancy in the otherwise serene background. The remaining young troll, the other crew of the two elder chieftains' watercraft, had accidentally tripped on one of the larger rocks haphazardly scattered about the shore. Lily watched him keenly for a moment, and she was relieved to see his neck free of bindings of any kind. He looked tired and hungry, a little scared, and very sad. He had probably lost more than one friend in the last week, after all, and his entire race had been under serious threat from a dangerous enemy. Lily wanted to do something for him, but was momentarily at a loss as to what might be done.

Deciding that offering food would be something both needed and welcome, Lily looked for the trusty Poplar and Yew, hoping the Wardens would be able to aid her in this little mission. Catching sight of them to her left, several feet beyond the end of the table amidst the spectra of the Court Guard, Lily waited until Yew's continually scanning gaze fell upon her. With nothing more than a subtle tilt of her head, the Fae warrior made his way to her as unobtrusively as possible. Poplar was right behind him, looking puzzled but at the ready until he too caught sight of Lily's attention on them.

They both knelt by her side and behind Vadom's chair, trying not to interrupt the proceedings as the spectrum charged with translating and negotiating began asking some prearranged questions of the chieftains.

"Yes, Your Highness?" Yew asked softly.

"Yew, I was wondering if we have any food to offer the young troll over by the boats? He just seems so downcast, I was hoping there was something we could do for him," Lily said quietly.

Though Lily had felt just a little uncertain at giving her attention to such a small matter when she was facing a table filled with much greater concerns, her worries were laid to rest at the respectful and even proud gazes of her Wardens. They didn't think she was doing anything unusual, but rather something good.

"Poplar and I can share our provisions with him, Your Highness," Yew replied readily.

"We will try to lift his spirits a little, Princess," Poplar added.

Lily smiled and whispered her thanks to them both, then watched as they inclined their heads to her, silently retreated, and made their way around the table toward the young troll. When it looked as though they were communicating with a combination of words and gestures, Lily returned her full focus to the conversation taking place at the table.

It didn't take long for her to catch up, as the diplomatic spectrum appeared to be asking questions of clarification at that point. While at first Lily thought they were plying the trolls for additional information, or perhaps testing the chieftains for consistency, she began to wonder if that was their primary motive after she caught their subtle glances in Alder's direction. Though he was obviously listening, Lily privately thought it was with only one ear on the conversation. What her *faelan* was really doing was thinking, and the Fae diplomats were giving him the time he needed to do so. Wondering if she could help, or if it would be best to remain quiet for now, Lily let the discussion ebb and flow around her, keeping one eye on her truemate all the while.

Finally, when she sensed that the trolls were growing restless, Lily turned her head a little to the side and laid her hand on Alder's forearm. He blinked, then looked over at her, a question in his eyes. Lily smiled what she hoped was a calm and reassuring smile for her *faelan*, then tilted her head ever so slightly toward the chieftains, raising her eyebrows in a question of her own at the same time. Alder regarded her steadily for a moment, then nodded, as though he had read the answer he needed in Lily's gaze. Turning to face the troll chieftains directly, Alder waited until the troll answering the most recent question fell silent. After a few moments passed, and every eye was upon him, the Silver Prince spoke.

"Chieftains of the Volcano Crescent, you have come to the western shore of the Fae Wood this morning to explain the on-going conflict between your people and ours, and to request a peaceful alliance with the inhabitants of the Wood. As the Prince of the Fae, I have heard your explanations for the martial engagements between our races that have occurred both recently and in the past, and I accept them as truth. With an enemy such as the xydolem in our midst, I also think it wisest to forge an alliance between trolls and fairies. Uniting our resources seems the surest way of countering this mutual foe.

"I will be in contact with both Silver Court and Golden Court today to tell our ruling monarchs and their Advisors what has been discussed this morning. When everyone is fully informed on the present situation and has had the opportunity to discuss the best course of action, we will send messengers to you in the Crescent, three days from now, regarding what we think our next steps ought to be. From there, I hope that we can effectively negotiate our response to the xydolem offensive and put in motion what must be done to protect our people and our homes."

When Alder paused and saw the open expressions of relief and rekindled hope in the faces of the chieftains, his tight posture relaxed just a little. Standing, he motioned for the other Fae at the table to do the same. As the troll leaders rose in response, Alder formally concluded the meeting.

"If there is anything further you wish to discuss, whether it be your priorities for dealing with the xydolem or other concerns, please speak with our diplomats before you go. While I do not want to end this discussion prematurely, I think it best for all seven of you to be back in the Crescent as soon as possible. No good can come from an extended absence of the trolls' clan leaders when the xydolem are so near. Thank you for coming here and for seeking peace with the Fae. May sun and rain both ever sustain you."

With a small bow, which the trolls reciprocated, Alder stepped back from the table and allowed the diplomatic spectrum to take charge of the final one-on-one discussions and the proper leave-taking for the visiting troll chieftains. Lily watched as Alder took a proud but grim-looking Captain Pine aside and began what was obviously a serious discussion with his *praetam*. Not wanting to interrupt, Lily turned to Vadom, who was still carefully watching over everything around them.

"I thought that went well, *Vapa*, don't you?"

"I do, *Vipina*. Though Alder had to make important judgments, I believe he chose the wisest course for all concerned. Let us hope that the xydolem will be dealt with as the situation requires, and that we can discover something of the being who controls them in the process."

Lily mulled over her *vapa*'s words for a moment, but upon seeing some of the trolls looking back at both her and Alder as they gradually returned to their boats, she decided to save detailed consideration of the morning's conference for later. Making her way around the table, Lily decided to check on the young troll whom Poplar and Yew had obviously befriended. Perhaps that strategic position would allow her to send the chieftains on their way with a little more fanfare than her practical truemate had imbued into the final proceedings.

When the Wardens saw her coming, they smiled and waved her over. Lily, with Vadom gliding silently by her side, came upon the trio by the watercraft moments later. It was readily apparent that the younger troll was in better spirits than he had been before, and Lily was sincerely glad. Though she didn't see the remnants of any food, she hoped he had eaten something, as there would probably be no stopping as he rowed all the way back across Molten Mirror.

"Princess, we have made the acquaintance of this young troll, and we'd be happy to introduce you to him before they have to leave," Poplar said easily, smiling his good-natured smile.

Lily returned the smile and nodded, turning expectantly toward the troll.

"Your Highness, allow me to make known to you Osniq of the Lava clan, son of Lava's current obsidian champion and grandson to the present chieftain," Yew said. "Osniq, this is Lily, Princess of the Fae, truemate of Prince Alder, daughter of the Golden King Oak, and a member of the Gildenthrone and Silverhall families."

Osniq smiled openly, black eyes flashing, then held out a hand at chest height before Lily. Unsure of what she was supposed to do in response, Lily slowly mirrored the gesture. Osniq's youthfully sincere smile grew a little wider.

"We shall grasp each other's forearms in friendship, Princess Lily. Then tap the other shoulder twice, as friends need reminders that they are not alone from time to time."

Lily grinned at Osniq's smooth explanation, then grasped his right forearm firmly, shaking once as she lifted her left hand and gently tapped his roundly muscular shoulder once, twice.

"It is a pleasure to meet you, Osniq of the Lava clan," Lily said in Ropazian, even as both of them returned their arms to their sides.

Osniq had spoken in the troll language, so Lily assumed that her Wardens had managed to convey to him that she would understand him regardless. Before Lily could determine how much of the Ropazian language Osniq knew, however, Alder was suddenly at her side. When she saw how intense his expression was, Lily realized that, perhaps, she shouldn't have actually touched the former rowing companion of a Void-bound troll when her truemate was in a state of heightened tension from being the royal representative at a conflict-driven meeting of races.

Lily tried to mitigate the situation by taking a step back from Osniq that simultaneously put her a step closer to her *vapa*. Surely that would help? Smiling in calm reassurance, Lily gave Alder her complete attention, waiting until his fiercely protective gaze flicked from Osniq back to her.

"*Faelan*, my Wardens thought I might like to meet a troll closer to my own age, as I asked them to check on him a little while ago. Osniq was simply teaching my *vapa* and me how trolls greet one another in friendship. It might be good for us to see the chieftains off in that way, don't you think?"

Alder looked into her eyes for another moment, then seemed to win some kind of internal struggle. She could practically hear his therianthrope growl in frustration. Feeling proud of her truemate and his level of control, Lily turned to face the young troll once again and made the introductions between Osniq and Alder. Though her *faelan* appeared to grip Osniq's forearm a little tighter than was necessary, Lily was happy when he pulled back after the requisite taps and immediately put a hand between her shoulder-blades. It felt almost like magic when he rubbed a few small circles there with his hand. Feeling something in her heart that seemed very much like contentment, Lily was inspired to extend the hand of friendship a little further for her new acquaintance.

"Osniq, I know that this is the first step of peace between our people and yours, but perhaps we can help set an example with our own new friendship. Perhaps you'd like to visit Alder and me sometime in the future? Though we haven't discussed our plans at length yet, I believe we will probably be at Silver Court for the present. Please let one of the messengers know if you'd like to stay with us as our guest and get to know the Fae better. I'm certain arrangements could be made, and I think, as you seem to have courage, that you could handle being a presence and a voice for the Crescent at court. I know that I would welcome another newcomer, being one to the Fae Wood myself."

Osniq appeared to catch the gist of Lily's words, for he was obviously both surprised and pleased by her invitation. Obsidian eyes flashing in excitement, his response was immediate.

"Princess Lily, though I must gain permission from my father and my chieftain before I accept your offer, it is very generous, and I hope to be able to give you an affirmative answer soon. Thank you so much for asking, it is truly an honor."

They shared happy grins, and in the moment that followed, everyone in their little group noticed that the chieftains and the fairy diplomats were starting to arrive at the row of boats beside them. Smiling once more at her new friend, Lily tilted her head at the clan leaders now ready to depart.

"Osniq, my truemate and I should give your chieftains one last farewell. I will simply tell you that I wish you a safe journey home, and that I hope to see you again soon."

"Thank you, Princess, I hope to be back," Osniq replied, unthinkingly offering his hand for her to shake once again.

When they had grasped forearms and tapped one another's shoulders with their good-byes, Osniq turned to the watercraft he had used to transport his grandfather and began preparing it for departure. Lily and Alder stepped forward to give each chieftain a similar farewell, surprising and evoking respect from every one of their new allies with the intrinsically trollish gesture. Finally, all of the visitors were back in their boats, though they left one craft behind. With one last wave, Lily and Alder stood with Vadom and all the other Fae on the shore of Molten Mirror, watching as the clan leaders of the Volcano Crescent made their way back to their imperiled home.

Lily noticed, as their allies rowed away on the thick, slate-gray surface of the lava lake, that a number of Court Guards were carefully loading the bowls of obsidian ornaments into the boat that remained on the shore by the Willows. Once all of the earthenware containers were snugged inside the craft, the diplomatic spectrum, along with Captain Pine, flew after the departing trolls, two of the diplomats carefully using their magic to propel the boat from above.

"I'm glad to see that a part of the troll warriors who were lost will be finding their way home soon," Lily said softly.

"I am, too," Alder replied. "From what the diplomats gathered, having those stones returned to them made a sizable impact on the chieftains. Apparently, every troll in the Crescent is given a piece of obsidian at birth, and their name and clan are etched onto the surface before the stone is placed in an ornament the troll never removes. The trolls believe that a part of their earth magic embeds itself in the obsidian over time, essentially becoming a part of the troll. We literally gave back a little piece of every warrior who died the other night, and now, perhaps, some of the survivors will have the naming stone of the loved ones they lost. I am glad your foresight allowed us to do this for the trolls, for I suspect that battalion of warriors is only the first of the casualties from the Blackstone clan that the Volcano Crescent will suffer before this xydolem trouble is over."

Lily turned Alder's words over in her mind, sifting what was saddening from what was comforting. Truly, the fact that the trolls each had a naming stone and treasured them was intriguing, special. She was happy, too, that it was her inner magic that had provided the chieftains solace in a moment of considerable grief. Absorbed in her thoughts, Lily hardly noticed when she and Alder fell into a companionable silence, both looking out at the great lake and the distant volcanoes that ringed its far shore.

After a time, Alder gently took Lily's hand in his own, though he kept his gaze on the barely rippling surface of Molten Mirror.

"*Faelani,* do you think I have done the right thing?"

Lily answered without pause, giving Alder's hand a small squeeze for emphasis.

"Yes, I do. I think we are very lucky to have the opportunity to turn one of our enemies into a much-needed ally, especially if the extent of the xydolem machinations are to be believed. Someone, somewhere, is a serious threat to the Fae and the Wood, and we will need all the help we can get to overcome such a foe."

"My parents will definitely disagree."

"My father may as well, but I do not think that changes the fact that you did what was best for our people and our home today, Alder."

Alder turned, then, to look directly into Lily's face. She met his stormy, glittering eyes, his steady gaze. After a few moments, Lily asked a serious question of her own.

"Do you feel I kept my promise to you, *faelan?*"

Her truemate smiled ruefully, and Lily felt her heart give an extra delightful beat.

"Considering I told you that I would be removing you from possible danger, I cannot help but take some responsibility for what you did contribute to that conflict with the Void-bound troll. I think I'd rather focus on your quick thinking, your talented solution, and your respect for my wishes all morning. *Faelani*, you were an asset and an anchor for me from beginning to end, and you have nothing but my gratitude for what you have done. I am the most fortunate of Fae to have found my mate in you, Lily."

Bubbles of happiness seemed to fill Lily's chest for a moment before they burst in joy. How lucky was she, the one who had been an outcast among the Outcasts, to have a Fae warrior, a prince— no, to have *Alder* say such things to her with such sincerity? Caught up in the nearly overwhelming intensity of her strange new feelings, Lily stepped closer and hugged Alder tightly. How wonderful this new life was becoming!

Lily stepped back after a moment, though she kept her hands at her *faelan*'s waist, just as he kept his loosely resting around her shoulders. Looking up at her truemate's face, Lily saw her own youthful enthusiasm smiling unabashedly back at her. Somehow, it was even better that Alder seemed to genuinely feel just as she did. In that instant, Lily thought they could take on the whole of Lamoranth, regardless of what it sent their way. She tucked that invincible feeling deep inside of her heart and her mind, knowing the memory could withstand any fear, and that it would endure much longer than the giddy bubbles that had given the powerful feeling its birth.

"Are you ready to go home now, Lily?"

Lily grinned at Alder's obvious reluctance to budge, given the question he had just posed.

"Yes, I'm ready."

Ready for her new home, ready for her new life, and ready for her new love.

EVERTUNDRA
ARRALDO
ICE PLAIN
MAP OF
LAMORANTH

MT BRIMSTONE
CAVE KINGDOM
MAGENTAY
CANYONS
JAPETA
JOQUOBON DESERT
VOLCANO
CRESCENT
Miles

Peninsula of the Misruler
Grandfather Mountains
Goblin Peaks
rest of
cients
The Waste
Ocean of Fintilles
Grasswikk
Air
nd Sky
Ropaz Grasslands
Northern Citadel
Zend
Village of Coven Dierdnom
Mother's Star
Ethic City
Wizentide
The Six Cities
Consort's Nook
Wizamoor
Goddess's Retreat
Wizulaan
Ford-Upon-Ward
Golden Court
River Ward
Molten Mirror Lake
Silver Court
Fae Wood
G

PRONUNCIATION GUIDE

Joquobon Desert

amadel—AHM-uh-dell
goffir—GOH-feer
Japeta—juh-PET-uh
Joquobon - JOE-quh-BOHN

Cave Kingdom

vipina—veh-PEEN-ah
vipin—VEH-pen
vapa—VAH-puh
vama—VAH-muh
vladi—v-LAY-dee
vu chiroptera—VOO chair-up-TERR-ah

Ropaz

Wikkenod—WICK-in-ODD
Wizulaan—WHIZ-oo-LAWN
Ropaz—ROE-paz

Fae Wood

faelani—fay-LAWN-ee
faelan—FAY-lawn
faelanzania—FAY-lawn-ZAHN-ya
praetam— PRAY-tahm
praetuu—PRAY-too
praetoh—PRAY-TOE
praetii—PRAY-TEE
piurteth—pure-TETH

Lamoranth

xydolem—ZY-doh-LIM
Magentay—muh-JEN-tay
Lamoranth—LAMB-or-ANTH
Arraldo—are-ALL-doh
Fintilles—fin-TILL-eez

ACKNOWLEDGMENTS

I'd like to take this opportunity to thank the people who offered not only encouragement, but a great deal of help in various ways as I traveled the long and winding road to publication:

My mom, Cecilia, for telling me I should be a writer instead of a doctor when I was in high school, and for backing that up in every way since, just because she knew it would make me truly happy.

Katie, Aaron, Josie, and Ezra for helping me find day jobs (especially the great nanny job! ;) Also, for a very helpful developmental edit, and for just all around being my New York family, thank you so much.

My step-mom, Jalen, for editing help, for being a great sounding board, and for lots of encouragement and gratuitous praise.

My brother, Toby, for demanding to read it, then liking it so much that he insisted I should just get it out there. Thanks for the push.

Julie, for volunteering to copy-edit my debut epic fantasy. I not only thank you, I applaud you!

My book designer, Brian Halley of Book Creatives, for creating such a beautiful cover, designing an elegant interior layout, and even drawing up a perfect map of Lamoranth—thank you for making my book stand out in the best way possible!

Finally, for all of the family and friends who encouraged me over the years that this endeavor has taken me, and never stopped believing that I would publish my big story eventually, thank you so much for your support and love. I love you all right back!

ABOUT THE AUTHOR

Hannah Lowry graduated from the University of Kansas with a B.A. in English, then departed for New York City in search of some excitement and adventure. She has spent the past several years working, writing, and having fun exploring the entire Northeast, occasionally journeying farther afield.

Lily of Lamoranth is her first novel, though it definitely will not be her last! For more information on both Hannah and her writing, please visit her website at www.lilythelegend.com.

Made in the USA
Lexington, KY
30 August 2015